Policy Documents and Reports

AAUP

American Association of University Professors

Policy Documents and Reports Eleventh Edition

American Association of University Professors | Washington, D.C.

Published by Johns Hopkins University Press | Baltimore

Disclaimer: The AAUP's policy statements and reports are intended to define fundamental professional values and standards for higher education. They have not been reviewed for conformance with state, local, or federal law, and they should not be construed as legal advice. To the extent that any statements include references to court proceedings or legal opinions, those references are informational only and do not constitute legal advice. Readers should seek appropriate legal or other professional advice regarding the current state of the law on a given topic and its application to specific facts and circumstances.

Johns Hopkins University Press
2715 North Charles Street
Baltimore, Maryland 21218-4363
www.press.jhu.edu

First published 1968
Eleventh edition 2015
Editor: Hans-Joerg Tiede

 (28)

ISBN-13: 978-1-4214-1637-3 (hardcover : alk. paper)
ISBN-10: 1-4214-1637-9 (hardcover : alk. paper)
ISBN-13: 978-1-4214-1638-0 (electronic)
ISBN-10: 1-4214-1638-7 (electronic)

Cataloging-in-Publication data is available from the Library of Congress.

A catalog record for this book is available from the British Library.

Special discounts are available for bulk purchases of this book. For more information, please contact Special Sales at 410-516-6936 or specialsales@press.jhu.edu.

Johns Hopkins University Press uses environmentally friendly book materials, including recycled text paper that is composed of at least 30 percent post-consumer waste, whenever possible.

Printed and bound in the United States by IBT/Hamilton

Contents

College and University Government

Professional Ethics

Faculty Status

Recruitment and Appointment

Contingent Appointments

Budgets, Salaries, and Benefits

Collective Bargaining

Work and Family

Discrimination

Students

Appendix: Investigative Procedures of the Association

Editor's Note

All statements collected in this volume are the most recent versions of these statements at the time of publication. The Association periodically revises policy statements. For the most recent versions of statements, see the AAUP website: http://www.aaup.org.

Several statements have been updated with additional statistical information or references to more recent court decisions, where appropriate. The AAUP's policy statements and reports are intended to define fundamental professional values and standards for higher education. They have not been reviewed for conformance with state, local, or federal law, and they should not be construed as legal advice. To the extent that any statements include references to court proceedings or legal opinions, those references are informational only and do not constitute legal advice. Readers should seek appropriate legal or other professional advice regarding the current state of the law on a given topic and its application to specific facts and circumstances.

Each section has an introduction that, for this centennial edition, provides some historical background of the Association's involvement in the topic of that section.

An attempt has been made to make references uniform across this edition of *Policy Documents and Reports*, also known as the AAUP Redbook. References to AAUP statements not in this edition are usually to the versions published in the *Bulletin of the American Association of University Professors* (1915–1955), the *AAUP Bulletin* (1956–1978), or *Academe* (1979–), including the annual special issue of *Academe*, which is published as the *Bulletin of the American Association of University Professors* (2010–), rather than to previous editions of the Redbook, since the three serial publications are now easily accessible via JSTOR (http://www.jstor.org) or the AAUP website. References to AAUP statements in this edition are given with page numbers to this edition; however, since the 1940 *Statement of Principles on Academic Freedom and Tenure* and

the *Statement on Government of Colleges and Universities* are cited in virtually all statements, they are referenced only when quoted verbatim.

In anticipation of the publication of the 1990 Redbook, statements that contained gender-specific language were updated to make the language gender-neutral. Previous editions of the Redbook indicated this in the headnote of each changed statement, here replaced by this general note. For a list of such statements, see "Gender-Specific Language Being Eliminated from Older Policy Documents," *Academe* 76 (May–June 1990): 36.

The titles of a few statements have been changed. These changes are indicated in the headnote. While several statements have at different times had the year of their origin as part of their title, only the 1940 *Statement* and the 1915 *Declaration of Principles on Academic Freedom and Academic Tenure* have done so consistently, and they are the only ones with years in their title in this edition. The following statements were shortened for inclusion in this or previous editions; they are listed here with a reference to the location of the full version:

"Accommodating Faculty Members Who Have Disabilities," *Bulletin of the American Association of University Professors*. Special issue, *Academe* 98 (July–August 2012): 30–42.

"Mandated Assessment of Educational Outcomes," *Academe* 77 (July–August 1991): 49–56.

"On Institutional Mergers and Acquisitions," *Academe* 68 (March–April 1982): 1a–9a.

"The Role of the Faculty in Conditions of Financial Exigency," *Bulletin of the American Association of University Professors*. Special issue, *Academe* 99 (July–August 2013): 118–47.

"The Use and Abuse of Faculty Suspensions," *Academe* 94 (November–December 2008): 45–59.

"The Work of Faculty: Expectations, Priorities, and Rewards," *Academe* 80 (January–February 1994): 35–48.

Introduction: AAUP Policies and Their Effective Use

The AAUP Redbook

The American Association of University Professors has issued *Policy Documents and Reports* since 1968. The first edition, with its spiral binding and red covers, had the distinctive features of an in-house production. The color has endured and has given the book its informal name: the Redbook. Subsequent editions published in the 1970s increased the number of policy statements included. The sixth edition, in 1984, was the first to be edited by longtime staff member B. Robert Kreiser and constituted a significant improvement over previous editions. It added an index and information from the legal staff of the AAUP's national office. It also added introductory material to each of the sections, which, since the first edition, were primarily organized to correspond to standing committees of the Association. These changes made the Redbook an actual book rather than simply a collection of individual policy statements, and while the current edition differs in several ways from previous ones, the debt it owes to Bob Kreiser's careful work on five editions of the Redbook from 1984 to 2006 cannot be overstated.

An important use, arguably the most important use, of the Redbook and of AAUP policy statements more generally is to inform college or university policies. Many institutions collect such policies in faculty handbooks (or manuals), and others use their language in collective bargaining contracts. Since policies governing the faculty may be adopted by systemwide or statewide governing boards, topics addressed in this introduction may be less applicable to campus-specific faculty handbooks, which in this case may only reflect local regulations. For this reason, the term "institutional regulations" is used here instead of "faculty handbook." The purpose of this introduction is to provide an overview of how to incorporate AAUP policies into institutional regulations and contracts, with a particular focus on the former. It provides a road map to the Redbook by giving pointers on where to find AAUP policy statements that contain relevant provisions on core topics and by explaining some of the central terminology. In addition, this introduction highlights some statements and reports that are new to this edition and several changes to those that were previously included.

Formulation of AAUP Policies

To understand the process by which the AAUP formulates and adopts policy statements, one must have some familiarity with those elements of the Association's governance structure involved in that process: the president, the governing Council, and the annual meeting.[1] The full role of each is described in the constitution of the Association, which is available on the AAUP's website.[2] Since the Association's founding in 1915, policy statements have been formulated by standing or special committees. Standing and special committees are appointed by the president.

Standing committee chairs, in turn, often appoint subcommittees, sometimes joined by well-known experts on the topic at hand. It is these subcommittees that most often research and draft statements. Once completed, a subcommittee statement is forwarded to the parent committee, which may approve it for publication during a public comment period. After the comment period, statements are revised, based on the comments received, before being approved in final form. Some statements are then adopted by the Council as AAUP policy. Finally, some statements are endorsed by annual meetings of the Association. As Matthew W. Finkin and Ralph S. Brown noted in a 1978 article, it is helpful to recognize and use the terminology of *approval, adoption,* and *endorsement* for the separate roles of different branches of the Association's governance structure in the process of formulating policies. The status of each statement and report in the Redbook with respect to this process is indicated in its headnote. Finkin and Brown also point out that some committee statements have been rejected by the Council or by the annual meeting, sometimes repeatedly, and that such statements are never included in the Redbook.[3]

The Association has sought to collaborate with other educational organizations on a number of its central statements, including, most notably, with the Association of American Colleges (now the Association of American Colleges and Universities) on the 1940 *Statement of Principles on Academic Freedom and Tenure* and the *Statement on Procedural Standards in Faculty Dismissal Proceedings* and with the Association of Governing Boards of Universities and Colleges and the American Council on Education on the *Statement* on *Government of Colleges and Universities*. The 1940 *Statement* was adopted by the Association of American Colleges and has been endorsed by more than two hundred educational organizations. The *Statement on Government* was jointly formulated with the other two organizations, the AAUP having adopted it as official policy and the others having commended it to the attention of their respective memberships. Headnotes of statements also indicate when statements result from such collaboration, and the 1940 *Statement* includes a list of educational organizations that have endorsed it.

The statements collected in the Redbook represent only a small sample of the policy work of the Association. Many additional statements on a range of topics have been published by the Association over the years. For AAUP statements not in the Redbook, references are provided to the serial publication of the Association: currently, the *Bulletin of the American Association of University Professors*. Because the Redbook contains the statements considered most central to the work of the Association, additions to and deletions from it have been subject to approval by the Council since 1994.

Also not included in the Redbook are the reports of investigative committees on violations of the Association's standards for academic freedom and tenure and for institutional governance. Such investigations may lead the annual meeting to impose *censure*, in the case of violations of academic freedom and tenure, or *sanction*, in the case of violations of governance standards. These investigations inform the development of AAUP policy, as do the mediative efforts of the Association's staff. Both the investigative reports and an annual report of the chair of Committee A on Academic Freedom and Tenure, which includes summaries of cases settled by staff mediation, are published in the *Bulletin of the American Association of University Professors*. Association procedures for conducting academic freedom and governance investigations are included in an appendix. Much more detailed procedures for the conduct of investigative committees were published in a handbook of the Association's Committee A in 1967.[4]

Throughout the history of the AAUP, a primary goal of the Association has been to encourage individual institutions to adopt its policy statements. While this introduction does not address the political question of how to bring about the adoption of AAUP policies at an institution, the central role of an AAUP chapter is to work in collaboration with institutional governance bodies to seek such an adoption. State

conferences of the Association should seek the adoption of AAUP policies by systemwide or statewide governance bodies.

Legal Status of Institutional and Association Regulations

The question of whether institutional regulations are contractual can arise in the context of disagreements over employment decisions by administrations or governing boards. The answer to the question differs from state to state and depends on specific circumstances. The AAUP maintains a guidebook that includes summaries of relevant court decisions by state and a list of references to law review articles.[5] As a matter of general principle, ensuring that initial appointment notices and regular reappointment notices contain references to the institutional regulations can be helpful in establishing their contractual status. Even where institutional regulations are not an enforceable contract, in the absence of a collective bargaining agreement, they are often the closest thing to a contract that faculty members have.

The role of AAUP statements in legal disputes over institutional regulations, and in particular the role of derivative statements issued by the AAUP in the context of interpreting its earlier policy documents, has been an issue of continuing interest in the higher education community.[6] AAUP principles are often cited in cases that appeal to "academic custom and usage" when interpreting institutional regulations. For a detailed, recent discussion of the concept of "academic custom and usage" and the role of AAUP statements in the legal context, see William A. Kaplin and Barbara A. Lee's *The Law of Higher Education*.[7]

AAUP Statements and Collective Bargaining Agreements

This introduction is chiefly devoted to the incorporation of AAUP policies into institutional regulations rather than into collective bargaining agreements. How institutional regulations interact with collective bargaining agreements depends on state law and the terms of the regulations and the collective bargaining agreements themselves. The AAUP generally encourages union chapters to use collective bargaining to provide an enforcement mechanism for the contents of institutional regulations. This can be accomplished by incorporating terms of the regulations into a collective bargaining agreement or making institutional regulations themselves subject to a collective bargaining agreement's grievance and arbitration procedures. Of course, sometimes regulations should not or cannot be incorporated into a contract. For example, state law may restrict certain topics from being included in the collective bargaining agreement. While collective bargaining agreements often either use language closely drawn from AAUP policy statements or explicitly refer to those statements, the incorporation of certain AAUP statements into collective bargaining agreements might be better avoided, because they "may unduly limit academic expression by setting rigid rules for professorial speech based on AAUP recommendations meant as counsels of prudence rather than absolute requirements."[8]

Institutional Regulations and Governance

The AAUP's principles of institutional governance apply to the formulation of policies in institutional regulations in two distinct ways: on the one hand, institutional regulations themselves should be the product of governance activities to which the AAUP's principles apply (the topic of this section); on the other, institutional regulations should contain statements regarding institutional governance which are consistent with AAUP principles (the topic of the next section).

In contrast to AAUP standards for the protection of academic freedom and tenure, which are detailed and specific, AAUP recommendations regarding institutional governance are general and conceptual. Given that governance practices can and do vary widely depending on institutional culture, mission, size, and public or private status, providing detailed blueprints for the conduct of shared governance is simply not practicable. And so, while specific model policies developed by the AAUP regarding academic freedom and tenure can be incorporated directly into institutional regulations, no comparable model institutional regulations exist for shared governance policies. Instead, the Association, at times in collaboration with other educational organizations, has established general principles of shared governance which are applicable to colleges and universities regardless of institutional differences.

The *Statement on Government of Colleges and Universities* is regarded by its supporters as the authoritative formulation of principles of governance for institutions of higher education in the United States. It identifies the three main components of institutional governance: the governing board, the faculty, and the president (which, in the statement, is a stand-in for the administration more generally). The statement recognizes the governing board as the final institutional authority regarding all decision making. However, it establishes expectations for the use of its final authority, in particular when its final authority is used to overturn a faculty recommendation, by identifying areas in which the other components of the institution have what the statement calls *primary responsibility* (a term that dates back to the AAUP's founding document, the 1915 *Declaration of Principles on Academic Freedom and Academic Tenure*).[9] The *Statement on Government* notes that "the faculty has primary responsibility for such fundamental areas as curriculum, subject matter and methods of instruction, research, faculty status, and those aspects of student life which relate to the educational process." It then explains what having primary responsibility means by providing an operational definition: when the faculty makes recommendations in its areas of primary responsibility, the "governing board and president should . . . concur with the faculty judgment except in rare instances and for compelling reasons which should be stated in detail." Thus, the statement identifies areas of specific faculty competence and notes that, while all faculty "decisions" are recommendations to the administration and the governing board which can be overturned, in the areas in which the faculty has specific competence, its judgment should normally be determinative.

Nevertheless, the *Statement on Government* recognizes that the administration and the governing board have the authority to overturn the faculty's judgment—for compelling reasons. The Committee on College and University Governance (formerly Committee T) subsequently explained how to interpret the concept of *compelling reasons*: "Committee T concluded that a compelling reason involves more than disagreement with faculty judgment but is not one that virtually commands a decision. Even if the administration and governing board are persuaded that the faculty judgment is incorrect, they should reverse it only on that rare occasion when they can provide convincing reasons for rejecting the faculty's presumed academic expertise. A compelling reason should be one which plainly outweighs persuasive contrary reasons."[10] Thus, the faculty should develop and approve policies that relate directly to its areas of primary responsibility ("curriculum, subject matter and methods of instruction, research, faculty status, and those aspects of student life which relate to the educational process"), subject to final approval by the administration and the governing board.[11] For other policies, the expectation for direct involvement of the faculty in policy formulation should be proportional to the relationship to the faculty's areas of primary responsibility. A large number of AAUP statements address the question of the appropriate faculty role in formulating policies in specific areas by explicating this relationship.

Institutional regulations should contain clear procedures for processing and approving changes to all regulations, with particular reference to the role of the faculty in that process. In addition, institutional regulations should describe the general role of the faculty in the governance of the institution. They should note the areas of primary responsibility of the faculty and, again, the general expectation of concurrence by the administration and the governing board with the faculty's judgment in these areas. Institutional regulations should also contain governance-related policies that comport with AAUP standards such as those outlined in the next section.

Governance-Related Institutional Regulations

Institutional regulations should include governance policies related to both the areas of primary responsibility and other areas that require meaningful participation of the faculty. This section discusses areas that have been identified by the Association as central to institutional governance (it does not, however, represent a complete listing of governance-related policies that institutional regulations should contain).

With the significant increase in faculty members holding contingent appointments, both full- and part-time, as well as the large variety of academic professionals, institutional regulations should clearly define who constitutes *the faculty* for the purpose of establishing eligibility to participate in governance and of determining applicability of different elements of academic due process. The main source for the AAUP's position on how to define faculty status is the *Joint Statement on Faculty Status of College and University Librarians*.[12] It notes that "where the role of college and university librarians . . . requires them to function essentially as part of the faculty, this functional identity should be recognized by granting of faculty status. Neither administrative responsibilities nor professional degrees, titles, or skills, per se, qualify members of the academic community for faculty status. The function of the librarian as participant in the processes of teaching, research, and service is the essential criterion of faculty status." This definition is further applied to the status of faculty with contingent appointments in the report *The Inclusion in Governance of Faculty Members Holding Contingent Appointments*,

which recommends the adoption of definitions of "faculty" which include those on contingent appointments.[13]

With respect to faculty governance bodies, the *Statement on Government* notes, "Agencies for faculty participation in the government of the college or university should be established at each level where faculty responsibility is present. An agency should exist for the presentation of the views of the whole faculty." Institutional regulations should contain governing documents of faculty governance bodies, such as the general faculty meeting or representative bodies, including senates or councils. Some of these documents—in particular, constitutions, bylaws, or standing rules—primarily relate to the role of these bodies as deliberative assemblies and thus should be based on the advice of parliamentary authorities such as *Robert's Rules of Order* or the *American Institute of Parliamentarians Standard Code of Parliamentary Procedure*.[14] Adopting the point of view that the purpose of faculty, senate, or council meetings is to conduct business as a deliberative assembly—that is, a group that meets for the purpose of conducting business by voting on proposals presented in the form of motions—is, arguably, one of the best ways to improve the effectiveness of the faculty's role in governance. It was, after all, AAUP founder Arthur Lovejoy who repeatedly noted that the role of the faculty in institutional governance is to be a legislative body.[15] Thus, familiarity with basic parliamentary procedure is helpful in drafting and revising elements of institutional regulations related to governance activities.

Since faculty members serving on governance bodies often are elected faculty *representatives*, establishing responsibilities of representatives to inform and seek input from their constituents is another important way to improve the faculty's role in institutional governance, especially in view of the apparent increase in administrative imposition of confidentiality requirements, both informally and through formal confidentiality agreements. The imposition of confidentiality requirements is more likely to occur in administrative searches and discussions of budgetary matters—areas in which the faculty does not have primary responsibility but which nevertheless require meaningful faculty participation because of their relationship to areas in which the faculty does have primary responsibility. In addition to the reports on these topics included in this edition of the Redbook, two recent reports of the Committee on Government of Colleges and Universities on these topics are not included here. These

reports give a more detailed overview of evaluations of administrators and on the responsibilities
of faculty representatives in searches, respectively.[16] Finally, governance regulations should
provide arrangements for faculty-board
communication.[17]

Academic Freedom, Tenure, and Due Process
Institutional policies should define academic
freedom and tenure and safeguard them through
regulations providing for academic due process.
The 1940 *Statement of Principles on Academic
Freedom and Tenure* has served as the foundational document defining academic freedom and
tenure in the United States since its original
formulation, as evidenced by its widespread
adoption by institutions and endorsement by
educational organizations. The AAUP has
subsequently issued many derivative statements
that provide applications and refinements of the
1940 *Statement*.

Many institutional regulations include the
1940 *Statement* and other AAUP statements, such
as the *Statement on Professional Ethics*, in their
entirety. While the Association is pleased to see
its policies incorporated verbatim, its main goal is
to see the adoption of the substance of its policies
rather than their exact formulations. (It should be
noted, however, that the Association's staff has
encountered situations in which AAUP policies in
institutional regulations were edited to state the
exact opposite of the original policy.)

While the 1940 *Statement* provides a definition
of both academic freedom and tenure, Committee
A subsequently endorsed the following compact
definition of academic freedom for inclusion in
institutional regulations: "Academic freedom is
the freedom to teach, both in and outside the
classroom, to conduct research and to publish the
results of those investigations, and to address any
matter of institutional policy or action whether or
not as a member of an agency of institutional
governance. Professors should also have the
freedom to address the larger community with
regard to any matter of social, political, economic,
or other interest, without institutional discipline
or restraint, save in response to fundamental
violations of professional ethics or statements that
suggest disciplinary incompetence."[18] In *For the
Common Good: Principles of American Academic
Freedom*, Matthew W. Finkin and Robert C. Post
provide a book-length discussion of the elements
of this conception of academic freedom.[19] The
subtitle of the book reflects the fact that the
AAUP's definition contains elements that are
specific to the historical development of academic

freedom in the United States. According to this
definition, academic freedom has four constitutive
elements: freedom of research and publication,
freedom in the classroom, freedom of extramural
utterance, and freedom of intramural utterance.
In addition to providing detailed explanations of
each of these elements, Finkin and Post discuss
multiple investigative reports that give specific
examples of the kind of "case law" that has been
developed by the AAUP in each of these areas.

"Academic Freedom, Tenure, and Due Process"
is the first section of this edition of the Redbook.
The first subsection, "Defining Academic Freedom
and Tenure," includes the 1940 *Statement* and
statements further explicating two of the four
constitutive elements: freedom in the classroom
and freedom of extramural utterance. Intramural
utterance—that is, speech on matters of institutional governance—has received increased
attention since the Supreme Court's *Garcetti v.
Ceballos* ruling. The ruling is discussed in detail
in *Protecting an Independent Faculty Voice*, the
report from which the above definition of
academic freedom is drawn. Both that report and
*On the Relationship of Faculty Governance to
Academic Freedom* are included in the section on
governance and provide further details on
intramural speech.[20] The AAUP encourages both
public and private institutions to safeguard speech
on matters of institutional governance by
adopting an appropriate definition of academic
freedom which explicitly includes such speech.[21]

Throughout its existence, the AAUP has
maintained that tenure is needed to protect
academic freedom. Tenure can be defined as an
"indefinite appointment terminable only for
cause." While the 1940 *Statement* included
mandatory retirement and termination for
financial exigency in addition to cause as possible
reasons for terminating tenure, policies specifying
a mandatory retirement age are no longer legal.
Subsequently, the Association recognized
program discontinuation as a legitimate reason as
well. Each of these reasons is discussed in detail
below.

Tenure, based on a probationary period of fixed
length, independent of academic rank, as defined
in the 1940 *Statement*, is in turn protected by
academic due process. The term *academic due
process* names procedures adapted to the higher
education environment to address negative
personnel decisions, specifically nonreappoint-
ments, dismissals, and terminations on grounds of
financial exigency or program discontinuance.
Grievance procedures and procedural safeguards
for the administration of sanctions other than

dismissal were subsequently added to expand the scope of academic due process.

The AAUP's *Recommended Institutional Regulations on Academic Freedom and Tenure* are designed to be adopted verbatim. First formulated in 1957, the *Recommended Institutional Regulations* have been regularly updated to reflect current AAUP policy. Regulations are numbered and are frequently referred to by number. When incorporating AAUP principles of academic due process into institutional regulations, it is important to distinguish the terminology employed in AAUP documents about adverse personnel decisions, which is quite specific and widely adopted in higher education. The central terms are summarized here.[22]

In the following discussion, faculty will be distinguished according to their tenure status, since, as William van Alstyne has noted, "the conferral of tenure means that the institution, after utilizing a probationary period of as long as six years in which it has had ample opportunity to determine the professional competence and responsibility of its appointees, has rendered a favorable judgment establishing a rebuttable presumption of the individual's professional excellence."[23]

1. Probationary and non-tenure-track faculty (but not tenured faculty) may be *nonreappointed* or have their appointments *nonrenewed*. That is, since their appointment is for a fixed term only, that appointment may be allowed to expire at its end. A denial of tenure is a specific kind of nonreappointment. In addition to providing timely notice of and, upon request, written reasons for nonreappointment, AAUP policy calls for procedural safeguards to protect against discrimination and violations of academic freedom. Most importantly, the burden of proof to demonstrate that a nonreappointment was based on discrimination or a violation of academic freedom is the faculty member's. In addition, a faculty member may request a review of a nonreappointment decision if the faculty member alleges that it was the result of inadequate consideration (including material procedural irregularities). For details, see Regulations 2 and 10, as well as the *Statement on Procedural Standards in the Renewal or Nonrenewal of Faculty Appointments*.[24]
2. Tenured, probationary, and non-tenure-track faculty may be *dismissed for cause*. The AAUP has detailed procedural standards that require a hearing before an elected faculty committee.

Briefly, the essential elements of a dismissal proceeding are as follows:

- A written statement of specific charges.
- A pretermination hearing before an elected body of peers.
- The burden of proof resting on the administration.
- The standard of proof based on clear and convincing evidence in the record as a whole.
- The faculty member's right to present evidence and cross-examine witnesses.
- The decision based on the record of the hearing.
- The faculty member's right to appeal to the governing board.

The AAUP maintains that "adequate cause for dismissal will be related, directly and substantially, to the fitness of faculty members in their professional capacities as teachers or researchers."[25] The Association has not specified what constitutes "cause," leaving it instead to institutions to formulate an appropriate definition consistent with the 1940 *Statement*. However, in 1973, the joint Commission on Academic Tenure in Higher Education of the AAUP and the Association of American Colleges recommended that dismissal for cause be restricted to "(a) demonstrated incompetence or dishonesty in teaching or research, (b) substantial and manifest neglect of duty, and (c) personal conduct which substantially impairs the individual's fulfillment of his [or her] institutional responsibilities."[26]

The relevant procedural details are specified in Regulation 5 and the *Statement on Procedural Standards in Faculty Dismissal Proceedings*.[27]

3. Tenured, probationary, and non-tenure-track positions may be *terminated* due to *financial exigency* or *program discontinuance*. It should be noted that some existing institutional regulations may contain provisions that permit terminations of appointments for financial exigency without defining "financial exigency." In the absence of such a definition, administrations or governing boards may declare financial exigencies in circumstances that fall short of what would be considered sufficient for such a declaration under AAUP-approved policies, so it is essential to define financial exigency in institutional regulations and in policies that specify the role of the faculty in such circumstances. Both financial exigency and program discontinuation are further

described in Regulation 4. For financial exigency, see specifically *The Role of the Faculty in Conditions of Financial Exigency* and *On Institutional Problems Resulting from Financial Exigency: Some Operating Guidelines*.[28]

The AAUP has made three important changes to the *Recommended Institutional Regulations* since the publication of the last edition of the Redbook, one of which specifically relates to the definition of financial exigency. Since some existing institutional regulations may contain previous versions of the regulations in full, these three changes are summarized here:

- Regulation 4c on terminations of appointments because of financial exigency has been amended to provide a fuller definition of "financial exigency." The rationale for the extended definition is provided in *The Role of the Faculty in Conditions of Financial Exigency*.
- A regulation on part-time faculty has been inserted as Regulation 13, and subsequent regulations have been renumbered. Existing institutional regulations may refer to specific regulations by number, and those numbered 13 or above should therefore be renumbered to reflect the current version of the *Recommended Institutional Regulations*.
- Previous versions of the *Recommended Institutional Regulations* contained a Regulation 4e, Termination because of Physical or Mental Disability. That regulation was withdrawn with the publication of the report *Accommodating Faculty Members Who Have Disabilities*.[29]

In addition to the central elements of academic due process outlined above, institutional regulations should contain grievance procedures and policies about the imposition of sanctions other than dismissal, such as fines, suspensions, and reassignments. For suspensions, in particular, see the report *The Use and Abuse of Faculty Suspensions*.[30] The Association's national office maintains sample grievance policies from several institutions, which can be provided on request.

Other Policies

In addition to policies on academic freedom and shared governance, which are central concerns of the Association, institutional regulations usually contain policies related to other matters of academic appointments and evaluation which are discussed in other sections of this edition of the Redbook.

The 2011 Dear Colleague letter of the US Department of Education's Office for Civil Rights has brought significant attention to policies related to sexual harassment and sexual assault. Two reports on those topics are included in the "Discrimination" section.[31] In addition to reports on each of these two topics, Committee A has noted the importance of providing academic due process protections to faculty members accused of sexual harassment.[32]

This edition of the Redbook includes an excerpt from another AAUP publication, a book-length 2014 study of academy-industry relationships which enumerates fifty-six principles to guide such relationships.[33] Included here are the versions of these principles reformulated for inclusion in institutional regulations and collective bargaining agreements. Several of these principles, however, are narrowly directed and thus applicable only to institutions with industrial ties.[34]

There are, of course, many specific policies that institutions will want to include in their institutional regulations which are not listed here. Some will depend on the nature and mission of the institution. For instance, medical schools will need certain kinds of policies that many other kinds of institutions do not require. Similarly, departments or programs may wish to adopt discipline-specific policies, such as statements on ethics, that have been formulated by professional organizations.

Practical Suggestions

Since institutional policies, by their nature, undergo regular review, how to organize them in a way that provides information about the status of updated policies is a matter of ongoing concern. The prevalent practice of distributing institutional regulations only in electronic form can make it difficult to date individual sections of policies. Institutional regulations should list the most recent date of change on each page or for each section. For certain kinds of institutional policies, it may be advisable to maintain a record of the changes within the document by providing dates of most recent changes with the policy. The institutional officer responsible for maintaining institutional regulations should provide an annual summary of changes to institutional regulations. Previous editions of the institutional regulations, as well as these summaries of changes, should be routinely archived to provide easy access to information about the development of the institutional policies. Access to the archives can be especially important when faculty members' conditions of employment have changed since their initial appointment.

Conclusion

The AAUP Redbook embodies the work for which the Association is most highly respected: its policy documents. These documents are developed through the collaborative efforts of the members of the Association's committees and its staff, and they are the result of a lengthy deliberative process that involves the higher education community, the governance arms of the Association, and outside experts. The formulation of policy statements and their adoption by institutions of higher education are central to the mission of the Association. On the occasion of the AAUP's centennial, it is worth recalling the goals set by the founders of the Association in the 1913 call for its organizational meeting: "The general purposes of such an Association would be to facilitate a more effective co-operation among the members of the profession in the discharge of their special responsibilities as custodians of the interests of higher education and research in America; to promote a more general and methodical discussion of problems relating to education in higher institutions of learning; to create means for the authoritative expression of the public opinion of college and university teachers; to make collective action possible; and to maintain and advance the standards and ideals of the profession."[35]

Notes

1. The other officers of the Association are the two vice presidents and the secretary-treasurer. Other than serving ex officio on the Council, they do not have a formal role in formulating AAUP policy.

2. http://www.aaup.org.

3. Ralph S. Brown Jr. and Matthew W. Finkin, "The Usefulness of AAUP Policy Statements," *AAUP Bulletin* 64 (March 1978): 5–11; on rejection, 6.

4. Louis Joughin, ed., *Academic Freedom and Tenure: A Handbook of the American Association of University Professors* (Madison: University of Wisconsin Press, 1969), 11–29.

5. AAUP, *Faculty Handbooks as Enforceable Contracts: A State Guide* (Washington, DC: AAUP, 2009), http://www.aaup.org/sites/default/files/files/Faculty%20Handbooks%20as%20Contracts%20Complete.pdf. In addition, see William A. Kaplin and Barbara A. Lee, *The Law of Higher Education*, 5th ed. (San Francisco: Jossey-Bass, 2014), 1:302–3, 543–68.

6. For example, see W. Todd Furniss, "The Status of 'AAUP Policy,'" *Educational Record* 59 (Winter 1978): 7–29, to which Finkin and Brown's "The Usefulness of AAUP Policy Statements" is a detailed reply.

7. Kaplin and Lee, *Law of Higher Education*, 1:556–59.

8. Ernst Benjamin, "The Collective Agreement: Redbook Principles," in *Academic Collective Bargaining*, ed. Ernst Benjamin and Michael Mauer (New York: Modern Language Association, 2006), 262. For further details, see Benjamin and Mauer generally; see Kaplin and Lee, *Law of Higher Education*, for a discussion of legal aspects of faculty collective bargaining.

9. AAUP, *Policy Documents and Reports*, 11th ed. (Baltimore: Johns Hopkins University Press, 2015), 3–12.

10. "Record of the Council Meeting: June 10, 11, and 13, 1993," *Academe* 79 (September–October 1993): 54.

11. At institutions that have all-university senates rather than faculty senates, the all-university senate should establish committees consisting of faculty only to make recommendations on matters that are in the primary responsibility of the faculty, and the all-university senate should concur in recommendations in areas of primary responsibility in the same manner that the administration and board should.

12. *Policy Documents and Reports*, 210–11.

13. Ibid., 197–209.

14. Henry M. Robert et al., *Robert's Rules of Order Newly Revised*, 11th ed. (Philadelphia: Da Capo Press, 2011). *American Institute of Parliamentarians Standard Code of Parliamentary Procedure* (New York: McGraw-Hill, 2012).

15. Arthur Lovejoy, "The Profession of the Professorate," *Johns Hopkins Alumni Magazine* 2 (November 1913–June 1914): 181–95. See also American Association of University Professors, *Report of the Committee of Inquiry on Conditions at the University of Utah* (July 1915), which was primarily written by Lovejoy.

16. "Confidentiality and Faculty Representation in Academic Governance," *Bulletin of the American Association of University Professors*. Special issue, *Academe* 99 (July–August 2013): 73–76. "Faculty Evaluation of Administrators," *Academe* 92 (September–October 2006): 101–8.

17. "Faculty Communication with Governing Boards: Best Practices," *Bulletin of the American Association of University Professors*. Special issue, *Academe* 100 (July–August 2014): 57–61.

18. "Protecting an Independent Faculty Voice: Academic Freedom after *Garcetti v. Ceballos*," *Policy Documents and Reports*, 126–29.

19. Matthew W. Finkin and Robert C. Post, *For the Common Good: Principles of American Academic Freedom* (New Haven, CT: Yale University Press, 2009).

20. *Policy Documents and Reports*, 123–25.

21. While the definition of academic freedom noted here explicitly includes intramural speech, the 1940 "Statement" is often taken to include it as well, because it ascribes to the faculty member the status of "officer of the institution." By contrast, the "Statement on Government" identifies intramural speech as a special case of extramural speech.

22. Some of the central terms described here are also explained in AAUP, *Navigating Faculty Appointments: Questions and Answers* (Washington,

DC: AAUP, 2009), http://www.aaup.org/sites/default/files/files/Navigating-Faculty-Appointments(1).pdf.

23. William van Alstyne, "Tenure: A Summary Explanation, and 'Defense,'" *AAUP Bulletin* 57 (September 1971): 329.

24. *Policy Documents and Reports*, 94–98.

25. "Recommended Institutional Regulations on Academic Freedom and Tenure," *Policy Documents and Reports*, 83.

26. *Faculty Tenure: A Report and Recommendations* (San Francisco: Jossey-Bass, 1973), 75.

27. *Policy Documents and Reports*, 91–93.

28. Ibid., 292–308, 309–10.

29. Ibid., 374–78.

30. Ibid., 105–13.

31. "Sexual Harassment: Suggested Policy and Procedures for Handling Complaints," ibid., 363–65. "Campus Sexual Assault: Suggested Policies and Procedures," ibid., 366–73.

32. "Due Process in Sexual-Harassment Complaints," *Academe* 77 (September–October 1991): 47.

33. AAUP, *Recommended Principles to Guide Academy-Industry Relationships* (Washington, DC: AAUP Foundation, 2014).

34. For further discussion, see ibid., 1–4.

35. "Call for the Meeting for Organization of a National Association of University Professors," *Bulletin of the American Association of University Professors* 2 (March 1916): 11–13.

Academic Freedom, Tenure, and Due Process

Events immediately before, during, and after the founding of the Association helped to set the AAUP on its path as the primary defender of academic freedom in American higher education. Johns Hopkins University philosopher Arthur O. Lovejoy and Columbia University economist E. R. A. Seligman, who had both conducted investigations into violations of academic freedom before the establishment of the AAUP, served as secretary of the Association and chair of its first Committee on Academic Freedom and Academic Tenure, respectively, dedicating themselves to the task of both defining and defending academic freedom throughout the founding year of the Association. The two crowning achievements of that year were the first investigation by the Association of a violation of academic freedom, at the University of Utah, and the presentation of the founding document of the AAUP: the 1915 *Declaration of Principles on Academic Freedom and Academic Tenure*.

The AAUP was founded at an organizational meeting held at the Chemists' Club in New York City on January 1 and 2, 1915. Seligman's chairmanship of a committee on academic freedom in the social sciences in 1914, briefly described in the introduction to the 1915 *Declaration*, was his impetus to propose at that meeting that the Association should take up the issue of academic freedom, which was approved. Lovejoy, who had been the primary force behind the movement to found the Association, famously took the initiative to travel to Utah upon learning in the press of the dismissal of multiple faculty members. A subcommittee consisting of Seligman, Lovejoy, and Princeton University economist Frank A. Fetter wrote the 1915 *Declaration*, which continues to serve as the intellectual foundation for the American conception of academic freedom to this day. Lovejoy's service on Committee A on Academic Freedom and Tenure extended until 1943.

Both the definition and the defense of academic freedom have been regular activities of the Association throughout its one-hundred-year history. Through its policy documents and reports and its investigations—and, since 1930, through the imposition of censure—the AAUP has made major contributions to the establishment of academic freedom and tenure throughout higher education in the United States. In order to obtain wider acceptance of its principles, the AAUP has cooperated with other educational organizations, efforts that culminated in the 1940 *Statement of Principles on Academic Freedom and Tenure*. The Association has also issued statements that further explain and expand the principles of the 1940 *Statement* and define the principles of academic due process.

While the Association has courageously defended academic freedom, it has also at times failed to do so. The report on *Academic Freedom in Wartime*, issued during World War I, represented an early retreat from the Association's principled declaration only two years before, and the AAUP failed to release any investigative reports from 1949 to 1954, during the height of the McCarthy era. In both cases the Association later reflected on these failures and sought to return to the principles that it has done so much to create and promulgate.

1915 Declaration of Principles on Academic Freedom and Academic Tenure

The report that follows was "accepted and approved" at the Second Annual Meeting as the *General Report of the Committee on Academic Freedom and Academic Tenure*. It has been published under the current title since at least 1943. The references exclusively to the male gender in this historic document have been left as they were.

Prefatory Note

At the December 1913 meetings of the American Economic Association, the American Political Science Association, and the American Sociological Society, a joint committee of nine faculty members was constituted to consider and report on the questions of academic freedom and academic tenure, so far as these affect university positions in these fields of study. At the December 1914 meeting of these three associations a preliminary report on the subject was presented by the joint committee.

At the meeting of the American Association of University Professors in January 1915, it was decided to take up the problem of academic freedom in general, and the president of the Association was authorized to appoint a committee of fifteen which should include, so far as the members were eligible, this joint committee of nine. The committee was therefore constituted as follows:

Edwin R. A. Seligman, Chairman, Columbia University (Economics)
Richard T. Ely, University of Wisconsin (Economics)
Frank A. Fetter, Princeton University (Economics)
James P. Lichtenberger, University of Pennsylvania (Sociology)
Roscoe Pound, Harvard University (Law)
Ulysses G. Weatherly, Indiana University (Sociology)
J. Q. Dealey, Brown University (Political Science)
Henry W. Farnam, Yale University (Political Science)
Charles E. Bennett, Cornell University (Latin)

Edward C. Elliott, University of Wisconsin (Education)
Guy Stanton Ford, University of Minnesota (History)
Charles Atwood Kofoid, University of California (Zoology)
Arthur O. Lovejoy, Johns Hopkins University (Philosophy)
Frederick W. Padelford, University of Washington (English)
Howard C. Warren, Princeton University (Psychology)

In view of the necessity of investigating an incident at the University of Pennsylvania, Professor Lichtenberger resigned in August 1915, and was replaced by Professor Franklin H. Giddings, Columbia University (Sociology). Professor Elliott, having been elected chancellor of the University of Montana, resigned in October. Professor Ford resigned in December, on account of inability to attend the meetings of the committee.

The committee of fifteen had scarcely been constituted when a number of cases of alleged infringement of academic freedom were brought to its attention. These cases were not only numerous, but also diverse in character, ranging from dismissals of individual professors to dismissal or resignation of groups of professors, and including also the dismissal of a university president, and the complaint of another university president against his board of trustees. The total number of complaints laid before the chairman of the committee during the year was eleven. As it was impossible for the committee to command the time or the amount of voluntary service necessary for dealing with all of these cases, those which seemed the most important were selected, and for each of these a subcommittee of inquiry was constituted. In the case of the University of Utah the special committee began work in April and published its report during the summer. In the case of controversies at the University of Colorado, the University of Montana, the University of Pennsylvania, and Wesleyan University, the committees of inquiry have their reports either completed or in an advanced stage of preparation. The general committee has had several meetings and has advised the committees of inquiry upon questions of principle and of method and procedure; but it has not, as a body, participated in the investigations of facts, and the committees of inquiry alone are responsible for their respective findings of fact. The general committee has, however, examined these special reports, and, accepting the findings of the subcommittees upon questions of fact, has approved their conclusions.

Three cases for which the committee was unable to secure investigating committees of this Association have been reported, after some preliminary inquiries, to the appropriate specialist societies; one case, arising at Dartmouth College, to the American Philosophical Association; one at Tulane University, to the American Physiological Society; and one at the University of Oklahoma, to the American Chemical Society.

The committee of fifteen has conceived it to be its duty to consider the problem of academic freedom as a whole and to present a report thereon. Such a report is herewith submitted.[1] The findings of special committees which have not already been printed will be presented in due course.

The safeguarding of a proper measure of academic freedom in American universities requires both a clear understanding of the principles which bear upon the matter, and the adoption by the universities of such arrangements and regulations as may effectually prevent any infringement of that freedom and deprive of plausibility all charges of such infringement. This report is therefore divided into two parts, the first constituting a general declaration of principles relating to academic freedom, the second presenting a group of practical proposals, the adoption of which is deemed necessary in order to place the rules and procedure of the American universities, in relation to these matters, upon a satisfactory footing.

I. General Declaration of Principles
The term "academic freedom" has traditionally had two applications—to the freedom of the teacher and to that of the student, *Lehrfreiheit* and *Lernfreiheit*. It need scarcely be pointed out that the freedom which is the subject of this report is that of the teacher. Academic freedom in this sense comprises three elements: freedom of inquiry and research; freedom of teaching within the university or college; and freedom of extramural utterance and action. The first of these is almost everywhere so safeguarded that the dangers of its infringement are slight. It may therefore be disregarded in this report. The second and third phases of academic freedom are closely related, and are often not distinguished. The third, however, has an importance of its own, since of late it has perhaps more frequently been the occasion of difficulties and controversies than has the question of freedom of intra-academic teaching. All five of the cases which have recently been investigated by committees of this Association have involved, at least as one factor, the right of university teachers to express their opinions freely outside the university or to engage in political activities in their capacity as citizens. The general principles which have to do with freedom of teaching in both these senses seem to the committee to be in great part, though not wholly, the same. In this report, therefore, we shall consider the matter primarily with reference to freedom of teaching within the university, and shall assume that what is said thereon is also applicable to the freedom of speech of university teachers outside their institutions, subject to certain qualifications and supplementary considerations which will be pointed out in the course of the report.

An adequate discussion of academic freedom must necessarily consider three matters: (1) the scope and basis of the power exercised by those bodies having ultimate legal authority in academic affairs; (2) the nature of the academic calling; and (3) the function of the academic institution or university.

1. Basis of Academic Authority
American institutions of learning are usually controlled by boards of trustees as the ultimate repositories of power. Upon them finally it devolves to determine the measure of academic freedom which is to be realized in the several institutions. It therefore becomes necessary to inquire into the nature of the trust reposed in these boards, and to ascertain to whom the trustees are to be considered accountable.

The simplest case is that of a proprietary school or college designed for the propagation of specific doctrines prescribed by those who have furnished its endowment. It is evident that in such cases the trustees are bound by the deed of gift, and, whatever be their own views, are obligated to carry out the terms of the trust. If a church or religious denomination establishes a college to be governed by a board of trustees, with the express understanding that the college will be used as an instrument of propaganda in the interests of the religious faith professed by the church or denomination creating it, the trustees have a right to demand that everything be subordinated to that end. If, again, as has happened in this country, a wealthy manufacturer establishes a special school in a university in order to teach, among other things, the advantages of a protective tariff, or if, as is also the case, an institution has been endowed for the purpose of propagating the doctrines of socialism, the situation is analogous. All of these are essentially proprietary institutions, in the moral sense. They do not, at least as regards one particular subject, accept the principles of freedom of inquiry, of opinion, and of teaching; and their purpose is not to advance knowledge by the unrestricted research and unfettered discussion of impartial investigators, but rather to subsidize the promotion of opinions held by the persons, usually not of the scholar's calling, who provide the funds for their maintenance. Concerning the desirability of the existence of such institutions, the committee does not wish to express any opinion. But it is manifestly important that they should not be permitted to sail under false colors. Genuine boldness and thoroughness of inquiry, and freedom of speech, are scarcely reconcilable with the prescribed inculcation of a particular opinion upon a controverted question.

Such institutions are rare, however, and are becoming ever more rare. We still have, indeed, colleges under denominational auspices; but very few of them impose upon their trustees responsibility for the spread of specific doctrines. They are more and more coming to occupy, with respect to the freedom enjoyed by the members of their teaching bodies, the position of untrammeled institutions of learning, and are differentiated only by the natural influence of their respective historic antecedents and traditions.

Leaving aside, then, the small number of institutions of the proprietary type, what is the nature of the trust reposed in the governing boards of the ordinary institutions of learning? Can colleges and universities that are not strictly bound by their founders to a propagandist duty ever be included in the class of institutions that we have just described as being in a moral sense proprietary? The answer is clear. If the former class of institutions constitutes a private or proprietary trust, the latter constitutes a public trust. The trustees are trustees for the public. In the case of our state universities this is self-evident. In the case of most of our privately endowed institutions, the situation is really not different. They cannot be permitted to assume the proprietary attitude and privilege, if they are appealing to the general public for support. Trustees of such universities or colleges have no moral right to bind the reason or the conscience of any professor. All claim to such right is waived by the appeal to the general public for contributions and for moral support in the maintenance, not of a propaganda, but of a non-partisan institution of learning. It follows that any university which lays restrictions upon the intellectual freedom of its professors proclaims itself a proprietary institution, and should be so described whenever it makes a general appeal for funds; and the public should be advised that the institution has no claim whatever to general support or regard.

This elementary distinction between a private and a public trust is not yet so universally accepted as it should be in our American institutions. While in many universities and colleges the situation has come to be entirely satisfactory, there are others in which the relation of trustees to professors is apparently still conceived to be analogous to that of a private employer to his employees; in which, therefore, trustees are not regarded as debarred by any moral restrictions, beyond their own sense of expediency, from imposing their personal opinions upon the teaching of the institution, or even from employing the power of dismissal to gratify their private antipathies or resentments. An eminent university president thus described the situation not many years since:

> In the institutions of higher education the board of trustees is the body on whose discretion, good feeling, and experience the securing of academic freedom now depends. There are boards which leave nothing to be desired in these respects; but there are also numerous bodies that have everything to learn with regard to academic freedom. These barbarous boards exercise an arbitrary power of dismissal. They exclude from the teachings of the university unpopular or dangerous subjects. In some states they even treat professors' positions as common political spoils; and all too frequently, in both state and endowed institutions, they fail to treat the members of the teaching staff with that high consideration to which their functions entitle them.[2]

It is, then, a prerequisite to a realization of the proper measure of academic freedom in American institutions of learning, that all boards of trustees should understand—as many already do—the full implications of the distinction between private proprietorship and a public trust.

2. *The Nature of the Academic Calling*

The above-mentioned conception of a university as an ordinary business venture, and of academic teaching as a purely private employment, manifests also a radical failure to apprehend the nature of the social function discharged by the professional scholar. While we should be reluctant to believe that any large number of educated persons suffer from such a misapprehension, it seems desirable at this time to restate clearly the chief reasons, lying in the nature of the university teaching profession, why it is in the public interest that the professorial office should be one both of dignity and of independence.

If education is the cornerstone of the structure of society and if progress in scientific knowledge is essential to civilization, few things can be more important than to enhance the dignity of the scholar's profession, with a view to attracting into its ranks men of the highest ability, of sound learning, and of strong and independent character. This is the more essential because the pecuniary emoluments of the profession are not, and doubtless never will be, equal to those open to the more successful members of other professions. It is not, in our opinion, desirable that men should be drawn into this profession by the magnitude of the economic rewards which it offers; but it is for this reason the more needful that men of high gift and character should be drawn into it by the assurance of an honorable and secure position, and of freedom to perform honestly and according to their own consciences the distinctive and important function which the nature of the profession lays upon them.

That function is to deal at first hand, after prolonged and specialized technical training, with the sources of knowledge; and to impart the results of their own and of their fellow-specialists' investigations and reflection, both to students and to the general public, without fear or favor. The proper discharge of this function requires (among other things) that the university teacher shall be exempt from any pecuniary motive or inducement to hold, or to express, any conclusion which is not the genuine and uncolored product of his own study or that of fellow specialists. Indeed, the proper fulfillment of the work of the professoriate requires that our universities shall be so free that no fair-minded person shall find any excuse for even a suspicion that the utterances of university teachers are shaped or restricted by the judgment, not of professional scholars, but of inexpert and possibly not wholly disinterested persons outside of their ranks. The lay public is under no compulsion to accept or to act upon the opinions of the scientific experts whom, through the universities, it employs. But it is highly needful, in the interest of society at large, that what purport to be the conclusions of men trained for, and dedicated to, the quest for truth, shall in fact be the conclusions of such men, and not echoes of the opinions of the lay public, or of the individuals who endow or manage universities. To the degree that professional scholars, in the formation and promulgation of their opinions, are, or by the character of their tenure appear to be, subject to any motive other than their own scientific conscience and a desire for the respect of their fellow experts, to that degree the university teaching profession is corrupted; its proper influence upon public opinion is diminished and vitiated; and society at large fails to get from its scholars, in an unadulterated form, the peculiar and necessary service which it is the office of the professional scholar to furnish.

These considerations make still more clear the nature of the relationship between university trustees and members of university faculties. The latter are the appointees, but not in any proper sense the employees, of the former. For, once appointed, the scholar has professional functions to perform in which the appointing authorities have neither competency nor moral right to intervene. The responsibility of the university teacher is primarily to the public itself, and to the judgment of his own profession; and while, with respect to certain external conditions of his vocation, he accepts a responsibility to the authorities of the institution in which he serves, in the essentials of his professional activity his duty is to the wider public to which the institution itself is morally amenable. So far as the university teacher's independence of thought and utterance is concerned—though not in other regards—the relationship of professor to trustees may be compared to that between judges of the federal courts and the executive who appoints them. University teachers should be understood to be, with respect to the conclusions reached and expressed by them, no more subject to the control of the trustees, than are judges subject to the control of the president, with respect to their decisions; while of course, for the same reason, trustees are no more to be held responsible for, or to be presumed to agree with, the opinions or utterances of professors, than the president can be assumed to approve of all the legal reasonings of the courts. A university is a great and indispensable organ of the higher life of a civilized community, in the work of which the trustees hold an essential and highly honorable place, but in which the faculties hold an independent place, with quite equal responsibilities—and in relation to purely scientific and educational questions, the primary responsibility. Misconception or obscurity in this matter has undoubtedly been a source of occasional difficulty in the past, and even in several instances during the current year, however much, in the main, a long tradition of kindly and courteous intercourse between trustees and members of university faculties has kept the question in the background.

3. The Function of the Academic Institution
The importance of academic freedom is most clearly perceived in the light of the purposes for which universities exist. These are three in number:

A. to promote inquiry and advance the sum of human knowledge;
B. to provide general instruction to the students; and
C. to develop experts for various branches of the public service.

Let us consider each of these. In the earlier stages of a nation's intellectual development, the chief concern of educational institutions is to train the growing generation and to diffuse the already accepted knowledge. It is only slowly that there comes to be provided in the highest institutions of learning the opportunity for the gradual wresting from nature of her intimate secrets. The modern university is becoming more and more the home of scientific research. There are three fields of human inquiry in which the race is only at the beginning: natural science, social science, and philosophy and religion, dealing with the relations of man to outer nature, to his fellow men, and to ultimate realities and values. In natural science all that we have learned but serves to make us realize more deeply how much more remains to be discovered. In social science in its largest sense, which is concerned with the relations of men in society and with the conditions of social order and well-being, we have learned only an adumbration of the laws which govern these vastly complex phenomena. Finally, in the spirit life, and in the interpretation of the general meaning and ends of human existence and its relation to the universe, we are still far from a comprehension of the final truths, and from a universal agreement among all sincere and earnest men. In all of these domains of knowledge, the first condition of progress is complete and unlimited freedom to pursue inquiry and publish its results. Such freedom is the breath in the nostrils of all scientific activity.

The second function—which for a long time was the only function—of the American college or university is to provide instruction for students. It is scarcely open to question that freedom of utterance is as important to the teacher as it is to the investigator. No man can be a successful teacher unless he enjoys the respect of his students, and their confidence in his intellectual integrity. It is clear, however, that this confidence will be impaired if there is suspicion on the part of the student that the teacher is not expressing himself fully or frankly, or that college and university teachers in general are a repressed and intimidated class who dare not speak with that candor and courage which youth always demands in those whom it is to esteem. The average student is a discerning observer, who soon takes the measure of his instructor. It is not only the character of the instruction but also the character of the instructor that counts; and if the student has reason to believe that the instructor is not true to himself, the virtue of the instruction as an educative force is incalculably diminished. There must be in the mind of the teacher no mental reservation. He must give the student the best of what he has and what he is.

The third function of the modern university is to develop experts for the use of the community. If there is one thing that distinguishes the more recent developments of democracy, it is the recognition by legislators of the inherent complexities of economic, social, and political life, and the difficulty of solving problems of technical adjustment without technical knowledge. The recognition of this fact has led to a continually greater demand for the aid of experts in these subjects, to advise both legislators and administrators. The training of such experts has, accordingly, in recent years, become an important part of the work of the universities; and in almost every one of our higher institutions of learning the professors of the economic, social, and political sciences have been drafted to an increasing extent into more or less unofficial participation in the public service. It is obvious that here again the scholar must be absolutely free not only to pursue his investigations but to declare the results of his researches, no matter where they may lead him or to what extent they may come into conflict with accepted opinion. To be of use to the legislator or the administrator, he must enjoy their complete confidence in the disinterestedness of his conclusions.

It is clear, then, that the university cannot perform its threefold function without accepting and enforcing to the fullest extent the principle of academic freedom. The responsibility of the university as a whole is to the community at large, and any restriction upon the freedom of the instructor is bound to react injuriously upon the efficiency and the morale of the institution, and therefore ultimately upon the interests of the community.

The attempted infringements of academic freedom at present are probably not only of less frequency than, but of a different character from, those to be found in former times. In the early period of university development in America the chief menace to academic freedom was ecclesiastical, and the disciplines chiefly affected were philosophy and the natural sciences. In more recent times the danger zone has been shifted to the political and social sciences—though we still have sporadic examples of the former class of cases in some of our smaller institutions. But it is precisely in these provinces of knowledge in which academic freedom is now most likely to be threatened, that the need for it is at the same time most evident. No person of intelligence believes that all of our political problems have been solved, or that the final stage of social evolution has been reached. Grave issues in the adjustment of men's social and economic relations are certain to call for settlement in the years that are to come; and for the right settlement of them mankind will need all the wisdom, all the good will, all the soberness of mind, and all the knowledge drawn from experience, that it can command. Toward this settlement the university has potentially its own very great contribution to make; for if the adjustment reached is to be a wise one, it must take due account of economic science, and be guided by that breadth of historic vision which it should be one of the functions of a university to cultivate. But if the universities are to render any such service toward the right solution of the social problems of the future, it is the first essential that the scholars who carry on the work of universities shall not be in a position of dependence upon the favor of any social class or group, that the disinterestedness and impartiality of their inquiries and their conclusions shall be, so far as is humanly possible, beyond the reach of suspicion.

The special dangers to freedom of teaching in the domain of the social sciences are evidently two. The one which is the more likely to affect the privately endowed colleges and universities is the danger of restrictions upon the expression of opinions which point toward extensive social innovations, or call in question the moral legitimacy or social expediency of economic conditions or commercial practices in which large vested interests are involved. In the political, social, and economic field almost every question, no matter how large and general it at first appears, is more or less affected by private or class interests; and, as the governing body of a university is naturally made up of men who through their standing and ability are personally interested in great private enterprises, the points of possible conflict are numberless. When to this is added the consideration that benefactors, as well as most of the parents who send their children to privately endowed institutions, themselves belong to the more prosperous and therefore usually to the more conservative classes, it is apparent that, so long as effectual safeguards for academic freedom are not established, there is a real danger that pressure from vested interests may, sometimes deliberately and sometimes unconsciously, sometimes openly and sometimes subtly and in obscure ways, be brought to bear upon academic authorities.

On the other hand, in our state universities the danger may be the reverse. Where the university is dependent for funds upon legislative favor, it has sometimes happened that the conduct of the institution has been affected by political considerations; and where there is a definite governmental policy or a strong public feeling on economic, social, or political questions, the menace to academic freedom may consist in the repression of opinions that in the particular political situation are deemed ultra-conservative rather than ultra-radical. The essential point, however, is not so much that the opinion is of one or another shade, as that it differs from the views entertained by the authorities. The question resolves itself into one of departure from accepted standards; whether the departure is in the one direction or the other is immaterial.

This brings us to the most serious difficulty of this problem; namely, the dangers connected with the existence in a democracy of an overwhelming and concentrated public opinion. The tendency of modern democracy is for men to think alike, to feel alike, and to speak alike. Any departure from the conventional standards is apt to be regarded with suspicion. Public opinion is at once the chief safeguard of a democracy, and the chief menace to the real liberty of the individual. It almost seems as if the danger of despotism cannot be wholly averted under any form of government. In a political autocracy there is no effective public opinion, and all are subject to the tyranny of the ruler; in a democracy there is political freedom, but there is likely to be a tyranny of public opinion.

An inviolable refuge from such tyranny should be found in the university. It should be an intellectual experiment station, where new ideas may germinate and where their fruit, though still distasteful to the community as a whole, may be allowed to ripen until finally, perchance, it may become a part of the accepted intellectual food of the nation or of the world. Not less is it a distinctive duty of the university to be the conservator of all genuine elements of value in the past thought and life of mankind which are not in the fashion of the moment. Though it need not be the "home of beaten causes," the university is, indeed, likely always to exercise a certain form of conservative influence. For by its nature it is committed to the principle that knowledge should precede action, to the caution (by no means synonymous with intellectual timidity) which is an essential part of the scientific method, to a sense of the complexity of social problems, to the practice of taking long views into the future, and to a reasonable regard for the teachings of experience. One of its most characteristic functions in a democratic society is to help make public opinion more self-critical and more circumspect, to check the more hasty and unconsidered impulses of popular feeling, to train the democracy to the habit of looking before and after. It is precisely this function of the university which is most injured by any restriction upon academic freedom; and it is precisely those who most value this aspect of the university's work who should most earnestly protest against any such restriction. For the public may respect, and be influenced by, the counsels of prudence and of moderation which are given by men of science, if it believes those counsels to be the disinterested expression of the scientific temper and of unbiased inquiry. It is little likely to respect or heed them if it has reason to believe that they are the expression of the interests, or the timidities, of the limited portion of the community which is in a position to endow institutions of learning, or is most likely to be represented upon their boards of trustees. And a plausible reason for this belief is given the public so long as our universities are not organized in such a way as to make impossible any exercise of pressure upon professorial opinions and utterances by governing boards of laymen.

Since there are no rights without corresponding duties, the considerations heretofore set down with respect to the freedom of the academic teacher entail certain correlative obligations. The claim to freedom of teaching is made in the interest of the integrity and of the progress of scientific inquiry; it is, therefore, only those who carry on their work in the temper of the scientific inquirer who may justly assert this claim. The liberty of the scholar within the university to set forth his conclusions, be they what they may, is conditioned by their being conclusions gained by a scholar's method and held in a scholar's spirit; that is to say, they must be the fruits of competent and patient and sincere inquiry, and they should be set forth with dignity, courtesy, and temperateness of language. The university teacher, in giving instruction upon controversial matters, while he is under no obligation to hide his own opinion under a mountain of equivocal verbiage, should, if he is fit for his position, be a person of a fair and judicial mind; he should, in dealing with such subjects, set forth justly, without suppression or innuendo, the divergent opinions of other investigators; he should cause his students to become familiar with the best published expressions of the great historic types of doctrine upon the questions at issue; and he should, above all, remember that his business is not to provide his students with ready-made conclusions, but to train them to think for themselves, and to provide them access to those materials which they need if they are to think intelligently.

It is, however, for reasons which have already been made evident, inadmissible that the power of determining when departures from the requirements of the scientific spirit and method have occurred, should be vested in bodies not composed of members of the academic profession. Such bodies necessarily lack full competency to judge of those requirements; their intervention can never be exempt from the suspicion that it is dictated by other motives than zeal for the integrity of science; and it is, in any case, unsuitable to the dignity of a great profession that the initial responsibility for the maintenance of its professional standards should not be in the hands of its own members. It follows that university teachers must be prepared to assume this responsibility for themselves. They have hitherto seldom had the opportunity, or perhaps the disposition, to do so. The obligation will doubtless, therefore, seem to many an unwelcome and burdensome one; and for its proper discharge members of the profession will perhaps need to acquire, in a greater measure than they at present possess it, the capacity for impersonal judgment in such cases, and for judicial severity when the occasion requires it. But the responsibility cannot, in this committee's opinion, be rightfully evaded. If this profession should prove itself unwilling to purge its ranks of the incompetent and the unworthy, or to prevent the freedom which it claims in the name of science from being used as a shelter for inefficiency, for superficiality, or for

9

uncritical and intemperate partisanship, it is certain that the task will be performed by others—by others who lack certain essential qualifications for performing it, and whose action is sure to breed suspicions and recurrent controversies deeply injurious to the internal order and the public standing of universities. Your committee has, therefore, in the appended "Practical Proposals," attempted to suggest means by which judicial action by representatives of the profession, with respect to the matters here referred to, may be secured.

There is one case in which the academic teacher is under an obligation to observe certain special restraints—namely, the instruction of immature students. In many of our American colleges, and especially in the first two years of the course, the student's character is not yet fully formed, his mind is still relatively immature. In these circumstances it may reasonably be expected that the instructor will present scientific truth with discretion, that he will introduce the student to new conceptions gradually, with some consideration for the student's preconceptions and traditions, and with due regard to character-building. The teacher ought also to be especially on his guard against taking unfair advantage of the student's immaturity by indoctrinating him with the teacher's own opinions before the student has had an opportunity fairly to examine other opinions upon the matters in question, and before he has sufficient knowledge and ripeness of judgment to be entitled to for many definitive opinion of his own. It is not the least service which a college or university may render to those under its instruction, to habituate them to looking not only patiently but methodically on both sides, before adopting any conclusion upon controverted issues. By these suggestions, however, it need scarcely be said that the committee does not intend to imply that it is not the duty of an academic instructor to give to any students old enough to be in college a genuine intellectual awakening and to arouse in them a keen desire to reach personally verified conclusions upon all questions of general concernment to mankind, or of special significance for their own time. There is much truth in some remarks recently made in this connection by a college president:

Certain professors have been refused reelection lately, apparently because they set their students to thinking in ways objectionable to the trustees. It would be well if more teachers were dismissed because they fail to stimulate thinking of any kind. We can afford to forgive a college professor what we regard as the occasional error of his doctrine,

especially as we may be wrong, provided he is a contagious center of intellectual enthusiasm. It is better for students to think about heresies than not to think at all; better for them to climb new trails, and stumble over error if need be, than to ride forever in upholstered ease in the overcrowded highway. It is a primary duty of a teacher to make a student take an honest account of his stock of ideas, throw out the dead matter, place revised price marks on what is left, and try to fill his empty shelves with new goods.[3]

It is, however, possible and necessary that such intellectual awakening be brought about with patience, considerateness, and pedagogical wisdom.

There is one further consideration with regard to the classroom utterances of college and university teachers to which the committee thinks it important to call the attention of members of the profession, and of administrative authorities. Such utterances ought always to be considered privileged communications. Discussions in the classroom ought not to be supposed to be utterances for the public at large. They are often designed to provoke opposition or arouse debate. It has, unfortunately, sometimes happened in this country that sensational newspapers have quoted and garbled such remarks. As a matter of common law, it is clear that the utterances of an academic instructor are privileged, and may not be published, in whole or part, without his authorization. But our practice, unfortunately, still differs from that of foreign countries, and no effective check has in this country been put upon such unauthorized and often misleading publication. It is much to be desired that test cases should be made of any infractions of the rule.[4]

In their extramural utterances, it is obvious that academic teachers are under a peculiar obligation to avoid hasty or unverified or exaggerated statements, and to refrain from intemperate or sensational modes of expression. But, subject to these restraints, it is not, in this committee's opinion, desirable that scholars should be debarred from giving expression to their judgments upon controversial questions, or that their freedom of speech, outside the university, should be limited to questions falling within their own specialties. It is clearly not proper that they should be prohibited from lending their active support to organized movements which they believe to be in the public interest. And, speaking broadly, it may be said in the words of a nonacademic body already once quoted in a publication of this Association, that "it is neither possible nor desirable to deprive a college professor of the political rights vouchsafed to every citizen."[5]

It is, however, a question deserving of consideration by members of this Association, and by university officials, how far academic teachers, at least those dealing with political, economic, and social subjects, should be prominent in the management of our great party organizations, or should be candidates for state or national offices of a distinctly political character. It is manifestly desirable that such teachers have minds untrammeled by party loyalties, unexcited by party enthusiasms, and unbiased by personal political ambitions; and that universities should remain uninvolved in party antagonisms. On the other hand, it is equally manifest that the material available for the service of the state would be restricted in a highly undesirable way, if it were understood that no member of the academic profession should ever be called upon to assume the responsibilities of public office. This question may, in the committee's opinion, suitably be made a topic for special discussion at some future meeting of this Association, in order that a practical policy, which shall do justice to the two partially conflicting considerations that bear upon the matter, may be agreed upon.

It is, it will be seen, in no sense the contention of this committee that academic freedom implies that individual teachers should be exempt from all restraints as to the matter or manner of their utterances, either within or without the university. Such restraints as are necessary should in the main, your committee holds, be self-imposed, or enforced by the public opinion of the profession. But there may, undoubtedly, arise occasional cases in which the aberrations of individuals may require to be checked by definite disciplinary action. What this report chiefly maintains is that such action cannot with safety be taken by bodies not composed of members of the academic profession. Lay governing boards are competent to judge concerning charges of habitual neglect of assigned duties, on the part of individual teachers, and concerning charges of grave moral delinquency. But in matters of opinion, and of the utterance of opinion, such boards cannot intervene without destroying, to the extent of their intervention, the essential nature of a university—without converting it from a place dedicated to openness of mind, in which the conclusions expressed are the tested conclusions of trained scholars, into a place barred against the access of new light, and precommitted to the opinions or prejudices of men who have not been set apart or expressly trained for the scholar's duties. It is, in short, not the absolute freedom of utterance of the individual scholar, but the absolute freedom of thought, of inquiry, of discussion and of teaching, of the academic profession, that is asserted by this declaration of principles. It is conceivable that our profession may prove unworthy of its high calling, and unfit to exercise the responsibilities that belong to it. But it will scarcely be said as yet to have given evidence of such unfitness. And the existence of this Association, as it seems to your committee, must be construed as a pledge, not only that the profession will earnestly guard those liberties without which it cannot rightly render its distinctive and indispensable service to society, but also that it will with equal earnestness seek to maintain such standards of professional character, and of scientific integrity and competency, as shall make it a fit instrument for that service.

II. Practical Proposals

As the foregoing declaration implies, the ends to be accomplished are chiefly three:

First: To safeguard freedom of inquiry and of teaching against both covert and overt attacks, by providing suitable judicial bodies, composed of members of the academic profession, which may be called into action before university teachers are dismissed or disciplined, and may determine in what cases the question of academic freedom is actually involved.

Second: By the same means, to protect college executives and governing boards against unjust charges of infringement of academic freedom, or of arbitrary and dictatorial conduct—charges which, when they gain wide currency and belief, are highly detrimental to the good repute and the influence of universities.

Third: To render the profession more attractive to men of high ability and strong personality by insuring the dignity, the independence, and the reasonable security of tenure, of the professorial office. The measures which it is believed to be necessary for our universities to adopt to realize these ends—measures which have already been adopted in part by some institutions—are four:

A. Action by Faculty Committees on Reappointments

Official action relating to reappointments and refusals of reappointment should be taken only with the advice and consent of some board or committee representative of the faculty. Your committee does not desire to make at this time any suggestion as to the manner of selection of such boards.

B. Definition of Tenure of Office

In every institution there should be an unequivocal understanding as to the term of each appointment; and the tenure of professorships and associate professorships, and of all positions above the grade of instructor after ten years of service, should be permanent (subject to the provisions hereinafter given for removal upon charges). In those state universities which are legally incapable of making contracts for more than a limited period, the governing boards should announce their policy with respect to the presumption of reappointment in the several classes of position, and such announcements, though not legally enforceable, should be regarded as morally binding. No university teacher of any rank should, except in cases of grave moral delinquency, receive notice of dismissal or of refusal of reappointment, later than three months before the close of any academic year, and in the case of teachers above the grade of instructor, one year's notice should be given.

C. Formulation of Grounds for Dismissal

In every institution the grounds which will be regarded as justifying the dismissal of members of the faculty should be formulated with reasonable definiteness; and in the case of institutions which impose upon their faculties doctrinal standards of a sectarian or partisan character, these standards should be clearly defined and the body or individual having authority to interpret them, in case of controversy, should be designated. Your committee does not think it best at this time to attempt to enumerate the legitimate grounds for dismissal, believing it to be preferable that individual institutions should take the initiative in this.

D. Judicial Hearings before Dismissal

Every university or college teacher should be entitled, before dismissal[6] or demotion, to have the charges against him stated in writing in specific terms and to have a fair trial on those charges before a special or permanent judicial committee chosen by the faculty senate or council, or by the faculty at large. At such trial the teacher accused should have full opportunity to present evidence, and, if the charge is one of professional incompetency, a formal report upon his work should be first made in writing by the teachers of his own department and of cognate departments in the university, and, if the teacher concerned so desires, by a committee of his fellow specialists from other institutions, appointed by some competent authority.

Notes

1. The committee has not hesitated to incorporate, by permission, a number of sentences from articles on the same subject published during this year by members of the committee or of the Association.

2. From "Academic Freedom," an address delivered before the New York Chapter of the Phi Beta Kappa Society at Cornell University, May 29, 1907, by Charles William Eliot, LL.D., President of Harvard University.

3. President William T. Foster in *The Nation*, November 11, 1915.

4. The leading case is *Abernethy v. Hutchison*, 3 L. J., Ch. 209. In this case, where damages were awarded, the court held as follows: "That persons who are admitted as pupils or otherwise to hear these lectures, although they are orally delivered and the parties might go to the extent, if they were able to do so, of putting down the whole by means of shorthand, yet they can do that only for the purpose of their own information and could not publish, for profit, that which they had not obtained the right of selling."

5. Report of the Wisconsin State Board of Public Affairs, December 1914.

6. This does not refer to refusals of reappointment at the expiration of the terms of office of teachers below the rank of associate professor. All such questions of reappointment should, as above provided, be acted upon by a faculty committee.

1940 Statement of Principles on Academic Freedom and Tenure

with 1970 Interpretive Comments

In 1915 the Committee on Academic Freedom and Academic Tenure of the American Association of University Professors formulated a statement of principles on academic freedom and academic tenure known as the 1915 *Declaration of Principles*, which was officially endorsed by the Association at its Second Annual Meeting held in Washington, D.C., December 31, 1915, and January 1, 1916.

In 1925 the American Council on Education called a conference of representatives of a number of its constituent members, among them the American Association of University Professors, for the purpose of formulating a shorter statement of principles on academic freedom and tenure. The statement formulated at this conference, known as the 1925 *Conference Statement on Academic Freedom and Tenure*, was endorsed by the Association of American Colleges (now the Association of American Colleges and Universities) in 1925 and by the American Association of University Professors in 1926.

In 1940, following a series of joint conferences begun in 1934, representatives of the American Association of University Professors and of the Association of American Colleges agreed on a restatement of the principles that had been set forth in the 1925 *Conference Statement on Academic Freedom and Tenure*. This restatement is known to the profession as the 1940 *Statement of Principles on Academic Freedom and Tenure*.

Following extensive discussions on the 1940 *Statement of Principles on Academic Freedom and Tenure* with leading educational associations and with individual faculty members and administrators, a joint committee of the AAUP and the Association of American Colleges met during 1969 to reevaluate this key policy statement. On the basis of the comments received, and the discussions that ensued, the joint committee felt the preferable approach was to formulate interpretations of the 1940 *Statement* from the experience gained in implementing and applying it for over thirty years and of adapting it to current needs.

The committee submitted to the two associations for their consideration *Interpretive Comments* that are included below as footnotes to the 1940 *Statement*.[1] These interpretations were adopted by the Council of the American Association of University Professors in April 1970 and endorsed by the Fifty-Sixth Annual Meeting as Association policy.

---

1. The Introduction to the Interpretive Comments notes: In the thirty years since their promulgation, the principles of the 1940 "Statement of Principles on Academic Freedom and Tenure" have undergone a substantial amount of refinement. This has evolved through a variety of processes, including customary acceptance, understandings mutually arrived at between institutions and professors or their representatives, investigations and reports by the American Association of University Professors, and formulations of statements by that association either alone or in conjunction with the Association of American

The purpose of this statement is to promote public understanding and support of academic freedom and tenure and agreement upon procedures to ensure them in colleges and universities. Institutions of higher education are conducted for the common good and not to further the interest of either the individual teacher or the institution as a whole.[2] The common good depends upon the free search for truth and its free exposition.

Academic freedom is essential to these purposes and applies to both teaching and research. Freedom in research is fundamental to the advancement of truth. Academic freedom in its teaching aspect is fundamental for the protection of the rights of the teacher in teaching and of the student to freedom in learning. It carries with it duties correlative with rights.[3]

Tenure is a means to certain ends; specifically: (1) freedom of teaching and research and of extramural activities, and (2) a sufficient degree of economic security to make the profession

_____

Colleges. These comments represent the attempt of the two associations, as the original sponsors of the 1940 "Statement," to formulate the most important of these refinements. Their incorporation here as Interpretive Comments is based upon the premise that the 1940 "Statement" is not a static code but a fundamental document designed to set a framework of norms to guide adaptations to changing times and circumstances.

Also, there have been relevant developments in the law itself reflecting a growing insistence by the courts on due process within the academic community which parallels the essential concepts of the 1940 "Statement"; particularly relevant is the identification by the Supreme Court of academic freedom as a right protected by the First Amendment. As the Supreme Court said in *Keyishian v. Board of Regents*, 385 US 589 (1967), "Our Nation is deeply committed to safeguarding academic freedom, which is of transcendent value to all of us and not merely to the teachers concerned. That freedom is therefore a special concern of the First Amendment, which does not tolerate laws that cast a pall of orthodoxy over the classroom."

2. The word "teacher" as used in this document is understood to include the investigator who is attached to an academic institution without teaching duties.

3. First 1970 comment: The Association of American Colleges and the American Association of University Professors have long recognized that membership in the academic profession carries with it special responsibilities. Both associations either separately or jointly have consistently affirmed these responsibilities in major policy statements, providing guidance to professors in their utterances as citizens, in the exercise of their responsibilities to the institution and to students, and in their conduct when resigning from their institution or when undertaking government-sponsored research. Of particular relevance is the "Statement on Professional Ethics" adopted in 1966 as Association policy (AAUP, *Policy Documents and Reports*, 11th ed. [Baltimore: Johns Hopkins University Press, 2015], 145–46).

attractive to men and women of ability. Freedom and economic security, hence, tenure, are indispensable to the success of an institution in fulfilling its obligations to its students and to society.

Academic Freedom

1. Teachers are entitled to full freedom in research and in the publication of the results, subject to the adequate performance of their other academic duties; but research for pecuniary return should be based upon an understanding with the authorities of the institution.

2. Teachers are entitled to freedom in the classroom in discussing their subject, but they should be careful not to introduce into their teaching controversial matter which has no relation to their subject.[4] Limitations of academic freedom because of religious or other aims of the institution should be clearly stated in writing at the time of the appointment.[5]

3. College and university teachers are citizens, members of a learned profession, and officers of an educational institution. When they speak or write as citizens, they should be free from institutional censorship or discipline, but their special position in the community imposes special obligations. As scholars and educational officers, they should remember that the public may judge their profession and their institution by their utterances. Hence they should at all times be accurate, should exercise appropriate restraint, should show respect for the opinions of others, and should make every effort to indicate that they are not speaking for the institution.[6]

_____

4. Second 1970 comment: The intent of this statement is not to discourage what is "controversial." Controversy is at the heart of the free academic inquiry which the entire statement is designed to foster. The passage serves to underscore the need for teachers to avoid persistently intruding material which has no relation to their subject.

5. Third 1970 comment: Most church-related institutions no longer need or desire the departure from the principle of academic freedom implied in the 1940 "Statement," and we do not now endorse such a departure.

6. Fourth 1970 comment: This paragraph is the subject of an interpretation adopted by the sponsors of the 1940 "Statement" immediately following its endorsement:

> If the administration of a college or university feels that a teacher has not observed the admonitions of paragraph 3 of the section on Academic Freedom and believes that the extramural utterances of the teacher have been such as to raise grave doubts concerning the teacher's fitness for his or her position, it may proceed to file charges under paragraph 4 of the section on Academic Tenure. In pressing such charges, the administration should remember that teachers are citizens and should be

Academic Tenure

After the expiration of a probationary period, teachers or investigators should have permanent or continuous tenure, and their service should be terminated only for adequate cause, except in the case of retirement for age, or under extraordinary circumstances because of financial exigencies.

In the interpretation of this principle it is understood that the following represents acceptable academic practice:

1. The precise terms and conditions of every appointment should be stated in writing and be in the possession of both institution and teacher before the appointment is consummated.
2. Beginning with appointment to the rank of full-time instructor or a higher rank,[7] the probationary period should not exceed seven years, including within this period full-time service in all institutions of higher education; but subject to the proviso that when, after a term of probationary service of more than three years in one or more institutions, a teacher is called to another institution, it may be agreed in writing that the new appointment is for a probationary period of not more than four years, even though thereby the person's total probationary period in the academic profession is extended beyond the normal maximum of seven years.[8] Notice should be given at least one year prior to the expiration of the probationary period if the teacher is not to be continued in service after the expiration of that period.[9]

---

accorded the freedom of citizens. In such cases the administration must assume full responsibility, and the American Association of University Professors and the Association of American Colleges are free to make an investigation.

Paragraph 3 of the section on Academic Freedom in the 1940 "Statement" should also be interpreted in keeping with the 1964 "Committee A Statement on Extramural Utterances," *Policy Documents and Reports*, 31, which states inter alia: "The controlling principle is that a faculty member's expression of opinion as a citizen cannot constitute grounds for dismissal unless it clearly demonstrates the faculty member's unfitness for his or her position. Extramural utterances rarely bear upon the faculty member's fitness for the position. Moreover, a final decision should take into account the faculty member's entire record as a teacher and scholar."

Paragraph 5 of the "Statement on Professional Ethics," *Policy Documents and Reports*, 146, also addresses the nature of the "special obligations" of the teacher:

> As members of their community, professors have the rights and obligations of other citizens. Professors measure the urgency of these obligations in the light of their responsibilities to their subject, to their students, to their profession, and to their institution. When they speak or act as private persons, they avoid creating the impression of speaking or acting for their college or university. As citizens engaged in a profession that depends upon freedom for its health and integrity, professors have a particular obligation to promote conditions of free inquiry and to further public understanding of academic freedom.

Both the protection of academic freedom and the requirements of academic responsibility apply not only to the full-time probationary and the tenured teacher, but also to all others, such as part-time faculty and teaching assistants, who exercise teaching responsibilities.

7. Fifth 1970 comment: The concept of "rank of full-time instructor or a higher rank" is intended to include any person who teaches a full-time load regardless of the teacher's specific title. [For a discussion of this question, see the "Report of the Special Committee on Academic Personnel Ineligible for Tenure," *AAUP Bulletin* 52 (September 1966): 280–82.]

8. Sixth 1970 comment: In calling for an agreement "in writing" on the amount of credit given for a faculty member's prior service at other institutions, the "Statement" furthers the general policy of full understanding by the professor of the terms and conditions of the appointment. It does not necessarily follow that a professor's tenure rights have been violated because of the absence of a written agreement on this matter. Nonetheless, especially because of the variation in permissible institutional practices, a written understanding concerning these matters at the time of appointment is particularly appropriate and advantageous to both the individual and the institution. [For a more detailed statement on this question, see "On Crediting Prior Service Elsewhere as Part of the Probationary Period," *Policy Documents and Reports*, 167–68.]

9. Seventh 1970 comment: The effect of this subparagraph is that a decision on tenure, favorable or unfavorable, must be made at least twelve months prior to the completion of the probationary period. If the decision is negative, the appointment for the following year becomes a terminal one. If the decision is affirmative, the provisions in the 1940 "Statement" with respect to the termination of service of teachers or investigators after the expiration of a probationary period should apply from the date when the favorable decision is made.

The general principle of notice contained in this paragraph is developed with greater specificity in the "Standards for Notice of Nonreappointment," endorsed by the Fiftieth Annual Meeting of the American Association of University Professors (1964) (*Policy Documents and Reports*, 99). These standards are:

> Notice of nonreappointment, or of intention not to recommend reappointment to the governing board, should be given in writing in accordance with the following standards:
> 1. *Not later than March 1 of the first academic year of service*, if the appointment expires at the end of that year; or, if a one-year appointment terminates during an academic year, at least three months in advance of its termination.

3. During the probationary period a teacher should have the academic freedom that all other members of the faculty have.[10]
4. Termination for cause of a continuous appointment, or the dismissal for cause of a teacher previous to the expiration of a term appointment, should, if possible, be considered by both a faculty committee and the governing board of the institution. In all cases where the facts are in dispute, the accused teacher should be informed before the hearing in writing of the charges and should have the opportunity to be heard in his or her own defense by all bodies that pass judgment upon the case. The teacher should be permitted to be accompanied by an advisor of his or her own choosing who may act as counsel. There should be a full stenographic record of the hearing available to the parties concerned. In the hearing of charges of incompetence the testimony should include that of teachers and other scholars, either from the teacher's own or from other institutions. Teachers on continuous appointment who are dismissed for reasons not involving moral turpitude should receive their salaries for at least a year from the date of notification of dismissal whether or not they are continued in their duties at the institution.[11]

---

2. *Not later than December 15 of the second academic year of service,* if the appointment expires at the end of that year; or, if an initial two-year appointment terminates during an academic year, at least six months in advance of its termination.
3. At least twelve months before the expiration of an appointment after two or more years in the institution.

Other obligations, both of institutions and of individuals, are described in the "Statement on Recruitment and Resignation of Faculty Members," *Policy Documents and Reports,* 153–54, as endorsed by the Association of American Colleges and the American Association of University Professors in 1961.

10. Eighth 1970 comment: The freedom of probationary teachers is enhanced by the establishment of a regular procedure for the periodic evaluation and assessment of the teacher's academic performance during probationary status. Provision should be made for regularized procedures for the consideration of complaints by probationary teachers that their academic freedom has been violated. One suggested procedure to serve these purposes is contained in the "Recommended Institutional Regulations on Academic Freedom and Tenure," *Policy Documents and Reports,* 79–90, prepared by the American Association of University Professors.

11. Ninth 1970 comment: A further specification of the academic due process to which the teacher is entitled under this paragraph is contained in the "Statement on Procedural Standards in Faculty Dismissal Proceedings," *Policy Documents and Reports,* 91–93, jointly approved by the

5. Termination of a continuous appointment because of financial exigency should be demonstrably bona fide.

Endorsers

Note: Groups that changed names subsequent to endorsing the statement are listed under their current names.

American Association of University Professors and the Association of American Colleges in 1958. This interpretive document deals with the issue of suspension, about which the 1940 "Statement" is silent.

The "Statement on Procedural Standards in Faculty Dismissal Proceedings" provides: "Suspension of the faculty member during the proceedings is justified only if immediate harm to the faculty member or others is threatened by the faculty member's continuance. Unless legal considerations forbid, any such suspension should be with pay." A suspension which is not followed by either reinstatement or the opportunity for a hearing is in effect a summary dismissal in violation of academic due process.

The concept of "moral turpitude" identifies the exceptional case in which the professor may be denied a year's teaching or pay in whole or in part. The statement applies to that kind of behavior which goes beyond simply warranting discharge and is so utterly blameworthy as to make it inappropriate to require the offering of a year's teaching or pay. The standard is not that the moral sensibilities of persons in the particular community have been affronted. The standard is behavior that would evoke condemnation by the academic community generally.

American Physiological Society 2006
National Women's Studies Association 2006
National Coalition for History 2006
Society for Military History 2006
Society for Industrial and Applied
    Mathematics 2006
Association for Research on Ethnicity and
    Nationalism in the Americas 2006
Society of Dance History Scholars.................. 2006
Association of Literary Scholars, Critics,
    and Writers 2006
National Council on Public History................ 2006
College Forum of the National Council of
    Teachers of English..................................... 2006
Society for Music Theory 2006
Society for Historians of American
    Foreign Relations.. 2006
Law and Society Association 2006
Society for Applied Anthropology.................. 2006
American Society of Plant Taxonomists......... 2006
Society for the History of Technology 2006
German Studies Association............................ 2006
Association of College and Research
    Libraries 2007
Czechoslovak Studies Association....................2007
American Educational Studies Association 2007
Southeastern Women's Studies Association .. 2009
American Academy for Jewish Research.........2014
American Association for Ukrainian
    Studies...2014
American Association of Italian Studies 2014
American Theatre and Drama Society 2014
Central European History Society...................2014
Central States Communication Association....2014
Chinese Language Teachers Association 2014
Coordinating Council for Women
    in History..2014
Ecological Society of America 2014
Institute for American Religious and
    Philosophical Thought 2014
Italian American Studies Association..............2014
Midwestern Psychological Association............2014
Modern Greek Studies Association..................2014
National Association of Professors
    of Hebrew..2014
National Council of Less Commonly
    Taught Languages 2014
Population Association of America..................2014
Society for Italian Historical Studies..............2014
Society for Psychophysiological Research.......2014
Society for Romanian Studies..........................2014
Society for Textual Scholarship.......................2014
Society for the History of Children and
    Youth...2014
Society for the Psychological Study
    of Social Issues..2014
Society for the Study of the Multi-Ethnic
    Literature of the United States....................2014
Society of Civil War Historians 2014
Society of Mathematical Psychology...............2014
Sociologists for Women in Society 2014
Urban History Association 2014
World History Association 2014
American Educational Research
    Association...2014
Labor and Working-Class History
    Association...2014
Paleontological Society 2014

19

Freedom in the Classroom

The report that follows, prepared by a subcommittee of the Association's Committee A on Academic Freedom and Tenure, was approved by Committee A in June 2007.

I. Introduction

The 1940 *Statement of Principles on Academic Freedom and Tenure* affirms that "teachers are entitled to freedom in the classroom in discussing their subject." This affirmation was meant to codify understandings of academic freedom commonly accepted in 1940. In recent years these understandings have become controversial. Private groups have sought to regulate classroom instruction, advocating the adoption of statutes that would prohibit teachers from challenging deeply held student beliefs or that would require professors to maintain "diversity" or "balance" in their teaching.[1] Committee A has established this subcommittee to assess arguments made in support of recent legislative efforts in this area.

II. The Contemporary Criticism

Critics charge that the professoriate is abusing the classroom in four particular ways: (1) instructors "indoctrinate" rather than educate; (2) instructors fail fairly to present conflicting views on contentious subjects, thereby depriving students of educationally essential "diversity" or "balance"; (3) instructors are intolerant of students' religious, political, or socioeconomic views, thereby creating a hostile atmosphere inimical to learning; and (4) instructors persistently interject material, especially of a political or ideological character, irrelevant to the subject of instruction. We address each of these charges in turn.

A. "Education, Not Indoctrination!"

The caption is taken from a statement of the Committee for a Better North Carolina, which in 2003 condemned the assignment of Barbara Ehrenreich's *Nickel and Dimed: On (Not) Getting By in America* to incoming students at the University of North Carolina at Chapel Hill. We agree, of course, that indoctrination is to be avoided, but the question is how education is to be distinguished from indoctrination.[2]

It is not indoctrination for professors to expect students to comprehend ideas and apply knowledge that is accepted within a relevant discipline. For example, it is not indoctrination for professors

of biology to require students to understand principles of evolution; indeed, it would be a dereliction of professional responsibility to fail to do so. Students must remain free to question generally accepted beliefs if they can do so, in the words of the 1915 *Declaration of Principles on Academic Freedom and Academic Tenure*, using "a scholar's method and . . . in a scholar's spirit."[3] But professors of logic may insist that students accept the logical validity of the syllogism, and professors of astronomy may insist that students accept the proposition that the earth orbits around the sun, unless in either case students have good logical or astronomical grounds to differ.

This process is instruction, not indoctrination. As John Dewey pointed out a century ago, the methods by which these particular conclusions have been drawn have become largely uncontested.[4] Dewey believed that it was an abuse of "freedom in the classroom" for an instructor to "promulgate *as truth* ideas or opinions which have *not* been tested," that is, which have not been accepted as true within a discipline.[5]

Dewey's point suggests that indoctrination occurs whenever an instructor insists that students accept *as truth* propositions that are in fact professionally contestable. If an instructor advances such propositions dogmatically, without allowing students to challenge their validity or advance alternative understandings, the instructor stands guilty of indoctrination.

Under this test, however, the Committee for a Better North Carolina could not possibly have known whether the assignment of Ehrenreich's *Nickel and Dimed*, which explores the economic difficulties facing low-wage workers in America, was an example of indoctrination or education. It is fundamental error to assume that the assignment of teaching materials constitutes their endorsement. An instructor who assigns a book no more endorses what it has to say than does the university library that acquires it. Assignment of a book attests only to the judgment that the work is worthy of discussion; it says nothing about the kind of discussion that the work will provoke or inspire. Classroom discussion of *Nickel and*

Dimed in North Carolina could have been conducted in a spirit of critical evaluation, or in an effort to understand the book in the tradition of American muckraking, or in an attempt to provoke students to ask deeper questions about their own ideas of poverty and class.

Even if the University of North Carolina's assignment of *Nickel and Dimed* were to be understood as in some sense endorsing the book, moreover, the charge of indoctrination would still be misplaced. Instructors indoctrinate when they teach particular propositions as *dogmatically* true. It is not indoctrination when, as a result of their research and study, instructors assert to their students that in their view particular propositions are true, even if these propositions are controversial within a discipline. It is not indoctrination for an economist to say to his students that in his view the creation of markets is the most effective means for promoting growth in underdeveloped nations, or for a biologist to assert her belief that evolution occurs through punctuated equilibriums rather than through continuous processes.

Indoctrination occurs when instructors dogmatically insist on the truth of such propositions by refusing to accord their students the opportunity to contest them. Indoctrination occurs when instructors assert such propositions in ways that prevent students from expressing disagreement. Vigorously to assert a proposition or a viewpoint, however controversial, is to engage in argumentation and discussion—an engagement that lies at the core of academic freedom. Such engagement is essential if students are to acquire skills of critical independence. The essence of higher education does not lie in the passive transmission of knowledge but in the inculcation of a mature independence of mind.

"Freedom in the classroom" is ultimately connected to freedom of research and publication. Freedom of research and publication is grounded in the exercise of professional expertise. Investigators are held to professional standards so that the modern university can serve as "an intellectual experiment station, where new ideas may germinate and where their fruit, though still distasteful to the community as a whole, may be allowed to ripen until finally, perchance, it may become part of the accepted intellectual food of the nation or of the world."[6] Academic freedom therefore includes the freedom to publish research results on controversial questions of public policy. A faculty committee at the University of Montana put it well in 1918:

> If professors of economics and politics can discuss none of these questions, their departments should not be permitted to continue in the University, for the very fact that we have faculty employed in these subjects implies that they must make a study of them and give the result of their investigations to the people of the state. It does not follow that their conclusions must be accepted, for the opinions of members of the faculty are worthy of consideration only so far as they are supported by indisputable facts and sound logic. In case their arguments are weak, the weakness can be detected and exposed.[7]

It follows that if an instructor has formed an opinion on a controversial question in adherence to scholarly standards of professional care, it is as much an exercise of academic freedom to test those opinions before students as it is to present them to the public at large. Josiah Royce stressed this point more than a century ago in response to the assertion of the regental right to control what is said in the classroom:

> Advanced instruction aims to teach the opinions of an honest and competent faculty member upon more or less doubtful questions. . . . The advanced instructor . . . has to be responsible not only for his manner of presenting his doctrines, but for the doctrines themselves, which are not admitted dogmas, but ought to be his personal opinions. But responsibility and freedom are correlatives. If you force me to teach such and such dogmas, then you must be responsible for them, not I. I am your mouthpiece. But if I am to be responsible for what I say, then I must be free to say just what I think best.[8]

Some instructors may prefer to dissect dispassionately every question presented, maintaining a studied agnosticism toward them all. Some may prefer to expound a preferred theory. Dewey regarded the choice of teaching style as a "personal" matter. One style may resonate better with some students than with others. Much depends on the "chemistry" of a particular class, as all seasoned instructors recognize. The fundamental point is that freedom in the classroom applies as much to controversial opinions as to studied agnosticism.[9] So long as opinion and interpretation are not advanced and insisted upon as dogmatic truth, the style of presentation should be at the discretion of the instructor.

B. Balance

Current charges of pedagogical abuse allege that instruction in institutions of higher education fails to exhibit a proper balance. It is said that instructors introduce political or ideological bias in their courses by neglecting to expose their students to contrary views or by failing to give students a full and fair accounting of competing points of view.

We note at the outset that in many institutions the contents of courses are subject to collegial and institutional oversight and control; even the text of course descriptions may be subject to approval. Curriculum committees typically supervise course offerings to ensure their fit with programmatic goals and their compatibility with larger educational ends (like course sequencing).[10] Although instructors are ethically obligated to follow approved curricular guidelines, "freedom in the classroom" affords instructors wide latitude to decide how to approach a subject, how best to present and explore the material, and so forth. An instructor in a course in English Romantic poetry is free to assign the poetry of the Harlem Renaissance so long as the course remains focused more on John Keats than on Countee Cullen.

To make a valid charge that instruction lacks balance is essentially to charge that the instructor fails to cover material that, under the pertinent standards of a discipline, is essential. There may be facts, theories, and models, particularly in the sciences, that are so intrinsically intertwined with the current state of a discipline that it would be unprofessional to slight or ignore them. One cannot now teach biology without reference to evolution; one cannot teach physical geology without reference to plate tectonics; one cannot teach particle physics without reference to quantum theory. There is, however, a large universe of facts, theories, and models that are arguably relevant to a subject of instruction but that need not be taught. Assessments of George Eliot's novel *Daniel Deronda* might be relevant to a course on her *Middlemarch*, but it is not a dereliction of professional standards to fail to discuss *Daniel Deronda* in class. What facts, theories, and models an instructor chooses to bring into the classroom depends upon the instructor's sense of pedagogical dynamics and purpose.

To urge that instruction be "balanced" is to urge that an instructor's discretion about what to teach be restricted. But the nature of this proposed restriction, when carefully considered, is fatally ambiguous. Stated most abstractly, the charge of lack of balance evokes a seeming ideal of neutrality. The notion appears to be that an instructor should impartially engage all potentially relevant points of view. But this ideal is chimerical. No coherent principle of neutrality would require an instructor in a class on constitutional democracy to offer equal time to "competing" visions of communist totalitarianism or Nazi fascism. There is always a potentially infinite number of competing perspectives that can arguably be deemed relevant to an instructor's subject or perspective, whatever that subject or perspective might be. It follows that the very idea of balance and neutrality, stated in the abstract, is close to incoherent.

The ideal of balance makes sense only in light of an instructor's obligation to present all aspects of a subject matter that professional standards would require to be presented. If a professor of molecular biology has an idiosyncratic theory that AIDS is not caused by a retrovirus, professional standards may require that the dominant contrary perspective be presented. Understood in this way, the ideal of balance does not depend on a generic notion of neutrality, but instead on how particular ideas are embedded in specific disciplines. This is a coherent idea of balance, and it suggests that balance is not a principle that can be invoked in the abstract but is instead a standard whose content must be determined within a specific field of relevant disciplinary knowledge.

There is another sense in which critics of higher education use the idea of "balance" to circle back to the question of indoctrination. It is hard to escape the impression that contemporary calls for "balance" imagine that an instructor's "freedom in the classroom" is merely the freedom to offer a neutral summary of the current state of a discipline, abjuring controversial and individual views. But this is to misunderstand the nature of higher education. More than fifty years ago, Edward C. Kirkland, a former chair of the AAUP's Committee A on Academic Freedom and Tenure, observed that departments of economics often housed professors of sharply conflicting views— views that simply could not be reconciled. It seemed to follow that some of them *had* to be teaching error. But, he concluded,

> Colleges and universities do not possess or teach the whole truth. They are engaged in the quest for truth. For that reason their scholars must be free to examine and test all facts and ideas, the unpleasant, the distasteful, and dangerous ones, and even those regarded as erroneous by a majority of their learned colleagues.[11]

If scholars must be free to examine and test, they must also be free to explain and defend their results, and they must be free to do so as much before their students as before their colleagues or the public at large. That is the meaning of "freedom in the classroom." To charge that university and college instruction lacks balance when it does more than merely summarize contemporary debates is fundamentally to misconstrue the nature of higher learning, which expects students to engage with the ideas of their professors. Instructors should not dogmatically teach their ideas as truth; they should not indoctrinate. But they can expect their students to respond to their ideas and their research. As students complete different courses taught by different professors, it is to be hoped that they will acquire the desire and capacity for independent thinking.

C. Hostile Learning Environment

Contemporary critics of the academy have begun to deploy the concept of a "hostile learning environment," which was first developed in the context of antidiscrimination law. The concept has been used in universities to support speech codes that suppress expression deemed offensive to racial, ethnic, or other minorities. The concept is now being used in an attempt to suppress expression deemed offensive on religious or political grounds.

The statement *On Freedom of Expression and Campus Speech Codes,* adopted as Association policy in 1994, acknowledges the need to "foster an atmosphere respectful of and welcoming to all persons."[12] An instructor may not harass a student nor act on an invidiously discriminatory ground toward a student, in class or elsewhere. It is a breach of professional ethics for an instructor to hold a student up to obloquy or ridicule in class for advancing an idea grounded in religion, whether it is creationism or the geocentric theory of the solar system.[13] It would be equally improper for an instructor to hold a student up to obloquy or ridicule for an idea grounded in politics, or anything else.

But the current application of the idea of a "hostile learning environment" to the pedagogical context of higher education presupposes much more than blatant disrespect or harassment. It assumes that students have a right not to have their most cherished beliefs challenged. This assumption contradicts the central purpose of higher education, which is to challenge students to think hard about their own perspectives, whatever those might be. It is neither harassment nor discriminatory treatment of a student to hold up to close criticism an idea or viewpoint the student has posited or advanced. Ideas that are germane to a subject under discussion in a classroom cannot be censored because a student with particular religious or political beliefs might be offended. Instruction cannot proceed in the atmosphere of fear that would be produced were a teacher to become subject to administrative sanction based upon the idiosyncratic reaction of

one or more students.[14] This would create a classroom environment inimical to the free and vigorous exchange of ideas necessary for teaching and learning in higher education.

D. Persistent Irrelevance

The 1940 *Statement of Principles* provides that teachers "should be careful not to introduce into their teaching controversial matter which has no relation to their subject." The origin of this admonition lies in the concern of the authors of the 1925 *Conference Statement on Academic Freedom and Tenure*[15] for immature youth or, more accurately, a concern by the administrators of small and often denominational colleges for potential adverse parental reaction to their children's exposure to thought contrary to the conventional pieties.[16] The admonition was reconsidered and addressed in an interpretive comment to the 1940 *Statement,* appended by the joint drafting organizations in 1970:

> The intent of this statement is not to discourage what is "controversial." Controversy is at the heart of the free academic inquiry which the entire statement is designed to foster. The passage serves to underscore the need for teachers to avoid persistently intruding material which has no relation to their subject.

The 1940 *Statement* should not be interpreted as excluding controversial matter from the classroom; any such exclusion would be contrary to the essence of higher education. The statement should be interpreted as excluding "irrelevant" matter, whether controversial or not.

The question, therefore, is how to determine whether material is "irrelevant" to classroom discussion. In some contexts, the meaning of "irrelevance" is clear. Students would have every right to complain if an instructor in ancient history dwelled on internecine conflict in her department or if an instructor in American literature engaged in lengthy digressions on his personal life. But such irrelevance is not the gravamen of the contemporary complaint.

The group calling itself Students for Academic Freedom (SAF), for example, has advised students that "your professor should not be making statements . . . about George Bush, if the class is not on contemporary American presidents, presidential administrations or some similar subject."[17] This advice presupposes that the distinction between "relevant" and "irrelevant" material is to be determined strictly by reference to the wording of a course description. Under this view, current events or personages are beyond the pale unless a course is specifically about them. But this interpretation of "relevance" is inconsistent with the nature of higher education, in which "all knowledge can be connected to all other knowledge."[18] Whether material is relevant to a better understanding of a subject cannot be determined merely by looking at a course description.

The profession has long recognized that the arbitrary lines suggested by SAF would confine instruction in ways that are pedagogically unsound. When George Parker, an assistant professor of religion and philosophy, was dismissed from Evansville College (Indiana) in 1948, in part for the introduction of "political discussion" into his classes—Parker was an ardent supporter of Henry Wallace and a sharp critic of Harry Truman—the Association's committee of inquiry discussed the 1940 *Statement*'s admonition as applied to Parker's classroom references:

> Aside from uncertainties as to what is "controversial" and what is "related," all experienced teachers realize that it is neither possible nor desirable to exclude rigidly all controversial subjects, or all topics upon which the teacher is not an expert. Many things introduced into the classroom— illustrative material or applications, overtones of significance, illuminating *obiter dicta*—may not be in the bond as far as the subject of the course is concerned, but these and kindred techniques may be of the essence of good teaching. Such techniques are readily distinguishable from calculated, overt "propaganda."[19]

The investigating committee's point still holds. Might not a teacher of nineteenth-century American literature, taking up *Moby Dick*, ask the class to consider whether any parallel between President George W. Bush and Captain Ahab could be pursued for insight into Melville's novel? Might not an instructor of classical philosophy, teaching Aristotle's views of moral virtue, present President Bill Clinton's conduct as a case study for student discussion? Might not a teacher of ancient history ask the class to consider the possibility of parallels between the Roman occupation of western Mesopotamia and the United States' experience in that part of the world two millennia later?[20] SAF would presumably sanction instructors for asking these types of questions, on the grounds that such questions are outside the purview of an official course description. But if an instructor cannot stimulate discussion and encourage critical thought by drawing analogies or parallels, the vigor and vibrancy of classroom discussion will be stultified. It was for doing just this that Professor Ralph Turner was dismissed from the University of Pittsburgh in 1934. The

Association's committee of investigation observed,

> Dr. Turner is a realist and one who looks at the facts of history realistically. He sought to make students understand that the historical persons of the past were real persons, possessing both virtues and vices and that they have their counterpart in others today. His choice of historical and present-day evidence and illustrations used in this comparative process was doubtless not always wise and caused some misunderstanding and criticism. In studying social conflicts and social traits he urged the students to observe those about them today, stressing the fact that the ever-shifting social processes are the stuff of history.
>
> Dr. Turner taught the Survey Course frankly from the viewpoint of common men and their status under different economic, social, and political conditions. Because of this fact he was regarded by some, including the Chancellor, as a propagandist. Also at times he jumped the gap between the past and the present in order to compare and contrast the past with the present. This procedure the Committee believes was not for the purpose of commenting on present-day conditions, as some criticism of his work implies, but rather to create in the minds of the students a consciousness of historical continuity and development.[21]

How an instructor approaches the material in classroom exposition is, absent breach of professional ethics, a matter of personal style, influenced, as it must be, by the pedagogical goals and classroom dynamics of a particular course, as well as by the larger educational objective of instilling in students the capacity for critical and independent thought. The instructor in Melville or classical philosophy or Roman history must be free to draw upon current persons and events just as Professor Turner did seventy years ago. Instructors must be free to employ a wide variety of examples in order to stimulate classroom discussion and thought. If allusions perform this function, they are not "irrelevant." They are pedagogically justified.

At root, complaints about the persistent interjection of "irrelevant" material concern the interjection of "controversial" material. The complaints are thus a variant of the charge that instructors have created a "hostile learning environment" and must be rejected for the reasons we have already discussed. So long as an instructor's allusions provoke genuine debate and learning that is germane to the subject matter of a course, they are protected by "freedom in the classroom."

In sum, contemporary critics of higher education argue that instructors must refrain from stating strong opinions, for doing so would both lack balance and constitute indoctrination; that instructors must not advance propositions germane to a subject if some students with deeply held religious or political beliefs might be offended, for doing so would create a hostile learning environment; and that instructors must abjure allusions to persons or events that advance discussion but that some students might fail to perceive to be clearly connected to a course description, for doing so would inject irrelevant material into the classroom. Such restrictions would excise "freedom in the classroom" from the 1940 *Statement*; they would conduce not to learning but to intellectual sterility.

III. The Modern Menace

We would be blinking at reality if we failed to acknowledge that recent challenges to "freedom in the classroom" are being advanced to further a particular political agenda. This is not the first time that universities have been suspected of harboring faculties who undermine established institutions and prevailing social values. Thomas Hobbes complained as far back as 1651 that university faculties "retain a relish of that subtile liquor . . . against the Civill Authority."[22]

According to a leading survey, faculty overwhelmingly subscribe to the proposition that it is wrong for instructors frequently to introduce "opinions on religious, political, or social issues clearly outside the realm of course topics" or to insist "that students take one particular perspective on course content."[23] Although contemporary critics of higher education have alleged that widespread abuse of the classroom is a fixture of the academic scene, the many legislative hearings and investigations nationwide have failed to substantiate the charge.[24] Nevertheless, with more than half a million full-time faculty in four-year colleges and universities teaching more than seven million students, it would seem statistically certain that sometime, somewhere, some instructor will step over the line.[25]

When that happens, sound professional standards of proper classroom conduct should be enforced in ways that are compatible with academic due process. Over the last century the profession has developed an understanding of the nature of these standards. It has also developed methods for enforcing these standards that allow for students to file complaints and that afford accused faculty members the right fully to be heard by a body of their peers. Close analysis of recent charges of classroom abuse demonstrates that these criticisms do not seek to vindicate professional standards, because they proceed on premises that are inconsistent with the mission and practice of higher education.

Calls for the regulation of higher education are almost invariably appeals to the coercive power of the state. In recent attempts to pass legislation to monitor and constrain faculty in the classroom lies a deep menace, which the architects of the American concept of academic freedom properly conceived as a potential "tyranny of public opinion."[26] American universities have been subject to this tyranny in the past. Walter Gellhorn observed in 1952 that the drive to root out communists was based on the assumption that "they will abuse their academic privileges by seeking to indoctrinate students."[27] Gellhorn noted that when the New York legislature declared in 1949 that communists ought not be permitted to teach because they disseminate propaganda, the legislature added that the propaganda "was frequently 'sufficiently subtle to escape detection in the classroom.' "[28]

Modern critics of the university seek to impose on university classrooms mandatory and ill-conceived standards of "balance," "diversity," and "respect." We ought to learn from history that the vitality of institutions of higher learning has been damaged far more by efforts to correct abuses of freedom than by those alleged abuses. We ought to learn from history that education cannot possibly thrive in an atmosphere of state-encouraged suspicion and surveillance.

Notes

1. Missouri House Bill No. 213 (introduced January 3, 2007) would have done both. It would have required each public institution of higher education to "ensure diversity," defined as "the foundation of a learning environment that exposes students to a variety of political, ideological, religious, and other perspectives, when such perspectives relate to the subject matter being taught or issues being discussed." It would also have required institutions to ensure that "conflicts between personal beliefs and classroom assignments that may contradict such beliefs can be resolved in a manner that achieves educational objectives without requiring a student to act against his or her conscience."

2. Committee A has endorsed what it calls the "nonindoctrination principle." See its 2003 statement, "Academic Bill of Rights," *Academe* 90 (January–February 2004): 79–81. See also the 1915 "Declaration of Principles on Academic Freedom and Academic Tenure," AAUP, *Policy Documents and Reports*, 11th ed. (Baltimore: Johns Hopkins University Press, 2015), 3–12, and "Joint Statement on Rights and Freedoms of Students," ibid., 381–86.

3. 1915 "Declaration of Principles," 9.

4. John Dewey, "Academic Freedom," *Educational Review* 23 (January 1902): 4.

5. Ibid., 4 (emphasis added), quoting William Rainey Harper's 1900 presidential address at the University of Chicago. It has been argued that indoctrination should be defined as promulgating as truth ideas or opinions that are not in fact true. Peter Wood, "Truths R Us," *Inside Higher Ed,* September 21, 2007, http://www .insidehighered.com/layout/set/print/views/2007/09/21 /wood.

Although this argument challenges what it calls the error of "disciplinary infallibility," it neglects to explain how the substance of truth is actually to be determined. Academic freedom would cease if arbiters of truth actually existed, because the views of such arbiters would override the professional autonomy of faculty. The most traditional and persuasive justification for academic freedom is that our best approximations of truth emerge only from the continuous and free exchange of ideas within the scholarly profession. When, as a result of this free exchange of ideas, the professional scholarly community accepts opinions or ideas as dogmatically and uncontroversially true, as is the case for many propositions within mathematics, it is not indoctrination for faculty to teach these propositions as true. It is indoctrination dogmatically to teach as truth ideas or opinions merely on the ground that they are asserted by some to be true.

6. 1915 "Declaration of Principles," 9.

7. "Committee on Academic Freedom: Statement on the Case of Professor Louis Levine of the University of Montana," *Bulletin of the American Association of University Professors* 5 (May 1919): 22.

8. Josiah Royce, "The Freedom of Teaching," *Overland Monthly* 2 (September 1883): 237.

9. For a defense of advocacy on pedagogical grounds, see Ernst Benjamin, "Some Implications of the Faculty's Obligation to Encourage Student Academic Freedom for Faculty Advocacy in the Classroom," in *Advocacy in the Classroom: Problems and Possibilities*, ed. Patricia Meyer Spacks (New York: St. Martin's, 1996), 302–14.

10. Some contemporary attacks on academic freedom center less on the claim of the instructor's bias than on the tendentiousness of the curriculum itself. See, for example, Lynne V. Cheney, *Academic Freedom* (Ashland, OH: John M. Ashbrook Center for Public Affairs, 1992). This wholesale assault on the freedom of the institution to construct the curriculum is beyond the scope of this report.

11. Edward C. Kirkland, "Academic Freedom in the Community," in *Freedom and the University*, Edgar N. Johnson et al. (Ithaca, NY: Cornell University Press, 1950), 115, 119.

12. *Policy Documents and Reports*, 361.

13. See, for example, http://www.fixedearth.com (accessed February 19, 2007).

14. This is discussed in "Academic Freedom and Tenure: The University of South Florida," *Bulletin of the American Association of University Professors* 50 (March 1964): 44–57. See also Mark Taylor, "The Devoted Student," *New York Times*, December 21, 2006.

15. "Conference on Academic Freedom and Tenure," *Bulletin of the American Association of University Professors* 11 (February 1925): 99–109.

16. See, for example, Lawrence J. Nelson, *Rumors of Indiscretion: The University of Missouri "Sex Questionnaire" Scandal in the Jazz Age* (Columbia: University of Missouri Press, 2003).

17. A placard, "Is Your Professor Using the Classroom as a Platform for Political Agendas? This Is a Violation of Your Academic Rights," accessed June 11, 2007 for this report, is, as of 2014, no longer posted at the SAF website, http://www.studentsforacademic freedom.org.

18. Conrad Russell, *Academic Freedom* (London: Routledge, 1993), 89.

19. "Academic Freedom and Tenure: Evansville College," *Bulletin of the American Association of University Professors* 35 (Spring 1949): 91–92.

20. Nicholas Kristof, "Et Tu George?," *New York Times*, January 23, 2007.

21. "Academic Freedom and Tenure: University of Pittsburgh," *Bulletin of the American Association of University Professors* 21 (March 1935): 247.

22. Thomas Hobbes, *Leviathan*, rev. 2nd ed., ed. Richard Tuck (Cambridge: Cambridge University Press, 1996), 237:

> It is therefore manifest, that the Instruction of the people, dependeth wholly, on the right teaching of Youth in the Universities. But are not (may some men say) the Universities of *England* learned enough already to do that? or is it you will undertake to teach the Universities? Hard questions. Yet to the first, I doubt not to answer; that till towards the later end of *Henry the eighth*, the Power of the Pope, was alwayes upheld against the Power of the Common-wealth, principally by the Universities; and that the doctrines maintained by so many Preachers, against the Soveraign Power of the King, and by so many Lawyers, and others, that had their education there, is a sufficient argument, that though the Universities were not authors of those false doctrines, yet they knew not how to plant the true. For in such a contradiction of Opinions, it is most certain, that they have not been sufficiently instructed; and 'tis no wonder, if they yet retain a relish of that subtile liquor, wherever they were first seasoned, against the Civill Authority.

23. John Braxton and Alan Bayer, *Faculty Misconduct in Collegiate Teaching* (Baltimore: Johns Hopkins University Press, 1999), 54, table 4.5, 46, table 4.2.

24. A Pennsylvania legislative committee held four public meetings throughout the state on this issue. Its investigation found that the one specific allegation of abuse, that a biology professor allegedly showed the Michael Moore film *Fahrenheit 9/11* to his class, never in fact occurred. Pennsylvania House of Representatives, *Report of the Select Committee on Academic Freedom in Higher Education Pursuant to House Resolution 177*, November 21, 2006.

25. The Missouri bill referred to at the outset (see note 1) was introduced because a student at Missouri State University complained of having been required as part of a class exercise in social work to sign a letter—by one press account to the state legislature, by another to a congressman—advocating the right of homosexuals to adopt children, a position with which

she disagreed on religious grounds. "Missouri State U. Settles Lawsuit Filed by Student," *St. Louis Post-Dispatch*, November 9, 2006; "Diversity and Academe," *St. Louis Post-Dispatch*, January 30, 2007. According to other students in the class, those who objected to signing the letter could opt for an alternative assignment. There has been no hearing on the matter. Erik Vance, "President at Missouri State U. Threatens to Shut Social-Work School after Scathing Report," *Chronicle of Higher Education*, April 20, 2007. The Missouri episode only underlines the importance of due process and a consequent suspension of judgment until the facts are found.

26. 1915 "Declaration of Principles," 8.

27. Walter Gellhorn, "A General View," in *The States and Subversion*, ed. Walter Gellhorn (Ithaca, NY: Cornell University Press, 1952), 358, 377.

28. Ibid., 379.

The Freedom to Teach

The following statement was approved by Committee A on Academic Freedom and Tenure in November 2013.

The freedom to teach includes the right of the faculty to select the materials, determine the approach to the subject, make the assignments, and assess student academic performance in teaching activities for which faculty members are individually responsible, without having their decisions subject to the veto of a department chair, dean, or other administrative officer. Teaching duties that are commonly shared among a number of faculty members require a significant amount of coordination and the imposition of a certain degree of structure, often involving a need for agreement on such matters as general course content, syllabi, and examinations.[1]

In a multisection course taught by several faculty members, responsibility is often shared among the instructors for identifying the texts to be assigned to students. Common course syllabi and examinations are also typical but should not be imposed by departmental or administrative fiat. The shared responsibility bespeaks a shared freedom, which trumps the freedom of an individual faculty member to assign a textbook that he or she alone considers satisfactory. The individual's freedom in other respects, however, remains undiluted. Individuals should be able to assign supplementary materials to deal with subjects that they believe are inadequately treated in the required textbook. Instructors also have the right to discuss in the classroom what they see as deficiencies in the textbook; doing so could turn out to be as effective in engaging the students as requiring them to use an alternate textbook. These principles apply equally to faculty in the tenure system and those with contingent appointments. Although, under these circumstances, the decisions of the group may prevail over the dissenting position of a particular individual, the deliberations leading to such decisions ought to involve substantial reflection and discussion by all those who teach the courses. The department should have a process for periodically reviewing curricular decisions and altering them based on a consensus of the appropriate teaching faculty, subject to review at other levels of governance.

Note

1. Substantially the same paragraph appears in "Academic Freedom in the Medical School" (AAUP, *Policy Documents and Reports*, 11th ed. [Baltimore: Johns Hopkins University Press, 2015], 71–72).

The Assignment of Course Grades and Student Appeals

The statement that follows was approved by the Association's Committee A on Academic Freedom and Tenure in June 1997 and further revised by Committee A in June 1998.

The American Association of University Professors regularly receives inquiries concerning the right of instructors to assign course grades to students, the right of students to challenge the assigned grades, and the circumstances and procedures under which student appeals should be made. The Association's Committee A on Academic Freedom and Tenure has approved the issuance of general guidelines on this subject. The following statement is intended to guide faculty members, administrators, and students with respect to the assignment of student grades and student appeals.

The Right of an Instructor to Assign Grades

The Association's *Statement on Government of Colleges and Universities* places primary responsibility with the faculty "for such fundamental areas as curriculum [and] subject matter and methods of instruction."[1] The assessment of student academic performance, it follows, including the assignment of particular grades, is a faculty responsibility. Recognizing the authority of the instructor of record to evaluate the academic performance of students enrolled in a course he or she is teaching is a direct corollary of the instructor's "freedom in the classroom" that the 1940 *Statement of Principles on Academic Freedom and Tenure* assures.[2] The faculty member offering the course, it follows, should be responsible for the evaluation of student course work and, under normal circumstances, is the sole judge of the grades received by the students in that course.

The Right of a Student to Appeal

According to the Association's *Statement on Professional Ethics*, "professors make every reasonable effort . . . to ensure that their evaluations of students reflect each student's true merit."[3] The academic community proceeds under the strong presumption that the instructor's evaluations are authoritative. At the same time, of course, situations do arise in which a student alleges that a grade he or she has received is wrong, and the *Joint Statement on Rights and Freedoms of Students* provides that "students should have protection through orderly procedures against prejudiced or capricious academic evaluation."[4] A suitable mechanism for appeal, one which respects both the prerogatives of instructors and the rights of students in this regard, should thus be available for reviewing allegations that inappropriate criteria were used in determining the grade or that the instructor did not adhere to stated procedures or grading standards.[5]

Under no circumstances should administrative officers on their own authority substitute their judgment for that of the faculty concerning the assignment of a grade. The review of a student complaint over a grade should be by faculty, under procedures adopted by faculty, and any resulting change in a grade should be by faculty authorization.

Procedures for Appeal

Committee A offers the following, not as a single procedure for grade appeals that all should follow, but as recommended procedural considerations.

1. A student who wishes to complain about a grade would be expected to discuss the matter first with the course instructor, doing so as soon as possible after receiving the grade.
2. The instructor should be willing to listen, to provide explanation, and to be receptive to changing the grade if the student provides convincing argument for doing so. (In most cases the discussion between the student and the instructor should suffice and the matter should not need to be carried further.)
3. If, after the discussion with the instructor, the student's concerns remain unresolved, the student might then approach the instructor's department chair or another member of the faculty who is the instructor's immediate administrative superior. That person, if he or she believes that the complaint may have merit, would be expected to discuss it with the

instructor. If the matter still remains unresolved, it should be referred to an ad hoc
faculty committee.

4. The ad hoc committee would ordinarily be
composed of faculty members in the instructor's
department or in closely allied fields. The
committee would examine available written
information on the dispute, would be available
for meetings with the student and with the
instructor, and would meet with others as it
sees fit.

5. If the faculty committee, through its inquiries
and deliberations, determines that compelling
reasons exist to change the grade, it would
request that the instructor make the change,
providing the instructor with a written
explanation of its reasons. Should the instructor decline, he or she should provide an
explanation for refusing.

6. The faculty committee, after considering the
instructor's explanation, and upon concluding
that it would be unjust to allow the original
grade to stand, may then recommend to the
department head or to the instructor's
immediate administrative superior that the
grade be changed. That individual will provide
the instructor with a copy of the recommendation and will ask the instructor to implement
it. If the instructor continues to decline, that
individual may then change the grade,

notifying the instructor and the student of this
action. Only that individual, upon the written
recommendation of the faculty committee,
should have the authority to effect a change in
grade over the objection of the instructor who
assigned the original grade.

Notes

1. AAUP, *Policy Documents and Reports,* 11th ed.
(Baltimore: Johns Hopkins University Press, 2015),
120.
2. Ibid., 14.
3. Ibid., 145.
4. Ibid., 382.
5. Institutions receiving federal funds are required
to provide procedures by which students can challenge
grades that they believe may have been tainted by
gender or disability discrimination. See, e.g., 34 CFR
Sections 106.8 and 104.7 and 28 CFR Section 35.107.
The *Revised Sexual Harassment Guidance,* issued by
the United States Department of Education's Office for
Civil Rights (OCR) in 2001, provides information on
the necessary components of such procedures. The OCR
guidance is available online at www.ed.gov/about/offices
/list/ocr/docs/shguide.pdf. Such grievance procedures
are also recommended to address allegations of race and
national origin discrimination. See *Protecting Students
from Harassment and Hate Crimes: A Guide for
Schools* (1999), 16. This publication, a joint effort of the
OCR and the National Association of Attorneys
General, is available online at www.ed.gov/offices/OCR
/archives/Harassment/harassment.pdf.

Committee A Statement on Extramural Utterances

The statement that follows was approved by the Association's Committee A on Academic Freedom and Tenure in October 1964. Its purpose is to clarify those sections of the 1940 *Statement of Principles on Academic Freedom and Tenure* relating to the faculty member's exercise of freedom of speech as a citizen.

The 1940 *Statement of Principles* asserts the right of faculty members to speak or write as citizens, free from institutional censorship or discipline. At the same time, it calls attention to the special obligations of faculty members arising from their position in the community: to be accurate, to exercise appropriate restraint, to show respect for the opinions of others, and to make every effort to indicate that they are not speaking for the institution. An interpretation of the 1940 *Statement*, agreed to at a conference of the Association of American Colleges[1] and the AAUP held on November 8, 1940, states that an administration may file charges in accordance with procedures outlined in the *Statement* if it feels that a faculty member has failed to observe the above admonitions and believes that the professor's extramural utterances raise grave doubts concerning the professor's fitness for continuing service.

In cases involving such charges, it is essential that the hearing should be conducted by an appropriate—preferably elected—faculty committee, as provided in Section 4 of the *Statement on Procedural Standards in Faculty Dismissal Proceedings*.[2] The controlling principle is that a faculty member's expression of opinion as a citizen cannot constitute grounds for dismissal unless it clearly demonstrates the faculty member's unfitness to serve. Extramural utterances rarely bear upon the faculty member's fitness for continuing service. Moreover, a final decision should take into account the faculty member's entire record as a teacher and scholar. In the absence of weighty evidence of unfitness, the administration should not prefer charges; and if it is not clearly proved in the hearing that the faculty member is unfit to continue, the faculty committee should make a finding in favor of the faculty member concerned.

Committee A asserts that it will view with particular gravity an administrative or board reversal of a favorable faculty committee hearing judgment in a case involving extramural utterances. In the words of the 1940 *Statement of Principles*, "the administration should remember that teachers are citizens and should be accorded the freedom of citizens." In a democratic society freedom of speech is an indispensable right of the citizen. Committee A will vigorously uphold that right.

Notes

1. Now the Association of American Colleges and Universities.

2. AAUP, *Policy Documents and Reports*, 11th ed. (Baltimore: Johns Hopkins University Press, 2015), 91–93.

Ensuring Academic Freedom in Politically Controversial Academic Personnel Decisions

The statement that follows is the executive summary of a longer report that was prepared by a subcommittee of the Association's Committee A on Academic Freedom and Tenure and approved by Committee A in June 2011.

Politically controversial cases involving college and university teachers spurred the founding of the AAUP and have recurred frequently thereafter. The Association has noted with special concern recent cases arising out of the war on terror, the conflict in the Middle East, and a resurgence of the culture wars in such fields as health and the environment. The Association's Committee A on Academic Freedom and Tenure accordingly formed a special subcommittee to report on the factors underlying the current problem, to review the history and character of politically controversial academic personnel decisions, to identify weaknesses in the principles and decision-making procedures that ensure academic freedom in politically controversial cases, and to recommend enhanced protections to ensure academic integrity in the conduct of such cases.

Because of the length and detail of the resulting report, the subcommittee has prepared this executive summary to make its recommended principles and procedures readily accessible both to the academic community and to the public, and to highlight the need for institutions to incorporate these principles and procedures into their own regulations. The full report notes the recent developments that have heightened the problem of political intrusion into the academic personnel process and fostered a climate inimical to academic freedom in which partisan political interests threaten to overwhelm professional judgment in academic personnel proceedings. It then provides a definition of political intrusion, an overview of the safeguards to academic freedom from political intrusion set forth in AAUP policy, and a reappraisal of past political intrusions in academic personnel decisions, including the challenges the Association has confronted in defending politically controversial professors. After this introduction, the main body of the report provides a detailed analysis and explanation of the principles necessary to guide academic decision making regarding politically controver-

sial personnel decisions and of the procedural safeguards required in the consideration of such decisions. A comprehensive list of these principles and safeguards concludes this executive summary, but readers who desire to understand fully the rationale for our recommendations should refer to the text of the entire report.

Current political threats to academic freedom have intensified with the rapid growth of the Internet and new media that have made it possible for talk-show hosts, bloggers, and well-funded interest groups to supplement the trustees, politicians, corporate and religious groups, and journalists who previously put untoward pressure on the university. At the same time, the need for faculty members to contribute their expertise to public discourse and policy debates has increased. The protection of their unfettered expression, including the ability to espouse highly controversial and unpopular views, is an essential social responsibility of universities and colleges. As the joint 1940 *Statement of Principles on Academic Freedom and Tenure* explains: "Institutions of higher education are conducted for the common good . . . [which] depends upon the free search for truth and its free exposition." The freedom that the common good requires, however, can be hard to maintain, as we have learned from such prior experiences as the dismissals of controversial professors and subsequent constraints on academic discourse during and after the two world wars. These events teach us that political restrictions on academic expression must not be countenanced— even when most faculty members support or at least acquiesce in them. To avoid a recurrence of such situations, the contemporary political pressures on the academic community must be countered by emphasizing how free universities contribute to the common good even as they create political tensions between the academy and society that require the protection of academic freedom.

Political intrusion, the report notes, usually arises out of controversies over political ideology, religious doctrine, social or moral perspectives, corporate practices, or public policy—not more narrowly professional disagreements and disputes among academics. It may arise from within as well as from without the university. Political intrusion from within may occur when members of the university who are sensitive to political concerns engage in self-censorship or when politically motivated academics violate or disregard sound academic principles and procedures. It may also come from outside the university when, for example, private corporations or public officials seek to persuade universities to terminate particular research activities, programs, or the services of the faculty members involved.

The AAUP's foundational 1915 *Declaration of Principles on Academic Freedom and Academic Tenure*[1] and its 1940 *Statement of Principles* established safeguards for academic freedom from political intrusion largely by protecting the rights of individual academics. As the McCarthy era drew to a close in 1956, the Association's report *Academic Freedom and Tenure in the Quest for National Security*[2] forcefully outlined the links between and among the academic freedom of the university, of the profession, and of individual professors. The 1956 report underscored the need for the mutual protection of the rights of all within the university community, an admonition that the subcommittee finds highly applicable to the obligation of tenured faculty members to protect the rights of those without tenure—an ever-increasing class of academics whose academic freedom has been eroded not so much by political intrusion as by the deterioration of the tenure system that the AAUP has championed since 1915 as the bulwark of academic freedom.

From its inception, even as the AAUP sought to protect academic freedom by strengthening tenure and instituting procedural protections, it struggled with the particular difficulties of defending faculty members embroiled in political controversy. Beginning with professional economists who ran afoul of the conservative business community in the Association's early days, the individuals who lost their positions for political reasons have been involved with some of the most controversial issues of their time. Whether by deviating from the hyperpatriotism of World War I, or refusing to answer questions about communism during the McCarthy era, or taking an unpopular stance toward the current conflict in the Middle East, the protagonists in these academic-freedom struggles have tested the limits of permissible dissent within the academic, as well as the broader, community. What makes the recent spate of politically controversial cases

particularly alarming is how many of them involve faculty members holding contingent appointments who can be dismissed without the procedural protections their tenured and tenure-track colleagues enjoy.

The AAUP has been responding to these new threats to academic freedom by releasing new policy statements emphasizing the rights of non-tenure-track faculty members and academic professionals and defending the integrity of the classroom. But even in cases where politically controversial individuals receive the full complement of AAUP-recommended procedural guarantees, there is increasing concern that mere adherence to due process or weak or substantively biased faculty committees may provide politicized decision making with a veneer of legitimacy. As the past century of political threats to academic freedom has revealed, although procedural protections—such as providing adequate notice, a statement of specific charges, and a hearing before one's peers—are crucial to the defense of academic freedom, they may not be sufficient in themselves, especially in cases where the dissenting faculty member confronts a strong mainstream consensus in support of repression.

The fundamental principle is that academic evaluation should be grounded on considerations that substantially affect the performance of academic responsibilities. This means especially that the selection and interpretation of course material should be assessed solely on the basis of educationally appropriate criteria and that the exclusion of controversial material on other than professional grounds stifles academic freedom and the opportunity for student learning. Since academic professionals are best prepared to distinguish professional from political or other extraneous concerns, the procedures recommended to implement these principles seek to ensure and give great weight to the findings of collegial committees.

We therefore recommend the following principles and procedures to enhance the protection of academic freedom in politically controversial academic personnel decisions:

Principles to Guide Decision Making regarding Politically Controversial Academic Personnel Decisions

The fundamental principle is that all academic personnel decisions, including new appointments and renewal of existing appointments, should rest on considerations that demonstrably pertain to the effective performance of the academic's professional responsibilities.

A. Assessing Charges of Indoctrination in the Classroom

1. Only the proven demonstration of the use of "dishonest tactics" to "deceive students"—not the political views, advocacy, or affiliations of the faculty member—may provide grounds for adverse action.
2. In a politically controversial proceeding, the admonition to tailor questions narrowly to permissible issues of academic fitness and to avoid any inquiry into political affiliations and beliefs is plainly imperative.
3. Neither the expression nor the attempted avoidance of value judgments can or should in itself provide a reasonable ground for assessing the professional conduct and fitness of a faculty member.
4. "So long as opinion and interpretation are not advanced and insisted upon as dogmatic truth, the style of presentation [in the classroom] should be at the discretion of the instructor" (*Freedom in the Classroom*[3]).
5. Whether a specific matter or argument is essential to a particular class or what weight it should be given is a matter of professional judgment, based on the standards of the pertinent disciplines and consistent with the academic freedom required if the disciplines themselves are to remain capable of critical self-reflection and growth.
6. Exclusion of controversial matter, whether under the persistent-intrusion clause of the 1970 Interpretive Comment 2 on the 1940 *Statement* or in the name of protecting students from challenges to their cherished beliefs, stifles the free discussion necessary for academic freedom.

B. Collegiality and Civility Are Not Appropriate Independent Criteria for Evaluation

The academic imperative is to protect free expression, not collegiality. In keeping with the general admonition that evaluation should focus on professional fitness, the statement *On Collegiality as a Criterion for Faculty Evaluation* maintains that whatever is pertinent with regard to collegiality should emerge through an evaluation based on the standard considerations of teaching, scholarship, and service.

C. Consideration of Extramural Speech in Politically Controversial Personnel Decisions

1. Consideration of the manner of expression is rarely appropriate to an assessment of academic fitness.
2. An administration should not discipline a faculty member for an off-campus statement that the faculty member could freely make on campus.
3. We find no basis upon which an institution might properly discipline a faculty member for extramural speech unless that speech implicates professional fitness.
4. We recommend, therefore, that institutions be especially careful in bringing charges shortly after controversial extramural expression and that, should disciplinary hearings be found necessary, the administration, board, and faculty all take special care to ensure full, fair, and equitable proceedings and judgments.
5. Academic institutions should take special care to ensure that the sanctions resulting from judicial determinations of criminal activity involving expressive conduct are not unnecessarily compounded by institutional sanction: for faculty, as for students, institutional authority should never be used merely to duplicate the functions of general laws. If, however, institutions are legally compelled to take such action, or if the faculty committee considers it pertinent to an evaluation of professional fitness, then academic hearings should be confined to the issue of whether the alleged conduct has substantially impaired the professional fitness of the academic appointee.

D. Compelled Political Declarations: Loyalty Oaths and Disclaimers

A faculty member's principled refusal to sign a loyalty oath should not be a justifiable reason for not appointing a faculty member or for terminating an appointment.

E. Civil Disobedience

In matters involving civil disobedience, as in disciplinary or other personnel proceedings generally, assessment of a particular charge of misconduct should be considered in the light of the faculty member's professional record considered as a whole. Institutions should be similarly cautious about imposing sanctions on the basis of inferences about a controversial individual's supposed lack of remorse and possible future activities.

Procedural Safeguards Required in the Consideration of Politically Controversial Academic Personnel Decisions

A. Sound and Fair Policies and Procedures

The institution should have in place sound and fair procedures consistent with AAUP-recommended standards. Faculty members and administrators should be familiar with these procedures and understand the need to safeguard academic freedom.

B. Measures to Deter Political Intrusion into Routine Personnel Processes

1. Complaints regarding alleged classroom statements forwarded by outside agencies or individuals should be generally ruled out of consideration in initiating or conducting personnel reviews.
2. When complaints regarding alleged classroom speech arise from or are promoted by student political groups, the complaints should be respected only to the extent merited by the complaints and only when they are based on evidence from students who were actually enrolled in the course or courses in which the alleged inappropriate conduct occurred and who were present to observe that conduct.
3. Established policies should provide for thorough professional review and care in the selection of outside expert reviewers. In the event of politically controversial reviews, special care should be taken to ensure that those external and internal academics invited to provide a professional evaluation are able and willing to conduct a review without regard to political concerns and in keeping with appropriate scholarly and disciplinary standards.

C. Measures to Ensure Dispassionate Review in Passionate Circumstances

1. Although some institution-specific faculty review procedures, such as those for hearings on charges of professional misconduct or sexual harassment, may not call for this preliminary consultation, the AAUP generally considers that such a faculty review is necessary in all cases and is essential prior to the filing of charges in any case arising from or in the midst of a political controversy.
2. To the extent that members of a preliminary consultative or hearing committee believe the process is too hasty or ill-considered, or the outcome predetermined, they must explain their views in the advice they provide to the president and firmly recommend that, if the hearing goes forward despite their recommendation, the administration should defer the proceeding until it can occur free of undue political constraints or, failing this, at least without injudicious haste and with all the essential procedural safeguards. If, or to the extent that, the president proceeds regardless of this advice, the public nature of the decision to proceed should relieve the committee of any

impediment to explaining publicly its concerns to and requesting support from the faculty senate or other faculty governance body that has the responsibility to scrutinize the process and to ensure that the faculty member involved receives all the procedural protections required for safeguarding academic freedom.

D. Weighing Charges

In politically controversial cases, the need for specific charges narrowly formulated with "reasonable particularity" does not relieve the committee or the governing board of the responsibility to weigh these charges in the light of the faculty member's "entire record as a teacher and scholar" (1970 Interpretive Comment 4 on the 1940 *Statement of Principles*).

E. Composition of Academic Hearing Committees

1. It is essential that the hearing committee be elected by the faculty or appointed by an appropriate elected faculty body.
2. In rare cases, experts from outside the university may be appointed to a hearing committee. They could be designated jointly by the administration and the accused faculty member, chosen separately by them, selected by the hearing committee, or engaged through some combination of these methods at the committee's discretion.

F. Confidentiality and Transparency

1. The committee should give great weight to the preference of the faculty member in these circumstances, both as to the openness of the hearing and the right to speak publicly on the issues. Of course, if the faculty member speaks out publicly or insists on an open hearing, the committee and the administration have a right to respond. The deliberations of the committee should be conducted in private.
2. The governing board would be well advised to follow the advice of the faculty committee, particularly in politically controversial cases in which academic freedom is at stake. If, after such consideration, the board nonetheless reaches a determination contrary to the recommendations of the hearing committee or increases the severity of sanctions, the board must provide the faculty committee and the individual with written, detailed, and compelling reasons for reversing or substantially altering the committee's recommendation.

G. Ensuring Substantive Due Process

The decision should be one that an experienced, informed, and disinterested academic might reach on the basis of clear and convincing evidence and the academic principles at issue, even if it is not the only possible such decision.

H. Obligations of the Hearing Committee

1. In politically controversial dismissal cases, a written, reasoned opinion is essential.
2. Substantive due process requires that the written reasons resulting from such academic proceedings be consistent with the evidence and with sound academic principles.

I. Obligations of the Administration and the Governing Board

In those politically controversial cases in which a governing board exercises its extraordinary authority to reverse or substantially alter the faculty recommendation, it is also imperative that the board fully meet its obligation to provide written compelling reasons stated in detail. The board's reasoning must be consistent with the basic requirement that "[a]dequate cause for a dismissal will be related, directly and substantially, to the fitness of faculty members in their professional capacities as teachers or researchers. Dismissal will not be used to restrain faculty members in their exercise of academic freedom or other rights of American citizens" (Regulation 5a of the *Recommended Institutional Regulations on Academic Freedom and Tenure*[4]).

Notes

1. AAUP, *Policy Documents and Reports*, 11th ed. (Baltimore: Johns Hopkins University Press, 2015), 3–12.
2. *AAUP Bulletin* 42 (Spring, 1956): 49–107.
3. *Policy Documents and Reports*, 21.
4. Ibid., 83.

Academic Freedom and Outside Speakers

The statement that follows, prepared by a subcommittee of the Association's Committee A on Academic Freedom and Tenure, was approved for publication by Committee A in July 2007.

Incidents in which colleges and universities have rescinded invitations issued to outside speakers have multiplied in recent years. Because academic freedom requires the liberty to learn as well as to teach, colleges and universities should respect the prerogatives of campus organizations to select outside speakers whom they wish to hear. The AAUP articulated this principle in 1967 in its Fifty-Third Annual Meeting, when it affirmed "its belief that the freedom to hear is an essential condition of a university community and an inseparable part of academic freedom," and that "the right to examine issues and seek truth is prejudiced to the extent that the university is open to some but not to others whom members of the university also judge desirable to hear."[1]

This principle has come under growing pressure. Citing an inability to guarantee the safety of outside speakers, or the lack of balance represented by the invitation of a college or university group, or the danger that a group's invitation might violate Section 501(c)(3) of the Internal Revenue Code, college and university administrators have displayed an increasing tendency to cancel or to withdraw funding for otherwise legitimate invitations to non-campus speakers. Committee A notes with concern that these reasons for canceling outside speakers are subject to serious abuse, and that their proper application should be limited to very narrow circumstances that only rarely obtain. Applied promiscuously, these reasons undermine the right of campus groups to hear outside speakers and thus contradict the basic educational mission of colleges and universities.

It is of course the responsibility of a college or university to guarantee the safety of invited speakers, and administrators ought to make every effort to ensure conditions of security in which outside speakers have an opportunity to express their views. The university is no place for a heckler's veto. In 1983, when unruly individuals on various campuses prevented United States Ambassador to the United Nations Jeane Kirkpatrick from addressing university audiences, Committee A reaffirmed "its expectation that all members of the academic community will respect the right of others to listen to those who have been invited to speak on campus and will indicate disagreement not by disruptive action designed to silence the speaker but by reasoned debate and discussion as befits academic freedom in a community of higher learning."[2] We have always been clear that colleges and universities bear the obligation to ensure conditions of peaceful discussion, which at times can be quite onerous. Only in the most extraordinary circumstances can strong evidence of imminent danger justify rescinding an invitation to an outside speaker.

Colleges and universities have also withdrawn invitations to outside speakers on the ground that such invitations reflect a lack of balance. This objection misunderstands the meaning of balance within a university setting. In the context of teaching, balance refers to the obligation of instructors to convey to students the state of knowledge, as warranted by a professional community of inquirers, in the field of learning to which a given course is devoted. There is no obligation to present ideas about "intelligent design" in a biology course, for example, because those ideas have no standing in the professional community of biologists. If invitations to outside speakers are extended within the context of teaching, they should be consistent with the obligations of professionalism. They should not be subject to an additional standard of balance that does not reflect professional standards.

Most invitations to outside speakers do not concern professional pedagogy of this kind, but reflect instead the interests of specific campus groups that are authorized by colleges and universities to learn by pursuing their own particular extracurricular activities. Invitations of this kind may raise a question about the overall contours of a university's extracurricular programming, but they ought not to be evaluated on an invitation-by-invitation basis. The spectrum of extracurricular activities sponsored by a college or university should be evaluated on the basis of its educational justifiability, rather than on the basis of a mechanical standard of balance that does not reflect educational objectives. So long as the range of a university's extracurricular programming is educationally justifiable, the specific invitations of particular groups should not be vetoed by university administrators because these invitations are said to lack balance. Campus groups should not be prevented from pursuing the very interests that they have been created to explore.

University administrators have also rescinded invitations to outside speakers who are politically controversial on the ground that during an election such invitations would violate the prohibition of section 501(c)(3) of the Internal Revenue Code, which provides that a charitable organization will qualify for a tax exemption only if it "does not participate in, or intervene in (including the publishing or distributing of statements), any political campaign on behalf of (or in opposition to) any candidate for public office." Before the 2004 presidential election, some institutions withdrew or objected to invitations to speakers identified with partisan political positions, including Michael Moore, a filmmaker critical of the Bush administration. In some cases, the initial invitations were issued by student organizations; in other cases, they were by members of a faculty body or as part of an invited speaker series.

Committee A is concerned that overly restrictive interpretations of Section 501(c)(3) have become an excuse for preventing campus groups from inviting politically controversial speakers. As was stated by the AAUP's Fifty-Second Annual Meeting, "the right to access to speakers on campus does not in its exercise imply in advance either agreement or disagreement with what may be said, or approval or disapproval of the speakers as individuals."[3] The idea that a university "participates" or "intervenes" in a political campaign by providing a forum to hear speakers who have something to communicate about issues of relevance to the campaign is thus fundamentally misplaced. The idea misconceives

the role and responsibility of a university, which is not to endorse candidates but to discuss issues of relevance to society.

The essentially educational role of a university has been recognized by the Internal Revenue Service, which has held that activities which might otherwise constitute prohibited political activities are to be understood, in the context of a college or university, as furthering the institution's educational mission. For this reason, a course in political campaign methods that requires students to participate in political campaigns of candidates of their choice does not constitute participation in a political campaign by the institution.[4]

Similarly, providing office space, financial support, and a faculty advisor for a campus newspaper that publishes students' editorial opinions on political matters does not constitute an attempt by the university to participate in political campaigns on behalf of candidates for public office.[5] Instead, the Internal Revenue Service has viewed these types of activities as serving the university's tax-exempt educational purposes.

As part of their educational mission, colleges and universities provide a forum for a wide variety of speakers. There can be no more appropriate site for the discussion of controversial ideas and issues than a college or university campus. Candidates for public office may speak on campus, as may their supporters or opponents, so long as the institution does not administer its speakers program in a manner that constitutes intervention in a campaign. Invitations made to outside speakers by students or faculty do not imply approval or endorsement by the institution of the views expressed by the speaker. Consistent with the prohibition on political activities, colleges and universities can specify that no member of the academic community may speak for or act on behalf of the college or university in a political campaign. Institutions may also clearly affirm that sponsorship of a speaker or a forum does not constitute endorsement of the views expressed.

Notes

1. "Fifty-Third Annual Meeting," *AAUP Bulletin* 53 (June 1967): 133–35.
2. "Report of Committee A, 1982–83," *Academe* 69 (September–October 1983): 6a–13a.
3. "Fifty-Second Annual Meeting," *AAUP Bulletin* 52 (June 1966): 205–8.
4. Revenue Ruling 72-512, 1972-2 *Cumulative Bulletin* 246.
5. Ibid.

Statement on Professors and Political Activity

The statement that follows was prepared by a subcommittee of the Association's Committee A on Academic Freedom and Tenure and approved by Committee A. It was adopted by the Association's Council in May 1969 and endorsed by the Fifty-Fifth Annual Meeting. It was endorsed in 1970 by the Association of American Colleges (now the Association of American Colleges and Universities). The governing bodies of the two associations, meeting in November 1989 and January 1990, respectively, eliminated five introductory paragraphs that were no longer applicable.

Introduction

The institutional regulations of many colleges and universities govern the participation of professors in political activity and public office holding. These regulations vary from absolute prohibitions against holding public office, campaigning for public office, or participating in the management of political campaigns, to requirements that professors engaging in such political activities merely inform administrative authorities in the college or university of their activities.

In view of the range and variety of institutional and legislative restrictions on political activities of professors, the American Association of University Professors and the Association of American Colleges believe there is a need for a definition of rights and obligations in this area. The following statement is offered as a guide to practice. It is hoped that colleges and universities will formulate and publish regulations consistent with these principles.

Statement

1. College and university faculty members are citizens, and, like other citizens, should be free to engage in political activities so far as they are able to do so consistently with their obligations as teachers and scholars.
2. Many kinds of political activity (e.g., holding part-time office in a political party, seeking election to any office under circumstances that do not require extensive campaigning, or serving by appointment or election in a part-time political office) are consistent with effective service as members of a faculty. Other kinds of political activity (e.g., intensive campaigning for elective office, serving in a state legislature, or serving a limited term in a full-time position) will often require that professors seek a leave of absence from their college or university.
3. In recognition of the legitimacy and social importance of political activity by professors universities and colleges should provide institutional arrangements to permit it, similar to those applicable to other public or private extramural service. Such arrangements may include the reduction of the faculty member's workload or a leave of absence for the duration of an election campaign or a term of office, accompanied by equitable adjustment of compensation when necessary.
4. Faculty members seeking leaves should recognize that they have a primary obligation to their institution and to their growth as educators and scholars; they should be mindful of the problem which a leave of absence can create for their administration, their colleagues, and their students; and they should not abuse the privilege by too frequent or too late application or too extended a leave. If adjustments in their favor are made, such as reduction of workload, they should expect the adjustments to be limited to a reasonable period.
5. A leave of absence incident to political activity should come under the institution's normal rules and regulations for leaves of absence. Such a leave should not affect unfavorably the tenure status of a faculty member, except that time spent on such leave from academic duties need not count as probationary service. The terms of a leave and its effect on the professor's status should be set forth in writing.

Academic Freedom and Artistic Expression

The statement that follows was adopted by the participants in the 1990 Wolf Trap Conference on Academic Freedom and Artistic Expression, sponsored by the American Association of University Professors, the American Council on Education, the Association of Governing Boards of Universities and Colleges, and the Wolf Trap Foundation. The statement was endorsed by the AAUP's Committee A on Academic Freedom and Tenure and by its Council at their meetings in June 1990.

Attempts to curtail artistic presentations at academic institutions on grounds that the works are offensive to some members of the campus community and of the general public occur with disturbing frequency. Those who support restrictions argue that works presented to the public rather than in the classroom or in other entirely intramural settings should conform to their view of the prevailing community standard rather than to standards of academic freedom. We believe that, "essential as freedom is for the relation and judgment of facts, it is even more indispensable to the imagination."[1] In our judgment academic freedom in the creation and presentation of works in the visual and the performing arts, by ensuring greater opportunity for imaginative exploration and expression, best serves the public and the academy.

The following proposed policies are designed to assist academic institutions to respond to the issues that may arise from the presentation of artistic works to the public and to do so in a manner that preserves academic freedom:

1. *Academic Freedom in Artistic Expression.* Faculty members and students engaged in the creation and presentation of works of the visual and the performing arts are as much engaged in pursuing the mission of the college or university as are those who write, teach, and study in other academic disciplines. Works of the visual and the performing arts are important both in their own right and because they can enhance our understanding of social institutions and the human condition. Artistic expression in the classroom, the studio, and the workshop therefore merits the same assurance of academic freedom that is accorded to other scholarly and teaching activities. Since faculty and student artistic presentations to the public are integral to their teaching, learning, and scholarship, these presentations merit no

less protection. Educational and artistic criteria should be used by all who participate in the selection and presentation of artistic works. Reasonable content-neutral regulation of the "time, place, and manner" of presentations should be developed and maintained. Academic institutions are obliged to ensure that regulations and procedures do not impair freedom of expression or discourage creativity by subjecting artistic work to tests of propriety or ideology.

2. *Accountability.* Artistic performances and exhibitions in academic institutions encourage artistic creativity, expression, learning, and appreciation. The institutions do not thereby endorse the specific artistic presentations, nor do the presentations necessarily represent the institution. This principle of institutional neutrality does not relieve institutions of general responsibility for maintaining professional and educational standards, but it does mean that institutions are not responsible for the views or the attitudes expressed in specific artistic works any more than they would be for the content of other instruction, scholarly publication, or invited speeches. Correspondingly, those who present artistic work should not represent themselves or their work as speaking for the institution and should otherwise fulfill their educational and professional responsibilities.

3. *The Audience.* When academic institutions offer exhibitions or performances to the public, they should ensure that the rights of the presenters and of the audience are not impaired by a "heckler's veto" from those who may be offended by the presentation. Academic institutions should ensure that those who choose to view an exhibition or attend a performance may do so without interference.

Mere presentation in a public place does not create a "captive audience." Institutions may reasonably designate specific places as generally available or unavailable for exhibitions or performances.

4. *Public Funding.* Public funding for artistic presentations and for academic institutions does not diminish (and indeed may heighten) the responsibility of the university community to ensure academic freedom and of the public to respect the integrity of academic institutions. Government imposition on artistic expression of a test of propriety, ideology, or religion is an act of censorship which impermissibly denies the academic freedom to explore, to teach, and to learn.

Note

1. Helen C. White, "Our Most Urgent Professional Task," *AAUP Bulletin* 45 (March 1959): 282.

Academic Freedom and Electronic Communications

This report was prepared by a subcommittee of the Association's Committee A on Academic Freedom and Tenure and initially published in 1997. A revised text was approved by Committee A and adopted by the Association's Council in November 2004. A revised and expanded text was approved by Committee A and adopted by the Association's Council in November 2013.

In November 2004, the Association's Council adopted *Academic Freedom and Electronic Communications*,[1] a report prepared by a subcommittee of Committee A on Academic Freedom and Tenure and approved by Committee A. That report affirmed one "overriding principle":

> Academic freedom, free inquiry, and freedom of expression within the academic community may be limited to no greater extent in electronic format than they are in print, save for the most unusual situation where the very nature of the medium itself might warrant unusual restrictions—and even then only to the extent that such differences demand exceptions or variations. Such obvious differences between old and new media as the vastly greater speed of digital communication, and the far wider audiences that electronic messages may reach, would not, for example, warrant any relaxation of the rigorous precepts of academic freedom.

This fundamental principle still applies, but developments since publication of the 2004 report suggest that a fresh review of issues raised by the continuing growth and transformation of electronic-communications technologies and the evolution of law in this area is appropriate. For instance, the 2004 report focused largely on issues associated with e-mail communications and the posting of materials on websites, online bulletin boards, learning-management systems, blogs, and listservs. Since then, new social media, such as Facebook, LinkedIn, Reddit, Tumblr, and Twitter, have emerged as important vehicles for electronic communication in the academy.

Already in 2004 it was clear that electronic communications could easily be forwarded to others at vastly greater speeds, with potentially profound implications for both privacy and free expression. As Robert M. O'Neil has written, "An electronic message may instantly reach readers across the country and indeed around the globe,

in sharp contrast to any form of print communication. Although a digital message, once posted, can be infinitely altered over time—another significant difference—the initial message may never be retracted once it has been sent or posted. Indeed, the first posting may remain accessible on 'mirror' sites despite all efforts to suppress, remove, and expunge it."[2] Electronic communications can be altered, or presented selectively, such that they are decontextualized and take on implicit meanings different from their author's original intent. With the advent of social media such concerns about the widespread circulation and compromised integrity of communications that in print might have been essentially private have only multiplied further.

Moreover, while the 2004 report assumed that electronic communications produced by faculty members in the course of their teaching and research were physically located on servers and computers owned and operated by their colleges and universities, today institutions increasingly employ technologies associated with cloud computing and other outsourcing strategies. These may involve relinquishing control to third-party services, storing data at multiple sites administered by several organizations, and relying on multiple services across the network—a shift that poses potentially profound challenges to academic freedom.

These changes have been magnified by the growing proliferation of new electronic-communications devices, such as smartphones and tablets. At Oakland University in Michigan, for example, the university's roughly 7,500 students now bring an average of 2.5 devices each to campus, while faculty members bring about two.[3] The desire of growing numbers of faculty members, staff members, and students to have access to communications and information on multiple devices, especially mobile devices, has increasingly driven institutions to create "BYOD" (bring-your-own-device) policies. By embracing individual consumer devices, an institution may better address the personal preferences of its faculty, staff, and students, offering not only increased mobility but also increased integration of their personal, work, and study lives. However, the increasing number of devices and the increasing demand for bandwidth from new applications may strain institutional resources in ways that might lead institutions to establish access restrictions that could adversely affect academic freedom.

More important, such practices can further blur boundaries between communications activities that are primarily extramural or personal and those that are related more directly to teaching and scholarship. Digital devices such as smartphones have also promoted increased interactivity between users and their devices, permitting users to create their own content but also to leave personal "footprints," which might be subject to surveillance.

As in 2004, "college and university policies that were developed for print and telephonic communications"—and policies developed for earlier modes of electronic communications—"may simply not fit (or may fit imperfectly) the new environment." *Faculty members need to understand more completely the implications for academic freedom of electronic-communications technologies, and they should be directly involved in the formulation and implementation of policies governing such technology usage.*

I. Freedom of Research and Publication

The 2004 report affirmed: "The basic precept in the 1940 *Statement of Principles on Academic Freedom and Tenure* that 'teachers are entitled to full freedom in research and in the publication of the results' applies with no less force to the use of electronic media for the conduct of research and the dissemination of findings and results than it applies to the use of more traditional media." As that report noted, however, access to materials in digital format may be subject to greater restrictions than would be the case with print-format materials.

A. Access to Information in Digital Format

Academic freedom is dependent on a researcher's ability not only to gain access to information but also to explore ideas and knowledge without fear of surveillance or interference. Historically, scholars have gained access to published and often to unpublished research materials through college and university libraries. Electronic-communications technologies have permitted

many libraries to offer access to a far broader array of materials than in the past through a wide variety of online databases. Some online catalogs, designed to replicate social media, now allow users to leave notations and reviews of cataloged materials that can be viewed around the world.

To be sure, as O'Neil has noted, "[a]lthough a university does to some degree control a scholar's recourse to print materials by its management of library collections, . . . the potential for limitation or denial of access is vastly greater when the institution maintains and therefore controls the gateway to the Internet."[4] Colleges and universities certainly are entitled to restrict access to their library resources, including electronic resources, to faculty members, staff members, students, and other authorized users, such as alumni and recognized scholars from other institutions, in accordance with policies adopted by the institution with the participation of the faculty. But the extent to which access to electronic materials may be limited is not always under the control of the library or even of the institution. Third-party vendors may seek to impose restrictions on access that go beyond those claimed by the institution itself, and such restrictions are rarely defined by faculty governance structures. Those vendors may also impose auditing requirements that are in tension with librarians' obligations to respect the confidentiality of patrons.

Concerns about access were heightened in early 2013 following the tragic suicide of open-access advocate Aaron Swartz. In 2011, a federal grand jury had indicted Swartz for the theft of millions of journal articles through the JSTOR account of the Massachusetts Institute of Technology. It was thought that Swartz had wanted to make all of those articles freely available. Authorities charged him with having used an MIT guest account, even though he did not have a legal right to do so. At the time of his death, Swartz faced millions of dollars in fines and legal costs and decades in prison if convicted. He reportedly had suffered from depression, but there was speculation that his legal troubles led to his suicide.

Although JSTOR declined to pursue action against Swartz, some charged that "MIT refused to stand up for Aaron and its own community's most cherished principles."[5] Ironically, however, it was MIT's relatively open policy of access to its network that enabled Swartz to obtain the downloaded materials. In its own subsequent investigation of the matter, MIT acknowledged that it had missed an opportunity to emerge as a leader in the national discussion on law and the

Internet. But the university denied having had any active role in his prosecution.[6]

Scholars have also debated whether Swartz's action was actually a kind of theft. "The 'property' Aaron had 'stolen,' we were told, was worth 'millions of dollars,'" wrote Harvard law professor Lawrence Lessig, "with the hint, and then the suggestion, that his aim must have been to profit from his crime. But anyone who says that there is money to be made in a stash of academic articles is either an idiot or a liar."[7]

The complicated copyright and other issues raised by the open-access movement are beyond the scope of this report. While the digital world has offered great promise to make information accessible to a global community, commercial forces have locked up most research behind paywalls and ever-more-restrictive licensing agreements. Faculty members who produce research in digital form frequently do not control how that research may be accessed and by whom. The AAUP's *Statement on Copyright* affirmed that "it has been the prevailing academic practice to treat the faculty member as the copyright owner of works that are created independently and at the faculty member's own initiative for traditional academic purposes."[8] Any consideration of open access must start from this principle.[9]

Often college and university libraries are themselves compelled to accede to the demands of outside vendors. Libraries and librarians can, however, promote open access to information by supporting institutional repositories, hosting open-access journals, and working with faculty members to promote the value of more open modes of scholarly communication. Libraries may also collaborate with others or work independently to develop a role as publisher both for new content and through digitization of material that is in the public domain or otherwise lawfully available for digitization.[10]

When resources are provided by third-party vendors, the library may also lose control over privacy and confidentiality. When a faculty member visits the library to read a book or a journal article, this activity takes place without triggering any recordkeeping or permissions issues. In the electronic journal and e-book environment, however, records of access and permissions may be critical to resolving issues concerning licensing and copyright infringement, and the existence of such records may compromise user confidentiality. Sometimes the identity of a person reading a resource is even embedded—both electronically and in text—in the journal article. Such features may violate state laws protecting the confidentiality of library circulation records.

The commitment of libraries and librarians to maximizing access to information and protecting user privacy and confidentiality should not change in the face of new technologies. The maintenance of usage logs for licensing reasons, for diagnosing technical problems, or for monitoring computer performance may be necessary, but libraries must strive to minimize such monitoring and to compile information as much as possible only in the aggregate. So, for example, when the library identifies a user as authorized to gain access to a journal held by another entity, it should indicate that the user is affiliated with the institution without sharing that user's identity.

Nevertheless, third-party vendors may gain access to user information, especially when these vendors offer research tools such as customized portals, saved searches, or e-mail alerts on research topics. How these vendors employ such information and who can gain access to it may be beyond the library's control. Librarians thus have a responsibility to educate users about the potential risks of using third-party tools.

Faculty members can also play a role in shaping the policies of publishers and online vendors regarding access to published research and monitoring of individual users through their roles as members of editorial boards and holders of managerial positions in academic societies and with private publishers. Faculty members in these positions can work with academic libraries to collaborate on cost-effective business models that encourage broad and confidential access to publications.

College and university libraries need to review existing policies on privacy and confidentiality to ensure that they have kept pace with practices and technologies in the library.[11] In addition, when negotiating contracts with vendors, librarians should require those vendors to protect user information to the same degree as if it were in the custody of a library. And, building on the success of laws in forty-eight states that protect the confidentiality of library users, as well as provisions of the Family Educational Rights and Privacy Act that protect the privacy of educational records, colleges and universities should advocate additional legislation that would provide the same level of protection to information held by third parties on behalf of libraries and their users, whether it is library-controlled information hosted on a server in another state, cloud-hosted information, or user-supplied information in a vendor's customizable portal.

The 2004 report noted that "in many disciplines, scholars may quite legitimately share material that would be deemed 'sexually explicit'—art, anatomy, psychology, etc. Such sharing is at least as likely to occur electronically as it has traditionally occurred in print. The difference in medium should no more affect the validity of such exchanges than it should justify a double standard elsewhere." AAUP policy elsewhere recognizes that academic freedom includes freedom of artistic expression "in visual and performing arts."[12] Increasingly, artistic expression that challenges conventional tastes and norms involves digital images, even more than images on canvas and film, or dance. It is thus vital to affirm that academic freedom applies to such novel modes of artistic expression as well as to traditional media. Nonetheless, the 2004 report on electronic communications noted that there may "be legitimate institutional interests in restricting the range of persons eligible to receive and gain access to such material—especially to ensure that minors are not targeted."

Although in 1968 the US Supreme Court recognized that material that is not legally obscene but is "harmful to minors" may be regulated, subsequent rulings have severely limited the application of this principle when it might affect access to such material by adults.[13] In this light, *institutional policy should make clear that faculty members in the course of their research have the right to gain access to and circulate electronically all legal materials, no matter how controversial, even if these might be considered "harmful to minors."*

In particular, colleges and universities should refrain from employment of so-called "filtering" software that limits access to allegedly "harmful" or even "controversial" materials. It is questionable whether such filters are appropriate or effective in school and public libraries, but they surely have no place in higher education facilities. Filters are especially insidious because users often cannot know whether they have been denied access to a site or resource.

B. Security versus Access

In recent years many university information-technology (IT) systems have come under sustained cyberattack, often from overseas. While these attacks have sometimes resulted in the theft of personal information, such as employee social security numbers, they also target faculty research materials, including patentable research, some with vast potential value, in areas as disparate as prescription drugs, computer chips, fuel cells, aircraft, and medical devices. Institu-

tions' infrastructure more generally has also been under threat. Some universities have experienced as many as one hundred thousand hacking attempts each day.[14]

The increased threat of hacking has forced many universities to rethink the basic structure of their computer networks. "A university environment is very different from a corporation or a government agency, because of the kind of openness and free flow of information you're trying to promote," said David J. Shaw, the chief information security officer at Purdue University. "The researchers want to collaborate with others, inside and outside the university, and to share their discoveries."[15]

While many corporate sites restrict resources to employees, university systems tend to be more open, and properly so. The most sensitive data can be housed in the equivalent of small vaults that are less accessible and harder to navigate, use sophisticated data encryption, and sometimes are not even connected to the larger campus network, particularly when the work involves dangerous pathogens or research that could turn into weapons systems.

Some universities no longer allow their professors to take laptops owned or leased by the university to certain countries. In some countries the minute one connects to a network, all data will be copied, or a program or virus will be planted on the computer in hopes that it will be transferred to a home network. Many institutions have become stricter about urging faculty members to follow federal rules that prohibit taking some kinds of sensitive data out of the country or have imposed their own tighter restrictions. Still others require that employees returning from abroad have their computers scrubbed by professionals before they may regain access to university servers.

These are genuine concerns, and universities are well advised to devote resources to protecting their electronic-communications networks. However, every effort should also be made to balance the need for security with the fundamental principles of open scholarly communication.

C. Scholarly Communication and Social Media

The advent of social media has raised some new questions about how scholars communicate about their research. For example, professors who present papers at scholarly conferences often use those occasions to try out new ideas and stimulate discussion. While they may be willing, even eager, to share unpolished or preliminary ideas with a closed group of peers, they may be less happy to have those in attendance broadcast these ideas through social media. Conference papers are often clearly labeled as "not for circulation." At some meetings, however, attendees at sessions have communicated to others electronically—and often instantaneously—through social media, e-mail, or blogs, reports and comments on papers and statements made by other conference presenters and attendees.[16]

Many academic conferences and some individual sessions have associated Twitter hash tags—at times suggested by the conference organizers. As a result, ideas and information that previously would have been controlled by the presenter and limited to a relatively small audience may quickly become accessible globally. Some have worried that reports on social media of conference proceedings might increase the likelihood that others could appropriate a presenter's new and original ideas before that individual has had an opportunity to develop them. While the concern may be speculative and the risk exaggerated, it is clear that new forms of social media and electronic-communications technologies can make research in progress both more accessible and more vulnerable to intellectual property theft. In effect, anyone with an Internet connection can function as a reporter publishing accounts of others' work.

"The debate over live tweeting at conferences is, in many ways, about control and access: who controls conference space, presentation content, or access to knowledge?" wrote one doctoral student. A professor responded with objections to sharing "other people's work without asking." For some the debate is generational. "I see this as a divide between older and newer forms of academic culture," wrote one younger scholar. "On the traditional model, you don't put an idea out there until it's fully formed and perfect."[17]

Of course, scholars have always debated each other's ideas and will continue to do so. However, *faculty members who use social media to discuss research should keep in mind the intellectual property rights of their colleagues as well as their own academic freedom to comment on and debate new ideas.*

II. Freedom of Teaching
According to the 1940 *Statement of Principles,* "teachers are entitled to freedom in the classroom in discussing their subject." But what constitutes a classroom? The 2004 report noted that "the concept of 'classroom' must be broadened" to reflect how instruction increasingly occurs through a "medium that clearly has no physical boundaries" and that "the 'classroom' must indeed encompass all sites where learning occurs."

If anything, the boundaries of the "classroom" have only expanded in the ensuing period. It is now more common than not for even the most traditional face-to-face classes to include material offered through online learning-management systems. And the rapid development and perhaps overhyped promise of totally online education, including the explosive growth of Massive Open Online Courses (MOOCs) frequently offered by for-profit private corporations, suggest that academic freedom in the online classroom is no less critical than it is in the traditional classroom.

This report is not the place to discuss all the myriad issues of academic freedom, shared governance, intellectual property, and institutional finances raised by the spread of online education. It is critical, however, to reiterate that *a classroom is not simply a physical space, but any location, real or virtual, in which instruction occurs and that in classrooms of all types the protections of academic freedom and of the faculty's rights to intellectual property in lectures, syllabi, exams, and similar materials are as applicable as they have been in the physical classroom.*

In August 2013, the administration reassigned the teaching duties of a tenured professor in Michigan after a student anonymously videotaped part of a ninety-minute lecture, a heavily edited two-minute version of which—described by some as an "anti-Republican rant"—was then aired on a conservative Internet site, on Fox News, and on YouTube, where it was viewed more than 150,000 times. In October 2013, a Wisconsin geography professor sent her students an e-mail message explaining that they could not gain access to census data to complete a required assignment because the "Republican/Tea Party–controlled House of Representatives" had shut down the government, thus closing the Census Bureau's website. After a student posted the message on Twitter, it appeared in a local newspaper and in national conservative media, resulting in numerous complaints to the university, which sent an e-mail message to the campus distancing the institution from the comment.[18]

These and similar incidents demonstrate that electronic media can expand the boundaries of the classroom in new and dramatic ways. And while classroom lectures, syllabi, and even an instructor's e-mail messages to students should be considered the intellectual property of the instructor, much of what teachers distribute to students in the classroom or write in e-mail messages may legally be redistributed by students for noncommercial uses under the "fair-use" principle. Moreover, copyright does not cover expression that is not reduced to "tangible" form, including extemporaneous utterances such as those of the Michigan professor, as it might in the case of a formal lecture, a PowerPoint presentation, or written material like a syllabus.

Surreptitious recording of classroom speech and activity may exert a chilling effect on the academic freedom of both professors and students.[19] Faculty also should be aware that electronic communications with students can easily be recirculated without the permission of either party.

It should be further noted that new teaching technologies and learning-management systems also allow faculty members and students to be monitored in new ways. Online teaching platforms and learning-management systems may permit faculty members to learn whether students in a class did their work and how long they spent on certain assignments. Conversely, however, a college or university administration could use these systems to determine whether faculty members were logging into the service "enough," spending "adequate" time on certain activities, and the like. Such monitoring should not be permitted without the explicit and voluntary permission of the instructor involved.

Some thorny issues also surround the proliferating use of plagiarism-detection software, such as Turnitin. The benefits (and limitations) of such services are often obvious, but many faculty members are unaware that these services keep databases of student papers, and although these papers apparently are not sold individually, the entire database can be and has been sold to third parties. This practice may raise copyright concerns beyond the scope of this report, but as one 2011 study concluded, it also raises "ethical issues because it denies students notice, access, and choice about the treatment of their personal information." That study proposed a "code of ethics" concerning the use of such services that faculty members may find helpful.[20]

While learning-management systems make it possible for faculty members to keep electronic teaching materials separate from scholarly, political, or personal materials often found on faculty websites, many instructors still frequently post course materials on websites alongside other content, some of which may be controversial. Students who encounter material they find disturbing while they are browsing through a faculty member's website in search of course materials may complain to the administration or even to the courts. While all legal material on faculty websites should enjoy the protections of academic freedom, instructors should exercise

care when posting material for courses on sites that also include potentially controversial noninstructional materials.

III. Access to Electronic-Communications Technologies

Colleges and universities commonly adopt formal electronic-communications policies, which define access to the institution's electronic-communications network and, through that network, to the Internet. Such policies generally try to balance the need, on the one hand, to protect the university's electronic resources from outside hacking and to safeguard confidential personal and research information and, on the other hand, to provide free access to authorized users. *Although security and liability concerns may result in legitimate constraints being placed on usage, in general no conditions or restrictions should be imposed on access to and use of electronic-communications technologies more stringent than limits that have been found acceptable for the use of traditional campus channels of communication.*

An institution may, for example, acceptably require each faculty user to obtain and enter a password or to change that password periodically. The university also has an interest in protecting its faculty, staff, and students from spam and in limiting how much bandwidth an individual may use to ensure that computing resources are not overburdened or squandered. However, wholesale bans on streaming video may constitute a violation of academic freedom. Some institutions have imposed limitations on access to streaming video and audio in student dormitories, both to prevent illegal downloading of copyrighted material and to avoid overburdening the network. But such efforts should not be extended to faculty members, who may need access to such sites and materials for their teaching or research. Moreover, restrictions that deny use for "personal matters" or limit usage to "official university business" can reduce productivity and are both unnecessary and problematic, as many private businesses have learned.

In an often well-intentioned effort to reduce spam and prevent the monopolization of bandwidth, some university IT offices have proposed policies under which users of institutional electronic-communications resources must seek advance permission to send messages to large groups of recipients. But even if such measures address the problems of spam and limited bandwidth—and it is questionable whether they do—they only create a much larger and more ominous academic freedom problem because they amount to de facto prior censorship. Similarly, provisions that have been proposed in some instances to bar communications that purportedly "interfere with the mission of the university" or that violate university policies amount to unwarranted censorship of free expression.

Some states have also barred public employees, including faculty members at public colleges and universities, from employing university electronic-communications resources—for example, a university e-mail account—for political campaigning. In such states, public colleges and universities must clearly define what constitutes such activity. While a public employee may reasonably be barred, for instance, from using a university website to run for public office or raise funds for a campaign, policies that discourage or prohibit, either explicitly or through imprecise or ill-defined language, faculty members, staff members, and students from expressing political preferences clearly violate fundamental principles of academic freedom and free expression.

Electronic resources should also be made available equally to all employees, including faculty members, for the purposes of union or other organizing activity. While the National Labor Relations Board has ruled that private employers may bar employees from using employer-owned e-mail accounts for non-work-related communications, if they do permit such activity they may not discriminate against union-related e-mail use nor can they bar the use of social media for discussion of working conditions.[21] Similarly, senate officers and other faculty representatives engaged in institutional governance activities should have free and unfettered access to university-controlled lists of faculty members they represent, and all faculty members should be able to comment electronically on governance issues without restriction or fear of disciplinary action.

In one 2014 incident, a faculty member in Colorado sent an e-mail message protesting proposed layoffs of faculty at his institution that offered a comparison with the 1914 Ludlow Massacre of striking Colorado miners. The university swiftly terminated the professor's access to the institution's e-mail system, charging that the message in question amounted to a violent threat. Although the administration later restored access, the faculty member's ability to distribute messages on listservs remained severely restricted. While institutions clearly have an obligation to protect members of the community from genuine threats of violence, overbroad interpretations of messages as constituting such

threats, as was surely the case in this instance, can violate academic freedom, especially if the accused is denied the protections of academic due process before any adverse action has been taken.[22]

The AAUP has upheld the right of faculty members to speak freely about internal college or university affairs as a fundamental principle of academic freedom that applies as much to electronic communications as it does to written and oral ones. This includes the right of faculty members to communicate with one another about their conditions of employment and to organize on their own behalf.

Frequently university policies attempt to delineate user "rights" and "responsibilities," but too often the emphasis of those policies is mainly on the latter. Administrations at some institutions appear to view computer and Internet access as a lower-order faculty perquisite that may be summarily terminated. Such views need to be rejected unequivocally. Access to campus computing facilities, and through them to the Internet, represents a vital component of faculty status for most scholars and teachers, especially as cost-cutting measures have caused libraries to rely more heavily on electronic instead of print journals. While it would be naive to suggest that circumstances might never warrant withdrawal or suspension of digital access, such access may be denied or limited only for the most serious of reasons (for example, creating and unleashing a destructive virus) and only after the filing of formal charges and compliance with rigorous disciplinary procedures that guarantee the protections of academic due process to the accused individual, even where the transgression may not be so grave as to warrant dismissal or suspension.

A university's policies must specify the infractions that might warrant such a sanction, recognizing only conduct that jeopardizes the system and the access of others. The policy should also prescribe the procedures to be followed in such a case. In exigent circumstances, a faculty member's computer access might be summarily and briefly suspended during an investigation of serious charges of abuse or misuse. Any such suspension should, however, be no longer than necessary to conduct the investigation and should be subject to prior internal faculty review.[23]

Indeed, *any restrictions that an institution may need to impose on access and usage must be narrowly defined and clearly and precisely stated in writing.* In addition, institutions should include in their electronic-communications policy a statement similar to that found in the University of California policy: "In general, the University cannot and does not wish to be the arbiter of the contents of electronic communications. Neither can the University always protect users from receiving electronic messages they might find offensive."[24]

IV. Outsourcing of Information Technology Resources

Many campuses have considered outsourcing the provision of noninstructional IT resources, such as e-mail servers and document storage. Outsourcing to a technology company can provide advantages to institutions, including lower cost and potentially better security, and help an institution focus on its core mission of education instead of on the provision of services.[25] Prior to the cloud outsourcing model, institutions operated in-house technical resources, and the information generated by their use remained within the confines of the institution. In many cloud models, however, it is assumed, sometimes without explicitly stating so, that the outside service provider can analyze how these resources are used for the provider's own benefit. Thus cloud services proceed from a fundamentally different set of assumptions from those that govern the same services that are provided in-house at institutions.

Electronic communications are vulnerable to a variety of threats. They may contain private or confidential information concerning the development of new drugs, classified research, export-controlled research, and advice to clients visiting institutionally operated legal clinics. They may be targets of government surveillance. Institutions also have special duties, including legal and ethical obligations, among others, to protect information about students.

Outsourcing presents several identifiable risks. Outsource providers may be motivated to offer services that they can develop and serve "at scale" and that do not require special protocols. These services may have been designed for businesses, and thus employees and the services themselves may not be tailored to the special context of higher education. In effect, outsourcing may undermine governance, as the provider may effectively set and change policy without consulting campus IT leadership or the faculty.[26]

Several approaches can strengthen an institution's posture on and commitment to academic freedom even in outsourced situations:

1. Institutions should formally involve the faculty in decisions to outsource core electronic-communications technologies.
2. The selection of an outsource provider must take into consideration other factors besides price, including institutional needs, legal and ethical obligations, and the norms and mission of the institution.
3. IT leadership should carefully evaluate the outsource provider's ability to gain access to content and traffic data. It is important to note that even if a provider promises not to circulate usage data to advertisers, that promise does not foreclose the analysis of electronic-communications data for other purposes, including commercial ones.
4. Faculty members should encourage campus IT leadership to collaborate with other institutions in jointly identifying problems and mitigating risks.
5. IT leadership should carefully evaluate the outside provider's uses, processing, and analysis of user content and transactional data. All uses of data should be reviewed by the institution and specifically authorized.
6. IT leadership should follow policy decisions and changes of outsource providers and notify faculty members when these decisions implicate governance issues.
7. IT leadership should consider technical approaches to reduce "vendor lock-in" and, where possible, to mask content and traffic data from these providers.
8. Contracts with outside vendors of electronic-communications services should explicitly reflect and be consistent with both internal institutional policies regarding such communications and applicable federal and state laws.

V. Unwarranted Inference of Speaking for or Representing the Institution

The 1940 *Statement of Principles* cautions that faculty members "should make every effort to indicate that they are not speaking for the institution" when in fact they are not doing so. The meaning of that constraint is clear enough in the print world. One may refer to one's faculty position and institution "for identification purposes only" in ways that create no tenable inference of institutional attribution. In the digital world, however, avoiding an inappropriate or unwarranted inference may be more difficult.

The very nature of the Internet causes attribution to be decontextualized. A statement made by a faculty member on a website or through e-mail or social media may be recirculated broadly, and any disclaimer that the institution bears no responsibility for the statement may be lost. What about statements made on Twitter, which limits communications to a mere 140 characters? It is hardly reasonable to expect a faculty member to indicate on every tweet that she or he is not speaking for the institution. And Facebook pages are part of a fixed template that does not allow for a banner disclaimer in a readily visible spot on an individual's main page.

In late 2012, a Florida professor posted on his blog a controversial statement expressing skepticism about official accounts concerning the murder of students at Sandy Hook Elementary School in Connecticut that year. The blog included this statement: "All items published herein represent the views of [the professor] and are not representative of or condoned by [the university]." Yet the administration claimed that even by mentioning his affiliation the professor had failed to distinguish adequately his personal views from those of the university and thereby damaged the institution. As a result, he was issued a formal reprimand.[27]

In a letter to the university president, the AAUP staff wrote that the professor "may indeed have posted highly controversial statements on his website; but it is such speech, in particular, that requires the protection of academic freedom. . . . In our time, when the Internet has become an increasingly important vehicle for free intellectual and political discourse around the world, the [university] administration's action, if allowed to stand, sets a precedent that potentially chills the spirited exchange of ideas—however unpopular, offensive, or controversial—that the academic community has a special responsibility to protect."

Institutions may reasonably take steps to avoid inferences of institutional attribution or agreement in ways that print communications might not warrant. Disclaimers may be useful, though their value is often exaggerated. However, the nature of electronic communication itself tends to decontextualize meaning and attribution, and *faculty members cannot be held responsible for always indicating that they are speaking as individuals and not in the name of their institution, especially if doing so will place an undue burden on the faculty member's ability to express views in electronic media.*

VI. Social Media

The 2004 report essentially assumed that electronic communications were either personal (if not wholly private), as with e-mail messages, or public (or open access), as with websites, blogs, or faculty home pages. The growth of social media calls such a distinction into question.

Faculty use of social media is increasing. In one survey of eight thousand faculty members, 70 percent of all those responding reported having visited a social-media site within the previous

month for personal use, a rate that rose to 84 percent when those who use social-media sites less frequently than monthly are added. Of greater relevance to the concerns of this report, more than 55 percent said they had made professional use of social media outside the classes they teach on at least a monthly basis, and 41 percent reported having used social media in their teaching.[28]

Social-media sites blur the distinction between private and public communications in new ways. Unlike blogs or websites, which are generally accessible to anyone with Internet access who goes in search of the site, social-media sites offer the appearance of a space that is simultaneously private and public, one that is on a public medium (the Internet) and yet defined by the user through invitation-only entry points, such as Facebook "friend" requests, and a range of user-controlled privacy settings.

The extent of the privacy of such sites, however, is at the least uncertain and limited, because it is dependent not only on the individual's privacy-setting choices and those of the members in the individual's network but also on the service provider's practices of analyzing data posted on the network. Moreover, social-media providers often modify their policies on privacy and access in ways that their users do not always fully comprehend. Faculty members may believe that their Facebook pages are more secure or private than a personal web page, but that is not necessarily true. The seemingly private nature of sites like Facebook, Flickr, or Pinterest can lead individuals to let their guard down more readily, because they may think they are communicating only to handpicked friends and family members, when in fact those friends and family members may be sharing their utterances with other unintended recipients without the individual's knowledge.[29] These sites are not closed portals, despite what their account controls may suggest. Likewise, an acquaintance may post private information about a faculty member's personal life without that faculty member's knowledge (or vice versa), and the viral nature of social-media sites may then make that comment more public than the original poster intended.

There is evidence that such concerns are not unwarranted. One prominent example was the 2010 case of a Pennsylvania professor who was suspended from her faculty position and escorted off campus by police after a student reported to the administration one of her Facebook status updates ("Had a good day today. Didn't want to kill even one student."). The professor alleged that she did not know that anyone other than her personal Facebook network could gain access to her status updates.

In another example, also from 2010, the administration at a Catholic theological seminary summarily dismissed an assistant professor of church history and languages who was also the library director, reportedly because of a comment he had posted on a former student's Facebook page a month earlier, predicting that "one day the Catholic Church will . . . approve of openly gay priests." In June 2013, an evolutionary psychology professor sparked an uproar after he told his Twitter followers that overweight students are not cut out for PhD programs. The professor quickly deleted the tweet, but he faced considerable criticism, especially after he tried to justify his comment by claiming it was part of a research project. The administration disciplined him for what he had written.[30]

In September 2013, the administration of Johns Hopkins University asked a professor, a prominent authority on Internet security and privacy issues, to remove a blog post, claiming that the post contained a link to classified information and used the logo of the National Security Agency (NSA) without authorization. The post was about NSA privacy debates and encryption engineering. The university has a number of ties with the NSA. The administration withdrew the request after the professor discussed it on Twitter and in the media.[31]

At the University of Kansas, also in September 2013, a journalism professor, responding to a shooting incident at the Washington Navy Yard in Washington, DC, tweeted a comment about gun control that many gun advocates found offensive. He was barraged with hate messages and death threats, and several legislators called for his dismissal. Although the university publicly reaffirmed its commitment to his freedom of speech, he was suspended to "avoid disruption." However, a suspension designed to protect a faculty member from potentially violent responses to a controversial statement can quite easily become a punishment for the content of the statement, which in this instance was clearly protected by both the First Amendment and principles of academic freedom.[32]

Many faculty members have decided that they will simply not join Facebook or similar sites. Others have decided that it would be improper ever to connect with a student on a social network. Most colleges and universities have yet to formulate policies regarding social-media usage by faculty members. At institutions where such policies exist, the focus is frequently on the university's reputation and not on the faculty's academic freedom. So, for instance, the University of South Carolina Upstate's "Social Media Policy and Procedure Guidelines" includes the following: "The purpose of the Social Media Policy is to ensure accuracy, consistency, integrity, and protection of the identity and image of the University of South Carolina Upstate by providing a set of required standards for social-media content from any department, school, facility, organization, entity, or affiliate."[33] It is unclear whether or to what extent this policy applies to individual faculty members.

The incident cited above at Kansas prompted the Kansas Board of Regents in December 2013 to adopt new rules under which faculty members and other employees may be suspended or dismissed for "improper use of social media." The new policy defined social media as "any facility for online publication and commentary" and covered but was "not limited to blogs, wikis, and social networking sites such as Facebook, LinkedIn, Twitter, Flickr, and YouTube." This definition could arguably include any message that appears electronically, including e-mail messages and online periodicals and books. The policy defined "improper use of social media" in extremely broad terms, including communications made "pursuant to . . . official duties" that are "contrary to the best interest of the university," as well as communication that "impairs discipline by superiors or harmony among co-workers, has a detrimental impact on close working relationships for which personal loyalty and confidence are necessary, impedes the performance of the speaker's official duties, interferes with the regular operation of the university, or otherwise adversely affects the university's ability to efficiently provide services."[34]

The AAUP quickly condemned the policy as "a gross violation of the fundamental principles of academic freedom that have been a cornerstone of American higher education for nearly a century. Not only faculty members, but students and members of the general public benefit from the free exchange of information and ideas that are at the heart of the academic enterprise, whether conducted orally, in print, or electronically."[35] In the face of widespread criticism, the board of regents agreed to work with campus leaders to revise the policy, but it was not withdrawn.

This report recommends that each institution work with its faculty to develop policies governing the use of social media. Any such policy must recognize that social media can be used to make extramural utterances and thus their use is subject to Association-supported principles of academic freedom, which encompass extramural utterances.

As Committee A previously noted regarding extramural utterances, "Professors should also have the freedom to address the larger community with regard to any matter of social, political, economic, or other interest, without institutional discipline or restraint, save in response to fundamental violations of professional ethics or statements that suggest disciplinary incompetence."[36]

Obviously, the literal distinction between "extramural" and "intramural" speech—speech outside or inside the university's walls—has little meaning in the world of cyberspace. But the fundamental meaning of extramural speech, as a shorthand for speech in the public sphere and not in one's area of academic expertise, fully applies in the realm of electronic communications, including social media.

VII. FOIA and Electronic Communications

In several recent instances, outside groups or governmental agencies have sought to obtain records of faculty members' electronic communications. In 2011, Virginia's attorney general Ken Cuccinelli demanded that the University of Virginia turn over all e-mail messages and other communications related to and produced by former professor Michael Mann, a prominent scientist of climate change, on the grounds that these were public records. The university successfully resisted the request, characterizing the investigation as "an unprecedented and improper governmental intrusion into ongoing scientific research," and charged Cuccinelli with targeting Mann because the attorney general "disagrees with his academic research regarding climate change."[37] But no sooner had this effort been thwarted, than a private group, the American Tradition Institute (ATI), filed a FOIA request that mirrored the attorney general's subpoena.

The AAUP and the Union of Concerned Scientists (UCS) filed a joint amicus brief in support of UVA and Professor Mann, urging that "in evaluating disclosure under FOIA, the public's right to know must be balanced against the significant risk of chilling academic freedom that FOIA requests may pose." ATI's request, the brief stated, "strikes at the heart of academic freedom and debate." ATI justified its broad intrusion by claiming that its purpose in seeking the records was to "open to public inspection the workings of a government employee, including the methods and means used to prepare scientific papers and reports that have been strongly criticized for technical errors." The AAUP-UCS brief argued, however, that "in the FOIA context, the public's right to information is not absolute and courts can

and do employ a balancing test to weigh the interest of the public's right to know against the equally important interests of academic freedom."[38]

Freedom of information laws are generally beneficial: they enhance public knowledge and debate on the workings of government agencies, including public universities. But as the AAUP-UCS amicus brief pointed out, in some situations a balance must be struck between competing interests. Likewise, the Supreme Court recognized as early as 1957 that politically motivated investigations of universities and scholars can have a chilling effect on academic freedom.[39] Allowing fleeting, often casual e-mail exchanges among scholars to be opened to inspection by groups bent on political attack implicates both privacy and academic freedom concerns. As Committee A previously noted in its report *Access to University Records*, "The presumption of confidentiality is strongest with respect to individual privacy rights; the personal notes and files of teachers and scholars; and proposed and ongoing research, where the dangers of external pressures and publicity can be fatal to the necessary climate of academic freedom."[40]

For example, in 2011, the Republican Party of Wisconsin filed a FOIA request with the University of Wisconsin, demanding that the university release e-mail messages from Professor William Cronon, then president of the American Historical Association, who had criticized the Republican governor's "assault on collective bargaining rights." The administration agreed to release some of Professor Cronon's e-mail messages, excluding "private e-mail exchanges among scholars that fall within the orbit of academic freedom and all that is entailed by it." The administration also excluded messages that contained student information and those "that could be considered personal pursuant to Wisconsin Supreme Court case law."

The University of Wisconsin's then-chancellor Carolyn Martin wrote:

When faculty members use e-mail or any other medium to develop and share their thoughts with one another, they must be able to assume a right to the privacy of those exchanges, barring violations of state law or university policy. Having every exchange of ideas subject to public exposure puts academic freedom in peril and threatens the processes by which knowledge is created. The consequence for our state will be the loss of the most talented and creative faculty who will choose to leave for universities where collegial exchange and the development of ideas can be undertaken without fear of premature exposure or reprisal for unpopular positions.

Unfortunately, this position has not always been endorsed by other authorities. In June 2012, the *American Independent News Network* sought documents relating to a study by Professor Mark Regnerus of the University of Texas at Austin. The university asserted that the documents were exempt from disclosure under a section of the Texas Education Code, which covers "technological and scientific information" developed by an institution that can be sold, traded, or licensed for a fee. Moreover, it asserted that the records contained information about third parties. The state attorney general's office rejected these claims, however, and in February 2013 the university released the requested records. By April 2013, the *American Independent* was reporting on material that Regnerus had received. A Florida court then ruled that the University of Central Florida also must share the e-mail messages of Professor James Wright, editor of the journal that published Regnerus's study. The court rejected the university's claims that the e-mail communications are not university records.[41]

It is apparent, then, that faculty members at public universities in Texas, Florida, and other states without scholarly exemption from public-records laws should be aware that titles of books they request from the library, peer-review comments they offer and solicit, and tentative ideas they share with colleagues may be matters for public scrutiny under state FOIA laws.[42]

In this light, faculty members should be advised to segregate, as much as possible, personal from professional correspondence and also segregate correspondence that concerns university business from other professional correspondence, such as work for scholarly publications and organizations. Moreover, given the uncertainty surrounding state FOIA laws, faculty members at public colleges and universities should consider the possibility that every e-mail message they send and receive might become public. Lastly, when such requests are made, faculty members should immediately seek the advice and support of their union (if one exists at their institution) or of legal counsel.

VIII. Defamation

Faculty blog posts, although public and open to all, may be targets of libel actions. In 2013, in separate incidents, two university librarians were sued by the Edwin Mellen Press and its founder, who claimed that negative comments about the press the librarians had posted on the Internet constituted libel. In the first case, Mellen sued an associate librarian at McMaster University in Ontario over a post he had written in 2010, when he was a member of the library faculty at Kansas State University, that described Mellen as a "vanity press" with "few, if any, noted scholars serving as series editors," benefiting largely from librarians not returning books sent for approval at "egregiously high prices." The librarian stated, "As a qualified and experienced librarian, I was sharing a professional opinion for consumption by peers."[43] Although Mellen dropped that suit, another suit by its founder continued. Mellen threatened legal action against the interim library dean at the University of Utah, after he criticized Mellen, in part for its action against the McMaster librarian. Mellen's threats prompted the Society for Scholarly Publishing to remove the Utah dean's posts from its blog, *The Scholarly Kitchen*. The Mellen Press's litigious behavior is clearly incompatible with principles of academic freedom.[44]

Because electronic communications are accessible almost instantaneously around the globe, scholars need to be aware that statements they post on blogs or websites or that they communicate by other electronic means may be subject to the laws of other countries. This fact was highlighted in 2013, when a publisher in India announced its intent to sue for libel a librarian at the University of Colorado at Denver, whose popular blog contains a running list of open-access journals and publishers he deems questionable or predatory. On the blog, the librarian accused the Indian publisher of spamming scholars with invitations to publish, quickly accepting their papers, then charging them a publishing fee of nearly $3,000 after a paper was accepted. A letter from the publisher's attorney sought $1 billion in damages and warned that the librarian could be imprisoned for up to three years under India's Information Technology Act.[45]

Such a suit would likely have little chance of success in US courts, but some other countries' libel laws are less stringent, although in India allegations of misuse of the Information Technology Act have led the Indian government to modify its rules to make them stricter. The all-too-common practice of pursuing libel judgments in other countries, most often England or Wales, where there is a presumption that derogatory statements are false, has been dubbed "libel tourism." In response, the US Congress in 2010 unanimously passed the SPEECH Act, which made foreign libel judgments unenforceable in US courts, unless those judgments are consistent with the First Amendment.[46] However, a judgment unenforceable in the United States might still be enforceable in the country where it was filed and which a scholar may need to visit. Those who not only communicate and publish in other countries but also travel there for research or teaching should be aware of the legal environment governing their expression in those countries.

IX. Privacy of Electronic Communications

Electronic communications have greatly enhanced the ability to teach, to learn, and to inquire. Such technologies have made collaboration over great distances much more efficient and enabled people to work effectively at any hour and in almost any place. At the same time, the structure of electronic-communications technologies can constrain inquiry. Such technologies are designed to document communications and thus amass records of intellectual activities. These records can distort interactions because electronic communications often lack the subtlety of in-person exchanges. They can also be used to investigate individuals in ways that were impossible just a decade ago. *Efforts to protect privacy in electronic communications are an important instrument for ensuring professional autonomy and breathing space for freedom in the classroom and for the freedom to inquire. Although privacy is framed as an individual right, group or associational privacy is also important to academic freedom and to ensuring a culture of trust at an institution.*

When Congress passed legislation to govern the privacy of e-mail and other electronic-communications technologies, these technologies were used primarily by businesses. As a result, some drew the conclusion that the degree of privacy appropriate to digital communications is substantially lower than that expected for traditional media. In the intervening years, however, the use of these technologies has blossomed among businesses and individuals alike.

The nature of a communications medium may take some toll on privacy. An institutional computing network legitimately "backs up" some portion of each day's e-mail traffic. IT staff members in the normal course of events have a technical degree of access to electronic messages that would be unthinkable for personnel in the university mailroom or the campus telephone network. By its very nature, electronic communication incurs certain risks that have no print counterpart—for example, the potential invasion of the system by hackers, despite the institution's best efforts to discourage and even prevent such intrusions. Some of these risks are simply part of

the reality of the digital age and a result of our extensive reliance on computer networks for the conduct of academic discourse. At the same time, some privacy risks are the product of business imperatives rather than technical necessities.

Privacy risks are likely to increase as institutions are called on to address more aggressively the security of college and university networks, as researchers increasingly use digital instead of printed resources, and as distance education and electronic-communications technologies are more generally relied on to execute institutional missions.

Faculty members also bear responsibility for protecting privacy in electronic communications. With the proliferation of BYOD policies, sensitive institutional data are sometimes stored on consumer-level devices. Thought must be given to the storage of student and research data on personal and portable devices in case these devices are compromised, lost, or stolen.

The sensitivity of academic communications and the wide range of scholarly purposes for which digital channels are used warrant a markedly higher level of protection. A fully responsive policy would reflect at least these criteria:

1. The policy should recognize the value of privacy as a condition for academic freedom and the benefits that privacy and autonomy bring to the individual, to groups, and to the culture of an institution. The institution should recognize that faculty members have a reasonable expectation of privacy in their electronic communications and traffic data.

2. The policy should clearly state that the university does not examine or disclose the contents of electronic communications and traffic data without the consent of the individual participating in the communication except in rare and clearly defined cases. Calls to examine electronic communications or transactional information should consider the special nature of the academy, weigh whether the examination would have disproportionately chilling effects on other individuals or the institution generally, and contemplate alternative or less invasive approaches to preserve privacy in communications.

3. Employees who operate and support electronic-communications resources regularly monitor transmissions for the purpose of ensuring reliability and security of those resources and services and, in that process, may observe certain transactional information or the contents of electronic communications. Except

in specifically defined instances or where required by law, they should not be permitted to seek out transactional information or contents when those are not germane to system operations and support or to disclose or otherwise use what they have observed.

4. Faculty members should be involved in the setting of institutional policies surrounding the monitoring of and access to content and traffic data in electronic communications. Policies on electronic communications should enumerate narrow circumstances where institutions can gain access to traffic logs and content unrelated to the technical operation of these services. If a need arises to get access to electronic-communications data, a designated university official should document and handle the request, and all parties to the communication should be notified in ample time for them to pursue protective measures—save in the rare case where any such delay would create imminent risk to human safety or university property. Accessed data may not be used or disseminated more widely than the basis for such exceptional action may warrant.

5. As reliance on electronic-communications technologies grows, more faculty online activities will be subject to being logged. Institutions are encouraged to use several strategies encapsulated by the idea of "privacy by design" to reduce the risk to free inquiry and association from this logging. These strategies include creating logs at the aggregate level, where individuals are not identifiable, when possible; carefully controlling access to these logs; removing identifying information from them; and deleting them according to some reasonable retention policy. These strategies must, of course, be balanced to accommodate legitimate security obligations.

Such principles as these, designed as they are to ensure the privacy of electronic communications, will require careful and extensive study by each institution and the tailoring of specific responses consistent not only with institutional needs and values but also with state and local law. At the same time, it must be acknowledged that whatever legal and policy protections may be available, all faculty members should recognize that in practice the privacy of electronic communications cannot always be protected. In addition to the issues raised previously about FOIA laws, faculty members need to recognize that even encrypted messages can be hacked and even the "safest" firewalls can be breached. Moreover, even the most sensitive and private e-mail messages, social-media postings, and texts can be forwarded to countless people instantaneously.

X. The Role of Faculty and Shared Governance

Some faculty members mistakenly believe that institutional IT policies are strictly under the purview of technology offices, which are thought to possess the requisite expertise to address network security, provision of bandwidth, outsourcing, and similar issues. But the interests of faculty members are not always consonant with those of IT offices. The latter may be charged, for example, with conserving resources, while faculty members need broad access to information and ideas.

Some technology offices may be tempted to employ software features "just because they can," without full consideration of their implications for academic freedom and learning. For example, recent learning-management software allows an institution to disable features that invade privacy. But some technology offices may have a cavalier attitude toward privacy or simply desire to offer all the "bells and whistles" available. Electronic communications are too important for the maintenance and protection of academic freedom to be left entirely to such offices. Faculty members must participate, preferably through representative institutions of shared governance, in the formulation and implementation of policies governing electronic-communications technologies.

However, in order for the faculty to play an active and constructive role in the development and execution of such policies, those faculty members who participate in such work need to become more informed about both the technical issues involved and the broader academic-freedom implications of their decisions. This report is designed to facilitate that process.

Specifically, we recommend the following:

1. Policies and practices regarding information technology should be within the purview of a representative faculty committee. Any new policy or major revision of an existing policy should be subject to approval by a broader faculty body such as a faculty senate.
2. The faculty committee may be drawn from the faculty senate or elected as an ad hoc committee by the faculty; its members should not be appointed by the administration.
3. Faculty members participating in the committee should be familiar with and informed about relevant developments in communications technology so that they are able to recognize potential conflicts with principles of academic freedom.

4. The members of the faculty committee should be provided with all relevant contracts and technical materials necessary to make informed decisions about policies governing electronic communications.

5. Whenever policies are proposed or administrative actions taken with respect to information technology that may directly or indirectly implicate academic freedom, faculty members must be consulted.

6. In those institutions with collective bargaining, faculty unions should seek to include in their collective bargaining agreements protections for academic freedom in electronic communications as described in this report.

Notes

1. *Academe* 91 (January–February 2005): 55–59.
2. Robert M. O'Neil, *Academic Freedom in the Wired World* (Cambridge, MA: Harvard University Press, 2008), 179–80.
3. Carl Straumsheim, "Device Explosion," *Inside Higher Ed*, September 5, 2013, http://www.insidehigh-ered.com/news/2013/09/05/wireless-devices-weigh-down-campus-networks.
4. O'Neil, *Academic Freedom in the Wired World*, 181.
5. Scott Jaschik, "Reacting to Aaron Swartz's Suicide," *Inside Higher Ed*, January 14, 2013, http://www.insidehighered.com/news/2013/01/14/academe-reacts-aaron-swartzs-suicide.
6. Colleen Flaherty, "Could Have Done More," *Inside Higher Ed*, July 31, 2013, http://www.insidehighered.com/news/2013/07/31/mit-releases-report-its-role-case-against-internet-activist-aaron-swartz.
7. Lawrence Lessig, "Prosecutor as Bully," *Lessig Blog*, January 12, 2013, http://lessig.tumblr.com/post/40347463044/prosecutor-as-bully.
8. AAUP, *Policy Documents and Reports*, 11th ed. (Baltimore: Johns Hopkins University Press, 2015), 264.
9. As of August 2013, more than 175 universities had endorsed open access. That month, for instance, the University of California Academic Senate adopted an open-access policy that will make research articles freely available to the public through eScholarship, California's open digital repository. The policy applies to all ten of the system's campuses with more than eight thousand tenured and tenure-track faculty members and will affect as many as forty thousand research papers a year. Faculty members can opt out or ask that their work be embargoed for a period of time, as many journal publishers require. In a departure from many other institutions' open-access policies, UC researchers will also be able to make their work available under commercial as well as noncommercial Creative Commons licenses. UC researchers get an estimated 8 percent of all US research money and produce 2 to 3 percent of peer-reviewed scholarly articles published worldwide every year. See "Open Access Gains Major Support in U. of California's

Systemwide Move," *Chronicle of Higher Education*, August 5, 2013.
10. One example of such a collaboration may be found at http://www.philosophersimprint.org/, an open-access online resource for philosophy scholarship, the mission of which is "to overcome [the] obstacles to the free electronic dissemination of scholarship."
11. For more on library privacy and confidentiality policies, see http://www.ala.org/offices/oif/statementspols/otherpolicies/rfidguidelines.
12. "Academic Freedom and Artistic Expression," *Policy Documents and Reports*, 40–41.
13. *Ginsberg* v. *New York*, 390 US 629 (1968). In 1997, the Court struck down the Communications Decency Act, and in 2009, it declined to review a decision by the US Court of Appeals for the Third Circuit striking down the Children's Online Protection Act. *Reno* v. *American Civil Liberties Union*, 521 US 844 (1997) and *ACLU* v. *Mukasey*, 534 F.3d 181 (3rd Cir. 2008), cert. denied, 555 US 1137 (2009).
14. Richard Pérez-Peña, "Universities Face a Rising Barrage of Cyberattacks," *New York Times*, July 16, 2013, http://www.nytimes.com/2013/07/17/education/barrage-of-cyberattacks-challenges-campus-culture.html.
15. Ibid.
16. Steve Kolowich, "The Academic Twitterazzi," *Inside Higher Ed*, October 2, 2012, http://www.insidehighered.com/news/2012/10/02/scholars-debate-etiquette-live-tweeting-academic-conferences.
17. Ibid.
18. Colleen Flaherty, "Not-So-Great Expectations," *Inside Higher Ed*, October 18, 2013, http://www.insidehighered.com/news/2013/10/18/professors-afforded-few-guarantees-privacy-internet-age.
19. The AAUP has been concerned with this issue since its 1915 *Declaration of Principles on Academic Freedom and Academic Tenure*, which stated, "Discussions in the classroom ought not to be supposed to be utterances for the public at large. They are often designed to provoke opposition or arouse debate." In the 1980s, a group called Accuracy in Academia encouraged students to record professors' classroom statements and send them to the organization to be tested for "accuracy." According to a 1985 statement the AAUP issued jointly with twelve other higher education associations, "The classroom is a place of learning where the professor serves as intellectual guide, and all are encouraged to seek and express the truth as they see it. The presence in the classroom of monitors for an outside organization will have a chilling effect on the academic freedom of both students and faculty members. Students may be discouraged from testing their ideas, and professors may hesitate before presenting new or possibly controversial theories that would stimulate robust intellectual discussion."
20. Bastiaan Vanacker, "Returning Students' Right to Access, Choice, and Notice: A Proposed Code of Ethics for Instructors Using Turnitin," *Ethics and Information Technology* 13 (2011): 327–38.
21. The Guard Publishing Company, d/b/a *The Register Guard*, 351 NLRB 1110 (2007), supplemental

decision, 357 NLRB No. 27 (2011); Hispanics United of Buffalo, Inc., 359 NLRB No. 37 (2012).

22. See http://aaupcolorado.org/2014/01/20 /colorado-conference-responds-to-csu-pueblo-president -lesley-di-mare-regarding-the-censure-of-professor-ti m-mcgettigan/ for more information about the Colorado incident.

23. AAUP-recommended procedures for the imposition of sanctions, whether minor or severe, may be found in Regulation 7 of the "Recommended Institutional Regulations on Academic Freedom and Tenure," *Policy Documents and Reports*, 85.

24. University of California Electronic Communica-tions Policy, http://policy.ucop.edu/doc/7000470 /ElectronicCommunications.

25. Outsourcing of instruction through online education offered by outside providers, however, is a quite different matter.

26. The abbreviation IT is used here and subse-quently in reference to those university offices and functions variously called "information technology," "instructional technology," or "institutional technology."

27. Scott Jaschik, "Reprimand for a Blog," *Inside Higher Ed*, April 12, 2013, http://www.insidehighered .com/news/2013/04/12/florida-atlantic-reprimands -professor-over-his-blog.

28. The survey was conducted by the Babson Survey Research Group on behalf of Pearson Learning Solutions. See Jeff Seaman and Hester Tinti-Kane, *Social Media for Teaching and Learning* (Boston: Pearson Learning Solutions, 2013), http://www .pearsonlearningsolutions.com/higher-education /social-media-survey.php.

29. Social-media communications may also be used by the social-media site itself for data-mining purposes.

30. Lauren Ingeno, "#Penalty," *Inside Higher Ed*, August 7, 2013, http://www.insidehighered.com/news /2013/08/07/fat-shaming-professor-faces-censure -university.

31. "Hopkins (Briefly) Asks Professor to Remove Blog Post," *Inside Higher Ed*, September 10, 2013, http://www.insidehighered.com/quicktakes/2013/09 /10/hopkins-briefly-asks-professor-remove-blog-post.

32. Scott Rothschild and Ben Unglesbee, "Professor Getting Death Threats over NRA Tweet, Colleagues Support His Free-Speech Rights," *Lawrence Journal-World*, September 23, 2013, http://www2.ljworld.com /news/2013/sep/23/firestorm-over-guths-comment -continues-university-/.

33. University of South Carolina Upstate, "Social Media Policy and Procedure Guidelines," https://www .uscupstate.edu/uploadedFiles/Offices/Communications /social/Social%20Media%20Policy%20Approved.pdf.

34. Kansas Board of Regents, "Policy Chapter II C Suspensions," http://www.kansasregents.org/policy_ chapter_ii_c_suspensions.

35. AAUP, "AAUP Statement on the Kansas Board of Regents Social Media Policy," http://www.aaup.org /file/KansasStatement.pdf.

36. "Protecting an Independent Faculty Voice: Academic Freedom after *Garcetti v. Ceballos*," *Policy Documents and Reports*, 126–29.

37. For a summary of key events in the Mann case, see http://www.aaup.org/our-programs/legal-program /legal-roundup-2012#iii.

38. Ibid.

39. *Sweezy v. New Hampshire*, 354 US 234, 250 (1957). ("The essentiality of freedom in the community of American universities is almost self-evident. . . . Scholarship cannot flourish in an atmosphere of suspicion and distrust.")

40. *Policy Documents and Reports*, 62.

41. Zachary M. Schrag, "Happy Goldfish Bowl to You, Professor," *Zachary M. Schrag* (blog), November 28, 2013, http://zacharyschrag.com/2013/11/28/happy -goldfish-bowl-to-you-professor/.

42. A recent survey of how state FOIA laws govern requests for material from public universities found that only twenty-five states offer various degrees of exception for academic materials, with the best statutes in Alaska, Pennsylvania, and Georgia. See Ryan C. Fairchild, "Giving Away the Playbook: How North Carolina's Public Records Law Can Be Used to Harass, Intimidate, and Spy," *North Carolina Law Review* 91 (2013): 2117–78. See also the memorandum about state FOIA laws available at http://www.law.gwu.edu/News /2013-2014events/Documents/ATIvUVA/State_FOI_ List.pdf.

43. Colleen Flaherty, "Price of a Bad Review," *Inside Higher Ed*, February 8, 2013, http://www.insidehigh ered.com/news/2013/02/08/academic-press-sues -librarian-raising-issues-academic-freedom.

44. Ry Rivard, "Call In the Lawyers," *Inside Higher Ed*, April 1, 2013, http://www.insidehighered.com/news /2013/04/01/mellen-press-continues-its-legal-maneuvers -against-critics.

45. Jake New, "Publisher Threatens to Sue Blogger for $1-Billion," *Chronicle of Higher Education*, May 15, 2013, https://chronicle.com/article/Publisher-Threatens -to-Sue/139243/.

46. 124 Stat. 2480–84. SPEECH is the acronym for "Securing the Protection of our Enduring and Estab-lished Constitutional Heritage."

Access to University Records

The report that follows was formulated by a subcommittee of Committee A on Academic Freedom and Tenure. It was approved by Committee A and adopted by the Council in November 1996. Legal citations in the report were updated in 2014.

"For the great majority of different records the public as a whole has a *right to know* what its government is doing."

Language of this kind, taken from the legislative history of the federal Freedom of Information Act (FOIA), expresses a view that has been applied in a number of jurisdictions to college and university documents either under federal law or under similar state statutes. Laws in every state give the public access to records of state government. A wide array of documents from public colleges and universities has been sought under these provisions. While in some states the records of public colleges and universities are largely shielded from public access, in others the laws have broader impact on institutions of higher education. The courts are often called upon to adjudicate claims of access. Among the kinds of documents from public colleges and universities that have been made available by court order are the following:

(i) names and addresses of respondents to a research survey about cigarette advertising;
(ii) filmstrips used in a college course on human sexuality;
(iii) peer review documents;
(iv) identity of donors;
(v) university legal bills;
(vi) copy of an unfunded grant proposal to NIH.[1]

Across the country results even in these categories may vary, depending on the terms and interpretation of different state laws.

There is nothing novel about courts deciding issues of access to information; indeed, it is an essential element in the process of permitting discovery by the parties in litigation. Pre-trial discovery often raises questions about what information must be disclosed to an opposing party. Similarly, labor law compels the sharing of certain information. A union generally has access to information of the employer relevant to satisfaction of the union's responsibilities. On a voluntary basis, members of a college or university community regularly exchange many types of information as they collaborate in advancing the institution's goals. So by court order, by operation of law, and by custom, an academic institution may disclose many of its records for specified purposes. These purposes include litigation, collective bargaining, and shared governance. The information is provided to individuals or groups that stand in defined relationships to the institution whether as litigants, unions, or faculty or student groups.

Public records acts, however, present a broader context because they provide *any* member of the public with access to documents that fall within the terms of the statute. No reason for requesting the information need be stated. FOIA and similar statutes have thus relieved the court of balancing the *need to know* of the one requesting access against the other party's desire to keep certain material partially or wholly confidential. Indeed, the assertion of a *right to know* gives conclusive weight to any requester's *want to know* and zero weight to an institution's *want to keep confidential*. This eliminates the distinction between *want* and *need* on the part of each party. FOIA and similar state statutes often contain exceptions. Depending on the state, these might include items such as employee personnel files or strategic materials connected with litigation or real estate transactions. For documents outside such enumerated exceptions, the statutes take no account of possible bases for confidentiality nor dangers of unlimited public access.

We do not address the legal status (state or federal) of requests for access to university documents. Our purpose, in response to a request from the AAUP Council, is to draft a statement of AAUP policy in respect to these matters. While there may be some differences between public and private institutions in this regard—for example, in taxpayers' legitimate interest in the expenditure of public funds—we do not find such differences material to the central issues of AAUP concern.

There are plainly situations in which a compelling case can be made for access by a limited audience to university documents that a university administration may not choose to make available unless compelled to do so. Some obvious examples: a staff member charged with misconduct must be in a position to know the source and nature of the charges made as well as the procedures followed by the administration in response to the complaint; a faculty member denied promotion, reappointment, or a salary increment who believes he or she has been discriminated against on some improper basis must be given access to certain documents with which to test this possibility; a faculty collective bargaining unit negotiating with an administration must have access to certain data with which to confront assertions by the university about its ability to provide salary or fringe benefit improvements; and any individual or group in litigation against the university needs to be able to discover facts with which to press claims.

Although means exist apart from freedom of information statutes by which access can be obtained in cases such as these, it is clear that a *generalized right of public access* to all university documents (provided, for example, by an unqualified FOIA) would serve all compelling needs and greatly reduce the efforts and outlays required to compel disclosure in particular situations. If no cost or potential dangers were associated with unqualified access to all university documents, independent of the nature of the request and of the requester's need to know, a general right of access would be both simple and efficient. Regrettably, this is not the case. While access confers benefits, it also carries costs and potential dangers, many of which apply with special force to an academic community by virtue of its essential, perhaps unique, mission to search for and disseminate truth by wide-ranging exploration of inchoate ideas and hypotheses, some of which may be seen as dangerous by others in the society. Sound policy requires a balancing of the benefits and costs of open access.

We believe that such a balancing does not lead to a strong presumption in favor of unlimited public access with respect to university documents.

The nature of the potential benefits and costs has been articulated in many places,[2] but at least a cursory review of some of them will be helpful.

Among the legitimate interests served by open public access to university documents are:

a. The increased ability to expose corrupt, biased, or otherwise improper behavior by institutions.
b. The beneficial pressure exerted on universities to fulfill their intended missions by the knowledge that failure to do so is likely to be exposed.
c. The incentive to university personnel to be more effective because their actions and decisions must survive public scrutiny.
d. The opportunity provided to a wise public for constructive input into university decisions.[3]
e. The lighter burden on all who seek access to university records.

Among the interests served by restrictions on access to university documents are:

a. The need to create and preserve a climate of academic freedom in the planning and conduct of research, free from harassment, public and political pressure, or premature disclosure of research in process.
b. The need to create a climate in which the university's teaching activities are unimpeded and open to innovation and in which controversial issues may be explored without externally imposed limits on what is said, read, or debated.
c. The gains to be achieved by the ability to collect information only available by assurance of confidentiality. This can apply in research in a variety of contexts. It can also apply to peer review and evaluation of the accomplishments of individuals who are being recruited, evaluated, retained, promoted, rewarded, discontinued, or discharged. Some evaluators require a promise of confidentiality except with respect to persons with a need to know; others will respond, but less helpfully, if confidentiality is not assured.
d. The recruitment of top-level administrators may, in some situations, be aided by assurances to potential candidates that their interest in the appointment will not be released to the public until such time as the candidate has entered the final stages of the search. Absent such assurances, some candidates, perhaps some of the most desirable, will simply refuse to be considered.
e. The need to avoid what has been called "the chilling effect" on what is explored and what is taught. Perceived threats of harassment, pressure, and adverse publicity may result from public disclosure. Teachers and scholars who observe others so treated in the conduct of their careers may modify what they teach and what they study.
f. The need to respect the privacy of teachers and scholars with respect to aspects of their private lives—such as marital status, outside income, sexual preferences, or medical records—that are irrelevant to their performance as teachers

and scholars, unless a compelling reason to breach that privacy has been established.

There is ample evidence that both the potential benefits and potential costs do occur in the academic setting. The balancing of benefits and costs of open access is not a once-and-for-all matter, because the considerations depend upon the nature of the document requested, the requester's need to know, and the breadth of disclosure to be made. To take easy extreme examples, there can be no question that students' requests for access to an examination that has been prepared but not yet given is without merit. Also lacking in merit would be an institution's refusal to provide anyone requesting it with information about the educational background of a teacher or summary data on the age, sex, and racial composition of its faculty. Few requests are so simply resolved, and thus what is required are some *rebuttable presumptions* that apply to different classes of requests, and an *internal procedure for evaluating competing claims*. We discuss each of these below.

Presumptions

Presumptions about the appropriateness of giving access to university documents depend both on the status of the requester and the nature of the information requested. A great variety of people and groups have at one time or another expressed a desire to know about material that universities do not routinely choose to make available. The status of those making the request is not irrelevant to the balancing that we believe to be appropriate. (It is irrelevant under FOIA and similar statutes.) Those requesting information include individual faculty members; faculty committees; faculty unions; students and student organizations; pressure groups from the community anxious to influence the nature of what is taught or researched;[4] companies and industry trade associations concerned that what is transpiring within the university will adversely (or beneficially) affect them or their competitors; representatives of the media, anxious to build circulation by exposing misbehavior, or merely catering to the curiosity of their clientele; and even lawyers seeking to define potential and profitable litigation against the university. Examples of each of these can be found.

The types of documents that are subject to requests for access are both numerous and varied. They range from simple requests for general information about faculty members' professional backgrounds and activities to the most searching demands for information about individuals'

personal lives. Some requests ask for details about promotion or disciplinary files of particular faculty members, and for the records of the deliberations of committees that have evaluated them. Requests may concern current ongoing research or outside activities of university staff. Other requests may seek documents giving detailed information about the origin and the use of university resources, including information about the identity of donors and the amount of payments to outside lawyers in particular cases.

One could conceptually cross-classify the nature of the requester and the nature of the information requested and create a grid with hundreds of "cells." One might then assign a particular presumption of openness or confidentiality to each. While for some cells the appropriate presumption may be self-evident, for many (indeed we believe most) there is need for a case-specific examination to balance the *need to know* against *the case for confidentiality*. A procedure by which this balancing can occur is also necessary.

These are not all matters of first impression for the professoriate and the Association; some of the relevant ground has been covered elsewhere and will not be retraced. The large topic of faculty access to faculty personnel files was the subject of a 1992 report and policy statement by Committees A and W, adopted by the Council. Its principal conclusions were: (1) faculty members should have unrestricted access to their own files including unredacted letters about them; (2) at the discretion of faculty appeals committees, faculty complainants should be given similar access to records of other faculty members for comparison purposes; and (3) faculty peer review committees should have open access to all such records. In addition, the desirability of open meetings legislation was the subject of a 1986 AAUP report.[5] While the Association has addressed the role of faculty in the selection of academic administrators, it has not analyzed the impact on such search processes of legally compelled disclosure to the public, notably including the media.[6] The Carnegie Commission for the Advancement of Teaching covered the latter subject in its useful report, *Choosing a College President: Opportunities and Constraints* (1990).[7] Further, we shall not discuss the rights of litigants to discovery of relevant documents, nor the requests by officially constituted professional associations or governmental review panels for data relevant to their investigations.

Despite these exclusions, much remains that might be discussed. In respect to the nature of the requester, it is useful to distinguish among four

types: (1) regularly constituted internal committees or bodies whose task is to review, evaluate,
or adjudicate matters concerning faculty status;
(2) other interested internal-to-the-university
persons or groups such as faculty unions, AAUP
chapters, student governments, or groups with a
particular interest, such as a faculty women's
caucus; (3) individual faculty members or *ad hoc*
student groups; (4) outside persons or groups,
however motivated.

In respect to the nature of the information
requested, for some classes of information the
presumption ought to be strong in favor of open
access, regardless of the requester's identity. This
would include information of the kind contained
in curricula vitae, information about published
research including access to nonconfidential
backup data, and summary information about
an institution including faculty composition,
workloads, curriculum, and salary levels. It would,
of course, also include information about fundamental institutional decisions once made and
effected, the procedures employed in making
these decisions, and the available channels of
appeal. At least summary information about
sources and uses of the institution's funds is
plainly appropriate for public institutions,
although perhaps less plainly for private ones.

At the other end of the spectrum are certain
kinds of information we believe should be
presumed confidential and thus not available to
any requester absent a determination of an
exceptional and compelling need to know. These
include personal information not contained in
curricula vitae such as family status, outside
income and assets, medical history, records of
library use, extramural affiliations, and political
or religious affiliations. Similarly, the deliberations, opinions voiced, individual votes, and
proceedings of faculty bodies should be presumed
to be private, in order not to chill full and candid
decision making. Of course, if a charge is made
that the basis for decisions is inappropriate, e.g.,
biased, these matters are the proper domain of a
grievance committee.

Even extending these lists of the easy presumptions would leave a vast array of requests for
which the extent and purpose of the requester's
need to know and the strength of the institution's
claim for confidentiality would be essential to
evaluating the request. Here, perhaps, some
weaker presumptions may be stated.

1. *Requests coming from regularly constituted
   internal bodies, such as review committees,
   grievance panels, and faculty senates.* We
   believe that there should be a rebuttable

presumption for open and unlimited access to
any university records upon showing by a
regularly constituted internal body of a
reasonable need to know. Examples include
budgetary information, material concerning
academic planning, and personnel information.
Disclosure may be subject to a pledge of
confidentiality with respect to information
that is not generally available for which either
privacy or confidentiality is claimed. (The
redaction of limited private or confidential
information can be a useful device.) The
process of shared governance must rest on a
premise of shared information. Those arguing
for nonrelease in these situations should bear
the burden of establishing a reasonable need to
keep confidential.

2. *Requests from other (nonofficial) internal
   groups.* We believe there should be no
   presumption either way, with the standard
   being that the specific need to know be
   balanced against the specific need for confidentiality and with due concern for the protection
   of individuals' privacy. The possibilities of a
   negotiated agreement on the extent and form
   of release of requested information should be
   explored, possibly utilizing the services of an
   ombudsman or mediator. On some occasions,
   the parties might agree upon limitations on
   the use and subsequent dissemination of the
   information. Narrowly tailored redaction
   might be considered.

3. *Requests from individual faculty members or
   student groups.* Requests of these kinds may
   be substantively similar to those discussed just
   above or may be indistinguishable from those
   of outsiders, discussed in the next section. For
   example, the treatment given to a faculty
   member or a group of students concerned with
   animal rights ought usually to be no different
   from that given to an outside group concerned
   with the same issue. On other issues, the
   concerns of individual professors or of student
   groups may be more analogous to the concerns
   of an official faculty body.[8] Thus, for example,
   a student group examining whether the
   university's curricular decisions were unduly responsive to the wishes of a generous
   outside benefactor ought generally to be
   treated no differently with respect to access to
   data from a faculty committee with the same
   concerns.

   Thus a first step in resolving such requests
   involves a determination whether the concern
   motivating the request is essentially an internal
   concern or an external one. This decision,
   rather than the mere fact of university

affiliation of the requester, usually ought to be controlling.

4. *Outside requesters.* We believe that considerations of privacy, academic freedom, and the desirable insulation of the university from outside pressures, as well as considerations of efficient operation of the educational enterprise, argue in favor of a *strong* or even *compelling* presumption against access to university documents for which a reasonable claim of confidentiality has been made. The presumption of confidentiality is strongest with respect to individual privacy rights; the personal notes and files of teachers and scholars; and proposed and ongoing research, where the dangers of external pressures and publicity can be fatal to the necessary climate of academic freedom. This presumption applies as well, but perhaps less conclusively, with respect to many other university records including, but not limited to, promotion and grievance files and disciplinary records.

Resolving Presumptions

There is a need for a mechanism to do the required balancing. Ultimately, of course, all such decisions are subject to judicial review and final determination under the laws of the relevant jurisdiction. However, we do not believe it is appropriate for universities or academic associations such as the AAUP simply to abdicate their responsibility to address the problem. Courts, in exercising judicial discretion, can and do give weight to appropriate internal procedures and findings and also to the standards of respected professional associations.

We recommend that academic institutions designate, or create, a joint administration/faculty committee with authority to receive and review requests for access to university records and to make recommendations in writing as to their disposition.

Such a committee should attempt the balancing we believe is required in a large number of cases. While balancing will have to be done within the applicable state and federal laws and internal rules, it may not be inappropriate for the committee to recognize that it might recommend differently if it were free of constraint. Beyond this, the balancing ought to be guided by precedents both of that institution and of the academic community. Considerations of privacy, of academic freedom, and of efficient conduct of the essential functions of an academic institution should not be subordinated to a generalized "right to know."

Notes

Editor's Note (2014): In the years since the initial publication of this report, the particular issue of whether public universities must provide access to faculty scholarship and communications related to that scholarship has been addressed by the courts. See, for example, *Cuccinelli v. Rector & Visitors of Univ. of Va.,* 283 Va. 420, 432 (2012) (rejecting the attorney general's efforts to obtain information related to scholarly research, holding that the university is not a "person" within the meaning of the Fraud Against Taxpayers Act and thus does not come within the purview of the attorney general's subpoena power under that statute). A current appeal before the Virginia State Supreme Court addresses the issue of whether the University of Virginia is required under the state FOIA to produce unpublished academic research and correspondence. *American Tradition Institute v. Rector & Visitors of Univ. of Va.,* Cir. Ct. No. CL-11-3236, *appeal granted* No. 130934 (Va. Sup. Ct. Sept. 23, 2013). The AAUP has filed an *amicus* brief in this case. Academic institutions also have been attempting to address this issue in internal policy documents. See, for example, UCLA Statement on the Principles of Scholarly Research and Public Records Requests, September 2012, available at https://www.apo.ucla.edu/resources/academic-freedom. Finally, scholars and lawyers also have evaluated the competing interests of academic freedom as balanced against the right of the public to information about public institutions. See generally Rachel Levinson-Waldman, *Academic Freedom and the Public's Right to Know,* ACS Issue Brief, at 19 (2011), available at http://www.acslaw.org/publications/issue-briefs/academic-freedom-and-the-public's-right-to-know-how-to-counter-the-chillin. The law in this area is evolving, and interested parties should consult legal counsel regarding the current state of the law.

1. See "Fischer v. The Medical College of Georgia and The R.J. Reynolds Tobacco Company: A Case Study of Constraints on Research" by Paul M. Fischer in *Academic Freedom: An Everyday Concern,* ed. Ernst Benjamin and Donald Wagner (1994) (tobacco advertising); *Russo v. Nassau County Community College,* 623 N.E. 2d 15 (N.Y. Apps. 1993) (sexuality teaching materials); *James v. Ohio State University,* 637 N.E. 2d 911 (Ohio Sup. Ct. 1994) (peer review documents); *Toledo Blade Co. v. University of Toledo Foundation,* 602 N.E. 2d 1159 (Ohio Sup. Ct. 1992) (donors to private foundation that served as main fund-raising arm of public university); "Rutgers Must Show Legal Bills," by Tia Swanson, *Home News and Tribune,* Jan. 5, 1996 (New Brunswick, N.J.); *Progressive Animal Welfare Society v. University of Washington,* 884 P.2d 592 (Wash. Sup. Ct. 1994) (*en banc*) (unfunded grant proposal).

2. For example, see "Access to Faculty Personnel Files," AAUP, *Policy Documents and Reports,* 11th ed. (Baltimore: Johns Hopkins University Press, 2015), 100–104.

3. The Association has previously addressed the need for faculty involvement in decisions, including decisions on the selection of academic administrators.

See "Faculty Participation in the Selection, Evaluation, and Retention of Administrators," ibid., 130–31, and the "Statement on Government of Colleges and Universities," 117.

4. Among these are supporters of animal rights, creationism, right to life, environmental protection, Americanism, and protection from pornography.

5. "On Open Meetings," *Academe* 72 (January–February 1986): 3a–4a.

6. See note 3 above.

7. The authors of the Carnegie study, Judith Block McLaughlin and David Riesman, served on the Association's subcommittee that addressed open meetings issues in 1986.

8. An individual professor seeking information about himself or herself presents, however, different considerations. See "Access to Faculty Personnel Files," note 2.

Academic Freedom at Religiously Affiliated Institutions: The "Limitations" Clause in the 1940 *Statement of Principles on Academic Freedom and Tenure*

The following report, approved under the title *The "Limitations" Clause in the 1940* Statement of Principles on Academic Freedom and Tenure: *Some Operating Guidelines* in 1999 by Committee A on Academic Freedom and Tenure, is a revision of a report initially approved for publication in November 1996.

Committee A reported in 1988 on the interpretive difficulty surrounding the provision in the 1940 *Statement of Principles,* that "[l]imitations of academic freedom because of religious or other aims of the institution should be clearly stated in writing at the time of the appointment."[1] This provision is commonly known as the "limitations" clause. In 1970, a set of Interpretive Comments on the 1940 *Statement* was adopted as Association policy, including the interpretive comment that "most church-related institutions no longer need or desire the departure from the principle of academic freedom implied in the 1940 *Statement,* and we do not now endorse such a departure." That interpretive comment left it unclear how the Association is to respond to an institution that does invoke the limitations clause in defense of a departure from the principles of academic freedom. In its 1988 report, Committee A held that the interpretive comment did not read the limitations clause out of the 1940 *Statement,* and thus did not imply that the Association would henceforth regard every resulting departure from the principles of academic freedom as by itself warranting Association censure. Committee A held that an institution that commits itself to a predetermined truth, and that binds its faculty accordingly, is not subject to censure on that ground alone. But Committee A also held that such an institution must not represent itself, without qualification, as an institution freely engaged in higher education: the institution must in particular disclose its restrictions on academic freedom to prospective members of the faculty. Committee A held, finally, that an institution is not subject to the academic freedom provisions of the 1940 *Statement*—a breach of which may result in censure—unless it does represent itself as an institution freely engaged in higher education.

Various sectarian institutions have been founded and are supported by sponsoring religious denominations for the training of their laity and clergy in the faith. So, too, have a number of institutions been established that are dedicated to the propagation of particular beliefs or schools of thought—in political economy (the Rand School was singled out for mention by Committee A in the 1920s), in clinical psychology, in early childhood pedagogy, and in the education and training of future leaders of the labor movement, to mention only a few. Institutions of this character function within a set of doctrines or beliefs, and they usually do not affirm a recognition of academic freedom, even subject to restriction. They unquestionably contribute to the pluralistic richness of the American intellectual landscape, but they are usually not institutions of a kind to which the academic freedom provisions of the 1940 *Statement* apply, and hence imposing censure on their administrations would usually not be appropriate.[2]

The usual is not the universal, however. When institutions dedicated to these or similar limited aims gain, or seek, broader recognition as seats of higher learning—e.g., by expanding their curricula, by identifying themselves as universities or colleges of liberal education, by awarding secular academic degrees, by securing regional or specialized accreditation, and by appealing to the public for support on those grounds—then we believe they are subject to the academic freedom provisions of the 1940 *Statement,* a breach of which may result in censure.

A further consideration is that somewhere between an institution committed to academic freedom and one that pervasively restricts its exercise lies an institution that provides academic freedom in most respects save for a carefully crafted core (or pocket) of credal or doctrinal conformity. This taxonomy corresponds roughly to the one used by the Danforth Commission on Church Colleges and Universities in 1965,[3] distinguishing among the "non-affirming college," the "defender-of-the-faith college," and—between them—the "free Christian (or Jewish) college" that may attach a religious preference in faculty appointment but that gives the faculty "wide freedom consistent with law and good taste." If "law and good taste" are taken to refer to ecclesiastical as well as civil-law restrictions, we believe that such an institution is appropriately viewed as subject to the academic freedom provisions of the 1940 *Statement*, and thus as one to which the limitations clause in particular was intended to apply.

As the Danforth Commission report also noted, many "non-affirming" institutions were originally created on strong doctrinal foundations; and, indeed, the prospect of movement from constraint to freedom pervades the Association's engagement with the issue. The 1922 Association of American Colleges proposal, cited in Committee A's 1988 report, referred to the toleration of restrictions as a "temporary concession." The 1970 interpretive comment quoted above spoke of change in the perceived needs and desires of church-related institutions; and it may be worthy of note that the AAUP did not investigate issues of academic freedom at an institution devoted to clerical education until the Concordia Seminary (Missouri) case in 1975, where, prior to the event under investigation, the institution had come to allow a good deal of academic freedom to flourish.[4]

In other words, movement from constraint to freedom is a historical characteristic of many church-related institutions, and a thoughtful argument could be made for the proposition that, as a pervasively sectarian or proprietary institution ordinarily outside the ambit of the Association's concern moves toward becoming more open, it moves as well toward bringing itself within the compass of the 1940 *Statement*; and that when it has done so to such an extent as to be considered primarily as a seat of unfettered learning, such limited restrictions as the institution retains will be subject to the 1940 *Statement*'s prescriptive requirements, including the limitations clause.

Accordingly, Committee A offers the following set of operating guidelines for Association treatment of a complaint: (1) at the outset by the Association's staff; (2) by the ad hoc committee of investigation, if one is appointed; and (3) by Committee A in considering the ad hoc committee's report.

Guideline One

When a complaint is received from a faculty member alleging a restriction on academic freedom because of a religious or other aim, the staff should decide whether, in its view, the institution is one at which adherence to the academic freedom provisions of the 1940 *Statement* is to be expected. Factors that the staff should consider include the institution's stated mission; its curriculum; its accreditation; its eligibility for tax support; its criteria for selection of its governing body, faculty, students, staff, and administration; and the ways in which it represents itself to the public in bulletins, catalogues, and other pronouncements.

If the staff concludes that the institution is not one at which adherence to the academic freedom provisions of the 1940 *Statement* is to be expected, the general secretary should decline to authorize an investigation.

Comment

The Association already draws an analogous distinction in the applicability of its provisions in that it declines to pursue cases arising at unaccredited institutions. No good reason exists, apart from ease of application, to permit determinations made by accrediting organizations, on which the Association has relatively little influence, to drive Association policy. (This is emphasized, perhaps, by the inclusion of proprietary and vocational "postsecondary education" within the realm of regional accreditation. Nor is state licensure by itself determinative, since the Association would not apply its processes to a "degree mill" authorized to award degrees under applicable state law.) It is only a next step to say that, despite regional accreditation and legal degree-granting authority, the Association's independent assessment of an institution may lead it to conclude that the institution does not purport to provide academic freedom and is not subject to the 1940 *Statement*.

It should be stressed in any event that if an institution is one at which adherence to the academic freedom provisions of the 1940 *Statement* is to be expected, the institution's invocation of the limitations clause does not absolve it of an obligation to afford due process in dismissal and nonreappointment actions as provided for in Association policies. On the contrary, the scope of the institution's limitation and the reasonable expectations of faculty members subject to it, the application of the limitation in the past, and the question whether it is being selectively applied for ulterior purposes are, among others, potential questions that may require a full hearing.

Guideline Two

Where the general secretary has authorized an investigation, the ad hoc committee should be charged with assessing whether or not the institution is subject to the provisions of the 1940 *Statement* in light of considerations of the kind pointed to in Guideline One. If it concludes that the institution is subject to those provisions, and if, further, the institution invoked the limitations clause, then the committee should assess how the limitation applies to the facts as found. Thus the ad hoc committee should consider the degree of specificity of the limitation and whether or not the institution afforded sufficient procedural safeguards to ensure that the application of its rules was adequately cabined.

Comment on the Clarity of the Proscription
It could be argued that an exact limitation is a practical impossibility; that no restrictive language could be devised that would at the same time anticipate future credal constraints or doctrinal disputes and meet a requirement that it be absolutely explicit.

Committee A sees the appropriate standard as not "absolutely explicit" (it is not even absolutely clear what that standard might require), but rather "adequately explicit." Thus, for example, a college's statement that it is "truly religious, but never denominational," that it is "positively and distinctly Christian in its influence, discipline, and instruction," is too broad, too inexact to constitute an acceptable limit on freedom of teaching. It does not provide a reasonable faculty member with clear enough information about—that is, fair warning of—what conduct is proscribed, and hence is not adequately explicit.

By contrast, a restriction on any teaching or utterance that "contradicts *explicit* principles of the [Church's] faith or morals," for example, is adequately explicit. It would, however, be incumbent on an institution adopting such a restriction to show that at the time of appointment, the institution and the faculty member knew precisely what those principles were. In a recent case, the institution required prospective faculty members to subscribe to a set of religious tenets, none of which explicitly proscribed conduct that could be taken as sympathetic to the civil rights of homosexuals; in taking action against a faculty member on grounds of conduct that was perceived as sympathetic to the civil rights of homosexuals, the governing board was bringing to bear on her a restriction of which she had not been given fair warning at the time of appointment.[5]

Adequate explicitness is plainly a matter of degree. Some institutions demand faithfulness to future teachings or doctrines that may be unascertained or unascertainable at the time and which may depart, subtly or radically, from those in effect at the time of appointment. A limitation drafted so broadly as to include any teaching, doctrine, or constraint subsequently promulgated would fail to meet the standard of adequate explicitness. But cases may arise where a restriction not imposed in express terms at the time of appointment can be viewed as covered by a broadly drafted rule because the restriction was reasonably anticipated.[6]

Guideline Three

Committee A is the body that decides, on the basis of the ad hoc committee's report, whether to recommend censure.

1. If Committee A concludes that the institution is not subject to the 1940 *Statement*'s requirement to afford academic freedom, it should not recommend censure.
2. If Committee A concludes that the institution is subject to the 1940 *Statement* but has not adhered to the terms of the limitations clause, then Committee A should presumably recommend censure.
3. If Committee A concludes that the institution is subject to the 1940 *Statement* and has adhered to the terms of the limitations clause, then Committee A should not recommend censure unless it concludes that the institution has failed to afford academic due process, or has violated some other key provision of the 1940 *Statement* or of derivative Association-supported standards.

Comment on Institutions for Clerical Education
Committee A said in its 1988 report: "Higher education is not catechesis, and this is no less true for professional clerical education than for any other professional calling." The committee may conclude, however, that a particular institution that is dedicated to training members of the clergy in the faith is outside the ambit of the Association's censure process, in light of Committee A's assessment of considerations of the kind pointed to in Guideline One.

If such an institution was one at which adherence to the academic freedom provisions of the 1940 *Statement* was to be expected, but has now ceased to be one—perhaps because of action by its governing board—the Association may wish to give notice to the profession and the public that the change has taken place.

Notes

1. "The 'Limitations' Clause in the 1940 'Statement of Principles,' " *Academe* 74 (September–October 1988): 52–58.

2. From its inception, the American Association of University Professors has found it necessary to distinguish between institutions of higher learning which are committed to academic freedom and those institutions where free inquiry is subordinated to a religious (or some other) mission. Committee A's seminal 1915 "Declaration of Principles on Academic Freedom and Academic Tenure," commenting on the latter institutions, stated,

> They do not, at least as regards one particular subject, accept the principles of freedom of inquiry, of opinion, and of teaching; and their purpose is not to advance knowledge by the unrestricted research and unfettered discussion of impartial investigators, but rather to subsidize the promotion of the opinions held by the persons, usually not of the scholar's calling, who provide the funds for their maintenance. . . . Genuine boldness

and thoroughness of inquiry, and freedom of speech, are scarcely reconcilable with the prescribed inculcation of a particular opinion upon a controverted question. (AAUP, *Policy Documents and Reports,* 11th ed. [Baltimore: Johns Hopkins University Press, 2015], 5).

3. Danforth Commission on Church Colleges and Universities, *Church-Sponsored Higher Education in the United States* (Washington, DC: American Council on Education, 1966).

4. "Academic Freedom and Tenure: Concordia Seminary," *AAUP Bulletin* 61 (April 1975): 49–59.

5. "Academic Freedom and Tenure: Nyack College," *Academe* 80 (September–October 1994): 73–79.

6. For example, Professor Ehlen at Concordia Seminary (Missouri) in 1975 could reasonably plead lack of adequate notice. But Professor Schmidt's claim at Concordia Theological Seminary (Indiana) in 1989 proved more troublesome; see "Academic Freedom and Tenure: Concordia Theological Seminary," *Academe* 75 (May–June 1989): 57–67.

On the Imposition of Tenure Quotas

This statement was approved by the Association's Committee A on Academic Freedom and Tenure and adopted by the Association's Council in October 1973.

Many institutions of higher education have had to consider ways of accommodating the number and composition of their faculty to a static or declining financial situation. The Association has developed criteria applicable where a reduction in faculty positions is contemplated because of financial exigency or discontinuance of a program.[1] This statement will concern itself with institutional policies designed to shape the overall composition of the faculty by limiting the number of tenured positions, and especially with those policies that establish a fixed maximum percentage of faculty who may possess tenure at a given time.[2]

The Association, while recognizing the concerns that motivate such quotas, opposes them. They are an unwise solution to the problem they purport to solve, and can have grave consequences for the institutions that adopt them. Moreover, they are not compelled, for other more nearly satisfactory alternatives are available.

Recognizing that tenure best protects academic freedom, but that it is usually undesirable to afford tenure automatically upon an individual's joining a faculty, the American Association of University Professors has supported the employment of a stated maximum probationary period, of sufficient but not excessive length, during which the academic qualifications and performance of newer faculty members can be evaluated in terms of institutional standards and expectations. Indeed, it is principally to provide each institution with a reasonable opportunity of assessing the skills of probationary appointees in terms of its tenure standards (and the availability of others whom it may also desire to consider for tenured appointment) that this Association has not favored policies of automatic tenure. However, to continue the service of faculty members beyond the maximum probationary period, while withholding tenure, presents an unwarranted hazard to their academic freedom.

Accordingly, institutions may properly set high standards for tenure, but they subvert the functions of tenure standards if they provide that, no matter how clearly nontenured faculty members meet any stated academic standard (and no matter how well they compare with the

tenured faculty and all others whom the institution is able to attract to that faculty), the system is such as to require their release from the very positions in which they have served with unqualified distinction. Holding faculty members in nontenured service, and then releasing them because a numerical limit on tenured positions prohibits their retention, has the effect of nullifying probation. All full-time appointments, excepting only special appointments of specified brief duration and reappointments of retired faculty members on special conditions, should be either probationary relating to continuous tenure or with continuous tenure.[3] To make appointments that are destined to lead to nonretention because of a fixed numerical quota of tenured positions, obviating any realistic opportunity for the affected individuals to be evaluated for tenure on their academic record, is to depart from a basic feature of the system of tenure and thus to weaken the protections of academic freedom.

A variation to nonretention because of a tenure quota, one which Committee A finds wholly inimical to the principles of academic freedom which tenure serves, is the policy adopted at a few institutions of withholding tenure from admittedly qualified candidates who have completed the maximum probationary period but retaining them in a kind of holding pattern, perpetually more vulnerable than their tenured colleagues to termination of services, unless and until the quota eases for them and they, too, are granted tenure. If they have fully earned an entitlement to tenure, there can be no justification for continuing them in a less favorable and more vulnerable status than their tenured colleagues.

Committee A, accordingly, opposes the adoption of tenure quotas for the following reasons:

1. If combined with the possibility of additional term contracts beyond the period of maximum probationary service plainly adequate to determine the individual's entitlement to tenure, the system indefensibly extends conditions of jeopardy to academic freedom.
2. Probation with automatic termination of appointment is not probation; those whom

quotas affect by automatically excluding them from consideration for tenure essentially are reduced to a terminal class of contract workers rendered incapable of full and equal faculty membership irrespective of the nature of the service they have given and irrespective of the professional excellence of that service.

3. In designating a portion of the probationary regular faculty as ineligible to continue, in order to cope with needs of staff flexibility and financial constraints, a quota system is a crude and unjust substitute for more equitable methods of academic planning.

Committee A, in registering its concern over the fixing of a maximum numerical percentage of tenured faculty, does not suggest that an institution should be unconcerned with appointment policies which will permit it to bring new members into its faculty with some regularity. A sound academic program needs elements not only of continuity but also of flexibility, which is served by the continuing opportunity to recruit new persons and to pursue new academic emphases. It is desirable for a faculty to include those recently arrived from the seminars of our graduate schools as well as those who are well established as scholars and teachers.

Such considerations of flexibility are often adduced in support of tenure quotas. But this misses two central points. First, the system of tenure does not exist as subordinate to convenience and flexibility. The protection of academic freedom must take precedence over the claimed advantages of increased flexibility.

Second, imposing a numerical limit on the percentage of tenured faculty disregards a range of other ways to attain a desired mix of senior and junior faculty. Indeed, it imposes an inequitable burden on a vulnerable portion of the faculty in a facile response to issues of academic staffing that should reflect far more comprehensive planning. Establishing fixed quotas may deprive the profession of a large part of the generation of scholars and teachers who currently populate the nontenured positions at our colleges and universities. It would be preferable by far to employ a variety of other measures—some affecting tenured faculty, others affecting probationary and nontenured faculty, and still others affecting prospective faculty members—to ensure that the necessary burdens of financial stringency and lack of growth are shared to some extent by all academic generations.

While opposing the imposition of tenure quotas, Committee A recognizes that the general proportion of a faculty on tenure can have an important long-range bearing on the nature and quality of an institution of higher education. Given a situation in which there is small prospect for significant growth in the total size of the faculty, considerations that merit attention include:

1. The desired distribution of tenured and nontenured faculty should be viewed as a long-term goal rather than a short-term solution. The ratio of tenured to nontenured faculty is itself the dynamic consequence of a complex of academic decisions and developments, each of which can be reconsidered. These include: (a) the rate of growth of the institution and its faculty; (b) the fraction of those appointed initially to tenured or probationary positions; (c) the use of visiting faculty members; (d) the use of graduate assistants; (e) the average length of the probationary period of nontenured faculty members who ultimately achieve tenure; (f) the fraction of nontenured faculty members who ultimately achieve tenure; (g) the institutional policy on retirement; and (h) the age distribution of the total faculty.

2. A satisfactory long-range plan may well imply that, along the way, the proportion of the faculty on tenure will at first increase and then, as the force of the plan takes effect, decrease. Just as the end of growth in the size of the faculty leads to a gradual increase in the proportion of those tenured, so the gradual aging of the present faculty will ultimately lead to a tendency for the proportion to decline. Most changes in academic personnel policies require some lag in time before full implementation and impact, and there is nothing disastrous in a temporary bulge in the percentage of faculty members on tenure. On the other hand, long-range injury to an institution may result from rigid and hasty application of any single presumed remedy, such as the imposition of a fixed quota.

3. It should be recognized that, in the short run, reducing the proportion of a faculty on tenure produces very little benefit by way of flexibility. It is only over a period of several years that a change in the proportion acquires pertinency. If an institution finds itself, at the beginning of development of a long-range plan, at or near a preferred distribution which it wishes generally to maintain, it may well be sensible to choose consciously to exceed the desired distribution temporarily while the steps necessary to return to that distribution take effect.

4. Equity and institutional morale demand that the probationary faculty not be made to bear all or almost all of the burden of satisfying the desired tenure ratio. Attractive accelerated retirement opportunities for senior tenured faculty present one possible alternative. Additionally, consideration may be given to planning carefully the proportion of teaching and research done by full-time and part-time tenured and probationary faculty, teaching assistants, and temporary appointees.

Foreclosing promotion to a tenured position because of a numerical quota is unacceptable. Stricter standards for the awarding of tenure can be developed over the years, with a consequent decrease in the probability of achieving tenure. But it is essential to distinguish a deliberate change in standards, retaining a positive probability of an individual's achieving tenure pursuant to well-defined criteria and adequate procedures for evaluation and review, from a situation in which the granting of tenure, for reasons unrelated to the individual's merits, is never a realistic possibility.

Notes

1. See Regulations 4c and 4d of the Association's "Recommended Institutional Regulations on Academic Freedom and Tenure," AAUP, *Policy Documents and Reports*, 11th ed. (Baltimore: Johns Hopkins University Press, 2015), 81–83. See also the Association's statement on "The Role of the Faculty in Budgetary and Salary Matters," ibid., 289–91, and "On Institutional Problems Resulting from Financial Exigency: Some Operating Guidelines," ibid., 309–10.

2. The Commission on Academic Tenure in Higher Education called for "policies relating to the proportion of tenured and nontenured faculty that will be compatible with the composition of [the institution's] present staff, its resources, and its future objectives." See *Faculty Tenure: A Report and Recommendations* (San Francisco: Jossey-Bass, 1973), 45–51, particularly the commission's recommendation, 50–51.

3. See Regulation 1b of the "Recommended Institutional Regulations on Academic Freedom and Tenure," *Policy Documents and Reports*, 80.

Academic Freedom in the Medical School

This statement was adopted by the participants in the Conference on Academic Values in the Transformation of Academic Medicine in May 1999. It was endorsed in June 1999 by the Association's Committee A on Academic Freedom and Tenure, adopted by the AAUP Council, and approved by the Eighty-Fifth Annual Meeting.

The term "academic freedom" refers to the freedom of college and university faculty to teach, to conduct research and publish the results, and to fulfill responsibilities as officers of an educational institution. Academic freedom is a core value in the American community of higher learning. Its protection is a crucial responsibility of university faculties, administrations, and governing boards. While academic freedom clearly safeguards the work of professors and their institutions, its primary purpose is to advance the general welfare. In the words of the seminal 1940 *Statement of Principles on Academic Freedom and Tenure,* "Institutions of higher education are conducted for the common good and not to further the interest of either the individual teacher or the institution as a whole. The common good depends upon the free search for truth and its free exposition."[1]

An administrative officer in academic medicine has recently observed that the issue of academic freedom, so central to the academic life of the university, "has rarely been debated within our nation's medical schools."[2] With the major changes that are currently in process in academic health centers—in the teaching of students, in the status of medical school faculty, and in the conditions under which these faculty members work—it is urgent that this topic now be addressed.

The modern medical school has many of the attributes of a complex, market-driven healthcare system with professors often acting as entrepreneurs in research and in patient care. It is marked by conflicting roles and responsibilities, both academic and nonacademic, for faculty members and administrators alike. The intense competition for private or governmental funding can affect the choice of research subjects, and in some instances, scientists in academic medicine are finding it difficult to secure funding for unorthodox research or research on matters that are politically sensitive. The growing reliance on the clinical enterprise at many medical schools, and the

resulting expansion of the number of professors who are engaged mainly in clinical work, may serve to divert the schools from their teaching mission, and may implicitly or explicitly dissuade professors from devoting their attention to such activities as graduate teaching or university service that are not income producing in nature. Further affecting the academic freedom of medical school faculty is the hospital pattern of hierarchical organization, with deans and department chairs—and often professional administrators who lack medical training or academic experience—making decisions that elsewhere in the university would be made collegially or left to individual professors. Academic freedom should be especially nurtured and supported because of the constraints surrounding medical research. Rules governing genetic research and engineering, debates about the beginning and end of human life, and disputes about the use of animals for research and experimentation are examples of matters that can profoundly affect the work of medical school professors. While society may require restraints on the pursuit of knowledge in these and other similarly sensitive areas, basic principles of academic freedom, in the medical school as elsewhere in an institution of higher learning, must be observed.

1. *Freedom to Inquire and to Publish.* The freedom to pursue research and the correlative right to transmit the fruits of inquiry to the wider community—without limitations from corporate or political interests and without prior restraint or fear of subsequent punishment—are essential to the advancement of knowledge. Accordingly, principles of academic freedom allow professors to publish or otherwise disseminate research findings that may offend the commercial sponsors of the research, potential donors, or political interests, or people with certain religious or social persuasions. As stated in a 1981 AAUP

report, however, "Academic freedom does not give its possessors the right to impose any risk of harm they like in the name of freedom of inquiry. It is no violation of any right . . . that falls into the cluster named by 'academic freedom' for a university to prevent a member of its faculty from carrying out research, at the university, that would impose a high risk of serious physical harm on its subjects, and that would in only minimal ways benefit either them or the state of knowledge in the field in question."[3] The pursuit of medical research should proceed with due regard for the rights of individuals as provided by National Institutes of Health and university protocols on the use of human and animal subjects. Any research plan involving such matters should be reviewed by a body of faculty peers or an institutional review board both before research is initiated and while it is being conducted. Any limitations on academic freedom because of the religious or other aims of an institution should be clearly stated in writing at the time of initial appointment.

2. *Freedom to Teach.* The freedom to teach includes the right of the faculty to select the materials, determine the approach to the subject, make the assignments, and assess student academic performance in teaching activities for which faculty members are individually responsible, without having their decisions subject to the veto of a department chair, dean, or other administrative officer. Teaching duties in medical schools that are commonly shared among a number of faculty members require a significant amount of coordination and the imposition of a certain degree of structure, and often involve a need for agreement on such matters as general course content, syllabi, and examinations. Often, under these circumstances, the decisions of the group may prevail over the dissenting position of a particular individual.

When faculty members are engaged in patient care, they have a special obligation to respect the rights of their patients and to exercise appropriate discretion while on rounds or in other non-classroom settings.

3. *Freedom to Question and to Criticize.* According to a 1994 AAUP statement, *On the Relationship of Faculty Governance to Academic Freedom,* faculty members should be free to speak out "on matters having to do with their institution and its policies," and they should be able "to express their professional opinions without fear of reprisal."[4] In speaking critically, faculty members should strive for accuracy and should exercise appropriate restraint. Tolerance of criticism, however, is a crucial component of the academic environment and of an institution's ultimate vitality. No attribute of the modern medical school that may distinguish it from other units within a university should serve as a pretext for abridging the role of the medical faculty in institutional governance, including, but not necessarily confined to, those areas specified in the AAUP's *Statement on Government of Colleges and Universities* as falling within the faculty's primary responsibility.[5]

Despite the serious challenges currently facing them, our institutions of academic medicine should respect and foster conditions that are essential to freedom of learning, freedom of teaching, and freedom of expression.

Notes

1. For a discussion of problems relating to academic medicine and the importance of tenure as a protection for academic freedom, see "Tenure in the Medical School," AAUP, *Policy Documents and Reports,* 11th ed. (Baltimore: Johns Hopkins University Press, 2015), 73–78.

2. N. Lynn Eckhert, "Time Is Ripe for Dialogue about Academic Freedom," *Academic Physician and Scientist* (July/August 1998): 3.

3. "Regulations Governing Research on Human Subjects," *Academe* 67 (December 1981): 367. In addition, see "Regulation of Research on Human Subjects: Academic Freedom and the Institutional Review Board," *Bulletin of the American Association of University Professors.* Special issue, *Academe* 99 (July–August 2013): 101–17.

4. *Policy Documents and Reports,* 124.

5. See also the derivative statement, "Faculty Participation in the Selection, Evaluation, and Retention of Administrators," ibid., 130–31.

Tenure in the Medical School

This report, approved in 1999 by the Association's Committee A on Academic Freedom and Tenure, is a revision of a report approved for publication by Committee A in November 1995.

Introduction and Background

This report and proposed policy statement result from ongoing concerns within the American Association of University Professors regarding the changing nature of academic medical centers in American higher education and the impact, evident or potential, of those changes on questions of faculty status and academic freedom within such centers.[1]

Until the early twentieth century, few medical schools were affiliated with universities, most being freestanding proprietary schools of varying standards. The faculty were largely physicians whose income was derived from the private practice of medicine and fees from students. Reforms in medical education early in this century were influenced by the Flexner report and fostered by the American Medical Association, and required the affiliation of medical schools with universities along European (particularly German) lines, with the concurrent establishment of basic-science departments for research and teaching.[2] The new university-affiliated medical schools developed full-time, salaried faculty, some of whom were not physicians but basic scientists by training, and their arrival coincided with the formation of the American Association of University Professors and the development of policies and standards relating to academic freedom and tenure.

The rapid post–World War II growth of medical schools resulted in major changes, including the increase in the number of medical students, curricular revision, augmented postgraduate medical training in clinical specialties (residency programs), greater emphasis on research and patient care, and the creation of non-tenure-track lines of full-time as well as part-time faculty. These expanded responsibilities required an expansion in the total number of faculty as well, and altered the relationship between the faculty and the medical school and also between the medical school and the university. Faculty salaries have become increasingly dependent on income from outside sources (e.g., research grants for faculty in basic-science departments and for non-physician scientists in clinical departments and fees from patient-care activities for physician faculty). Academic advancement and tenure have become increasingly based on scholarly research and publications, and less on teaching and service.

Medical schools have a unique status among institutions of higher learning. Whether state or private, they are large institutions which, with few exceptions, are part of or affiliated with universities. They encompass diverse educational and research interests ranging from molecular biology to preventive medicine. They rely on affiliated hospitals and clinics for patients for medical practice and teaching of students, postgraduates (residents), and fellows.

If medical schools are very different from the universities with which they are affiliated, they are also very different institutions from what they were three decades ago. Then a medical school looked a lot more like the rest of the university. Its revenues came from the same combination of sources, but the proportions of that income were very different from what they are now. Revenue now comes from tuition and fees, state and local governments, federal funds (research and other income), endowment, contract research, and medical services.

The number of medical students has not grown in recent years, but that number is about double that of thirty-five years ago.[3] The number of faculty members, however, has grown dramatically over that period of time. Today there are about 75,000 faculty members in medical schools. A very substantial number of the newly added faculty members are appointed to full-time positions in clinical departments, but most of their responsibilities are in billable patient care and clinical teaching (supervising medical students in practice settings). The balance between income-generating patient services and the teaching of students weighs heavily on the side of the former. The rapid growth in the number of clinical faculty members, a number about ten times as large as thirty-five years ago, is almost entirely due to its role in producing revenue, as the number of students has only doubled since then.

Because of the volatility of the environment in which medical schools function, now and in the future, it is especially appropriate that the role of tenure as the guarantor of academic freedom in these institutions receives examination. Faculty members in medical schools face problems with respect to tenure different from those faced by faculty members in other parts of the university. The expectation that tenured faculty members create their own salaries from the provision of medical services or research grants will cause increasing problems as resources become scarcer. For example, reliance on external funding for salary support poses special problems for non-physician tenured and tenure-track faculty researchers in clinical departments. If these faculty members lose research grant support, they cannot turn to medical practice to earn a salary. Their vulnerability is greater than that of tenured physician faculty members who can teach medical specialties and who can earn income by medical practice, as well as that of tenured faculty members in basic-science departments who can teach in their academic specialties.

As a provider of health care, a medical school needs income derived from the clinical services to provide a large share of the salaries of the physician faculty. Physicians who provide patient care include tenure-track and tenured faculty, non-tenure-track faculty, and resident and subspecialty physicians in training. The non-tenure-track physician faculty, who are not necessarily required to be scholars and may do little teaching, provide much of the care of patients, whose fees add to the income of the medical school.

The modern medical school, in short, has the attributes of a business enterprise with largely individual entrepreneurial activities in both patient care and research. Those faculty members so involved are counted on to bring in funds not only to underwrite salaries for supporting personnel, laboratory equipment and supplies, and those indirect costs necessary to maintain the infrastructure of the enterprise, but also to underwrite faculty salaries, including in many cases a portion of the salaries of tenured faculty members. Academic advancement of faculty in basic-science departments and non-physician faculty in clinical departments is disproportionately dependent upon scholarly research as compared with teaching and service, and the research in turn is disproportionately dependent on salary support from research grants. The heavy dependence on external funding for salary

support can divert faculty dedication and effort away from teaching and university service toward research or patient care to maintain their income and status.

The challenges facing the medical school have been succinctly stated by the president of the Association of American Medical Colleges (AAMC), Dr. Jordan J. Cohen:

> The existence of tenure in medical schools represents a linkage to the broader academic culture of the university, with its traditional devotion to a free exchange of ideas without threat of economic penalty. Yet medical schools, because of their increased involvement in the real world of health-care delivery, are also linked to the corporate culture, with its brutal devotion to productivity without guarantees of economic security. The clash of these cultures is reaching deafening proportions and will challenge the most adroit academic administrators. If medical schools are to succeed, they must avoid the Scylla of an ivory-tower disregard of new competitive realities and the Charybdis of a corporate sellout of academic values.[4]

In this report Committee A has attempted to maintain an awareness of precisely those twin dangers.

Issues with Respect to Association Policy

The general concern of Committee A is whether medical schools support, or are prepared in the near and long-term future to support, the policies and procedures relating to academic freedom, tenure, and due process that have been promulgated by the AAUP since its founding. The need for a review of Association policy is suggested by the questions raised by some medical school administrators and faculty about the validity of and need for tenure, along with instances of abridgment of academic freedom and due process in medical schools. Among the issues we have noted are (1) the appearance of de facto departures from standards, for example, in regard to the application of the probationary period; (2) the increasing use of non-tenurable full-time as well as part-time faculty; (3) in some, though not all, medical schools, an apparently inadequate role for medical school faculty in institutional governance, particularly in terms of faculty status, working conditions, and curriculum; and (4) a concern about possible intrusion by outside agents (e.g., state legislatures, Congress, licensing authorities) on governance and curriculum.

Although there is no doubt that the intensity of debate regarding the future of tenure in medical schools is considerably heightened as a result of the pressures we have been outlining, recent studies indicate that tenure in some form remains at the core of the faculty staffing policies of such schools.[5] The issue of tenure is more dramatically highlighted in the drop in the proportion of clinical faculty with tenure or on the tenure track.[6] Within the tenure track, there is growing belief that a six-year probationary period may be inadequate "for basic-science faculty to establish themselves as independent investigators, especially given the competition for research funding." If tenure is suffering erosion, it has not yet endured a frontal attack.

But even where the presence of tenure suggests the reassuring persistence of the system, there is solid evidence that the financial assurances of that system are being defined in a more limited way: that is, in connection with the percentage of institutional "hard money" in the tenure line. Unlike the situation in other academic units in modern American colleges and universities, it is not uncommon in medical schools to have tenure guarantees attached to, say, 20 or 30 percent of a faculty member's full-time appointment, with the remainder of the salary dependent on the procurement of external funding. Inasmuch as the 1940 *Statement of Principles on Academic Freedom and Tenure,* drafted and endorsed by the AAUP and the Association of American Colleges and Universities and carrying the endorsement of more than 240 educational and professional associations, links tenure not only to "freedom of teaching and research and of extramural activities," but also to "a sufficient degree of economic security to make the profession attractive to men and women of ability," there would seem to be involved in appointments of the sort just described a very real question as to precisely what tenure means under conditions that protect only a portion of the faculty member's income. A reasonable interpretation of the 1940 *Statement* would seem to imply that the ability of the faculty member to defend academic freedom, his or her own or the principle in general, is linked to whether the salary is adequate to the maintenance of financial independence.[7]

At the same time, the enormous diversity of medical-school programs and of the variety of faculty who teach in them suggests that certain kinds of appointments were not foreseen by, and in any case not intended to fall within the ambit of, the 1940 *Statement.* In contrast to academic faculty of the sort envisioned by that statement, academic physicians deal directly with the general public (patients) in an income-producing environment. Their relationship to the institution with which they are affiliated is therefore fundamentally unlike that of the full-time teachers and

investigators who are described in the statement. We acknowledge that no policy adopted by the Association with respect to the academic culture of medical schools can command the adherence of those schools without taking into account the nature of the medical enterprise. Nonetheless, we believe that existing Association policy can convincingly address many of those realities.[8]

The subcommittee acknowledges that medical schools to some extent, and increasingly, partake of the nature of corporate as well as academic enterprise. (Here we would content ourselves with noting that corporations are not by definition incapable of offering appropriate guarantees of appointment.) Association policy must be flexible enough to address this question in a principled manner while being persuasive in terms of policy guidance to those engaged in the daily work of medical education. We also believe, however, that the presence of income-generating activities in no way weakens the claim of faculty members in those schools to the protections of academic freedom and tenure consistent with the particular role that a given faculty member plays. To the extent that medical schools, and academic health centers, are academic institutions, and that an appointment in them is subject to those expectations that apply to tenured and tenure-track appointments in other disciplinary areas of the university, we see no basis for conceding that such appointments are immune from the application of Association standards. To the extent that an appointment in, for example, a teaching hospital, with perhaps peripheral instructional duties and the expectation of the generation of clinical income, is essentially that of a practitioner, we do not assert that the award of tenure is necessarily appropriate. Rather, we would argue that such classes of faculty should enjoy academic freedom, including, but not restricted to, the right to speak on institutional policy, and that they should be provided with protections against the application of unreasonable or capricious sanctions, such as precipitate dismissal, without the opportunity for a hearing, during a stated term of appointment. An important part of the responsibility for ensuring these conditions lies with the tenured faculty of the institution, in the context of a sound system of shared governance.

For the goal of quality to be implemented in a qualitatively sound way, the faculty members who offer medical education under substantially the same expectations of performance applicable to tenure-track faculty in other disciplines at that institution must have the same opportunity to benefit from freedom of inquiry, in teaching, research, and clinical practice, that ensures high quality in other areas of the academic enterprise. This includes the customary assurances of peer review and the right of appeal (rather than the mere delegation of review to officers of the medical-school administration), a probationary period consonant with AAUP standards, a level of participation in the governance of the medical school appropriate to the particular kind of faculty appointment, and sufficient economic security to provide a safeguard for the exercise of academic freedom by all faculty.[9] There should be collegial development of policies regarding laboratory space, clinical and other work assignments, research and space resources, and procedures that encourage the resolution of differences through peer review. In short, after giving all due allowance to the specific realities of the teaching and research environment in medical schools, we do not believe that they are so peculiar as to warrant placing all faculty in such schools beyond the academic pale, that is, outside the generally accepted standards set forth in the 1940 *Statement* and derivative policies of this Association.

Statement of Policy

1. The multiple purposes of an academic medical school have led to a variety of academic appointments—tenured, tenure-track, and non-tenurable—in which teaching, research, service, clinical practice, and patient care are given different weights and emphases. To the extent that these functions are all designated by traditional academic titles, however modified (e.g., clinical associate professor), they warrant the assumption of faculty status that brings the holders of those titles within the ambit of applicable Association policies and procedures, and hence the protections appropriate to a particular status.

2. Where the configuration of duties is such as to suggest the advisability of an appointment in a non-tenure-track position, a starting point for considering the obligations of the medical school may be found in the Association's 1993 report, *The Status of Non-tenure-track Faculty,* for all classes of faculty, full or part time. Where the exigencies of particular kinds of faculty appointments may require exceptions to the standards set forth in that document, those exceptions should be specified after meaningful consultation with the appropriate faculty bodies in the medical school.

3. The Association has never countenanced the creation of large classes of faculty in categories other than tenured, tenure track, and visiting (or other appointments designated as short term with a terminus understood by both parties to the contract). To the extent that a faculty appointment at a medical school resembles a traditional academic appointment, with clearly understood obligations in teaching, research, and service, the burden of proof on the institution is greater to justify making the appointment to a non-tenure-track position.

4. Tenure in a medical school should normally be awarded to a faculty member on the basis of the probationary period as defined in the 1940 *Statement, viz:*

    Beginning with appointment to the rank of full-time instructor or a higher rank, the probationary period should not exceed seven years, including within this period full-time service in all institutions of higher education; but subject to the proviso that when, after a term of probationary service of more than three years in one or more institutions, a teacher is called to another institution, it may be agreed in writing that the new appointment is for a probationary period of not more than four years, even though thereby the person's total probationary period in the academic profession is extended beyond the normal maximum of seven years. Notice should be given at least one year prior to the expiration of the probationary period if the teacher is not to be continued after the expiration of that period.[10]

    We note a number of devices in the medical-school setting to lengthen the probationary period, for example, by allowing adequate time for persons in clinical positions to seek board certification, time devoted to patient care rather than research. While the complexities with respect to clinical practice may make such arrangements not only useful, but also beneficial to the clinical faculty member, we see no reason to consider the extension of such a practice to researchers in the basic sciences when expectations for the award of tenure conform to those extant in connection with appointments elsewhere in the university.

5. The sources of funding for positions in academic medical schools vary perhaps more greatly than in other units of the university, with the faculty member being expected in many cases to make up a designated portion of his or her salary from patient care or research. The 1940 *Statement of Principles* stipulates that tenure is a means not only to academic freedom, but also to "a sufficient degree of economic security to make the profession attractive to men and women of ability." Except, as is sometimes the case, where the

reward of rank and tenure is purely honorific, all tenured and tenure-track faculty should be guaranteed an assured minimum salary adequate to the maintenance of support at a level appropriate to faculty members in the basic sciences, and not merely a token stipend, on a formula to be determined by the administration and board of trustees after consultation with a representative body of the faculty. The unilateral administrative abrogation of a portion of that salary, absent a prior understanding as to the extent of its guarantee, may reasonably be interpreted not as an exercise of fiduciary responsibility but as an attack on the principle of tenure. While the same minimum may not apply in the case of non-tenure-track faculty, those faculty should have a clearly understood and contractually enforceable expectation of a stipulated salary that cannot be unilaterally or arbitrarily abridged during the appointment period. Although the extent of economic security may be subject to interpretation, due process must be assured for all faculty regardless of the nature of the appointment.

6. Since medical schools, whether freestanding or part of a larger institution, demonstrably engage many of their faculty in the traditional areas of teaching and research, the participation of the faculty in governance is as essential to educational quality in the medical school context as in any other part of the university. According to the Association's *Statement on Government of Colleges and Universities,*

> The faculty has primary responsibility for such fundamental areas as curriculum, subject matter and methods of instruction, research, faculty status, and those aspects of student life which relate to the educational process. On these matters the power of review or final decision lodged in the governing board or delegated by it to the president should be exercised adversely only in exceptional circumstances, and for reasons communicated to the faculty.

The level of faculty participation, of course, may be adjusted in individual cases to take into account such considerations as the tenurable or non-tenurable nature of the appointment, as well as full- or part-time status, though we suggest that a functional definition of the faculty member's role ought to be the chief determinant. We have seen no compelling argument why the faculty of such schools should exercise a more limited influence in those schools than do faculty elsewhere in higher education, especially since in an

academic health center a large portion of the budget may be generated by faculty in the form of clinical income as well as external grants. Key to the role of medical faculty, for the purposes of the present report, is the opportunity to define the terms and conditions of faculty employment, including such appointments as are necessary to meet institutional needs, and procedures for the award of tenure under Association-supported standards.

Conclusion

The Association has long held that academic tenure is not merely, or even most importantly, a form of job security, but rather an instrument for the protection of "the common good." In serving that function, a system of tenure, properly applied, is a guarantor of educational quality. We question whether any institution of higher education or one of its components, whether the purpose be undergraduate, graduate, or professional education, can provide such educational quality without that reasonable assurance of stability that helps ensure the commitment of its faculty members to freedom of inquiry in teaching and research and to the preparation of its students.

Notes

1. Much of the background section of this report has been adopted freely (and with thanks) from a 1994 report by an AAUP Task Force on Medical Schools.

2. Abraham Flexner, *Medical Education in the United States and Canada* (Boston: Merrymount Press, 1910; Carnegie Foundation for the Advancement of Teaching, Bulletin #4); Lester S. King, *American Medicine Comes of Age, 1840–1920* (Chicago: American Medical Association, 1984); Paul Starr, *The Social Transformation of American Medicine* (New York: Basic Books, 1982).

3. Robert F. Jones, *American Medical Education: Institutions, Programs, and Issues* (Washington, DC: Association of American Medical Colleges, 1992), 10.

4. Jordan J. Cohen, "Academic Medicine's Tenuous Hold on Tenure," *Academic Medicine* 70 (1995): 294.

5. The conclusion of Robert F. Jones and Susan C. Sanderson, "Tenure Policies in U.S. and Canadian Medical Schools" (*Academic Medicine* 69 [1994]: 772–78), is that "medical schools have adapted tenure policies to allow themselves flexibility in meeting their academic and clinical missions. The forces driving schools to fashion unique faculty appointment arrangements are not dissipating. Tenure is likely to continue in the academic medical center of the future but to play a diminished role."

6. "In 1983, 30,856 clinical faculty were listed on the FRS [Association of American Medical Colleges Faculty

Roster System], with 59 percent in tenure streams. . . . By 1993, the number of clinical faculty listed on the FRS had nearly doubled, to 58,607. Only 47 percent were in tenure streams: 26 percent with tenure and 21 percent on track" (Jones and Sanderson, "Tenure Policies," 773).

7. Practices vary widely with respect to the percentage of clinical appointments that may be tenured, and in some cases the tenured portion may be so negligible as to be of little concern to the clinical faculty member. The situation has become much more complex since the time of the 1940 "Statement," and its framers doubtless would not have envisioned the complexities that have emerged. We suggest using a basic-science salary line as a guidepost for determining salary guarantees for clinical faculty members. The faculty of the particular school should be involved in arriving at a specific recommendation. Creative approaches not overtly at odds with existing Association policy seem possible. Thus, one school represented on the subcommittee has adopted a commitment to support such a faculty member at the fiftieth percentile at his or her academic rank as reported annually by the AAMC, or the present salary of the individual, whichever is less.

8. Although dealing primarily with term contracts in the area of sponsored research, the Association's "Report of the Special Committee on Academic Personnel Ineligible for Tenure" (*AAUP Bulletin* 52 [September 1966]: 280–82) acknowledges a category of employment, "contract research teams," to which "traditional concepts of academic freedom and tenure do not apply." It also argues, however, that "whenever academic institutions designate full-time researchers as faculty members, either by formal appointment or by conferring the titles of instructor, assistant or associate professor, or professor, those researchers should have all the rights of other faculty members." In the case of faculty members whose title is modified by the designation "clinical," this issue now presents itself in a new light which we believe needs to be addressed here. More reluctantly, but with the awareness that the Association must nonetheless take account of changing realities, AAUP's Committee on Part-Time and Non-tenure-track Appointments has developed, and the Association's Council (1993) approved, a document setting forth the basic protections that should be applied to non-tenure-track faculty: "The Status of Non-tenure-track Faculty" (*Academe* 79 [July–August 1993]: 39–46; see Statement of Policy, point 2, in this document).

9. In medical schools, the extent of the inclusion in departmental and faculty governance structures will depend on the extent to which the particular faculty member has responsibility for organizational or instructional matters that go beyond the specific, part-time instructional function for which he or she was appointed. For example, representation on a faculty curriculum committee by a part-time clinical faculty member who has been asked to organize student rotations in primary-care physicians' offices might seem reasonable. Likewise, the inclusion of a full-time non-tenure-track researcher on a faculty research committee might be deemed appropriate.

10. See also the Association's "Standards for Notice of Nonreappointment," AAUP, *Policy Documents and Reports*, 11th ed. (Baltimore: Johns Hopkins University Press, 2015), 99.

Recommended Institutional Regulations on Academic Freedom and Tenure

The *Recommended Institutional Regulations on Academic Freedom and Tenure* set forth, in language suitable for use by an institution of higher education, rules that derive from the chief provisions and interpretations of the 1940 *Statement of Principles on Academic Freedom and Tenure* and of the *Statement on Procedural Standards in Faculty Dismissal Proceedings*. The *Recommended Institutional Regulations* were first formulated by Committee A on Academic Freedom and Tenure in 1957. A revised and expanded text, approved by Committee A in 1968, reflected the development of Association standards and procedures. Texts with further revisions were approved by Committee A in 1972, in 1976, in 1982, in 1990, in 1999, in 2005, in 2006, in 2009, and in 2013. Three particularly noteworthy changes since the last edition of *Policy Documents and Reports* are the new definition of "financial exigency" in Regulation 4c, the elimination of a regulation entitled "Termination Because of Physical or Mental Disability," which is further explained in the report "Accommodating Faculty Members Who Have Disabilities," and the addition of Regulation 13 entitled "Part-Time Faculty Appointments."

The current text, adopted by the Council as AAUP policy, is based upon the Association's continuing experience in evaluating regulations actually in force at particular institutions. It is also based upon further definition of the standards and procedures of the Association over the years. The Association will be glad to assist in interpretation of the regulations or to consult about their incorporation in, or adaptation to, the rules of a particular college or university.

Foreword

These regulations are designed to enable the [named institution] to protect academic freedom and tenure and to ensure academic due process. The principles implicit in these regulations are for the benefit of all who are involved with or are affected by the policies and programs of the institution. A college or university is a marketplace of ideas, and it cannot fulfill its purposes of transmitting, evaluating, and extending knowledge if it requires conformity with any orthodoxy of content and method. In the words of the United States Supreme Court, "Teachers and students must always remain free to inquire, to study and to evaluate, to gain new maturity and understanding; otherwise our civilization will stagnate and die."

1. Statement of Terms of Appointment

a. The terms and conditions of every appointment to the faculty will be stated or confirmed in writing, and a copy of the appointment document will be supplied to the faculty member. Any subsequent extensions or modifications of an appointment, and any special understandings or any notices incumbent upon either party to provide, will be stated or confirmed in writing, and a copy will be given to the faculty member.

b. With the exception of special appointments clearly limited to a brief association with the institution, and reappointments of retired faculty members on special conditions, all full-time faculty appointments are of two kinds: (1) probationary appointments; (2) appointments with continuous tenure.

c. Except for faculty members who have tenure status, every person with a teaching or research appointment of any kind will be informed each year in writing of the renewal of the appointment and of all matters relative to eligibility for the acquisition of tenure.

2. Probationary Appointments

a. Probationary appointments may be for one year, or for other stated periods, subject to renewal. The total period of full-time service prior to the acquisition of continuous tenure will not exceed ____ years,[1] including all previous full-time service with the rank of instructor or higher in other institutions of higher learning, except that the probationary period may extend to as much as four years, even if the total full-time service in the profession thereby exceeds seven years; the terms of such extension will be stated in writing at the time of initial appointment.[2] Scholarly leave of absence for one year or less will count as part of the probationary period as if it were prior service at another institution, unless the individual and the institution agree in writing to an exception to this provision at the time the leave is granted.

b. The faculty member will be advised, at the time of initial appointment, of the substantive standards and procedures generally employed in decisions affecting renewal and tenure. Any special standards adopted by the faculty member's department or school will also be transmitted. The faculty member will be advised of the time when decisions affecting renewal or tenure are ordinarily made and will be given the opportunity to submit material believed to be helpful to an adequate consideration of the faculty member's circumstances.

c. Regardless of the stated term or other provisions of any appointments, written notice that a probationary appointment is not to be renewed will be given to the faculty member in advance of the expiration of the appointment as follows: (1) not later than March 1 of the first academic year of service if the appointment expires at the end of that year; or, if a one-year appointment terminates during an academic year, at least three months in advance of its termination; (2) not later than December 15 of the second academic year of service if the appointment expires at the end of that year; or, if an initial two-year appointment terminates during an academic year, at least six months in advance of its termination; (3) at least twelve months before the expiration of an appointment after two or more years of service at the institution.

d. The institution will normally notify faculty members whose appointments are being renewed of the terms and conditions of their renewals by March 15, but in no case will such information be given later than ____.[3]

e. When a decision not to renew an appointment has been reached, the faculty member involved will be informed of that decision in writing by the body or individual making the decision; the faculty member will be advised upon request of the reasons which contributed to that decision. The faculty member may request a reconsideration by the body or individual making the decision.

f. If the faculty member so requests, the reasons given in explanation of the nonrenewal will be confirmed in writing.

g. Insofar as the faculty member alleges that the decision against renewal was based on inadequate consideration, the committee[4] that reviews the faculty member's allegation will determine whether the decision was the result of adequate consideration in terms of the relevant standards of the institution. The review committee will not substitute its judgment on the merits for that of the body or individual that made the decision. If the review committee believes that adequate consideration was not given to the faculty member's qualifications, it will recommend reconsideration by the body or individual that made the decision, indicating the respects in which it believes the consideration may have been inadequate. It will provide copies of its findings to the faculty member, the body or individual that made the decision, and the president or other appropriate administrative officer.

3. Termination of Appointment by Faculty Members

Faculty members may terminate their appointments effective at the end of an academic year, provided that they give notice in writing at the earliest possible opportunity, but not later than May 15, or thirty days after receiving notification of the terms of appointment for the coming year, whichever date occurs later. Faculty members may properly request a waiver of this requirement of notice in case of hardship or in a situation where they would otherwise be denied substantial professional advancement or other opportunity.

4. Termination of Appointments by the Institution

a. Termination of an appointment with continuous tenure, or of a probationary or special appointment before the end of the specified term, may be effected by the institution only for adequate cause.

b. If termination takes the form of a dismissal for cause, it will be pursuant to the provisions specified in Regulation 5.

Financial Exigency[5]

c. (1) Termination of an appointment with continuous tenure, or of a probationary or special appointment before the end of the specified term, may occur under extraordinary circumstances because of a demonstrably bona fide financial exigency, i.e., a severe financial crisis that fundamentally compromises the academic integrity of the institution as a whole and that cannot be alleviated by less drastic means.

[Note: Each institution in adopting regulations on financial exigency will need to decide how to share and allocate the hard judgments and decisions that are necessary in such a crisis.

As a first step, there should be an elected faculty governance body, or a body designated by a collective bargaining agreement, that participates in the decision that a condition of financial exigency exists or is imminent and that all feasible alternatives to termination of appointments have been pursued, including expenditure of one-time money or reserves as bridge funding, furloughs, pay cuts, deferred-compensation plans, early-retirement packages, deferral of nonessential capital expenditures, and cuts to noneducational programs and services, including expenses for administration.[6]

Judgments determining where within the overall academic program termination of appointments may occur involve considerations of educational policy, including affirmative action, as well as of faculty status, and should therefore be the primary responsibility of the faculty or of an appropriate faculty body.[7] The faculty or an appropriate faculty body should also exercise primary responsibility in determining the criteria for identifying the individuals whose appointments are to be terminated. These criteria may appropriately include considerations of length of service.

The responsibility for identifying individuals whose appointments are to be terminated should be committed to a person or group designated or approved by the faculty. The allocation of this responsibility may vary according to the size and character of the institution, the extent of the terminations to be made, or other considerations of fairness in judgment. The case of a faculty member given notice of proposed termination of appointment will be governed by the following provisions.]

(2) Before any proposals for program discontinuance on grounds of financial exigency are made, the faculty or an appropriate faculty body will have opportunity to render an assessment in writing of the institution's financial condition.

[Note: Academic programs cannot be defined ad hoc, at any size; programs should be recognized academic units that existed prior to the declaration of financial exigency. The term "program" should designate a related cluster of credit-bearing courses that constitute a coherent body of study within a discipline or set of related disciplines. When feasible, the term should designate a department or similar administrative unit that offers majors and minors.]

(i) The faculty or an appropriate faculty body will have access to at least five years of audited financial statements, current and following-year budgets, and detailed cash-flow estimates for future years.

(ii) In order to make informed recommendations about the financial impact of program closures, the faculty or an appropriate faculty body will have access to detailed program, department, and administrative-unit budgets.

(iii) Faculty members in a program being considered for discontinuance because of financial exigency will promptly be informed of this activity in writing and provided at least thirty days in which to respond to it. Tenured, tenure-track, and contingent faculty members will be informed and invited to respond.

(3) If the administration issues notice to a particular faculty member of an intention to terminate the appointment because of financial exigency, the faculty member will have the right to a full hearing before a faculty committee. The hearing need not conform in all respects with a proceeding conducted pursuant to Regulation 5, but the essentials of an on-the-record adjudicative hearing will be observed. The issues in this hearing may include the following:

(i) The existence and extent of the condition of financial exigency. The burden will rest on the administration to prove the existence and extent of the condition. The findings of a faculty committee in a previous proceeding involving the same issue may be introduced.

(ii) The validity of the educational judgments and the criteria for identification for termination; but the recommendations of a faculty body on these matters will be considered presumptively valid.

(iii) Whether the criteria are being properly applied in the individual case.

(4) If the institution, because of financial exigency, terminates appointments, it will not at the same time make new appointments, except in extraordinary circumstances where a serious distortion in the academic program would otherwise result. The appointment of a faculty member with tenure will not be terminated in favor of retaining a faculty member without tenure, except in extraordinary circumstances where a serious distortion of the academic program would otherwise result.

(5) Before terminating an appointment because of financial exigency, the institution, with faculty participation, will make every effort to place the faculty member concerned in another suitable position within the institution.

(6) In all cases of termination of appointment because of financial exigency, the faculty member concerned will be given notice or severance salary not less than as prescribed in Regulation 8.

(7) In all cases of termination of appointment because of financial exigency, the place of the faculty member concerned will not be filled by a replacement within a period of three years, unless the released faculty member has been offered reinstatement and at least thirty days in which to accept or decline it.

Discontinuance of Program or Department for Educational Reasons[8]

d. Termination of an appointment with continuous tenure, or of a probationary or special appointment before the end of the specified term, may occur as a result of bona fide formal discontinuance of a program or department of instruction. The following standards and procedures will apply.

(1) The decision to discontinue formally a program or department of instruction will be based essentially upon educational considerations, as determined primarily by the faculty as a whole or an appropriate committee thereof.

[Note: "Educational considerations" do not include cyclical or temporary variations in enrollment. They must reflect long-range judgments that the educational mission of the institution as a whole will be enhanced by the discontinuance.]

(2) Faculty members in a program being considered for discontinuance for educational considerations will promptly be informed of this activity in writing and provided at least thirty days in which to respond to it. Tenured, tenure-track, and contingent faculty members will be invited to participate in these deliberations.

[Note: Academic programs cannot be defined ad hoc, at any size; programs must be recognized academic units that existed prior to the decision to discontinue them. The term "program" should designate a related cluster of credit-bearing courses that constitute a coherent body of study within a discipline or set of related disciplines. When feasible, the term should designate a department or similar administrative unit that offers majors and minors.]

(3) Before the administration issues notice to a faculty member of its intention to terminate an appointment because of formal discontinuance of a program or department of instruction, the institution will make every effort to place the faculty member concerned in another suitable position. If placement in another position would be facilitated by a reasonable period of training, financial and other support for such training will be proffered. If no position is available within the institution, with or without retraining, the faculty member's appointment then may be terminated, but only with provision for severance salary equitably adjusted to the faculty member's length of past and potential service, an amount which may well exceed but not be less than the amount prescribed in Regulation 8.

[Note: When an institution proposes to discontinue a program or department of instruction based essentially on educational considerations, it should plan to bear the costs of relocating, training, or otherwise compensating faculty members adversely affected.]

(4) A faculty member who contests a proposed relocation or termination resulting from a discontinuance has a right to a full hearing before a faculty committee. The hearing need not conform in all respects with a proceeding conducted pursuant to Regulation 5, but the essentials of an on-the-record adjudicative hearing will be observed. The issues in such a hearing may include the institution's failure to satisfy any of the conditions specified in Regulation 4d. In the hearing, a faculty determination that a program or department is to be discontinued will be considered presumptively valid, but the burden of proof on other issues will rest on the administration.

Review

e. In cases of termination of appointment, the governing board will be available for ultimate review.

5. Dismissal Procedures

a. Adequate cause for a dismissal will be related, directly and substantially, to the fitness of faculty members in their professional capacities as teachers or researchers. Dismissal will not be used to restrain faculty members in their exercise of academic freedom or other rights of American citizens.[9]

b. Dismissal of a faculty member with continuous tenure, or with a special or probationary appointment before the end of the specified term, will be preceded by (1) discussions between the faculty member and appropriate administrative officers looking toward a mutual settlement; (2) informal inquiry by the duly elected faculty committee [insert name of committee], which may, if it fails to effect an adjustment, determine whether in its opinion dismissal proceedings should be undertaken, without its opinion being binding upon the president; (3) a statement of charges, framed with reasonable particularity by the president or the president's delegate.

c. A dismissal, as defined in Regulation 5a, will be preceded by a statement of charges, and the individual concerned will have the right to be heard initially by the elected faculty hearing committee [insert name of committee].[10] Members deeming themselves disqualified for bias or interest will remove themselves from the case, either at the request of a party or on their own initiative. Each party will have a maximum of two challenges without stated cause.[11]

(1) Pending a final decision by the hearing committee, the faculty member will be suspended, or assigned to other duties in lieu of suspension, only if immediate harm to the faculty member or others is threatened by continuance. Before suspending a faculty member, pending an ultimate determination of the faculty member's status through the institution's hearing procedures, the administration will consult with the Faculty Committee on Academic Freedom and Tenure [or whatever other title it may have] concerning the propriety, the length, and the other conditions of the suspension. A suspension that is intended to be final is a dismissal and will be treated as such. Salary will continue during the period of the suspension.

(2) The hearing committee may, with the consent of the parties concerned, hold joint prehearing meetings with the parties in order to (i) simplify the issues,

(ii) effect stipulations of facts,

(iii) provide for the exchange of documentary or other information, and

(iv) achieve such other appropriate prehearing objectives as will make the hearing fair, effective, and expeditious.

(3) Service of notice of hearing with specific charges in writing will be made at least twenty days prior to the hearing. The faculty member may waive a hearing or may respond to the charges in writing at any time before the hearing. If the faculty member waives a hearing, but denies the charges or asserts that the charges do not support a finding of adequate cause, the hearing tribunal will evaluate all available evidence and rest its recommendation upon the evidence in the record.

(4) The committee, in consultation with the president and the faculty member, will exercise its judgment as to whether the hearing should be public or private.

(5) During the proceedings the faculty member will be permitted to have an academic adviser and counsel of the faculty member's choice.

(6) At the request of either party or the hearing committee, a representative of a responsible educational association will be permitted to attend the proceedings as an observer.

(7) A verbatim record of the hearing or hearings will be taken, and a copy will be made available to the faculty member without cost, at the faculty member's request.

(8) The burden of proof that adequate cause exists rests with the institution and will be satisfied only by clear and convincing evidence in the record considered as a whole.

(9) The hearing committee will grant adjournments to enable either party to investigate evidence as to which a valid claim of surprise is made.

(10) The faculty member will be afforded an opportunity to obtain necessary witnesses and documentary or other evidence. The administration will cooperate with the hearing committee in securing witnesses and in making available documentary and other evidence.

(11) The faculty member and the administration will have the right to confront and cross-examine all witnesses. Where the witnesses cannot or will not appear, but the committee determines that the interests of justice require admission of their statements, the committee will identify the witnesses, disclose their statements, and, if possible, provide for interrogatories.

(12) In the hearing of charges of incompetence, the testimony will include that of qualified faculty members from this or other institutions of higher education.

(13) The hearing committee will not be bound by strict rules of legal evidence and may admit any evidence which is of probative value in determining the issues involved. Every possible effort will be made to obtain the most reliable evidence available.

(14) The findings of fact and the decision will be based solely on the hearing record.

(15) Except for such simple announcements as may be required, covering the time of the hearing and similar matters, public statements and publicity about the case by either the faculty member or administrative officers will be avoided so far as possible until the proceedings have been completed, including consideration by the governing board of the institution. The president and the faculty member will be notified of the decision in writing and will be given a copy of the record of the hearing.

(16) If the hearing committee concludes that adequate cause for dismissal has not been established by the evidence in the record, it will so report to the president. If the president rejects the report, the president will state the reasons for doing so, in writing, to the hearing committee and to the faculty member and provide an opportunity for response before transmitting the case to the governing board. If the hearing committee concludes that adequate cause for a dismissal has been established, but that an academic penalty less than dismissal would be more appropriate, it will so recommend, with supporting reasons.

6. Action by the Governing Board

If dismissal or other severe sanction is recommended, the president will, on request of the faculty member, transmit to the governing board the record of the case. The governing board's review will be based on the record of the committee hearing, and it will provide opportunity for argument, oral or written or both, by the principals at the hearing or by their representatives. The decision of the hearing committee will either be sustained or the proceedings returned to the committee with specific objections. The committee will then reconsider, taking into account the stated objections and receiving new evidence, if necessary. The governing board will make a final decision only after study of the committee's reconsideration.

7. Procedures for Imposition of Sanctions Other Than Dismissal

a. If the administration believes that the conduct of a faculty member, although not constituting adequate cause for dismissal, is sufficiently grave to justify imposition of a severe sanction, such as suspension from service for a stated period, the administration may institute a proceeding to impose such a severe sanction; the procedures outlined in Regulation 5 will govern such a proceeding.

b. If the administration believes that the conduct of a faculty member justifies imposition of a minor sanction, such as a reprimand, it will notify the faculty member of the basis of the proposed sanction and provide the faculty member with an opportunity to persuade the administration that the proposed sanction should not be imposed. A faculty member who believes that a major sanction has been incorrectly imposed under this paragraph, or that a minor sanction has been unjustly imposed, may, pursuant to Regulation 16, petition the faculty grievance committee for such action as may be appropriate.

8. Terminal Salary or Notice

If the appointment is terminated, the faculty member will receive salary or notice in accordance with the following schedule: at least three months, if the final decision is reached by March 1 (or three months prior to the expiration) of the first year of probationary service; at least six months, if the decision is reached by December 15 of the second year (or after nine months but prior to eighteen months) of probationary service; at least one year, if the decision is reached after eighteen months of probationary service or if the faculty member has tenure.[12]

This provision for terminal notice or salary need not apply in the event that there has been a finding that the conduct which justified dismissal

involved moral turpitude. On the recommendation of the faculty hearing committee or the president, the governing board, in determining what, if any, payments will be made beyond the effective date of dismissal, may take into account the length and quality of service of the faculty member.

9. Academic Freedom and Protection against Discrimination

a. All members of the faculty, whether tenured or not, are entitled to academic freedom as set forth in the 1940 *Statement of Principles on Academic Freedom and Tenure*, formulated by the Association of American Colleges and Universities and the American Association of University Professors.

b. All members of the faculty, whether tenured or not, are entitled to protection against illegal or unconstitutional discrimination by the institution, or discrimination on a basis not demonstrably related to the faculty member's professional performance, including but not limited to race, sex, religion, national origin, age, disability, marital status, or sexual orientation.

10. Complaints of Violation of Academic Freedom or of Discrimination in Nonreappointment

If a faculty member on probationary or other nontenured appointment alleges that a decision against reappointment was based significantly on considerations that violate (a) academic freedom or (b) governing policies on making appointments without prejudice with respect to race, sex, religion, national origin, age, disability, marital status, or sexual orientation, the allegation will be given preliminary consideration by the [insert name of committee], which will seek to settle the matter by informal methods. The allegation will be accompanied by a statement that the faculty member agrees to the presentation, for the consideration of the faculty committee, of such reasons and evidence as the institution may allege in support of its decision. If the difficulty is unresolved at this stage and if the committee so recommends, the matter will be heard in the manner set forth in Regulations 5 and 6, except that the faculty member making the complaint is responsible for stating the grounds upon which the allegations are based and the burden of proof will rest upon the faculty member. If the faculty member succeeds in establishing a prima facie case, it is incumbent upon those who made the decision against reappointment to come forward with evidence in support of their decision. Statistical evidence of improper discrimination may be used in establishing a prima facie case.

11. Administrative Personnel

The foregoing regulations apply to administrative personnel who hold academic rank, but only in their capacity as faculty members. Administrators who allege that a consideration that violates academic freedom or governing policies against improper discrimination, as stated in Regulation 10, significantly contributed to a decision to terminate their appointment to an administrative post or not to reappoint them are entitled to the procedures set forth in Regulation 10.

12. Political Activities of Faculty Members

Faculty members, as citizens, are free to engage in political activities. Where necessary, leaves of absence may be given for the duration of an election campaign or a term of office, on timely application, and for a reasonable period of time. The terms of such leave of absence will be set forth in writing, and the leave will not affect unfavorably the tenure status of a faculty member, except that time spent on such leave will not count as probationary service unless otherwise agreed to.[13]

13. Part-Time Faculty Appointments[14]

a. The terms and conditions of every appointment to a part-time nontenured faculty position will be stated in writing, including the length of service. A copy of the appointment document will be provided to the part-time faculty member.

b. In a case of dismissal before the end of the period of appointment, the administration will set forth cause for the action, and the faculty member will have the right to a hearing before a faculty committee.[15]

c. In a case of nonreappointment, if a part-time faculty member establishes a prima facie case, to the satisfaction of a duly constituted faculty committee, that considerations that violate academic freedom or governing policies against improper discrimination, as stated in Regulation 10, significantly contributed to his or her nonretention, it is incumbent on those who made the decision to come forward with evidence in support of that decision.

d. After having been reappointed beyond an initial term, a part-time faculty member who is subsequently notified of nonreappointment will be advised upon request of the reasons that contributed to the decision. Upon the faculty member's further request, the reasons will be confirmed in writing. The faculty member will be afforded opportunity for review of the decision by a faculty committee.

e. For part-time faculty members who have served for three or more terms within a span of three years, the following additional protections of academic due process apply:

(1) Written notice of reappointment or nonreappointment will be issued no later than one month before the end of the existing appointment. If the notice of reappointment is to be conditioned, for example, on sufficiency of student enrollment or on financial considerations, the specific conditions will be stated with the issuance of the notice.

(2) If the faculty member notified of nonreappointment alleges that the decision was based significantly on considerations that violate academic freedom or governing policies against improper discrimination, the allegation will be subject to review in the manner set forth in Regulation 10.

(3) When the part-time faculty member is denied reappointment to an available assignment (one with substantially identical responsibilities assigned to another part-time faculty member with less service), if the nonreappointed faculty member alleges that the decision was based on inadequate consideration, the allegation will be subject to review by a faculty body. If this body, while not providing judgment on the merits of the decision, finds that the consideration has been inadequate in any substantial respects, it will remand the matter for further consideration accordingly.[16]

f. Prior to consideration of reappointment beyond a seventh year, part-time faculty members who have taught at least twelve courses or six terms within those seven years shall be provided a comprehensive review with the potential result of (1) appointment with part-time tenure where such exists, (2) appointment with part-time continuing service, or (3) nonreappointment. Those appointed with tenure shall be afforded the same procedural safeguards as full-time tenured faculty. Those offered additional appointment without tenure shall have continuing appointments and shall not be replaced by part-time appointees with less service who are assigned substantially identical responsibilities without having been afforded the procedural safeguards associated with dismissal as set forth above in section b.

14. Graduate Student Employees

a. The length, terms, and conditions of every university appointment of a graduate student employee will be stated in writing at the time of the initial appointment. A copy of the appointment document will be supplied to the appointee.[17]

b. The graduate student employee on recurring appointments will be advised at the time of initial appointment of the substantive standards, expectations, and procedures generally employed at the institution in decisions affecting renewal and of any special standards adopted by the graduate student employee's department or school. The graduate student employee will be advised of the time when decisions affecting renewals are made and will be given the opportunity to submit material believed to be helpful to an adequate consideration of his or her circumstances.

c. In a case of dismissal before the end of the period of an academic or professional appointment, the graduate student employee will be provided with a statement of reasons for the action and will have the right to a pretermination hearing before a duly constituted committee. The hearing need not conform in all respects with a proceeding conducted pursuant to Regulation 5, but the essentials of an on-the-record adjudicative hearing will be observed. In such a hearing, the administration will have the burden of showing adequate cause for dismissal.[18] Adequate cause for a dismissal will be related, directly and substantially, to the fitness of the graduate student employee in his or her professional capacity regarding teaching, research, or other academic duties. Dismissal will not be used to restrain graduate student employees in their exercise of academic freedom or constitutional rights.

d. Written notice of reappointment or nonreappointment will be issued to graduate student academic or professional employees no later than one month before the end of the existing appointment.

e. Graduate student academic or professional employees who are notified of nonreap-pointment will be advised upon request of the reasons that contributed to the decision. Upon the employee's further request, the reasons will be confirmed in writing. The employee will be afforded the opportunity for review of the decision by a duly constituted committee.

f. In a case of nonreappointment, if a graduate student academic or professional employee establishes a prima facie case to the satisfaction of a duly constituted committee that considerations that violate academic freedom or governing policies against improper discrimination based on race, sex, national origin, age, disability, marital status, or sexual orientation significantly contributed to his or her nonretention, it is incumbent on those who made the decision to come forward with evidence in support of that decision.

g. If a graduate student employee who is denied reappointment to an available academic or professional position alleges that the decision was based on inadequate consideration, the allegation will be subject to review by a duly constituted body.[19] If this body, while not providing judgment on the merits of the decision, finds that the consideration has been inadequate in any substantial respects, it will remand the matter, recommending to the department that it assess the merits once again, this time remedying the inadequacies of its prior consideration.[20]

h. Graduate student academic or professional employees will have access to the faculty grievance committee, as specified in Regulation 16.

15. Other Academic Staff

a. In no case will a member of the academic staff who is not otherwise protected by the preceding regulations that relate to dismissal proceedings be dismissed without having been provided with a statement of reasons and an opportunity to be heard before a duly constituted committee.[21] (A dismissal is a termination before the end of the period of appointment.)

b. With respect to the nonreappointment of a member of such academic staff who establishes a prima facie case to the satisfaction of a duly constituted committee that considerations that violate academic freedom or governing policies against improper discrimination as stated in Regulation 10, significantly contributed to the nonreappointment, the academic staff member will be given a statement of reasons by those responsible for the nonreappointment and an opportunity to be heard by the committee.

16. Grievance Procedure

If any faculty member alleges cause for grievance in any matter not covered by the procedures described in the foregoing regulations, the faculty member may petition the elected faculty grievance committee [here name the committee] for redress. The petition will set forth in detail the nature of the grievance and will state against whom the grievance is directed. It will contain any factual or other data that the petitioner deems pertinent to the case. Statistical evidence of improper discrimination, including discrimination in salary, may be used in establishing a prima facie case. The committee will decide whether or not the facts merit a detailed investigation; if the faculty member succeeds in establishing a prima facie case, it is incumbent upon those who made the decision to come forward with evidence in support of their decision. Submission of a petition will not automatically entail investigation or detailed consideration thereof. The committee may seek to bring about a settlement of the issue(s) satisfactory to the parties. If in the opinion of the committee such a settlement is not possible or is not appropriate, the committee will report its findings and recommendations to the petitioner and to the appropriate administrative officer and faculty body, and the petitioner will, upon request, be provided an opportunity to present the grievance to them. The grievance committee will consist of three [or some other number] elected members of the faculty. No officer of the administration will serve on the committee.

Note on Implementation

The *Recommended Institutional Regulations* here presented will require for their implementation a number of structural arrangements and agencies. For example, the *Regulations* will need support by

1. channels of communication among all the involved components of the institution and between them and a concerned faculty member;
2. definitions of corporate and individual faculty status within the college or university government and of the role of the faculty in decisions relating to academic freedom and tenure; and

3. appropriate procedures for the creation and operation of faculty committees, with particular regard to the principles of faculty authority and responsibility.

The forms which these supporting elements assume will of course vary from one institution to another. Consequently, no detailed description of the elements is attempted in these *Recommended Institutional Regulations*. With respect to the principles involved, guidance will be found in the Association's *Statement on Government of Colleges and Universities*.

Notes

1. Under the 1940 "Statement of Principles on Academic Freedom and Tenure," this period may not exceed seven years. However, the Association's 2001 "Statement of Principles on Family Responsibilities and Academic Work" (AAUP, *Policy Documents and Reports*, 11th ed. [Baltimore: Johns Hopkins University Press, 2015], 339–46) provides that "a faculty member be entitled to stop the clock or extend the probationary period, with or without taking a full or partial leave of absence, if the faculty member (whether male or female) is a primary coequal caregiver of newborn or newly adopted children," that "institutions allow the tenure clock to be stopped for up to one year for each child, and . . . that faculty be allowed to stop the clock only twice, resulting in no more than two one-year extensions of the probationary period."

2. The exception here noted applies only to an institution where the maximum probationary period exceeds four years.

3. April 15 is the recommended date.

4. This committee, which can be the grievance committee noted in Regulation 16, is to be an elected faculty body. Similarly, the members of the committees noted in Regulations 4c(3), 4d(4), 10, and 13 are to be elected. A committee of faculty members appointed by an elected faculty body can substitute for a committee that is elected directly.

5. See "The Role of the Faculty in Conditions of Financial Exigency," *Policy Documents and Reports*, 292–308. The definition of "financial exigency" offered in that report and adopted here is intended to be more responsive to actual institutional conditions and extends the standard of exigency to situations not covered by Committee A's previous definition.

6. See "The Role of the Faculty in Budgetary and Salary Matters," *Policy Documents and Reports*, 289–91, especially the following passages:

> The faculty should participate both in the preparation of the total institutional budget and (within the framework of the total budget) in decisions relevant to the further apportioning of its specific fiscal divisions (salaries, academic programs, tuition, physical plant and grounds, and so on). The soundness of resulting decisions should be enhanced if an elected representative committee of the faculty participates in deciding on the overall allocation of institutional resources and the proportion

to be devoted directly to the academic program. This committee should be given access to all information that it requires to perform its task effectively, and it should have the opportunity to confer periodically with representatives of the administration and governing board. . . .

Circumstances of financial exigency obviously pose special problems. At institutions experiencing major threats to their continued financial support, the faculty should be informed as early and specifically as possible of significant impending financial difficulties. The faculty—with substantial representation from its nontenured as well as its tenured members, since it is the former who are likely to bear the brunt of the reduction—should participate at the department, college or professional school, and institution-wide levels in key decisions as to the future of the institution and of specific academic programs within the institution. The faculty, employing accepted standards of due process, should assume primary responsibility for determining the status of individual faculty members.

7. See "Statement on Government of Colleges and Universities," *Policy Documents and Reports*, 117–22, especially the following passage: "Faculty status and related matters are primarily a faculty responsibility; this area includes appointments, reappointments, decisions not to reappoint, promotions, the granting of tenure, and dismissal. The primary responsibility of the faculty for such matters is based upon the fact that its judgment is central to general educational policy."

8. When discontinuance of a program or department is mandated by financial exigency of the institution, the standards of Regulation 4c above will apply.

9. For cause relating to physical or mental disability, see "Accommodating Faculty Members Who Have Disabilities," *Policy Documents and Reports*, 374–78.

10. This committee should not be the same as the committee referred to in Regulation 5b(2).

11. Regulations of the institution should provide for alternates or for some other method of filling vacancies on the hearing committee resulting from disqualification, challenge without stated cause, illness, resignation, or other reason.

12. For renewable term appointments not specifically designated as probationary for tenure, see "The Applicability of the 'Standards for Notice of Nonreappointment' to All Full-Time Faculty on Renewable Term Appointments," *Academe* 81 (September–October 1995): 51–54, which states,

While academic institutions commonly adhere to the Association's *Standards for Notice of Nonreappointment* with respect to faculty appointments that they recognize as probationary, in many cases they have not considered those standards to be applicable to those full-time faculty members whose service under non-tenure-track appointments has involved more than "a brief association with the institution" and who continue to serve on annual appointments that are indefinitely renewable at the discretion of the administration. Typically, although the terms of their appointments may stipulate that they

are for one year only, the faculty members are given reason to expect that, so long as they perform creditably and so long as enough courses remain available, the appointments will be renewed. Frequently, however, at or near the end of an academic year, these individuals are suddenly notified that their appointments are not in fact being renewed for the following year. Despite what may have been an extended affiliation with the institution, the faculty members are not viewed as entitled to the notice of nonreappointment that would be given to colleagues who hold appointments designated as probationary.

Committee A considers all full-time faculty members holding renewable term appointments, whatever their title or status, to be entitled to notice of nonreappointment as called for in the Association's recommended standards. We do not view it as necessary, or indeed as equitable, to deprive full-time "non-tenure-track" faculty members of the safeguards that the standards for notice are intended to provide.

13. See "Statement on Professors and Political Activity," *Policy Documents and Reports*, 39.

14. This regulation does not apply to faculty members with reduced loads who are tenured or probationary for tenure and who have the protections of academic due process which are provided in Regulations 2, 4, 5, 6, 7, and 8. It does apply to all other faculty members whose appointments are less than full-time, whatever their rank or title and whether they are paid on a pro-rata, a per-course, or any other basis.

15. As stated in Regulation 5a, "Adequate cause for a dismissal will be related, directly and substantially, to the fitness of faculty members in their professional capacities as teachers or researchers. Dismissal will not be used to restrain faculty members in their exercise of academic freedom or other rights of American citizens."

16. See "Statement on Procedural Standards in the Renewal or Nonrenewal of Faculty Appointments," *Policy Documents and Reports*, 94–98, especially the following passages:

It is easier to state what the standard "adequate consideration" does not mean than to specify in detail what it does. It does not mean that the review committee should substitute its own judgment for that of members of the department on the merits of whether the candidate should be reappointed or given tenure. The conscientious judgment of the candidate's departmental colleagues must prevail if the invaluable tradition of departmental autonomy in professional judgments is to prevail. The term "adequate consideration" refers essentially to procedural rather than to substantive issues: Was the decision conscientiously arrived at? Was all available evidence bearing on the relevant performance of the candidate sought out and considered? Was there adequate deliberation by the department over the import of the evidence in the light of the relevant standards? Were irrelevant and improper standards excluded from consideration? Was the decision a bona fide exercise of professional academic judgment? These are the kinds of questions suggested by the standard "adequate consideration."

If, in applying this standard, the review committee concludes that adequate consideration was not given, its appropriate response should be to recommend to the department that it assess the merits once again, this time remedying the inadequacies of its prior consideration.

17. Universities assume responsibilities when they accept graduate students with a promise of financial support. Graduate student employees have a legitimate expectation of fulfillment of the promise unless legitimate cause to terminate support is shown. If the cause relates to the graduate student employee's work and/or academic performance or progress, the employee should be given sufficient time and opportunity to redress the concern.

18. According to the Association's "Statement on Collective Bargaining" (*Policy Documents and Reports*, 323–24), "Participation in a strike or other work action does not by itself constitute grounds for dismissal or nonreappointment or for imposing other sanctions against faculty members."

19. For comment on the term "adequate consideration," see note 16, supra.

20. Nonreappointment conditioned on inadequate academic performance as a graduate student may be reviewed in the manner provided in Committee A's statement "The Assignment of Course Grades and Student Appeals," in *Policy Documents and Reports*, 29–30.

21. Each institution should define with particularity who are members of the academic staff.

Statement on Procedural Standards in Faculty Dismissal Proceedings

The following statement was prepared by a joint committee representing the Association of American Colleges (now the Association of American Colleges and Universities) and the American Association of University Professors and was approved by these two associations at their annual meetings in 1958. It supplements the 1940 *Statement of Principles on Academic Freedom and Tenure* by providing a formulation of the "academic due process" that should be observed in dismissal proceedings. The exact procedural standards here set forth, however, "are not intended to establish a norm in the same manner as the 1940 *Statement of Principles on Academic Freedom and Tenure,* but are presented rather as a guide."

Introductory Comments

Any approach toward settling the difficulties which have beset dismissal proceedings on many American campuses must look beyond procedure into setting and cause. A dismissal proceeding is a symptom of failure; no amount of use of removal process will help strengthen higher education as much as will the cultivation of conditions in which dismissals rarely, if ever, need occur.

Just as the board of control or other governing body is the legal and fiscal corporation of the college, the faculty is the academic entity. Historically, the academic corporation is the older. Faculties were formed in the Middle Ages, with managerial affairs either self-arranged or handled in course by the parent church. Modern college faculties, on the other hand, are part of a complex and extensive structure requiring legal incorporation, with stewards and managers specifically appointed to discharge certain functions.

Nonetheless, the faculty of a modern college constitutes an entity as real as that of the faculties of medieval times, in terms of collective purpose and function. A necessary precondition of a strong faculty is that it have first-hand concern with its own membership. This is properly reflected both in appointments to and in separations from the faculty body.

A well-organized institution will reflect sympathetic understanding by trustees and teachers alike of their respective and complementary roles. These should be spelled out carefully in writing and made available to all. Trustees and faculty should understand and agree on their several functions in determining who shall join and who shall remain on the faculty. One of the prime duties of the administrator is to help preserve understanding of those functions. It seems clear on the American college scene that a close positive relationship exists between the excellence of colleges, the strength of their faculties, and the extent of faculty responsibility in determining faculty membership. Such a condition is in no way inconsistent with full faculty awareness of institutional factors with which governing boards must be primarily concerned.

In the effective college, a dismissal proceeding involving a faculty member on tenure, or one occurring during the term of an appointment, will be a rare exception, caused by individual human weakness and not by an unhealthful setting. When it does come, however, the college should be prepared for it, so that both institutional integrity and individual human rights may be preserved during the process of resolving the trouble. The faculty must be willing to recommend the dismissal of a colleague when necessary. By the same token, presidents and governing boards must be willing to give full weight to a faculty judgment favorable to a colleague.

One persistent source of difficulty is the definition of adequate cause for the dismissal of a faculty member. Despite the 1940 *Statement of Principles on Academic Freedom and Tenure* and subsequent attempts to build upon it, considerable ambiguity and misunderstanding persist throughout higher education, especially in the respective conceptions of governing boards, administrative officers, and faculties concerning this matter. The present statement assumes that individual institutions will have formulated their own definitions of adequate cause for dismissal, bearing in mind the 1940 *Statement* and standards that have developed in the experience of academic institutions.

This statement deals with procedural standards. Those recommended are not intended to establish a norm in the same manner as the 1940 *Statement of Principles on Academic Freedom and Tenure,* but are presented rather as a guide to be used according to the nature and traditions of particular institutions in giving effect to both faculty tenure rights and the obligations of faculty members in the academic community.

Procedural Recommendations

1. *Preliminary Proceedings concerning the Fitness of a Faculty Member.* When reasons arise to question the fitness of a college or university faculty member who has tenure or whose term appointment has not expired, the appropriate administrative officers should ordinarily discuss the matter with the faculty member in personal conference. The matter may be terminated by mutual consent at this point; but if an adjustment does not result, a standing or ad hoc committee elected by the faculty and charged with the function of rendering confidential advice in such situations should informally inquire into the situation, to effect an adjustment, if possible, and, if none is effected, to determine whether in its view formal proceedings to consider the faculty member's dismissal should be instituted. If the committee recommends that such proceedings should be begun, or if the president of the institution, even after considering a recommendation of the committee favorable to the faculty member, expresses the conviction that a proceeding should be undertaken, action should be commenced under the procedures that follow. Except where there is disagreement, a statement with reasonable particularity of the grounds proposed for the dismissal should then be jointly formulated by the president and the faculty committee; if there is disagreement, the president or the president's representative should formulate the statement.

2. *Commencement of Formal Proceedings.* The formal proceedings should be commenced by a communication addressed to the faculty member by the president of the institution, informing the faculty member of the statement formulated, and also informing the faculty member that, at the faculty member's request, a hearing will be conducted by a faculty committee at a specified time and place to determine whether he or she should be removed from the faculty position on the grounds stated. In setting the date of the hearing, sufficient time should be allowed the faculty member to prepare a defense. The faculty member should be informed, in detail or by reference to published regulations, of the procedural rights that will be accorded. The faculty member should state in reply whether he or she wishes a hearing, and, if so, should answer in writing, not less than one week before the date set for the hearing, the statements in the president's letter.

3. *Suspension of the Faculty Member.* Suspension of the faculty member during the proceedings is justified only if immediate harm to the faculty member or others is threatened by the faculty member's continuance. Unless legal considerations forbid, any such suspension should be with pay.

4. *Hearing Committee.* The committee of faculty members to conduct the hearing and reach a decision should be either an elected standing committee not previously concerned with the case or a committee established as soon as possible after the president's letter to the faculty member has been sent. The choice of members of the hearing committee should be on the basis of their objectivity and competence and of the regard in which they are held in the academic community. The committee should elect its own chair.

5. *Committee Proceeding.* The committee should proceed by considering the statement of grounds for dismissal already formulated, and the faculty member's response written before the time of the hearing. If the faculty member has not requested a hearing, the committee should consider the case on the basis of the obtainable information and decide whether the faculty member should be removed; otherwise, the hearing should go forward. The committee, in consultation with the president and the faculty member, should exercise its judgment as to whether the hearing should be public or private. If any facts are in dispute, the testimony of witnesses and other evidence concerning the matters set forth in the president's letter to the faculty member should be received.

The president should have the option of attendance during the hearing. The president may designate an appropriate representative to assist in developing the case; but the committee should determine the order of proof, should normally conduct the questioning of witnesses, and, if necessary, should secure the presentation of evidence important to the case.

The faculty member should have the option of assistance by counsel, whose functions should be similar to those of the representative chosen by the president. The faculty member should have the additional procedural rights set forth in the 1940 *Statement of Principles on Academic Freedom and Tenure,* and should have the aid of the committee, when needed, in securing the attendance of witnesses. The faculty member or the faculty member's counsel and the representative designated by the president should have the right, within reasonable limits, to question all witnesses who testify orally. The faculty member should have the opportunity to be confronted by all adverse witnesses. Where unusual and urgent reasons move the hearing committee to withhold this right, or where the witness cannot appear, the identity of the witness, as well as the statements of the witness, should nevertheless be disclosed to the faculty member. Subject to these safeguards, statements may, when necessary, be taken outside the hearing and reported to it. All of the evidence should be duly recorded. Unless special circumstances warrant, it should not be necessary to follow formal rules of court procedure.

6. *Consideration by Hearing Committee.* The committee should reach its decision in conference, on the basis of the hearing. Before doing so, it should give opportunity to the faculty member or the faculty member's counsel and the representative designated by the president to argue orally before it. If written briefs would be helpful, the committee may request them. The committee may proceed to decision promptly, without having the record of the hearing transcribed, where it feels that a just decision can be reached by this means; or it may await the availability of a transcript of the hearing if its decision would be aided thereby. It should make explicit findings with respect to each of the grounds of removal presented, and a reasoned opinion may be desirable. Publicity concerning the committee's decision may properly be withheld until consideration has been given to the case by the governing body of the institution. The president and the faculty member should be notified of the decision in writing and should be given a copy of the record of the hearing. Any release to the public should be made through the president's office.

7. *Consideration by Governing Body.* The president should transmit to the governing body the full report of the hearing committee, stating its action. On the assumption that the governing board has accepted the principle of the faculty hearing committee, acceptance of the committee's decision would normally be expected. If the governing body chooses to review the case, its review should be based on the record of the previous hearing, accompanied by opportunity for argument, oral or written or both, by the principals at the hearing or their representatives. The decision of the hearing committee should either be sustained or the proceeding be returned to the committee with objections specified. In such a case the committee should reconsider, taking account of the stated objections and receiving new evidence if necessary. It should frame its decision and communicate it in the same manner as before. Only after study of the committee's reconsideration should the governing body make a final decision overruling the committee.

8. *Publicity.* Except for such simple announcements as may be required, covering the time of the hearing and similar matters, public statements about the case by either the faculty member or administrative officers should be avoided so far as possible until the proceedings have been completed. Announcement of the final decision should include a statement of the hearing committee's original action, if this has not previously been made known.

Statement on Procedural Standards
in the Renewal or Nonrenewal
of Faculty Appointments

The statement that follows, a revision of a statement originally adopted in 1971, was approved by the Association's Committee A on Academic Freedom and Tenure, adopted by the Association's Council in November 1989, and endorsed by the Seventy-Sixth Annual Meeting.

Except for special appointments clearly designated at the outset as involving only a brief association with the institution, all full-time faculty appointments are either with continuous tenure or probationary for tenure. Procedures bearing on the renewal or nonrenewal of probationary appointments are this statement's concern.

The Probationary Period: Standards and Criteria

The 1940 *Statement of Principles on Academic Freedom and Tenure* prescribes that "during the probationary period a teacher should have the academic freedom that all other members of the faculty have." The Association's *Recommended Institutional Regulations on Academic Freedom and Tenure*[1] prescribe further that "all members of the faculty, whether tenured or not, are entitled to protection against illegal or unconstitutional discrimination by the institution, or discrimination on a basis not demonstrably related to the faculty member's professional performance. . . ." A number of the rights of nontenured faculty members provide support for their academic freedom and protection against improper discrimination. They cannot, for example, be dismissed before the end of a term appointment except for adequate cause that has been demonstrated through academic due process—a right they share with tenured members of the faculty. If they assert that they have been given notice of nonreappointment in violation of academic freedom or because of improper discrimination, they are entitled to an opportunity to establish their claim in accordance with Regulation 10 of the *Recommended Institutional Regulations*. They are entitled to timely notice of nonreappointment in accordance with the schedule prescribed in the statement on *Standards for Notice of Nonreappointment*.[2] Lacking the reinforcement of tenure, however, academic freedom and protection against improper

discrimination for probationary faculty members have depended primarily upon the understanding and support of their tenured colleagues, the administration, and professional organizations, especially the American Association of University Professors. In the *Statement on Government of Colleges and Universities*, the Association has asserted that "faculty status and related matters are primarily a faculty responsibility; this area includes appointments, reappointments, decisions not to reappoint, promotions, the granting of tenure, and dismissal." Collegial deliberation of the kind envisioned by the *Statement on Government* will minimize the risk of a violation of academic freedom, of improper discrimination, and of a decision that is arbitrary or based on inadequate consideration.

Frequently, young faculty members have had no training or experience in teaching, and their first major research endeavor may still be uncompleted at the time they start their careers as college teachers. Under these circumstances, it is particularly important that there be a probationary period—a maximum of seven years under the 1940 *Statement of Principles on Academic Freedom and Tenure*—before tenure is granted. Such a period gives probationary faculty members time to prove themselves, and their colleagues time to observe and evaluate them on the basis of their performance in the position rather than on the basis only of their education, training, and recommendations.

Good practice requires that the institution (department, college, or university) define its criteria for reappointment and tenure and its procedures for reaching decisions on these matters. The 1940 *Statement of Principles* prescribes that "the precise terms and conditions of every appointment should be stated in writing and be in the possession of both institution and teacher before the appointment is consummated."

Moreover, fairness to probationary faculty members prescribes that they be informed, early in their appointments, of the substantive and procedural standards that will be followed in determining whether or not their appointments will be renewed or tenure will be granted.

The Association accordingly recommends:

1. *Criteria and Notice of Standards*
   Probationary faculty members should be advised, early in their appointment, of the substantive and procedural standards generally accepted in decisions affecting renewal and tenure. Any special standards adopted by their particular departments or schools should also be brought to their attention.

The Probationary Period:
Evaluation and Decision

The relationship of the senior and junior faculty should be one of colleagueship, even though nontenured faculty members know that in time they will be judged by their senior colleagues. Thus the procedures adopted for evaluation and possible notification of nonrenewal should not endanger this relationship where it exists, and should encourage it where it does not. Nontenured faculty members should have available to them the advice and assistance of their senior colleagues; and the ability of senior colleagues to make a sound decision on renewal or tenure will be enhanced if an opportunity is provided for a regular review of the candidate's qualifications. A conjunction of the roles in counseling and evaluation may be productive: for example, an evaluation, whether interim or at the time of final determination of renewal or tenure, should be presented in such a manner as to assist nontenured faculty members as they strive to improve their performance.

Any recommendation regarding renewal or tenure should be reached by an appropriate faculty group in accordance with procedures approved by the faculty. Because it is important to both the faculty member and the decision-making body that all significant information be considered, the candidate should be notified that a decision is to be made regarding renewal of appointment or the granting of tenure and should be afforded an opportunity to submit material that the candidate believes to be relevant to the decision.

The Association accordingly recommends:

2. a. *Periodic Review*
   There should be provision for periodic review of a faculty member's situation during the probationary service.

b. *Opportunity to Submit Material*
Probationary faculty members should be advised of the time when decisions affecting renewal and tenure are ordinarily made, and they should be given the opportunity to submit material that they believe will be helpful to an adequate consideration of their circumstances.

Observance of the practices and procedures outlined above should minimize the likelihood of reasonable complaint if nontenured faculty members are given notice of nonreappointment. They will have been informed of the criteria and procedures for renewal and tenure; they will have been counseled by faculty colleagues; they will have been given an opportunity to have all material relevant to their evaluation considered; and they will have a timely decision representing the views of faculty colleagues.

Notice of Reasons

Since 1971 it has been the Association's position, reached after careful examination of advantages and disadvantages, that nontenured faculty members notified of nonreappointment should, upon request, receive a statement of the reasons for the decision. In reaching this position, the Association considered the needs both of the institution and of the individual faculty member.

A major responsibility of the institution is to recruit and retain the best-qualified faculty within its goals and means. In a matter of such fundamental importance, the institution, through the appropriate faculty agencies, must be accorded the widest latitude consistent with academic freedom, equal opportunity, and the standards of fairness. The Association recognized that the requirement of giving reasons could lead, however erroneously, to an expectation that the decision-making body must justify its decision. A notice of nonreappointment could thus become confused with dismissal for cause, and under these circumstances the decision-making body could become reluctant to reach adverse decisions that might culminate in grievance procedures. As a result there was some risk that the important distinction between tenure and probation would be eroded.

Weighed against these important institutional concerns, however, were the interests of the individual faculty members. They could be honestly unaware of the reasons for a negative decision, and the decision could be based on a judgment of shortcomings which they could easily remedy if informed of them. A decision not to renew an appointment could be based on erroneous information which the faculty member could readily correct if informed of the basis for the decision. Again, the decision could be based on considerations of institutional policy or program development that have nothing to do with the faculty member's professional competence, and if not informed of the reasons, the faculty member could mistakenly assume that a judgment of inadequate performance has been made. In the face of a persistent refusal to supply the reasons, a faculty member may be more inclined to attribute improper motivations to the decision-making body or to conclude that its evaluation has been based upon inadequate consideration. If the faculty member wished to request a reconsideration of the decision, or a review by another body, ignorance of the reasons for the decision would create difficulties both in reaching a decision whether to initiate such a request and in presenting a case for reconsideration or review.

The Association's extensive experience with specific cases since 1971 has confirmed its conclusion that the reasons in support of the faculty member's right to be informed outweigh the countervailing risks. Every notice of nonreappointment, however, need not be accompanied by a written statement of the reasons for nonreappointment. It may not always be to the advantage of the faculty member to be informed of the reasons for nonreappointment, particularly in writing. The faculty member may be placed under obligation to divulge them to the appointing body of another institution if it inquired. Similarly, a written record is likely to become the basis for continuing responses by the faculty member's former institution to prospective appointing bodies.

At many institutions, moreover, the procedures of evaluation and decision may make it difficult, if not impossible, to compile a statement of reasons that precisely reflects the basis of the decision. When a number of faculty members participate in the decision, they may oppose a reappointment for a variety of reasons, few or none of which may represent a majority view. To include every reason, no matter how few have held it, in a written statement to the faculty member may misrepresent the general view and damage unnecessarily both the morale and the professional future of the faculty member.

In many situations, of course, a decision not to reappoint will not reflect adversely upon the faculty member. An institution may, for example, find it necessary for financial or other reasons to restrict its offerings in a given department. The acquisition of tenure may depend not only upon satisfactory performance but also upon a long-term opening. Nonrenewal in these cases does not suggest a serious adverse judgment. In these

situations, providing a statement of reasons, either written or oral, should pose no difficulty, and such a statement may in fact assist the faculty member in searching for a new position.

Should the faculty member, after weighing the considerations cited above, decide to request the reasons for the decision against reappointment, the reasons should be given. The faculty member also should have the opportunity to request a reconsideration by the decision-making body.

The Association accordingly recommends:

3. *Notice of Reasons*
   In the event of a decision not to renew an appointment, the faculty member should be informed of the decision in writing, and, upon request, be advised of the reasons which contributed to that decision. The faculty member should also have the opportunity to request a reconsideration by the body or individual that made the decision.

Written Reasons

Having been given orally the reasons that contributed to the decision against reappointment, the faculty member, to avoid misunderstanding, may request that they be confirmed in writing. The faculty member may wish to petition the appropriate faculty committee, in accordance with Regulation 10 of the Association's *Recommended Institutional Regulations,* to consider an allegation that the reasons given, or other reasons that were not stated, constitute a violation of academic freedom or improper discrimination. The faculty member may wish to petition a committee, in accordance with Regulation 16 of the *Recommended Institutional Regulations,* to consider a complaint that the decision resulted from inadequate consideration and was therefore unfair. The faculty member may believe that a written statement of reasons might be useful in pursuing a professional career.

If the department chair or other appropriate institutional officer to whom the request is made believes that confirming the oral statement in writing may be damaging to the faculty member on grounds such as those cited earlier in this statement, it would be desirable for that officer to explain the possible adverse consequences of confirming the oral statement in writing. If, in spite of this explanation, the faculty member continues to request a written statement, the request should be honored.

The Association accordingly recommends:

4. *Written Reasons*
   If the faculty member expresses a desire to petition the grievance committee (such as is

described in Regulations 10 and 16 of the Association's *Recommended Institutional Regulations*), or any other appropriate committee, to use its good offices of inquiry, recommendation, and report, or if the request is made for any other reason satisfactory to the faculty member alone, the reasons given in explanation of the nonrenewal should be confirmed in writing.

Review Procedures: Allegations of Violation of Academic Freedom or of Discrimination

The best safeguard against a proliferation of grievance petitions on a given campus is the observance of sound principles and procedures of academic freedom and tenure and of institutional government. Observance of the procedures recommended in this statement—procedures that would provide guidance to nontenured faculty members, help assure them of a fair professional evaluation, and enlighten them concerning the reasons contributing to key decisions of their colleagues—should contribute to the achievement of harmonious faculty relationships and the development of well-qualified faculties.

Even with the best practices and procedures, however, faculty members will at times think that they have been improperly or unjustly treated and may wish another faculty group to review a decision of the faculty body immediately involved. The Association believes that fairness to both the individual and the institution requires that the institution provide for such a review when it is requested. The possibility of a violation of academic freedom or of improper discrimination is of vital concern to the institution as a whole, and where either is alleged it is of cardinal importance to the faculty and the administration to determine whether substantial grounds for the allegation exist. The institution should also be concerned to see that decisions respecting reappointment are based upon adequate consideration, and provision should thus be made for a review of allegations by affected faculty members that the consideration has been inadequate.

Because of the broader significance of a violation of academic freedom or of improper discrimination, the Association believes that the procedures to be followed in these two kinds of complaints should be kept separate from a complaint over adequacy of consideration. Regulation 10 of the *Recommended Institutional Regulations* provides a specific procedure for the review of complaints of academic freedom violation or of discrimination:[3]

If a faculty member on probationary or other nontenured appointment alleges that a decision against reappointment was based significantly on considerations that violate (1) academic freedom or (2) governing policies on making appointments without prejudice with respect to race, sex, religion, national origin, age, disability, marital status, or sexual orientation, the allegation will be given preliminary consideration by the [insert name of committee], which will seek to settle the matter by informal methods. The allegation will be accompanied by a statement that the faculty member agrees to the presentation, for the consideration of the faculty committee, of such reasons and evidence as the institution may allege in support of its decision. If the difficulty is unresolved at this stage, and if the committee so recommends, the matter will be heard in the manner set forth in Regulations 5 and 6, except that the faculty member making the complaint is responsible for stating the grounds upon which the allegations are based, and the burden of proof will rest upon the faculty member. If the faculty member succeeds in establishing a prima facie case, it is incumbent upon those who made the decision against reappointment to come forward with evidence in support of their decision. Statistical evidence of improper discrimination may be used in establishing a prima facie case.

The Association accordingly recommends:

5. *Petition for Review Alleging an Academic Freedom Violation or Improper Discrimination* Insofar as the petition for review alleges a violation of academic freedom or improper discrimination, the functions of the committee that reviews the faculty member's petition should be the following:
   a. to determine whether or not the notice of nonreappointment constitutes on its face a violation of academic freedom or improper discrimination;
   b. to seek to settle the matter by informal methods;
   c. if the matter remains unresolved, to decide whether or not the evidence submitted in support of the petition warrants a recommendation that a formal proceeding be conducted in accordance with Regulations 5 and 6 of the *Recommended Institutional Regulations*, with the burden of proof resting upon the complaining faculty member.

Review Procedures: Allegations of Inadequate Consideration

Complaints of inadequate consideration are likely to relate to matters of professional judgment, where the department or departmental agency should have primary authority. For this reason, the basic functions of the review committee should be to determine whether the appropriate faculty body gave adequate consideration to the faculty member's candidacy in reaching its decision and, if the review committee determines otherwise, to request reconsideration by that body.

It is easier to state what the standard "adequate consideration" does not mean than to specify in detail what it does. It does not mean that the review committee should substitute its own judgment for that of members of the department on the merits of whether the candidate should be reappointed or given tenure.[4] The conscientious judgment of the candidate's departmental colleagues must prevail if the invaluable tradition of departmental autonomy in professional judgments is to prevail. The term "adequate consideration" refers essentially to procedural rather than to substantive issues: Was the decision conscientiously arrived at? Was all available evidence bearing on the relevant performance of the candidate sought out and considered? Was there adequate deliberation by the department over the import of the evidence in light of the relevant standards? Were irrelevant and improper standards excluded from consideration? Was the decision a bona fide exercise of professional academic judgment? These are the kinds of questions suggested by the standard "adequate consideration."

If, in applying this standard, the review committee concludes that adequate consideration was not given, its appropriate response should be to recommend to the department that it assess the merits once again, this time remedying the inadequacies of its prior consideration.

An acceptable review procedure, representing one procedural system within which such judgments may be made, is outlined in Regulation 16 of the *Recommended Institutional Regulations*, as follows:

> If any faculty member alleges cause for grievance in any matter not covered by the procedures described in the foregoing regulations, the faculty member may petition the elected faculty grievance commit-tee [here name the committee] for redress. The petition will set forth in detail the nature of the grievance and will state against whom the grievance is directed. It will contain any factual or other data which the petitioner deems pertinent to the case. Statistical evidence of improper discrimination, including discrimination in salary, may be used in establishing a prima facie case. The committee will

decide whether or not the facts merit a detailed investigation; if the faculty member succeeds in establishing a prima facie case, it is incumbent upon those who made the decision to come forward with evidence in support of their decision. Submission of a petition will not automatically entail investigation or detailed consideration thereof. The committee may seek to bring about a settlement of the issue satisfactory to the parties. If in the opinion of the committee such a settlement is not possible or is not appropriate, the committee will report its findings and recommendations to the petitioner and to the appropriate administrative officer and faculty body, and the petitioner will, upon request, be provided an opportunity to present the grievance to them. The grievance committee will consist of three [or some other number] elected members of the faculty. No officer of administration will serve on the committee.

The Association accordingly recommends:

6. *Petition for Review Alleging Inadequate Consideration*
   Insofar as the petition for review alleges inadequate consideration, the functions of the committee which reviews the faculty member's petition should be the following:
   a. to determine whether the decision was the result of adequate consideration, with the understanding that the review committee should not substitute its judgment on the merits for that of the body or individual that made the decision;
   b. to request reconsideration by the faculty body when the committee believes that adequate consideration was not given to the faculty member's qualifications (in such instances, the committee should indicate the respects in which it believes that consideration may have been inad-equate); and
   c. to provide copies of its report and recom-mendation to the faculty member, the body or individual that made the decision, and the president or other appropriate adminis-trative officer.

Notes
1. AAUP, *Policy Documents and Reports*, 11th ed. (Baltimore: Johns Hopkins University Press, 2015), 85.
2. Ibid., 99.
3. Faculties processing complaints under Regula-tions 10 and 16 may wish to secure the further advice of the Association's Washington office.
4. As used here, "department" may refer to any institutional body or individual responsible for making a recommendation or decision on reappointment.

Standards for Notice of Nonreappointment

The statement that follows was approved by the Association's Committee A on Academic Freedom and Tenure, adopted by the Association's Council in October 1963, and endorsed by the Fiftieth Annual Meeting in 1964.

Because a probationary appointment, even though for a fixed or stated term, carries an expectation of renewal, the faculty member should be explicitly informed of a decision not to renew an appointment, in order that the faculty member may seek a position at another college or university.[1] Such notice should be given at an early date, since a failure to secure another position for the ensuing academic year will deny the faculty member the opportunity to continue in the profession. The purpose of this statement is to set forth in detail, for the use of the academic profession, those standards for notice of nonreappointment which the Association over a period of years has actively supported and which are expressed as a general principle in the 1940 *Statement of Principles on Academic Freedom and Tenure*.

The Standards for Notice

Notice of nonreappointment, or of intention not to recommend reappointment to the governing board, should be given in writing in accordance with the following standards:

1. Not later than March 1 of the first academic year of service, if the appointment expires at the end of that year; or, if a one-year appointment terminates during an academic year, at least three months in advance of its termination.
2. Not later than December 15 of the second academic year of service, if the appointment expires at the end of that year; or, if an initial two-year appointment terminates during an academic year, at least six months in advance of its termination.
3. At least twelve months before the expiration of an appointment after two or more years in the institution.

Note

1. For renewable term appointments not specifically designated as probationary for tenure, see "The Applicability of the 'Standards for Notice of Nonreappointment' to All Full-Time Faculty on Renewable Term Appointments," *Academe* 81 (September–October 1995): 51–54, which states,

> While academic institutions commonly adhere to the Association's *Standards for Notice of Nonreappointment* with respect to faculty appointments that they recognize as probationary, in many cases they have not considered those standards to be applicable to those full-time faculty members whose service under non-tenure-track appointments has involved more than "a brief association with the institution" and who continue to serve on annual appointments that are indefinitely renewable at the discretion of the administration. Typically, although the terms of their appointments may stipulate that they are for one year only, the faculty members are given reason to expect that, so long as they perform creditably and so long as enough courses remain available, the appointments will be renewed. Frequently, however, at or near the end of an academic year, these individuals are suddenly notified that their appointments are not in fact being renewed for the following year. Despite what may have been an extended affiliation with the institution, the faculty members are not viewed as entitled to the notice of nonreappointment that would be given to colleagues who hold appointments designated as probationary.
>
> Committee A considers all full-time faculty members holding renewable term appointments, whatever their title or status, to be entitled to notice of nonreappointment as called for in the Association's recommended standards. We do not view it as necessary, or indeed as equitable, to deprive full-time "non-tenure-track" faculty members of the safeguards that the standards for notice are intended to provide.

Access to Faculty Personnel Files

This report, approved in 1999 jointly by the Association's Committee A on Academic Freedom and Tenure and its Committee on Women in the Academic Profession (Committee W), is a briefer version of a report initially approved by the two committees in 1992, adopted by the Association's Council in June of that year, and endorsed by the Seventy-Eighth Annual Meeting.

Access by faculty members to their own personnel files and to the files of colleagues has been a significant issue for the academic profession. The long-standing practice on many campuses of confidentiality of such files has been tested by state "sunshine" laws, by court decisions requiring disclosure of personnel files in certain litigation situations, and by concern about racial and gender discrimination in faculty personnel decisions. The issue of confidentiality was perhaps most significantly highlighted in the 1990 decision of the United States Supreme Court in *University of Pennsylvania v. EEOC*, 493 US 182. There, the Court unanimously held that the Equal Employment Opportunity Commission, investigating a charge of employment discrimination in violation of Title VII of the 1964 Civil Rights Act, is entitled to secure, through the issuance of a subpoena, faculty personnel files relevant to the case, including files of faculty members other than the complaining party. (The Court left unresolved the question whether the personnel files to be turned over to the agency might be in redacted form, i.e., edited so as to avoid disclosure of the identity of the evaluator.)

The Court in *University of Pennsylvania* rejected the university's claim that it had a privilege, rooted in the First Amendment and in more general notions of academic freedom, to shield such files against the agency's demands for disclosure. It held that the only limitations upon what had to be disclosed were those that usually obtain when enforcing administrative subpoenas, i.e., the relevance of the requested material and the burden to the defendant. Lower courts appear to agree that the same scope of discovery granted to the EEOC applies to actions brought under Title VII by private litigants.

In view of the ability of faculty members in many personnel disputes to have access to personnel files, through judicial or administrative directives, colleges and universities should give further attention to the question whether they should voluntarily make such files available

through their own internal regulations, particularly those setting forth procedures for peer review by faculty committees. Committees A and W of the American Association of University Professors have considered the circumstances and conditions under which faculty members should be afforded access to their own personnel records and to the records of others. The attentions of the two committees were focused upon four questions. Although issues of access to personnel files may be raised in other situations, we believe that the answers to these questions deal with the central issues and provide guidance for other situations that might arise. This report, after recounting the four questions, will set forth "the case for openness" and "the case for confidentiality," and will summarize the conclusions of Committees A and W on each of the questions.

1. When, and in what form, should faculty members have access to materials in their own personnel files?
2. When, and in what form, should faculty members have access to general information about other faculty members, such as is normally contained in a curriculum vitae?
3. When, and in what form, should faculty peer-review committees have access to the files of faculty complainants and of other faculty members whose files are relevant for comparison?
4. When, and in what form, should faculty peer-review committees make available to a faculty complainant the personnel files of other faculty members?

The Case for Openness

A central argument in support of greater access to faculty personnel files is that knowledge that one's evaluation of the work of a faculty member—whether at one's own institution or at another institution—might be accessible to that person will induce greater care and responsibility on the part of the commentator. The knowledge that one's assessment will be shielded from the scrutiny of the faculty member being discussed could encourage careless and unsubstantiated commentary. In too many instances, confidentiality has been known to foster invidiously discriminatory assessments. The AAUP's tradition of academic freedom and faculty governance relies upon a standard of professionalism that should enable faculty members to be willing to be held accountable for their judgments. To suggest that collegiality requires total secrecy would undermine this concept.

It can also be argued that affording a faculty member access to evaluations of his or her work is further justified by the great professional and personal consequences of decisions about reappointment, promotion, or tenure. Quite apart from cases of suspected discrimination, access could be a means of ensuring not only greater care in evaluation but also simple fairness to the faculty member being assessed, for that person is commonly in the best position to comment upon or to rebut the critical comments of others, whose judgment may be a product of misinformation, misunderstanding, or disciplinary bias.

Proponents of openness assert that the benefits of access to personnel files are particularly great in situations in which a faculty member claims to have been the victim of invidious discrimination in violation of law. The same would be true when a claim is made that norms of the academy have been violated because a faculty member has been punished for exercising academic freedom or because procedures have not afforded thorough or fair consideration of the faculty member's status.

Another important reason for greater openness derives from long-standing AAUP policies relating to the providing of reasons and peer review in certain cases of challenged personnel decisions. The AAUP has long supported the right of a faculty member to receive, upon request, a written statement of reasons for the denial of reappointment or tenure. AAUP policy has also long endorsed intramural review by an independent faculty body of allegations that a decision on faculty status has been tainted by violations of academic freedom or by invidious discrimination or resulted from inadequate consideration.

Thus proponents of openness argue that a faculty member's right to reasons is surely vacuous if there is no effective correlative right to ascertain whether those reasons are substantiated by materials in the faculty member's personnel file, including the assessments of faculty peers. Just as surely, it would seem, the role of peer review is undermined if a faculty committee impaneled to assess a colleague's claims relating to

academic freedom, discrimination, or inadequate consideration—or institutional claims of inferior performance in teaching or scholarship—cannot have full access to relevant personnel information. In many such cases, relevant information will include not only assessments of the faculty complainant but also assessments of his or her colleagues, particularly those in the same discipline who are alleged by the complainant to have received preferential treatment.

Another basis for increased access is the decision of the Supreme Court in *University of Pennsylvania v. EEOC*. Faculty complainants have recourse to the courts and to administrative agencies for legal redress on a variety of contractual, statutory, and constitutional theories, and the likelihood is great that they will be able through litigation to secure discovery of relevant personnel materials, their own and in many cases those of faculty colleagues. The institution should therefore be willing to make such materials available voluntarily through intramural procedures. Doing so would help ensure that faculty grievances may be resolved fairly, expeditiously, and inexpensively without the felt necessity of initiating legal proceedings. Coincidentally, doing so would allow for primary emphasis upon resolution of such disputes, best suited to internal collegial assessment, where the AAUP would have them resolved—before faculty peer-review committees rather than before a judicial or administrative decision maker lacking in understanding of the values and criteria intrinsic to the academy.

Those who emphasize the values of confidentiality of faculty files argue that the objectives just articulated may be all but fully achieved by providing a faculty complainant or a faculty appeals committee with personnel information in either summary or redacted form. Summaries, however, will typically fail to capture the detail, nuance, and tone that are often of the greatest importance in conveying the writer's views and that must, in the interests of fairness and accuracy, be communicated to faculty members as well. Moreover, a serious issue may well arise as to the scholarly competence or objectivity of the person assigned the task of reducing personnel assessments to summary form.

Similar flaws, although perhaps of a somewhat lesser order of magnitude, may obtain when material is made accessible only in redacted form. Very often, the probative force of evaluative comments may be either enhanced by the scholarly credentials of the evaluator, or diluted or indeed altogether discredited by that individual's known scholarly (and in some cases even personal) biases. To delete information about the source of evaluative comments may serve to deprive an aggrieved faculty member and peer-review panels of much that might bear upon the weight of the faculty member's claim—that might show in some instances that the claim is particularly weak, but in others that it is quite credible.

The Case for Confidentiality

Perhaps the most weighty argument in support of confidentiality of faculty personnel files is that such confidentiality is the only way to ensure complete candor in the evaluation of candidates for appointment, reappointment, promotion, and tenure. Honest evaluations are at the core of the personnel decision-making process and are indispensable to the quality of an academic institution. Evaluators, whether internal or external, who know that the faculty candidate (or contentious third parties) will have relatively unfettered access to evaluations are likely to be a good deal less candid in their assessments. Revealing the identity of evaluators along with their critical comments may bias the process toward letters of appraisal that are less reliable, and thus less useful.

Proponents of confidentiality see no justification for providing fewer safeguards of confidentiality to the comments of internal reviewers than to the comments of those at other institutions. The adverse impact of open access would be at least as great. Evaluations from within departments may be most seriously affected. Lack of confidentiality may either result in less-than-candid assessments, as already noted, or create the risk, at least as discomfiting, that candidly critical assessments will strain internal collegial relationships and seriously undermine morale and community.

Confidentiality as a safeguard for candid assessments of quality is not unique to personnel files; it characterizes other pertinent processes within the academy. For example, reputable university presses and peer-reviewed journals routinely rely upon confidential processes of evaluation. Even more pertinently, faculty deliberations that culminate in personnel decisions are all but universally conducted in private; and many institutions have secret ballots on such matters as a further means of ensuring uninhibited assessments.

The advocates of open access to personnel files, particularly for the aggrieved faculty member, must conclude that any sacrifice of candor is outweighed by a more urgent and pervasive need to uncover distortions and biases, whether intentional or inadvertent, by colleagues and extramural evaluators. The advocates of confidentiality, however, challenge this assumption of distortion and bias. They view it as incompatible with a paradigm of faculty professionalism that relies instead on faculty integrity, respect, collegiality, and self-discipline. Indeed, they view the AAUP's traditional commitment to academic freedom and faculty self-governance as ultimately founded upon such a paradigm.

This is not to say that confidentiality cannot be abused. Of course it can. It is only to argue that, on the whole, faculty members can and should be trusted to discharge their evaluative responsibilities with integrity and seriousness of purpose, that confidentiality will contribute to a freer, franker, and better process of evaluation, and that in the long run this benefit will outweigh the predictable costs of abuse.

It can be argued that even if this benign paradigm of professionalism is thought naive—or, more pertinently, even if it has unquestionably been shown to fail in particular instances of demonstrable discrimination (or violation of academic freedom)—it does not follow that we must discard all restraints upon disclosure of faculty personnel files. Although openness is a value, it is not an absolute value. Its desirability depends upon its impact on other significant values, such as privacy, collegiality, and the promotion of the general academic enterprise. The question, therefore, is one of balance. A far better balance might be struck through the endorsement of intermediate levels of disclosure. Such a balance would recognize the need to root out distortion and bias but would also honor traditional attributes of faculty professionalism.

Some advocates of confidentiality assert that most of the benefits of openness recounted above can be attained—without undue sacrifice of the benefits that derive from confidentiality—if faculty files were to be made available in redacted form. Others would go further and claim that the benefits of openness could be attained even if faculty files were to be made available not at any time on demand, but only in the case of an adverse personnel decision, and, in those cases in which it would suffice and can be done readily and fairly, through the preparation of summaries. Such forms of intermediate levels of disclosure would enable faculty members independently to review the basis for, and if desired to comment upon, personnel decisions that affect them.

Although proponents of confidentiality would concede that special situations arise in which claims of discrimination cannot be sustained without access to unredacted files, they would argue that these situations are infrequent when measured against the thousands of personnel decisions made on college and university campuses each year, and that these relatively rare occasions can in any event be easily accommodated by creating mechanisms to grant unredacted access in appropriate circumstances.

In keeping with the idea that confidentiality of files should be compromised only sparingly, and only in a manner carefully tailored to the exigencies of the case, one can surely make a stronger claim for access, in summary or redacted form, to the files of an aggrieved faculty member than for access to the files of third persons. Access by a faculty complainant to the files of colleagues presents the problems relating to candor and collegiality noted above, and it also creates new problems by impairing the colleagues' interests in privacy and by possibly engendering intramural divisiveness.

Conclusions

1. *Committees A and W have concluded that faculty members should, at all times, have access to their own files, including unredacted letters, both internal and external.*

The committees determined that, for the reasons elaborated above in the section titled "The Case for Openness," such access promotes care and accuracy in evaluations, and also provides faculty members a fair opportunity to learn of and respond to critical evaluations. Such access is therefore likely to discourage evaluations that are based upon improper disciplinary, gender, or racial bias, and to facilitate access to proof of such bias. The identity of the writer should be known, because this information will be of pervasive importance in assessing the weight to be given to such evaluations. An individual who is uncertain whether grounds exist for contesting an adverse personnel decision cannot know if there is a basis for appeal unless he or she knows not only the official stated reasons for such a decision but also the substance of the letters of evaluation, internal and external, as well as their authorship.

2. *Committees A and W have concluded that a faculty member should be afforded access upon request to general information about other faculty members such as is normally contained in a curriculum vitae.*

The members of the two committees believe that faculty members should surely know as much about their colleagues as does the general public. Institutions of higher education gather curricula vitae from faculty members at regular intervals, often in the context of yearly salary reviews as well as in reviews for reappointment, tenure, and promotion. There is little reason not to share this information within the university community when it is generally available. A wider distribution of this kind of material could benefit those who are unsure of how their work compares with that of others, and it could serve the larger good of keeping faculty members abreast of each other's work.

3. *Committees A and W have concluded that, for purposes of comparison, files of a faculty complainant and of other faculty members should be available in unredacted form to faculty appeals committees to the extent that such committees deem the information relevant and necessary to the fair disposition of the case before them.*

At the heart of AAUP policies regarding such core issues as academic freedom, due process, antidiscrimination, and faculty governance is the role of peer-review committees in the appeal of adverse personnel decisions. It is essential that such committees, initially in deciding whether a faculty claim has sufficient merit to warrant a formal hearing, and subsequently in deciding at a hearing the relevance and weight to be given to various materials in faculty personnel files, be permitted to examine all materials that might arguably be relevant. Those essential powers of faculty appeals committees would be untenably hobbled if an administrative official could unilaterally determine that certain materials are not relevant to a faculty claim, or that relevant materials are too sensitive to be reviewed by the committee in unedited form. Although there is always a risk that unedited sensitive material might be improperly "leaked" to the aggrieved faculty member or to others, Committees A and W believe that AAUP-recommended policies on disclosure should be shaped by an assumption of responsible and professional behavior by peer-review committee members. Because relevance is the central criterion for access by a peer-review committee, it follows that in appropriate cases the committee should be afforded access to materials contained in the personnel files of faculty members other than the complainant. Such recourse to third-party files, however, is likely to be the exception rather than the rule; it will not likely be relevant in a wide variety of faculty grievances, including cases in which violation of academic freedom or inadequate consideration is alleged. Committees A and W recognize that the practice on a significant number of campuses relating to disclosure to peer-review committees is considerably more restrictive than that advocated here. Nonetheless, the recommendation of the committees is thought particularly warranted, for two reasons. First, as already noted, a movement toward access for such committees is very much consistent with, if not indeed dictated by, core AAUP-recommended policies on faculty governance and peer review. Second, a faculty member whose appeal is markedly hampered by the committee's inability to secure meaningful access to materials (including relevant third-party materials) will often be able to secure such materials by pressing his or her case in an administrative or judicial forum; all parties would be better served—as would the concept of peer review—if comparable access could be secured through more expeditious and less expensive intramural procedures. (Relatedly, given the fact that personnel files are subject to discovery in formal legal proceedings, it is unlikely that their availability to peer-review committees under limited circumstances, as an effective alternative to or precursor of formal legal proceedings, would materially increase any inclination on the part of peer evaluators to be less than candid or to refrain from commenting altogether.)

4. *Committees A and W have concluded that a faculty appeals committee should make available to the aggrieved faculty member, in unredacted form and without prejudging the merits of the case, all materials the appeals committee deems relevant to the complaint, including personnel files of other faculty members, having due regard for the privacy of those who are not parties to the complaint.*

If a faculty appeals committee determines that certain material, even from third-party files, is relevant to the claims made by an aggrieved faculty member, there would normally be little or no justification for withholding that material from the faculty complainant pursuing intramural procedures. Indeed, it is difficult to contemplate a system

> of academic due process and peer review in which a faculty complainant should be required to present his or her case while being denied an opportunity to examine material that the faculty hearing body has determined to be relevant to the case.

The wisdom of providing access in intramural proceedings is reinforced by the likelihood that most such material, because of the determination of relevance by a peer-review panel, would

ultimately be discoverable in any event by the faculty complainant in a formal legal proceeding. Because the scrutiny of third-party files will ordinarily be regarded as relevant only in those cases in which discrimination is alleged, such cases are the most likely to generate agency or court directives to disclose such material.

Moreover, because Committees A and W also believe that such discrimination cases tend particularly to call for disclosure of the source of evaluations in order to assess the credibility or bias of the evaluator, they believe that such evaluations—including those relating to relevant faculty members other than the complainant—should be communicated to the complainant unedited and unredacted.

Given the importance of the privacy interests of the faculty members whose files might be turned over to an aggrieved colleague, Committees A and W emphasize that a claim of privacy for such files should be honored, barring a strong reason to the contrary. The only legitimate reason for not doing so is the need to use those files as comparators when judging whether a faculty complainant has been discriminated against or otherwise unfairly treated. The faculty appeals committee should have the authority to make the determination of reasonable need to disclose such information to a faculty complainant, and to take steps to minimize the risks of further disclosure.

Committees A and W recognize that some colleges and universities, while willing to abide by most of the principles suggested in this report, would prefer to carve out an exception with regard to the disclosure of evaluations in unredacted form, especially if the evaluations were originally solicited under an explicit or implicit assurance of confidentiality. Even apart from the issue of redaction, we appreciate that the recommendations made here go beyond the practices regarding access to personnel files that are common in many colleges and universities. We believe, however, that the AAUP can make a contribution by setting forth the strong affirmative reasons that warrant such openness while urging institutions to move forthrightly in that direction.

The Use and Abuse of Faculty Suspensions

The report that follows is excerpted from a longer report of the same title, which was prepared by a subcommittee of Committee A on Academic Freedom and Tenure and approved for publication by Committee A in August 2008.

I. Background

This subcommittee was charged with reviewing and analyzing the large number of AAUP cases and complaints involving suspension from teaching or research as a sanction imposed on faculty members, and the additional sanction of expulsion or banishment from the entire campus or from certain areas and activities. Although the suspension of a faculty member from some or all duties is not a new phenomenon, it has been increasingly common in recent years; and although Association policy severely limits its use, it appears to have become almost a routine recourse for administrations seeking to discipline faculty members regardless of the seriousness of the alleged cause. The subcommittee has reviewed the development of Association policy since the issuance of the 1940 *Statement of Principles on Academic Freedom and Tenure,* some forty published Committee A reports, a limited number of university task-force reports that examined the use of suspension, and other available material.[1]

Suspension has been defined in different ways both in institutional regulations and by administrations at the time the penalty is imposed on the faculty member. Sometimes, as we will show, administrators decline to use the term and claim that in fact what they are imposing is not a suspension at all. An examination of some of these claims will be useful in restating the central tenets of Association policy. In addition, suspension has sometimes been employed as a sanction independent of dismissal, here termed "freestanding" suspension (see Section IV).

Historically, suspension has been regarded in Association policy as a severe sanction second only to dismissal, because it has been seen primarily in terms of removal of a faculty member from teaching. As one case report put it, "Barring a teacher from his classroom inflicts ignominy upon the teacher and is destructive to the morale of the academic community."[2] An eloquent statement on the adverse effects of suspension, one that has been cited in several subsequent Committee A investigations, was the finding of the investigating committee in the 1966 case of St. John's University:

> The profession's entire case for academic freedom and its attendant standards is predicated upon the basic right to employ one's professional skills in practice, a right, in the case of the teaching profession, which is exercised not in private practice but through institutions. To deny a faculty member this opportunity without adequate cause, regardless of monetary compensation, is to deny him his basic professional rights. Moreover, to a good teacher, to be involuntarily idle is a serious harm in itself. One has only to think of the famous teachers of the past, beginning with Socrates, to realize what a serious injury it would have been to these men to have been denied the right to teach. In the case of the teachers at St. John's, denial of their classrooms was, in itself, serious injury. To inflict such injury without due process and, therefore, without demonstrated reason, destroys the academic character of the University.[3]

In the forty-two years since the publication of the St. John's report, removal from teaching duties is not necessarily the primary or relevant issue in all cases of suspension. The reason for this is that the increasing complexity of faculty work has come to include many more duties than teaching. The more duties a faculty member has, the more there are to suspend him or her from. Moreover, the greater the influence of campus legal counsel in protecting the university from liability, the more reasons can be found for imposing a suspension. As researchers, for example, faculty members often have relationships beyond their institutions that could be compromised by suspension. The relationship of researchers to outside funding agencies, both public and private (including corporate sponsors), is increasingly complicated (some might say vexed) by stringent reporting requirements and restraints posed by the need to avoid conflict of interest. E-mail and computing services, the first of these entirely unknown in 1966 and the second still in a relatively primitive form, now are essential components of almost any aspect of faculty work. Faculty research in the sciences funds graduate student positions or involves access to and oversight of a laboratory that by the nature of the project may be subject to federal and state regulations dealing with such questions as biohazards or animal care. In addition, today's workplace protections against sexual harassment and provisions for the disabled were never envisioned by the formulators of the 1940 *Statement*, let alone the 1915 *Declaration of Principles on Academic Freedom and Academic Tenure*.[4]

It is not surprising under these circumstances that increasingly the Association is dealing with cases that involve partial suspensions, in which the faculty member is blocked from some duties or locations, but not others. The placing of physical constraints short of entire banishment from campus through denial of access to a library, computer center, or e-mail seriously impedes faculty work. That work can be even more seriously affected when the faculty member is barred from his or her office, studio, or laboratory even when not barred from setting foot on the entire campus. Removal from even a single class can, of course, pose serious complications for the faculty member's standing as a teacher.

Whether a suspension is partial or total, whether or not it is accompanied by expulsion or banishment from the campus, in many cases administrations, often acting on advice of their legal counsel, do not seem, or care, to grasp the severe effects that suspension can have, not only on the reputation—and morale—of an accused faculty member, but also on his or her ability to contest the intended sanction. Suspension usually implies an extremely negative judgment, for which the basis remains untested in the absence of a hearing, even though an administration may claim that it is saving the faculty member embarrassment. That potential embarrassment must be risked (or at least the faculty member should be permitted to risk it) if the individual is to have a chance of clearing his or her name.[5] Beyond that, suspension may create a prejudicial atmosphere totally out of proportion to the alleged offense and undeserved in the light of the professor's previous record (see the 1970 report on the case at Alfred University).

II. The Development of Association Policy
The 1940 *Statement of Principles* is silent on the question of suspension, but the St. John's investigating committee found it "reasonable to construe" the statement "as applying to suspension from all academic duties," since such an action is "tantamount to summary dismissal within the

meaning of the statement." Association policy on suspension derives explicitly from recommendation number 3 of the joint *Statement on Procedural Standards in Faculty Dismissal Proceedings*:[6] "Suspension of the faculty member during [dismissal] proceedings is justified only if immediate harm to the faculty member or others is threatened by the faculty member's continuance. Unless legal considerations forbid, any such suspension should be with pay." The 1970 *Interpretive Comments* on the 1940 *Statement* added that "[a] suspension which is not followed by either reinstatement or the opportunity for a hearing is in effect a summary dismissal in violation of academic due process."

The fullest expansion of these points, which links suspension to a subsequent dismissal proceeding, is found in the *Recommended Institutional Regulations on Academic Freedom and Tenure*[7] (1968 and subsequent revisions, hereafter cited as *RIR*), section 5c(1):

> Pending a final decision by the hearing committee, the faculty member will be *suspended or assigned to other duties in lieu of suspension, only if immediate harm* to the faculty member or others is threatened by continuance. Before suspending a faculty member, pending an ultimate determination of the faculty member's status through the institution's hearing procedures, the administration will consult with the Faculty Committee on Academic Freedom and Tenure [or whatever other title it may have] concerning the propriety, the length, and the other conditions of the suspension. A suspension that is intended to be final is a dismissal and will be treated as such. Salary will continue during the period of the suspension. (Emphasis added.)

The 1971 *Report of the Joint Committee on Faculty Responsibility*,[8] the Association's first extensive discussion of sanctions short of dismissal, listed eight such sanctions in ascending order of severity, of which the eighth, "suspension from service for a stated period, without other prejudice," is the most severe.[9] "If the alleged offense is believed serious enough to warrant suspension without pay for a stated period, it is clear that a considerable measure of academic due process must be provided (for example, informal conference, screening committee, written statement of charges, regularized faculty committee, complete transcript, right to counsel, right of cross examination, etc.)."[10] As a result of this report, *RIR* 7a was added in 1971, providing (in language much more exacting than the report) for suspension as a sanction separate from dismissal but requiring the same standard of due process:

If the administration believes that the conduct of a faculty member, although not constituting adequate cause for dismissal, is sufficiently grave to justify imposition of a severe sanction such as *suspension from service for a stated period*, the administration may institute a proceeding to impose such a severe sanction; the procedures outlined in Regulation 5 [governing dismissals] will govern such a proceeding. (Emphasis added.)

In short, the development of Association policy originally saw suspension as preceding potential dismissal; after 1971 it also recognized the possible levying of suspension as a freestanding sanction. The first of these types of suspension occupies the bulk of the cases we survey here, and can be broadly classified either as a *prehearing* suspension, in which suspension with pay is imposed until a dismissal hearing can be held, or a *pretermination* suspension, in which suspension, albeit not a freestanding sanction, is levied without any commitment to holding a formal dismissal hearing and may indeed be regarded as self-sufficient for the institution's purposes, leading to termination immediately or at the end of the faculty member's term of appointment. In either case, however, depending on the circumstances (including indefinite and nondefinitive suspension prolonged over several academic terms), such an action may be seen as tantamount to a dismissal for cause, as will be repeated several times in this report.

III. Definitional Issues in Association Policy and Case History

Five key definitional issues underlie *RIR* 5c(1), and in this section the subcommittee treats them in the order in which they are treated in that regulation.

A. The Meaning of Suspension

As we have said, removal from classroom or laboratory duties has been at the core of the development of Association policy and case reports, although suspension in a broader context is understood to figure, and usually has figured, in such cases. The report of the investigating committee on St. John's University pointed out that removal from teaching is the severest of sanctions, whether resulting from dismissal or from potentially temporary suspension. This position is unequivocally restated in the 1995 report of the investigating committee concerning a nonreappointment case at the University of Southern California, which argued that the mere continuance of the faculty member in some duties did not negate the underlying fact of suspension:

Suspending a faculty member is a very serious sanction. The provision on suspension in the USC Faculty Handbook [which tied suspension only to the initiation of dismissal proceedings, like earlier AAUP policy, and which invoked the standard of "immediate harm"] is plainly intended to make suspension difficult. If assignment to some duty, however trivial, were to mark faculty members as not suspended, accomplishing the purpose for which an administration might wish to suspend a faculty member would be easy. The threat to academic freedom of interpreting suspension in this way is obvious.

The investigating committee went on to say that even at a research university, where research may carry as much weight as teaching, "suspending [faculty members] from teaching is suspending them, and the committee believes that the term is so understood by faculty members across the country, whether at research universities or at institutions engaged primarily in teaching." Additionally, if the reason alleged for suspension is the best interest of the students, such an action is "a devastating indictment of a faculty member. Its impact is no less devastating if the faculty member continues to be assigned nonteaching duties."[11]

The italicized language in the following quotations from Association policy seems somewhat less emphatic, and could conceivably lead to confusion. Thus *RIR* 5c(1) describes the faculty member as *"suspended or assigned to other duties in lieu of suspension,"* which might seem to imply that suspension from classroom duties is not really a suspension—or tantamount to dismissal—if other duties, either preexisting or newly imposed, are still expected.[12] *RIR* 7a and the Association's 1971 joint subcommittee report on faculty responsibility both speak of *suspension from service*, which seems to imply, on the contrary, that suspension involves all aspects of the faculty member's duties. In some cases, however, administrators appear to have seized on circumstances that they believe render the designation "suspension" moot, not least because if the administration's action is not really suspension, the level of due process need not accord with Association-supported standards or indeed, sometimes, with the standards set forth in the institution's own stated regulations.

Resistance to calling the action a suspension can be particularly prevalent in cases that involve continued payment of salary to the faculty member during the period of suspension, as if the mere fact of pay were sufficient to absolve the administration of impropriety, but it is also the case in reassignments when the faculty member is removed from the classroom.[13]

Despite the changes in academic work that we have noted, suspension still probably continues to be understood, especially by the public, primarily to mean suspension from teaching. Under no circumstances, however, does an assignment to other duties alter the fact that the faculty member has been suspended, unless the consent of the faculty member to the reassignment pending a hearing has been sought and granted. Nor does the continuation of the faculty member in other ongoing activities, such as committee service, alter that fact. Still, the apparent discordance or inconsistency between *RIR* 5c(1) and 7a needs to be resolved. Finally, and fittingly in terms of what we have said about the altered character of faculty duties, the term "suspension" may be equally appropriate in the case of a faculty member who does little or no teaching but who is removed from those duties that are directly related to his or her professional fitness, for example, the director of a research institute or a librarian.[14]

B. Immediate Harm

RIR 5c(1) speaks of the threat of immediate harm to oneself or others as a precondition to suspending a faculty member. But unlike suspension, which is capable of legislative definition, "immediate harm" is a much more problematic, if not elusive, concept; administrations that have invoked it as a justification for suspension have given it what, to say the least, are very broad interpretations.

In many of the cases we have reviewed, the administration did not attempt to justify a prehearing or pretermination suspension on the basis of "immediate harm." In one case, the reason for suspension was the distribution of an essay as required reading in an advanced writing course, an essay that the president found offensive. The professor was subsequently reinstated with "a censure for poor judgment in this instance."[15] Where some mention of the concept, if not the exact term, occurred, it was frequently attached to vague, trivial, or even faintly comical charges: "inefficiency," "neglect of academic duty," holding students or colleagues up for public contempt, and the authorship of two anonymous letters critical of the president; "teaching deficiencies" that were "harmful to the institution" and to "the immature and impressionable minds of undergraduates"; "employing an attorney and contemplating litigation"; the distribution of a satire of a required fall faculty workshop as well as the conduct of a course in social processes that students claimed would require them to under-

take projects that might lead to their arrest if they were to get good grades; and both the giving of advice to students to go to other colleges and the fact of declining enrollments in the faculty member's discipline.[16] In this last case, "When the investigating committee pointed out to [the president] that the standard implies more direct and tangible harm, he suggested that [the faculty member's] emotional condition posed possible harm to students and faculty."[17] Elsewhere, three dismissed faculty members notified of suspension with pay were charged with "repeated disregard for institutional objectives, policies, and/or authority." They were told that their "continued and repeated conduct constitutes a continual threat to the operation of the college as well as a threat to the board of regents in their statutory authority."[18] One suspension was based on a reference in the college handbook to the need to uphold the institution's "good name and reputation," which in the words of the investigating committee was "so loose and so open to differing interpretations as to be nearly meaningless. It could be used to justify the suspension of members of the faculty who say or do anything of which the administration does not approve."[19]

Whether or not recourse to suspension may in some cases be necessary under circumstances that involve immediate harm to a faculty member or others, it is clear that none of the foregoing charges could be construed as involving immediate harm in the rigorous sense that Association-recommended policy implies. If, in predismissal cases, there is no invocation, let alone evidence, of immediate harm, there should be no suspension to begin with.

The problem is not only how to delimit the concept of "immediate harm," but also what is meant by "others." Who and what are these others? Are they living, breathing human beings, or are they abstractions referring to institutional self-interest or administrative dignity? It is relatively easy to establish what immediate harm is not, as our examples, ranging from the risible to the sinister, testify. At least one investigating committee, however, has offered suggestions on what it might be: namely, disruption of, or the encouragement of anyone else to disrupt or otherwise impede, another individual's performance of university duties; making it difficult for the university to administer any of its programs or facilities; or using the classroom to espouse, gratuitously and irrelevantly, any views relating to the political and religious causes and controversies to which the faculty member is committed outside the classroom.[20] A quite different kind of case might be one in which a qualified medical opinion was obtained that actual physical danger to self and others existed when a faculty member had been behaving irrationally, was making serious threats against others on campus, and was known to have access to weapons. The large majority of the AAUP's published case reports seem to concur with the point that "harm" is meant to be understood as physical (a 2003 investigating committee report on the University of South Florida suggests that harm could include the physical obstruction of the orderly conduct of academic business), and they all agree that "others" refers to people and not to institutional reputation, the general good of the institution, or fears of hypothetical developments such as the fear of litigation that an investigating committee thought might have figured in another case.[21] The concept of immediate harm is inextricably bound up with the gravity of the charges, and the grounds for suspension should therefore be as stringent as those for dismissal. A perceived emergency tends too often to set the stage for a suspension, not only of the faculty member, but also of academic due process itself.

This being said, however, it seems unrealistic to confine the justification for suspensions exclusively to a narrow concept of "physical harm." A more mundane reason for suspension might be a legitimate fear that a disaffected faculty member is impairing the ability of his or her colleagues to carry out their business, for example, by being repeatedly disruptive in department meetings, making it impossible to carry out the work of the department. A professor's inability to handle a chaotic classroom situation might also raise concerns about immediate harm to the students in that class. Or there might be good reason for concluding that a researcher's handling of grant money is so irresponsible as to jeopardize continuance of the grant. In such cases the harm done by the faculty member may be real and immediate, but not physically threatening. Still, it needs to be emphasized that suspension from duties for these kinds of reasons also requires the affordance of academic due process to the accused faculty member.

C. Consultation with a Faculty Committee
RIR 5c(1) stipulates that before an administration suspends a faculty member, it should consult with an appropriate faculty committee charged with handling issues of academic freedom and tenure "as to the propriety, the length, and the other conditions of the suspension." The requirement of consultation reflects the fact that realistically a genuine and immediate threat of harm can hardly

be demonstrated in a timely manner through a full due process hearing. When, as seems increasingly to be the case, suspension is justified either by invoking the threat of immediate harm or by relying on some verbal formula that falls far short of that but is nonetheless taken as self-justifying, such a justification is used to trump the necessity, desirability, or even the possibility of consulting with a faculty body. The language of the provision and its placement under Regulation 5 presupposes that the context is one of pending dismissal proceedings preceded by a statement of charges. In the situations considered in this report, however, suspension tends to take place before any formal charges are filed, and may or may not be followed later by a dismissal proceeding.[22]

Faculty consultation of the sort envisioned in this situation may be regarded not only as an appropriate exercise of faculty responsibilities in a matter affecting faculty status but also as a prudent measure on the part of the administration.

D. Suspension with Pay
While Association-supported policy specifies continued payment of salary (unless otherwise forbidden by law) in all circumstances in which a suspension is a prehearing sanction, the AAUP has never argued that pay alone is sufficient, whether as a matter of relief, as a way to obviate the potential stain of a suspension, or as a benevolent action that expunges any further obligations on the part of the administration. Continuance of salary is not only an essential ingredient of decent treatment, but even more fundamentally also a recognition that a final determination on the guilt or innocence of the accused faculty member has not yet been reached through a hearing. Moreover, if the subject faculty member is without a salary, mounting a defense against charges is much more difficult, if not impossible.

This subcommittee takes no heart from the fact that in many, if not most, of the cases we examined, the suspended faculty member remained on salary. We suggest, rather, that this practice often reflects one of two less than benign assumptions (and possibly both): first, that continuance of salary relieves an administration from the necessity of a faculty hearing because the adverse action supposedly can no longer be described as a suspension; second, that the continued payment of salary provides a contractual hedge in the event of litigation.[23] In cases of freestanding suspension, however, where the matter has been examined deliberatively in a proceeding in accordance with Association-recommended standards of academic due process, suspension without pay may be deemed an appropriate punitive sanction.

E. Expulsion or Banishment

If the continuation of a faculty member in his or her duties poses such a serious threat to the safety of self or others, for the faculty member's own protection, as well as that of others, physical removal from the campus may be the only reasonable or responsible course of action. As we noted in the introduction to this report, Association policy nowhere sorts out actions like "quarantine," "exile," "banishment," or "expulsion."

The routinization of the practice of banishment suggests an intention to add insult to injury. When the effect of suspension is not only to remove the faculty member from teaching duties but also to deny him or her access to the material needed to prove that the charges are groundless and wrongful, such a practice is doubly intolerable. It may be that some instances of banishment have resulted from a misapplication of business practices that might be appropriate in the corporate sector but not in an educational institution. In a business, a disgruntled employee who has been fired could conceivably use his or her office computer to transmit private corporate information to a competitor. In a college or university, such an interest is not likely to be at stake. But unless the threat of immediate harm is so exigent as to require the faculty member not only to be suspended but also to be absent from campus—and we think the standard in that case should be of high magnitude indeed—or unless there is demonstrable evidence that the faculty member's office itself contains material or information that poses a high risk to campus security, we see no grounds to support banishment as a sanction superimposed on the suspension itself.

IV. Suspension as an Independent Sanction (Freestanding Suspension)

It is well attested in the Association's case history that suspension without a hearing, or a hearing indefinitely deferred, is tantamount to dismissal.[24] Regulation 7a envisions a deliberative proceeding in cases in which the immediate-harm standard is not likely to apply. One might argue, for example, that a serious academic offense (for example, scientific misconduct) was not grounds for dismissal in light of the individual's total record, and certainly not for the application of the "immediate-harm standard," but nonetheless sufficiently serious to justify the imposition of a severe sanction.

A University of New Hampshire case offers the kind of situation in which freestanding suspension might conceivably have been the object of a disciplinary proceeding. In that case, a faculty member in the Department of English was suspended, initially without pay, and told to undergo weekly counseling for at least a year at his own expense with "a professional psychotherapist approved by the university" for having allegedly violated a policy on sexual harassment by using sexually charged metaphors to describe the nature of establishing a topic in technical writing. "Shadow sections" were set up for the students who were upset by what they regarded as his inappropriate sexual innuendoes. The reprimand that went with the suspension required that in addition to undergoing mandatory counseling the professor (1) reimburse the university for the cost of those sections, (2) not retaliate against the students who had filed charges, and (3) apologize in writing, by a specified date, to the protesting students for having created a "hostile and offensive academic environment." Since he denied the factual basis of the charges that led to these sanctions, the faculty member refused to comply. In this case, suspension was initially imposed but put in abeyance pending a faculty hearing on the procedures. Though the faculty committee was to find that the professor's grievance had merit and that he had not been granted the opportunity to prepare a defense, three weeks before the committee issued its report he learned that he would not be scheduled to teach any classes during the fall semester, though his salary and benefits would continue. The four conditions attached to the reprimand became part of the conditions on which the suspension would be removed. Although the administration is not on record as having at any time threatened formal dismissal, the sanction ultimately became one of suspension without pay, which, in the absence of the faculty member's compliance, the investigating committee assumed correctly was tantamount to a dismissal for cause. Had a body of the faculty been convened in a due process hearing to render judgment on the matter, under AAUP policy any formal recommendation that might have emerged, up to and including suspension without pay (a suspension with a stated date by which it would be lifted), should have been the end of the matter, absent an appeal by the faculty member to the administration and ultimately the governing board if the recommendation were unfavorable.[25] One lesson of the New Hampshire case, applicable to prehearing suspensions as well as freestanding suspensions, would seem to be that a suspension must be for a stated term and at its end be considered to have met the conditions of the punishment exacted; it cannot be premised on a suspension of indefinite duration requiring the performance of certain duties (particularly undergoing mandatory counseling, which the professor resisted because its acceptance amounted to a coerced admission of guilt) to be satisfied without becoming a dismissal for cause.[26]

V. Effects of Suspension on the Faculty Member

More needs to be said about how suspension may not only cause psychological damage but also compromise the ability of the faculty member to respond.

Quite aside from the long-range effects of a suspension on an individual's record, more immediate complications may create a climate in which a faculty member, already placed on the defensive, can then be targeted for engaging in further "misbehavior" that in fact might be a consequence of the act of suspension itself.

The attachment of conditions for removal from suspension further contributes to a hostile climate in which the fairness of any subsequent judicial proceeding—if there is one—is seriously compromised. Sometimes the conditions seem to have no other purpose than that of humiliation. In one egregious instance, a professor was replaced as the course instructor but ordered by the dean to continue to attend the class and listen to the new teacher until further notice, an action triggered by student complaints over his grades. In this instance, the dean repeatedly interrupted the faculty member, took over the class, and "treated [him] like an errant schoolboy in front of his classes" prior to the suspension.[27] Sometimes a condition may be imposed even if dismissal has been decided upon anyway and is attached to the expiration of the faculty member's existing contract. Thus at one community college, two professors were given notice of nonreappointment fifteen months in advance but suspended from teaching during the final academic year, allegedly because of declining enrollments in the business department. Subsequently, letters were sent to the two faculty members reaffirming the suspension decision but warning that "any conduct which, in the college's opinion, is detrimental to the interests of its operation, will result in the cessation of the salary-benefit continuation plan."[28] The investigating committee judged this as an indication of motives for the suspension other than declining enrollments, but the conditions surrounding the suspension, threatening termination if even one misstep (as defined by the administration) occurred, are of the kind that contribute to an intolerable atmosphere for faculty members already under the normal pressures consequent upon termination of services.

VI. Concluding Comments

This subcommittee has provided an examination of historical experience within the AAUP and what can be drawn from it by way of policy discussion. Such a discussion might turn on the question whether there are changes in campus climate sufficient to call for a review, from the ground up, of at least the rhetorical adequacy of current AAUP policy. Certainly new technologies such as e-mail and computing have extended the potentially damaging effects of suspension actions since the days when access to the classroom was the principal, if not the only, issue. But to come at the matter from a different angle, we also report in the wake of heightened campus tensions ranging from fatal gunfire in a classroom to threatening graffiti that cause an entire campus to shut down. Does the Association have an affirmative obligation to counsel administrations on how they might resist public pressure for quick action lest another tragic or threatening instance were to occur for which they would be held accountable? The fact is—and one could argue that this has always been the case—that classical academic freedom issues are not always in play in a suspension action, notably in an emergency situation. The irrational behavior of a faculty member who endangers his or her colleagues because he or she has access to dangerous biological agents may require quick administrative action in the first instance, with faculty follow-up. Some may believe that such cases involve questions of degree, not kind; others may disagree and believe either that new policy is needed or that, at the very least, existing policy needs to be recast in such a way as to acknowledge legitimate safety concerns more clearly and to take into account the intense nature of public pressure on those whose oversight of an institution includes direct responsibility for public safety. We will be content if this report begins that discussion.

Notes

1. According to a staff memorandum, the Association, since its founding in 1915, has published nearly 120 reports in which suspension has figured as an element in the case, beginning with 1917 and 1919 reports on the University of Montana. It should also be borne in mind that literally thousands of complaints and cases involving suspension have been dealt with by the Association over nearly a century that never

reached the investigative stage, much less became the subject of a published report.

2. "Academic Freedom and Tenure: College of the Ozarks," *AAUP Bulletin* 49 (Winter 1963): 358.

3. "Academic Freedom and Tenure: St. John's University (New York)," *AAUP Bulletin* 52 (Spring 1966): 18–19.

4. AAUP, *Policy Documents and Reports*, 11th ed. (Baltimore: Johns Hopkins University Press, 2015), 3–12.

5. See "Academic Freedom and Tenure: St. Mary's College (California)," *AAUP Bulletin* 62 (Spring 1976): 73: "The investigating committee disagrees sharply with the assertion that a unilateral administrative decision not to offer a hearing can be in the best interests of a faculty member. A formal hearing can result, in some cases, in embarrassment and even stigmatization for the faculty member involved. The waiver of dismissal proceedings, however, lies not within the discretion of the administration but . . . [that] of the affected faculty member." The same can be said for hearings on suspension. The severity of the sanction is underlined in the case of Armstrong State College, where the administration attempted to argue that, since a suspended faculty member's appointment had not been renewed prior to the suspension, the suspension itself was of negligible importance. The investigating committee objected: "The fact of nonrenewal does not in itself imply adverse judgment with regard to an individual faculty member's fitness to teach. The enforced separation of a teacher from his classroom, however, is an action of severity, to be taken only for serious and pressing reasons, with significant professional damage to the individual's future in teaching" ("Academic Freedom and Tenure: Armstrong State College [Georgia]," *AAUP Bulletin* 58 [Spring 1972]: 74).

6. *Policy Documents and Reports*, 91–93.

7. Ibid., 79–90.

8. *AAUP Bulletin* 57 (December 1971): 524–27.

9. The first seven are as follows: "a. An oral reprimand; b. A written reprimand; c. A recorded reprimand; d. Restitution (e.g., payment for damage done to individuals or to the institution); e. Loss of prospective benefits for a stated period (e.g., suspension of 'regular' or 'merit' increase in salary, suspension of promotion eligibility); f. A fine; g. Reduction in salary for a stated period."

10. Donna R. Euben and Barbara A. Lee, "Faculty Discipline: Legal and Policy Issues in Dealing with Faculty Misconduct," *Journal of College and University Law* 32, no. 2 (2006): 241–308, offers a longer list of lesser sanctions more elaborate than the Association's, prefacing it with the workplace idea of "progressive discipline," in which behavior, when repeated, may be subject to increasingly severe degrees of sanction. The Association appears never to have dealt formally with this issue, perhaps in part not only because by its nature academic work is less repetitive than work in some other settings, but also because many cases involve faculty members not heretofore charged with any kind of misconduct whose actions suddenly give offense to

an administration. College and university files doubtless contain instances of reprimands accompanied by the threat of more serious penalties if the behavior is repeated (the principal author of this report is aware of such an instance at his own institution), but predictably many such instances may be assumed to have flown under the Association's radar. The Euben and Lee article has provided valuable information from legal sources for some of the issues we deal with here.

11. "Academic Freedom and Tenure: University of Southern California," *Academe* 81 (November–December 1995): 47–48.

12. This runs contrary to actual case history, though one of the most egregious cases reported avoids the term "suspension" in describing what happened. At Texas A&M University, the professor, a tenured faculty member with sixteen years of experience and a promotion to full professor two years before the events, was placed on "probation" and reassigned to research duties under conditions so intolerable as to make it difficult, if not impossible, for him to carry them out ("Academic Freedom and Tenure: Texas A&M University," *AAUP Bulletin* 53 [Winter 1967]: 379–80). The research assignment was extended a second year with the promise (unfulfilled at the time of the report) of "a proper hearing on his fitness to assume a full-time teaching position." At Armstrong State College, a faculty committee majority found that a mandatory leave constituted a suspension not provided for in the college's own statutes, a view with which the investigating committee concurred. A minority of the same faculty committee took a different view because the faculty member could still perform committee and department assignments.

13. We return to the issue of suspension with pay in Section III.D. With respect to definitional issues in investigations, see "Academic Freedom and Tenure: Adelphi University," *AAUP Bulletin* 53 (Autumn 1967): 285, where the investigating committee "reject[ed] flatly the [administration's] effort to draw a distinction between a suspension and a 'terminal leave of absence with salary.'" The committee wryly noted that "the distinction appears to be no more than an effort to borrow the happy connotations which the phrase 'terminal leave' carries in military service to mask removal from the classroom, in this case on flimsy charges and without a hearing." At Meharry Medical College, handbook guidelines broadly comporting with AAUP-supported standards for suspension were circumvented by the administration's declaring the affected faculty members to be on "administrative leave with pay" ("Academic Freedom and Tenure: Meharry Medical College [Tennessee]," *Academe* 90 [November–December 2004]: 73).

14. An interesting twist on these cases is offered by the Loma Linda University report, involving clinical professors of medicine who, although deriving their income chiefly from practice, nonetheless were in the investigating committee's judgment entitled to be treated as faculty because they took on such traditional faculty duties as teaching, research, and training of interns. See "Academic Freedom and Tenure: Loma

Linda University," *Academe* 78 (May–June 1992): 42–49.

15. "Academic Freedom and Tenure: University of South Florida," *AAUP Bulletin* 50 (Spring 1964): 54.

16. "College of the Ozarks," 358; "Adelphi University," 281; "Academic Freedom and Tenure: Amarillo College," *AAUP Bulletin* 53 (Autumn 1967): 300; "Academic Freedom and Tenure: Elmira College," *AAUP Bulletin* 61 (Spring 1975): 66–70; "Academic Freedom and Tenure: Birmingham-Southern College," *Academe* 65 (May 1979): 237.

17. "Birmingham-Southern College," 237.

18. "Academic Freedom and Tenure: Oklahoma College of Osteopathic Medicine and Surgery," *Academe* 71 (May–June 1985): 39.

19. "Academic Freedom and Tenure: Philander Smith College," *Academe* 90 (January–February 2004): 61.

20. "Academic Freedom and Tenure: University of South Florida," *Academe* 89 (May–June 2003): 67. In a recently publicized incident at Saint Xavier University (Chicago), the campus was closed temporarily because of a graffito threatening violence on a specific date. If an incident like this led to the identification of a faculty malefactor, the demonstration of immediate harm to institutional operation would conceivably be a relatively easy matter. As it happens, a student was subsequently charged.

21. "Academic Freedom and Tenure: University of New Hampshire," *Academe* 80 (November–December 1994): 76.

22. At the University of New Hampshire, the faculty member argued that cancelation of his fall teaching schedule, prior to the issuance of the report of a hearing panel studying his grievance, made it unlikely that he could receive a fair hearing.

23. "Courts generally rule that suspension with pay does not trigger constitutional due process concerns at public institutions" (Euben and Lee, "Faculty Discipline," 277). The same line of reasoning has led to the argument, in *Simonson v. Iowa State University*, 603

N.W.2d 557, 559 (Iowa 1999), that paid administrative leave "did not trigger due process protections under the state and federal constitutions because [the professor] was not deprived of any economic benefits" (278).

24. A reasonably typical case is that of the King's College, in which suspension with pay for a terminal year was followed neither by reinstatement nor by opportunity for a hearing ("Academic Freedom and Tenure: The King's College [New York]," *Academe* 76 [July–August 1990]: 45–52). Also relevant are cases, like a number of the ones we have reviewed, involving nontenured faculty members who have been given notice of nonreappointment and then had a terminal suspension added to that notice, even though their salary may have been continued.

25. The case was complicated by the fact that it was heard ultimately by mixed faculty-student-staff committees; in one case the chair was a student.

26. The New Hampshire case was ultimately resolved in the courts, which found that the sanctions against the professor, taken as a whole, constituted "more than a de minimis deprivation of [the faculty member's] due process rights," and that his suspension without pay provided an independent basis for a preliminary injunction on the grounds of prior and continuing irreparable harm to the faculty member (*Silva v. New Hampshire*, 888 F. Supp. 293 (D.N.H. 1994); Euben and Lee, "Faculty Discipline," 281). See also Euben and Lee's discussion of a related case, *Delahoussaye v. Board of Supervisors of Community and Technical Colleges*, 906 So. 2d 646 (La. Ct. App. 2005); the two cases together seem to provide evidence encouraging institutions to continue the payment of salary to a suspended faculty member in order to avoid claims of economic damage.

27. "Academic Freedom and Tenure: Tennessee State University," *Academe* 73 (May–June 1987): 43.

28. "Academic Freedom and Tenure: Dean Junior College (Massachusetts)," *Academe* 77 (May–June 1991): 28.

College and University Government

Included among the possible activities of the Association in the call for the organizational meeting in 1915 was the study of "the function of faculties in university government." The Committee on the Place and Function of Faculties in University Government and Administration (now known as the Committee on College and University Governance) was appointed in the spring of 1917 and published its first statement in 1920. The statement, authored under the chairmanship of Ohio State University philosopher J. A. Leighton, contained both specific recommendations for the conduct of institutional government and a survey of practices at more than sixty institutions. The specific recommendations addressed the relationship between the faculty and the governing board, the faculty and the president, and the faculty and deans; the role of the faculty in the determination of educational policies and in the preparation of the budget; and the government of departments. In some places, most notably on the question of faculty membership on governing boards, the committee was unable to agree on a single recommendation.

Beginning in 1936, the committee again surveyed governance practices, and it issued refinements to its earlier recommendations in 1938. The committee's 1938 report, authored under the chairmanship of Cornell University philosopher George H. Sabine, concluded with the following observation:

> The immediately practical problems in university government are, first, to regularize the faculty's share in making and executing educational policy and, second, to find the means for creating representative institutions which will make such sharing real. The ideal . . . is to fuse together administration and the educational tasks of the university as respectively means and end. . . . There can be no question of claiming democracy at the cost of efficiency. The claim is rather that, except by agencies representing the common convictions of the teaching profession, there can be no university government which is in any large sense efficient. If this purpose is kept steadily in view, there can be no permanent clash of interests between teachers and administrative officers, since both are united in a common purpose.
>
> Some such conception of university government is inherent in the avowed purposes and the historical development of this Association, which stands upon the assumption that the combination of teaching and investigation in our institutions of higher learning constitutes a profession. From this point of view a university or a college is in essence a group of scholars cooperating in an educational task, and conducting that task essentially by discussion and mutual conviction. The future of university education, and incidentally the future of this Association, depends upon our ability to find the kind of institutions in which our conception can be embodied and to give to the government of universities a form such that cooperative scholarship may find therein its organs.

In the period from 1958 to 1964, the committee issued a series of drafts of principles, which led to efforts toward a joint statement in 1963, first with the American Council on Education and then also with the Association of Governing Boards of Universities and Colleges. The culmination of these efforts was the *Statement on Government of Colleges and Universities*. This statement, with its call for joint effort among the different components of institutional government and its specification of areas of primary responsibility for governing boards, administrations, and faculties, remains the Association's central policy document relating to academic governance. It has been supplemented over the years by a series of derivative policy statements, many of which are included here.

While investigations of violations of academic freedom have been conducted by the Association since its founding year and have frequently commented, by necessity, on the prevailing governance climate at the investigated institution, investigations of governance violations seem to have originated in 1957. Since 1991, the AAUP has used the practice of sanctioning institutions for infringement of governance standards. In recent years, the Association has published reports on institutions in which the governing board and administration unilaterally suspended faculty senates (Idaho State University, Rensselaer Polytechnic Institute), in which the governing board forced the resignation of a university president without faculty consultation (University of Virginia), and in which the administration failed to involve the faculty in curricular and budgetary decisions under circumstances that ultimately led to the closing of a college (Antioch University).

Statement on Government of Colleges and Universities

The statement that follows is directed to governing board members, administrators, faculty members, students, and other persons in the belief that the colleges and universities of the United States have reached a stage calling for appropriately shared responsibility and cooperative action among the components of the academic institution. The statement is intended to foster constructive joint thought and action, both within the institutional structure and in protection of its integrity against improper intrusions.

It is not intended that the statement serve as a blueprint for governance on a specific campus or as a manual for the regulation of controversy among the components of an academic institution, although it is to be hoped that the principles asserted will lead to the correction of existing weaknesses and assist in the establishment of sound structures and procedures. The statement does not attempt to cover relations with those outside agencies that increasingly are controlling the resources and influencing the patterns of education in our institutions of higher learning: for example, the US government, state legislatures, state commissions, interstate associations or compacts, and other interinstitutional arrangements. However, it is hoped that the statement will be helpful to these agencies in their consideration of educational matters.

Students are referred to in this statement as an institutional component coordinate in importance with trustees, administrators, and faculty. There is, however, no main section on students. The omission has two causes: (1) the changes now occurring in the status of American students have plainly outdistanced the analysis by the educational community, and an attempt to define the situation without thorough study might prove unfair to student interests, and (2) students do not in fact at present have a significant voice in the government of colleges and universities; it would be unseemly to obscure, by superficial equality of length of statement, what may be a serious lag entitled to separate and full confrontation. The concern for student status felt by the organizations issuing this statement is embodied in a note, "On Student Status," intended to stimulate the educational community to turn its attention to an important need.

This statement was jointly formulated by the American Association of University Professors, the American Council on Education (ACE), and the Association of Governing Boards of Universities and Colleges (AGB). In October 1966, the board of directors of the ACE took action by which its Council "recognizes the statement as a significant step forward in the clarification of the respective roles of governing boards, faculties, and administrations" and "commends it to the institutions which are members of the Council." The Council of the AAUP adopted the statement in October 1966, and the Fifty-Third Annual Meeting endorsed it in April 1967. In November 1966, the executive committee of the

117

AGB took action by which that organization also "recognizes the statement as a significant step forward in the clarification of the respective roles of governing boards, faculties, and administrations" and "commends it to the governing boards which are members of the Association."

1. Introduction

This statement is a call to mutual understanding regarding the government of colleges and universities. Understanding, based on community of interest and producing joint effort, is essential for at least three reasons. First, the academic institution, public or private, often has become less autonomous; buildings, research, and student tuition are supported by funds over which the college or university exercises a diminishing control. Legislative and executive governmental authorities, at all levels, play a part in the making of important decisions in academic policy. If these voices and forces are to be successfully heard and integrated, the academic institution must be in a position to meet them with its own generally unified view. Second, regard for the welfare of the institution remains important despite the mobility and interchange of scholars. Third, a college or university in which all the components are aware of their interdependence, of the usefulness of communication among themselves, and of the force of joint action will enjoy increased capacity to solve educational problems.

2. The Academic Institution: Joint Effort

a. Preliminary Considerations

The variety and complexity of the tasks performed by institutions of higher education produce an inescapable interdependence among governing board, administration, faculty, students, and others. The relationship calls for adequate communication among these components, and full opportunity for appropriate joint planning and effort.

Joint effort in an academic institution will take a variety of forms appropriate to the kinds of situations encountered. In some instances, an initial exploration or recommendation will be made by the president with consideration by the faculty at a later stage; in other instances, a first and essentially definitive recommendation will be made by the faculty, subject to the endorsement of the president and the governing board. In still others, a substantive contribution can be made when student leaders are responsibly involved in the process. Although the variety of such approaches may be wide, at least two general conclusions regarding joint effort seem clearly warranted: (1) important areas of action involve at one time or another the initiating capacity and decision-making participation of all the institutional components, and (2) differences in the weight of each voice, from one point to the next, should be determined by reference to the responsibility of each component for the particular matter at hand, as developed hereinafter.

b. Determination of General Educational Policy

The general educational policy, i.e., the objectives of an institution and the nature, range, and pace of its efforts, is shaped by the institutional charter or by law, by tradition and historical development, by the present needs of the community of the institution, and by the professional aspirations and standards of those directly involved in its work. Every board will wish to go beyond its formal trustee obligation to conserve the accomplishment of the past and to engage seriously with the future; every faculty will seek to conduct an operation worthy of scholarly standards of learning; every administrative officer will strive to meet his or her charge and to attain the goals of the institution. The interests of all are coordinate and related, and unilateral effort can lead to confusion or conflict. Essential to a solution is a reasonably explicit statement on general educational policy. Operating responsibility and authority, and procedures for continuing review, should be clearly defined in official regulations.

When an educational goal has been established, it becomes the responsibility primarily of the faculty to determine the appropriate curriculum and procedures of student instruction.

Special considerations may require particular accommodations: (1) a publicly supported institution may be regulated by statutory provisions, and (2) a church-controlled institution may be limited by its charter or bylaws. When such external requirements influence course content and the manner of instruction or research, they impair the educational effectiveness of the institution.

Such matters as major changes in the size or composition of the student body and the relative emphasis to be given to the various elements of the educational and research program should involve participation of governing board, administration, and faculty prior to final decision.

c. Internal Operations of the Institution

The framing and execution of long-range plans, one of the most important aspects of institutional responsibility, should be a central and continuing concern in the academic community.

Effective planning demands that the broadest possible exchange of information and opinion should be the rule for communication among the components of a college or university. The channels of communication should be established and maintained by joint endeavor. Distinction should be observed between the institutional system of communication and the system of responsibility for the making of decisions.

A second area calling for joint effort in internal operation is that of decisions regarding existing or prospective physical resources. The board, president, and faculty should all seek agreement on basic decisions regarding buildings and other facilities to be used in the educational work of the institution.

A third area is budgeting. The allocation of resources among competing demands is central in the formal responsibility of the governing board, in the administrative authority of the president, and in the educational function of the faculty. Each component should therefore have a voice in the determination of short- and long-range priorities, and each should receive appropriate analyses of past budgetary experience, reports on current budgets and expenditures, and short- and long-range budgetary projections. The function of each component in budgetary matters should be understood by all; the allocation of authority will determine the flow of information and the scope of participation in decisions.

Joint effort of a most critical kind must be taken when an institution chooses a new president. The selection of a chief administrative officer should follow upon a cooperative search by the governing board and the faculty, taking into consideration the opinions of others who are appropriately interested. The president should be equally qualified to serve both as the executive officer of the governing board and as the chief academic officer of the institution and the faculty. The president's dual role requires an ability to interpret to board and faculty the educational views and concepts of institutional government of the other. The president should have the confidence of the board and the faculty.

The selection of academic deans and other chief academic officers should be the responsibility of the president with the advice of, and in consultation with, the appropriate faculty.

Determinations of faculty status, normally based on the recommendations of the faculty

groups involved, are discussed in Part 5 of this statement; but it should here be noted that the building of a strong faculty requires careful joint effort in such actions as staff selection and promotion and the granting of tenure. Joint action should also govern dismissals; the applicable principles and procedures in these matters are well established.[1]

d. External Relations of the Institution

Anyone—a member of the governing board, the president or other member of the administration, a member of the faculty, or a member of the student body or the alumni—affects the institution when speaking of it in public. An individual who speaks unofficially should so indicate. An individual who speaks officially for the institution, the board, the administration, the faculty, or the student body should be guided by established policy.

It should be noted that only the board speaks legally for the whole institution, although it may delegate responsibility to an agent. The right of a board member, an administrative officer, a faculty member, or a student to speak on general educational questions or about the administration and operations of the individual's own institution is a part of that person's right as a citizen and should not be abridged by the institution.[2] There exist, of course, legal bounds relating to defamation of character, and there are questions of propriety.

3. The Academic Institution: The Governing Board

The governing board has a special obligation to ensure that the history of the college or university shall serve as a prelude and inspiration to the future. The board helps relate the institution to its chief community: for example, the community college to serve the educational needs of a defined population area or group, the church-controlled college to be cognizant of the announced position of its denomination, and the comprehensive university to discharge the many duties and to accept the appropriate new challenges which are its concern at the several levels of higher education.

The governing board of an institution of higher education in the United States operates, with few exceptions, as the final institutional authority. Private institutions are established by charters; public institutions are established by constitutional or statutory provisions. In private institutions the board is frequently self-perpetuating; in public colleges and universities the present membership of a board may be asked to suggest candidates for appointment. As a whole and individually, when the governing board confronts the problem of succession, serious attention should be given to obtaining properly qualified persons. Where public law calls for election of governing board members, means should be found to ensure the nomination of fully suited persons, and the electorate should be informed of the relevant criteria for board membership.

Since the membership of the board may embrace both individual and collective competence of recognized weight, its advice or help may be sought through established channels by other components of the academic community. The governing board of an institution of higher education, while maintaining a general overview, entrusts the conduct of administration to the administrative officers—the president and the deans—and the conduct of teaching and research to the faculty. The board should undertake appropriate self-limitation.

One of the governing board's important tasks is to ensure the publication of codified statements that define the overall policies and procedures of the institution under its jurisdiction.

The board plays a central role in relating the likely needs of the future to predictable resources; it has the responsibility for husbanding the endowment; it is responsible for obtaining needed capital and operating funds; and in the broadest sense of the term it should pay attention to personnel policy. In order to fulfill these duties, the board should be aided by, and may insist upon, the development of long-range planning by the administration and faculty. When ignorance or ill will threatens the institution or any part of it, the governing board must be available for support. In grave crises it will be expected to serve as a champion. Although the action to be taken by it will usually be on behalf of the president, the faculty, or the student body, the board should make clear that the protection it offers to an individual or a group is, in fact, a fundamental defense of the vested interests of society in the educational institution.[3]

4. The Academic Institution: The President
The president, as the chief executive officer of an institution of higher education, is measured largely by his or her capacity for institutional leadership. The president shares responsibility for the definition and attainment of goals, for administrative action, and for operating the communications system that links the components of the academic community. The president represents the institution to its many publics. The president's leadership role is supported by delegated authority from the board and faculty.

As the chief planning officer of an institution, the president has a special obligation to innovate and initiate. The degree to which a president can envision new horizons for the institution, and can persuade others to see them and to work toward them, will often constitute the chief measure of the president's administration.

The president must at times, with or without support, infuse new life into a department; relatedly, the president may at times be required, working within the concept of tenure, to solve problems of obsolescence. The president will necessarily utilize the judgments of the faculty but may also, in the interest of academic standards, seek outside evaluations by scholars of acknowledged competence.

It is the duty of the president to see to it that the standards and procedures in operational use within the college or university conform to the policy established by the governing board and to the standards of sound academic practice. It is also incumbent on the president to ensure that faculty views, including dissenting views, are presented to the board in those areas and on those issues where responsibilities are shared. Similarly, the faculty should be informed of the views of the board and the administration on like issues.

The president is largely responsible for the maintenance of existing institutional resources and the creation of new resources; has ultimate managerial responsibility for a large area of nonacademic activities; is responsible for public understanding; and by the nature of the office is the chief person who speaks for the institution. In these and other areas the president's work is to plan, to organize, to direct, and to represent. The presidential function should receive the general support of board and faculty.

5. The Academic Institution: The Faculty
The faculty has primary responsibility for such fundamental areas as curriculum, subject matter and methods of instruction, research, faculty status, and those aspects of student life which relate to the educational process.[4] On these matters the power of review or final decision lodged in the governing board or delegated by it to the president should be exercised adversely only in exceptional circumstances, and for reasons communicated to the faculty. It is desirable that the faculty should, following such communication, have opportunity for further consideration and further transmittal of its views to the president or board. Budgets, personnel limitations, the time element, and the policies of other groups, bodies, and agencies

having jurisdiction over the institution may set limits to realization of faculty advice.

The faculty sets the requirements for the degrees offered in course, determines when the requirements have been met, and authorizes the president and board to grant the degrees thus achieved.

Faculty status and related matters are primarily a faculty responsibility; this area includes appointments, reappointments, decisions not to reappoint, promotions, the granting of tenure, and dismissal. The primary responsibility of the faculty for such matters is based upon the fact that its judgment is central to general educational policy. Furthermore, scholars in a particular field or activity have the chief competence for judging the work of their colleagues; in such competence it is implicit that responsibility exists for both adverse and favorable judgments. Likewise, there is the more general competence of experienced faculty personnel committees having a broader charge. Determinations in these matters should first be by faculty action through established procedures, reviewed by the chief academic officers with the concurrence of the board. The governing board and president should, on questions of faculty status, as in other matters where the faculty has primary responsibility, concur with the faculty judgment except in rare instances and for compelling reasons which should be stated in detail.

The faculty should actively participate in the determination of policies and procedures governing salary increases.

The chair or head of a department, who serves as the chief representative of the department within an institution, should be selected either by departmental election or by appointment following consultation with members of the department and of related departments; appointments should normally be in conformity with department members' judgment. The chair or department head should not have tenure in office; tenure as a faculty member is a matter of separate right. The chair or head should serve for a stated term but without prejudice to reelection or to reappointment by procedures that involve appropriate faculty consultation. Board, administration, and faculty should all bear in mind that the department chair or head has a special obligation to build a department strong in scholarship and teaching capacity.

Agencies for faculty participation in the government of the college or university should be established at each level where faculty responsibility is present. An agency should exist for the presentation of the views of the whole faculty. The structure and procedures for faculty participation should be designed, approved, and established by joint action of the components of the institution. Faculty representatives should be selected by the faculty according to procedures determined by the faculty.[5]

The agencies may consist of meetings of all faculty members of a department, school, college, division, or university system, or may take the form of faculty-elected executive committees in departments and schools and a faculty-elected senate or council for larger divisions or the institution as a whole.

The means of communication among the faculty, administration, and governing board now in use include: (1) circulation of memoranda and reports by board committees, the administration, and faculty committees; (2) joint ad hoc committees; (3) standing liaison committees; (4) membership of faculty members on administrative bodies; and (5) membership of faculty members on governing boards. Whatever the channels of communication, they should be clearly understood and observed.

On Student Status

When students in American colleges and universities desire to participate responsibly in the government of the institution they attend, their wish should be recognized as a claim to opportunity both for educational experience and for involvement in the affairs of their college or university. Ways should be found to permit significant student participation within the limits of attainable effectiveness. The obstacles to such participation are large and should not be minimized: inexperience, untested capacity, a transitory status which means that present action does not carry with it subsequent responsibility, and the inescapable fact that the other components of the institution are in a position of judgment over the students. It is important to recognize that student needs are strongly related to educational experience, both formal and informal.

Students expect, and have a right to expect, that the educational process will be structured, that they will be stimulated by it to become independent adults, and that they will have effectively transmitted to them the cultural heritage of the larger society. If institutional support is to have its fullest possible meaning, it should incorporate the strength, freshness of view, and idealism of the student body.

The respect of students for their college or university can be enhanced if they are given at least these opportunities: (1) to be listened to in the classroom without fear of institutional reprisal for the substance of their views, (2) freedom to discuss questions of institutional policy and operation, (3) the right to academic due process when charged with serious violations of institutional regulations, and (4) the same right to hear speakers of their own choice as is enjoyed by other components of the institution.

Notes

1. See the 1940 "Statement of Principles on Academic Freedom and Tenure," AAUP, *Policy Documents and Reports*, 11th ed. (Baltimore: Johns Hopkins University Press, 2015), 13–19, and the "Statement on Procedural Standards in Faculty Dismissal Proceedings," ibid., 91–93. These statements were jointly adopted by the Association of American Colleges (now the Association of American Colleges and Universities) and the American Association of University Professors; the 1940 "Statement" has been endorsed by numerous learned and scientific societies and educational associations.

2. With respect to faculty members, the 1940 "Statement of Principles on Academic Freedom and Tenure" reads, "College and university teachers are citizens, members of a learned profession, and officers of an educational institution. When they speak or write as citizens, they should be free from institutional censorship or discipline, but their special position in the community imposes special obligations. As scholars and educational officers, they should remember that the public may judge their profession and their institution by their utterances. Hence they should at all times be accurate, should exercise appropriate restraint, should show respect for the opinions of others, and should make every effort to indicate that they are not speaking for the institution" (ibid., 14).

3. Traditionally, governing boards developed within the context of single-campus institutions. In more recent times, governing and coordinating boards have increasingly tended to develop at the multi-campus regional, systemwide, or statewide levels. As influential components of the academic community, these supra-campus bodies bear particular responsibility for protecting the autonomy of individual campuses or institutions under their jurisdiction and for implementing policies of shared responsibility. The American Association of University Professors regards the objectives and practices recommended in the "Statement on Government" as constituting equally appropriate guidelines for such supra-campus bodies, and looks toward continued development of practices that will facilitate application of such guidelines in this new context. [Preceding note adopted by the AAUP's Council in June 1978. See also "Statewide Boards of Higher Education: The Faculty Role," *Academe* 70 (May–June 1984): 16a.]

4. With regard to student admissions, the faculty should have a meaningful role in establishing institutional policies, including the setting of standards for admission, and should be afforded opportunity for oversight of the entire admissions process. [Preceding note adopted by the Council in June 2002.]

5. The American Association of University Professors regards collective bargaining, properly used, as another means of achieving sound academic government. Where there is faculty collective bargaining, the parties should seek to ensure appropriate institutional governance structures which will protect the right of all faculty to participate in institutional governance in accordance with the "Statement on Government." [Preceding note adopted by the Council in June 1978.]

On the Relationship of Faculty Governance to Academic Freedom

This statement was approved in May 1994 by the Association's Committee on College and University Governance (Committee T). In June 1994 it was approved by Committee A on Academic Freedom and Tenure and adopted by the Association's Council.

Since its founding in 1915, the AAUP has been actively engaged in developing standards for sound academic practice and in working for their acceptance throughout the community of higher education. Two aspects of an institution's academic practice have been of particular concern to the Association ever since: the rights and freedoms of individual faculty members and the role of the faculty in institutional governance. The fundamental principles describing the rights and freedoms that an institution should accord to its individual faculty members are set forth in the 1940 *Statement of Principles on Academic Freedom and Tenure;* those principles have been further developed in more recent Association statements and reports that bring the principles to bear on specific issues having to do with faculty status. The fundamental principles describing the proper role of faculty members in institutional governance are set forth in the *Statement on Government of Colleges and Universities;* those principles, too, have been further developed in more recent Association statements and reports.

Although the Association established Committee A in 1915, its initial year, to attend to issues of academic freedom and tenure, and created Committee T the following year to address issues of institutional "government," the AAUP has not spoken explicitly to the links between its principles in these two basic areas. Thus, the 1940 *Statement of Principles* describes faculty members as "officers of an educational institution," but it is silent about the governance role they should carry out in light of their being officers of the institution. The *Statement on Government* describes the role in institutional government that faculty should be accorded, but it does not speak to the bearing of that role on the rights and freedoms of individual faculty members.[1]

Historical and contemporary links can be clearly seen, however. This statement will suggest that a sound system of institutional governance is a necessary condition for the protection of faculty rights and thereby for the most productive exercise of essential faculty freedoms. Correspondingly, the protection of the academic freedom of faculty members in addressing issues of institutional governance is a prerequisite for the practice of governance unhampered by fear of retribution.[2]

An institution's system of governance is the structure according to which authority and responsibilities are allocated to the various offices and divisions within the institution. How should that authority be allocated? Conducting the academic enterprise requires carrying out a complex array of tasks by the various components of the institution. The *Statement on Government* singles out three major institutional components—the governing board, the administration, and the faculty—and describes their respective responsibilities, that is, the tasks for which each is primarily responsible. Being responsible for carrying out a task is one thing, however, and having authority over the way in which the task is carried out is quite another. The *Statement on Government* connects them in the following general principle, enunciated at the outset: "differences in the weight of each voice, from one point to the next, should be determined by reference to the responsibility of each component for the particular matter at hand. . . ." Thus degrees of authority should track directness of responsibility.

For example, since the faculty has primary responsibility for the teaching and research done in the institution, the faculty's voice on matters having to do with teaching and research should be given the greatest weight. From that idea flow more specific principles regarding the faculty's role, as expressed in the *Statement on Government.* Since such decisions as those involving choice of method of instruction, subject matter to be taught, policies for admitting students, standards of student competence in a discipline, the maintenance of a suitable environment for learning, and standards of faculty competence bear directly on the teaching and research conducted in the institution, the faculty should have primary authority over decisions about such matters—that is, the administration should "concur with the faculty judgment except in rare instances and for compelling reasons which should be stated in detail." Other decisions bear less directly on the teaching and research conducted in the institution; these include, for instance, decisions about the institution's long-range objectives, its physical and fiscal resources, the distribution of its funds among its various divisions, and the selection of its president. But these decisions plainly can have a powerful impact on the institution's teaching and research, and the *Statement on Government,* therefore, declares that the decision-making process must include the faculty, and that its voice on these matters must be accorded great respect.

In short, the *Statement on Government* derives the weight of the faculty's voice on an issue—that is, the degree to which the faculty's voice should be authoritative on the issue—from the relative directness with which the issue bears on the faculty's exercise of its various institutional responsibilities.

There are at least three reasons why the faculty's voice should be authoritative across the entire range of decision making that bears, whether directly or indirectly, on its responsibilities. For each of these reasons it is also essential that faculty members have the academic freedom to express their professional opinions without fear of reprisal.

In the first place, this allocation of authority is the most efficient means to the accomplishment of the institution's objectives. For example, as the *Statement on Government* maintains, "the educational effectiveness of the institution" is the greater the more firmly the institution is able to protect this allocation of authority against pressures from outside the institution. Moreover, scholars in a discipline are acquainted with the discipline from within; their views on what students should learn in it, and on which faculty members should be appointed and promoted, are therefore more likely to produce better teaching and research in the discipline than are the views of trustees or administrators. More generally, experienced faculty committees—whether constituted to address curricular, personnel, or other matters—must be free to bring to bear on the issues at hand not merely their disciplinary competencies, but also their first-hand understanding of what constitutes good teaching and research generally, and of the climate in which those endeavors can best be conducted.

The second reason issues from the centrality of teaching and research within the array of tasks carried out by an academic institution: teaching and research are the very purpose of an academic institution and the reason why the public values and supports it. This means that the faculty, who are responsible for carrying out those central tasks, should be viewed as having a special status within the institution. The Association has taken this view from its earliest days. Its first statement, the 1915 *Declaration of Principles,*[3] declares that members of a faculty "are the appointees, but not in any proper sense the employees," of the trustees; they are partners with the trustees, and, as the 1915 *Declaration* states, the office of faculty member should be—indeed, it is in the public interest that the office of faculty member should be—"one both of dignity and of independence." Allocation of authority to the faculty in the areas of its responsibility is a necessary condition for the faculty's possessing that dignity and exercising that independence.

The third reason is the most important in the present context: allocation of authority to the faculty in the areas of its responsibility is a necessary condition for the protection of academic freedom within the institution. The protection of free expression takes many forms, but the issue emerges most clearly in the case of authority over faculty status.

The academic freedom of faculty members includes the freedom to express their views (1) on academic matters in the classroom and in the conduct of research, (2) on matters having to do with their institution and its policies, and (3) on issues of public interest generally, and to do so even if their views are in conflict with one or another received wisdom. Association policy documents over the years before and since the adoption of the 1940 *Statement of Principles* have described the reasons why this freedom should be accorded and rights to it protected. In the case (1) of academic matters, good teaching requires developing critical ability in one's students and an understanding of the methods for resolving disputes within the discipline; good research requires permitting the expression of contrary views in order that the evidence for and against a hypothesis can be weighed responsibly. In the case (2) of institutional matters, grounds for thinking an institutional policy desirable or undesirable must be heard and assessed if the community is to have confidence that its policies are appropriate. In the case (3) of issues of public interest generally, the faculty member must be free to exercise the rights accorded to all citizens.[4]

Protecting academic freedom on campus requires ensuring that a particular instance of faculty speech will be subject to discipline only where that speech violates some central principle of academic morality, as, for example, where it is found to be fraudulent (academic freedom does not protect plagiarism and deceit). Protecting academic freedom also requires ensuring that faculty status turns on a faculty member's views only where the holding of those views clearly supports a judgment of competence or incompetence.

It is in light of these requirements that the allocation to the faculty—through appropriate governance processes and structures—of authority over faculty status and other basic academic matters can be seen to be necessary for the protection of academic freedom. It is the faculty—not trustees or administrators—who have the experience needed for assessing whether an instance of faculty speech constitutes a breach of a central principle of academic morality, and who have the expertise to form judgments of faculty competence or incompetence. As AAUP case reports have shown, to the extent that decisions on such matters are not in the hands of the faculty, there is a potential for, and at times the actuality of, administrative imposition of penalties on improper grounds.

A good governance system is no guarantee that academic freedom will flourish. A governance system is merely a structure that allocates authority, and authority needs to be exercised if even the most appropriate allocation of it is to have its intended effects. Faculty members must be willing to participate in the decision-making processes over which a sound governance system gives them authority. As the Association's *Statement on Professional Ethics* says, faculty members must "accept their share of faculty responsibilities for the governance of their institution." If they do not, authority will drift away from them, since someone must exercise it, and if members of the faculty do not, others will.

The second possible source of concern is more subtle. Even with a sound governance system in place and with a faculty active in self-government and operating under rules and regulations protective of academic freedom, dysfunctions that undermine academic freedom may still occur: subtle (or not so subtle) bullying on the part of

the faculty itself, a covertly enforced isolation, a disinclination to respect the views of the offbeat and cranky among its members. That is to say, given appropriate formal protections, such incivilities may not issue in clear-cut violations of academic freedom, but a faculty member's academic freedom may nevertheless be chilled.[5]

In sum, sound governance practice and the exercise of academic freedom are closely connected, arguably inextricably linked. While no governance system can serve to guarantee that academic freedom will always prevail, an inadequate governance system—one in which the faculty is not accorded primacy in academic matters—compromises the conditions in which academic freedom is likely to thrive. Similarly, although academic freedom is not a sufficient condition, it is an essential one for effective governance. Thus, the earliest principles formulated by the Association, those of 1915 and 1916, are most likely to thrive when they are understood to reinforce one another. Under those conditions, institutions of higher education will be best served and will in turn best serve society at large.

Notes

1. The "Statement on Government" does, however, quote from the 1940 "Statement of Principles" (AAUP, *Policy Documents and Reports*, 11th ed. [Baltimore: Johns Hopkins University Press, 2015], 122, n. 2).

2. Also relevant are the Association's "Statement on Professional Ethics," ibid., 145–46, and "A Statement of the Association's Council: Freedom and Responsibility," *AAUP Bulletin* 56 (December 1970): 375–76.

3. 1915 "Declaration of Principles on Academic Freedom and Academic Tenure," *Policy Documents and Reports*, 3–12.

4. In this connection, several policy statements have particular relevance, including the "Committee A Statement on Extramural Utterances," ibid., 31, and the "Statement on Professors and Political Activity," ibid., 39.

5. According to "A Statement of the Association's Council: Freedom and Responsibility," "Membership in the academic community imposes on students, faculty members, administrators, and trustees an obligation to respect the dignity of others, to acknowledge their right to express differing opinions, and to foster and defend intellectual honesty, freedom of inquiry and instruction, and free expression on and off the campus" (375).

Protecting an Independent Faculty Voice: Academic Freedom after *Garcetti v. Ceballos*

The statement that follows is the executive summary of a longer report that was prepared by a subcommittee of the Association's Committee A on Academic Freedom and Tenure and approved by Committee A in June 2009. Legal citations in the report were updated in 2014.

Most faculty may be unaware that a recent Supreme Court decision, *Garcetti v. Ceballos* (2006),[1] and several subsequent lower-court rulings applying that decision to higher education pose a serious threat to academic freedom and the ability of faculty in public institutions to partici-pate freely in academic governance. The serious-ness of this threat led the AAUP's Committee A on Academic Freedom and Tenure to form a subcommittee to examine the potential impact of the *Garcetti* decision and to suggest actions to be taken in both public and private colleges and universities to preserve academic freedom even in the face of judicial hostility or indifference. Because of the length and detailed legal analysis of its report, the subcommittee has also prepared this executive summary to make its general findings more readily accessible and to highlight its call for action outside the limited confines of the courts. The full report begins with an overview of the historical development of the principle of academic freedom in the United States. It then provides a substantial analysis of the legal precedents concerning both academic freedom, in particular, and the more general limits on the free speech rights of public employ-ees, the issue addressed in the *Garcetti* case, before concluding with a series of recommended steps that faculty and administrators should take to safeguard academic freedom.

In *Garcetti v. Ceballos*, the Supreme Court allowed a Los Angeles district attorney's office to discipline a deputy district attorney for having criticized his supervisors' actions; the Court ruled that when public employees speak "pursuant to their official duties, the employees are not speaking as citizens for First Amendment purposes, and the Constitution does not insulate their communications from employer discipline." Although the majority expressly left open whether its ruling should apply to "speech related to scholarship and teaching" in public colleges and universities, subsequent decisions in the lower

federal courts concerning faculty speech have disregarded this reservation and now threaten to diminish severely the constitutional protection of the academic freedom of professors whose engagement in governance, as well as their teaching and research, is considered part of their "official duties."

The drafters of the AAUP's 1915 *Declaration of Principles on Academic Freedom and Academic Tenure*,[2] which has provided a basis for the American understanding of academic freedom, did not rely upon the Constitution or statutes to make their case. At the time, faculty members at both private and public institutions were largely governed by the common law of master and servant; that is, the institution had authority and control over the faculty. Hence, most governing boards and presidents had the legal power to dismiss faculty members, who were at-will employees, for their economic, political, social, or religious views and for their criticisms of the institution. The authors of the *Declaration* argued that, for universities to advance knowledge and train students to think for themselves, faculty not only had to possess disciplinary expertise but also needed to be free from the control of their governing board and administration. The *Declaration*'s authors explained that "[u]niversity teachers should be understood to be, with respect to the conclusions reached and expressed by them, no more subject to the control of the trustees than are judges subject to the control of the president." The assertion and exercise of these liberties confronted the master-servant model head on. As the 1915 *Declaration* put it, faculty members are "appointees" of the governing boards "but not in any proper sense the employees."

By the late 1930s, the principles of academic freedom in teaching, research, and publication had become generally accepted in most of public and nondenominational private higher education, and they were codified in the 1940 *Statement of Principles on Academic Freedom and Tenure*, the joint formulation of the AAUP and the Association of American Colleges (now the Association of American Colleges and Universities). This development occurred outside the context of the law and the constitutional right to free speech.

One aspect of academic freedom asserted in the 1940 *Statement* is the role of the faculty member in institutional life as a citizen or an "officer" of the institution. The academic freedom of a faculty member pertains to both (1) speech or action taken as part of the institution's governing and decision-making processes (for example, within a faculty committee or as part of a grievance filing) and (2) speech or action that is critical of institutional policies and of those in authority and takes place outside an institution's formal governance mechanisms (such as e-mail messages sent to other faculty members). In its 1994 statement *On the Relationship of Faculty Governance to Academic Freedom*,[3] the AAUP affirmed the inextricable connection between academic freedom in teaching and research and the free and effective participation of faculty in institutional governance.

Although the principle of academic freedom developed outside the law, beginning in the 1950s the Supreme Court began to interpret the First Amendment to include some protections for academic freedom for faculty at public institutions. In *Keyishian v. Board of Regents* (1967),[4] a majority of the Court recognized academic freedom as a First Amendment interest. The subcommittee report emphasizes, however, that such protection did not extend to private institutions, since First Amendment protections apply only to restrictions on speech by arms of government. Moreover, the First Amendment protections provided to faculty at public institutions, while often quite helpful, never fully incorporated the AAUP's understanding of the scope of academic freedom.

Soon after the *Keyishian* ruling, the Supreme Court began to hand down a series of decisions addressing public employee speech more broadly. In *Pickering v. Board of Education* (1968),[5] the Court strengthened the free speech rights of public employees by qualifying the long-standing legal doctrine that the First Amendment did not restrain the government when it functioned as an employer. That doctrine had been encapsulated by Oliver Wendell Holmes in 1892, when he stated that a policeman "may have a constitutional right to talk politics, but he has no constitutional right to be a policeman." In *Pickering*, a case decided in favor of a public employee's free speech rights, the Supreme Court balanced the interests of a public employee "as a citizen, in commenting upon

matters of public concern," against "the interests of the State, as an employer, in promoting the efficiency of the public services it performs through its employees." In subsequent decisions regarding public employee speech prior to *Garcetti*, the Court began to limit employee speech protection to a more restricted definition of matters of "public concern," so *Garcetti* ought not to have been a total surprise.

The threat to academic freedom implicit in *Garcetti's* pinched reading of public employees' free speech right became explicit in three subsequent lower-court decisions. In *Hong v. Grant* (2007),[6] a district judge, citing *Garcetti* and ignoring the Supreme Court's reservation for speech related to teaching and research, ruled that the University of California "is entitled to unfettered discretion when it restricts statements an employee makes on the job and according to his professional responsibilities." Such responsibilities included participation in institutional governance. Appeals courts in both *Renken v. Gregory* (2008)[7] and *Gorum v. Sessoms* (2009)[8] adopted similarly restrictive interpretations of faculty free speech rights. As of this writing, the *Hong* decision is on appeal, and the AAUP has filed an amicus brief.[9]

The subcommittee report notes the irony that, based on the broad definition of "official duties" employed in these post-*Garcetti* rulings, only faculty speech on topics beyond the speaker's expertise may be constitutionally protected and that there now may exist a "negative or inverse correlation between the scope of a professor's (or a faculty's) role in shared governance and the breadth of potential protection for expressive activity . . . . In brief, as the cases stand now, one could argue that the less of a stake you have in your institution's shared governance, the freer you are (as a First Amendment matter) to criticize how it is governed, and vice versa."

Based on its review of relevant cases, the subcommittee report reiterates the imperative of making the case for academic freedom at both public and private institutions, not as a matter of law, but as a principle vital to the effective functioning of institutions of higher learning. While supporting efforts to shape the law through amicus curiae briefs, the report focuses on how the academic community can best preserve and protect academic freedom in light of the threat posed by the post-*Garcetti* legal context. The report urges faculty groups to minimize the dangers of recent court rulings and avert their recurrence, including through efforts to make administrators and governing boards aware of the risks to institutional health and to higher education generally if they use the *Hong-Renken-Gorum* doctrine to curtail intramural faculty speech.

The subcommittee also calls upon AAUP chapters and faculty senates at both public and private colleges and universities to develop policy statements at the institutional level that will explicitly incorporate protections for faculty speech on institutional academic matters and governance, such as the amendments recently adopted by the Board of Regents of the University of Minnesota. At the moment, most institutions have policy statements that recognize academic freedom as it pertains to teaching, research, and publication, but typically, such statements do not refer to speech relating to governance. The report concludes by providing the Minnesota language and two other draft policy statements as examples of language that might be incorporated into faculty handbooks or other institutional regulations to clarify that academic freedom protects faculty speech about institutional academic matters and governance as well as teaching, research, and extramural statements:

1. Academic Freedom and Academic Responsibility sections of the Academic Freedom and Responsibility policy of the University of Minnesota, as amended by the board of regents on June 12, 2009:

   Academic freedom is the freedom to discuss all relevant matters in the classroom, to explore all avenues of scholarship, research, and creative expression, and to speak or write without institutional discipline or restraint on matters of public concern as well as on matters related to professional duties and the functioning of the University. Academic responsibility implies the faithful performance of professional duties and obligations, the recognition of the demands of the scholarly enterprise, and the candor to make it clear that when one is speaking on matters of public interest, one is not speaking for the institution.

2. Subcommittee proposal option 1:

   Academic freedom is the freedom to teach, both in and outside the classroom, to conduct research and to publish the results of those investigations, and to address any matter of institutional policy or action whether or not as a member of an agency of institutional governance. Professors should also have the freedom to address the larger community with regard to any matter of social, political, economic, or other interest, without institutional discipline or restraint, save in response to fundamental violations of professional ethics or statements that suggest disciplinary incompetence.

3. Subcommittee proposal option 2:

   Academic freedom is the freedom to teach, both in and outside the classroom, to research and to publish the results of those investigations, and to address any matter of institutional policy or action whether or not as a member of an agency of institutional governance. Professors should also have the freedom to speak to any matter of social, political, economic, or other interest to the larger community, subject to the academic standard of conduct applicable to each.

Notes

Editor's Note (2014): Courts continue to weigh the question of whether the *Garcetti* decision applies to speech related to scholarship and teaching in public colleges and universities, with no definitive holding to date from the US Supreme Court. For example, in *Demers v. Austin*, 746 F.3d 402 (9th Cir. 2014), a Ninth Circuit panel, quoting *Grutter v. Bollinger*, 539 US 306, 329 (2003), held that the *Garcetti* holding did not apply to "speech related to scholarship or teaching" on the grounds that the Supreme Court has "long recognized that, given the important purpose of public education and the expansive freedoms of speech and thought associated with the university environment, universities occupy a special niche in our constitutional tradition." The Fourth Circuit applied similar reasoning in rejecting the application of *Garcetti* to academic speech in a university setting. See *Adams v. Trs. of the Univ. of N.C.-Wilmington*, 640 F.3d 550, 562 (4th Cir. 2011) ("We are . . . persuaded that *Garcetti* would not apply in the academic context of a public university as represented by the facts of this case."). Other courts have applied *Garcetti* in cases involving academic speech in a university setting. See, e.g., *Savage v. Gee*, 665 F.3d 732 (6th Cir. 2012) (applied *Garcetti* in a case involving the Head of Reference and Library Instruction at Ohio State University); *Renken v. Gregory*, 541 F.3d 769 (7th Cir. 2008) (held that the administration of grants was part of a tenured professor's official duties and dismissed the First Amendment retaliation claim pursuant to *Garcetti*).

1. 547 US 410 (2006).
2. AAUP, *Policy Documents and Reports*, 11th ed. (Baltimore: Johns Hopkins University Press, 2015), 3–12.
3. Ibid., 123–25.
4. 385 US 589 (1967).
5. 391 US 563 (1968).
6. 516 F. Supp. 2d 1158 (C.D. Cal. 2007). This decision was affirmed by the Ninth Circuit in *Hong v. Grant*, 403 Fed. Appx. 236 (9th Cir. Cal. 2010). However, because the Ninth Circuit ruled that the defendants were immune from suit, the court did not take up the merits of Professor Hong's First Amendment claims. Instead, the court decided to "leave the question of whether faculty speech such as Hong's is protected under the First Amendment for consideration

in another case." In 2011 the Ninth Circuit held that the *Garcetti* analysis did not apply to academic speech. See *Demers* discussed in the Editor's Note supra.

7. 541 F.3d 769 (7th Cir. 2008).
8. 561 F.3d 179 (3d Cir. 2009).

9. As previously noted, the *Hong* decision was affirmed on appeal on alternate grounds, but the underlying holding of the District Court was subsequently repudiated by the Ninth Circuit's decision in *Demers*. See discussion in note 6 and the Editor's Note.

Faculty Participation in the Selection, Evaluation, and Retention of Administrators

The statement that follows, a revision and expansion of the 1974 statement on *Faculty Participation in the Selection and Retention of Administrators*, was prepared by the Association's Committee on College and University Governance. It was adopted by the Association's Council in June 1981 and endorsed by the Sixty-Seventh Annual Meeting.

The Association's *Statement on Government of Colleges and Universities* rests largely upon the conviction that interdependence, communication, and joint action among the constituents of a college or university enhance the institution's ability to solve educational problems. As one facet of this interdependence, the Statement on Government asserts the expectation that faculty members will have a significant role in the selection of academic administrators, including the president, academic deans, department heads, and chairs. As a corollary, it is equally important that faculty members contribute significantly to judgments and decisions regarding the retention or nonretention of the administrators whom they have helped select.

The Selection of Administrators

The *Statement on Government* emphasizes the primary role of faculty and board in the search for a president. The search may be initiated either by separate committees of the faculty and board or by a joint committee of the faculty and board or of faculty, board, students, and others, and separate committees may subsequently be joined. In a joint committee, the numbers from each constituency should reflect both the primacy of faculty concern and the range of other groups, including students, that have a legitimate claim to some involvement. Each major group should elect its own members to serve on the committee, and the rules governing the search should be arrived at jointly. A joint committee should determine the size of the majority that will be controlling in making an appointment. When separate committees are used, the board, with which the legal power of appointment rests, should either select a name from among those submitted by the faculty committee or should agree that no person will be chosen over the objections of the faculty committee.

The role of the faculty in the selection of an administrator other than a president should reflect the extent of legitimate faculty interest in the position. In the case of an academic administrator whose function is mainly advisory to a president or whose responsibilities do not include academic policy, the faculty's role in the search should be appropriate to its involvement with the office. Other academic administrators, such as the dean of a college or a person of equivalent responsibility, are by the nature of their duties more directly dependent upon faculty support. In such instances, the composition of the search committee should reflect the primacy of faculty interest, and the faculty component of the committee should be chosen by the faculty of the unit or by a representative body of the faculty. The person chosen for an administrative position should be selected from among the names submitted by the search committee. The president, after fully weighing the views of the committee, will make the final choice. Nonetheless, sound academic practice dictates that the president not choose a person over the reasoned opposition of the faculty.

The Evaluation of Administrators

Institutions should develop procedures for periodic review of the performance of presidents and other academic administrators. The purpose of such periodic reviews should be the improvement of the performance of the administrator during his or her term of office. This review should be conducted on behalf of the governing board for the president, or on behalf of the appointing administrator for other academic administrators. Fellow administrators, faculty, students, and others should participate in the review according to their legitimate interest in the result, with faculty of the unit accorded the primary voice in the case of academic administrators. The governing board or appointing administrator should publish a summary of the review, including a statement of actions taken as a result of the review.

The Retention of Administrators

A more intensive review, conducted near the end of a stated term of administrative service, may be an appropriate component of the decision to retain or not to retain an administrator. When used for such a purpose, the review should include such procedural steps as formation of an ad hoc review committee, with different constituencies represented according to their legitimate interest in the result; consideration of such added data as the administrator's self-assessment and interviews with appropriate administrators and faculty and students; and submission of a report and recommendations, after the subject administrator has had an opportunity to comment on the text, to the board or appointing administrator. The board or appointing administrator should accept the recommendations of the review committee, except in extraordinary circumstances and for reasons communicated to the committee with an opportunity for response by the concerned parties prior to a final decision. The report should be made public, except for such sections as the board or appointing administrator and the review committee agree to be confidential, together with an account of actions taken as a result of the review.

All decisions on retention and nonretention of administrators should be based on institutionalized and jointly determined procedures which include significant faculty involvement. With respect to the chief administrative officer, the *Statement on Government* specifies that the "leadership role" of the president "is supported by delegated authority from the board and faculty." No decision on retention or nonretention should be made without an assessment of the level of confidence in which he or she is held by the faculty. With respect to other academic administrators, sound practice dictates that the president should neither retain an administrator found wanting by faculty standards nor arbitrarily dismiss an administrator who meets the accountability standards of the academic community. In no case should a judgment on retention or nonretention be made without consultation with all major constituencies, with the faculty involved to a degree at least co-extensive with its role in the original selection process.

The president and other academic administrators should in any event be protected from arbitrary removal by procedures through which both their rights and the interests of various constituencies are adequately safeguarded.

The Role of the Faculty in the Accrediting of Colleges and Universities

The statement that follows was approved by the Association's Committee on Accrediting of Colleges and Universities, adopted by the Association's Council in April 1968, and endorsed by the Fifty-Fourth Annual Meeting.

Institutional evaluation is a joint enterprise between institutions of higher education and the accrediting commissions of regional associations. For their most effective work the accrediting commissions require the cooperative effort of qualified faculty members and administrators, who should be encouraged by their colleges and universities to participate in the work of the commissions. Within a college or university, the nature of the accrediting process requires common enterprise among the faculty, the administration, and to some extent the governing board. The appraisal of the academic program should be largely the responsibility of faculty members. They should play a major role in the evaluation of the curriculum, the library, teaching loads and conditions, research, professional activities, laboratories and other academic facilities, and faculty welfare and compensation, all in relation to the institution's objectives and in the light of its financial resources. To higher education generally, faculty members may exercise a special responsibility as the segment of the educational community that is in the best position to recognize and appraise circumstances affecting academic freedom, faculty tenure, the faculty role in institutional government, and faculty status and morale. This statement presents standards for the expression of faculty interest and responsibility in the accreditation process.

Recommended Standards for Institutions of Higher Education

1. Primary responsibility for the preparation of the academic aspects of the self-evaluation should rest with a committee composed largely of faculty members and responsible to the faculty as a whole. Additions or deletions should be made only after consultation with the authors of the sections of the report that are affected.
2. The self-evaluation should include a description of

   a. conditions of academic freedom and tenure (including provisions for academic due process);
   b. conditions of faculty participation in institutional government (including provisions for the orderly handling of grievances and disputes); and
   c. faculty status and morale (including working conditions and total compensation). Significant differences of opinion in these and other areas should be reflected in the self-evaluation.
3. The completed self-evaluation should be made available to the entire faculty prior to its submission to the accrediting commission and should be subject to amendment in the light of faculty suggestions.
4. Representatives of the faculty, including members of appropriate faculty committees, should be available to meet with the visiting committee to discuss questions of faculty concern.
5. The report of the visiting committee should be made available to the entire faculty.
6. The faculty should be fully informed of the accrediting commission's actions after an evaluation and should be kept abreast of all significant developments and issues arising between the accrediting commission and the institution. It should participate, as in the self-evaluation, in any subsequent activities regarding the institution's accreditation.

Recommended Standards for the Regional Accrediting Commissions

1. Regular visiting committees should include full-time teaching or research faculty members.
2. A formally adopted institutional policy on academic freedom and tenure, consistent with the major provisions of the 1940 *Statement of Principles on Academic Freedom and Tenure,* should be a condition for accreditation.

3. Reports by regular visiting committees should take explicit account of
   a. conditions of academic freedom and tenure (including provisions for academic due process);
   b. conditions of faculty participation in institutional government (including provisions for the orderly handling of grievances and disputes); and
   c. faculty status and morale (including working conditions and total compensation).

   The reports should describe any significant shortcomings in these areas.

4. When significant shortcomings have been found in the areas listed above, the commissions should deal with these as with similar shortcomings in other areas, endeavoring to secure improvement and applying appropriate sanctions in the absence of improvement within a reasonable time.

5. A gross violation of academic freedom, tenure, or due process should, unless promptly corrected, lead to action looking toward withdrawal of accreditation.

The Faculty Role in the Reform of Intercollegiate Athletics: Principles and Recommended Practices

This report was approved for publication by the Association's Committee on Teaching, Research, and Publication in October 2002.

Introduction

Athletics first appeared on American college campuses as an intramural activity, a much-needed recreational complement to academic life. During the past century this form of athletics, usually organized by students and overseen by faculty, was gradually transformed on many campuses into a highly commercial, increasingly professional enterprise whose control, audience, and venues became ever more divorced from campus life. The subsequent record of excesses, exploitation, and abuses in intercollegiate athletics proved impervious to repeated efforts at substantive reform.

A decade ago, concerned about these abuses and their increasingly corrosive impact on the core academic mission of American institutions of higher education, the AAUP published two reports on the subject: *The Role of the Faculty in the Governance of College Athletics: A Report of the Special Committee on Athletics* and the *Statement on Intercollegiate Athletics*.[1] Both reports described the major problems in intercollegiate sports that were judged to require substantive reform and offered recommendations to improve the educational experiences of college athletes. The reports argued that Association-supported standards of governance in colleges and universities, and the need to protect and preserve traditional educational values and academic standards, demanded more active faculty engagement with and oversight of intercollegiate athletics programs than had previously been the case. The reports went on to call for reforms in admissions and financial aid practices, closer faculty monitoring of college athletes' educational experiences and academic progress, and better management of the financial operations of the athletics program.

In the decade that has passed since those reports were written, a large and growing body of literature has continued to detail the baleful influence of intercollegiate athletics on higher education.[2] Many of the same academic and financial improprieties—and lack of accountability—that occasioned the earlier AAUP reports are still present, some in more extreme forms. The Association has been especially concerned about the continuing preferential treatment of athletes with regard to admissions and scholarship aid, disappointing graduation records for athletes, and ethical breaches of academic standards by coaches, students, administrators, and faculty. The problems associated with intercollegiate athletics have involved not only the quality of education offered to athletes but also the effects of bad practices on the academic wellbeing of the student body at large. They have also included exploitation and abuses of students by coaches, practice and contest schedules incompatible with commitments to academic priorities, improper intervention in academic matters by athletics administrators and staff, undue reliance on sports programs for institutional status, subordination of the academic progress of college athletes to the demands of athletics, and outside interference by overzealous alumni and boosters in college and university governance. For many years such issues were thought to be problems only at major institutions with big-time sports programs—in particular, institutions with Division IA football and basketball teams. Recently, however, as some smaller institutions have coveted the potential revenues and public notice associated with high-profile sports programs, the temptation for these institutions to promote athletics has been intense and at times irresistible. The problems noted above exist, to a greater or lesser extent, at most institutions that engage in competitive intercollegiate athletics.

Across the spectrum of higher education, budgetary allocations made to intercollegiate sports have continued to rise exponentially, often at the expense of academic programs. Moreover, the allocation of spending within athletics programs may unfairly disadvantage some college athletes, with programs for women and non-revenue-producing sports in general suffering. The escalating commercialization of intercollegiate athletics and the lack of transparency in policies and their implementation have contributed to the erosion of the role of the athlete as a student.

The abuses and scandals in intercollegiate athletics programs that continue to beset the academic community have prompted the Association to examine this subject again and to offer this report. Though addressed primarily to the faculty, the report seeks to provide guidance to all campus constituents on the principles that should inform sound institutional policy governing intercollegiate athletics. The report also recommends practices that can strengthen the particular role of the faculty in institutional governance, provide an agenda for faculty action, and significantly improve the educational climate not only for the college athletes most immediately affected but also for the entire academic community. Some of the recommendations involve the development of greater consensus among the faculty as well as between the faculty and other campus constituents about the importance of ensuring that athletics programs are conducted with integrity and that students who are athletes receive a solid education and fair treatment. These proposals are offered to temper, if not entirely to cure, the excesses of intercollegiate athletics. Absent better practices, we believe, the stature of higher education is diminished and athletically gifted students are done a singular disservice.

Efforts at Reform

The best-known efforts at reform of intercollegiate athletics have been initiated by organizations beyond our college and university campuses. The most notable of these external groups is the Knight Foundation Commission on Intercollegiate Athletics. The commission, which includes leaders from higher education, business, and athletics, issued its first report on sports reform in 1991. That report, *Keeping the Faith with the Student-Athlete*, focused on the primary responsibility of college and university presidents to ensure the appropriate educational and ethical operation of their institutions' athletics programs. Although there have been isolated cases of presidentially led institutional reform, the general situation has, if anything, deteriorated rather than improved, prompting the Knight Commission to issue in 2001 a second report on athletics reform, *A Call to Action: Reconnecting College Sports and Higher Education*. It argues that academic values and

competitive athletics may be in irreconcilable conflict and concludes that "if it proves impossible to create a system of intercollegiate athletics that can live honorably within the American college and university, then responsible citizens must join with academic and public leaders to insist that the nation's colleges and universities get out of the business of big-time sports." Whereas the commission's 1991 report focused primarily on the role of the president in athletics reform, the 2001 report emphasizes the role of the institution's trustees: "Presidents cannot act on an issue as emotional and highly visible as athletics without the unwavering public support of their boards."[3]

Notably missing from these and most other reform efforts, at least until recently, has been the collective voice of the faculty. The situation has begun to change. The AAUP, in its earlier statements, urged faculty participation in the cause of reform. On most campuses, however, advocacy of significant change in college athletics has been mostly limited to individual faculty members; the faculty as a whole has been largely disengaged or indifferent.

We have been heartened by the actions that some faculty members have taken recently to raise their voices and assert their governance responsibilities as they relate to intercollegiate athletics. The Drake Group, a national alliance of more than one hundred faculty members from across the country, was established in 1999 with the stated aim of "closing the ever-widening gap between athletics and education" and "working to restore and defend academic integrity in college sports."[4] The alliance has issued a series of position statements and attracted considerable media attention to the cause of faculty-initiated reform. More recently, a number of faculty senates at institutions in the Pacific-10 Conference have adopted resolutions decrying the commercialization of college athletics and condemning the use of scarce resources to fund lavish sports facilities as well as the intensified competition for recruiting and retaining athletes. Similar efforts have also been undertaken by faculty governance leaders at universities in the Committee on Institutional Cooperation (CIC), a group comprising Big Ten Conference institutions and the University of Chicago, which in November 2001 endorsed a resolution on intercollegiate athletics that they agreed to propose to their respective faculty senates. The resolution calls on "the faculties of CIC institutions [to] join with colleagues in the Pac10 conference in urging the presidents, faculty athletics committees, and faculty conference representatives of Big-Ten conference schools and of other institutions engaged in intercollegiate athletics, to join in a concerted effort" to deal with the problems that have been identified. Several of the CIC campus senates responded positively to this call.

The increasing prominence of faculty senates as vehicles for faculty engagement in sports reform is a particularly promising development. As one commentator has observed, "The size and legitimacy of a senate offers a much stronger voice for faculty."[5]

Despite the serious problems we have identified, the AAUP, recognizing that intercollegiate sports can benefit both students and institutions, continues to believe that meaningful and constructive reform can and should be pursued. The Association appreciates that not all campuses will be prepared to endorse every one of the principles set forth in this report or to implement all of the recommended standards and procedures described below. We hope, however, that faculty members will evaluate their own campus practices and, where appropriate, work toward implementation of these recommendations.

Principles and Recommendations

Under generally accepted principles of academic government, the "faculty has primary responsibility for such fundamental areas as curriculum, subject matter and methods of instruction, . . . and those aspects of student life which relate to the educational process."[6] The faculty, it follows, is properly involved in all matters with significant educational implications and has an obligation to ensure academic primacy in an institution's athletics programs. It further follows that "the faculty has primary responsibility for those aspects of an athlete's experience that involve education. Thus, it is the faculty's duty to ensure that the athlete has a full opportunity to participate in the educational process, and that a proper balance is achieved between the athletic and educational experiences." Indeed, the preservation of integrity in the college athlete's academic life is directly dependent upon the faculty's ability to assert its primacy in "defining and monitoring the educational experiences of athletes," while reducing "the pressures in college sports that would subvert the athlete's educational effort." This goal "can be achieved only by removing all decision making that relates to academic matters from the commercial incentives that otherwise affect the daily functioning of the athletics department." In short, colleges and universities must make certain that college athletes remain students first, and that they have available, and are able to take full advantage of, the same

opportunities for intellectual development and personal growth as other students. Therefore, it should be the responsibility of the institution to have the decisions that affect their lives as students made by those who know them as students—the faculty.[7]

If principles are to have their desired effect, they must culminate in practice. We recognize that the internal functioning of an institution's athletics program is subject to a range of external rules and standards promulgated by athletics conferences and by regulatory bodies such as the National Collegiate Athletic Association (NCAA), the National Association of Intercollegiate Athletics, and the National Junior College Athletic Association. In some cases, however, these rules represent minimum standards, and we believe that it is the responsibility of members of the faculty to work to strengthen these standards, consistent with the mission of their particular institution. We focus on the overall faculty role in governance as it relates to intercollegiate athletics, with particular emphasis on the areas of admissions and financial aid, academic standards and support services, and finances.

Faculty Governance and Athletics

As noted above, generally accepted principles of shared (or collaborative) governance call for the faculty to play a substantial role in determining educational policy and in resolving educational problems within the academic institution. The nature and degree of the faculty's involvement will vary depending on the particular issues or area of concern. Given the seriousness of the concerns that have been raised about intercollegiate athletics programs, we believe that mechanisms should be established to enable the faculty to participate meaningfully in the formulation of an institution's overall athletics policy and that the faculty, through its senate (or a similar institution-wide, elected representative faculty body) ought to place the oversight of athletics programs squarely within its purview and be prepared to devote the time and energy necessary to accomplish what needs doing. We also believe, following the Association's 1989 report titled *The Role of the Faculty in the Governance of College Athletics*, that "the athletics department should not be allowed to function as a separate entity," and that "the goal of structural reform in the governance of college sports should be to integrate athletics more fully into the educational mission of the institution."[8] To this end, we urge consideration of the following recommendations.

The Association's *Statement on Intercollegiate Athletics* recommends that a committee elected by the faculty should monitor the compliance with policies relating to admission, the progress toward graduation, and the integrity of the course of study of students who engage in intercollegiate athletics. This committee should report annually to the faculty on admissions, on progress toward graduation, and on graduation rates of athletes by sport. Further, the committee should be charged with seeking appropriate review of cases in which it appears that faculty members or administrators have abused academic integrity in order to promote athletic programs.[9]

We agree, and we recommend that this duly constituted faculty body have a direct and formal relationship with the senate. We further recommend the following:

1. Reports presented to the senate should include financial information relating to the athletics program. The senate may need to appoint ad hoc faculty committees to examine data and determine whether or not the institution is realizing its goals and maintaining academic standards consonant with the institution's educational mission.
2. Reports should provide academic profiles of college athletes in comparison to the rest of the student body.
3. In addition to receiving regular informational reports on the institution's athletics program, the senate should make recommendations where appropriate, and legislate when possible, on athletics policies affecting academic standards. Legislative actions should be taken by the senate to ensure that academic standards for college athletes are comparable to those for the rest of the student body.
4. The faculty member designated to serve as the institution's representative to external agencies like the athletics conference or the NCAA should enjoy the general support of the faculty. Accordingly, the senate should have a significant advisory role in the presidential appointment of the individual who serves in that capacity.
5. The athletics representative should be kept fully informed about all aspects of the institution's athletics program. The representative should, in turn, provide regular reports to the administration and the senate on his or her activities.
6. The senate should adopt legislation prohibiting the faculty athletics representative and any other faculty members involved in oversight responsibilities for athletics from accepting special benefits, such as paid trips to games.[10]

7. The senate should have a direct and formal relationship with a committee charged with oversight responsibility for the institution's athletics program. This committee should be composed of a majority of faculty and academic administrators, and its chair should be a faculty member who is elected by the faculty senate. The committee should include the athletics director and other university administrators with applicable governance authority (for example, the director of admissions) and the faculty athletics representative as ex officio members.
8. The athletics director should serve as a resource for the senate and respond to inquiries from the faculty. He or she should prepare periodic reports on the operation of the athletics program.
9. The athletics department should be required to submit a report on compliance with Title IX to the faculty senate for review, comment, and possible approval on an annual basis.

Admissions and Financial Aid

"With regard to student admissions," according to a recently adopted footnote to the Association's *Statement on Government of Colleges and Universities*, "the faculty should have a meaningful role in establishing institutional policies, including the setting of standards for admission, and should be afforded opportunity for oversight of the entire admissions process." The faculty's central role in establishing policies on admissions as well as on financial aid entails faculty responsibility for ensuring adherence to these policies with regard to college athletes. To this end we make the following recommendations:

1. Faculty should exercise their principal responsibility for formulation of admissions requirements for educational programs, ensuring that the academic integrity of the admissions process is not compromised by pressure to produce winning teams.
2. Faculty should ensure that applicants for admission are treated fairly, and that those admitted have the preparation deemed necessary for academic success. In particular, admissions standards for athletes should be comparable to and consistent with those for other students.
3. Faculty should ensure that financial-aid standards for athletes are comparable to those for other students, and that the aid is administered by the institution's financial-aid office. In accordance with existing AAUP policy, faculty should also ensure that continuation of

need-based aid to students who drop out of athletic competition or complete their athletic eligibility will be conditioned only on their remaining academically and financially qualified.[11] Other financial aid to athletes should be continued so long as they are students in good academic standing and are meeting the obligations consistent with accepting the aid.

4. Faculty should ensure that athletes on financial aid receive adequate support to cover their living expenses as well as their educational expenses.

5. Faculty, working through the senate and with members of the athletics committee, should monitor compliance with policies relating to admissions, insisting on full disclosure of information necessary to discharge this function.

6. Faculty should work within their own institutions and assist in lobbying the NCAA to change regulations in order to ensure that scholarship recipients enjoy the same financial opportunities as other students.

Academic Standards and Support Services

Colleges and universities have an obligation to create appropriate opportunities and conditions for students—athletes and nonathletes alike—to pursue their educational goals. Primary responsibility for creating and maintaining those opportunities and conditions should rest with the faculty, which sets general academic policy, oversees the curriculum, teaches the courses, assesses student academic performance, and recommends the conferral of degrees. Athletics programs should carry out their activities in a manner that is respectful of the faculty's right to teach as well as the student's right to learn. Achievement of these aims, we believe, will require adherence to the recommendations that follow.

1. Consistent with principles of academic freedom, control over how courses are taught and how students are evaluated, including the assignment of grades, should rest exclusively with the faculty and not be delegated to noninstructional staff.[12]

2. Athletics programs should structure their activities so that participants have the same opportunities as other students to pursue a recognized degree program, as determined by the faculty, and to choose courses and schedules that are consistent with their making normal progress toward fulfilling degree requirements and completing those requirements within a reasonable period of time. The

faculty should guard against courses or degrees whose main purpose is to keep athletes academically eligible to participate in intercollegiate sports.

3. Athletics programs should schedule their activities so as to conform with the academic calendar and to minimize intrusions on the classroom and pressures on athletes' academic obligations. In particular, athletic events and team travel should be arranged to permit participants to meet the academic standards set by the faculty for all students in their courses, including attendance, completion of assignments, and evaluations. Athletics schedules should also respect campus-wide study and examination periods.

4. Policies governing class absences for athletes involved in intercollegiate sports should be approved by the faculty. The athletics program should be required to provide statistics on such absences to the faculty senate and its relevant committees through regular yearly reports to those bodies.

5. Faculty have a responsibility to ensure that athletes obtain appropriate advising and other assistance in meeting their academic obligations. Whatever the special needs of athletes, the support programs for tutoring and instruction in study skills available to them should be the same as those offered to nonathletes. Athletes should be accorded no favoritism or special treatment in the affordance of counseling or academic support services.

6. Faculty should ensure that any academic support unit that is charged with advising athletes should be established and overseen by the faculty and report to an academic officer.

Finances

Intercollegiate athletics, especially on campuses that have "high-profile" programs, with their ever-mounting costs of new facilities and coaches' salaries, requires a major allocation of financial resources. Examples of skewed or misplaced fiscal priorities abound. The faculty is properly concerned about decisions respecting the allocation of institutional resources in the context of more general institutional needs and goals, and it has a vital role to play in assessing the budgetary implications of decisions concerning the overall size and scope of the athletics program. Institutions of higher education, with their sundry programs and auxiliary enterprises, have as their principal mission the discovery, transmission, and preservation of knowledge in the service of the larger society. In furtherance of their mission, most colleges and universities are supported by public funds, whether through grants, tax exemptions, or direct government appropriations, and they are expected, in turn, to exercise proper stewardship of this public trust. Faculty members have an important role to play in advising administrators and trustees on the integrity of athletics programs, thereby helping to ensure the public's trust and its continuing support. The faculty is but one voice in the budgetary process, but that voice is a vital one. Colleges and universities must handle accounting matters in a manner that does not raise questions about the institution's fundamental mission and purpose. Therefore, members of the faculty must acquire the information they need to monitor the educational and financial aspects of their institution's athletics programs.

Meaningful accountability in the financing of college athletics requires full disclosure of financial information and openness of debate. Since a great deal of money is involved—either on the credit or the debit side of college and university budgets—the issues of finance are critical. Resources invested in athletics enterprises should be justified by the general purposes of the educational institution and not by measures of (potential or actual) financial return or profit. In carrying out their legitimate functions, institutions have a fiduciary responsibility to ensure that resources are used judiciously and appropriately in the public trust and in compliance with legal and ethical obligations of nondiscrimination. Transparency in reporting revenues and expenditures, including the compensation of coaches and athletics directors, is essential. The athletics program should therefore be required to submit its annual budget to the faculty senate for review and comment.

The need for sound handling of financial matters related to sports leads us to urge consideration of the following recommended standards and procedures:

1. Athletics programs and enterprises within the athletics department should be fully integrated into the control and governance structures of the institution, and those responsible for these areas should be held accountable for their budgetary actions in accordance with the institution's educational mission.
2. Cost-cutting measures should be considered along with revenue-enhancing strategies in balancing the athletics budget line in a manner consonant with the institution's educational priorities. Athletics personnel and programs should not be exempt from institutional

retrenchment plans. The assets and operational costs of the athletics program should be included in determining whether a state of financial exigency exists in an institution and in implementing the remedies necessary to alleviate such a fiscal emergency. Consistent with Association-supported standards, which require meaningful faculty involvement in decisions relating to retrenchment, recommendations made by the faculty should incorporate revenues and expenditures of the athletics program.[13]
3. Commercial activities sponsored by the athletics program must be consistent with the institution's educational mission.
4. The choice of athletes' uniforms, shoes, or other equipment should not be based on any financial arrangements or contracts between vendors and the institution, the athletics department, or individual coaches. College athletes should not be employed for purposes of commercial advertisement or marketing.
5. Institutions should refuse to sign contracts with apparel or equipment manufacturers, or allow coaches or other members of the athletics program to sign contracts, that contain "nondisparagement" clauses. Such clauses, which typically prohibit college or university personnel from making any critical remarks about the company, its policies, or its products, are inconsistent with principles of academic freedom.[14]
6. The athletics program should follow accepted accounting and auditing procedures implemented by the institution that accurately record internal and external sources of income (including general-fund appropriations), reflect operational and deferred expenses, and identify indebtedness.
7. The athletics program should bear the same share of indirect costs as other programs and departments, and these costs should be recorded in its budget.
8. Gifts for the purpose of endowing positions on athletics teams or staff positions in the athletics program should be received and managed through the institution's central financial office and disbursed with the purpose of supporting the academic progress of students and the educational mission of the institution.
9. Athletics program personnel, including coaches, should not use campus facilities for personal gain, and they should eschew endorsements and other personal contracts with third parties that would compromise or conflict with their responsibilities to college

athletes or the institution. Athletics personnel who seek outside employment while they are under contract with the institution should be governed by the same provisions that apply to the institution's academic and support staff. The terms of any internal or external contracts should be fully disclosed.

10. Financial arrangements with booster clubs should be open to scrutiny by the campus community.

11. Allocation of financial resources among men's and women's athletics programs should reflect: (a) the recognized educational benefits of these programs common to each gender; and (b) the intent of federal legislation addressing gender equity. In particular, reduction of the size of men's teams in revenue-producing sports should be considered as an alternative to the abolition of teams in nonrevenue-producing sports.

12. The faculty senate should review and comment on contracts between the athletics program and commercial enterprises when such contracts have a potential impact on the academic life or educational experiences of college athletes.

Conclusions

"Universities must be judged by their achievements as academic institutions, not as sports franchises," observed Indiana University president Myles Brand, president of the NCAA (2003–2009), in 2001. We need, he added, "to make certain that athletics programs enhance and support the larger academic mission of the university."[15]

Given the principles and the recommended practices set forth above to implement change, what can be done to ensure that they are enacted and enforced? As the 2001 Knight Commission report states, "Change will come, sanity will be restored, only when the higher education community comes together to meet collectively the challenges its members face." As for the faculty's role in this process, on some campuses a fundamental reordering of the structures and practices of institutional governance may be needed before the faculty can begin to assume its appropriate responsibility for the oversight of the institution's athletics program. However, in those institutions with a strong tradition and practice of shared governance, campus-wide recognition of and dedication to these principles as part of institutional governance should make it much easier for the faculty, if it is willing to become engaged, to assume its appropriate role in athletics reform. We hasten to add that, as was observed in

The Role of the Faculty in the Governance of College Athletics, "It is doubtful that faculty efforts alone will be sufficient to refocus the priorities of major athletics programs. On the other hand, faculties are in a unique position to advocate adherence to meaningful academic standards."[16]

Enactment and enforcement of the requisite reforms to establish a proper balance between sports and education will require members of the faculty—working as much as possible with supportive, or at least sympathetic, administrators, trustees, and athletics program staff, including coaches—to invest time and energy in this project. We urge the adoption by faculty senates of resolutions embodying the principles set forth here, and we call upon administrations to work with the faculty to implement policies consistent with the practices recommended in this report. We also encourage individual faculty members to continue to speak out with independence and candor about the issues we have addressed. At the same time, we want to emphasize the need for institutions to ensure that faculty members who do bring public attention to these matters and who actively work for reform are afforded protections against retaliation for exercising their academic freedom.

As with the efforts undertaken by the Drake Group and by a number of faculty senates at Pac-10 and Big Ten universities, faculty members at one institution may find it useful to form coalitions with members of senates at other institutions and with other external groups who share the same principles and goals in order to promote these recommended practices and assist in advancing the reform of intercollegiate athletics programs. But ultimately faculty must take responsibility at their own institutions for the proper functioning of athletics programs and the appropriate treatment of college athletes as students.

Notes

1. "The Role of the Faculty in the Governance of College Athletics," *Academe* 76 (January–February 1990): 43–47; "Statement on Intercollegiate Athletics," AAUP, *Policy Documents and Reports,* 11th ed. (Baltimore: Johns Hopkins University Press, 2015), 389–90.

2. Among the most important recent books on the subject, see James L. Duderstadt, *Intercollegiate Athletics and the American University: A University President's Perspective* (Ann Arbor: University of Michigan Press, 2000); Allen L. Sack, Ellen J. Staurowsky, and Kent Waldrep, *College Athletes for Hire: The Evolution and Legacy of the NCAA's Amateur Myth* (New York: Praeger, 1998); James L. Shulman and

William G. Bowen, *The Game of Life: College Sports and Educational Values* (Princeton, NJ: Princeton University Press, 2001); Murray Sperber, *Beer and Circus: How Big-Time College Sports Is Crippling Undergraduate Education* (New York: Holt, 2000); Rick Telander, Richard Warch, and Murray Sperber, *The Hundred Yard Lie: The Corruption of College Football and What We Can Do to Stop It* (Champaign: University of Illinois Press, 1996); and John R. Thelin, *Games Colleges Play: Scandal and Reform in Intercollegiate Athletics* (Baltimore: Johns Hopkins University Press, 1994).

3. In its 2001 report, in a section titled "The Need to Act Together," the Knight Commission notes that "Faculty, too, have a critical role to play. Above all, they must defend the academic value of their institutions." John S. and James L. Knight Foundation, "A Call to Action," 25 (http://www.knightcommission.org/images /pdfs/2001_knight_report.pdf). See also the Knight Commission's 2010 report, "Restoring the Balance: Dollars, Values, and the Future of College Sports" at http://www.knightcommission.org/restoringthebalance.

4. http://thedrakegroup.org/.

5. John R. Gerdy, "Athletic Victories, Educational Defeats," *Academe* 88, no. 1 (January–February 2002): 35.

6. "Statement on Government of Colleges and Universities," *Policy Documents and Reports*, 120.

7. The quoted passages are from "The Role of the Faculty in the Governance of College Athletics," 45.

8. Ibid., 44.

9. "Statement on Intercollegiate Athletics," 389.

10. The section headed "Conflicts of Interest," ibid., 390, provides that "paid-for trips to games, and other special benefits for faculty, administrators, or members of governing boards involved in the oversight of athletics, whether offered by the university or by outside groups, create conflicts of interest and should be eliminated."

11. Ibid, 389.

12. See "The Assignment of Course Grades and Student Appeals," *Policy Documents and Reports*, 29–30.

13. See Regulation 4c of the "Recommended Institutional Regulations on Academic Freedom and Tenure," ibid., 79–90, and "On Institutional Problems Resulting from Financial Exigency: Some Operating Guidelines," ibid., 309–10.

14. See, for example, W. Lee Hansen, ed., *Academic Freedom on Trial: 100 Years of Sifting and Winnowing at the University of Wisconsin Madison* (Madison: University of Wisconsin Press, 1998), 11.

15. "Presidents Have Cause, Means to Reduce Arms," *NCAA News*, February 12, 2001.

16. "The Role of the Faculty in the Governance of College Athletics," 44.

Professional Ethics

From its earliest years, the Association has recognized that the privileges associated with faculty status create a corresponding obligation to observe suitable professional and ethical standards. In his introductory address to the first meeting of the Association in 1915, President John Dewey proclaimed that one of the Association's priorities would be the development of "professional standards . . . which will be quite as scrupulous regarding the obligations imposed by freedom as jealous of the freedom itself." A Committee on University Ethics was one of the AAUP's original standing committees, and Professor Dewey served as its first chair.

The 1940 *Statement of Principles on Academic Freedom and Tenure* declares that academic freedom "carries with it duties correlative with rights." These duties are described in the documents that follow, beginning with the Association's basic *Statement on Professional Ethics*. Other statements provide guidance on particular ethical situations.

The Association maintains a standing Committee on Professional Ethics. The Association views questions involving propriety of conduct as best handled within the framework of individual institutions by reference to an appropriate faculty body. While the Association's good offices are available for advice and mediation, its function in the area of ethics is primarily educative: to inform members of the higher education community about principles of professional ethics and to encourage their observance.

Statement on Professional Ethics

The statement that follows was originally adopted by the Association's Council in April 1966 and endorsed by the Fifty-Second Annual Meeting as Association policy. Revisions were made and approved by the Association's Council in 1987 and 2009.

Introduction

From its inception, the American Association of University Professors has recognized that membership in the academic profession carries with it special responsibilities. The Association has consistently affirmed these responsibilities in major policy statements, providing guidance to professors in such matters as their utterances as citizens, the exercise of their responsibilities to students and colleagues, and their conduct when resigning from an institution or when undertaking sponsored research. The *Statement on Professional Ethics* that follows sets forth those general standards that serve as a reminder of the variety of responsibilities assumed by all members of the profession.

In the enforcement of ethical standards, the academic profession differs from those of law and medicine, whose associations act to ensure the integrity of members engaged in private practice. In the academic profession the individual institution of higher learning provides this assurance and so should normally handle questions concerning propriety of conduct within its own framework by reference to a faculty group. The Association supports such local action and stands ready, through the general secretary and the Committee on Professional Ethics, to counsel with members of the academic community concerning questions of professional ethics and to inquire into complaints when local consideration is impossible or inappropriate. If the alleged offense is deemed sufficiently serious to raise the possibility of adverse action, the procedures should be in accordance with the 1940 *Statement of Principles on Academic Freedom and Tenure,* the *Statement on Procedural Standards in Faculty Dismissal Proceedings,*[1] or the applicable provisions of the Association's *Recommended Institutional Regulations on Academic Freedom and Tenure.*[2]

The Statement

1. Professors, guided by a deep conviction of the worth and dignity of the advancement of knowledge, recognize the special responsibili-ties placed upon them. Their primary responsi-bility to their subject is to seek and to state the truth as they see it. To this end professors devote their energies to developing and improving their scholarly competence. They accept the obligation to exercise critical self-discipline and judgment in using, extend-ing, and transmitting knowledge. They practice intellectual honesty. Although professors may follow subsidiary interests, these interests must never seriously hamper or compromise their freedom of inquiry.

2. As teachers, professors encourage the free pursuit of learning in their students. They hold before them the best scholarly and ethical standards of their discipline. Professors demonstrate respect for students as individuals and adhere to their proper roles as intellectual guides and counselors. Professors make every reasonable effort to foster honest academic conduct and to ensure that their evaluations of students reflect each student's true merit. They respect the confidential nature of the relation-ship between professor and student. They avoid any exploitation, harassment, or discrimina-tory treatment of students. They acknowledge significant academic or scholarly assistance from them. They protect their academic freedom.

3. As colleagues, professors have obligations that derive from common membership in the community of scholars. Professors do not discriminate against or harass colleagues. They respect and defend the free inquiry of associ-ates, even when it leads to findings and conclusions that differ from their own. Professors acknowledge academic debt and strive to be objective in their professional judgment of colleagues. Professors accept their share of faculty responsibilities for the governance of their institution.

4. As members of an academic institution, professors seek above all to be effective teachers and scholars. Although professors observe the stated regulations of the institu-tion, provided the regulations do not contra-

vene academic freedom, they maintain their right to criticize and seek revision. Professors give due regard to their paramount responsibilities within their institution in determining the amount and character of work done outside it. When considering the interruption or termination of their service, professors recognize the effect of their decision upon the program of the institution and give due notice of their intentions.

5. As members of their community, professors have the rights and obligations of other citizens. Professors measure the urgency of these obligations in the light of their responsibilities to their subject, to their students, to their profession, and to their institution. When they speak or act as private persons, they avoid creating the impression of speaking or acting for their college or university. As citizens engaged in a profession that depends upon freedom for its health and integrity, professors have a particular obligation to promote conditions of free inquiry and to further public understanding of academic freedom.

Notes

1. AAUP, *Policy Documents and Reports*, 11th ed. (Baltimore: Johns Hopkins University Press, 2015), 91–93.

2. Ibid., 79–90.

Statement on Plagiarism

The statement that follows was approved for publication by the Association's Committee on Professional Ethics, adopted by the Association's Council in June 1990, and endorsed by the Seventy-Sixth Annual Meeting.

The main practical activity of the American Association of University Professors, since its founding, has concerned restraints upon the right of faculty members to inquire, to teach, to speak, and to publish professionally. Yet throughout its existence, the Association has emphasized the responsibilities of faculty members no less than their rights. Both rights and responsibilities support the common good served by institutions of higher education which, in the words of the 1940 *Statement of Principles on Academic Freedom and Tenure*, "depends upon the free search for truth and its free exposition."[1]

In its *Statement on Professional Ethics*, the Association has stressed the obligation of professors to their subject and to the truth as they see it, as well as the need for them to "exercise critical self-discipline and judgment in using, extending, and transmitting knowledge."[2] Defending free inquiry by their associates and respecting the opinions of others, in the exchange of criticism and ideas, professors must also be rigorously honest in acknowledging their academic debts. In the light of recent concerns within and outside of the academic profession, it has seemed salutary to restate these general obligations with respect to the offense of plagiarism.

Definition

The offense of plagiarism may seem less self-evident in some circles now than it did formerly. Politicians, business executives, and even university presidents depend on the ideas and literary skills of committees, aides, and speech-writers in the many communications they are called on to make inside and outside their organizations. When ideas are rapidly popularized and spread abroad through the media, when fashion and the quest for publicity are all around us, a concern with protecting the claims of originality may seem to some a quaint survival from the past or even a perverse effort to deter the spread of knowledge.

Nevertheless, within the academic world, where advancing knowledge remains the highest calling, scholars must give full and fair recognition to the contributors to that enterprise, both for the substance and for the formulation of their findings and interpretations. Even within the academic community, however, there are complexities and shades of difference. A writer of textbooks rests on the labors of hundreds of authors of monographs who cannot all be acknowledged; the derivative nature of such work is understood and even, when it is well and skillfully done, applauded. A poet, composer, or painter may "quote" the creation of another artist, deliberately without explanation, as a means of deeper exploration of meaning and in the expectation that knowledgeable readers, listeners, or viewers will appreciate the allusion and delight in it. There are even lapses—regrettable but not always avoidable—in which a long buried memory of something read surfaces as a seemingly new thought.

But none of these situations diminishes the central certainty: taking over the ideas, methods, or written words of another, without acknowledgment and with the intention that they be credited as the work of the deceiver, is plagiarism. It is theft of a special kind, for the true author still retains the original ideas and words, yet they are diminished as that author's property and a fraud is committed upon the audience that believes those ideas and words originated with the deceiver. Plagiarism is not limited to the academic community but has perhaps its most pernicious effect in that setting. It is the antithesis of the honest labor that characterizes true scholarship and without which mutual trust and respect among scholars is impossible.

Precepts

Every professor should be guided by the following:

1. In his or her own work the professor must scrupulously acknowledge every intellectual debt—for ideas, methods, and expressions—by means appropriate to the form of communication.

2. Any discovery of suspected plagiarism should be brought at once to the attention of the affected parties and, as appropriate, to the profession at large through proper and effective channels—typically through reviews in or communications to relevant scholarly journals. The Association's Committee on Professional Ethics stands ready to provide its good offices in resolving questions of plagiarism, either independently or in collaboration with other professional societies.

3. Professors should work to ensure that their universities and professional societies adopt clear guidelines respecting plagiarism, appropriate to the disciplines involved, and should insist that regular procedures be in place to deal with violations of those guidelines. The gravity of a charge of plagiarism, by whomever it is made, must not diminish the diligence exercised in determining whether the accusation is valid. In all cases the most scrupulous procedural fairness must be observed, and penalties must be appropriate to the degree of offense.[3]

4. Scholars must make clear the respective contributions of colleagues on a collaborative project, and professors who have the guidance of students as their responsibility must exercise the greatest care not to appropriate a student's ideas, research, or presentation to the professor's benefit; to do so is to abuse power and trust.

5. In dealing with graduate students, professors must demonstrate by precept and example the necessity of rigorous honesty in the use of sources and of utter respect for the work of others. The same expectations apply to the guidance of undergraduate students, with a special obligation to acquaint students new to the world of higher education with its standards and the means of ensuring intellectual honesty.

Conclusion

Any intellectual enterprise—by an individual, a group of collaborators, or a profession—is a mosaic, the pieces of which are put in place by many hands. Viewed from a distance, it should appear a meaningful whole, but the long process of its assemblage must not be discounted or misrepresented. Anyone who is guilty of plagiarism not only harms those most directly affected but also diminishes the authority and credibility of all scholarship and all creative arts, and therefore ultimately harms the interests of the broader society. The danger of plagiarism for teaching, learning, and scholarship is manifest, the need vigorously to maintain standards of professional integrity compelling.

Notes

1. AAUP, *Policy Documents and Reports*, 11th ed. (Baltimore: Johns Hopkins University Press, 2015), 14.

2. Ibid., 145.

3. On the question of due process for a faculty member who is the subject of disciplinary action because of alleged plagiarism, see Regulations 5 and 7 of the Association's "Recommended Institutional Regulations on Academic Freedom and Tenure," ibid., 79–90.

Consensual Relations between Faculty and Students

The statement that follows was approved by the Association's Committee on Women in the Academic Profession, adopted by the Association's Council in June 1995, and endorsed by the Eighty-First Annual Meeting.

Sexual relations between students and faculty members with whom they also have an academic or evaluative relationship are fraught with the potential for exploitation. The respect and trust accorded a professor by a student, as well as the power exercised by the professor in an academic or evaluative role, make voluntary consent by the student suspect. Even when both parties initially have consented, the development of a sexual relationship renders both the faculty member and the institution vulnerable to possible later allegations of sexual harassment in light of the significant power differential that exists between faculty members and students.

In their relationships with students, members of the faculty are expected to be aware of their professional responsibilities and to avoid apparent or actual conflict of interest, favoritism, or bias. When a sexual relationship exists, effective steps should be taken to ensure unbiased evaluation or supervision of the student.

Faculty Status

Throughout most of the first half of the twentieth century, security of tenure, where it existed at all, was tied to academic rank, most often to that of full professor. Reporting on a survey of some three hundred institutions in 1931, Committee A on Academic Freedom and Tenure noted that almost no faculty members at the rank of instructor were appointed with a presumption or with an explicit understanding of permanent tenure, while about 40 percent of assistant and associate professors and about 60 percent of full professors were. More assistant professors than associate professors were initially appointed with a fixed term. A separate survey found that instructors and assistant professors made up about half of the faculty in most institutions in 1940.[1] While faculty at a lower rank could be promoted to a higher rank and thus achieve a more permanent measure of tenure, crucially, there was no definite period after which a review for promotion, and thus tenure, would have to take place. Consequently, a large percentage of the professoriate was on quasi-contingent appointments throughout that period of time.

A significant innovation of the 1940 *Statement of Principles on Academic Freedom and Tenure* over previous statements of the Association was the establishment of a probationary period of fixed length "with appointment to the rank of full-time instructor or a higher rank."

Following the increasing adoption of the 1940 *Statement*, the Association responded to concerns over full-time appointments to ranks ineligible for tenure with the creation of a special committee, which reported in 1966. The committee asserted categorically that "anyone who does an instructor's work should be given appropriate rank and privileges." Consequently, the committee refused "to grant that, for purposes of the 1940 *Statement*, there is any such thing as a full-time teacher at a rank below that of instructor." It has been the continuing position of the Association that, with limited exceptions, "all full-time faculty appointments are of two kinds: (1) probationary appointments; (2) appointments with continuous tenure."

Nevertheless, the reliance on faculty members holding contingent appointments has been increasing. The Association has responded to this trend with a number of policy statements collected here, together with other statements related to faculty appointments.

Note
1. Paul C. Reinert, *Faculty Tenure in Colleges and Universities from 1900 to 1940* (St. Louis: Saint Louis University Press, 1946), 34.

Statement on Recruitment and Resignation of Faculty Members

The statement printed below was adopted by the Association of American Colleges (now the Association of American Colleges and Universities) in January 1961 with the following reservations as set forth in a preamble prepared by that association's Commission on Academic Freedom and Tenure:

1. No set of principles adopted by the Association can do more than suggest and recommend a course of action. Consequently, the present statement in no way interferes with institutional sovereignty.
2. The commission realizes that the diversity of practice and control that exists among institutions of higher learning precludes any set of standards from being universally applicable to every situation.
3. The statement is concerned only with minimum standards and in no way seeks to create a norm for institutions at which "better" practices already are in force.
4. The commission recognizes the fact that "emergency" situations will arise and will have to be dealt with. However, it urges both administration and faculty to do so in ways that will not go counter to the spirit of cooperation, good faith, and responsibility that the statement is seeking to promote.
5. The commission believes that the spirit embodied in the proposed statement is its most important aspect.

In view of these reservations, the Council of the American Association of University Professors in April 1961 voted approval of the statement without adopting it as a binding obligation. Endorsement of the statement in this form was voted by the Forty-Seventh Annual Meeting.

Mobility of faculty members among colleges and universities is rightly recognized as desirable in American higher education. Yet the departure of a faculty member always requires changes within the institution and may entail major adjustments on the part of faculty colleagues, the administration, and students in the faculty member's field. Ordinarily a temporary or permanent successor must be found and appointed to either the vacated position or the position of a colleague who is promoted to replace the faculty member. Clear standards of practice in the recruitment and in the resignations of members of existing faculties

should contribute to an orderly interchange of personnel that will be in the interest of all.

The standards set forth below are recommended to administrations and faculties, in the belief that they are sound and should be generally followed. They are predicated on the assumption that proper provision has been made by employing institutions for timely notice to probationary faculty members and those on term appointments, with respect to their subsequent status. In addition to observing applicable requirements for notice of termination to probationary faculty members, institutions should make provision for notice to all faculty members, not later than March 15 of each year, of their status the following fall, including rank and (unless unavoidable budgetary procedures beyond the institution forbid) prospective salary.

1. Negotiations looking to the possible appointment for the following fall of persons who are already faculty members at other institutions, in active service or on leave of absence and not on terminal appointment, should be begun and completed as early as possible in the academic year. It is desirable that, when feasible, the faculty member who has been approached with regard to another position inform the appropriate officers of his or her institution when such negotiations are in progress. The conclusion of a binding agreement for the faculty member to accept an appointment elsewhere should always be followed by prompt notice to the faculty member's current institution.

2. A faculty member should not resign, in order to accept other employment as of the end of the academic year, later than May 15 or thirty days after receiving notification of the terms of continued employment the following year, whichever date occurs later. It is recognized, however, that this obligation will be in effect only if institutions generally observe the time factor set forth in the following paragraph for new offers. It is also recognized that emergen-

cies will occur. In such an emergency the faculty member may ask the appropriate officials of the institution to waive this requirement; but the faculty member should conform to their decision.

3. To permit a faculty member to give due consideration and timely notice to his or her institution in the circumstances defined in paragraph one of these standards, an offer of appointment for the following fall at another institution should not be made after May 1. The offer should be a "firm" one, not subject to contingencies.

4. Institutions deprived of the services of faculty members too late in the academic year to permit their replacement by securing the members of other faculties in conformity to these standards, and institutions otherwise prevented from taking timely action to recruit from other faculties, should accept the necessity of making temporary arrangements or obtaining personnel from other sources, including new entrants to the academic profession and faculty personnel who have retired.

5. Except by agreement with their institution, faculty members should not leave or be solicited to leave their positions during an academic year for which they hold an appointment.

The Ethics of Recruitment and Faculty Appointments

In 1990, the Council of Colleges of Arts and Sciences (CCAS) established a Commission on Recruitment Ethics to consider the continuing experiences of colleges and universities in recruiting faculty members to their campuses. The commission prepared a draft statement for discussion at the CCAS's national meeting in 1991. Subsequently, the commission asked the American Association of University Professors to review the draft statement and to consider working with it in promulgating a joint statement. In February 1992, a joint committee representing the commission and the Association met in Washington. The commission's original draft statement was revised in light of comments by the members of the joint committee.

This statement was adopted by the CCAS in November 1992. The statement was approved for publication by the Association's Committee on Professional Ethics in December 1992 and adopted by the Association's Council in June 1993.

The standards set forth below are intended to apply to the recruitment and appointment of faculty members in colleges and universities. They are directed to administrators and faculty members in the belief that they will promote the identification and selection of qualified candidates through a process that promotes candor and effective communication among those who are engaged in recruitment. The standards are offered not as rules to serve every situation, but with the expectation that they will provide a foundation for appropriate practices. The spirit of openness and shared responsibility that these standards are intended to convey is also applicable to considerations of affirmative action in the recruitment of faculty.[1]

The Announcement of a Faculty Position

1. Prior to announcing a faculty vacancy, there should be agreement among all responsible parties on each major element of the position (e.g., rank, salary, and eligibility for tenure), how the position relates to the department's (or the equivalent unit's) likely needs for the future, the expectations concerning the professional work of the faculty member(s) being recruited, and the resources that will be provided to help the faculty member(s) meet those expectations.

2. An institution that announces a search should be genuinely engaged in an open process of recruitment for that position. Descriptions of vacant positions should be published and distributed as widely as possible to reach all potential candidates. The procedure established for reviewing applicants and for selecting final candidates should be consistent with the institution's announced criteria and commitment to a fair and open search.

3. All announcements for faculty positions should be clear concerning rank, the length of the appointment, whether the position is with tenure or carries eligibility for tenure, whether the availability of the position is contingent upon funding or other conditions, teaching and research expectations, and requisite experience and credentials. Criteria and procedures for reappointment, promotion, and tenure at the institution, as well as other relevant information, should be made available to all interested candidates upon request.

4. Interested candidates should have at least thirty days from the first appearance of the announcement to submit their applications.

Confidentiality, Interviews, and the Final Decision

1. Institutions should respect the confidentiality of candidates for faculty positions. The institution may contact references, including persons who are not identified by the candidate, but it should exercise discretion when doing so. An institution should not make

public the names of candidates without having given the candidates the opportunity to withdraw from the search.

2. Those who participate in the interview should avoid any discriminatory treatment of candidates. All communications with the candidates concerning the position should be consistent with the information stated in the announcement for the position.

3. Candidates for faculty positions should disclose in a timely fashion conditions that might materially bear upon the institution's decision to offer the appointment (for example, requirements for research funds, unusual moving costs, a delayed starting date, or the intention to retain an affiliation at the institution with which the candidate is currently associated).

4. If candidates request information about the progress of the search and the status of their candidacy, they should be given the information.

5. The institution's decision about which candidate will be offered the position should be consistent with the criteria for the position and its duties as stated in the announcement of the vacancy. If the selection of the final candidates will be based on significant changes in the criteria for the position or its duties as stated in the original announcement, the institution should start a new search.

The Offer and Acceptance

1. The institution may wish to provide informal notification to the successful candidate of its intention to offer an appointment, but the formal offer itself should be an unequivocal letter of appointment signed by the responsible institutional officer. "Oral offers" and "oral acceptances" should not be considered binding, but communications between the successful candidate and those representing the institution should be frank and accurate, for significant decisions are likely to be based on these exchanges. The written offer of appointment should be given to the candidate within ten days of the institution's having conveyed an intention to make the offer; a candidate should be informed promptly if the offer is not to be forthcoming within ten days.

2. The terms of an offer to an individual should be consistent with the announcement of the position. Each of the following should be stated clearly in the letter offering an appointment: (a) the initial rank; (b) the length of the appointment; (c) conditions of renewal; (d) the salary and benefits; (e) the duties of the

position; (f) as applicable, whether the appointment is with tenure, the amount of credit toward tenure for prior service, and the maximum length of the probationary period; (g) as applicable, the institution's "startup" commitments for the appointment (for example, equipment and laboratory space); (h) the date when the appointment begins and the date when the candidate is expected to report; (i) the date by which the candidate's response to the offer is expected, which should not be less than two weeks from receipt of the offer; and (j) details of institutional policies and regulations that bear upon the appointment. Specific information on other relevant matters also should be conveyed in writing to the prospective appointee.

3. An offer of appointment to a faculty member serving at another institution should be made no later than May 1, consistent with the faculty member's obligation to resign, in order to accept other employment, no later than May 15.[2] It is recognized that, in special cases, it might be appropriate to make an offer after May 1, but in such cases there should be an agreement by all concerned parties.

4. The acceptance of a position is a written, affirmative, and unconditional response sent by the candidate to the institution no later than the date stated in the offer of appointment. If the candidate wishes to accept the offer contingent upon conditions, those conditions should be specified and communicated promptly in writing to the institution which is offering the position.

5. If the candidate wishes to retain an affiliation with his or her current institution, that circumstance should be brought promptly to the attention of the current institution and the recruiting institution.

6. Individuals who accept an appointment should arrive at the institution in sufficient time to prepare for their duties and to participate in orientation programs.

Notes

1. For specific considerations of affirmative action in the recruitment of faculty, see the AAUP's "Affirmative-Action Plans: Recommended Procedures for Increasing the Number of Minority Persons and Women on College and University Faculties," AAUP, *Policy Documents and Reports*, 11th ed. (Baltimore: Johns Hopkins University Press, 2015), 157–63.

2. See the "Statement on Recruitment and Resignation of Faculty Members," issued jointly by the AAUP and the Association of American Colleges (now the Association of American Colleges and Universities), ibid., 153–54.

Affirmative-Action Plans: Recommended Procedures for Increasing the Number of Minority Persons and Women on College and University Faculties

The report that follows was approved by the Association's Committee on Women in the Academic Profession and adopted by the Association's Council in June 1983. Legal citations in the report were updated in 2014.

What is sought in the idea of affirmative action is essentially the revision of standards and practices to ensure that institutions are in fact drawing from the largest marketplace of human resources in staffing their faculties and a critical review of appointment and advancement criteria to ensure that they do not inadvertently foreclose consideration of the best-qualified persons by untested presuppositions which operate to exclude women and minorities.

Affirmative Action in Higher Education: A Report by the Council Committee on Discrimination

Since this report was issued in 1973, the commitment of the American Association of University Professors to affirmative action in higher education has remained strong. Our concern has been heightened, in fact, by a number of worrisome trends:

1. Although some faculty members have vigorously supported affirmative action, faculty members have too often abrogated their traditional role in institutional policy formulation and implementation by allowing administrators to assume major responsibility for affirmative-action requirements.
2. The administrations of many institutions have promulgated rules that not only intrude into the academic decision-making process, but also are counterproductive to the aims of affirmative action.
3. Insufficient progress has been made in removing the vestiges of discrimination and achieving equality.
4. Failure of many universities and colleges to end discriminatory policies and practices or to provide effective internal means of redress has led faculty members to resort to federal agencies and the courts. At the same time, enforcement activities have been viewed as unwarranted interference with institutional autonomy.
5. Criticism of affirmative action—from litigation attacking the use of race as a criterion in student admissions policies to political initiatives restricting the consideration of diversity as a factor in hiring at public institutions—has been widespread. Affirmative action has provided a handy target for the critics of government regulation of academic institutions, although other aspects of government regulation may in fact be far more intrusive and expensive to implement.

AAUP Policies

In view of these concerns, now is an appropriate time for the AAUP not only to reaffirm its stand in support of affirmative action, but also to suggest ways that affirmative action might be implemented in such a fashion as to be both effective and consonant with AAUP standards. The AAUP has long endorsed the principle of nondiscrimination, and the 1973 report of the Council Committee on Discrimination saw affirmative action as a necessary corollary to that principle.[1]

Although affirmative action involves the identification of groups, such identification need not and should not imply a remedy that sacrifices individual rights to purported group entitlements. The AAUP has consistently supported the rights of individuals, advocating that an individual receive neither more nor less favorable treatment simply because of his or her race or sex.[2]

We believe that the following forms of affirmative action are consistent with the principle of nondiscrimination in the protection of individual rights.

1. Examination of policies to be certain that they are scrupulously nondiscriminatory in principle and in practice, followed by corrective action where needed. Included would be a review of recruitment practices to ensure all qualified candidates for a position an opportunity to be considered fairly; to eliminate stereotyping assumptions, such as a belief that women with young children will be unable to devote themselves adequately to their profession; and to provide adequate internal grievance procedures for those who perceive that they have been the victims of discrimination.

2. *Examination of policies and procedures that, while facially neutral, have an adverse impact on women or minorities.* Whenever possible, they should be eliminated or replaced by less exclusionary policies designed to accomplish the same legitimate purpose.[3] The goal is to do away with gratuitous barriers to the fair consideration of women and minorities. Examples would be the narrowing of anti-nepotism policies or the liberalization of childbearing and child-rearing leave policies. Another, less direct, action might be provision for day-care facilities, the absence of which tends to have a heavier impact on women than on men.

3. *Race- or sex-sensitive selectivity.* Awareness of race or sex in the appointment and retention process reaches a more difficult concept, but one that we believe was affirmatively addressed by the 1973 committee and by the AAUP's amicus brief in the Bakke case.[4] It is contemplated that in the interest of "diversity" a faculty might make the academic judgment that it would be desirable to have more men or more women or more black or more white persons among the faculty or student body. Such a judgment raises a delicate matter in that we must ensure that the call for diversity does not itself lead to a violation of individual rights. It also raises the question of what types of considerations may appropriately be taken into account in the development and application of assessment criteria.

At church-related institutions (although probably not at public institutions), for example, a religious affiliation may be considered in providing a degree of homogeneity in institutional values. With respect to political views, on the other hand, the AAUP would not endorse the right of a faculty to make judgments based on diversity criteria, nor could a public institution do so legally. At the same time there are some considerations that faculty might quite properly take into account in order to achieve a certain heterogeneity they might view as beneficial to the stated purpose of the college or university. Institutional diversity may, in itself, be an appropriate goal. Under certain circumstances it

can be sound policy to avoid appointing large numbers of PhDs from a single institution, apart from the merits of individual candidates, and an age mix may also be sought in a manner consistent with nondiscrimination principles.

Affirmative action may thus permit the inclusion of sex or race among a number of characteristics assessed in a potential candidate— along with his or her publications, area of specialization, academic credentials, and so on. Sound academic practice requires that these criteria provide the basis for a complex assessment of relative merit and not merely establish a large pool of minimally qualified candidates. Nonetheless, it is frequently the case that the selection process produces a group of two or more highly rated candidates who are viewed as approximately equivalent. In such circumstances, and in the interests of diversity, affirmative-action considerations might control the final selection. This type of selectivity is still consistent with the principle of nondiscrimination in that, as a matter of faculty judgment, the decision may be made that more males are needed in a predominantly female department or more whites at a predominantly black institution.[5] It should be kept in mind, however, that what is permissible or desirable in race- or sex-sensitive selectivity in the appointment process differs from what may be permissible in subsequent personnel decisions.[6]

4. *The establishment of achievable goals for the appointment of women and minority faculty members.* A " 'goal' is nothing more or less than an expectation of what an institution has reason to suppose will result under conditions of nondiscrimination."[7] The setting of goals in an affirmative-action plan does not guarantee representation for the groups for whom the goals are set, but it does serve as a useful monitoring device consistent with the principle of nondiscrimination and the rights of individuals.

Despite recognition of past and continuing discrimination in higher education and the slow progress in achieving a more diverse faculty in terms of race and sex, the AAUP does not support affirmative action that would set rigid quotas in the appointment of faculty members. We recognize that special efforts may be needed to attract and retain women and minority faculty members. It is our position, however, that if the first three means of implementing affirmative action described above were fully implemented at colleges and universities, there would be no need to mandate appointments from underrepresented groups. Where the principle of nondiscrimination is truly operative, the expectation is that all groups, where large enough units were considered, would achieve adequate representation.[8] The focus of our concern, in light of our equal concern for the rights of individual candidates, must necessarily fall on the decision-making process and how to make it as nondiscriminatory as possible within the academic setting. It is important that faculty members take the initiative in the establishment of numerical goals as well as in other aspects of affirmative action; if, however, individual departments are unwilling to accept responsibility, then there must be effective means within the institution to ensure that provisions are made for equality of opportunity.

The AAUP recognizes that a fundamental commitment to nondiscrimination and equal opportunity requires the careful development and vigorous implementation and monitoring of affirmative-action plans designed to meet the needs and standards of the academic community. In line with the types of affirmative action described above, affirmative-action plans may include a wide range of lawful and academically sound corrective policies and procedures employed to overcome the effects of past or present barriers to equal employment opportunity. We believe that such plans are essential not only to ensure that equal opportunity is realized, but also to remove those vestiges of past discrimination that would otherwise perpetuate indefinitely the disadvantages of unequal treatment.

The second assumption on which these procedures are founded is that primary responsibility for affirmative action should reside within the academic community and especially with the faculty. Members of the academic community frequently regard affirmative action as a bureaucratic intrusion and respond with merely cosmetic formal compliance. We ought instead to recognize that outside pressure, though at times intrusive and insensitive, is sometimes required to stimulate the reform of long-standing discriminatory policies and procedures. We need, in fact, to reexamine long-standing policies to ascertain whether there are some facially neutral policies that have an adverse impact on women or minority persons without providing a substantial contribution to academic excellence. We need to integrate affirmative-action efforts into the routine conduct of personnel decisions through established procedures for peer review and collegial governance. While the primary responsibility lies within the institutions, we recognize that their policies and judgments cannot be exempted from administrative and judicial scrutiny and review. The right to institutional autonomy does not include the right to violate the law. The role of the government should, however, vary inversely with the efforts of the academic community to implement the principles of nondiscrimination.

Affirmative-Action Plans

1. Designing the Plan

Consonant with principles of sound academic governance,[9] the faculty should play a major role in formulating an institution's affirmative-action plan. To the extent that persons affected participate in the development and ratification of a plan, the document's acceptability will be enhanced.

The content of affirmative-action plans should be sensitive to classifications requiring academic expertise. Attention must also be paid to institutional policies governing tenure and promotion and fringe benefits and salary, and to any other area of professional life where vestiges of bias may persist. The most difficult aspect of plan development is the formulation of goals and timetables that not only are realistic, but also will serve as an incentive to maximum effort in providing equality of opportunity. Realism requires an honest recognition of diminishing resources, shrinking enrollments, and the limits of the candidate pool available to a specific institution and in specific disciplines or professional fields.

The existence of a formal document which sets forth the institution's commitment to equal-opportunity obligations, including goals, timetables, and procedures for the rectification of inequities, should be publicized. Incorporating the plan in faculty, staff, and student handbooks ensures its availability and facilitates its use as a ready reference.

2. Implementing the Plan

a. The Affirmative-Action Office

(1) The institution should establish an affirmative-action office.

(2) An affirmative-action officer for faculty should be a person selected by a representative committee on which faculty members have a major role; it is preferable that the person selected have had faculty experience in order to ensure an understanding of the role of faculty and to foster cooperation.

(3) The affirmative-action officer should have power of effective oversight of search and appointment procedures for faculty and academic administrative positions and their implementation. For example, the affirmative-action officer should have the authority, upon determining that a department's search for candidates has not been adequate, to defer an appointment

pending appropriate faculty and administrative review.

(4) The affirmative-action officer should play a role in the normal personnel-action procedures of the institution, including promotion, tenure, and salary determinations. Timely reviews of individual actions should be complemented by public disclosure through periodic reports on the overall situation at the institution with respect to personnel decisions affecting faculty status.

(5) The administration of an institution's affirmative-action program should encourage and provide a mechanism for faculty participation. Support from members of the faculty and the administration is of the utmost importance. A committee established by the appropriate institutional governing body should be responsible for promoting the policies established in the institution's affirmative-action plan and for periodic review of the plan once adopted. An institution-wide committee would be able to see to the integration of the affirmative-action plan into the personnel decision-making process and the coordination of equal-opportunity activities on campus.

(6) A charge for implementation of the affirmative-action plan should be given by the president of the institution to the affirmative-action officer and to the committee that has oversight responsibilities. This charge should be communicated to the faculty, staff, and students.

b. *Recruitment*

(1) A plan for the recruitment of minority persons and women should be developed by each department and approved by the affirmative-action officer.

(2) Departments should establish search committees that would work in consultation with the department chairperson and other members of the department toward meeting departmental goals in appointing minority persons and women.

(3) Plans for recruitment should include advertising in appropriate professional publications, in newsletters of minority or women's groups, and in publications of minority and women's caucuses or professional organizations. If a search is to be internal only, announcements should be circulated only internally. The deadline for applications should allow for a reasonable period of time after the announcement appears.

(4) Descriptions of vacant positions should be clear concerning teaching load, research expectation, departmental duties, and other responsibilities. Written criteria and procedures for reappointment, promotion, and tenure at the institution should be available for all interested candidates.

(5) Search committees should ask minority and women's caucuses of professional organizations for suggestions of candidates.

(6) Department chairpersons in graduate programs should be asked to call the opening to the attention of their current students or recent graduates.

(7) Search committees should consider going beyond those institutions from which faculty at the institution have been traditionally recruited. Consistent use of the same few institutions may perpetuate a pattern of discrimination in faculty hiring. In addition to broadening the base of sources from which candidates are seriously considered and appointed, the regularly recruited institutions should be asked to submit names of all qualified candidates.

(8) Search committees should contact the minority and women graduates (or men in departments where there are few men) and present and former members of the department for suggestions of possible candidates.

(9) Departments might well consult with the appropriate minority and women's groups on campus to secure their aid in recruitment efforts.

(10) Women and minority candidates who have recently acquired their professional training, after having been absent from formal academic pursuits for some years, should be judged with other recently trained persons for the same positions.

(11) In recruiting for faculty, the standards should be the same for all candidates. White males should not be considered on "promise" and all others, of comparable education and accomplishments, on "achievement." Search committees should be sensitive in reading letters of reference for indications of bias.

(12) The fact that the pool of minority persons and women candidates for a particular vacancy is small should not be used as an excuse for not attempting to recruit for such candidates.

c. *Screening of Candidates*

(1) Search committees should make every effort to include among the applicants a

diversity of candidates. After receipt of candidates' credentials and accompanying letters of recommendation, search committees should invite applicants—men and women, majority and minority—to the campus for interviews.

(2) When feasible, the affirmative-action officer and/or members of the appropriate minority or women's group on campus should be invited to meet with the minority or women candidates. It is important for the candidates to know that there are current faculty members who are minority persons or women.

d. *Appointments*

(1) Appointments should be made on the basis of individual merit. Careful consideration should be given to the criteria traditionally used for merit to be certain that they serve to further academic excellence. It is especially important to reconsider any facially neutral policies that have an adverse impact on affirmative-action efforts that is disproportionate to their contribution to the determination of merit. The need for an institution to justify a criterion as appropriate rises in direct proportion to its exclusionary effect.

(2) Offers to minority and women candidates should be made as attractive as possible; for example, appointment to full-time probationary or tenured positions, arranging course assignments in an area of the candidate's specialty, or a part-time appointment when mutually desirable or advantageous. This last item requires special attention because of the tendency to relegate women involuntarily to part-time or irregular positions on the faculty.

(3) Reports on faculty personnel decisions should include information on the department's search for minority and women candidates, interviews held, and the basis for a final choice.

e. *Professional Advancement*

(1) Criteria for reappointment, promotion, or tenure should have been made clear to the candidate at the time of his or her appointment. They should be reviewed with the appointee on a regular basis afterwards.

(2) Sexual or racial qualifications for reappointment, promotion, or the granting of tenure should not be introduced. Although a decision to seek diversity may be a legitimate factor in the appointment process, denial of retention or advancement because of this consideration is inappropriate and

often a breach of stated criteria and expectations. While it is understood that needs of institutions change, a redefinition of criteria and/or the imposition of requirements substantially different from those stated at the time of the initial appointment are suspect and should be carefully examined for their potentially discriminatory impact.

(3) As in the case of all new appointees, care should be taken not to appoint a woman or minority candidate to a position for which she or he is marginally qualified and then to provide no opportunity for professional development, such as a lightened teaching load to enable access to further study or research opportunities. Without support for professional development that is made available to all new appointees equitably, these faculty members often are denied reappointment. The cycle is likely to be repeated with their replacements. Where this occurs, there may be the appearance of a viable affirmative-action program without the reality of one.

(4) Because the number of minority and women faculty members at most institutions is small, it is important that they be made to feel welcome at the institution and educated into practical professional concerns. They should be given advice, if needed, on appropriate journals for the publication of scholarly papers, on obtaining grant support, and on participation in professional meetings and conferences.

(5) An institution can provide various incentives for the professional development of faculty members in junior academic positions, including postdoctoral opportunities in those fields historically closed to women and minorities, early leaves or sabbaticals, summer research grants, and funds for attendance at professional meetings. Because women and minority persons have traditionally been excluded in disproportionate numbers from such support, special encouragement may be required to ensure their participation.

f. *Retrenchment*

In those situations where an administration moves to terminate the positions of faculty members on continuous appointment on grounds of financial exigency or discontinuance of program, Regulation 4c of the Association's Recommended Institutional Regulations on Academic Freedom and Tenure recognizes that "judgments determining where within the overall academic program termination of appointments may occur involve considerations of educational policy, including affirmative action, as well as of faculty status."[10] That is, special care should be taken that the burden of retrenchment does not fall inequitably on those for whom affirmative action was taken. The same careful scrutiny must be given to retrenchment criteria as to those used in appointment, promotion, and tenure.

3. Monitoring the Plan

Through its governance structure, the faculty is best qualified to ensure that the letter and spirit of affirmative action are followed in the search for new appointees, as well as in promotion, retention, and tenure decisions. Furthermore, it is essential that the faculty, in conjunction with the administration, establishes and implements appropriate grievance procedures. Information regarding nondiscrimination policies, and notice of the recourse available should they not be followed, should be distributed to the faculty. Grievance committees should have access to the files and statements on which disputed decisions have been based, and, upon request, the faculty member should be provided an explanation of decisions affecting his or her status on the faculty.

Conclusions

Progress in the appointment and professional advancement of women and minority persons in higher education has been exceedingly slow. There are few minority and women faculty members in most academic fields; those there are tend to be concentrated in the lower academic ranks and in part-time and temporary positions. Unequal treatment of the underrepresented groups continues. The AAUP's surveys of faculty compensation consistently show a gap in salary between men and women faculty members.[11] It is clear that discrimination has not been eliminated, and effective affirmative-action plans are necessary. We urge a greater commitment—psychologically, ideologically, and materially—to the basic principles of affirmative action, and to the implementation and monitoring of affirmative-action plans, so as to approach real equality of opportunity.

Notes

Editor's Note (2014): In the decades since this report initially was published, courts have continued to address the issue of whether affirmative-action plans are constitutionally permissible and whether such plans should be subject to strict scrutiny versus intermediate scrutiny. In developing affirmative-action plans,

institutions must ensure that they consult with their own legal counsel for laws currently in effect. Additionally, it must be noted that courts, including the US Supreme Court, have addressed the use of diversity as a factor in higher education student admissions directly and have only alluded to its use in higher education hiring decisions with no specific resolution of the constitutionality of such use. Finally, adoption of an affirmative-action plan should include a legal review of current laws with respect to the need to explore race-neutral alternatives to achieve diversity before using race-conscious approaches.

1. This committee report endorsed federal guidelines establishing numerical goals and timetables and asked institutions to "review the effects and the assumptions of stated or unstated standards of appointment and advancement, to provide statistical forecasts under an affirmative-action plan, and to monitor equal protection provisions" ("Affirmative Action in Higher Education: A Report by the Council Committee on Discrimination," *AAUP Bulletin* 59 [June 1973]: 178–83).

2. This is the basis of the AAUP's position on pension benefits that similarly situated men and women should receive equal periodic benefits. To give each man more in benefits to make up for the fact that more men die early means that men and women who in fact live the same number of years will be treated differently. The Supreme Court in *Los Angeles Department of Water and Power v. Manhart*, 435 US 702 (1978), found this difference in treatment to be an illegal preference for group rights over individual rights. Limited federal legislation guaranteeing group entitlement has been upheld by the Supreme Court in *Fullilove v. Klutznick*, 448 US 448 (1980), but there is no general constitutional provision for group rights, which would, for example, provide for representational voting as is done by some governments. While the AAUP recognizes, as does federal law, the right of religious institutions to formulate appointment policies based on religious affiliation, it has never endorsed a policy of guaranteed representation of certain groups in employment. *Editor's Note* (2014): Readers should note that the case law in this area has evolved over the decades and that there have been numerous cases since *Fullilove v. Klutznick*, 448 US 448 (1980), that have addressed this issue. Independent legal review is necessary for the current status of the law in this area.

3. See "Affirmative Action in Higher Education."

4. The AAUP's amicus curiae brief in *Regents of the University of California v. Bakke*, 438 US 265 (1978). In this brief the AAUP took the position that when (a) a faculty was convinced on the merits that racial heterogeneity was in fact relevant to conditions of its own professional excellence, and when (b) failure to "count" race might necessarily frustrate that possibility to improve its excellence, then it might consider race in deciding on admissions. Justice Powell found this position to be the sole basis on which it was constitutional for a public university to make any use of race. This position has been reiterated subsequently in other amicus briefs filed by the AAUP, including *Gratz v.*

Bollinger and *Grutter v. Bollinger*, challenging the admissions policies and practices at the University of Michigan, and *Smith v. University of Washington Law School*, challenging affirmative action in law-school admissions.

5. While the body of this statement refers rather consistently to women and minorities, because that is where the problem usually is, it is recognized that, in some cases, affirmative action may be desirable to increase the number of men or whites on the faculty. Again, that would be an academic judgment by the faculty.

6. See 2e, Professional Advancement (2).

7. "Affirmative Action in Higher Education," 182.

8. We recognize the great difficulties in eliminating the historical effects of discrimination; nonetheless, we believe that these historical disabilities can be remedied through a truly nondiscriminatory system without the imposition of mandatory quotas or a double standard that would merely perpetuate the myth of inferiority.

9. See "Statement on Government of Colleges and Universities," AAUP, *Policy Documents and Reports*, 11th ed. (Baltimore: Johns Hopkins University Press, 2015), 117–22.

10. Ibid., 81.

11. See, e.g., "Annual Report on the Economic Status of the Profession, 1999–2000," *Academe* 86 (March–April 2000).

Verification and Trust: Background Investigations Preceding Faculty Appointment

This report was approved for publication by the Association's Committee A on Academic Freedom and Tenure in June 2004 and adopted by the Association's Council in November 2004.

Many employers in the United States have been initiating or expanding policies requiring background checks of prospective employees. The ability to perform such checks has been abetted by the growth of computerized databases and of commercial enterprises that facilitate access to personal information. Employers now have ready access to public information that had heretofore been difficult to collect without an expenditure of considerable effort and money—criminal records, litigation history, worker-compensation claims, marriage records, bankruptcy liens, court judgments, and more. They also have ready access to private information—credit-card history, airline use, certain telephone records, bank-account histories, pharmacy records, and even records of medical visits. The ready availability of these data creates the serious possibility of promiscuous, unfair, and perhaps even abusive investigations, and yet access to these data is subject to few legal limits.[1] Systematic inquiry into such personal information is nevertheless commonly understood to constitute a serious and harmful intrusion upon an individual's privacy.

Higher education has not been immune to the siren call for background information. Legislation mandating background checks for all employees of certain public institutions (which may include all or some public institutions of higher education) has been adopted in at least one state. The purchasing consortium of the Committee on Institutional Cooperation (made up of the Big Ten universities and the University of Chicago) now makes available at a discount the services of a background-checking company; it is for each participating institution to decide whether and how these services will be used. Some colleges and universities have initiated or expanded background investigations of candidates for faculty appointments. This interest in background checks has arisen despite the absence of any systematic study of the need for the information such checks might produce. The interest within higher education was especially stimulated by the extraordinary discovery in 2003 that a respected member of the faculty at Pennsylvania State University had for decades been on parole for murders he committed in another state when he was a teenager. The misrepresentation of faculty credentials or experience is not totally foreign to higher education.[2] But such sensational incidents are fortunately few, and almost all can be avoided if faculty search committees exercise reasonable care.

Because colleges and universities are now considering extensive and intrusive background checks with an urgency that seems quite out of proportion to the actual problems facing the academy, the AAUP's Committee A on Academic Freedom and Tenure appointed a subcommittee to consider the question of the standards that should guide academic institutions in the implementation of background checks.

Fortunately, we need not write on a clean slate. Almost three decades ago, the Privacy Protection Study Commission, created by the federal Privacy Act of 1974, addressed the tension between individual privacy and institutional needs for information in the context of employment.[3] It focused on two central issues of relevance here: the scope of background investigations and the procedures employed when such investigations are conducted. It concluded, rightly in our estimation, that the former must be guided by a norm of proportionality and the latter by concerns for both accuracy and fairness. We believe these governing principles to be applicable to higher education, and we address them below.

Scope of Investigation

Because colleges and universities must repose a high degree of trust in their faculties, they are justified in attempting to ascertain whether candidates are worthy of that trust. For this reason, they ordinarily charge search committees with the responsibility of conducting thorough checks of a candidate's references and of interviewing a candidate's present and former colleagues. Search committees should take this responsibility very seriously. To ensure the accuracy of a candidate's curriculum vitae, search committees also check educational credentials, prior employment, professional experience, and the like. No doubt such reference checks entail some compromise of the privacy of candidates, but it is justified in light of reasonable institutional needs.

We recommend that this principle of proportionality be preserved. The privacy of a candidate should be compromised only as necessary in order to secure information that may ensure that applicants are qualified to meet the particular obligations of specific positions. Thus, for example, appointments involving access to federally classified data may require government approval, which may justify background investigations of sufficient scope to ensure that a candidate will meet government standards. Similarly, appointments requiring the bonding of an appointee may require a background check of sufficient scope as to satisfy a bonding authority.

Our primary recommendation is that the principle of proportionality prohibits the adoption of a general policy of searching the criminal records, if any, of all applicants for all faculty positions. The mere fact of an applicant's having been swept up into the criminal-justice system is not, by itself, relevant to his or her suitability for a faculty position. For example, many faculty members, as students, were convicted of civil disobedience during the civil-rights struggle, and others were later arrested in protest of the Vietnam War.

While it is possible that a search of criminal records might disclose information that could reasonably be thought to have a negative bearing on a particular candidate's suitability for a faculty position, such a discovery must surely be rare. At the same time, the moral cost of adopting a general policy of requiring such searches in order to identify the rare special case is great. Undertaking such searches is highly invasive of an applicant's privacy and potentially very damaging. The probative value of criminal records is often small, because such records are notoriously imprecise. They contain information that ranges from arrest to indictment, from conviction to deferred prosecution and deferred sentencing, from completion of probation to the expunging of conviction. Context is often all important to understand this information, and context is never

supplied. Casting a wide net in order to acquire such information in the hope that it might turn up matters of relevance to an appointment that is under consideration would risk great damage for small and speculative gain, and it would cede unacceptable discretion to those entrusted with assessing the significance of this information in the absence of a proper context. It also raises possible legal concerns about the exercise of due care in the secure maintenance and deployment of this information. Such concerns led the Privacy Protection Study Commission to recommend that only criminal-justice information "directly relevant to a specific employment decision" be acquired by employers.[4]

We agree. We recognize that there may be instances in which the nature of a particular appointment might justify an investigation of the criminal record of an applicant. For example, some states require criminal checks of persons to be employed in specific capacities, most notably in child care. But we conclude that for an ordinary faculty appointment, the likely benefits of a background criminal investigation of an applicant are dwarfed by the grave invasions of privacy caused by such investigations, as well as by the great potential of such investigations to facilitate the misuse of sensitive information. Such investigations are accordingly inconsistent with the principle of proportionality.

To enforce the general principle that the scope of a background check be limited by the specific requirements of a particular position, we recommend that whenever a college or university contemplates pursuing background checks that are more extensive than those now customary within the academy, it should specify the information it seeks and explain the reasons it believes such information is necessary. We hope this requirement of transparency will provoke discussion that will help to ensure that academic institutions do not unduly and unnecessarily expand the scope of background checks.

Concerns for Fairness and Accuracy

We do not in this report assess the procedures that accompany the forms of reference checking that are now commonly applied to candidates for ordinary faculty positions. We instead address the very different concerns for fairness and accuracy that arise when institutions of higher education seek to conduct extensive background investigations of sensitive information, including criminal records. Positive law already offers useful guidance on the question of proper procedures. The federal Fair Credit Reporting Act governs the procedures that employers must use when they retain businesses to conduct background checks. In summary: (a) the candidate must be informed of the proposed background check and authorize it in writing; (b) the candidate must be given a copy of the final report; and (c) no adverse action may be taken on the basis of the report unless and until the prospective employee has had an opportunity to contest or clarify its accuracy. There is much technical complexity in this law that we find unnecessary to consider. Suffice it to say, we recommend that these basic elements be adopted as governing principles whether a background investigation is conducted by a third party or by an academic institution itself.

Following a search, records should be discarded except with regard to successful candidates. If the report is to remain in a candidate's file, it should be corrected to remove all inaccuracies. All irrelevant personally identifiable information in a faculty member's file should be destroyed; relevant but harmful information should be kept confidential, perhaps in files segregated on that basis (if state law allows), and kept for a period no longer than justified by institutional need.

Notes

1. These limits are set out in Matthew Finkin, *Privacy in Employment Law,* 2nd ed. (Washington, DC: BNA Books, 2003), chap. 4.

2. This assertion is based on the subcommittee's request for a review of the prevalence of cases of misrepresentation or wrongful nonrepresentation in the Association's files. The staff reported a case of what today would be called "identity theft," an episode occurring more than two decades ago, that would have been headed off by more careful screening by normal means. Occasionally, such cases have reached the courts. For example, *Fuller v. DePaul University,* 12 N.E.2d 213 (Ill. App. 1938), in which a professor at a Catholic university had concealed the fact that he had been a priest and was dismissed, and *In Re Hadzi-Antich,* 497 A.2d 1062 (D.C. App. 1985), in which a former law professor who falsified his resume in applying for a teaching position was subject to sanction by the bar.

3. US Privacy Protection Study Commission, *Personal Privacy in an Information Society* (Washington, DC, 1977), chap. 6.

4. *Personal Privacy,* 246.

On Crediting Prior Service Elsewhere as Part of the Probationary Period

The statement that follows was approved by the Association's Committee A on Academic Freedom and Tenure and adopted by the Association's Council in June 1978.

The 1940 *Statement of Principles on Academic Freedom and Tenure* defines the probationary period for faculty members as follows:

> Beginning with appointment to the rank of full-time instructor or a higher rank, the probationary period should not exceed seven years, including within this period full-time service in all institutions of higher education; but subject to the proviso that when, after a term of probationary service of more than three years in one or more institutions, a teacher is called to another institution, it may be agreed in writing that the new appointment is for a probationary period of not more than four years, even though thereby the person's total probationary period in the academic profession is extended beyond the normal maximum of seven years. Notice should be given at least one year prior to the expiration of the probationary period if the teacher is not to be continued in service after the expiration of that period.[1]

The underlying objective of the foregoing provision is to recognize university teaching as a profession in which, after a limited probationary period to demonstrate professional competence in their positions, faculty members achieve tenure in order to protect academic freedom and provide a reasonable degree of economic security. Tenure in the profession as a whole, rather than at a particular institution, is not a practical possibility, since a faculty appointment is at a given institution. Nevertheless, to the extent that experience anywhere provides relevant evidence about competence, excessive probation can occur not only at one institution but also through failure to grant any probationary credit for service at one or more previous institutions.

The 1940 *Statement* recognizes, however, that, because there is great diversity among institutions, not all experience is interchangeable, and that an institution may properly wish to determine whether an individual meets its standards for permanent appointment by on-the-spot experience. Thus a minimum probationary period, up to four years, at a given institution is a reasonable arrangement in appointing a person with prior service. It meets a reasonable demand of institutions that wish to make considered decisions on tenure based on performance at those institutions, and the needs of individuals who wished to obtain appointments that might not otherwise have been available to them because of insufficient time for evaluation.

The Association has long had complaints, primarily from research-oriented institutions, that the mandated counting of prior service elsewhere made it risky for them to offer appointments to unproved persons whose teaching experience was in a nonresearch setting or incidental to completion of graduate degree requirements. The Association's response has been to insist that the institutions and the individuals concerned should bear these risks, rather than allow for probationary service that exceeds four years at the current institution with the total probationary years in excess of seven.

One consequence of the above, however, is that if an institution adheres to the provision for crediting prior service it is less likely to appoint persons with countable prior service but without demonstrated competence in their current position. Thus avoidance of excessive probation may result, particularly in a "buyer's" market, in unemployability. A second consequence is that institutions sometimes simply disassociate themselves from the 1940 *Statement* in the matter. Each consequence is unfortunate, and either suggests that departures from the existing proviso, to adjust to its changed impact, be allowed under certain circumstances.

Nevertheless, the Association continues to take the position that the 1940 *Statement*'s provision for crediting prior service is sound, and it urges adherence to this position. It is particularly opposed to belated arrangements not to count prior service that are made in order to avoid an impending decision on tenure. The Association recognizes, however, that in specific cases the interests of all parties may best be served through agreement at the time of initial appointment to allow for more than four years of probationary service at the current institution (but not exceeding seven years), whatever the prior service elsewhere. Significantly different current responsibilities or a significantly different institutional setting can be persuasive factors in deciding that it is desirable to provide for a fuller current period of probation. In these specific cases, if the policy respecting the probationary period has been approved by the faculty or a representative faculty body, the Association will not view an agreement not to credit prior service as a violation of principles of academic freedom and tenure warranting an expression of Association concern.

In dealing with previous service, the 1940 *Statement*'s admonition that "the precise terms and conditions of every appointment should be stated in writing and be in the possession of both institution and teacher before the appointment is consummated" is particularly important. The years of previous service to be credited should be determined and set forth in writing at the time of initial appointment.

The previous service that should be taken into account is full-time faculty service at an institution of higher education that was accredited or was an official candidate for accreditation by a recognized United States accrediting agency.

Questions on whether to take into account previous service that occurred many years in the past, or previous service in a distinctly different area, should be referred to an appropriate faculty committee at the time of initial appointment.

Note

1. According to the 1970 Interpretive Comment Number 5, "The concept of 'rank of full-time instructor or a higher rank' is intended to include any person who teaches a full-time load regardless of the teacher's specific title" (AAUP, *Policy Documents and Reports*, 11th ed. [Baltimore: Johns Hopkins University Press, 2015], 15).

Senior Appointments with Reduced Loads

The statement that follows was approved by the Association's Committee on Women in the Academic Profession in April 1987 and by the Association's Committee A on Academic Freedom and Tenure in June 1987.

In its 1980 report on the *Status of Part-Time Faculty*,[1] Committee A noted that the 1940 *Statement of Principles on Academic Freedom and Tenure* "refers, with respect to tenure, only to those appointed to full-time service." The concept of tenure rested on a view of part-time service as occasional, adjunct, and cost-effective in terms of flexibility; it assumed no ongoing institutional commitment; and it assumed that part-time faculty members were properly relieved of responsibility for the institution's academic program.

Committee A's 1980 report reflected a significant change in perceptions of the nature of part-time service. Citing the 1973 recommendation of the Commission on Academic Tenure in Higher Education,[2] the report agreed that institutions should "consider modifying their tenure arrangements in order to permit part-time faculty service under appropriate conditions to be credited toward the award of tenure, and to permit tenured positions to be held by faculty members who for family or other appropriate reasons cannot serve on a full-time basis. "While Committee A recognized that many part-time faculty members are not potential candidates for tenure, it recommended that colleges and universities "consider creating a class of regular part-time faculty members, consisting of individuals who, as their professional career, share the teaching, research, and administrative duties customary for faculty at their institution, but who for whatever reason do so less than full time." This class of part-time faculty, the report concluded, "should have the opportunity to achieve tenure and the rights it confers."

Additional benefit would be derived from policies and practices that open senior academic appointments to persons with reduced loads and salaries without loss of status.

In the light of Committee A's recommendation, a senior appointee might choose, for whatever reason, to reduce proportionately his or her overall duties at the institution. If the faculty member were tenured, there would be no loss of the protections of due process and the other entitlements that accrue with tenure;[3] if the faculty member were nontenured, the policy might permit continuance with an "opportunity to achieve tenure and the rights it confers."

These appointments would not normally be made available if the individual were seeking reduction of the academic commitment in order to accept a teaching position elsewhere. Criteria for professional advancement, including promotion in rank, should be the same for all faculty appointees, whether they serve full time or with reduced loads. Where there is mutual agreement among the faculty member, the department, and the college or university administration, opportunity should exist for a faculty member to move from a full to a reduced load and back to full-time status, depending on the needs of the individual and the institution.

These modified appointments would help meet the special needs of individual faculty members, especially those with child-rearing and other personal responsibilities, as well as those seeking a reduced workload as a step toward retirement. A more flexible policy for senior appointments (whether tenured or nontenured) would increase the opportunities available both to individuals and to institutions with respect to faculty appointments.

Notes

1. *Academe* 67 (February–March 1981): 29–39.
2. Commission on Academic Tenure in Higher Education, *Faculty Tenure: A Report and Recommendations* (San Francisco: Jossey-Bass, 1973).
3. Where the action to reduce a full-time tenured faculty member to part-time status is mandated by a declared financial exigency or discontinuance of program, AAUP policy calls for the preservation of the protections of tenure and for continuance of salary on a pro-rata basis. (See Committee A report on "Academic Freedom and Tenure: Eastern Oregon State College," *Academe* 68 [May–June 1982]: 1a–8a, for further discussion of this issue.)

Contingent Appointments and the Academic Profession

The statement that follows was prepared by a joint subcommittee of the Association's Committee on Contingent Faculty and the Profession (formerly the Committee on Part-Time and Non-tenure-track Appointments) and Committee A on Academic Freedom and Tenure and adopted by the Association's Council in November 2003. Statistical information in the report was updated in 2014.

Ten years ago, the Association addressed the conditions and status of part-time and non-tenure-track faculty in a thoroughly documented report.[1] Since that time, faculty work has become more fragmented, unsupported, and destabilized. Faculty members are now classified in a growing number of categories with new titles and with distinct responsibilities, rights, and privileges.[2]

The proportion of faculty who are appointed each year to tenure-line positions is declining at an alarming rate. Because faculty tenure is the only secure protection for academic freedom in teaching, research, and service, the declining percentage of tenured faculty means that academic freedom is increasingly at risk. Academic freedom is a fundamental characteristic of higher education, necessary to preserve an independent forum for free inquiry and expression, and essential to the mission of higher education to serve the common good. This report examines the costs to academic freedom incurred by the current trend toward overreliance on part- and full-time non-tenure-track faculty.

A common thread runs through earlier statements and reports on the topic of part-time and non-tenure-track appointments. Some of these statements, which were adopted by the Association's committees and Council over the last three decades, are described in an addendum following this report. They acknowledge the economic and managerial pressures that have been presented—in good economic times and bad—as justification for a constantly increasing reliance on part- and full-time non-tenure-track appointments. But they also clearly articulate the dangers to the quality of American higher education that are inherent in this trend.

Consistent with the Association's earlier statements, this report and its recommendations proceed from the premise that faculty in higher education must have academic freedom protected by academic due process. It emphasizes the importance of preserving for all faculty the integrity of the profession, founded on the interaction of research, teaching, and service, and it offers recommendations for institutions and academic departments that are undertaking to restabilize their faculties by increasing the proportion of full-time tenure-line appointments.

While this statement emphasizes the necessity of correcting the growing dependence on contingent faculty appointments, the Association recognizes the significant contrast between current practices and the recommendations on faculty work offered here as necessary for the well-being of the profession and the public good. Therefore, the statement both offers guidelines by which institutions and faculties can plan and implement gradual transitions to a higher proportion of tenurable positions and, at the same time, affirms the development of intermediate, ameliorative measures by which the academic freedom and professional integration of faculty currently appointed to contingent positions can be enhanced by academic due process and assurances of continued employment.

Definition of Contingent Faculty

The term "contingent faculty" includes both part- and full-time faculty who are appointed off the tenure track. The term calls attention to the tenuous relationship between academic institutions and the part- and full-time non-tenure-track faculty members who teach in them. For example, teachers hired to teach one or two courses for a semester, experts or practitioners who are brought in to share their field experience, and whole departments of full-time non-tenure-track English composition instructors are all "contingent faculty." The term includes adjuncts, who are generally compensated on a per-course or hourly basis, as well as full-time non-tenure-track faculty who receive a salary.

For purposes of a policy discussion, these faculty cannot be separated neatly into two groups—part time and full time—based on the number of hours they work. Some faculty members are classified by their institutions as "part time," even though they teach four or five courses per term.[3] Whether these faculty members teach one class or five, the common characteristic among them is that their institutions make little or no long-term commitment to them or to their academic work. The fact that many non-tenure-track faculty are personally committed to academic careers, even while putting together a patchwork of teaching opportunities in one or more institutions in order to sustain themselves, has become all but irrelevant in institutional practice.

A small percentage of part-time faculty bring the benefit of expertise in a narrow specialty to add depth or specificity to the course offerings otherwise available at an institution.[4] Another small percentage are practitioners of a profession such as law, architecture, or business and bring their direct experience into the classroom in a class or two each week. While many individuals with such appointments may find the conditions of part-time academic employment acceptable, their situation is the exception rather than the norm, and therefore should not serve as the primary model for a policy discussion.[5] The vast majority of non-tenure-track faculty, part and full time, do not have professional careers outside of academe, and most teach basic core courses rather than narrow specialties.[6]

Graduate students who teach classes fall along a spectrum. At one end is the student who teaches a reasonable number of classes as part of his or her graduate education. At the other end is the person who teaches independently, perhaps for many years, but not in a probationary appointment, while he or she completes a dissertation. To the extent that a person functions in the former group, as a graduate student, his or her teaching load should be carefully structured to further—not frustrate—the completion of his or her formal education. To the extent that a person functions in the latter group, undertaking independent teaching activities that are similar in nature to those of regular faculty, the term "contingent

faculty" should apply. (For a more detailed discussion, see the AAUP's *Statement on Graduate Students.*[7])

Postdoctoral fellowships, particularly in the humanities, are being used in new ways that, in effect, create a new employment tier prior to a tenure-track appointment. The concept of "contingent faculty" includes postdoctoral fellows who are employed off the tenure track for periods of time beyond what could reasonably be considered the extension and completion of their professional training. Institutions' increased reliance on postdocs to handle their teaching and research needs tends to delay the access of these individuals to appropriate security in the profession, and to create yet another requirement for new PhDs seeking tenure-line appointments, thereby undermining reasonable expectations of long-term institutional commitments to new faculty.

Nontenured Majority

At most universities and colleges, the number of tenure-track positions now available is insufficient to meet institutional teaching and research needs. To staff essential courses, most institutions hire both part- and full-time faculty off the tenure track on short-term contracts and in other less formal arrangements.

Ten years ago, the Association reported that non-tenure-track appointments accounted for about 58 percent of all faculty positions in American higher education.[8] As of 1998, such appointments still accounted for nearly three out of five faculty positions, in all types of institutions.[9] In community colleges, more than three out of five positions are part-time non-tenure-track positions, and 35 percent of all full-time positions are off the tenure track. Non-tenure-track appointments make up an even larger proportion of new appointments. Through the 1990s, in all types of institutions, three out of four new faculty members were appointed to non-tenure-track positions.[10]

The number of *full-time* non-tenure-track appointments is growing even faster than the number of *part-time* non-tenure-track appointments. Full-time appointments off the tenure track were almost unknown a generation ago; in 1969, they amounted to 3.3 percent of all full-time faculty positions.[11] But between 1992 and 1998, the number of full-time non-tenure-track faculty increased by 22.7 percent, from 128,371 to 157,470. During that same period, the number of part-time non-tenure-track faculty increased by only 9.4 percent, from 360,087 to 393,971, and the number of full-time tenure-line faculty increased by less than 1 percent. By 1998, full-time non-tenure-track faculty comprised 28.1 percent of all full-time faculty and 16 percent of all faculty. Part-time non-tenure-track faculty comprised 95 percent of all part-time faculty, and 40 percent of all faculty.[12]

"Non-regular" appointments, including both part-time faculty and the rapidly growing group of full-time non-tenure-track faculty, have become the norm.[13] These appointments require only minimal commitment from the institution, and they result in a predictably high level of faculty turnover. Most non-tenure-track appointments are very brief in duration, lasting for only one or two terms. Only a quarter of all part-time faculty appointments extend beyond two terms. Full-time non-tenure-track faculty serve most frequently in one-year appointments.[14]

Women are more strongly represented among part-time faculty than among full-time faculty. As of 1998, 48 percent of all part-time faculty were female, while only 36 percent of all full-time faculty were female.[15] Women who do hold full-time positions are more strongly represented among lecturer and instructor positions, with little opportunity for tenure. As of 2000, women made up 55 percent of lecturers, 58 percent of instructors, 46 percent of assistant professors, 36 percent of associate professors, and only 21 percent of full professors.[16] Although the participation of women in the academic profession is increasing overall, the increase comes at a time when opportunities for full-time tenured positions are declining.

The minimal institutional commitment and relatively rapid turnover that characterize appointments of part- and full-time contingent faculty mean that few faculty members are available for long-term institutional and curricular planning, for mentoring newer faculty, and for other collegial responsibilities such as peer reviews of scholarship and evaluations for reappointment and tenure. The faculty as a whole is less stable when its members are increasingly unable to support these key academic activities.

Diminishing Investment in Education

The diminishing level of institutional commitment to a stable, full-time, tenured faculty might suggest that higher education is a fading value in our society—that perhaps there are fewer students, flagging interest in completing degrees, and lower enrollment in graduate studies. In fact, the opposite is true. Between 1976 and 1999, student enrollment in degree-granting institutions grew by 34 percent. During that time, the number of bachelor's degrees conferred increased

by 31 percent, master's degrees by 41 percent, and doctoral degrees by 35 percent.[17] But instead of increasing proportionately the number of full-time tenured and tenure-track faculty positions needed to teach these students and mentor these graduates, since 1976 institutions have increased the number of part-time faculty by 119 percent and the number of full-time non-tenure-track faculty by 31 percent.[18] Most of these contingent faculty members teach undergraduates.[19]

During part of this period of rapid enrollment growth, colleges and universities, especially public institutions, experienced serious budgetary pressures. In 1980, state governments supported almost a third (31 percent) of the cost of higher education in public institutions, with the rest of the higher education budget depending on tuition and fees (21 percent), federal appropriations (15 percent), sales and services (21 percent), gifts and endowments (7 percent), and other sources, including local governments.[20] By 1996, the burden had shifted considerably, with state budgets offering just 23 percent of the necessary support. The federal government also reduced its share of support, to 12 percent, and income from other sources stayed about the same. This left tuition and fees as the sole source for 28 percent of the revenue. Recent budget constraints in nearly every state have further strained the support of public institutions.

As budgets tightened and tuition and fees increased through the 1980s and 1990s, institutions set new priorities. But even with substantial increases in student enrollments, many institutions chose to allocate proportionately less to their instructional budgets, and instead to increase spending on physical plants, new technologies and technology upgrades, and administrative costs. In 1998, the congressionally appointed National Commission on the Cost of Higher Education confirmed that investments in faculty had decreased in recent years, even as tuitions rose.[21] In their testimony and comments to the commission, representatives of public and private institutions described pressures to compete for students by investing heavily in recreational facilities, updated dormitories, and the latest computer technologies. Institutions made up for these heavy expenditures by reducing instructional budgets, which they accomplished by hiring more contingent faculty instead of making a commitment to tenure-line faculty. While this choice may have improved the infrastructure on many campuses, it has undoubtedly imposed a cost on the quality of instruction. Though incoming students may find finer facilities, they are also likely to find fewer full-time faculty with adequate time, professional support, and resources available for their instruction.

Costs of Increased Contingency

The dramatic increase in the number and proportion of contingent faculty in the last ten years has created systemic problems for higher education. Student learning is diminished by reduced contact with tenured faculty members, whose expertise in their field and effectiveness as teachers have been validated by peer review and to whom the institution has made a long-term commitment. Faculty governance is weakened by constant turnover and, on many campuses, by the exclusion of contingent faculty from governance activities. Inequities and physical distance among potential colleagues undermine the collegial atmosphere of academic institutions and hamper the effectiveness of academic decision making. The integrity of faculty work is threatened as parts of the whole are divided and assigned piecemeal to instructors, lecturers, graduate students, specialists, researchers, and even administrators. Academic freedom is weakened when a majority of the faculty cannot rely on the protections of tenure. The following paragraphs examine each of these problems as an educational cost that institutions incur when they choose not to invest adequately in their instructional missions.

Quality of Student Learning

Most educators agree that maintaining the quality of student learning is a major challenge for higher education. Recent studies have identified informal interactions with faculty outside the classroom, which "positively influence persistence, college graduation, and graduate school enrollments" of students, as one of the strongest positive factors contributing to student learning.[22] Unfortunately, part-time faculty members, who are typically paid by the course, are discouraged by their employment arrangements from spending time outside of class with students or on student-related activities, whether in office hours and less formal interactions or in class preparation and grading papers. In addition, the practice of paying very low wages to adjuncts pressures many to support themselves by seeking multiple course assignments on multiple campuses, thus further limiting their opportunities to interact with students. Full-time faculty generally spend 50 to 100 percent more time per credit hour on instruction, in and out of the classroom, than do part-time faculty.[23] However, as a diminishing number of full-time tenured and tenure-track faculty must take on

additional institutional responsibilities that are not typically shared with contingent faculty, including faculty governance and institutional support of various kinds, tenure-track faculty may find that they are also pressed for time to spend with students outside of class. Students clearly bear the direct impact of reductions in institutional instructional budgets. The Association's 1986 statement *On Full-Time Non-tenure-track Appointments*[24] cautions:

> We question whether the intellectual mission of a college or university is well served when the institution asserts that certain basic courses are indispensable for a liberal education but then assigns responsibility for those courses to faculty members who are deemed replaceable and unnecessary to the institution. Indeed, we believe that an institution reveals a certain indifference to its academic mission when it removes much of the basic teaching in required core courses from the purview of the regular professoriate.

Because of increased reliance on contingent faculty, students entering college now are less likely than those of previous generations to interact with tenured or tenure-track professors who, in turn, are fully engaged in their respective academic disciplines. It is the professional involvement of faculty in academic disciplines that ensures the quality, currency, and depth of the content being offered to students. But now, because of the time constraints imposed on contingent faculty, especially part-time faculty, teachers of undergraduate courses are less likely to be informed about the latest developments in an academic discipline and to be challenged by recent research and writing. It is difficult for part-time faculty to be flexible and responsive to students' interests and abilities when they lack class preparation time and are required to deliver courses according to a predetermined curriculum. Contingent faculty, especially part-time faculty, are less likely than their tenure-line colleagues to have professional support such as office space, personal computers, and professional development opportunities. Because they lack resources and compensated time, contingent faculty may not be able to assign and supervise complex and meaningful projects.[25] Students of contingent faculty may have diminished opportunity to reach beyond the limits of the course outline and the classroom, with their instructor's support, to encounter a passion for scholarship and freedom of inquiry. Moreover, the heavy use of contingent faculty in fundamental first- and second-year undergraduate courses tends to separate tenure-track faculty from the introductory teaching that is critical to their understanding of the student body and of the basic questions that new students ask about their disciplines. This reduced contact with undergraduate students makes it more difficult for tenure-track faculty to sustain the cohesion and effectiveness of the curriculum. Finally, as the Association's 1993 statement *The Status of Non-tenure-track Faculty* points out, faculty with non-tenure-track appointments "serve with their academic freedom in continuous jeopardy." It is therefore not surprising, the statement notes, that "the more cautious among them are likely to avoid controversy in their classrooms" and thus to deprive their students of that quintessential college experience.

Equity among Academic Colleagues
Inequities begin in the appointment process. Appointments of full-time tenure-track faculty typically follow rigorous national searches, which include a review of the candidate's scholarly record, an assessment of teaching potential, and consideration of other attributes by faculty in the department offering the appointment. Contingent faculty, by contrast, are often appointed in hurried circumstances. Department chairs select likely candidates from a local list, reviewing their curricula vitae and perhaps their past student evaluations. Faculty in most contingent positions are rarely reviewed and evaluated during their appointments, and little care is taken to enhance their professional development and advancement. In many institutions, evaluations are the responsibility of the busy dean or chair who appointed the individual, and may be neglected unless complaints or problems arise. By contrast, in other institutions, contingent faculty are constantly evaluated, sometimes by faculty members with much less experience, or even by graduate students.

Economic differences provide an even sharper contrast between part-time contingent faculty and tenured faculty. While part-time faculty who teach in professional and vocational schools or programs are likely to hold full-time positions outside the academy, those who teach in core liberal arts fields such as English, foreign languages, history, and mathematics are more likely to rely on their teaching for their livelihood. This means that a sizeable corps of college teachers lacks access to employment benefits, including health insurance and retirement plans.[26] To support themselves, part-time faculty often must teach their courses as piecework, commuting between institutions, preparing for courses on a grueling timetable, striving to create and evaluate appropriately challenging assignments, and

making enormous sacrifices to maintain interaction with their students. A large gap in working conditions exists even between the most experienced part-time faculty members and newly appointed tenure-track faculty members.

Contingent faculty, both part and full time, are constantly confronted with reminders of their lack of status in the academic community. The isolation of contingent faculty from opportunities to interact with their tenured or tenure-track colleagues and to participate in faculty governance, professional development, and scholarly pursuits promotes divisions and distinctions that undermine the collegial nature of the academic community. Taken together, these inequities weaken the whole profession and diminish its capacity to serve the public good.

Integrity of Faculty Work
Higher education achieves its unique standing in our society because it is characterized by original research, teaching that is grounded in scholarly disciplines, and service to the larger community, all supported and protected by academic freedom. Institutions rely on the professional responsibility of the faculty to maintain a strong commitment to student learning and to the development of scholarship. Indeed, the Association's founding statement, the 1915 *Declaration of Principles on Academic Freedom and Academic Tenure,*[27] describes the public purposes of a college or university as teaching, scholarship, and service. The relative emphasis placed on teaching, scholarship, and service by a faculty member varies according to the terms of his or her appointment and academic discipline and the type of institution at which he or she works. But although emphases vary, these functions are not completely divisible. Faculty work cannot be sliced cleanly into component parts without losing the important connections that make up the whole. For example, while teaching may be the primary mission of certain types of institutions or programs, teaching faculty recognize the need to engage in scholarly work in order to remain current and effective as teachers in their respective disciplines. Similarly, research universities support original research, but research faculty typically share new information and insights with the university community by teaching in a graduate program and by consulting with academic colleagues. In all types of institutions, faculty share a responsibility for academic decision making. Faculty participation in governance structures is an essential feature of higher education, ensuring that programs and courses are of high quality and are academic in nature.

Faculty also serve the university or college in many ways, such as by acting as faculty advisers to student organizations, providing information to prospective students and their parents, and supporting student activities. Finally, the university's ability to be of service to the community at large depends on the availability of faculty to share their academic knowledge outside of academe. Services ranging from providing economic development advice to local governments and community organizations to advising local schools on college preparatory courses tie the university or college to the larger community, and help to inform the institution's research and teaching functions.

Tenured and tenure-track faculty are expected to engage to some extent in teaching, scholarship, and service, and their salaries and teaching loads reflect that expectation. Faculty holding contingent appointments, on the other hand, are rarely compensated for time spent on shared governance or other service. The professional development and scholarly accomplishments of contingent faculty are often viewed as irrelevant or simply ignored.

To maintain the quality of higher education, faculty must stay in contact with other scholars in their disciplines. Contingent appointments frustrate such involvement and hamper original research because they are unstable and because they rarely include institutional support for scholarly activities and professional development. Scholarship requires continuity. It is particularly difficult for faculty members with contingent appointments to engage in scholarly work when the conditions of their appointments vary from year to year (or even term to term). Access to scholarly resources such as libraries, collections, or laboratories varies widely with different types of appointments. Even full-time non-tenure-track appointments, arguably more stable than part-time appointments, leave little time for scholarly development, because faculty with these appointments tend to teach many more classes than tenured or tenure-track faculty. In doctoral institutions, full-time non-tenure-track faculty teach 50 percent more hours than tenure-track faculty, and in other four-year institutions, 15 percent more.[28]

To support the essential mission of higher education, faculty appointments, including contingent appointments, should incorporate all aspects of university life: active engagement with an academic discipline, teaching or mentoring of undergraduate or graduate students, participation in academic decision making, and service on campus and to the surrounding community.

Faculty who are appointed to less-than-full-time positions should participate at least to some extent in the full range of faculty responsibilities. For all faculty members in contingent positions, this participation should be supported by compensation and institutional resources and recognized in the processes of evaluation and peer review.

Academic Freedom
Academic freedom in colleges and universities is essential to the common good of a free society. Academic freedom rests on a solid base of peer review and as such is the responsibility of the entire profession. The profession protects academic freedom through a system of peer review that results in institutional commitment to faculty members. Faculty peers make careful judgments in the appointment process, conduct ongoing reviews that may lead to reappointments, and make evaluations that may determine the completion of the probationary period and the beginning of continuous tenure. Individual faculty members can exercise their professional inquiry and judgment freely because peer review affirms their competence and accomplishments in their fields.

By contrast, the attenuated relationship between the contingent faculty member and his or her department or institution can chill the climate for academic freedom. Currently, neither peer review nor academic due process operates adequately to secure academic freedom for most contingent faculty members. The lack of adequate protection for academic freedom can have visible results. Contingent faculty may be less likely to take risks in the classroom or in scholarly and service work. The free exchange of ideas may be hampered by the specter of potential dismissal or nonrenewal for unpopular utterances. In this chilling atmosphere, students may be deprived of the robust debate essential to citizenship. They may be deprived of rigorous and honest evaluations of their work. Likewise, faculty may be discouraged from explorations of new knowledge and experimentation with new pedagogies. Perhaps most important, institutions may lose the opportunity to receive constructive criticism of academic policies and practices from a significant portion of the academic community.

To secure academic freedom for the entire profession, and to ensure the highest quality in teaching and research, the responsibilities of faculty peers in the appointment and evaluation of colleagues for contingent faculty positions should resemble those for appointments on the tenure track. Faculty members appointed and reappointed to contingent positions should receive conscientious and thorough peer reviews in which they can demonstrate their effectiveness; their successive reappointments would then validate their record of competence and accomplishments in their respective fields.

Resting securely on a base of peer review, academic freedom is best guaranteed by tenure and academic due process. We here affirm long-standing Association policy that, with carefully circumscribed exceptions, all full-time appointments are of two kinds: probationary appointments and appointments with continuous tenure. According to the joint 1940 *Statement of Principles on Academic Freedom and Tenure,* "[a]fter the expiration of a probationary period, teachers or investigators should have permanent or continuous tenure, and their services should be terminated only for adequate cause . . . or under extraordinary circumstances because of financial exigencies."[29] For full-time faculty the probationary period should not exceed seven years, and those who are reappointed beyond seven years should be recognized as having the protections that would accrue with tenure—termination only for adequate cause and with due process.

To protect academic freedom and to ensure the highest quality in college and university education, colleges and universities need the stability of a tenured faculty. The Association's 1993 report *The Status of Non-tenure-track Faculty* urges: "Whenever possible, the regular academic instruction of students should be the responsibility of faculty members who are responsible for the curriculum and participate in the governance of the institution, and to whom the institution is willing to make the commitment of tenure." Where the ideal is not immediately reachable, faculties and administrations should both adopt concrete plans to increase the proportion of positions that are protected by tenure, and in the interim develop and implement practical safeguards for academic freedom for all faculty, and assurances of conscientious peer review and continued employment of well-qualified faculty, in order to maintain the quality of the education offered at the institution. This transitional phase should include at least these three elements:

1. Part- and full-time contingent faculty should be provided opportunities to move into tenured positions (part or full time), the requirements for which should be defined, as always, by faculty peers.
2. Part-time faculty, after a reasonable opportunity for successive reviews and reappointments, should have assurances of continued employment. (For examples of measures that

provide such assurances, see the recommendations on tenure and academic due process in the following section of this report and the 1979 summary, *Academic Freedom and Due Process for Faculty Members Who Serve Less Than Full Time.*[30])
3. Faculty and administrators should exercise great care in recruiting and appointing new faculty, for any position, to ensure that new faculty may have some prospect of eventually achieving tenure. Finally, it is important to note that tenure can be granted at any professional rank (or without rank); the Association does not link tenure with a particular faculty status. The professor in a research university, whose appointment includes a significant responsibility for original research, should not be the sole or primary model for tenurable academic work. A faculty member whose position focuses primarily on teaching, supported by sufficient opportunity for scholarship and service, is also engaged in tenurable academic work. Just as there are different emphases in the range of faculty appointments in research universities, comprehensive universities, liberal arts colleges, and community colleges, all of which define tenurable faculty work, so, too, there may be different models for tenurable faculty work within a single institution.

Recommendations on Faculty Work

The work of faculty comprises an integrated whole; segmenting that work threatens the quality of higher education, undermines the reliability and effectiveness of academic decision making, undercuts the necessary protections of academic freedom, and imposes an unacceptable cost on student learning. The increased reliance of the academy on faculty whose academic freedom is not protected diminishes the professional autonomy and the intellectual independence of all faculty—essential elements of the mission of higher education. Knowing from long experience that academic freedom thrives in a relationship of commitment and responsibility between faculty and their institutions, the Association makes the following recommendations.

Faculty Work as an Integrated Whole

Faculty appointments, part or full time, should be structured to involve, at least to some extent, the full range of faculty responsibilities, including teaching activities both in and outside the classroom, scholarly pursuits such as contributions to an academic discipline or maintenance of professional currency, and service that ensures that academic decisions are well informed by the experience and expertise of all faculty and that the wider community shares in the benefits of the knowledge fostered by the university community.

Peer Review
Collegial support of academic freedom for the profession requires conscientious and thorough reviews of the work of all faculty members, including contingent faculty. Reviews should be conducted by faculty peers and should be structured to permit faculty members to demonstrate their competence and accomplishments in their respective fields. The records of reviews should validate faculty members' effectiveness in their positions. Appointment, review, and reappointment processes should incorporate accepted practices of academic due process, and should give careful attention to the quality of education that the faculty member contributes to the institution.

Tenure and Academic Due Process
Teaching, scholarship, and service must be protected by academic freedom and due process. For faculty with full-time appointments, academic freedom must be protected by tenure following a reasonable probationary period. For faculty with full-time appointments, regardless of their titles, the probationary period should not exceed seven years. In addition, all part-time faculty, after appropriate successive reviews for reappointments, should have assurance of continuing employment. Such assurance can be provided through a variety of measures, some of which were recommended by the Association in 1993. Examples include longer terms of appointment, opportunities for advancement through ranks, due-process protections (described below), recognition of seniority (such as first opportunities for reappointment and course selection), conscientious peer evaluation, earlier notices of reappointment, and opportunities to appeal nonreappointment.

The Association affirms as partial protections of academic freedom for part-time faculty the following specific due-process provisions set forth in 1979: written terms and conditions of appointments, modifications, and extensions; a written statement of reasons and an opportunity to be heard before a duly constituted committee prior to involuntary termination during a period of appointment; access to a duly elected faculty grievance committee; and a statement of reasons and a hearing before a duly constituted faculty committee for nonreappointment, if the faculty member makes a prima facie case of an academic freedom violation or improper discrimination.

Shared Governance
Curricular and other academic decisions benefit from the participation of all faculty, especially those who teach core courses. Governance responsibilities should be shared among all faculty at an institution, including those appointed to less-than-full-time positions. Although part-time faculty have proportionately less time available for governance responsibilities, their appointments should provide for appropriate participation and compensation. Faculty and administrators in each institution, program, or department should together determine the appropriate modes and levels of participation in governance for part-time faculty, considering issues such as voting rights, representation, and inclusion in committees and governance bodies, with the primary aim of obtaining the best wisdom and cooperation of all colleagues in the governance of their institutions. Participation in shared governance requires vigilant support of academic freedom and the protections of due process. In order to protect the right and the responsibility of nontenured as well as tenured faculty to participate freely and effectively in faculty governance, it is incumbent on all faculty to protect the exercise of academic freedom by their colleagues in faculty governance processes.

Compensation
All faculty work should be compensated fairly. Positions that require comparable work, responsibilities, and qualifications should be comparably compensated, taking into account variations by discipline, seniority, and departmental priorities. As the Association recommended in 1993, compensation for part-time appointments, including those in which faculty are currently paid on a per-course or per-hour basis, should be the applicable fraction of the compensation (including benefits) for a comparable full-time position.[31] Although the variety of responsibilities and qualifications required of each position may make comparability difficult to determine, it is the responsibility of duly constituted faculty bodies to meet this challenge.

Limitations of Contingent Appointments
Recognizing that current patterns of faculty appointment depart substantially from the ideal, the Association affirms its 1980 and 1993 recommendations that no more than 15 percent of the total instruction within an institution, and no more than 25 percent of the total instruction within any department, should be provided by faculty with non-tenure-track appointments.

For the long-term good of institutions and their students, the use of non-tenure-track appointments should be limited to specialized fields and emergency situations. Faculty who hold such special and emergency appointments should have the protections of academic freedom, due process, and fair compensation as described above. Special appointments refer, for example, to sabbatical replacements, substitutes for leaves of absence, or limited "artist-in-residence" appointments. Special appointments should not exceed a small percentage of all faculty appointments, and the Association's allowance for special appointments should not be construed as an endorsement of the thousands of full-time non-tenure-track faculty appointments that now comprise over 30 percent of all full-time faculty positions.

Flexible Scheduling
Within the context of tenure, a certain amount of flexibility in scheduling is an appropriate response to the needs of faculty at various career stages. The Association affirms the recommendation made in the 1987 statement *Senior Appointments with Reduced Loads*[32] for opportunities "for faculty member[s] to move from a full to a reduced load and back to full-time status, depending on the needs of the individual and the institution." Modified appointments—possibly with reduced workloads and salary, but without loss in status—might serve faculty members at various stages of life or career. The Association's 2001 *Statement of Principles on Family Responsibilities and Academic Work* recommends, among other accommodations for faculty who are new parents, adjustments in the probationary period at the request of the faculty member.[33]

These recommendations speak to all faculty—tenured, tenure track, and contingent. They urge a renewal of the conception of faculty work as an integrated whole that fits with and supports the mission of higher education for the public good. They urge an integration of principles of academic freedom and due process in the work of all faculty, and recommend inclusion of all faculty in the academic work of the institution. The Association recognizes the gap between these recommendations and current practices. This gap must be bridged in two ways: (1) by developing concrete mechanisms to integrate contingent faculty into the academic work of their institutions and to protect the academic freedom of faculty currently appointed to contingent positions, and (2) by increasing the proportion of positions protected by tenure. We offer below some practical guidelines for transitions to an improved ratio of tenured faculty. Each plan for transition, of

course, must be customized to a particular institution, as developed by administrations and all faculty working together collegially.

Transition from Current to Best Practices
Transitions happen gradually. The professoriate's transition from a body composed mainly of full-time tenure-line faculty to a body composed mainly of contingent faculty occurred over several decades. Now, some institutions seek to recover the stability and quality of instruction lost in that transition. Some simply seek to improve the ratio of tenure-line faculty in one or more departments. Such changes do not have to be precipitate and jarring to institutions, to students, or to faculty members who were appointed on a contingent basis and have, nonetheless, tried to build an academic career. Both faculty and administrators participated in the decisions that have resulted in heavy reliance on contingent faculty, especially for undergraduate teaching. Both faculty and administrators now share the responsibility for reducing such reliance while minimizing the costs of change to current contingent faculty.

A transition to a stable, mostly tenured or tenure-eligible faculty can be accomplished by relying primarily on attrition, retirements, and the appointment of more faculty to meet the needs of the increasing number of students expected in coming decades. Plans for conversion should be addressed by duly constituted faculty bodies that invite the participation of contingent faculty.

Instructional budgets, of necessity, compete for funds with other college and university priorities. Students, alumni, parents, and local legislators may be among the first to recognize the value of investments that strengthen the quality of undergraduate education and may assist in identifying the resources necessary for a transition.

For example, in 2001, the California legislature passed a resolution to increase the percentage of tenured and tenure-track faculty in the California State University system to 75 percent over an eight-year period. A systemwide working group adopted a plan that outlined a goal of improving the ratio of tenured and tenure-track faculty by 1.5 percent each year. The plan anticipated that many faculty holding non-tenure-track lecturer positions would apply successfully for newly created tenure-track positions, and that the remaining replacements of lecturer positions with tenure-track positions could be handled through attrition and retirements of lecturers. To meet the goal, the state undertook to conduct between

1,800 and 2,000 annual searches for new tenure-track faculty. The cost of recruiting, appointing, and compensating the new positions was estimated to be between $4.8 and $35 million in each of the eight years, which reflected an increase of 0.18 percent to 1.3 percent in the systemwide budget.[34]

At Western Michigan University, the faculty successfully bargained for a contract that offered tenurable positions to a group of "faculty specialists" including health specialists and teachers in the College of Aviation. Because the faculty union and the institution had moved incrementally toward this step, first regularizing the positions by adopting position descriptions and promotional ranks and agreeing on some due-process provisions, and then offering job security with four-year reviews, the cost of the transition to the tenure track was negligible.[35]

These two examples demonstrate that institutions committed to high-quality undergraduate education can plan appropriate steps to reduce their reliance on temporary faculty.

Preparation for a Transition
We make the following recommendations for systems, institutions, departments, or programs preparing to make a transition from an unstable academic environment characterized by overreliance on contingent faculty appointments to a stable academic environment characterized by a predominantly tenure-line faculty.

Assess the current situation. How many faculty members in each department are currently appointed off the tenure track? How many of such appointments are needed to serve the long-term best interests of the students and the institution? The current ratio of contingent faculty to tenured and tenure-track faculty should serve as a benchmark. As a transition begins, the institution or department should seek to reduce that ratio.

Define and describe the goal. Faculty and administrators should consider the end result sought. Different profiles of tenurable positions, with varied emphases given to teaching, research, and service as integral parts of faculty work, might suit the mission and work of different departments, programs, or institutions. Each department, program, or institution should consider which profiles best fit its long-term needs. For example, the work of some tenured faculty, particularly at the undergraduate level, may emphasize teaching or service, while the work of others may emphasize research and graduate education. Some faculty may be eligible for tenure as specialists, as clinical instructors, or in other positions that vary from conventional

faculty ranks of assistant, associate, and full professor.

To determine the number of tenured positions needed for each department, program, or institution, faculty and administrators should begin with the premise that core and advanced courses should be taught by faculty who have the protection of academic freedom, secured by tenure and academic due process, as well as the ability to participate fully in their profession and in the collegial environment of the academy. Duly constituted faculty bodies should determine the full complement of tenured and tenure-track faculty needed in a department, program, or institution. The number of tenure lines in the budget of an institution or statewide system should reflect at least the number of faculty needed to teach the students enrolled in core and advanced courses offered on a continuing basis. Budget constraints and other concerns may prevent the immediate realization of a full complement of tenured faculty. Nevertheless, the goal should be defined.

Consider appropriate criteria for tenure. A duly constituted body of faculty peers should determine tenure qualifications and requirements for each type of appointment. When a position is made "tenurable," the relative emphasis on teaching, scholarship, and service necessary for that position, and therefore the qualifications that should be emphasized in tenure criteria for that position, may vary among departments and programs and among types of appointments.

Stabilize the situation. Having made a commitment to reduce reliance on a contingent teaching force, institutions should avoid appointing new contingent faculty during the transition. New contingent appointments, if any, should be limited to candidates whose qualifications, after a probationary period, are likely to meet the institution's standards for tenure in the type of position being filled, in anticipation of eventual tenure eligibility. Such appointments should be made only in the context of a definite timetable, coupled with the commitment of appropriate resources, to convert the positions to tenure-track positions. Institutions should not rotate contingent faculty members through various types of appointments for the purpose of avoiding professional commitments to them.

Institutions should also avoid the proliferation of new types of contingent appointments and the proliferation of new names for existing types of appointments. Such proliferation increases the instability of the faculty and damages the careers of individual faculty members who are rotated through a variety of non-tenure-track positions.

Design a deliberate approach. Plans for a transition to a primarily tenured and tenure-track faculty should be structured to ensure the least possible disruption to student learning and faculty careers. A transition can be achieved through an incremental approach that relies in large part on the voluntary attrition of faculty holding contingent appointments. Contingent faculty, especially those who have been reappointed several times, should be included in faculty decision-making processes about the conversion of positions or the creation of new positions.

Faculty may determine that, during a period of transition, individuals currently holding teaching-only positions or other positions not presently recognized as tenurable may be "grandfathered" into tenured or tenurable positions. Based on their existing qualifications and consistently demonstrated effectiveness in their current work responsibilities, full-time non-tenure-track faculty who are reappointed for a period of time that is equivalent to the probationary period for tenure-track faculty should be recognized as being entitled, in their current positions, to the protections that would accrue with tenure. Part-time faculty whose effective academic service and accomplishments lead to successive reappointments should be accorded assurances of continued employment. (See the recommendations on tenure and academic due process, above.) When the "grandfathered" positions become vacant through attrition or retirement, new candidates can be recruited according to qualifications that faculty peers determine are necessary in the long term for the tenure-track positions.

When institutions create new tenurable positions in order to increase the proportion of tenured and tenure-track faculty, part- and full-time contingent faculty who have experience, length of service, and a record of accomplishments should be welcomed as applicants for such new positions. Because some of these faculty may have been serving ably in similar positions for many years, faculty peers should design an appropriate probationary period for tenure that takes into account their individual qualifications and experience.

Recognize costs and plan for necessary resources. Just as overreliance on contingent faculty has long-term costs to students and institutions, transition to a full-time tenured and tenure-eligible faculty has immediate costs. These costs represent an appropriate investment, primarily in undergraduate education. They are offset somewhat by the diminished administrative expense of handling high turnover among faculty teaching essential courses, but nevertheless

may be significant, especially in times of tight budgets.

Converting full-time non-tenure-track positions to tenurable positions represents the smallest increase in expenditures, as the compensation for full-time contingent faculty is only marginally less than for assistant professors overall. But, as noted earlier, full-time contingent faculty typically carry a heavier teaching load than assistant professors on the tenure track (50 percent heavier in research institutions, 15 percent heavier in other four-year institutions). To integrate these positions fully into the profession, these full-time teachers would need to be relieved of some teaching duties to allow time for scholarship and service, even if their positions continue to emphasize teaching as a primary activity. However, as is suggested by the examples of the California State University system and Western Michigan University, incremental budget increases may be sufficient to accommodate a conversion from contingency to stability.

Converting part-time positions to full-time tenurable positions presents a greater economic challenge. Part-time faculty are typically paid by the course, at roughly half the cost of full-time equivalent replacements.[36] In addition, the institution typically incurs little or no financial liability for employment benefits for part-time faculty. The costs of a transition toward full-time tenure-track appointments can be spread out over time by such incremental steps as restructuring per-course appointments into fractional half-time or full-time appointments, with proportionate pay and benefits. Some part-time appointments, particularly of specialists and professional practitioners, may be appropriate to continue over a long term. In such cases, tenure eligibility for the part-time position, with proportionate compensation, should be considered.

Consistent with these recommendations, there are at least two ways to begin a transition from an unstable academic environment characterized by overreliance on contingent faculty appointments to a stable academic environment characterized by a predominantly tenure-line faculty. One option is for institutions to convert the tenure-eligible status of faculty members currently holding contingent appointments. Another option is for the institution to create new tenure-eligible positions, recruiting broadly for these positions and gradually phasing out contingent positions.

Conversion of Status

Faculty and administrators at an institution may consider changing the status of existing positions from non-tenure-track to tenure line. The tenure-line positions can be either part or full time, depending on the needs of the department or program. When status is changed, the individuals holding the positions are offered a probationary period for tenure, and the following guidelines should be followed:

1. Faculty should consider the work to be undertaken by those holding newly converted positions. Formerly non-tenure-track positions may need to be restructured or rearranged to allow the faculty members in such positions to assume the full range of faculty responsibilities, appropriate to the position, and to be compensated and recognized for those responsibilities.
2. The experience and accomplishments of faculty members who have served in contingent positions at the institution should be credited in determining the appropriate length and character of a probationary period for tenure in the converted position.
3. If the requirements of the position change when it becomes a tenure-line position, the faculty member in the position should be given time and appropriate professional-development support during a probationary period to enable him or her to meet the new requirements.

Creation of New Positions
Faculty and administrators at an institution may decide to create new tenure-track positions while reducing the number of new appointments of contingent faculty. When this is done, the following guidelines should be followed:

1. Faculty should reconsider the academic work to be undertaken by those holding both new and existing tenure-line positions. Faculty responsibilities may need to be restructured or rearranged in order to ensure that undergraduate as well as graduate courses are appropriately staffed.
2. When colleges and universities create new tenure-track positions, they should advertise widely to generate a diverse pool of applicants.
3. Experienced, effective, and qualified faculty members currently holding contingent appointments should be encouraged to apply for the new tenure-track positions. In the selection and appointment process, faculty and administrators should recognize the value of continuity in teaching and familiarity with the institution's programs as desirable criteria. Contingent faculty members should be given fair and careful consideration when new tenure-eligible positions are created, and their experience and accomplishments should be

taken into account. Certainly, faculty charged with the selection of new colleagues should scrupulously avoid discrimination against applicants currently employed in contingent positions. In the context of a transition, faculty members who have served many years in contingent appointments should have the option of continuing in the same position, with the same qualifications and responsibilities.
4. When institutions replace part-time positions with full-time positions, and/or contingent positions with tenure-track positions, they should create timetables that rely, insofar as possible, on attrition and voluntary terminations, in order to introduce the least possible disruption in the work lives of contingent faculty members who have served the institution well over a period of years.
5. Plans for transition should be multi-year plans, including a realistic assessment of the resources needed to accomplish the change, and the steps necessary to commit the appropriate resources.

Conclusion
The integrity of higher education rests on the integrity of the faculty profession. To meet the standards and expectations appropriate to higher education, faculty need to incorporate teaching, scholarship, and service in their work, whether they serve full time or less than full time. The academic freedom that enlivens and preserves the value of academic work is protected by a responsible and reasonable commitment between the university or college and the faculty member. For the good of higher education and the good of society as a whole, this commitment must be preserved for all faculty. But the majority of faculty members now work without such a commitment from their institutions, and therefore without adequate protection of academic freedom.

This report has identified some of the real costs of overreliance on part-time and non-tenure-track faculty: costs to the quality of student learning, to equity among academic colleagues, to the integrity of faculty work, and to academic freedom. These costs are now borne primarily by students and by contingent faculty. In the long term, however, the cost of cutting corners on education will be borne by society as a whole as it gradually loses its independent academic sector.

For the good of institutions, of the educational experiences of students, and of the quality of education, the proportion of tenured and tenure-track faculty should be increased. Institutions that are now experimenting with ways to increase the proportion of tenured and tenure-track faculty are finding that the way back is complicated and somewhat treacherous. The guidelines for transition presented here do not offer a complete blueprint; they are intended instead as a beginning diagram or sketch to assist faculty and administrators who have made a commitment to change the structure of their faculty appointment and reappointment processes. Many details described in this report are left to the judgment of faculty members working within their institutional governance structures. Good-faith efforts to strengthen the commitment between institutions and the faculty members who carry out their academic missions will improve the quality of education offered at these institutions while preserving the integrity of the academic profession.

Addendum: Previous Reports on Contingent Faculty

Over the past few decades, the Association and its committees have issued a number of statements and reports on part-time and non-tenure-track faculty. In 1979, at the request of the Committee on Women in the Academic Profession, Committee A on Academic Freedom and Tenure created a summary entitled *Academic Freedom and Due Process for Faculty Members Who Serve Less Than Full Time.* The text of the summary follows:

> The 1940 *Statement of Principles on Academic Freedom and Tenure* calls for academic freedom for all who are engaged in teaching or research, and Committee A's *Recommended Institutional Regulations on Academic Freedom and Tenure* includes provisions for due process for all faculty members, including those who serve less than full time. Regulation 1a specifies that "the terms and conditions of every appointment to the faculty will be stated or confirmed in writing, and a copy of the appointment document will be supplied to the faculty member. Any subsequent extensions or modifications of an appointment, and any special understandings, or any notices incumbent upon either party to provide, will be stated or confirmed in writing and a copy will be given to the faculty member." Regulation 14a, which would be applicable to part-time faculty in any case where Regulations 5 and 6 [on dismissal for cause] may not be, calls for a "statement of reasons and an opportunity to be heard before a duly constituted committee" prior to involuntary termination before the end of a period of appointment. Under Regulation 14b, a part-time faculty member who alleges a violation of academic freedom, or improper discrimination in the context of a nonreappointment, can, upon establishing a

prima facie case before a duly constituted committee, receive a statement of reasons from those responsible for the nonreappointment and an opportunity to be heard by the committee. Under Regulation 15, part-time as well as full-time faculty members may seek redress from an elected faculty grievance committee.[37]

A note following the text of the 1979 summary adds: "In addition to academic freedom and due process, Association policies applicable to faculty members serving less than full time include the statement on *Leaves of Absence for Child-Bearing, Child-Rearing, and Family Emergencies,* which recommends that a temporary reduction in workload be made available to faculty members with family responsibilities; and [the] statement on *Senior Appointments with Reduced Loads* which proposes that 'senior academic appointments and tenure [be open] to persons other than those giving full-time service.' "[38]

Other early statements, such as *The Status of Part-Time Faculty,* issued in 1980 by Committee A, draw a clear line between faculty members who serve less than full time and faculty members who have a workload "equivalent to that of full-time faculty."[39] Faculty members in the latter group are "entitled regardless of . . . specific title, to the rights and privileges of . . . full-time faculty members," including consideration for tenure after a probationary period. Setting aside that group, the 1980 report then focuses on part-time faculty. Citing a "common concern for academic quality," the report recommends that attention be given to "appropriate review of the qualifications of part-time faculty members, their participation in the planning and implementation of the curriculum, their availability to students for advice and counseling, their ability to keep current in their respective fields, and the chilling effect on their teaching which lack of the protections of academic due process may engender." Thus, the 1980 report acknowledges the professional nature of all faculty work and urges that all faculty, part time as well as full time, be included in all aspects of the work of the profession.

The 1980 report also addresses, for the first time, the issue of tenure for part-time faculty, proposing that colleges and universities "consider creating a class of regular part-time faculty members" who could qualify for tenure in less-than-full-time appointments. The 1987 statement *Senior Appointments with Reduced Loads* clarifies that such arrangements might be useful not only for faculty members seeking a reduced workload as a step toward retirement but also for those seeking to balance family and professional responsibilities. The statement recommends that "opportunity should exist for the faculty member to move from a full to a reduced load and back to full-time status, depending on the needs of the individual and the institution."

In 1986, in a report titled *On Full-Time Non-tenure-track Appointments,* Committee A described the efforts of a subcommittee to assess the "current dimensions" of the practice of appointing full-time non-tenure-track faculty and to analyze the adverse implications of the continuing proliferation of these appointments. The 1986 report also addresses the stated reasons for such appointments and their observable effects on higher education. Institutions defend non-tenure-track appointments primarily in terms of cost savings and flexibility, but the report observes that direct savings were possible in the short term and only at an "inordinately high cost to the quality of the entire academic enterprise." The assertion that non-tenure-track faculty appointments were needed for flexibility to meet changing student demand, the subcommittee reported, was belied by the extensive (and, we could say now, continuing and long-term) use of such appointments in core academic courses, especially in the humanities.

The 1986 report notes that the proliferation of non-tenure-track appointments created a divided faculty, in which a large proportion of teachers was not involved in curricular and academic decision making, not supported in scholarship, and neither compensated nor recognized for advising and other services that make up the whole of faculty work. The committee surmises that this situation undermined the attractiveness and economic security of the academic profession, and sent a message that prospective faculty members would be wise to seek careers in commercial and other sectors.

In 1993, the Association adopted as policy *The Status of Non-tenure-track Faculty.* That report, written at a time when about half of all faculty appointments in American higher education were off the tenure track, takes a fresh look at non-tenure-track faculty, both part and full time, as a group. The report catalogues the increase of both kinds of appointments, the exploitation of faculty in such positions, and the accelerating negative effects of these practices on higher education. Several topics are addressed with greater specificity than in previous statements. These include the need for job security, benefits, and opportunities for advancement; the need for participation in governance; and the conversion of part-time appointments to tenure-track positions. The basic premise of the 1993 report is the necessity for the replacement of contingent positions with tenured positions for most faculty. Then, as now, the Association was unwilling to assent to the establishment of a subordinate tier of faculty members, without full status and responsibility within the academy.

Notes

1. "The Status of Non-tenure-track Faculty," *Academe* 79 (July–August 1993): 39–46.

2. Douglas McGray, "Title Wave," *New York Times,* August 4, 2002. McGray notes that "the Army has fewer titles to classify soldiers (twenty-four from private through general) than a typical research university has to classify teachers (forty from teaching fellow to professor emeritus, at Harvard)."

3. Long-standing Association policy determines full-time status by the individual's functions in the institution, not by his or her title. The "1970 Interpretive Comments" to the 1940 "Statement of Principles on Academic Freedom and Tenure" states, "The concept of 'rank of full-time instructor or a higher rank' is intended to include any person who teaches a full-time load, regardless of the teacher's specific title." Many part-time faculty teach at several institutions, so that their aggregate amount of work equals or exceeds the equivalent of a full-time load. Even so, their relationship to each institution is that of a part-time faculty member.

4. For example, instruction in the performance of an unusual musical instrument or in the application of a particular computer program to a specific industry.

5. This report does not address the complexities of "clinical" faculty appointments in disciplines such as law, social work, and health sciences. The Association addressed clinical appointments in medical schools in "Tenure in the Medical School" (1995), in AAUP, *Policy Documents and Reports,* 11th ed. (Baltimore: Johns Hopkins University Press, 2015), 73–78. That report states, in part, "To the extent that a faculty appointment at a medical school resembles a traditional academic appointment, with clearly understood obligations in teaching, research, and service, the burden of proof on the institution is greater to justify making the appointment a non-tenure-track position." This provision may well be applicable to clinical appointments in other disciplines.

6. "Part-Time Instructional Faculty and Staff: Who They Are, What They Do, and What They Think," National Center for Education Statistics (NCES), US Department of Education (http://nces.ed.gov/pubs2002 /2002163u.pdf). See Tables 4, 18, and 31. According to Table 18, part-time instructors rely on income from their academic work for up to 44 percent of their total income. The original source of much of the data used in this statement is the 1999 National Study of Postsecondary Faculty, which may systematically underrepresent the number of part-time faculty. Faculty are included in the survey only when information on them is available through a central institutional list; when

they are available at the same institution for a period of several months, perhaps extending over two terms; and when they can be reached through the institution to complete the survey. Adjunct faculty who teach one or two courses at a time on several different campuses may be unlikely to meet these three conditions.

7. *Policy Documents and Reports*, 387–88.

8. By fall 2011, an estimated 71 percent of all faculty positions were off the tenure track. In community colleges, 70 percent of faculty positions were part time, and 45 percent of full-time positions were off the tenure track (John W. Curtis, *The Employment Status of Instructional Staff Members in Higher Education, Fall 2011*, American Association of University Professors, April 2014: 13, Table 7).

9. "Part-Time Instructional Faculty and Staff," Tables 1 and 12.

10. Martin J. Finkelstein and Jack H. Schuster, "Assessing the Silent Revolution: How Changing Demographics Are Reshaping the Academic Profession," *AAHE Bulletin* (October 2001): 5, Figure 2. A majority of full-time appointments were off the tenure track in 1993, 1995, and 1997, as are virtually all part-time appointments. In a subsequent work, Schuster and Finkelstein documented that more than half of new full-time appointments were off the tenure track from 1993 through 2003, with the proportion of non-tenure-track appointments rising through the period (Jack H. Schuster and Martin J. Finkelstein, *The American Faculty: The Restructuring of Academic Work and Careers* [Baltimore: Johns Hopkins University Press, 2006], 194, Figure 7.1). Figures for 2009 from the US Department of Education indicate that 58 percent of new full-time appointments in that year were off the tenure track.

11. Ibid., 5.

12. "Part-Time Instructional Faculty and Staff," Tables 1 and 12. As of fall 2011, non-tenure-track faculty members composed 40.0 percent of the full-time faculty and 19.4 percent of all faculty members. Part-time faculty composed 51.4 percent of the faculty (John W. Curtis, *The Employment Status of Instructional Staff Members in Higher Education, Fall 2011*, American Association of University Professors, April 2014: 13, Table 7).

13. Finkelstein and Schuster, "Assessing the Silent Revolution," 5.

14. "Part-Time Instructional Faculty and Staff," Table 13. See also John W. Curtis and Saranna Thornton, "Here's the News: The Annual Report on the Economic Status of the Profession, 2012–13," *Academe* 99 (March–April 2013): 4–19.

15. "Part-Time Instructional Faculty and Staff," Table 6. "Full-time faculty" includes tenured, tenure-track, and non-tenure-track faculty. In fall 2011, 52.5 percent of part-time faculty members were women, while women composed 44.2 percent of full-time faculty members (John W. Curtis, *The Employment Status of Instructional Staff Members in Higher Education, Fall 2011*, American Association of University Professors, April 2014: 23, Table 12).

16. Marcia Bellas, *AAUP Faculty Salary and Faculty Distribution Fact Sheet, 2000–01* (2002). In academic year 2012–13, women made up 56 percent of full-time lecturers, 61 percent of instructors, 51 percent of assistant professors, 43 percent of associate professors, and 29 percent of full professors (unpublished analysis from the AAUP "Annual Report on the Economic Status of the Profession," *Academe* 99 [March–April 2013]).

17. "Digest of Education Statistics 2001," NCES, US Department of Education (http://nces.ed.gov/pubs2002/2002130.pdf), Tables 172 and 247. Between fall 1976 and fall 2012, total enrollment in degree-granting institutions grew by 87 percent. Between 1976–77 and 2011–12, the number of bachelor's degrees awarded increased by 80 percent, master's degrees by 67 percent, and doctoral degrees by 78 percent ("Digest of Education Statistics 2013," NCES, US Department of Education [http://nces.ed.gov/programs/digest/], Tables 303.10 and 318.40).

18. "Fall Staff in Postsecondary Institutions, 1997," NCES, US Department of Education (http://nces.ed.gov/pubs2000/2000164.pdf)—committee calculations from the data. Between 1976 and 2011, the number of part-time faculty members increased by 286 percent. From 1976 to 2011, the number of full-time non-tenure-track faculty members grew by 259 percent (John W. Curtis and Saranna Thornton, "Losing Focus: The Annual Report on the Economic Status of the Profession, 2013–14," *Academe* 100 [March–April 2014]: 7, Figure 1).

19. "Part-Time Instructional Faculty and Staff," Table 30.

20. "Digest of Education Statistics 2001," Table 330. Many colleges, including public colleges, sell some of their services locally and internationally. This category may also include fees for the use of facilities, conference income, and the like. A direct comparison with earlier years is difficult, because the categories used for financial reporting have changed. In fiscal year 2011–12, public colleges and universities obtained approximately 22 percent of total revenues from state governments, 21 percent from tuition and fees, and 17 percent from the federal government ("Digest of Education Statistics 2013," Table 333.10).

21. National Commission on the Cost of Higher Education, *Straight Talk about College Costs and Prices* (Washington, DC: Oryx Press, 1998).

22. Ernst Benjamin, "How Over Reliance on Contingent Appointments Diminishes Faculty Involvement in Student Learning," *Peer Review* (February 2002): 4–10. Benjamin discusses studies by Alexander Astin, George Kuh, Ernest Pascarella, and Patrick Terenzini.

23. Ernst Benjamin, "Reappraisal and Implications for Policy and Research" [of excessive reliance on contingent appointments], *New Directions for Higher Education* 123 (October 2003): 79–113. According to Benjamin, full-time contingent faculty spend about the same amount of time on instructional activities as tenured and tenure-track faculty, but for contingent faculty, more of that time is spent in teaching. Thus, the

time available for interaction with students, and for preparation and assessment outside of class, is significantly lower on a per-credit basis than it is for probationary tenure-track faculty. Benjamin's tables are based on data from the 1999 National Study of Postsecondary Faculty and include all work hours, paid and unpaid, attributed to an institution by part-time faculty. For full-time faculty, "nonclassroom instructional time" includes time for grading papers, preparing courses, developing new curricula, advising or supervising students, and working with student organizations or intramural activities.

24. *Policy Documents and Reports*, 190–96.

25. For examples, see "Part-Time Instructional Faculty and Staff," Tables 36–39 and 40–47.

26. Ernst Benjamin, "Variations in the Characteristics of Part-Time Faculty by General Fields of Instruction and Research," *New Directions for Higher Education* 104 (December 1998): 45–59.

27. *Policy Documents and Reports*, 3–12.

28. Benjamin, "Reappraisal and Implications for Policy and Research."

29. The 1940 "Statement" also allowed termination of tenured appointments "in the case of retirement for age," which has now been superseded by federal law.

30. The summary is included in "Previous Reports on Contingent Faculty," at the end of this report. It was originally published in the "Report of Committee A, 1978–79," *Academe* 65 (September 1979): 293–303.

31. "The Status of Non-tenure-track Faculty." Essential benefits include health-care insurance, life insurance, and retirement contributions.

32. *Policy Documents and Reports*, 169.

33. Ibid., 339–46.

34. Office of the Chancellor, California State University, "A Plan to Increase the Percentage of Tenured and Tenure-Track Faculty in the California State University," July 2002. To put this figure in context, in the same year, CSU considered a systemwide computer upgrade that would have cost $160 million.

35. Information on Western Michigan University's contract is drawn from Gary Mathews, "Contract Issues Continue to Percolate and Brew," *WMU-AAUP Advocate* (October 2002); Piper Fogg, "Widening the Tenure Track," *Chronicle of Higher Education*, January 3, 2003; and Article 20 of the WMU-AAUP contract, WMU-AAUP website at http://www.wmuaaup.net/.

36. Benjamin, "Reappraisal and Implications for Policy and Research."

37. The references to specific regulations are to the 1976 "Recommended Institutional Regulations on Academic Freedom and Tenure," *AAUP Bulletin* 62 (August 1976): 184–91. The addition of Regulation 13 in 2007 has both superseded the recommendations here and caused regulations numbered 13 and above to be renumbered as 14 and above. See "Recommended Institutional Regulations on Academic Freedom and Tenure," *Policy Documents and Reports*, 79–90.

38. "Leaves of Absence for Child-Bearing, Child-Rearing, and Family Emergencies" has been superseded by the 2001 "Statement of Principles on Family Responsibilities and Academic Work," *Policy Documents and Reports*, 339–46.

39. *Academe* 67 (February–March 1981): 29–39. Another example is a 1978 Committee A report, "On Full-Time Non-tenure-track Appointments," superseded by the 1986 report cited above. See *AAUP Bulletin* 64 (September 1978): 267–73.

Tenure and Teaching-Intensive Appointments

This report was prepared by a subcommittee of the Committee on Contingency and the Profession. The parent committee approved publication of this final report in 2010. The full report contained two appendices, which have been omitted here. Statistical information in the report was updated in 2014.

I. The Collapsing Faculty Infrastructure

The past four decades have seen a failure of the social contract in faculty employment. The tenure system was designed as a big tent, aiming to unite a faculty of tremendously diverse interests within a system of common professional values, standards, and mutual responsibilities.[1] It aimed to secure reasonable compensation and to protect academic freedom through continuous employment.[2] Financial and intellectual security enabled the faculty to carry out the public trust in both teaching and research, sustaining a rigorous system of professional peer scrutiny in hiring, evaluation, and promotion. Today the tenure system has all but collapsed.

Before 1970, as today, most full-time faculty appointments were teaching-intensive, featuring teaching loads of nine hours or more per week. Nearly all of those full-time teaching-intensive positions were on the tenure track. This meant that most faculty who spent most of their time teaching were also campus and professional citizens, with clear roles in shared governance and access to support for research or professional activity.[3]

Today, most faculty positions are still teaching intensive, and many of those teaching-intensive positions are still tenurable. In fact, the proportion of teaching-intensive to research-intensive appointments has risen sharply.[4] However, the majority of teaching-intensive positions have been shunted outside of the tenure system. This has in most cases meant a dramatic shift from "teaching-intensive" appointments to "teaching-only" appointments, featuring a faculty with attenuated relationships to campus and disciplinary peers. This seismic shift from "teaching-intensive" faculty within the big tent of tenure to "teaching-only" faculty outside of it has had severe consequences for students as well as faculty themselves, producing lower levels of campus engagement across the board and a rising service burden for the shrinking core of tenurable faculty.

The central question we have to face in connection with this historic change is real and unavoidable: Should more classroom teaching be done by faculty supported by the rigorous peer scrutiny of the tenure system? Most of the evidence says yes, and a host of diverse voices agree. This view brings together students, faculty, legislators, the AAUP, and even many college and university administrators. At some institutions, however, particularly at large research universities, the tenure system has already been warped to the purpose of creating a multitier faculty. In order to avoid this, as E. Gordon Gee of Ohio State University puts it, individuals must have available to them "multiple ways to salvation" inside the tenure system. Tenure was not designed as a merit badge for research-intensive faculty or as a fence to exclude those with teaching-intensive commitments.

By 2007, almost 70 percent of faculty members were employed off the tenure track.[5] Many institutions use contingent faculty appointments throughout their programs; some retain a tenurable faculty in their traditional or flagship programs while staffing others—such as branch campuses, online offerings, and overseas campuses—almost entirely with faculty on contingent appointments. Faculty serving on a contingent basis generally work at significantly lower wages, often without health coverage and other benefits, and in positions that do not incorporate all aspects of university life or the full range of faculty rights and responsibilities. The tenure track has not vanished, but it has ceased to be the norm. This means that the majority of faculty work in subprofessional conditions, often without basic protections for academic freedom.

Some of these appointments, particularly in science and medicine, are research intensive or research only, and the faculty in these appointments often work under extremely troubling conditions. However, the overwhelming majority of non-tenure-track appointments are teaching only or teaching intensive. Non-tenure-track faculty and graduate students teach the majority of classes at many institutions, commonly at shockingly low rates of pay.

This compensation scheme has turned the professoriate into an irrational economic choice, denying the overwhelming majority of individuals the opportunity to consider college teaching as a career. This form of economic discrimination is deeply unfair, both to teachers and to their students; institutions that serve the economically marginalized and the largest proportion of minority students, such as community colleges, typically employ the largest numbers of non-tenurable faculty.[6] As the AAUP's 2009 Report on the Economic Status of the Profession points out, the erosion of the tenure track rests on the "fundamentally flawed premise" that faculty "represent only a cost, rather than the institution's primary resource." Hiring faculty on the basis of the lowest labor cost and without professional working conditions "represents a disinvestment in the nation's intellectual capital precisely at the time when innovation and insight are most needed."

A broad and growing front of research shows that the system of permanently temporary faculty appointments has negative consequences for student learning.[7] Mindful that their working conditions are their students' learning conditions, many faculty holding contingent appointments struggle to shield students from the consequences of an increasingly unprofessional workplace. Faculty on contingent appointments frequently pay for their own computers, phones, and office supplies, and dip into their own wallets for journal subscriptions and travel to conferences to stay current in their fields. Some struggle to preserve academic freedom. However heroic, these individual acts are no substitute for professional working conditions.

We are at a tipping point. Campuses that overuse contingent appointments show higher levels of disengagement and disaffection among faculty, even those with more secure positions.[8] We see a steadily shrinking minority, faculty with tenure, as increasingly unable to protect academic freedom, professional autonomy, and the faculty role in governance for themselves—much less for the contingent majority. At many institutions, the proportion of faculty with tenure is below 10 percent, and too often tenure has become the privilege of those who are, have been, or soon will be administrators.

II. It Is Time to Stabilize the Faculty
In opposition to this trend, a new consensus is emerging that it is time to stabilize the crumbling faculty infrastructure. Concerned legislators and some academic administrators have joined faculty associations in calling for dramatic reductions in the reliance on contingent appointments, commonly urging a maximum of 25 percent.[9] Across the country, various forms of stabilization have been attempted by administrators and legislators, proposed by faculty associations, or negotiated at the bargaining table.

Many stabilization efforts focus on winning employment security for full-time faculty serving on contingent appointments, a fast-growing class of appointment. In some cases, such positions effectively replace tenure lines; in others, they represent a more welcome consolidation of part-time contingent appointments. Increasingly, however, teachers and researchers in both full- and part-time contingent positions are seeking and receiving provisions for greater stability of employment: longer appointment terms, the expectation or right of continuing employment, provisions for orderly layoff, and other rights of seniority. These rights have been codified in a variety of contract language, ranging from "instructor tenure" to "continuing" or "senior lectureship" to certificates of continuing employment.

As faculty hired into contingent positions seek and obtain greater employment security, often through collective bargaining, it is becoming clear that academic tenure and employment security are not reducible to each other. A potentially crippling development in these arrangements is that many—while improving on the entirely insecure positions they replace—offer limited conceptions of academic citizenship and service, few protections for academic freedom, and little opportunity for professional growth. These arrangements commonly involve minimal professional peer scrutiny in hiring, evaluation, and promotion.

III. Conversion to Tenure Is the Best Way to Stabilize the Faculty
The Committee on Contingency and the Profession believes that the best way to stabilize the faculty infrastructure is to bundle the employment and economic securities that activist faculty on contingent appointments are already winning for themselves with the rigorous scrutiny of the tenure system. The ways in which contingent teachers and researchers are hired, evaluated, and promoted often bypass the faculty entirely and

are generally less rigorous than the intense review applied to faculty in tenurable positions.

Several noteworthy forms of conversion to tenure have been implemented or proposed at different kinds of institutions. The most successful forms are those that retain experienced, qualified, and effective faculty, as opposed to those that convert positions while leaving behind the faculty currently in them. As the AAUP emphasized in its 2003 policy document *Contingent Appointments and the Academic Profession*, stabilization of positions can and should be accomplished without negative consequences for current faculty and their students.

The best practice for institutions of all types is to convert the status of contingent appointments to appointments eligible for tenure with only minor changes in job description. This means that faculty hired contingently with teaching as the major component of their workload will become tenured or tenure-eligible primarily on the basis of successful teaching.[10] (Similarly, faculty serving on contingent appointments with research as the major component of their workload may become tenured or eligible for tenure primarily on the basis of successful research.) In the long run, however, a balance is desirable. Professional development and research activities support strong teaching, and a robust system of shared governance depends upon the participation of all faculty, so even teaching-intensive tenure-eligible positions should include service and appropriate forms of engagement in research or the scholarship of teaching.

In some instances faculty serving on a contingent basis will prefer a major change in their job description with conversion to tenure eligibility. For example, some faculty in teaching-intensive positions might prefer to have research as a larger component of their appointments. While the employer should not impose this major change in job description on the faculty member seeking tenure eligibility, the AAUP encourages the employer to accommodate the faculty member. However, faculty themselves should not perpetuate the false impression that tenure was invented as a merit badge for research-intensive appointments.

Finally, stabilizing the faculty infrastructure means substantially transforming the circumstances of teachers and researchers serving part time (about half of the faculty nationwide). Many faculty members serving part time might prefer full-time employment. Stabilizing this group means consolidating part-time work into tenure-eligible, full-time, and usually teaching-intensive positions—through attrition, not layoffs.

For faculty who wish to remain in the profession on a part-time basis over the long term, *we recommend as best practice fractional positions, including fully proportional pay, that are eligible for tenure and benefits, with proportional expectations for service and professional development.*[11]

The proliferation of contingent appointments will continue if institutions convert select appointments to the tenure track while continuing to hire off the tenure track elsewhere. *We urge that conversion plans include discontinuance of any new off-track hiring, except where such hires are genuinely for special appointments of brief duration.*

Tenure was conceived as a right rather than a privilege. As the 1940 *Statement of Principles* observed, the intellectual and economic securities of the tenure system must be the bedrock of any effort by higher education to fulfill its obligations to students and society.

Notes

1. With respect to faculty tenure, the Association holds to the following tenets: (1) with the exception of brief special appointments, all full-time faculty appointments should be either tenured or probationary for tenure ("Statement on Procedural Standards in the Renewal or Nonrenewal of Faculty Appointments," AAUP, *Policy Documents and Reports*, 11th ed. [Baltimore: Johns Hopkins University Press, 2015], 94–98); (2) the probationary period should not exceed seven years (1940 "Statement of Principles on Academic Freedom and Tenure"); (3) tenure can be granted at any professional rank (1970 Interpretive Comment 5 on the 1940 "Statement"); (4) tenure-line positions can be part time as well as full time (Regulation 13 of the "Recommended Institutional Regulations on Academic Freedom and Tenure," *Policy Documents and Reports*, 79–90); (5) faculty appointments, including part-time appointments in most cases, should incorporate all aspects of university life and the full range of faculty responsibilities ("Contingent Appointments and the Academic Profession," ibid., 170–85); and (6) termination or nonrenewal of an appointment requires affordance of requisite academic due process ("Recommended Institutional Regulations," ibid., 79–90).

2. The 1940 "Statement of Principles on Academic Freedom and Tenure" characterizes the tenure system as a "means to certain ends; specifically: (1) freedom of teaching and research and of extramural activities, and (2) a sufficient degree of economic security to make the profession attractive to men and women of ability. Freedom and economic security, hence tenure, are indispensable to the success of an institution in fulfilling its obligations to its students and to society." That statement has now been endorsed by more than two hundred academic organizations.

3. As of 1970, roughly three-fourths of all faculty were in the tenure stream and 78 percent of all faculty

were full-time; in 1969, only 3.2 percent of full-time appointments were nontenurable. Among all full-time appointments in 1969, teaching-intensive faculty (with nine or more hours a week of teaching) outnumbered research-intensive faculty (with six or fewer hours a week of teaching) in a ratio of 1.5:1, accounting for 60 percent of the total number of full-time appointments. See Jack H. Schuster and Martin J. Finkelstein, *The American Faculty: The Restructuring of Academic Work and Careers* (Baltimore: Johns Hopkins University Press, 2006), 41 (Table 3.2, "American Faculty by Employment Status, 1970–2003"), 174 (Table 6.1, "Non-tenure-eligible Faculty, 1969–1998,"), 97 (Table 4.4, "Ratio of High to Low Teaching Loads among Full-Time Faculty, 1969–1998").

4. By 1998, among full-time faculty, the ratio of teaching-intensive appointments to research-intensive ones had risen significantly from 1.5:1 to 2:1, or from about 60 percent to 67 percent of the total. This was accomplished, as Schuster and Finkelstein document, "largely by the resort to 'teaching only' appointments" (99). However, the percentage of all faculty who were in teaching-intensive appointments rose much more sharply, largely because of a massive increase in teaching-intensive part-time appointments (ibid.).

5. "On the Brink: The Annual Report on the Economic Status of the Profession, 2008–09," *Academe* 95 (March–April 2009): 24 (Figure 4, "Trends in Faculty Status, 1975–2007").

6. *American Faculty*, 43–47.

7. Some recent and notable research articles on this topic are Ernst Benjamin, "How Over-Reliance upon Contingent Appointments Diminishes Faculty Involvement in Student Learning," *Peer Review* 5 (Fall 2002): 4–10; Ronald Ehrenberg and Liang Zhang, "Do Tenured and Tenure-Track Faculty Matter?," *Journal of Human Resources* 40 (Summer 2005): 647–59; Paul Umbach, "How Effective Are They? Exploring the Impact of Contingent Faculty on Undergraduate Education," *Review of Higher Education* 30 (Winter 2007): 91–123; M. Kevin Eagan Jr. and Audrey J. Jaeger, "Closing the Gate: Part-Time Faculty Instruction in Gatekeeper Courses and First-Year Persistence," *New Directions for Teaching and Learning* 115 (Fall 2008): 39–53; Audrey J. Jaeger, "Contingent Faculty and Student Outcomes," *Academe* 94 (November–December 2008): 42–43; Paul D. Umbach, "The Effects of Part-Time Faculty Appointments on Instructional Techniques and Commitment to Teaching," paper presented at the 33rd Annual Conference of the Association for the Study of Higher Education, Jacksonville, November 5–8, 2008; A. J. Jaeger and M. K. Eagan, "Unintended Consequences: Effects of Exposure to Part-Time Faculty on Associate's Degree Completion," *Community College Review* 36 (January

2009): 167–94; M. K. Eagan and A. J. Jaeger, "Part-Time Faculty at Community Colleges: Implications for Student Persistence and Transfer," *Research in Higher Education* 50 (March 2009): 168–88. These newspaper articles provide a summary of current research: Karin Fischer, "Speaker Says Adjuncts May Harm Students," *Chronicle of Higher Education*, November 18, 2005; Scott Jaschik, "Evaluating the Adjunct Impact," *Inside Higher Ed*, November 6, 2008; David Moltz, "The Part-Time Impact," *Inside Higher Ed*, November 16, 2009. For a different point of view, see Scott Jaschik, "What Adjunct Impact?," *Inside Higher Ed*, May 3, 2010.

8. P. Umbach and R. Wells, "Understanding the Individual and Institutional Factors That Affect Part-Time Community College Faculty Satisfaction," paper presented at the 2009 Annual Meeting of the American Educational Research Association, San Diego, April 13–17, 2009.

9. See, for example, California Assembly Bill 1725, http://www.eric.ed.gov/ERICWebPortal/recordDetail ?accno=ED425764, and Assembly Concurrent Resolution 73, http://www.leginfo.ca.gov/pub/01-02/bill/asm /ab_0051-0100/acr_73_bill_20010924_chaptered.pdf, as well as the American Federation of Teachers' Faculty and College Excellence (FACE) campaign, http://www .aftface.org.

10. For part-time contingent faculty, the AAUP's 2006 addition to its "Recommended Institutional Regulations on Academic Freedom and Tenure" (*Policy Documents and Reports*, 86, Regulation 13) urges that "prior to consideration of reappointment beyond a seventh year, part-time faculty members who have taught at least twelve courses or six terms within those seven years . . . be provided a comprehensive review with a view toward (1) appointment with part-time tenure where such exists, (2) appointment with part-time continuing service, or (3) non-reappointment. Those appointed with tenure shall be afforded the same procedural safeguards as full-time tenured faculty." The 2003 statement "Contingent Appointments and the Academic Profession" recommends, "The experience and accomplishments of faculty members who have served in contingent positions at the institution should be credited in determining the appropriate length and character of a probationary period for tenure in the converted position."

11. At least since the publication of its 1980 statement "The Status of Part-Time Faculty," *Academe* 67 (February–March 1981): 29–39, the AAUP has recommended that colleges consider creating a class of "regular part-time faculty members, consisting of individuals who, as their professional career, share the teaching, research, and administrative duties customary for faculty at their institution . . . [and] the opportunity to achieve tenure and the rights it confers."

On Full-Time Non-tenure-track Appointments

This report, prepared by a subcommittee of the Association's Committee A on Academic Freedom and Tenure, was approved by Committee A in June 1986. Statistical information in the report was updated in 2014.

Introduction

Regulation 1b of the Association's *Recommended Institutional Regulations on Academic Freedom and Tenure*[1] provides that, "with the exception of special appointments clearly limited to a brief association with the institution, and reappointments of retired faculty members on special conditions, all full-time faculty appointments are of two kinds: (1) probationary appointments; (2) appointments with continuous tenure." As the authors of Committee A's 1978 report *On Full-Time Non-tenure-track Appointments* concluded,

> We think that the very limited exceptions allowed by Regulation 1b are the most that should be allowed. The teacher with tenure is a teacher whose service can be terminated only for adequate cause; and we think that every full-time teacher should either have that status or be a candidate for it—save for those who fall under the exceptions allowed by Regulation 1b, in particular, those who are visitors, or temporary replacements, or for whose subjects the institution in good faith expects to have only a short-term need.[2]

Since 1978, regularly funded fixed-term, annually renewable, or indefinite full-time tenure-ineligible appointments (some of them with rather eccentric or unorthodox titles), running parallel to, and in many cases replacing, traditional tenure-track positions, have remained a persistent phenomenon in American colleges and universities. At some institutions and in certain disciplinary fields the number of faculty members appointed to such non-tenure-track positions is continuing to grow. The AAUP has recognized that these non-tenure-track appointments do considerable damage both to principles of academic freedom and tenure and to the quality of our academic institutions—not to mention the adverse consequences for the individuals serving in such appointments.

The subcommittee's task has been to examine and assess the current dimensions of this staffing practice and the arguments made in its support; to review the findings and recommendations of the 1978 subcommittee report on this subject; and to analyze the implications that the continuing proliferation of these appointments may have for the future of higher education.

The Scope and Extent of the Problem

Informed discussion of the issues raised by the use of non-tenure-track positions must begin with an analysis of the scope and extent of the problem. Looking at the academic profession as a whole, we have examined data on individual faculty *members* as well as on *positions* at institutions that, taken together, provide an overview of the current situation. The data on *persons* come from a sample survey of 5,000 faculty members conducted by the Carnegie Foundation for the Advancement of Teaching in spring 1984 (a similar national survey was also conducted in 1975). The data on *positions*, collected in connection with the preparation of the AAUP's Annual Report on the Economic Status of the Profession, comprise some 163,000 full-time appointments for each of the past two academic years (1984–86) at approximately 800 academic institutions that provided tenure information. According to the Carnegie survey, between 10.6 percent and 12.6 percent of full-time faculty were not on a tenure track (nor "covered for job security" by a collective bargaining agreement) in the spring of 1984.[3] The AAUP data indicate that nearly 10 percent of all full-time positions included in the surveys were non-tenure-track.[4]

The data on hand reveal increasing uniformity in the number of non-tenure-track positions across ranks and types of institution, suggesting that the practice may well be on the way toward becoming entrenched. Indeed, according to the most recent available data from the National Research Council, between 25 percent and 40 percent of all first-time junior faculty appointments in 1981 were to non-tenure-eligible positions.[5] In addition, data from the 1975 and

1984 Carnegie surveys suggest that most types of institutions experienced an increase (often quite substantial) in the proportion of nontenured faculty members who were serving in a full-time capacity but were not eligible for tenure.

The available data show that among women included in the 1984–85 AAUP compensation survey, 16.5 percent, or 6,816, served in non-tenure-track positions. These data suggest that between 40 and 45 percent of all non-tenure-track positions surveyed were filled by women—a striking statistic when one considers that women held only 25 percent of the total number of full-time faculty positions covered in the survey. Of the more than 8,000 positions held by women at the instructor and nonprofessorial ranks, more than half were in non-tenure-track positions.[6]

The subcommittee has examined several recent studies that surveyed the incidence of full-time faculty members serving in non-tenure-track appointments. A 1984 American Council on Education survey of full-time faculty in the humanities found that the number and proportion of "core humanities" faculty outside the tenure system has increased, while the proportion eligible for tenure, but not yet tenured, has fallen. Only 40 percent of the new "core humanities" appointments made in the 1982–83 academic year were to tenured or tenure-track positions. In political science, according to an American Political Science Association survey, over 30 percent of all new full-time faculty members during the 1983–84 and 1984–85 academic years received non-tenure-track appointments.

Although data for other fields are hard to come by, the creation and expansion of non-tenure-eligible positions are clearly not limited to faculty in the humanities and social sciences. They are also quite common in the natural sciences and in rapidly expanding fields like computer science. In many professional schools as well, particularly in the health sciences and in schools of law, new appointments to tenure-ineligible clinical positions appear to be the norm rather than the exception.

In sum, the available data support the view that a far-from-negligible class of more or less permanent "temporary" faculty, a disproportionate number of them women, has become an established feature of American higher education.

Stated Reasons for the Use of Non-tenure-track Appointments

Numerous forms of appointment exist for faculty members who serve in non-tenure-track positions. The authors of the Association's 1978 report

usefully distinguished three principal types of non-tenure-track teachers:

> The first hold indefinitely renewable appointments: the faculty members are appointed for one or more years and are told that their appointments may be renewed—no limit is placed on the number of possible renewals. The second hold "limited renewable" appointments: the faculty members are told that their (usually one-year) appointments may be renewed so many times only. . . . The third occupy "folding chairs": the faculty member's initial appointments (usually for two or three years) are explicitly terminal—no renewal is possible under any circumstances.

The data reported in the surveys cited above do not separate out or distinguish among these various kinds of tenure-ineligible appointments. Whatever the type of non-tenure-track position utilized, however—whether renewable indefinitely, renewable until a stated maximum duration is reached, or fixed-term "folding chair"—the same general arguments have been advanced over the years in justification of these appointments, above all the flexibility they afford the institution in terms of financial investment and programmatic commitments.

Faced with the possibility (and the reality) of shifts in student interests and declining enrollments as well as cutbacks in federal, state, and foundation support, colleges and universities have looked to less costly alternatives to traditional staffing patterns and have seized upon the full-time non-tenure-track position as one of the most convenient of these alternatives. The argument is frequently made that, because individuals appointed to such positions are typically engaged only to teach lower-level classes and thus have attenuated responsibilities as compared with tenure-track faculty members who are also expected to do research and institutional service, the institution is justified in paying them lower salaries and/or giving them heavier teaching loads. Additional savings can accrue by not providing non-tenure-track faculty with normal merit pay increases and fringe benefits—such as institutional research grants, travel subsidies, professional meeting allowances, and sabbaticals. In the case of other benefits (e.g., pensions), there may be a waiting period before the individual attains eligibility. Moreover, most non-tenure-track faculty usually do not achieve the higher salaries based on seniority and promotion through the ranks that tenure-track and tenured faculty would; their opportunities for advancement tend to be limited even if they are reappointed for many years. In addition, if the non-tenure-track faculty are not engaged in research, there are significant ancillary cost savings: fewer demands on the institution for secretarial and research assistance, library and computer facilities, equipment, and office and laboratory space.

Along with financial savings, institutions have found the use of full-time non-tenure-track appointments attractive for their promised contribution to administrative and programmatic flexibility. Colleges and universities can cut or transfer positions without conforming with the standards for notice or the normal procedures for evaluation of performance that are required for regular probationary faculty. New programs can be instituted without requiring a long-term commitment to funding a particular faculty member whose skills and expertise may not be needed should the innovation prove to be of only transient interest. An institution thus can explore student demand for a discipline or field not currently represented among the tenured or tenure-track faculty. The classification of positions as tenure ineligible also enables colleges and universities that are concerned that too high a percentage of the faculty holds tenure to keep down the number of those who enter the tenured ranks.

A complementary argument is that as regular full-time positions are vacated in traditional fields, full-time slots should be filled only on a non-tenure-track basis, because either declining enrollments may be expected in the particular field or expanding enrollments may occur in other fields. It is argued that in fields of declining enrollments, especially where an oversupply of potential faculty appointees exists, the institution does not need to offer very attractive positions. Conversely, in fields where there is a shortage of faculty and high student demand, it is argued either that no one in those fields needs long-term security or that no one really qualified is available, and thus that the position should be filled only on a temporary basis with whoever can be found.

Non-tenure-track appointments do indeed appear to afford an institution greater flexibility. They carry no continued institutional commitment to the support of a program or to the employment of an individual, no matter how excellent either might be. Notwithstanding the oft-made assertion that non-tenure-track appointments are being used primarily to enable institutions to hedge their long-term support for certain positions as opposed to particular individuals, however, the subcommittee doubts that "flexibility" is actually an objective in many non-tenure-

track appointments that are currently being made. In fact, a substantial proportion of these appointments are being made in fields that are central to the institution's academic program, with assignment to courses in which continued enrollment is virtually guaranteed. In addition, we must question whether any real flexibility is achieved when a significant number of those who serve in non-tenure-track positions are reappointed indefinitely year after year—attaining de facto tenure without a formal judgment about their qualifications ever having been made.

Adverse Effects of These Appointments

It seems clear that the expanded use of full-time non-tenure-track appointments can be an expedient answer to fiscal and enrollment problems facing colleges and universities—if saving money is the key consideration. But, in the judgment of this subcommittee, the savings realized are at an inordinately high cost to the quality of the entire academic enterprise. In the remainder of this report we turn to an examination of the serious adverse repercussions of non-tenure-track appointments for individual faculty members, for scholarship and learning, for students, and for institutions of higher learning themselves. In the discussion that follows, the subcommittee has relied upon a variety of sources, some more impressionistic than others, but we have confidence in the accuracy of the picture that has emerged.

1. *Effects on the Non-tenure-track Faculty Members Themselves.* The most immediate adverse impact of non-tenure-track appointments, of course, is on those occupying these positions. What seems to have developed at many colleges and universities in the United States is a class of insecure full-time faculty members whose status is inferior to that of both their tenure-eligible and their tenured colleagues and whose role in some respects does not differ from that of teaching assistants. They find themselves frequently at the margins of departmental and institutional life. In many cases they are neither required nor expected—and often not permitted—to advise students, to play a role in faculty personnel and budgetary matters, or to participate in the development of curricula and the formulation and implementation of academic policy. They are, as the 1978 report on this subject observed, denied "full and equal faculty membership irrespective of the nature of the service they have given and irrespective of the professional excellence of that service." They tend to receive less desirable teaching assignments, larger classes, and heavier teaching loads. Their compensation tends to

remain low, no matter how well they perform their circumscribed role. Indeed, a rigorous periodic review of their performance may not occur at all.

The appointment of full-time faculty members with attenuated responsibilities serves to develop an underclass, precluded from participation in faculty governance by rule and, in too many cases, from scholarly pursuits and other professional activities by necessity. These faculty members are faced with precarious employment prospects, and hence an uncertain professional future, and are generally without the time, status, and opportunity—or the rewards—to develop themselves professionally as teachers and scholars. Because many of them are appointed to "teach-only" positions, they cannot develop the habits of the professional academic, especially the regular and ongoing pursuit of new knowledge and the periodic revision of their courses. They are often forced to endure recurrent slights from their senior colleagues, who, in the words of one non-tenure-track appointee, "seem to take it for granted that people who accept temporary appointments are somehow deficient or suspect academically."[7] They frequently work in unprofessional and "anti-professional" conditions, relatively cut off from collegial stimulation and support, disconnected from other members of the profession (and the discipline) beyond the department, and lacking both access to institutional resources necessary for building a research career and the incentive or the pressure to become productive scholars. Many are overworked and are necessarily distracted by the constant, time-consuming (and expensive) preoccupation of pursuing their next position. Even those with relatively long-term contracts, who stay in one place for an extended period and are thus able to avoid the disruptions in their work and their lives that attend frequent moves, rarely have opportunities for research, because of heavy teaching loads. They have little in the way of research and other assistance, facilities, or travel money; at some institutions they cannot serve as principal investigator or project director on a grant, even in those cases where research is part of their academic responsibilities. They are rarely eligible for sabbaticals or even for leaves without pay for professional development.

Individuals who hold indefinitely renewable appointments and who function like regular and ongoing full-time faculty members, but who have no prospect of tenure because of the way their position happens to be defined, serve with their academic freedom in continuous jeopardy. As the authors of the Association's 1978 report observed,

"The teachers who must go, hat in hand, every year (or every two years, or every three years) indefinitely into the future, to ask if they may stay, are not teachers who can feel free to speak and write the truth as they see it." Not surprisingly, the more cautious among them are likely to avoid controversy in their classes or with the deans and department heads on whose good will they are dependent for periodic reappointment. The institution may express its commitment to protect their academic freedom, but to those whose appointment may not be renewed solely at the administration's discretion such a commitment may seem of little value—and best not tested. Moreover, as the numbers of non-tenure-track faculty members increase, their freedom is placed in greater jeopardy. The contagion of insecurity restricts unorthodox thinking, while the rising number of non-tenure-track faculty reduces the cadre of those faculty members—notably those with tenure—who are uninhibited in advocating changes in accepted ideas and in the policies and programs of the institutions at which they serve.

2. *Effects on Students and the Learning Process.* As one critic has observed, the extensive use of full-time non-tenure-track appointments "not only compromises individual working lives and individual careers, but [also] contributes to the dysfunctioning of our colleges and universities as organizations."[8] At a time marked by calls for excellence and more rigorous standards in higher education, the abuse of non-tenure-track appointments can undermine academic standards and lead to the erosion of the quality of undergraduate education. It is difficult to develop a coherent curriculum, maintain uniform standards for evaluating students' performance, or establish continuity between and among courses when major academic responsibilities are divided among "transient" and regular faculty, especially when they have relatively little interaction with one another. Students are denied a stable learning environment and consistent quality instruction by continuous "rotating-out" of faculty. Temporary faculty are less likely to be deeply concerned about or interested in the future of the institution that currently employs them, thus contributing to an institutional environment that discourages students' involvement in learning outside the classroom. Even if these faculty members are interested or concerned, and many are, they may not have the time or the opportunity to develop an institutional memory. They are also less likely to have the time—or the inclination—to direct their creative energies into innovative approaches to teaching or to keep abreast of current develop-

ments in their field. Students are likely to be shortchanged in still other ways. Non-tenure-track appointees tend to be assigned to lower-division, undergraduate teaching, often in large lecture classes, and consigned to nothing but routine pedagogy, to their systematic or total exclusion from other courses and levels of courses. According to one observer, "assigning [temporary] faculty to introductory-level courses often creates divisions within a department: those who teach low-prestige 'service' courses to freshmen and sophomores, and those who teach high-prestige upper-division and graduate courses. Such a division implies that the professional standing of the [regular] faculty is unnecessary for teaching 'service' courses," that is, courses that introduce students to an academic discipline.[9] This practice denies freshmen and sophomores the best possible instruction from regular faculty members; compromises academic standards; and raises questions about how seriously a particular department or an entire institution views its teaching function. It is also self-defeating, because the service courses often attract (or repel) potential candidates for advanced courses in the discipline. There is a pressing need for energetic, dedicated, and respected teachers to staff introductory classes in which students can learn the critical thinking and writing skills they must have to succeed in college and beyond. According to the report issued by the National Institute of Education (NIE) Study Group on the Conditions of Excellence in American Higher Education, *Involvement in Learning: Realizing the Potential of American Higher Education*,[10] "When most freshmen courses are taught by low-paid, low-status instructors, students quickly get the message that the department cares little about the large and diverse group of students in its lower-division courses." The NIE report goes on to recommend that "colleges assign as many of their finest instructors as possible to courses [that have] large numbers of first-year students."

We question whether the intellectual mission of a college or university is well served when the institution asserts that certain basic courses are indispensable for a liberal education but then assigns responsibility for those courses to faculty members who are deemed replaceable and unnecessary to the institution. Indeed, we believe that an institution reveals a certain indifference to its academic mission when it removes much of the basic teaching in required core courses from the purview of the regular professoriate. Far from "realizing the potential of American higher education" (the goal of the NIE report), this practice is virtually guaranteed to erode the quality and cohesiveness of a college's academic programs and to make the institution less attractive to prospective students.

3. *Effects on Institutional Morale and Academic Governance.* The presence of large numbers of temporary faculty members who must anxiously concern themselves from year to year with their status within the institution and the profession is hard on morale—theirs and that of everyone around them. In addition, for the institution as a whole the excessive use of non-tenure-track appointments, by creating a divided, two-class faculty, erodes collegiality and sound governance practices. As we have seen, temporary appointees are not fully integrated into the life of the institution: they are often treated like second-class citizens, mere "contract workers," disenfranchised from collegiate and departmental governance and often isolated from their colleagues.

The fact that many of their colleagues are running so fast just to stay in place in dead-end jobs also affects the current generation of tenure-track faculty members. More of the student advising, committee work, and other administrative duties will fall on them if their non-tenure-track colleagues have attenuated responsibilities and are excluded from the governance process. These burdens impinge upon their time for research and professional development. Moreover, the atmosphere will be less generally supportive of scholarly pursuits, to everyone's loss.

4. *Effects on the Future of the Profession.* Professors Howard R. Bowen and Jack H. Schuster, authors of the recently published book, *American Professors: A National Resource Imperiled*, state that their study was prompted by concern about the ability of "the higher education community . . . to recruit and retain excellent faculty not only in the immediate future but also over the next twenty-five years, when the replacement of the vast majority of the present faculties will be necessary."[11] That task, involving the recruitment of some 500,000 new faculty members, will not be an easy one, if recent experience is any guide. The NIE's report on excellence notes that the proportion of entering college freshmen planning to become college teachers dropped from 1.8 percent in 1966 to .25 percent in 1982, an 89 percent decline that, in the words of the report, "bodes ill for the future of higher education." Bowen and Schuster point to the fact that "an increasing proportion of doctoral candidates are finding employment in nonacademic industries and professions"; in particular, "higher education has become a steadily less

attractive magnet . . . [for] exceptionally talented people such as Rhodes Scholars, members of Phi Beta Kappa, and honor graduates of prestigious institutions." Bowen and Schuster also "see great danger of a steady and growing drain of the ablest people now in the profession," for they are finding significantly more lucrative and professionally more rewarding and challenging career options that will utilize their considerable skills to a greater degree. The increasing incidence and abuse of non-tenure-track appointments, at the very time when many of the brightest and most talented young men and women are abandoning any thought of pursuing a career in higher education, runs counter to efforts to "recruit, encourage, and develop talents of the highest caliber" and may well contribute to the growing flight from the profession of disappointed and frustrated junior faculty and eventually to a critical shortage of qualified college faculty members in the next generation. Given all the other ways in which colleges and universities are gradually losing their power to compete for current and future faculty talent, the continuing proliferation of these temporary positions—filled by underpaid instructors with low status and no job security—seems shortsighted and counterproductive, "undermin[ing] the attractiveness of careers in higher education both to incumbents and to potential new entrants," who may be irretrievably lost to the professoriate.[12]

Bowen and Schuster have cited the "concern of faculty [with] the tendency of colleges and universities to shift institutional risk to faculty members by resorting to expedients that undermine faculty career opportunities. One of these is to employ an increasing proportion of non-tenure-track faculty. . . . All of these practices tend to impair the attractiveness of the profession to younger faculty and to prospective faculty members."

According to the NIE study, "Faculty are the core of the academic work force, and their status, morale, collegiality, and commitment to their institutions are critical to student learning. When we allow support for such a critical component of the enterprise to erode to the point at which the profession itself has become less attractive to our brightest students, we are compromising the future of higher learning in America."

Institutions of higher education have a responsibility to nurture talent, but the continued widespread use of non-tenure-track appointments may well destroy the careers of young faculty members, reduce the attractiveness of the profession for those fortunate enough to be able to enter it in the first place, undermine academic tenure, and threaten academic freedom. The general academic community—administrators, trustees, and faculty members alike—has a shared responsibility to foster, not to stifle, the development of a new generation of talented young scholars willing and able to fill the positions that will become available in the decades ahead.

Conclusions

The dangers to academia that were discussed in the Association's 1978 report *On Full-Time Non-tenure-track Appointments* have been shown in recent years to be extensive and serious. Higher education has come to rely increasingly on the services of faculty members who hold appointments in full-time, regularly funded positions that may be renewed indefinitely from year to year but provide no expectation of tenure after the successful completion of a fixed period of probationary service. The persistence, and in some cases expansion, of this class of faculty members, especially where they have teaching responsibilities at the core of an institution's regular academic program, jeopardizes the foundations upon which the basic 1940 *Statement of Principles on Academic Freedom and Tenure* rests. Individuals who are offered full-time service only on non-tenure-track lines lack the financial, intellectual, and pedagogical security needed for the profession to be an attractive career choice for young scholars. Moreover, and of even greater importance, faculty members who hold such positions lack the security without which academic freedom and the right to pursue one's own contributions in research and teaching are but illusions.

Like the authors of the Association's statement *On the Imposition of Tenure Quotas*, this subcommittee recognizes that a "sound academic program needs elements not only of continuity but also of flexibility, which is served by the continuing opportunity to recruit new persons and to pursue new academic emphases." At the same time, however, we share the concerns expressed in that statement regarding the too-facile invocation of considerations of flexibility, whether it is in support of tenure quotas or, as in this case, in defense of non-tenure-track appointments: "The system of tenure does not exist as subordinate to convenience and flexibility. The protection of academic freedom must take precedence over the claimed advantages of increased flexibility."[13]

While responsibility for the substantial increase in the extent to which our colleges and universities are staffed by non-tenure-track teachers rests primarily with administrative officers concerned both to save money and to retain a maximum degree of "managerial flexibility," other institutional constituencies must also bear some responsibility for this state of affairs. In particular, at many institutions senior faculty members have acquiesced in and even encouraged the appointment of large numbers of tenure-ineligible faculty members, perhaps out of a desire to free themselves for their own research and for teaching upper-division and graduate courses or in the belief that the resulting savings would leave more funding for their salaries and benefits. Ultimately, however, the general development of a more-or-less permanent two-tier system brings with it a class consciousness that affects the faculty's perception of itself, the students' perception of the faculty, and the outside world's perception of academe. By their relative lack of concern for their temporary colleagues and their tacit approval of the two-class system in hopes of maintaining and enhancing their own positions, these tenure-track and tenured faculty members may eventually bring to an end the cherished characteristics of their way of life.

Unfortunately, the problem as identified and discussed in 1978 has become more serious. In an era of financial stringency and of diminished national commitment to the development and expansion of higher education, the utilization of tenure-ineligible faculty positions has seemed an attractive strategy. Demographic uncertainties about the size of the college-age population in the future, along with uncertainties about which kinds of colleges and universities will be popular choices, reinforce the desire to have a large, insecure, and impermanent academic labor pool. We believe, however, that the reasons which have been advanced for the use of tenure-ineligible full-time faculty appointments are without merit and that, for the sake of higher education, of academic freedom, and of the professional security and future of coming generations of scholars and their students, the abuse of these appointments should be stopped.

Notes

Editor's Note (2014): The AAUP Research Office has regularly updated statistics on the profound shift toward contingent appointments over the past three decades. The most recent information can be found in the research section of the AAUP website (http://www .aaup.org/our-work/research). The newer data support the conclusions of the section entitled "The Scope and Extent of the Problem" as drafted in 1986, and in most respects the statistics have dramatically worsened.

1. AAUP, *Policy Documents and Reports,* 11th ed. (Baltimore: Johns Hopkins University Press, 2015), 79–90.

2. *AAUP Bulletin* 64 (September 1978): 273.

3. The lower estimate assumes that all faculty members who held an acting or visiting appointment had tenure at the institution from which they were visiting.

4. For 2004–5, the corresponding figures were 367,931 full-time faculty appointments at 1,416 institutions, with 20.5 percent of the positions non-tenure track. These figures include institutions that do not have a system of academic tenure.

5. *Departing the Ivy Halls* (Washington, DC: National Academy of Sciences, 1983).

6. For 2004–5, the corresponding figures were as follows: 27.9 percent of women held non-tenure-track positions (39,442 individuals); 52.3 percent of all non-tenure-track positions surveyed were filled by women; women held 38.3 percent of the total number of full-time faculty positions. Of the 30,354 positions held by women at the instructor and other non-professorial ranks, 81.4 percent were in non-tenure-track positions. This proportion was 80.4 percent for men as well.

7. Barbara K. Townsend, "Outsiders Inside Academe: The Plight of the Temporary Teachers," *Chronicle of Higher Education,* May 28, 1986, 72.

8. Martin Finkelstein, "Life on the 'Effectively Terminal' Tenure Track," *Academe* 72 (January–February 1986): 36.

9. Maxine Hairston, "We're Hiring Too Many Temporary Instructors," *Chronicle of Higher Education,* April 17, 1985, 80.

10. Study Group on the Conditions of Excellence in American Higher Education, *Involvement in Learning: Realizing the Potential of American Higher Education* (Washington, DC: National Institute of Education, 1984).

11. Howard R. Bowen and Jack H. Schuster, "Outlook for the Academic Profession," *Academe* 71 (September–October 1985): 9–15.

12. Bowen and Schuster, "Outlook for the Academic Profession."

13. *Policy Documents and Reports,* 69.

The Inclusion in Governance of Faculty Members Holding Contingent Appointments

The report that follows was prepared by a joint subcommittee of the Association's Committee on Contingency and the Profession and the Committee on College and University Governance, was approved by both parent committees, and was adopted as policy by the AAUP Council at its November 2012 meeting. Statistical information in the report was updated in 2014.

I. Introduction

As the AAUP has documented time and again, the proportion of faculty appointments that are "contingent"—lacking the benefits and protections of tenure and a planned long-term relationship with an institution—has increased dramatically over the past few decades and continues to increase. While awareness of the problem is also growing, its magnitude is obscured by institutional practices that assign teachers and researchers to many different employment statuses, some of which do not use the word "faculty": lecturers, senior lecturers, adjuncts, instructors, non-tenure-track faculty, non-senate faculty, unranked faculty, postdocs, visiting faculty, professors of practice, research assistants, teaching assistants, co-adjutants, affiliates, specialists, clinical faculty, and so on. Using a broad definition of faculty that includes graduate-student employees as well as full- and part-time instructors regardless of title, the AAUP has calculated that by 2009—the latest year for which national data are available—75.6 percent of US faculty appointments were off the tenure track and 60.5 percent of US faculty appointments were part-time appointments off the tenure track, including graduate-student employee appointments. These figures underrepresent postdoctoral fellows, a growing category of appointment on some campuses and in some disciplines. Though many people inside and outside of higher education think of tenure-track appointments as the norm, in reality tenure-track faculty are a dwindling minority on American campuses: while in 1975, tenure-track faculty accounted for 45.1 percent of the instructional staff, by 2009 they accounted for only 24.4 percent.[1]

The structures of faculty governance, however, as well as AAUP policies on the subject, tend to assume a faculty that is primarily full time and on the tenure track. The participation in institutional and departmental governance of faculty holding contingent appointments is uneven, with some institutions encouraging it, some allowing it, and some barring it.

Because of this disconnection between the realities of faculty status and prevailing practices and policies of the profession, two AAUP standing committees, the Committee on Contingency and the Profession and the Committee on College and University Governance, established this joint subcommittee to study the issues and develop Recommendations for the inclusion in governance of faculty holding contingent appointments.

In order to get a better sense of the range of existing practices, the subcommittee developed an informal survey requesting information on various aspects of existing practices regarding the participation of contingent faculty in governance: eligibility to serve, the existence of seats in institutional governance bodies reserved for such faculty, policies to ensure academic freedom, compensation for service, and Recommendations about how to improve the current situation. A pilot version of the survey was distributed at the August 2010 Conference of the Coalition of Contingent Academic Labor, and a revised version was distributed to eight hundred faculty senate leaders during the 2010–11 academic year. The subcommittee received 125 responses from senate leaders, most (88.7 percent) of whom were at either doctoral or comprehensive institutions; in many cases, the responses were only partial, with respondents skipping some questions. While the survey's informal nature, its concentration on certain types of institutions, and many incomplete responses mean that its findings cannot be reliably generalized, the responses received were illuminating. Indeed, one of the most frustrating aspects of the survey, the high number of "not sure" responses from senate leaders to questions about policies at their own institutions, suggests that better training of faculty leaders is sorely needed.

The survey responses indicated, not surprisingly, that faculty in part-time, postdoctoral, or graduate-student employee positions are less often included in governance than their full-time non-tenure-track colleagues. Three-quarters of respondents indicated that at their institution, full-time non-tenure-track faculty are eligible to serve in governance roles. Only about a quarter indicated that part-time faculty are eligible, and the percentages reporting eligibility for graduate-student employees (5.8 percent) and postdoctoral fellows (2.9 percent) were extremely low. The majority (63.7 percent) indicated that their institution does not have seats in governance bodies reserved for contingent faculty members. A majority of respondents who reported that at least some faculty holding contingent appointments are eligible to serve in governance also reported limits on such eligibility or service: 43.1 percent reported limits on the number of full-time non-tenure-track faculty who are allowed to serve; 37.6 percent reported that such faculty must possess particular qualifications, such as a specified minimum teaching load or a certain type of appointment, in order to participate; and 67.9 percent reported that there are specific types of governance activities from which non-tenure-track faculty are barred (in most cases, committees that deal with personnel issues).

A substantial majority of respondents (88 percent) indicated that non-tenure-track faculty are not compensated for their service in governance; 43 percent, however, said that service is taken into consideration in evaluation.

A majority—62.4 percent—indicated that their institution has policies to ensure academic freedom and shared governance rights for non-tenure-track faculty. However, the responses did not give a clear picture of the nature and enforceability of these policies (in part because the question was overly broad). In short, the current state of affairs couples a steadily rising proportion of faculty on contingent appointments with a system in which such faculty are only sometimes included in departmental and institutional governance structures.

This state of affairs is problematic, first, because it undermines faculty professionalism, the integrity of the academic profession, and the faculty's ability to serve the common good. The Association's 2003 statement *Contingent Appointments and the Academic Profession* thoroughly discussed the many ill effects of contingent appointments generally, ranging from sharply diminished protections for academic freedom to exploitative working conditions to the lack of a consistent faculty presence for students.[2] The

effect of contingency on governance is to cut off many faculty members from participation in an integral part of faculty work. The fact that a large percentage of faculty do not participate in governance activities is alarming in the context of a larger trend toward "unbundling" faculty work—an extreme instance of which can be seen in online or for-profit institutions that pay one "employee" to design a curriculum and then employ a cadre of part-time "employees" to deliver the material, with little permissible variation or exercise of professional judgment and no job security. Sometimes, tests or other learning assessments are written or administered by yet another part-time "employee."

The current state of affairs is also problematic because it undermines equity among academic colleagues. The causes and repercussions of a system in which some faculty receive vastly more compensation, privilege, autonomy, evaluation, information, professional support, and respect than others extend far beyond governance. But the routine exclusion of some faculty from department meetings, curricular planning, and other governance activities does much to foster the sense of inequity. On the other side of the divide, the proportion of full-time or tenure-track faculty appointments in some departments and institutions is dwindling, and those who hold such appointments are overburdened with governance responsibilities as the pool of colleagues eligible to share this work shrinks.

Perhaps most important is that the exclusion of so many faculty from governance activities undercuts the ability of the faculty to carry out its responsibilities in this area. When half or more of the faculty at an institution may not participate in meetings of the faculty senate, when decisions about revisions to a course are made without input from those who teach it, or when the majority of a department's faculty has no voice in the selection of its chair, something is amiss. While these problems are by no means universal—governance structures vary widely both among institutions and among academic units within an institution—they are widespread. And as the percentage of tenure-track faculty at an institution dwindles, any governance system that relies primarily upon them to represent the faculty's views becomes less representative, less effective, and more easily bypassed.

While the exclusion from governance of faculty holding contingent appointments is problematic, their inclusion is also problematic. For unsalaried part-time faculty, participating in departmental or institutional governance often means putting in many additional hours for little or no compensation. Such faculty often get no formal recognition or credit for governance activities (and, depending on the type of activity, may even have it counted against them). Faculty on term contracts cannot be assured that they will be able to complete long-term projects. At some institutions, faculty holding contingent appointments may have different qualifications or job duties from their tenure-track colleagues, raising questions about their ability to contribute meaningfully—if at all—to tenure-track hiring, promotion, and tenure decisions. Most problematic is the fact that, by definition, contingent faculty are not protected by tenure and so may be particularly vulnerable to retaliation for actions or positions taken in carrying out governance duties; for the same reason, they may be more susceptible to pressure from administrators or other faculty than are tenure-track faculty.

The difficulties of including faculty who hold contingent appointments in governance activities are not trivial, and we discuss them in detail in what follows. However, we conclude that, on the whole, the exclusion from governance of faculty with contingent appointments is the greater danger to the integrity of the profession and the quality of higher education. In order for the faculty's voice to be heard and for the faculty to retain its ability to contribute substantially to academic decision making, the expectation of service in governance must be expanded beyond tenured and tenure-track faculty as it has been expanded in the past: a century ago senior faculty members generally were the sole participants in university governance. In what follows, we discuss aspects of faculty participation in governance and make recommendations for how such participation can be broadened.

II. Relevant AAUP Policies

Recommendations for the participation in governance of faculty holding contingent appointments must grow from the circumstances of higher education today, discussed above, and also from AAUP policies and principles, discussed in this section. The AAUP, along with other higher education organizations, has long asserted that academic freedom, due process, and shared governance are indispensable to the mission of colleges and universities to serve the common good. Association policy statements provide the basis for guidelines to enable faculty holding contingent appointments to participate effectively in college and university governance while being protected from threats of retaliation or intimidation.

The joint 1940 *Statement of Principles on Academic Freedom and Tenure*, formulated with what is now the Association of American Colleges and Universities and endorsed by more than two hundred educational organizations and disciplinary societies, identifies the components of academic freedom for faculty as "full freedom in research and in the publication of the results," "freedom in the classroom in discussing their subject," and freedom to "speak and write as citizens" (freedom in extramural utterances).[3] The 1940 *Statement* identifies tenure as the means by which academic freedom is best protected and outlines the safeguards of academic due process that tenure affords. Thus, full-time faculty members should serve a probationary period not to exceed seven years; at the conclusion of this period, faculty who have met the institution's stated criteria should be granted "permanent or continuous tenure." The statement further identifies the procedural safeguards that accompany tenure.

Importantly for this report on faculty holding contingent appointments, the 1940 *Statement* asserts that a probationary faculty member "should have the academic freedom that all other members of the faculty have."[4] Interpretive Comments appended to the statement in 1970 observe that "the 1940 *Statement* is not a static code but a fundamental document designed to set a framework of norms to guide adaptations to changing times and circumstances." The fourth Interpretive Comment, concerning extramural utterances, asserts that "[b]oth the protection of academic freedom and the requirements of academic responsibility apply not only to the full-time probationary and the tenured teacher, but also to all others, such as part-time faculty and teaching assistants, who exercise teaching responsibilities."[5] Thus, the 1940 *Statement* with its 1970 Interpretive Comments is careful to establish its adaptability to changing conditions and to apply its principles to faculty members beyond the full-time tenured and tenure-track faculty.

The *Statement on Government of Colleges and Universities*, jointly formulated in 1966 by the AAUP, the American Council on Education, and the Association of Governing Boards of Universities and Colleges, assigns to the various components of colleges and universities different degrees of authority in institutional governance, depending upon the responsibilities of those components. So, for example, the statement assigns to faculty joint responsibility with the administration and the governing board for the formulation of general educational policy, planning, physical resources, budgeting, presidential searches, and external relations. However, because of its special responsibilities—and expertise—in the teaching and research functions of an academic institution, the faculty has "primary responsibility for such fundamental areas as curriculum, subject matter and methods of instruction, research, faculty status, and those aspects of student life that relate to the educational process." Since the faculty has primary responsibility in these areas, its decisions should only rarely be overridden by the administration and only for "compelling reasons which should be stated in detail." The statement observes that "[a]gencies for faculty participation in the government of the college or university should be established at each level where faculty responsibility is present. An agency should exist for the presentation of the views of the whole faculty."[6]

The Association's 1994 statement *On the Relationship of Faculty Governance to Academic Freedom* establishes the reciprocal relationship of faculty governance and academic freedom: "[A] sound system of institutional governance is a necessary condition for the protection of faculty rights and thereby for the most productive exercise of essential faculty freedoms. Correspondingly, the protection of the academic freedom of faculty members in addressing issues of institutional governance is a prerequisite for the practice of governance unhampered by fear of retribution." The statement warns that faculty must participate in the structures of their governance systems because "if they do not, authority will drift away from them, since someone must exercise it, and if members of the faculty do not, others will."[7]

With the publication in 2003 of *Contingent Appointments and the Academic Profession*, the Association addressed the full range of issues posed by the proliferation of non-tenure-track or "contingent" faculty appointments. Among those appointments the statement included full- and part-time faculty, adjuncts, postdoctoral fellows, and graduate-student employees who "undertak[e] independent teaching activities that are similar in nature to those of regular faculty." The 2003 statement recommends that contingent appointments include "the full range of faculty responsibilities": teaching, scholarship, and service. Also recommended is the protection of academic freedom through tenure or, for part-time faculty after successive reappointments, the "assurance of continuing employment."[8] The statement recommends extending shared governance responsibilities to "all faculty at an institution, including those appointed to less-than-full-time positions."

As noted above, the AAUP has described the 1940 *Statement* as "not a static code" but rather a document that sets forth norms that can guide changes in changing circumstances. It views academic freedom and academic responsibility as applicable not only to tenured and probationary faculty members but to "all others . . . who exercise teaching responsibilities." The 1994 statement on faculty governance and academic freedom articulates the necessary reciprocal relationship between academic freedom and academic governance and urges faculty to participate in governance to prevent the loss of those powers of governance to the administration. The 2003 statement on contingent appointments recommends that such appointments include service as well as teaching and research. The statement also advocates the extension of shared governance responsibilities and opportunities to "all faculty," including part-time faculty.

Drawing upon these earlier policy documents, we set forth here the principles that form the basis of the recommendations in this report:

1. "Faculty" should be defined inclusively rather than exclusively; faculty status should not be limited to those holding tenured or tenure-track appointments.
2. Faculty members who hold contingent appointments should be afforded responsibilities and opportunities in governance similar to those of their tenured and tenure-track colleagues.
3. Faculty governance must be exercised to be real.
4. Academic freedom and governance reinforce each other. While governance work helps to support faculty status, a secure faculty is a prerequisite for free participation in governance.
5. All faculty members should be afforded academic freedom and due-process protections, whether they hold tenured, tenure-track, or contingent appointments.

III. Recommendations
We make the following recommendations for including faculty members holding contingent appointments in governance.

A. Definition of Faculty
In some AAUP policy documents, ambiguity results from a tendency to treat the concept of "faculty" as if its definition were self-evident. For example, the *Statement on Government*'s assertion that "[f]aculty representatives should be selected by the faculty according to procedures

determined by the faculty" begs the question of who the faculty are. Does a system in which only tenured or tenure-track faculty can decide upon election procedures that apply only to tenured or tenure-track faculty meet the standard of fairness?

Our informal survey asked respondents about which appointments are included in their institution's definition of faculty and found that while almost all institutions, as would be expected, include in the definition those who hold full-time tenure-track appointments, practice is split on full-time non-tenure-track faculty (84.5 percent include them), part-time non-tenure-track faculty (69.8 percent), graduate-student employees (9.5 percent), and postdoctoral fellows (6 percent). Defining "faculty" is no simple task, given variations in job duties and overlap between academic and administrative duties. Luckily, it has already been attempted, in the *Joint Statement on Faculty Status of College and University Librarians*, adopted by the AAUP's Council in 1973:

> Librarians perform a teaching and research role inasmuch as they instruct students formally and informally and advise and assist faculty in their scholarly pursuits. Librarians are also themselves involved in the research function; many conduct research in their own professional interests and in the discharge of their duties.
>
> Where the role of college and university librarians . . . requires them to function essentially as part of the faculty, this functional identity should be recognized by the granting of faculty status. Neither administrative responsibilities nor professional degrees, titles, or skills, per se, qualify members of the academic community for faculty status. The function of a librarian as participant in the processes of teaching and research is the essential criterion of faculty status.[9]

We base our definition of faculty on the *Joint Statement on Faculty Status of College and University Librarians*, adding to it the proviso that participation in the processes of teaching and research must be professional in nature (therefore, for example, a student conducting student-level research would not qualify). The definition clearly includes individuals appointed as teachers, whether full or part time, on or off the tenure track. But a number of difficult-to-classify appointment types still exist, prominent among them graduate-student employees, postdoctoral fellows, and administrators.

The terms and conditions of graduate-student employment vary widely, from staffing a desk to working in a laboratory to designing and teaching one or more courses independently, and several

factors play into a determination of which graduate-student employees qualify as faculty: status as a "participant in the processes of teaching and research," independent exercise of professional judgment, and activity that is not conducted primarily for the graduate student's own education. Employment consisting of nonacademic tasks does not meet this standard, nor does activity, even if in support of teaching or research, that does not require professional judgment—for example, enrolling subjects in clinical trials or making photocopies for a course packet—nor does work that is academic but not independent in nature: tutoring undergraduates, grading papers or tests in courses taught primarily by someone else, running discussion sections, and doing lab work requiring skill and judgment in a research project designed and run by someone else. Engagement in teaching and research activities that do require professional judgment may still not qualify the graduate student as a contingent faculty member if the primary purpose of those activities is to educate the student—for example, independently teaching a limited number of courses or receiving financial support (commonly termed a "fellowship") from the university to conduct research toward a degree. Individuals engaged in these activities may have a claim to representation in institutional governance as students or staff members, but those claims do not fall under the purview of this report. At the other end of the spectrum, as *Contingent Appointments and the Academic Profession* describes it, is "the person who teaches independently, perhaps for many years, but not in a probationary appointment, while he or she completes a dissertation." The statement clearly identifies such persons as faculty: "To the extent that a person functions in [this] group, undertaking independent teaching activities that are similar in nature to those of regular faculty, the term 'contingent faculty' should apply."[10] By extension, it would also apply to the analogous group among research-oriented graduate-student employees: those who secure funding either from the university or from an outside granting agency to conduct research independently while at the same time providing essential work for a lab.

The 2003 statement also includes in its definition of contingent faculty "postdoctoral fellows who are employed off the tenure track for periods of time beyond what could reasonably be considered the extension and completion of their professional training."[11] Postdoctoral fellowships, like research-oriented graduate-student employment, are ideally training programs, providing for a brief period of mentored research preparatory to an academic or scientific career. Comprehensive data on length of postdoctoral appointments do not exist, but it is certain that many now continue far longer than required for training purposes and are often exploited for the cheap labor that they provide to universities. According to the National Postdoctoral Association, the average post-doc is in his or her early thirties, works more than fifty hours a week, and earns a median salary of $42,000 a year (below the median wage of individuals who hold bachelor's degrees), despite the fact that postdocs, by definition, hold terminal degrees.[12] While postdocs may perform fairly routine laboratory work, they also typically focus at least some of the time on their own research and publications. Many postdocs thus meet the criteria for being defined as "faculty." These would include the relatively small number of postdocs outside of the sciences, where "post-doctoral fellow" is often another euphemism for "non-tenure-track, short-term faculty member."

Classification is also difficult when administrative and teaching or research duties overlap in the same individual. In these instances we believe that those individuals who hold such appointments should be defined as "faculty" if their primary responsibility is teaching or research, rather than administration.

Recommendation 1: Institutional policies should define as "faculty" and include in governance bodies at all levels individuals whose appointments consist primarily of teaching or research activities conducted at a professional level. These include (1) tenured faculty, (2) tenure-track faculty, (3) full- and part-time non-tenure-track teachers and researchers, (4) graduate-student employees and postdoctoral fellows who are primarily teachers or researchers, and (5) librarians who participate substantially in the process of teaching or research. Those individuals whose primary duties are administrative should not be defined as faculty.

B. Eligibility to Serve on and Vote in Elected Governance Bodies

The question arises whether restrictions should be placed on the participation of contingent faculty in governance. Reasons advanced in favor of restrictions include the limited knowledge of the institution that contingent faculty are supposed to have because of their short-term contracts; the fact that some individuals may teach "on the side" while having primary careers in another field; the possibility that, either because they teach at multiple institutions or because they hold other jobs, faculty on part-time contingent appointments have looser ties to the institution than their full-time counterparts; the logistical difficulties posed by part-time and short-term appointments; and the possibility that faculty on contingent appointments are beholden to department chairs or administrators for their continued employment and may therefore be likely to seek to please these individuals in the exercise of governance activities.

On the first reason, we note that many faculty members who hold contingent appointments, despite the fact that those appointments are often contractually short term, serve in the same departments for years or decades and may have considerable experience—a good deal more than the recently appointed tenure-track faculty members who are usually permitted to serve in governance. Of course, it is also true that many contingent appointments are genuinely short term, and it may be the case that newly appointed individuals serving in such positions are unable to contribute usefully to certain aspects of departmental or institutional governance.

We therefore see no reason why an institution or a department, if it wishes, should not establish a time-in-service threshold for certain governance activities—for example, one year of service before a new faculty member is eligible to run for the faculty senate. This concern, however, applies equally to all faculty—full and part time, tenure track and contingent—and thus any restriction should apply equally to all faculty as well. If such a requirement for full-time faculty were expressed in calendar time (for instance, a year), it would have to be translated into terms (for instance, two semesters) for part-time faculty, in order to avoid excluding those who teach intermittently. It should also be noted that many contingent faculty have more multi-institutional experience than their tenure-track colleagues and that this experience is valuable in all governance functions as well as in other roles, such as teaching and research.

The second reason (having a primary career in another field) we recognize as the more serious concern, although a rarer case than some suppose. Many faculty members serving in contingent appointments are in fact career academics: retirees from tenured appointments or individuals who have been unable to secure tenure-track appointments but work full time or nearly full time in academia, often by piecing together part-time jobs. The classic depiction of the part-time faculty member as a practicing patent attorney or cellist who offers his or her specialized expertise on the side is a relative rarity. Such cases, however, do exist, and there are institutions or departments where many, perhaps a majority, of the faculty are individuals without much academic experience or interest, who would identify themselves primarily not as faculty but as members of some other profession who happen to be teaching a course. The possible danger, then, is that if faculty members on part-time appointments are granted full participation in governance activities, the faculty whose primary profession is not academic would outnumber and could outvote other faculty.

The third reason (weak ties to and investment in the particular institutions) is predicated on a similar concern. In both of these cases, we conclude that (a) some governance participation is appropriate, (b) the assumption of major leadership roles may be inappropriate but is unlikely to occur, and (c) faculty governance systems have for decades dealt with similar issues as they pertain to full-time tenured faculty, without resorting to barring them from governance service. Since the part-time faculty in question here do teach courses, they are members of the faculty, are experienced with their courses and their students, and should be involved in curricular planning and similar work. While it would likely not be appropriate for a person who either has another career or teaches at several institutions and has little interest in the one in question to assume a major faculty leadership role, such a person would be unlikely to stand for election to an important governance role and would be unlikely to get elected. Finally, we reiterate that these concerns also pertain to full-time tenure-line faculty. Institutions have found ways to accommodate "star" faculty who come in once a week to teach a graduate seminar, faculty who have little interest in their institution, and faculty with substantial clinical practices or consulting businesses without denying them a role in the system of faculty governance.

The fourth reason, logistical difficulties, is at once trivial and confounding. Such difficulties might include the running of elections with so many individuals whose status keeps changing and about whom information is not reliably available; the possibility that short-term faculty would not be around to see out the work they started (for example, to finish a yearlong committee project or serve a whole term in an elected office); and the challenges of scheduling meetings with part-time faculty members who are on campus only one day a week, or at night, or, in the case of those teaching online, not at all. We conclude, however, that these logistical difficulties should not be used as an excuse to exclude a wide swath of faculty from institutional governance. And the difficulties, while daunting, can be surmounted. Given the variety of governance

structures and types of faculty appointments, it is impossible to offer exact prescriptions, but we would suggest that faculty and administrators look at three areas when creating a plan to ensure a governance role for faculty on contingent appointments.

First, poor institutional practices should be remedied. Examples include inadequate record-keeping systems that would make it difficult to determine eligibility for governance service or to contact part-time faculty at an institution, many short-term contracts resulting in a high faculty turnover, and such abysmally low compensation that part-time faculty cannot afford to add another duty.

Second, the institution or department should look at how similar logistical difficulties have been surmounted to accommodate the busy schedules of tenured and tenure-track faculty. For example, what has happened when a tenure-track faculty member goes on leave midway through a multiyear committee project?

Third, the institution or department should consider systems that have been developed at other institutions specifically to incorporate large numbers of part-time faculty into governance.

The final reason often advanced for excluding faculty on contingent appointments from governance—that they may feel beholden to the department chairs or administrators who hire and reappoint them and thus may not exercise independence in governance matters—should be taken seriously. Therefore, as we discuss below, the hiring, reappointment, and firing of such faculty should not be invested in a single person without provisions for due process. And all institutions should be fully committed to the processes that ensure academic freedom for all faculty.

In sum, the basic requirements for and means of participating in governance activities that apply to contingent faculty should be as parallel as possible to those that apply to full-time tenure-track faculty. Participation on some governance bodies, such as committees responsible for awarding research grants or establishing a graduate-level curriculum, may require particular expertise that not all faculty—whether tenure track or contingent—possess. Service on such committees may thus be dependent on expertise but not on whether a faculty member holds a contingent or a tenure-track appointment. The details of how parallels between the treatment of contingent and tenure-track faculty can best be maintained should be left to the faculty in each institution, but with the participation of all faculty, as defined in Recommendation 1.

A corollary to this argument is that there should be no need to reserve special seats in governance bodies for contingent faculty. Reserving seats might be an appropriate transitional mechanism designed to ensure that contingent faculty have at least some representation in governance, but it will be unnecessary when they are included as full participants. However, we recognize that most institutions and departments have not yet begun to achieve full parity; thus, for some institutions, reserving a certain number of seats for faculty on contingent appointments may be a necessary step forward.

This report seeks to define faculty and to determine eligibility for participating in governance by describing faculty members' functions. As noted earlier, the AAUP states that librarians have faculty status insofar as they share the "functional identity" of teaching and scholarly research. This report consequently defines as having faculty status and being eligible to participate in governance bodies those persons who teach and conduct research at a professional, scholarly level. This report similarly defines as having faculty status those graduate-student employees who participate as teachers or academic researchers, who exercise independent professional judgment, and whose activities are not primarily directed toward their own education. A corollary of our definitions is that an individual whose appointment and activities are primarily administrative should not be considered a member of the faculty for governance purposes.

Thus, this report has carefully defined faculty using AAUP criteria. No AAUP policy or document that refers to faculty does so in a way that recommends a differential authority to one group of faculty over another. Therefore, accepting fractional voting for contingent faculty participation in shared governance could set an unfortunate and discriminatory precedent in the AAUP. As noted above, the fourth Interpretive Comment to the 1940 *Statement* asserts that all faculty members should have the same protections of academic freedom and the same academic responsibilities as tenure-track faculty members. AAUP annual election rules allot full voting rights to part-time and non-tenure-track faculty as well as to tenured and tenure-track faculty. Yet the allocation of governance seats in many faculty governance bodies, as reflected in our survey of faculty senates, commonly gives one or two seats to all faculty on contingent appointments regardless of their numbers or their professional qualifications, undermining equity and invidiously reducing those faculty members to second-class status without regard to any specific

professional function that they might serve or qualifications that they might possess as faculty members.

Recommendation 2: Eligibility for voting and holding office in institutional governance bodies should be the same for all faculty regardless of full- or part-time status. Institutions may wish to establish time-in-service eligibility requirements; if the eligibility requirement for full-time faculty is expressed in calendar time (for instance, a year), it would have to be translated into terms (for instance, two semesters) applicable to part-time faculty in order to accommodate those who teach intermittently.

Recommendation 3: While reserving a specified number of seats for contingent faculty may be adopted as a transitional mechanism to ensure at least some contingent faculty representation in institutional governance bodies, ideally there should be no minimum or maximum number of seats reserved in institutional governance bodies where representation of contingent faculty is appropriate, as described elsewhere in this report.

Recommendation 4: All members of the faculty, defined on the basis of their primary function as teachers or researchers and assuming that they meet any time-in-service requirements, should be eligible to vote in all elections for institutional governance bodies on the basis of one person, one vote.

C. Participation in Evaluation

The *Statement on Government of Colleges and Universities* asserts that faculty status and related matters are primarily a faculty responsibility; according to the statement, "this area includes appointments, reappointments, decisions not to reappoint, promotions, the granting of tenure, and dismissal. . . . Determinations in these matters should first be by faculty action through established procedures."[13] Faculty have both a right to be evaluated by other faculty and a responsibility to evaluate their peers ("evaluation" is used here in its broadest sense, referring to all procedures used to determine the employability of a faculty member). This standard is widely implemented in the academy for selection, reappointment, tenure, and promotion decisions relating to full-time tenure-track faculty; deviations from this standard often signal major violations of shared governance in institutions of higher learning. However, it is quite common for faculty serving in contingent appointments to be hired by department chairs or administrators without the participation of faculty bodies and neither permitted to participate in the evaluation of other faculty nor thoroughly evaluated themselves. It is worrisome that in many instances the evaluation of contingent faculty is performed with little or no input from any faculty body. The Association's *Statement on Teaching Evaluation* speaks directly about this: "Evaluation of teaching in which an administrator's judgment is the sole or determining factor is contrary to policies set forth in the *Statement on Government of Colleges and Universities. . . .* Faculty members should have a primary, though not exclusive, role in evaluating an individual faculty member's performance as teacher. . . . [T]he faculty's considered judgment should constitute the basic recommendation to the next level of responsibility."[14] Worse than evaluation conducted solely by one chair or administrator is the not-uncommon case of contingent faculty who are evaluated entirely on the strength of student-satisfaction surveys; here, the decision makers are essentially students. These practices clearly do not conform to AAUP-supported standards. We conclude, then, that the basic requirements for and means of evaluation of faculty should be as nearly parallel as possible for contingent faculty and full-time tenure-track faculty. Indeed, faculty serving in contingent appointments should participate in evaluating their peers (other faculty serving in contingent appointments) in the same fashion that full-time tenure-track faculty participate in the evaluation of their peers.

Reasons that have been advanced against allowing contingent faculty to participate in the evaluation of their peers include their possible dependence on department chairs and administrators for continued employment (which might undermine their ability to exercise independent judgment) and possible conflicts of interest stemming from competition for work. With regard to the former, we argue that if procedures for the hiring and reappointment of contingent faculty mirrored those that apply to full-time tenure-track faculty, this dependence would be diminished, since reappointment would be based on objective criteria, not the will of a single individual. With respect to the latter, conflicts of interest exist among both the full-time tenure-track and the contingent faculty and should not be used as a reason to bar just one group from participating in evaluation. Participation in evaluation of peers should be based not on tenure status but on the expertise necessary to carry out the assigned duties. Very often, the expertise necessary to competently evaluate contingent faculty belongs primarily to other contingent faculty, because the stratification in many departments results in contingent and tenure-track faculty teaching, on the whole, different kinds of courses.

If changes to a curriculum affect contingent faculty who teach, say, English composition, the effects of those changes can best be communicated by those who have experienced them. Many of the best evaluators of teachers of these courses will be other teachers of these courses, regardless of faculty status. Again, the details of how the parallels between the evaluation procedures for faculty holding contingent and tenure-track appointments can best be maintained and the establishment of appropriate criteria for contingent faculty to participate in the evaluation of their peers should be left to the faculty in each institution—with the participation of all faculty, as defined in Recommendation 1.

Whether faculty serving in contingent appointments should contribute to the evaluation of tenure-track faculty—by, for example, sitting on a promotion and tenure committee—is a different question. According to the *Statement on Government*, "The primary responsibility of the faculty for such matters is based upon the fact that its judgment is central to general educational policy. Furthermore, scholars in a particular field or activity have the chief competence for judging the work of their colleagues."[15] At some institutions, the job duties of faculty serving in contingent and tenure-track appointments differ little, and participation of the former in the evaluation of the latter might be entirely appropriate. For example, at some community colleges where the majority of faculty, regardless of status, primarily teach and teach the same sorts of classes, there would seem to be no reason why a contingent faculty member could not usefully contribute to promotion decisions. At other institutions, however, the job duties associated with the two types of appointments may differ considerably, with tenure-track faculty expected to engage in substantial research and scholarship activities in which faculty serving in contingent appointments have no official responsibilities. While we note that (a) many contingent faculty might still be active researchers and well able to judge the research efforts of their tenure-track colleagues and (b) the degree of specialization in some research institutions means that it is not uncommon for tenure-track faculty to judge scholarship that they are not particularly well equipped to understand, we still conclude that it is reasonable for institutions to restrict faculty on contingent appointments from participating in the evaluation of tenured and tenure-track faculty.

Recommendation 5: While faculty on contingent appointments may be restricted from participating in the evaluation of tenured and tenure-track faculty, faculty on contingent appointments should have the opportunity to contribute to the evaluation of other contingent faculty.

D. Requirement of and Compensation for Service
So far, this report has focused mainly on the eligibility of faculty on contingent appointments to serve in governance roles. With a few limitations, we have concluded that they should be allowed to so serve. There is an additional caveat. Permissible participation in governance can easily become expected or presumed to be expected. That is, faculty on contingent appointments may be pressured to participate by the assumption that participation is a hidden qualification for advancement. Thus, it is essential that department bylaws or guidelines, as well as the contracts of faculty on contingent appointments, make clear the voluntary and unremunerated nature of participation.

We now take up the other side of the question: whether faculty on contingent appointments should be expected or required to serve in such roles. The primary objections to such an expectation are (1) that faculty on contingent appointments may not wish to serve; (2) that, where academic freedom is inadequately protected, they might put themselves at risk when freely expressing opinions in governance activities and that the dependence of contingent faculty on chairs or administrators for their continued employment might undermine their ability to make independent judgments for the good of the department or university; and (3) that the pay structures of part-time appointments, in particular, rarely include compensation for service.

The first of these considerations is relatively trivial. There is no reason to suppose that a disinclination to participate in governance activities is any more widespread among faculty holding contingent appointments than it is among those holding tenure-line appointments. AAUP policy holds that certain aspects of institutional governance are properly the responsibility of the faculty, so faculty must fulfill those responsibilities.

The second consideration is very serious and has implications both for the faculty themselves and for the integrity of the governance system. Since contingent faculty by definition have little job security, they are at greater risk than others of retaliation if their speech or actions in the context of governance displease administrators or other faculty members. In addition, faculty on contingent appointments, particularly part-time faculty, often have no recourse if they believe they have

been subject to retaliation. Because of these precarious working conditions, they may be susceptible to pressure, whether real or imagined, to vote or act in a certain way, thus compromising the integrity of the governance process.

Despite the seriousness of these considerations, the solution is not to bar some faculty from service but to better protect the academic freedom of those serving in governance roles. And, indeed, this is the path advocated by the AAUP with regard to other groups of faculty. Like contingent faculty, tenure-track (but untenured) faculty may be susceptible to retaliation and pressure, but the AAUP does not advocate excluding them from governance activities. In light of the 2006 US Supreme Court decision in *Garcetti v. Ceballos* and subsequent court decisions that threaten the exercise of academic freedom in governance activities at public universities (by ruling that the government can restrict speech related to "official duties"), the Association's Recommendation has been that institutions adopt specific policy language designed to ensure the continued protection of academic freedom and shared governance.[16] This policy language should protect the academic freedom of all faculty serving in governance roles, whether they hold tenure-line or contingent appointments. In addition to adopting policies in this area if none exist, the AAUP further recommends that institutions examine existing policies to make sure that they explicitly extend protections for academic freedom to all faculty, regardless of status or appointment category. The third consideration, compensation, is also serious. Both full- and part-time contingent appointments typically carry lower compensation than do tenure-line appointments, and part-time faculty compensation is often very low and explicitly tied only to classroom hours.[17] Suddenly requiring faculty on part-time appointments to put in many additional hours for the same low pay is indefensible. However, again we must conclude that the appropriate response is not to keep contingent faculty from carrying out governance responsibilities but to provide adequate support so that they can do so. One way of doing this, in line with the piecemeal manner in which most part-time faculty are currently paid, would be to pay directly for governance work—a faculty member earning $2,000 apiece to teach two courses would be awarded a further specific sum to serve on a committee or in the faculty senate. This approach has drawbacks, however: the difficulty of determining the relative cash values of different governance tasks, the possibility that faculty would be drawn to particular committees or to stand for election to the faculty senate out of financial need rather than a true inclination to do the work, and the possibility that faculty would be inclined to vote in accordance with the wishes of whoever appointed them in order to increase the chance of keeping the position or being reappointed. In the 2003 statement *Contingent Appointments and the Academic Profession*, the Association recommended that "faculty appointments, including contingent appointments, . . . incorporate all aspects of university life: active engagement with an academic discipline, teaching or mentoring of undergraduate or graduate students, participation in academic decision making, and service on campus and to the surrounding community." The statement continues: "[T]his participation should be supported by compensation and institutional resources and recognized in the processes of evaluation and peer review."[18] We reaffirm these Recommendations and further recommend that the best way to provide compensation is by structuring appointments to include an expectation of and compensation for service, but without tying a particular dollar amount to a particular service task, with the understanding that the basic principle of equal pay for equal work and for work of equal value should be the goal.

Recommendation 6: All faculty members, regardless of their status or appointment type, should, in the conduct of governance activities, be explicitly protected by institutional policies from retaliation in the form of discipline, nonreappointment, dismissal, or any other adverse action. Such institutional policies could include incorporation of appropriate language into faculty handbooks, bylaws, or other regulations. All faculty members should be able to vote or abstain freely, without compulsion and without the necessity of defending their decision to vote or to abstain.

Recommendation 7: Faculty holding contingent appointments should be compensated in a way that takes into consideration the full range of their appointment responsibilities, which should include service. Where such compensation does not exist, its absence should not be used to exclude faculty on contingent appointments from voluntarily serving in governance. Faculty on contingent appointments should not be required, expected, or pressured to participate in activities that are not included as compensated responsibilities under the terms and conditions of their appointments. The Association discourages compensation for service tasks that are not explicitly a component of an appointment.

Recommendation 8: Where service is explicitly a component of the appointment, participation in service should be included as part of the evaluation of a faculty member on a contingent appointment. If service in a governance role is not explicitly a component of the appointment, it may be recognized as an additional positive factor in the evaluation if the faculty member voluntarily participates in it, but a lack of service should not be considered a negative factor in the evaluation.

IV. Conclusion

We recognize that as long as a significant portion of the faculty has virtually no security of employment and many are involuntarily employed part time, the question of how to include all faculty in governance, especially as elected or voting representatives, is one without a fully satisfactory answer. This is especially true in nonunionized situations where no enforceable contract exists that prohibits retaliation for protected activities. However, faculty members should not be excluded from participation in governance because of the appointment conditions over which they have little control. The inclusion in governance roles of faculty who hold contingent appointments has problematic aspects, but it is crucial to establishing strong faculty governance. The governance system must be protected by the most rigorous possible commitment in spirit, in writing, and in fact to prevent retaliation against all those who voice opinions in the governance process that may offend those with more power.

Full and meaningful integration of faculty in shared governance is possible only where academic freedom is protected by tenure or tenure-like terms and conditions of employment. Thus, efforts to implement the Recommendations put forth through this statement will ideally go hand in hand with efforts to convert contingent faculty appointments into appointments that are tenured or tenure track or that involve eligibility for continuing service, regardless of whether the faculty member's assignments are full or part time, teaching or research intensive.[19] The faculty must be able to exercise its collective voice freely and fully if it is to effectively determine the course of higher education. Toward this goal, democracy and active voluntarism must be combined with a culture of faculty solidarity across all ranks and classifications.

Notes

1. "It's Not Over Yet: The Annual Report on the Economic Status of the Profession, 2010–11," *Academe* 97 (March–April 2011): 7, Figure 1. Another appropriate term for the broad category that includes graduate student employees is "instructional staff." In 2011, 76.4 percent of instructional staff appointments were off the

tenure track and 60.8 percent were either part-time faculty members or graduate student employees. The proportion of those individuals in tenured or tenure-track positions had declined to 23.5 percent (John W. Curtis, *The Employment Status of Instructional Staff Members in Higher Education, Fall 2011*, American Association of University Professors, April 2014: 8, Table 5).

2. AAUP, *Policy Documents and Reports*, 11th ed. (Baltimore: Johns Hopkins University Press, 2015), 170–85.

3. Ibid., 14. Another aspect of academic freedom implied in the 1940 "Statement," but not stated explicitly, relates to faculty members' role in governance as "officers" of the institution. According to the executive summary of a 2009 AAUP report, which draws upon the Association's 1994 statement "On the Relationship of Faculty Governance to Academic Freedom" (ibid., 123–25; discussed below), "The academic freedom of a faculty member pertains to both (1) speech or action taken as part of the institution's governing and decision-making processes (for example, within a faculty committee or as part of a grievance filing) and (2) speech or action that is critical of institutional policies and of those in authority and takes place outside an institution's formal governance mechanisms (such as e-mail messages sent to other faculty members)" ("Protecting an Independent Faculty Voice: Academic Freedom after *Garcetti v. Ceballos*," ibid., 126–29).

4. Ibid., 16.

5. Ibid., 14–15.

6. Ibid., 121.

7. Ibid., 125.

8. Ibid., 171, 176, 177. Regulation 13 (on "Part-Time Faculty Appointments") of the "Recommended Institutional Regulations on Academic Freedom and Tenure" (ibid., 79–90) sets forth additional procedural protections for holders of part-time appointments. These include a written statement of the terms and conditions of every appointment; a written statement of cause, with an opportunity for a faculty hearing, when the faculty member is to be dismissed before an appointment expires; a written statement upon request of reasons for nonreappointment, with the opportunity for review of the decision by a faculty body; and, for those retained beyond seven years of service, an evaluation potentially leading to tenure where part-time tenure is granted or to a continuing appointment with procedural safeguards against replacement by another part-time faculty member.

9. *AAUP Bulletin* 59 (June 1973): 266–67. A subsequently modified version, with language that differs from the quoted language, can be found in *Policy Documents and Reports*, 210–11.

10. *Policy Documents and Reports*, 171.

11. Ibid.

12. National Postdoctoral Association, "Fact Sheet," updated December 12, 2013, http://www.nationalpostdoc .org/images/stories/Documents/Other/NPA-fact-sheet -dec-2013.pdf.

13. *Policy Documents and Reports*, 121.

14. Ibid., 221.

15. Ibid., 121.

16. "Protecting an Independent Faculty Voice: Academic Freedom after *Garcetti v. Ceballos*," ibid., 126–29.

17. The AAUP's Annual Report on the Economic Status of the Profession consistently finds that annual compensation for full-time contingent appointments is lower even than that of assistant professors, though some faculty on full-time contingent appointments may have more job seniority than associate or full professors. In the most recent survey, 2011–12, the combined averages were as follows: assistant professor, $66,564; no rank, $61,939; lecturer, $54,202; instructor, $47,847 ("A Very Slow Recovery: The Annual Report on the Economic Status of the Profession, 2011–12," *Academe* 98 [March–April 2012]: 21). The National Institutes of Health establishes "stipend" levels for postdoctoral fellows (*Ruth L. Kirschstein National Research Service Award [NRSA] Stipends, Tuition/Fees and Other Budgetary Levels Effective for Fiscal Year 2012*, Bethesda: National Institutes of Health, released January 20, 2012, updated May 8, 2013, http://grants .nih.gov/grants/guide/notice-files/NOT-OD-12-033 .html), which are followed by many institutions; in 2011, they ranged from $38,496 for a beginning postdoc to $53,112 for a postdoc with seven or more years of experience. Comprehensive national data on compensation for part-time faculty are not available, but smaller surveys and publicly available information such as collective bargaining agreements and published institutional salary information indicate that pay is typically much lower than the corresponding portion of a full-time salary at the same institution, and access to substantial benefits programs is rare. Part-time faculty are often explicitly compensated just for teaching or for classroom hours. Available information suggests that graduate-student employee compensation often exceeds compensation for part-time faculty at the same institution, but many graduate-student employees already report working more than the number of hours suggested by their institutions as the norm.

In 2013–14 the average salary for assistant professors was $69,848; for unranked full-time faculty members, $65,622; lecturers, $55,890; and instructors, $49,963. Note that the proportions off the tenure track in these positions are 23.4 percent, 74.2 percent, 98.9 percent, and 90.9 percent, respectively (John W. Curtis and Saranna Thornton, "Losing Focus: The Annual Report on the Economic Status of the Profession, 2013–14," *Academe* 100 [March–April 2014]: 25, survey report Table 4; 34, Table 11). The 2012–13 AAUP report also provides extensive analysis on salaries of full-time non-tenure-track faculty members from the 2010 survey conducted by the Coalition on the Academic Workforce (John W. Curtis and Saranna Thornton, "Here's the News: The Annual Report on the Economic Status of the Profession, 2012–13," *Academe* 99 [March–April 2013]).

The most recent notice on postdoctoral stipend levels from the National Institutes of Health (http://grants .nih.gov/grants/guide/notice-files/NOT-OD-14-046

.html) set the levels for fiscal year 2014 as a range from $42,000 for an individual with no "relevant postdoctoral experience" to $55,272 for an individual with seven years of experience or more.

Data on part-time faculty pay are still not available on a comprehensive national basis, but the large survey carried out by the Coalition on the Academic Workforce in fall 2010 provides the best recent information. Overall, part-time faculty members were paid a median wage of $2,700 for a three-credit course in fall 2010. Only 22.6 percent of part-time faculty respondents to that survey indicated they had access to health benefits through their academic employer (Coalition on the Academic Workforce, *A Portrait of Part-Time Faculty Members*, 2012: 10, 13).

The Oklahoma State University Office of Institutional Research & Information Management tabulated results from 46 universities during the 2012–13 academic year and found a mean stipend paid to graduate assistants of $15,294, exclusive of any tuition waivers. The Oklahoma State report does not provide any information on workloads for graduate assistants (Office of Institutional Research & Information Management, Oklahoma State University *2012–2013 Graduate Assistant Stipend Survey*, https://irim.okstate .edu/Publications).

18. *Policy Documents and Reports*, 175.

19. The following AAUP documents address conversion of contingent to permanent status: "Contingent Appointments and the Academic Profession," Regulation 13 of the "Recommended Institutional Regulations," and "Tenure and Teaching-Intensive Appointments," ibid., 186–89.

LIBRARIANS AND ACADEMIC PROFESSIONALS

Joint Statement on Faculty Status of College and University Librarians

The statement that follows was prepared by the Joint Committee on College Library Problems, a national committee representing the Association of College and Research Libraries (ACRL), the Association of American Colleges (now the Association of American Colleges and Universities), and the American Association of University Professors. The statement was endorsed by the board and annual meeting of the ACRL, a division of the American Library Association, in 1972. It was reaffirmed by the ACRL board in June 2001 and 2007. It was adopted by the Council of the American Association of University Professors in April 1973 and endorsed by the Fifty-Ninth Annual Meeting. Additional revisions were made by a joint subcommittee of the ACRL and the AAUP in June 2012; the revised text was adopted by the AAUP's Council and the ACRL in 2012.

As the primary means through which students and faculty gain access to the storehouse of organized knowledge, the college and university library performs a unique and indispensable function in the educational process. This function will grow in importance as students assume greater responsibility for their own intellectual and social development. Indeed, all members of the academic community are likely to become increasingly dependent on skilled professional guidance in the acquisition and use of library resources as the forms and numbers of these resources multiply, scholarly materials appear in more languages, bibliographical systems become more complicated, and library technology grows increasingly sophisticated. The librarian who provides such guidance plays a major role in the learning process.

The character and quality of an institution of higher learning are shaped in large measure by the nature and accessibility of its library resources as well as the expertise and availability of its librarians. Consequently, all members of the faculty should take an active interest in the operation and development of the library. Because the scope and character of library resources should be taken into account in such important

academic decisions as curricular planning and faculty appointments, librarians should have a voice in the development of the institution's educational policy.

Librarians perform a multifaceted role within the academy. It includes not only teaching credit courses but also providing access to information, whether by individual and group instruction, selecting and purchasing resources, digitizing collections, or organizing information. In all of these areas, librarians impart knowledge and skills to students and faculty members both formally and informally and advise and assist faculty members in their scholarly pursuits. They are involved in the research function and conduct research in their own professional interests and in the discharge of their duties. Their scholarly research contributes to the advancement of knowledge valuable to their discipline and institution.

In addition, librarians contribute to university governance through their service on campus-wide committees. They also enhance the reputation of the institution by engaging in meaningful service and outreach to their profession and local communities.

Where the role of college and university librarians, as described in the preceding paragraphs, requires them to function essentially as part of the faculty, this functional identity should be recognized by granting of faculty status. Neither administrative responsibilities nor professional degrees, titles, or skills, per se, qualify members of the academic community for faculty status. The function of the librarian as participant in the processes of teaching, research, and service is the essential criterion of faculty status.

College and university librarians share the professional concerns of faculty members. Academic freedom is indispensable to librarians in their roles as teachers and researchers. Critically, they are trustees of knowledge with the responsibility of ensuring the intellectual freedom of the academic community through the availability of information and ideas, no matter how controversial, so that teachers may freely teach and students may freely learn. Moreover, as members of the academic community, librarians should have latitude in the exercise of their professional judgment within the library, a share in shaping policy within the institution, and adequate opportunities for professional development and appropriate reward.

Faculty status entails for librarians the same rights and responsibilities as for other members of the faculty. They should have corresponding entitlement to rank, promotion, tenure, compensation, leaves, and research funds.

Librarians should be offered the opportunity to have either academic-year appointments with salary and benefits commensurate with those of other faculty members or calendar-year appointments with additional compensation for summer work as is customary for faculty members who take on summer teaching assignments. As with faculty members in other academic departments on campus, librarians should be responsible for the development of their promotion and tenure criteria. Because of the special teaching role of librarians, criteria and standards may differ from traditional classroom faculty, but they must be comparable in rigor and content. Promotion and tenure guidelines should be approved by whatever faculty body is responsible for the establishment of promotion and tenure procedures and policy. Faculty librarians should go through the same process of evaluation as other faculty members.[1]

On some campuses, adequate procedures for extending faculty status to librarians have already been established. These procedures vary from campus to campus because of institutional differences. In the development of such procedures, it is essential that the general faculty or its delegated agent determine the specific steps by which any professional position is to be accorded faculty rank and status. In any case, academic positions that are to be accorded faculty rank and status should be approved by the senate or the faculty at large before submission to the president and to the governing board for approval.

With respect to library governance, it is to be presumed that the governing board, the administrative officers, the library faculty, and representatives of the general faculty will share in the determination of library policies that affect the general interests of the institution and its educational program. In matters of internal governance, the library will operate like other academic units with respect to decisions relating to appointments, promotions, tenure, and conditions of service.[2]

Notes

1. See the 1940 "Statement of Principles on Academic Freedom and Tenure," AAUP, *Policy Documents and Reports*, 11th ed. (Baltimore: Johns Hopkins University Press, 2015), 13–19; the "Statement on Procedural Standards in Faculty Dismissal Proceedings," ibid., 91–93; and the "Statement of Principles on Leaves of Absence," ibid., 317–18.

2. See the "Statement on Government of Colleges and Universities," ibid., 117–22.

College and University Academic and Professional Appointments

This report was prepared by the Association's Committee on Academic Professionals. It was adopted by the Council in November 2002 as Association policy. Statistical information in the report was updated in 2014.

For many years, professional appointees who are not members of the faculty have shared in the academic work of our colleges and universities, including teaching and research. These colleagues often have advanced training and wide experience and perform critical educational roles with students; in many cases, their academic credentials are commensurate with those of faculty. Yet, although they have shared the professional and academic work, many have not been accorded the rights and protections appropriate to their positions.

Over the last decade or so, changes in the medical and health sciences and in student services, in the development of new corporate relationships, and in the use of new technologies, have resulted in the creation of more narrowly specialized and defined positions. Many of these new positions, though professional in nature, lack essential protections of professional autonomy. The Association seeks to ensure sound personnel policies for all faculty and professional appointees, for it believes that these colleagues should share in those personnel policies and protections that are essential to the full exercise of academic and professional judgment and expertise in our colleges and universities. Recognition of these basic rights contributes to the college or university mission by enhancing staff performance, providing a better learning environment for students, and contributing to the welfare of the community.

The terms "academic professional" and "professional appointee" are difficult to define, because different types of institutions and different campuses classify positions in a variety of ways. But the term "professional" carries recognizable characteristics, including advanced education and training, accountability to one's peers in a discipline or profession, accepted standards and practices for the profession, and the necessity for the exercise of independent judgment and expertise.

Data from the 1999 Fall Staff Survey of the National Center for Education Statistics (NCES)

reveal that faculty constitute little more than a third of university and college personnel. Of the remaining two-thirds, about 30 percent are classified as "professional staff." This category includes "technical and paraprofessional" staff; executive, administrative, or managerial personnel; "other professionals"; and graduate assistants.[1] This statement addresses the rights and protections appropriate to full-time academic and professional staff, other than graduate assistants and senior administrators, as defined by the NCES "professional" category and described by the characteristics named above. Examples of staff appointments that may be considered professional appointments are academic advisers, academic-services officers, extension-program coordinators, financial-aid officers, archivists, career counselors, psychologists, and university-press editors. There are also many professional and technical positions in learning or testing centers, research centers, laboratories, medical facilities, allied health centers, computing centers, and other areas.

The Association has afforded membership eligibility to professional appointees in collective bargaining chapters since 1972. Eligibility was not accorded on the basis of a definition or list, but simply on the basis of a "community-of-interest" determination leading to their incorporation in AAUP-affiliated bargaining units by state and federal labor-board decisions. In 1992 the AAUP extended voting membership to similar academic and professional staff regardless of representation. The inclusion of these colleagues as AAUP members heightens the need for the Association to address the issue of protections for professional appointees.

AAUP policies vary substantially both in foundation and in scope of application. The broadest principles apply to all college or university staff, while others apply more narrowly to professional or academic staff, or indeed only to instructional and research faculty. Although it is not feasible here to sort through the full range of AAUP policies in detail and to anticipate their specific application to particular groups of university staff, it is important to formulate some general understandings and guidelines to protect the professional autonomy and security of all professionals regardless of classification.

Many AAUP policies derive in part from broad civic principles and, therefore, apply not only to faculty but also to any employee or citizen. Employees, generally, may have various rights involving freedom of expression and association, democratic participation, nondiscrimination, and due process that are applicable independent of status. AAUP principles derived from general rights also apply regardless of status. But many AAUP policies arise from more specific principles, and these policies involve more specific application.

Accordingly, it is important to consider the manner in which more specific principles, especially those pertaining to the professional and academic nature of faculty work, shape AAUP policies. Similarly, it is necessary to recognize distinctions in the procedures that apply to faculty and to other professionals, and even among professionals. Even among different groups of faculty, the AAUP already recognizes differences in the applicable policies and standards. What is essential, however, is that AAUP policies promote equity and fairness for all professional appointees.

Faculty members and other professional appointees in the academy share similar and overlapping commitments and frequently work with each other on academic and administrative responsibilities. An increasing number of professionals teach academic classes and advise students on their curricular and career choices. These overlapping responsibilities create a community of interest that extends in some measure to such issues as academic governance, affirmative action, academic due process, and, where applicable, collective bargaining. It may prove useful to explore briefly each of these issues.

Issues

Academic freedom for faculty rests on the academic nature of our profession. The Association's 1915 *Declaration of Principles on Academic Freedom and Academic Tenure*[2] elucidates the specifically professional underpinnings of academic freedom, stating that "the scholar has professional functions to perform in which the appointing authorities have neither competency nor moral right to intervene." The need, expressed here and elsewhere, to protect professional expertise is a vital component of the claim to academic freedom and a component even of the

claim to the protections of tenure set forth in the 1940 *Statement of Principles on Academic Freedom and Tenure,* when it calls for "a sufficient degree of economic security to make the profession attractive to men and women of ability." The need to ensure professionalism is shared with others, such as health professionals employed in academic institutions, who, like faculty, need due-process protections to safeguard professional independence and sufficient economic security to justify a long-term investment in professional education and development.

Nonetheless, the 1940 *Statement* pertains to academic freedom and tenure. The controversial nature of the academic process of "the free search for truth and its free expression" is the foundation of the academic profession's unique claim to the due-process protections afforded by tenure. This was manifest to the authors—the Association of College and Research Libraries, the Association of American Colleges (now the Association of American Colleges and Universities), and the AAUP—of the *Joint Statement on Faculty Status of College and University Librarians.*[3] They reasoned:

> Neither administrative responsibilities nor professional degrees, titles, or skills, per se, qualify members of the academic community for faculty status. *The function of the librarian as participant in the process of teaching and research is the essential criterion of faculty status. . . . Academic freedom, for example, is indispensable to [college and university] librarians, because they are trustees of knowledge with the responsibility of ensuring the availability of information and ideas, no matter how controversial, so that teachers may freely teach and students may freely learn.* (Emphasis added.)

Therefore, the joint statement calls for librarians who are involved in teaching and research to have faculty status and the corresponding faculty rights and responsibilities, including tenure. University and college staff who do not share the academic responsibilities entailed in teaching and research are nonetheless entitled to appropriate job security and due process, but not necessarily to the specific guarantees and procedures of tenure. Nor need these professionals experience the unusually long probationary period and demanding evaluation associated with the recognition of tenure.

AAUP policies regarding institutional governance entail similar distinctions. Many management theorists recognize the general value of employee participation in some levels of decision making, and many university administrators support consultation of faculty along with other "concerned groups." The AAUP assertion of faculty primacy in matters of academic policy and decisions regarding faculty status is narrower but reaches further. The *Statement on Government of Colleges and Universities* states: "The primary responsibility of the faculty for such matters is based upon the fact that its judgment is central to general educational policy." Thus the claim of primacy pertains narrowly to academic policy.

Participation in academic governance generally depends on the nature of the appointee's professional training and experience in educational matters. The *Joint Statement on Faculty Status of College and University Librarians* observes that "as members of the academic community, librarians should have latitude in the exercise of their professional judgment within the library [and] a share in shaping policy within the institution." It should be noted that, as in the case of faculty status and tenure, the application to librarians of the AAUP's governance policies reflects their academic as well as their general professional responsibilities. So, too, these recommendations reasonably apply to other essentially academic appointees. All professional appointees are entitled to full participation in nonacademic governance bodies.

The AAUP's standards in the area of affirmative-action policy are also grounded in the academic responsibilities of the faculty. The AAUP's commitment to special measures intended to ensure equal opportunity should apply throughout the college or university, in order to enable the institution to carry out this academic mission. When the AAUP advocates in the 1973 statement *Affirmative Action in Higher Education*[4] that an institution should deliberately take account of race, ethnicity, and gender with a view to affirmative efforts to increase the participation of previously underrepresented groups, the recommendation is grounded not in the generic purpose of providing commensurate job opportunities but in the educational value of diversity: "a recognition of the richness which a variety of intellectual perspectives and life experiences can bring to the program." More specifically, the Association's subsequent 1983 statement *Affirmative-Action Plans*[5] sought to base its recommendation on the US Supreme Court's recognition of diversity as an educational consideration by reasoning that "in the interests of 'diversity' a faculty might make the *academic* judgment that it might be desirable to have more men or women or more black or more white persons among the faculty or student body" (emphasis added).

The AAUP is broadly committed to the concept of "due process," but the Association's recommended policies involving academic due process are often specific to faculty. For example, notice requirements for reappointment and nonrenewal are based on the rhythm of the academic year. Appeal procedures in the event of nonreappointment should distinguish complaints involving alleged discrimination or violation of academic freedom from those alleging inadequate consideration. Although both procedures place the burden of proof on the grievant, those involving academic qualification also call for substantial deference to peer decisions. In the absence of a collective bargaining contract, the AAUP relies on academic peer review rather than external arbitration or adjudication as the primary procedure to resolve complaints or appeals regarding nonrenewal, dismissal, or termination on grounds of program elimination or financial exigency.

Overall, in determining the appropriate protections to be afforded to professionals in the academy, there are at least two questions to be asked in examining a particular professional position: To what extent is the presumption of academic freedom or professional autonomy central to the effective functioning of the person in that position? To what extent does this role require institutional safeguards for its proper exercise? In sum, to the extent that a community of interest with faculty is functionally evident in the tasks undertaken by nonfaculty professionals, the Association recognizes a common ground and a specific obligation to support their concerns.

With a view to safeguarding the quality of academic decision making and in contrast to the possible preferences of many employers, the AAUP calls for faculty involvement in making decisions that may lead to the termination of faculty appointments. Where such procedures are applicable to noninstructional professionals, particular consideration must be given to the delineation of an appropriate peer group. Depending upon the profession, the employee may be involved in a professional organization that provides peer reviews or consultations on the professional judgments of members. Due process procedures can be designed to ensure that a professional staff member is not dismissed or otherwise disciplined for exercising professional expertise or judgment. The AAUP's general commitment to the opportunity for collective bargaining for those who so choose may resolve some of these due-process issues. That is, professionals may, where they have the opportunity to engage in collective bargaining and elect to do so, pursue due process directly through the establish-

ment of grievance and arbitration procedures—
even where AAUP policy prefers peer review.

Recommendations

The AAUP urges colleges and universities to
develop and maintain reasonable and fair
employment policies. All employees, regardless of
academic or professional status, deserve suitable
terms and conditions of employment. Recognition
of these basic rights contributes to the college or
university mission by enhancing staff performance, providing a better learning environment
for students, and contributing to the welfare of
the community. For professionals, the AAUP
recommends, and will seek to ensure, that
universities and colleges provide appropriate
terms and conditions of appointment. These
include, but are not limited to, the following:

1. The terms and conditions of each appointment
   should be stated in writing, and a copy of the
   appointment document and any subsequent
   revisions should be provided to the appointee.
2. All college and university personnel procedures should include appropriate safeguards to
   ensure nondiscrimination and equal opportunity; in the case of primarily academic
   appointments, universities and colleges are
   encouraged to pursue especially vigorous
   efforts to recruit and retain women and
   minorities in the interests of educational
   diversity.
3. Salaries for all appointees should be sufficient
   to support and educate a family in, or in
   reasonable proximity to, the college or
   university community; and salaries of
   professional appointees should be sufficient to
   attract men and women of ability to the
   profession. Compensation should include
   provision for affordable health care and secure
   retirement.
4. Professionals, like other staff, should be afforded a healthy and safe working
   environment.
5. Promotion or other career-advancement
   opportunities should be available based on
   professional and academic qualifications,
   ability, and achievement.
6. Term appointments should include reasonable
   notice of nonrenewal; after a period of
   probation, professional appointees should have
   an opportunity to obtain appropriate security
   of employment.
7. Professionals should have access to a fair and
   reasonable grievance procedure and opportunities for review of allegedly improper
   discipline, nonrenewal, or termination. In the
   case of continuing appointments, discipline
   and discharge should entail demonstration of
   just cause in a due-process hearing. In collegial
   work environments, due process includes an
   opportunity for peer participation in the
   review process.
8. Professionals should have the opportunity to
   participate in institutional policy formulation
   and, when appropriate, collegial personnel
   decisions; those with academic responsibilities
   should have the commensurate opportunity to
   participate in the formulation of academic
   policy. Professionals should have the opportunity to participate in appropriate shared-
   governance bodies.
9. Professionals should be afforded the necessary sphere of autonomous decision making
   within which they can exercise their best
   professional judgment; those with significant
   academic responsibilities should have
   academic freedom in the discharge of those
   responsibilities and in their civic lives. Of
   course, colleges and universities should
   recognize the free-expression rights of all of
   their employees.
10. Professional appointees should have the right
    to choose to participate in collective
    bargaining.

Notes

1. At the time of publication, the most recent data
from NCES are for fall 2011. Those data indicate that
the proportion of faculty has grown from 36 percent of
all employees in 1999 to 39 percent in 2011, while the
proportion of other professionals, using the categories
noted in the original statement, has grown from 39 to
42 percent during the same period. It should also be
noted that most of the growth in faculty positions
during the period has come through part-time
appointments, while the opposite is true for the "other
professional" category.

2. AAUP, *Policy Documents and Reports*, 11th ed.
(Baltimore: Johns Hopkins University Press, 2015),
3–12.

3. *AAUP Bulletin* 59 (June 1973): 266–67. A
subsequently modified version, with language that
differs from the quoted language, can be found in *Policy
Documents and Reports*, 210–11.

4. *AAUP Bulletin* 59 (June 1973): 178–83.

5. *Policy Documents and Reports*, 157–63.

Evaluation of Faculty Members

The Association first addressed the proper evaluation of teaching in 1933, when the Committee on College and University Teaching issued a lengthy report that identified the need for "some systematic plan whereby the quality of teaching can be determined in a more dependable way." The committee commented specifically on the use of student evaluations, which it noted had begun to be employed by institutions "during recent years." The committee observed,

> Too much reliance, in any event, should not be placed upon student opinion with respect to the quality of the teaching that is given to them. For occasionally a teacher achieves a high place in the estimation of his students by doing most of their work for them, by solving all the difficult problems, and by making the subject matter of his course so clear to them that no appreciable intellectual exertion on their own part is demanded. When knowledge comes easily there are some students who put this down as the result of good teaching. To locate the easy teacher is a matter of simple arithmetic, but he often turns out to be a poor teacher. Undergraduates, moreover, are prone to be unduly influenced by a teacher's personal appearance, his mannerisms if he has any, his interest in their student activities, and other things which have little or no relation to the real effectiveness of his classroom work. Frequently it happens, moreover, that students do not appreciate, until years after they have gone out into the world, how much they owe to certain teachers whose work did not impress them as undergraduates.

The committee also commented on the concerns that were raised at the time about the possible protection of tenure for the incompetent, concerns that were eventually to lead to the kinds of proposals addressed in the report on post-tenure review included here. Noting that the Association had never intervened in dismissals resulting from demonstrable incompetence, the committee warned that

> it is well to remember that security of tenure . . . cannot be purchased without price. Any arrangement which is effective in giving peace of mind to those professors whom a college strongly desires to retain must inevitably afford shelter for an occasional teacher whose retention is not so clearly desirable. It is the belief of the committee that a free hand in the dismissal of any teacher whom the college administration is minded to dismiss would break the morale of faculties and would result in poorer rather than better teaching.

Statement on Teaching Evaluation

This statement was prepared by the Association's Committee on Teaching, Research, and Publication. It was adopted by the Association's Council in June 1975 and endorsed by the Sixty-First Annual Meeting.

In response to a chronic need for arriving at fair judgments of a faculty member's teaching, the Association sets forth this statement as a guide to proper teaching evaluation methods and their appropriate uses in personnel decisions. This statement confines itself to the teaching responsibilities of college and university professors and is not intended as the definitive statement on reviewing and weighing all aspects of a faculty member's work. In addressing itself to teaching, the statement has no intention of minimizing the importance of other faculty responsibilities. There is a need for assessment of a teacher's scholarship both more precise and more extensive than commonly employed. There is a need to define service and the value attached to it, as well as to review carefully the kind and quality of service performed by faculty members. Additional guidance in the complex task of reviewing faculty service is to be found in other Association documents: the *Statement on Procedural Standards in the Renewal or Nonrenewal of Faculty Appointments,*[1] the *Recommended Institutional Regulations on Academic Freedom and Tenure,*[2] the *Statement on Government of Colleges and Universities*, and the *Statement on Faculty Workload.*[3]

Colleges and universities properly aspire to excellence in teaching. Institutional aspirations, however, have not often led to practices that clearly identify and reward teaching excellence, and the quality of teaching is not in fact the determining consideration in many decisions on retention, promotion, salary, and tenure. The aspirations of faculty members are often frustrated, because they must wrestle with diverse obligations—commonly identified as *teaching, research*, and *service*—placed upon them by the profession at large, the scholarly discipline, the institution, and their own varied interests. Establishing a positive relationship between the institution's and the department's aspirations and the individual's competencies and aims is one outcome of fair and thorough faculty review procedures.

1. Institutional Values and Policies
Making clear the expectations the institution places upon the teacher and providing the conditions and support necessary to excellent teaching are primary institutional obligations. It is a first order of business that institutions declare their values and communicate them with sufficient clarity to enable colleges and departments to set forth specific expectations as to teaching, research, and service, and to make clear any other faculty obligations. Both institution-wide and college or department policies on promotion, salary, and tenure should be written and subject to periodic review, a process in which faculty members must play a central part.

2. Expectations, Criteria, and Procedures
At the college or department level the expectations as to teaching, the weighting of teaching in relation to other expectations, and the criteria and procedures by which the fulfillment of these expectations is to be judged should be put in writing and periodically reviewed by all members of the college or department. This policy statement should specify the information that is to be gathered for all faculty members, the basic procedures to be followed in gathering it, and the time schedule for various aspects of the review process. Such information should include firsthand data from various sources, including students, and should emphasize the primacy of faculty colleague judgments of teaching effective-

ness at the first level of review and recommendation.

3. Adequate Evaluation Data

Casual procedures, a paucity of data, and unilateral judgments by department chairs and deans too often characterize the evaluation of teaching in American colleges and universities. Praiseworthy and systematic efforts to improve the processes of teaching evaluation have moved toward identifying characteristics of effective teaching and recognizing and weighting the multiple aspects of an individual teacher's performance. A judicious evaluation of a college professor as teacher should include: (a) an accurate factual description of what an individual does as a teacher, (b) various measures of the effectiveness of these efforts, and (c) fair consideration of the relation between these efforts and the institution's and the department's expectations and support. An important and often overlooked element of evaluating teaching is an accurate description of a professor's teaching. Such a description should include the number and level and kinds of classes taught, the numbers of students, and out-of-class activities related to teaching. Such data should be very carefully considered both to guard against drawing unwarranted conclusions and to increase the possibilities of fairly comparing workloads and kinds of teaching, of clarifying expectations, and of identifying particulars of minimum and maximum performance. Other useful information might include evidence of the ability of a teacher to shape new courses, to reach different levels and kinds of students, to develop effective teaching strategies, and to contribute to the effectiveness of the individual's and the institution's instruction in other ways than in the classroom. The gathering of such data can promote a careful consideration of both the institution's and the department's values. If a department, for example, places great value upon teaching large numbers of lower-level students, that value should be reflected in the judgments about teachers who perform such tasks effectively. Too often, even at the simple point of numbers and kinds of students taught, departments and institutions operate on value assumptions seldom made clear to the faculty.

Another kind of data that should be systematically gathered and examined by the teacher's colleagues includes course syllabi, tests, materials, and methods employed in instruction. Care should be taken that such scrutiny not inhibit the teacher, limit the variety of effective teaching styles, or discourage purposeful innovation. Evidence of a concern for teaching and teaching competence demonstrated in publications, attendance at meetings, delivery of lectures, and consulting should also be included among the essential information to be reviewed.

4. Assessing the Effectiveness of Instruction

Student learning. Evaluation of teaching usually refers to efforts made to assess the effectiveness of instruction. The most valid measure is probably the most difficult to obtain, that is, the assessment of a teacher's effectiveness on the basis of the learning of his or her students. On the one hand, a student's learning is importantly influenced by much more than an individual teacher's efforts. On the other, measures of before-and-after learning are difficult to find, control, or compare. From a practical point of view, the difficulties of evaluating college teaching on the basis of changes in student performance limit the use of such a measure. The difficulties, however, should not rule out all efforts to seek reliable evidence of this kind.

Teaching performance. Evaluating teaching on the basis of teaching performance also presents difficulties in measurement, but the large body of research into the reliability and validity of carefully applied performance measures supports the practical usefulness of these data. Data on teaching performance commonly come from trained observers, faculty colleagues, and students.

Student perceptions. Student perceptions are a prime source of information from those who must be affected if learning is to take place. Student responses can provide continuing insights into a number of the important dimensions of a teacher's efforts: classroom performance, advising, and informal and formal contacts with students outside of class. A variety of ways are available to gather student opinion, ranging from informal questioning of individual students about details of a specific course to campus-wide questionnaires.

Faculty members should be meaningfully involved in any systematic efforts to obtain student opinion. Cooperation among students, faculty, and administration is necessary to secure teaching performance data that can be relied upon. No one questionnaire or method is suitable to every department or institution. Different kinds of questionnaires can be useful in assessing different kinds of courses and subject matters and in meeting the need for information of a particular kind. However, a common instrument covering a range of teachers, departments, and subject matter areas has the great advantage of affording meaningful comparative data. The important consideration is to obtain reliable data over a range of teaching assignments and over a period of time. Evaluations in which results go only to the individual professor may be of use in improving an individual teacher's performance, but they contribute little to the process of faculty review. Student input need not be limited by course evaluations. Exit interviews, questionnaires to alumni, and face-to-face discussion are other ways in which student feedback can be profitably gathered.

Classroom visitation. Because of the usefulness of having firsthand information about an individual's teaching effectiveness, some institutions have adopted a program of classroom visitation. There are various ways of having colleagues visit classrooms, but such visits do not necessarily yield reliable data. Careful observations over a period of time may, however, be useful in evaluating instruction and in fostering effective teaching. Clearly, there must be an understanding among the visitors and the visited upon such matters as who does the visiting, how many visits are made, what visitors look for, what feedback is given to the visited, and what other use is made of the information.

Self-evaluation. Some institutions draw upon self-evaluation as an element in assessing teaching. The limitations on self-evaluation are obvious, and neither the teacher nor the institution should be satisfied with self-evaluation alone. However, faculty members as individuals or as members of committees can assist colleagues in making the kind of self-evaluation which constitutes a contribution to improving and evaluating teaching. Arousing an interest in self-examination, structuring self-evaluations so that they might afford more reliable data, and giving faculty members the opportunity to assess their own teaching effectiveness and to add their own interpretation of student ratings and classroom visitations can increase the usefulness of self-evaluation as a part of the review process.

Outside opinions. Some institutions seek outside opinions and judgments as to a professor's competence. Reliable outside judgments about an individual's teaching, however, are difficult to secure. It would be a mistake to suppose that a college teacher's scholarly reputation is an accurate measure of teaching ability. Visiting teams from the outside, given ample time to observe the teacher, to talk with students, and to examine relevant data, might prove a useful, though expensive, means of improving the quality of evaluation. Information and opinions from faculty members in other departments and from persons outside the university should be sought when an individual's teaching assignment and the informant's firsthand knowledge appear to justify their use.

5. Procedures

The emphasis in evaluation should be upon obtaining firsthand evidence of teaching competence, which is most likely to be found among the faculty of a department or college and the students who receive instruction. Evaluation of teaching in which an administrator's judgment is the sole or determining factor is contrary to policies set forth in the *Statement on Government of Colleges and Universities.*

The institution's commitment to teaching should be manifested in concrete ways. For example, some institutions have adopted policies that make recommendations for promotion unacceptable unless they provide strong and convincing evidence of teaching competence. Combining the systematic evaluation of teaching with direct efforts to assist teachers in developing their effectiveness is another example of institutional commitment. It is the responsibility of the institution and the colleges, departments, or other instructional divisions to establish and maintain written policies and procedures that ensure a sound basis for individual judgments fairly applied to all.

Faculty members should have a primary, though not exclusive, role in evaluating an individual faculty member's performance as teacher. Factual data, student opinion, and colleague judgments should be central in the formal procedures for review which should involve faculty discussion and vote. Those being evaluated should be invited to supply information and materials relevant to that evaluation. If the department does not have final authority, the faculty's considered judgment should constitute the basic recommendation to the next level of responsibility, which may be a college-wide or university-wide faculty committee. If the chair's recommendation is contrary to that of the department faculty, the faculty should be informed of the chair's reasons prior to the chair's submitting his or her recommendation and that of the faculty and should be given an opportunity to respond to the chair's views.

The dean's function, where separate from that of a chair or division head, is typically one of review and recommendation either in the dean's own person or through an official review body at that level. If the recommendation at this level is contrary to that of the department chair or faculty, opportunity should be provided for discussion with the chair or faculty before a formal recommendation is made.

Final decisions should be made in accordance with the *Statement on Government of Colleges and Universities:* "The governing board and president should, on questions of faculty status, as in other matters where the faculty has primary responsibility, concur with the faculty judgment except in rare instances and for compelling reasons which should be stated in detail."[4] Procedures in accordance with the Association's *Recommended Institutional Regulations on Academic Freedom and Tenure* and the *Statement on Procedural Standards in the Renewal or Nonrenewal of Faculty Appointments* should be provided to handle faculty grievances arising from advancement recommendations.

6. Some Further Implications

The responsible evaluation of teaching does not serve advancement procedures alone. It should be wisely employed for the development of the teacher and the enhancement of instruction. Both of these aims can be served by the presence of a faculty committee charged with the overall responsibility of remaining conversant with the research in evaluating teaching and of providing assistance in maintaining sound policies and procedures in reviewing faculty performance. The full dimensions of teaching should not be slighted in the desire to arrive at usable data and systematic practices. Though teaching can be considered apart from scholarship and service, the general recognition of these three professional obligations suggests that the relationships are important. The kind of teaching that distinguishes itself in colleges and universities is integral with scholarship, has a way of getting outside classroom confines, and may exemplify the highest meaning of service. A judicious evaluation system would recognize the broad dimensions of teaching, be sensitive to different kinds and styles of instruction, and be as useful in distinguishing superior teaching from the merely competent as in identifying poor teaching.

Notes

1. AAUP, *Policy Documents and Reports,* 11th ed. (Baltimore: Johns Hopkins University Press, 2015), 94–98.

2. Ibid., 79–90.

3. Ibid., 237–40.

4. Ibid., 121.

Observations on the Association's Statement on Teaching Evaluation

The following observations were approved for publication by the Association's Committee on Teaching, Research, and Publication in May 2005 on the occasion of the thirtieth anniversary of the adoption in 1975 of the *Statement on Teaching Evaluation*. These observations were adopted by the Association's Council in November 2005.

Introduction

The *Statement on Teaching Evaluation* remains sound policy, and its guidance "for arriving at fair judgments of a faculty member's teaching" continues to be invaluable.[1] The world of higher education has changed significantly, however, since the publication of the statement. The proportion of faculty appointments that are non-tenure track, full time as well as part time, has grown to more than 60 percent of all faculty appointments;[2] student evaluations of teaching are increasingly relied upon in decisions about renewal, tenure, promotion, and salary increases; new computer-based tools have been developed to administer, disseminate, and interpret student evaluations of teaching; and corporate forms of governance are threatening to become prevalent in higher education. In light of these new and important changes to higher education, we thought it desirable to bring forth these comments.

Observations

The *Statement on Teaching Evaluation* was published in 1975 "as a guide to proper teaching evaluation methods and their appropriate uses in personnel decisions." It recommends that colleges and universities and their academic departments have clear, written policies about expectations concerning teaching, and provide support for meeting those expectations. The statement emphasizes that descriptions of a professor's teaching and data about the teaching obtained from other sources must be accurate. It cautions that "the full dimensions of teaching should not be slighted in the desire to arrive at usable data and systematic practices." The statement further recommends that the faculty member being assessed have a meaningful role in the evaluation process, and it calls for faculty members to have the primary, although not the exclusive, role in evaluating an individual faculty member's

performance as a teacher. Last, it urges that "factual data, student opinion, and colleague judgments should be central in the formal procedures for review, which should involve faculty discussion and vote."

Since the statement's publication, a growing body of scholarship, supplemented by extensive experience, has developed regarding effective teaching and learning strategies, the role of teaching centers in assisting faculty to enhance their teaching, and the evaluation of teaching by faculty peers and students. Both this scholarship and experience show that faculty members share pedagogical and evaluation materials with colleagues; that self evaluation, assessment by teams of faculty members, and student evaluations provide a regular flow of data that facilitates continual improvement in teaching; and that technology has contributed new tools with which teachers may assess and improve their teaching and conduct student evaluations. In addition, the dissemination of evaluations of teaching can provide students with useful information with which to plan their course of study, and offers faculty peers and administrators a richer body of material on which to base judgments of professional merit.

Two key issues identified in the 1975 statement continue, however, to trouble the evaluation of teaching: how best to ensure that evaluations of teaching provide accurate information about the effectiveness of teaching and how to ensure that faculty have the primary responsibility for devising and implementing teaching evaluations. We will offer the following comments on these two issues, and will then turn to an issue of academic freedom.

The expanding use of, and reliance on, teaching evaluations since 1975 have given rise to an abundance of data about classroom performance. Although survey instruments, data collection, and methods for disseminating information vary within and across institutions, several common areas of concern exist with regard to the type, quality, and accuracy of the data collected. One concern involves the practice of relying solely on numerically based student evaluations. Although survey forms that call for numerical evaluations have the advantage of offering a common instrument that can provide comparative data, in many places they have become the dominant, or even sole, component of the evaluation of teaching and tend to displace less standardized and more individualized forms. We encourage the inclusion of a section that invites students to provide written comments relevant to a particular course and a particular instructor.

A second concern is that numerically based evaluations are sometimes misunderstood and therefore misinterpreted, resulting in erroneous conclusions about the absolute and relative merit of faculty members. The data employed are often ill-suited for the type of statistical analysis carried out, being neither continuous in nature nor useful for making the fine distinctions on which rewards are often based. For example, teachers with numerical ratings falling below a certain percentile obtained by the entire faculty, such as 50 or even 90, may be rated as inadequate. Such a use of relative position as an absolute measure of merit overlooks the possibility that the majority of faculty in some departments or institutions will be ranked as "superior," so that some or even all of those in the department or institution with evaluations below the mean may in fact be good teachers. In other departments, most faculty will be ranked as "poor," and some or even all of those ranked above the mean may be poor teachers.

Another problem is the belief that judgments can be made about the relative merit of faculty members despite response rates of students that may vary widely from one class to another. If the response rate by students in one class is higher than 90 percent while in another class of the same size the response rate is 50 percent, no comparison of the sets of responses is statistically valid.

Beyond these concerns about the interpretation of numerical data, a growing body of evidence suggests that student evaluations create pressures that work against educational rigor. Rather than exclusively measure teaching effectiveness, evaluations tend also to measure the influence of personal style, gender, and other matters extraneous to the quality of teaching. One possible way to offset such influences is to include questions directed at student self evaluation in evaluations of teaching (for example, did the student dedicate sufficient time to coursework?).

There is also evidence suggesting that the use of student evaluations in faculty personnel decisions may produce incentives to weaken or dilute course content and contribute to grade inflation. The pressure to do so can be acute for probationary faculty and especially for part- and full-time non-tenure-track faculty who are subject to nonreappointment at the discretion of the administration. These faculty members may come under pressure to give higher grades than students deserve to improve their teaching-evaluation scores. The pressure could be diminished in several ways: through evaluations with specific criteria for faculty members on renewable term appointments; through appointment and reappointment decisions based on criteria specific to the positions; and through opportunities for faculty on renewable term appointments, part- or full-time, to move into tenured or tenurable positions.[3]

The faculty should have primary responsibility for developing reliable methods for evaluating teaching, which should distinguish between questions that are appropriately answered by students and those that are appropriately addressed by peers. The numerical scores that students give instructors on evaluations should be interpreted with valid statistical methods, and, as noted above, a comments section should be included in the instrument.

A separate set of concerns arises as a result of shifts from collegial forms of academic governance, with the emphasis on consultation and participation, to corporate, top-down managerial styles. The corporate model has brought a tendency to judge the success of teaching and teachers in numerical terms, and by the redefinition of education as a commodity that universities are expected to sell and that students, as paying customers, are expected to consume. A potentially troubling effect of this approach to education is that it can create pressure on faculty members to please students rather than to educate them. In this context, teaching evaluations may be seen less as a guide for improving teaching and more as an important marketing tool because they may enhance the image of the institution as responsive to student opinions. Online capabilities may then extend the use of teaching evaluations beyond their traditional scope and purpose. Thus it is not unknown for links to teaching evaluations to be provided in online course catalogues, or for class-by-class, year-by-year evaluation scores to be posted on the Web and thus made available to all faculty and students. Since these measures do not require permission of the instructor, faculty oversight of the evaluation process can be compromised. We urge faculty members to take an active role in formulating and adopting policies that specify the proper use and dissemination of student evaluations of teaching, including the purpose and scope of their online availability.

The relationship between faculty members and those in positions of institutional authority, including department chairs, has also changed. In collective bargaining situations, consideration should be given to including contractual provisions to restrain the potential for administrators to extend their role in the evaluation process by requiring a single approach or evaluative method of the faculty within a department or school, or by mandating the inclusion of certain quantifiable features of evaluation, such as timetables for improvement and specified educational outcomes.

With regard to the role of administrators in the evaluation process, the *Statement on Teaching Evaluation* states, "Emphasis in evaluation should be upon obtaining firsthand evidence of teaching competence, which is most likely to be found among the faculty of a department or college and the students who receive instruction. Evaluation of teaching in which an administrator's judgment is the sole or determining factor is contrary to policies set forth in the *Statement on Government of Colleges and Universities*." We reaffirm the primacy of the faculty in the evaluation of teaching and recommend that institutional evaluation policies preserve the essential role of peer evaluation of courses and teaching performance.

The increasingly important role that technology has assumed in the instruction of virtually all disciplines has raised an issue of academic freedom: the widespread expectation that instructors use particular forms of technology in their courses. Evaluation questionnaires often ask about the use of technology in the learning experience (for example, how many assignments used Web-based resources, or how often did the instructor use the smart workstation for lecture demonstrations?). The inclusion of such questions seems to suggest that faculty members are expected to use these technologies in their classrooms, even though they may have no pedagogical reason to do so. Instructors should be free to determine the extent to which they employ technology in their classrooms according to their professional assessment of its benefits and costs to instruction in a particular subject matter.

The authors of the 1975 statement advocated the evaluation of teaching for the "development of the teacher and the enhancement of instruction." Instructors may accomplish these purposes in several ways. One is to make more extensive use

of the teaching portfolio. Because the portfolio typically contains a statement of teaching philosophy, copies of syllabi, sample corrected work and other course materials, and summaries of student evaluations of the faculty member's teaching, it goes beyond exclusive reliance on student ratings in the evaluation of teaching. Teaching centers have also proved valuable. They provide faculty members with access to fellow teachers or mentors of recognized quality, to courses and workshops on pedagogical matters, to assistance in videotaping of classes, and to libraries with relevant literature. We encourage the use of classroom visitation by peers on a regular basis with advance notice of such visits. We recognize that the logistics of implementing peer evaluation, with at least two or three visits to each class for each evaluation, may be cumbersome. Recognition of the practical difficulties, however, does not relieve members of the profession of their obligation to ensure the quality of teaching, or their responsibility to evaluate teaching performance according to knowledge both of the subject matter and of teaching methods that students may not possess. With respect to guidelines for classroom visitation, we reiterate those outlined in the 1975 statement: "There must be an understanding among the visitors and the visited upon such matters as who does the visiting, how many visits are made, what visitors look for, what feedback is given to the visited, and what other use is made of the information."

In conclusion, institutions, departments, and faculty members should ensure that the evaluations of teaching promote and sustain excellence of teaching and education, that faculty be primarily responsible for devising systems of evaluation and monitoring their use, and that the development and implementation of teaching evaluation methods be consistent with principles of academic freedom and shared governance.

Notes

1. Since the publication of the 1975 "Statement on Teaching Evaluation" (AAUP, *Policy Documents and Reports,* 11th ed. [Baltimore: Johns Hopkins University Press, 2015], 219–22), the Association has addressed the issue of college teaching in additional policy statements. Published statements in *Policy Documents and Reports* include "The Work of Faculty: Expectations, Priorities, and Rewards" (1993), 241–44; "The Assignment of Course Grades and Student Appeals" (1997), 29–30; and the "Statement on Faculty Workload with Interpretive Comments" (2000), 237–40.

2. Another term for the broad category that includes graduate student employees is "instructional staff." In 2011, 76.4 percent of instructional staff appointments

were off the tenure track and 60.8 percent were either part-time faculty members or graduate student employees.

3. The proportion of those individuals in tenured or tenure-track positions had declined to 23.5 percent (John W. Curtis, *The Employment Status of Instructional Staff Members in Higher Education, Fall 2011*, American Association of University Professors, April 2014: 8, Table 5).

On these and related issues, see the report on "Contingent Appointments and the Academic Profession" in *Policy Documents and Reports*, 170–85.

On Collegiality as a Criterion for Faculty Evaluation

The statement that follows was approved by the Association's Committee A on Academic Freedom and Tenure and adopted by the Association's Council in November 1999.

In evaluating faculty members for promotion, renewal, tenure, and other purposes, American colleges and universities have customarily examined faculty performance in the three areas of teaching, scholarship, and service, with service sometimes divided further into public service and service to the college or university. While the weight given to each of these three areas varies according to the mission and evolution of the institution, the terms are themselves generally understood to describe the key functions performed by faculty members.

In recent years, Committee A has become aware of an increasing tendency on the part not only of administrations and governing boards but also of faculty members serving in such roles as department chairs or as members of promotion and tenure committees to add a fourth criterion in faculty evaluation: "collegiality."[1] For the reasons set forth in this statement, we view this development as highly unfortunate, and we believe that it should be discouraged.

Few, if any, responsible faculty members would deny that collegiality, in the sense of collaboration and constructive cooperation, identifies important aspects of a faculty member's overall performance. A faculty member may legitimately be called upon to participate in the development of curricula and standards for the evaluation of teaching, as well as in peer review of the teaching of colleagues. Much research, depending on the nature of the particular discipline, is by its nature collaborative and requires teamwork as well as the ability to engage in independent investigation. And committee service of a more general description, relating to the life of the institution as a whole, is a logical outgrowth of the Association's view that a faculty member is an "officer" of the college or university in which he or she fulfills professional duties.[2]

Understood in this way, collegiality is not a distinct capacity to be assessed independently of the traditional triumvirate of teaching, scholarship, and service. It is rather a quality whose value is expressed in the successful execution of these three functions. Evaluation in these three areas will encompass the contributions that the virtue of collegiality may pertinently add to a faculty member's career. The current tendency to isolate collegiality as a distinct dimension of evaluation, however, poses several dangers. Historically, "collegiality" has not infrequently been associated with ensuring homogeneity, and hence with practices that exclude persons on the basis of their difference from a perceived norm. The invocation of "collegiality" may also threaten academic freedom. In the heat of important decisions regarding promotion or tenure, as well as other matters involving such traditional areas of faculty responsibility as curriculum or academic hiring, collegiality may be confused with the expectation that a faculty member display "enthusiasm" or "dedication," evince "a constructive attitude" that will "foster harmony," or display an excessive deference to administrative or faculty decisions where these may require reasoned discussion. Such expectations are flatly contrary to elementary principles of academic freedom, which protect a faculty member's right to dissent from the judgments of colleagues and administrators.

A distinct criterion of collegiality also holds the potential of chilling faculty debate and discussion. Criticism and opposition do not necessarily conflict with collegiality. Gadflies, critics of institutional practices or collegial norms, even the occasional malcontent, have all been known to play an invaluable and constructive role in the life of academic departments and institutions. They have sometimes proved collegial in the deepest and truest sense. Certainly a college or university replete with genial Babbitts is not the place to which society is likely to look for leadership. It is sometimes exceedingly difficult to distinguish the constructive engagement that characterizes true collegiality from an obstructiveness or truculence that inhibits collegiality. Yet the failure to do so may invite the suppression of dissent. The very real potential for a distinct criterion of "collegiality" to cast a pall of stale uniformity places it in direct tension with the value of faculty diversity in all its contemporary manifestations.

Relatively little is to be gained by establishing collegiality as a separate criterion of assessment. A fundamental absence of collegiality will no doubt manifest itself in the dimensions of teaching, scholarship, or, most probably, service, though here we would add that we all know colleagues whose distinctive contribution to their institution or their profession may not lie so much in service as in teaching and research. Professional misconduct or malfeasance should constitute an independently relevant matter for faculty evaluation. So, too, should efforts to obstruct the ability of colleagues to carry out their normal functions, to engage in personal attacks, or to violate ethical standards. The elevation of collegiality into a separate and discrete standard is not only inconsistent with the long-term vigor and health of academic institutions and dangerous to academic freedom, it is also unnecessary.

Committee A accordingly believes that the separate category of "collegiality" should not be added to the traditional three areas of faculty performance. Institutions of higher education should instead focus on developing clear definitions of teaching, scholarship, and service, in which the virtues of collegiality are reflected. Certainly an absence of collegiality ought never, by itself, to constitute a basis for nonreappointment, denial of tenure, or dismissal for cause.

Notes

1. At some institutions, the term "collegiality" or "citizenship" is employed in regulations or in discussions of institutional practice as a synonym for "service." Our objection is to the use of the term "collegiality" in its description of a separate and additional area of performance in which the faculty member is to be evaluated.

2. The locus classicus for this term is the 1940 "Statement of Principles on Academic Freedom and Tenure": "College and university teachers are citizens, members of a learned profession, and officers of an educational institution" (AAUP, *Policy Documents and Reports*, 11th ed. [Baltimore: Johns Hopkins University Press, 2015], 14).

Post-tenure Review: An AAUP Response

The following report, approved in June 1999 by the Association's Committee A on Academic Freedom and Tenure, was adopted that month by the Council and endorsed by the Eighty-Fifth Annual Meeting.

Introduction

The Association's existing policy on post-tenure review, approved by Committee A and adopted by the Council in November 1983, is as follows:

> The Association believes that periodic formal institutional evaluation of each post-probationary faculty member would bring scant benefit, would incur unacceptable costs, not only in money and time but also in dampening of creativity and of collegial relationships, and would threaten academic freedom.
>
> The Association emphasizes that no procedure for evaluation of faculty should be used to weaken or undermine the principles of academic freedom and tenure. The Association cautions particularly against allowing any general system of evaluation to be used as grounds for dismissal or other disciplinary sanctions. The imposition of such sanctions is governed by other established procedures, enunciated in the 1940 *Statement of Principle on Academic Freedom and Tenure* and the *Statement on Procedural Standards in Faculty Dismissal Proceedings* that provide the necessary safeguards of academic due process.

By the mid-1990s, new forms of post-tenure review were appearing: a significant number of legislatures, governing boards, and university administrators were making such reviews mandatory; others were in various stages of consideration. For this reason it has become necessary not only to *reaffirm* the principles of the 1983 statement, but also to provide standards that can be used to assess the review process when it is being considered or implemented. This report accordingly offers practical recommendations for faculty at institutions where post-tenure review is being considered or has been put into effect.

The principles guiding this document are these: Post-tenure review ought to be aimed not at accountability, but at faculty development. Post-tenure review must be developed and carried out by faculty. Post-tenure review must not be a reevaluation of tenure, nor may it be used to shift the burden of proof from an institution's administration (to show cause for dismissal) to the individual faculty member (to show cause why he or she should be retained). Post-tenure review must be conducted according to standards that protect academic freedom and the quality of education.

Definition of Terms

Because post-tenure review is used to mean many things, it is important to define our understanding of the term. Lurking within the phrase are often two misconceptions: that tenured faculty are not already recurrently subject to a variety of forms of evaluation of their work, and that the presumption of merit that attaches to tenure should be periodically cast aside so that the faculty member must bear the burden of justifying retention. Neither assumption is true. Although it would perhaps be best to utilize a term other than post-tenure review, most alternative expressions (such as periodic evaluation of tenured faculty) do not clearly enough dispel the misconceptions, and the more familiar term has become so widely adopted in academic parlance that it would only create additional confusion were it not used here.

Post-tenure review is a system of periodic evaluation that goes beyond the many traditional forms of continuous evaluation utilized in most colleges and universities. These traditional forms of evaluation vary in their formality and comprehensiveness. They include annual reports for purposes of determining salary and promotion, reviews for the awarding of grants and sabbaticals, and reviews for appointment to school and university committees, graduate faculties, interdisciplinary programs, and professorial chairs and learned societies. More narrowly focused reviews include course-by-course student teaching evaluations, peer review and wider public scrutiny of scholarly presentations and publications, and both administrative and collegial observation of service activities. Faculty members are also evaluated in the course of the program reviews required for regional or specialized accreditation and certification of undergraduate and graduate programs.

What post-tenure review typically adds to these long-standing practices is a formalized additional layer of review that, if it is not simply redundant, may differ in a number of respects: the frequency and comprehensiveness of the review, the degree of involvement by faculty peers, the use of self-evaluations, the articulation of performance objectives, the extent of constructive "feedback," the application of innovative standards and principles, and the magnitude of potential sanctions. At its most draconian, post-tenure review aims to reopen the question of tenure; at its most benign, it formalizes and systematizes long-standing practices. In this report, we use the term post-tenure review to refer to the variety of practices that superimpose a more comprehensive and systematic structure on existing processes of evaluation of tenured faculty.

Post-tenure Review and Academic Freedom: A General Caution

Post-tenure review should not be undertaken for the purpose of dismissal. Other formal disciplinary procedures exist for that purpose. If they do not, they should be developed separately, following generally accepted procedures.[1]

Even a carefully designed system of post-tenure review may go awry in a number of ways of serious concern to the Association. Many, though not all, proponents of post-tenure review purportedly seek to supplement preexisting ways of reviewing the performance of tenured faculty with a system of managerial accountability that could ensure faculty productivity, redirect faculty priorities, and facilitate dismissal of faculty members whose performance is deemed unsatisfactory. Despite assurances by proponents that they do not so intend, the substitution of managerial accountability for professional responsibility characteristic of this more intrusive form of post-tenure review alters academic practices in ways that inherently diminish academic freedom.

The objectionable change is not that tenured faculty would be expected to undergo periodic evaluation. As noted here, they generally do—and they should. Nor is there any claim that tenure must be regarded as an indefinite entitlement. Tenured faculty are already subject to dismissal for incompetence, malfeasance, or failure to perform their duties, as well as on grounds of bona fide financial exigency or program termination. Nor is the issue, as many faculty imagine, simply who controls the evaluation. Faculty members as well as administrators can and do err.

Rather, the most objectionable feature of many systems of post-tenure review is that they ease

the prevailing standards for dismissal and diminish the efficacy of those procedures that ensure that sanctions are not imposed for reasons violative of academic freedom. Some proponents of post-tenure review, motivated by a desire to facilitate the dismissal of tenured faculty, seek to substitute less protective procedures and criteria at the time of post-tenure review. But demanding procedures and standards are precisely what prevent dismissal for reasons violative of academic freedom.

If the standard of dismissal is shifted from "incompetence" to "unsatisfactory performance," as in some current proposals, then tenured faculty must recurrently "satisfy" administrative officers rather than the basic standards of their profession. In addition, some forms of post-tenure review shift the burden of proof in a dismissal hearing from the institution to the tenured faculty member by allowing the institution to make its case simply by proffering the more casually developed evaluation reports from earlier years. Effectively the same concerns arise when the stipulated channel for challenging substantively or procedurally unfair judgments in the course of post-tenure review is through a grievance procedure in which the burden of proving improper action rests with the faculty member.

Academic freedom is not adequately protected in any milieu in which most faculty members bear the burden of demonstrating a claim that their dismissal is for reasons violative of their academic freedom. The heightened protection of the tenured faculty is not a privilege, but a responsibility earned by the demonstration of professional competence in an extended probationary period, leading to a tenured position with its "rebuttable presumption of professional excellence."[2] It chills academic freedom when faculty members are subjected to revolving contracts or recurrent challenge after they have demonstrated their professional competence.

When post-tenure review substitutes review procedures for adversarial hearing procedures, or diverse reappointment standards for dismissal standards, it creates conditions in which a host of plausible grounds for dismissal may cloak a violation of academic freedom. Innovative research may be dismissed as unproven, demanding teaching as discouraging, and independence of mind as a lack of collegiality. The lengthy demonstration of competence that precedes the award of tenure is required precisely so that faculty are not recurrently at risk and are afforded the professional autonomy and integrity essential to academic quality.

We recognize that some tenured faculty members may, nonetheless, fail to fulfill their professional obligations because of incompetence, malfeasance, or simple nonperformance of their duties. Where such a problem appears to exist, "targeted" review and evaluation should certainly be considered, in order to provide the developmental guidance and support that can assist the faculty member to overcome those difficulties. Should it be concluded, however, that such developmental assistance is (or is likely to be) unavailing, the remedy lies not in a comprehensive review of the entire faculty, nor in sacrificing the procedural protections of the tenured faculty member, but in an orderly application of long-standing procedures such as those in the Association's *Recommended Institutional Regulations on Academic Freedom and Tenure* (Regulations 5–7) for the imposition of sanctions up to and including dismissal.

In other cases, faculty members may voluntarily agree to redirect their work or to accept early-retirement incentives as a consequence, for example, of a decision to redirect departmental priorities. But the use of sanctions pursuant to individual reviews to induce the resignation of programmatically less "desirable" faculty members or to redirect otherwise competent faculty endeavors may well have deleterious consequences for academic freedom. The prohibition of the use of major sanctions to redirect or reinvigorate faculty performance without a formal finding of inadequacy does not mean that administrators and colleagues have no less demanding recourse to bring about improvement. Although academic acculturation will ordinarily have provided a sufficient incentive, the monetary rewards or penalties consequent on salary, promotion, and grant reviews can and do encourage accommodation to institutional standards and professional values.

Even on campuses where there is not thought to be a problem with so-called "deadwood" or incompetent faculty members, many proponents of post-tenure review, as well as those who adopt it in the hope of forestalling more comprehensive and blatant attacks on tenure, sometimes envision such review as a means for achieving larger management objectives such as "downsizing," "restructuring," or "reengineering." Individual faculty reviews should, however, focus on the quality of the faculty member's work and not on such larger considerations as programmatic direction. Downsizing may be properly accomplished through long-term strategic planning and, where academically appropriate, formal program discontinuance (with tenured faculty subject to termination of appointment only if reasonable efforts to retrain and reassign them to other suitable positions are unsuccessful).

It might be thought that the untoward impact on academic freedom and tenure may thus be eliminated by implementing a system of post-tenure review that has no explicit provision for disciplinary sanctions. Even here, however, where the reviews are solely for developmental ends, there is a natural expectation that, if evidence of deficiency is found, sanctions of varying degrees of subtlety and severity will indeed follow, absent prompt improvement. Hence, even the most benign review may carry a threat, require protections of academic due process, and inappropriately constrain faculty performance. This point warrants further elaboration.

A central dimension of academic freedom and tenure is the exercise of professional judgment in such matters as the selection of research projects, teaching methods and course curricula, and evaluations of student performance. Those who have followed recent attacks on faculty workloads know that the issue rapidly shifted from the allegation that faculty did not work enough (which, it turned out, they plainly did) to the allegation that faculty did not do the right sort of work. Some proponents of post-tenure review will thus not be content with the identification of the few "slackers" already known to their colleagues by other means, nor even with the imposition of a requirement of faculty cooperation and institutional loyalty. They also want faculty members to give back some portion of their ability to define their own work and standards of performance. For example, increased emphasis on students' evaluations of teaching may lead to the avoidance of curricular experimentation or discourage the use of more demanding course materials and more rigorous standards. Periodic review that is intended not only to ensure a level of faculty performance (defined by others than faculty) but also to shape that performance accordingly, and regardless of tenure, is a most serious threat to academic freedom.

Another consequence of the misapplication of the managerial model to higher education is the ignoring of another important dimension of academic freedom and tenure: time, the time required to develop and complete serious professional undertakings. Shortening the time horizon of faculty, so as to accord with periodic reviews, will increase productivity only artificially, if at all. More frequent and formal reviews may lead faculty members to pick safe and quick, but less potentially valuable, research projects to minimize the risk of failure or delayed achievement.

By way of summary, then, of the Association's principal conclusions, well-governed universities already provide a variety of forms of periodic evaluation of tenured faculty that encourage both responsible performance and academic integrity. Those forms of post-tenure review that diminish the protections of tenure also unambiguously diminish academic freedom, not because they reduce job security but because they weaken essential procedural safeguards. The only acceptable route to the dismissal of incompetent faculty is through carefully crafted and meticulously implemented procedures that place the burden of proof on the institution and that ensure due process. Moreover, even those forms of post-tenure review that do not threaten tenure may diminish academic freedom when they establish a climate that discourages controversy or risk-taking, induces self-censorship, and in general interferes with the conditions that make innovative teaching and scholarship possible. Such a climate, although frequently a product of intervention by trustees or legislators, may instead regrettably flow on occasion from unduly intrusive monitoring by one's faculty peers.

Comprehensive post-tenure review is thus a costly and risky innovation, which may fail either to satisfy ill-informed critics on the one hand or to protect professional integrity on the other. If managerially imposed, it may be a poor substitute for the complex procedures colleges and universities have crafted over the years to balance professional responsibility and autonomy. On the other hand, if designed and implemented by the faculty in a form that properly safeguards academic freedom and tenure and the principle of peer review, and if funded at a meaningful level, it may offer a way of evaluating tenured faculty which supports professional development as well as professional responsibility. To that end, we offer the following guidelines and standards.

Guidelines for Deciding Whether to Establish a Formal System of Post-tenure Review

1. It is the obligation of the administration and governing board to observe the principle, enunciated in the Association's *Statement on Government of Colleges and Universities,* that the faculty exercises primary responsibility for faculty status and thus the faculty is the appropriate body to take a leadership role in designing additional procedures for the evaluation of faculty peers. Faculty representatives involved in the development of those procedures should be selected by the faculty according to procedures determined by the faculty.[3]

2. Any discussion of the evaluation of tenured faculty should take into account procedures that are already in place for that purpose: e.g., annual merit reviews of teaching, scholarly productivity, and service; comprehensive consideration at the time of promotion to professor and designation to professorial chairs; and programmatic and accreditation reviews that include analyses of the qualifications and performance of faculty members in that program. The discussion should elicit convincing data on what it is that existing procedures fail to address. The questions for faculty bodies include:
   a. What are the problems that are calling for this particular solution? Are they of a degree that requires more elaborate, or more focused, procedures for enhancing faculty performance?
   b. If the answer to the latter question is yes, would it be possible to devise a system of post-tenure review on the basis of existing procedures—for example, a five-year review that is "piggybacked" onto the annual reviews? It should be noted that this system may serve a constructive purpose for those departments that do not do an adequate job in their annual review.
   c. Is the projected post-tenure review confined to developmental purposes, or is it being inappropriately projected as a new and easier way of levying major sanctions up to and including dismissal?

3. If the institution does not already have in place standards for dismissal-for-cause proceedings, it should adopt such procedural standards as are set forth in existing Association policy statements rather than move to post-tenure review as an alternative dismissal route.[4]

4. Just as the Association has never insisted on a single model of faculty governance but only on the underlying premises that should guide a college or university in respect to that governance, so here any particular form of post-tenure review will depend on the characteristics of the institution: its size, its mission, and the needs and preferences of the faculty, as well as on the resources that the institution can bring to bear in the area of faculty development. Again, the questions to be asked include, but are not necessarily limited to:
   a. whether the review should be "blanket" for all tenured faculty or focused on problematic cases;
   b. whether a review can be activated at the request of an individual faculty member for

purposes that he or she would regard as constructive;

c. whether a cost-benefit analysis shows that institutional resources can adequately support a meaningful and constructive system for post-tenure review without damage to other aspects of the academic program and to the recognition of faculty merit, since the constructiveness of such a system depends not only on the application of these standards but also on the ability to support and sustain faculty development.

5. Any new system of post-tenure review should initially be set up on a trial basis and, if continued, should itself be periodically evaluated with respect to its effectiveness in supporting faculty development and redressing problems of faculty performance, the time and cost of the effort required, and the degree to which in practice it has been effectively cordoned off—as it must be if it is to be constructive—from disciplinary procedures and sanctions.

Minimum Standards for Good Practice If a Formal System of Post-tenure Review Is Established

1. Post-tenure review must ensure the protection of academic freedom as defined in the 1940 *Statement of Principles.* The application of its procedures, therefore, should not intrude on an individual faculty member's proper sphere of professional self-direction, nor should it be used as a subterfuge for effecting programmatic change. Such a review must not become the occasion for a wide-ranging "fishing expedition" in an attempt to dredge up negative evidence.

2. Post-tenure review must not be a reevaluation or revalidation of tenured status as defined in the 1940 *Statement.* In no case should post-tenure review be used to shift the burden of proof from the institution's administration (to show cause why a tenured faculty member should be dismissed) to the individual faculty member (to show cause why he or she should be retained).

3. The written standards and criteria by which faculty members are evaluated in post-tenure review should be developed and periodically reviewed by the faculty. The faculty should also conduct the actual review process. The basic standard for appraisal should be whether the faculty member under review discharges conscientiously and with professional competence the duties appropriately associated with his or her position, not whether the

faculty member meets the current standards for the award of tenure as those might have changed since the initial granting of tenure.

4. Post-tenure review should be developmental and supported by institutional resources for professional development or a change of professional direction. In the event that an institution decides to invest the time and resources required for comprehensive or "blanket" review, it should also offer tangible recognition to those faculty members who have demonstrated high or improved performance.

5. Post-tenure review should be flexible enough to acknowledge different expectations in different disciplines and changing expectations at different stages of faculty careers.

6. Except when faculty appeals procedures direct that files be available to aggrieved faculty members, the outcome of evaluations should be confidential, that is, confined to the appropriate college or university persons or bodies and the faculty member being evaluated, released otherwise only at the discretion, or with the consent of, the faculty member.

7. If the system of post-tenure review is supplemented, or supplanted, by the option of a formal development plan, that plan cannot be imposed on the faculty member unilaterally, but must be a product of mutual negotiation. It should respect academic freedom and professional self-direction, and it should be flexible enough to allow for subsequent alteration or even its own abandonment. The standard here should be that of good faith on both sides—a commitment to improvement by the faculty member and to the adequate support of that improvement by the institution—rather than the literal fulfillment of a set of nonnegotiable demands or rigid expectations, quantitative or otherwise.

8. A faculty member should have the right to comment in response to evaluations, and to challenge the findings and correct the record by appeal to an elected faculty grievance committee[5] or she should have the same rights of comment and appeal concerning the manner in which any individualized development plan is formulated, the plan's content, and any resulting evaluation.

9. In the event that recurring evaluations reveal continuing and persistent problems with a faculty member's performance that do not lend themselves to improvement after several efforts, and that call into question his or her ability to function in that position, then other possibilities, such as a mutually agreeable

reassignment to other duties or separation, should be explored. If these are not practicable, or if no other solution acceptable to the parties can be found, then the administration should invoke peer consideration regarding any contemplated sanctions.[6]

10. The standard for dismissal or other severe sanction remains that of adequate cause, and the mere fact of successive negative reviews does not in any way diminish the obligation of the institution to show such cause in a separate forum before an appropriately constituted hearing body of peers convened for that purpose. Evaluation records may be admissible but rebuttable as to accuracy. Even if they are accurate, the administration is still required to bear the burden of proof and demonstrate through an adversarial proceeding not only that the negative evaluations rest on fact, but also that the facts rise to the level of adequate cause for dismissal or other severe sanction. The faculty member must be afforded the full procedural safeguards set forth in the *Statement on Procedural Standards in Faculty Dismissal Proceedings* and the *Recommended Institutional Regulations on Academic Freedom and Tenure*, which include, among

other safeguards, the opportunity to confront and cross-examine adverse witnesses.

Notes

1. These procedures are set forth in the 1940 "Statement of Principles on Academic Freedom and Tenure," the "Statement on Procedural Standards in Faculty Dismissal Proceedings," and the Association's "Recommended Institutional Regulations on Academic Freedom and Tenure." These documents appear in AAUP, *Policy Documents and Reports*, 11th ed. (Baltimore: Johns Hopkins University Press, 2015), 13–19, 91–93, and 79–90.

2. See William Van Alstyne, "Tenure: A Summary, Explanation, and 'Defense,'" *AAUP Bulletin* 57 (September 1971): 328–33; and Matthew W. Finkin, "The Assault on Faculty Independence," *Academe* 83 (July–August 1997): 16–21.

3. Here, and in other guidelines and standards set forth below, the procedures, in addition to conforming with established AAUP-supported standards, should also conform to the applicable provisions of any collective bargaining agreement.

4. For the applicable policy statements, see note 1.

5. See Regulation 16, "Recommended Institutional Regulations," *Policy Documents and Reports*, 88.

6. See Regulations 5–7, "Recommended Institutional Regulations," ibid., 83–85.

Faculty Work

The Committee on the Normal Amount of Teaching and Research observed in its report to the 1930 annual meeting that it was necessary "in considering the teaching load to include every phase of it that takes the professor's time and energy, not merely the hours the professor punches on the classroom time-clock." The committee also pointed out that "the professor as a class is expected as part of his duties to engage in numerous 'outside activities.'" At the time, it was common for research to be considered as one of the many unremunerated "outside activities" rather than as part of faculty workload. Given the many demands on professors' time, the committee responded to administrators' calls for increased teaching loads: "It is not a question of whether the professor can teach more hours; it is a question of whether for the best good of himself and his work he ought to do so." The committee's main concern was the lowering of quality which accompanies the increase of quantity in teaching.

Enumerating "the multifarious extra-curricular activities in which college teachers sometimes engage," the Committee on College and University Teaching in its 1932 report identified "the giving of extension and correspondence courses, outside speaking engagements which professors are urged to make as a service to the institution, professional work closely related to a teacher's field of scholarship (such as the editing of a scientific periodical), remunerated outside employment (such as serving as an industrial consultant), and evening classes such as are held in some metropolitan institutions." The committee recommended that "extension courses, correspondence courses, and evening classes, as well as committee work within the institution if it is of any considerable amount, should be counted as part of the weekly teaching load and should be paid for within the teacher's regular salary rather than as extra compensation."

While the reports of the two committees cited here show the constancy of some of the concerns about faculty workload over the past eighty years, other concerns have changed during that time. The mention of "correspondence courses" in 1932 gave way to a *Statement on Instructional Television* in 1969, the subject of which in turn was radically superseded by online and distance learning, addressed in a report included here.

Statement on Faculty Workload with Interpretive Comments

This statement was approved by the Association's Committee on Teaching, Research, and Publication in April 1968. It was adopted by the Association's Council in October 1969 and endorsed by the Fifty-Sixth Annual Meeting.

Introduction

No single formula for an equitable faculty workload can be devised for all of American higher education. What is fair and works well in the community college may be inappropriate for the university, and the arrangement thought necessary in the technical institute may be irrelevant in the liberal arts college.

This is not to say, however, that excessive or inequitably distributed workloads cannot be recognized as such. In response to the many appeals received in recent years, therefore, this Association wishes to set forth such guidelines as can be applied generally, regardless of the special circumstances of the institution concerned:

1. A definition of maximum teaching loads for effective instruction at the undergraduate and graduate levels.
2. A description of the procedures that should be followed in establishing, administering, and revising workload policies.
3. An identification of the most common sources of inequity in the distribution of workloads.

Maximum Teaching Loads

In the American system of higher education, faculty "workloads" are usually described in hours per week of formal class meetings. As a measurement, this leaves much to be desired. It fails to consider other time-consuming institutional duties of the faculty member, and, even in terms of teaching, it misrepresents the true situation. The teacher normally spends far less time in the classroom than in preparation, conferences, grading of papers and examinations, and supervision of remedial or advanced student work. Preparation, in particular, is of critical importance, and is probably the most unremitting of these demands; not only preparation for specific classes or conferences, but that more general preparation in the discipline, by keeping up with recent developments and strengthening one's grasp on older materials, without which the faculty member will soon dwindle into ineffec-

tiveness as scholar and teacher. Moreover, traditional workload formulations are at odds with significant current developments in education emphasizing independent study, the use of new materials and media, extracurricular and off-campus educational experiences, and interdisciplinary approaches to problems in contemporary society. Policies on workload at institutions practicing such approaches suggest the need for a more sophisticated discrimination and weighting of educational activities.

This Association has been in a position over the years to observe workload policies and faculty performance in a great variety of American colleges and universities, and in its considered judgment the following maximum workload limits are necessary for any institution of higher education seriously intending to achieve and sustain an adequately high level of faculty effectiveness in teaching and scholarship:

For undergraduate instruction, a teaching load of twelve hours per week, with no more than six separate course preparations during the academic year.

For instruction partly or entirely at the graduate level, a teaching load of nine hours per week.

This statement of *maximum* workload presumes a traditional academic year of not more than thirty weeks of classes. Moreover, it presumes no unusual additional expectations in terms of research, administration, counseling, or other institutional responsibilities. Finally, it presumes also that means can be devised within each institution for determining fair equivalents in workload for those faculty members whose activities do not fit the conventional classroom lecture or discussion pattern: for example, those who supervise laboratories or studios, offer tutorials, or assist beginning teachers.

Preferred Teaching Loads

Even with the reservations just enunciated, however, it would be misleading to offer this statement of maximum loads without providing some guidelines for a preferable pattern. This Association has observed in recent years a steady reduction of teaching loads in American colleges and universities noted for the effectiveness of their faculties in teaching and scholarship to norms that can be stated as follows:

For undergraduate instruction, a teaching load of nine hours per week.

For instruction partly or entirely at the graduate level, a teaching load of six hours per week.

The Association has observed also that in the majority of these institutions further reductions have become quite usual for individuals assuming heavier-than-normal duties in counseling, program development, administration, research, and many other activities. In a smaller number, moreover, even lower teaching loads have been established generally, for all faculty members.

It must be recognized that achievement of nine- or six-hour teaching loads may not be possible at present for many institutions. The Association believes, nevertheless, that the nine- or six-hour loads achieved by our leading colleges and universities, in some instances many years ago, provide as reliable a guide as may be found for teaching loads in any institution intending to achieve and maintain excellence in faculty performance.

Procedures

The faculty should participate fully in the determination of workload policy, both initially and in all subsequent reappraisals. Reappraisal at regular intervals is essential, in order that older patterns of faculty responsibility may be adjusted to changes in the institution's size, structure, academic programs, and facilities. Current policy and practices should be made known clearly to all faculty members, including those new to the institution each year.

The individual may have several quite different duties, some of which may be highly specialized, and the weight of these duties may vary strikingly at different times during the year. It is important, therefore, that individual workloads be determined by, or in consultation with, the department or other academic unit most familiar with the demands involved. Those responsible should be allowed a measure of latitude in making individual assignments, and care should be taken that all of the individual's services to the institution are considered.

Common Sources of Inequity in the Distribution of Workloads

1. *Difficulty of Courses.* No two courses are exactly alike, and some differences among individual loads are therefore to be expected within a common twelve-hour, nine-hour, or six-hour policy. Serious inequity should be avoided, however, and the most frequent sources of difficulty are easily identified.

   a. The number of different course preparations should be considered, not only the total class hours per week.

   b. Special adjustments may be appropriate for the faculty member introducing a new course or substantially revising an older course. This is a matter of institutional self-interest as well as of equity; if the new course has been approved as likely to strengthen the institution's program, all appropriate measures should be taken to ensure its success.

   c. Extreme differences in scope and difficulty among courses should not be overlooked merely because contention might be provoked on other less obvious imbalances. The difference in difficulty among some courses is so pronounced that no faculty member concerned would deny the existence of the discrepancy. Such imbalances may occur among courses in different disciplines as well as those within the same discipline. In some subjects the advanced course is the more demanding; in others, the introductory course. One course may entail constant student consultation; another may entail a heavy burden of paperwork. At least the more obvious discrepancies should be corrected.

   d. The size of the classes taught should also be considered. The larger class is not always more demanding than the smaller class; but it does not follow that the question of class size can safely be ignored. In a given institution there will be many generally comparable courses, and for these the difficulty will probably be directly proportionate to the number of students involved. In some institutions aware of this problem, faculty workload is now measured in terms of student-instruction load, or "contact hours," as well as in the conventional classroom or credit hours. Regardless of the institution's particular circumstances, it should be possible by formal or informal means to avoid serious inequities on these four major points.

2. *Research.* Increasingly each year undergraduate as well as graduate institutions specify "research" as a major responsibility of the faculty. Lack of clarity or candor about what constitutes such "research" can lead to excessive demands on the faculty generally or on part of the faculty. If the expectation is only of that "general preparation" already described, no additional reduction in faculty workload is indicated. Usually, however, something beyond that general preparation is meant: original, exploratory work in some special field of interest within the discipline. It should be recognized that if this is the expectation, such research, *whether or not it leads to publication,* will require additional time. It is very doubtful that a continuing effort in original inquiry can be maintained by a faculty member carrying a teaching load of more than nine hours; and it is worth noting that a number of leading universities desiring to emphasize research have already moved or are now moving to a six-hour policy. If it is original work that is expected, but the institution fails to state candidly whether in practice scholarly publication will be regarded as the only valid evidence of such study, the effect may well be to press one part of the faculty into "publishing research" at the expense of a "teaching research" remainder. Neither faculty group will teach as well as before.

In short, if research is to be considered a *general* faculty responsibility, the only equitable way to achieve it would seem to be a *general* reduction in faculty workload. If the expectation is that some but not all of the faculty will be publishing scholars, then that policy should be candidly stated and faculty workloads adjusted equitably in accordance with that expectation.

3. *Responsibilities Other Than Teaching and Research.* Although faculty members expect as a matter of course to serve in student counseling, on committees, with professional societies, and in certain administrative capacities, a heavy commitment in any of these areas, or service in too many of these areas at once, will of course impair the effectiveness of the faculty member as teacher and scholar. A reduction in workload is manifestly in order when an institution wishes to draw heavily on the services of an individual in these ways, or when with its approval the individual is engaged in community or government service. No universally applicable rule can be advanced here but, as suggested earlier, the faculty unit

responsible for individual assignments should take all such additional service into full consideration. Often, the determination of an appropriate reduction in workload depends on nothing more complex than an estimate of the hours that these additional duties will require.

2000 Interpretive Comments
The interpretive comments that follow were approved by the Association's Committee on Teaching, Research, and Publication in March 2000. They were adopted by the Association's Council in June 2000 and endorsed by the Eighty-Sixth Annual Meeting.

The world of higher education has changed significantly since the Association issued its *Statement on Faculty Workload* in 1969. While the number of faculty members in the profession has increased considerably, the proportion who hold positions that are with tenure or probationary for tenure has decreased significantly. Colleges and universities are meeting their instructional needs by increasing their reliance on part-time, adjunct, or full-time non-tenure-track faculty members and on new technologies. The increased reliance on various types of non-tenure-track faculty has added to the workload of tenured and tenure-track faculty, who must assume additional administrative and governance responsibilities. In reviewing the *Statement on Faculty Workload,* we have looked at how these changes affect the work of faculty in what was already a complex and diversified academic workplace.

The Association's recommendations regarding workload were developed, according to the *Statement on Faculty Workload,* in order to ensure and sustain an "adequately high level of faculty effectiveness in teaching and scholarship." That statement recommended *maximum* and *preferred* teaching loads, and offered differing workload recommendations based on whether or not the instruction was offered at the undergraduate or the graduate level. We reaffirm the need to distinguish between *maximum* and *preferred* loads, but we believe that differences in workload should reflect the differing research and instructional expectations for faculty members at different kinds of academic institutions. We believe that institutional expectations concerning the amount of research a faculty member is required to conduct are a more useful determinant than whether instruction is offered at the undergraduate or the graduate level.

The 1969 *Statement* noted that no single formula for an equitable faculty workload could be devised for all of American higher education. Still, we note that the various segments of higher education have all recently undergone similar changes in the pattern of faculty appointments and in the nature of technological innovations.

This committee has also examined the application of the 1969 *Statement* in the context of the rapidly growing community college segment of American higher education.

Maximum Teaching Loads

1. *Community Colleges.* Community college teaching loads have typically exceeded the maximum of twelve hours per week that the 1969 *Statement* recommended for undergraduate instruction. We believe that the recommended maximum load should remain the twelve hours recommended in the original statement. The academic and instructional responsibilities and obligations involved in educating the diverse range of students who attend community colleges are no less demanding than those at other institutions of higher education. Although the expectations for research and service in the two-year sector may differ in particulars from those in other sectors of higher education, the professional demands are equivalent.

2. *Part-Time Faculty.* Many institutions have converted full-time faculty appointments to positions held by part-time faculty or graduate assistants. We observe with concern that recent institutional practice has led to a multitier system of appointments that provide part-time faculty members little opportunity to conduct research or to participate in professional development.

    We recommend that part-time faculty appointments not be based, as they commonly are, solely on course or teaching hours. Activities that extend well beyond classroom time—including maintaining office hours, participating in collegial curricular discussions, preparing courses, and grading examinations and essays—should be recognized. These faculty duties should be defined, and the part-time faculty members who engage in

these activities should be compensated and supported professionally based on pro-rata or proportional performance of an equivalent full-time position.[1]

3. *Graduate Teaching Assistants.* The teaching loads of graduate assistants should permit those who hold these positions to meet their own educational responsibilities as well as to meet the needs of their students. We therefore see merit in an institution's setting a limit on the amount of work it assigns to graduate assistants, generally recommended not to exceed twenty hours per week, so that they are not hindered in completing their own degree requirements.[2]

Distance Education

No examination of teaching loads today would be complete without consideration of how distance education has affected the work of faculty members who engage in it. Since faculty members have primary responsibility for instruction, the curricular changes needed to implement new technologies—including course design, implementation, review, and revision—require substantial faculty participation. Institutions should provide training as well as support for those faculty members expected to implement new instructional technologies. Consideration should also be given to the matter of increases in contact hours in the real or asynchronous time required to achieve interactive learning and student accessibility.[3] The increased time in course preparation and the demands of interactive electronic communication with individual students call for a reduction in the maximum classroom hour assignment.

Notes

1. See "The Status of Non-tenure-track Faculty," *Academe* 79 (July–August 1993): 39–46.
2. See "Statement on Graduate Students," AAUP, *Policy Documents and Reports*, 11th ed. (Baltimore: Johns Hopkins University Press, 2015), 387–88.
3. For a detailed examination of these issues, see "Statement on Online and Distance Education," ibid., 254–56.

The Work of Faculty: Expectations, Priorities, and Rewards

This statement, excerpted from a longer report of the same title, was approved by the Association's Committee on Teaching, Research, and Publication in December 1993.

Introduction

What is it that college and university faculty members really do? Much of the confusion surrounding the current debate over faculty workload stems from misconceptions about how faculty spend their time, particularly outside of the classroom. People making policy decisions need to understand the multiple components of faculty work and to take account of the diversity within the American higher education system, a rich variety that militates against the development of simple or uniform standards applicable to all types of institutions.

The purpose of this report is to assess the current state of public discussion regarding the duties and obligations of the professoriate: to look at recent debates about the size and nature of faculty workloads; to offer clarification of the roles of teaching, scholarship, and service for faculty, their institutions, and the public welfare; and to set the problems of the academy against the backdrop of public debates about the costs and benefits of higher education.

In 1969, the Association addressed the question of faculty workloads and the appropriate balance between teaching and research. The statement[1] that was adopted by the AAUP's Council defined maximum and preferred teaching loads in terms of classroom contact hours; advocated collegial procedures for establishing, administering, and revising workload policies; and identified common sources of inequity in the distribution of workloads.

The world changes: the problems of the 1990s differ dramatically from those of 1969. In this report we now address these issues by directing attention to total faculty workload, rather than classroom hours. We approach the question of balance through definitions of teaching, scholarship, and service that emphasize the great variety of activities so embraced; we urge the integration of all the components of academic activity. We do this in the face of external pressures upon the academy and in acknowledgment of the need to reassess our profession and our priorities and to communicate to the general public our understanding of our work and its value, while emphasizing the immense variety of institutions of higher education and the wide range of their problems, resources, and academic and public missions.

Conclusions and Recommendations

We offer these conclusions and recommendations . . . with the forceful reminder that no single answer to any of the complex questions we have examined can possibly fit all institutions in the diverse world of colleges and universities.

1. *Faculty workload combines teaching, scholarship, and service; this unity of components is meant to represent the seamless garment of academic life, and it defines the typical scholarly performance and career.* Higher education works best when faculty members teach with enthusiasm, engage in scholarly activities and research, and are deeply committed to collegial, community, and professional service. All of these are vital components of the work of faculty. Ideally they reinforce each other, to the benefit of students and institutions and as major motives and sources of satisfaction in the life and career of each faculty member.

   We distort the enterprise of higher education if we attempt to separate these endeavors, or to define them as essentially competitive rather than as complementary.

2. *Faculty workload and hours in the classroom are not the same thing.* The general public tends to equate the number of hours spent in the classroom—the contact-hour teaching load—with a faculty member's workload, which properly should be seen as the aggregate of hours devoted to all the forms and demands of teaching, of scholarship and research and publication, and of the many varieties of professional service. Not only does a mere tally and consideration of "teaching hours" ignore

members of the faculty who teach in laboratories, or in settings other than within the traditional classroom (as in studios, small-group tutorials, field work, or clinics); it also distorts the nature of academic work by minimizing the value of the integrated career and the synergistic nature of experience and judgment that come from engagement in the multiple dimensions of faculty work.

Data[2] show that on average faculty members routinely work somewhere between 45 and 55 hours per week. Workload should be thought of as total professional effort, which includes the time (and energy) devoted to class preparation, grading student work, curriculum and program deliberations, scholarship (including, but not limited to, research and publication), participation in governance activities, and a wide range of community services, both on and off campus.

3. *External mandates of workload and productivity are not an effective or desirable means of enhancing the quality or cost-effectiveness of higher education.* We believe that nothing of any value, insofar as the quality of higher education is at issue, is likely to result from extramural efforts to define workload or to determine an appropriate mixture among types of professional activity, whether we refer to individuals or to institutions. Many such attempts at external supervision and demands for accountability rest on an unsupported idea that heavier teaching loads are the solution to the current budgetary ills of higher education. We find no reason to think that more hours of student-teacher classroom contact are the road to better higher education. Nor does any convincing logic indicate that closer supervision of faculty performance will raise productivity and cut costs.

It is not difficult to understand why such externally imposed remedies are widely advocated for the problems that beset higher education. However, they neither blend with nor add to higher education's ongoing efforts to improve educational quality and to broaden access to institutions of higher learning.

4. *Teaching is a basic activity of the professoriate, and institutional reward systems should reflect the fundamental importance of effective teaching.* Teaching—which includes laboratory instruction, academic advising, training graduate students in seminars and individualized research, and various other forms of educational contact in addition to instructing undergraduates in the classroom—should be given very high priority in all institutions of higher education. Surveys and interviews indicate that faculty members derive great satisfaction from teaching well and from working closely with students. Expectations of teaching effectiveness should be high, and those who meet them should be rewarded for their success—as for other noteworthy contributions—as part of the regular reward system of colleges and universities.

We worry that efforts to offer special rewards to a few faculty members for superior teaching may in some instances be substituted for broader and deeper institutional commitment to teaching and to the educational welfare of the students. Such rewards are well earned and come as a welcome signal of institutional concern. But, by themselves, such individualized rewards can become mere tokens and can even detract from efforts to direct scarce and contested resources toward an across-the-board enrichment of education, especially of bread-and-butter undergraduate teaching and student needs. The culture of each institution should expect the vast majority of its faculty—at all ranks—to engage in serious teaching as well as in educational planning, just as it should interpret the many forms of teacher-student interaction as dimensions of its pedagogical mission.

5. *Research, generally understood to mean discovery and publication, should be related to a broader concept of scholarship that embraces the variety of intellectual activities and the totality of scholarly accomplishments. Though discovery and publication are the core of scholarly endeavor, scholarship seen in its many forms offers a wider context within which to weigh individual contributions.* Innovative and integrative research are essential to research and graduate institutions as well as the capstone of many faculty careers. But scholarship can also mean work done to further the application and integration or synthesis of knowledge, and new directions in pedagogy clearly fall on both sides of the line between what we see as teaching and what can be classified as scholarship. In addition, work in the creative and performing arts, in applied fields of academe, and in areas that demand practical training, is also—by the working definitions of the needs and traditions of such areas—often best classified as research. By enlarging the perspective through which we judge scholarly achievement, we more accurately define the many ways in which intellectual inquiry shapes the path of scholarly pursuits and of our complex and

interrelated roles as teachers and researchers in a multitude of institutional and disciplinary settings.

We believe that all faculty members—regardless of institution and regardless of workload—should involve themselves as fully as possible in creative and self-renewing scholarly activities. We enjoin all institutions to commit a suitable share of resources to encourage faculty to engage in the scholarship appropriate to their careers and to each institution's mission. Each institution should create and interpret its system of rewards to reinforce the efforts of all members of its faculty who are striving to contribute. The responsibility of providing opportunities for such creativity falls upon administrators as well as upon faculty members themselves, and we especially point to the responsibility of senior faculty to encourage and support the scholarly development of their junior colleagues.

6. *In a public climate that, in recent years, has posited a competition between teaching and research, and that is inclined to blame the latter for a perceived decline in the quality of the education available to undergraduates, we need to affirm our support for research.* Eliminating research from the majority of our campuses, and relegating it to an elite few, would cost our country dearly. It would also deal a heavy blow to the morale of the professoriate as well as to the status of higher education as a profession that attracts a stream of gifted and dedicated young men and women.

Major reductions in research would also ultimately lead to a decline in the quality of teaching. We would find it more difficult to prepare a new generation of graduate students and researchers, and our collective loss would extend to the humanistic and social enhancements as well as to the material gains that have come to our society through the advancement of knowledge. The arguments offered against academic research—that if faculty members did less research they could teach more—disregard the quality of teaching that students would receive were professors to become mere transmitters of received information, rather than explorers and discoverers. We must pay tribute to the many ways in which research informs teaching within the world of higher education, just as it serves society beyond the walls of the academy.

7. *The "ratcheting up" of expectations is detrimental to students as well as to faculty.* Public calls for more faculty time in the classroom have not been balanced by reduced demands, on the part of educational administrators and even by faculty peers, regarding faculty publications and service. The current and highly publicized calls for a "renewed" emphasis on teaching, combined with the long fiscal crisis in the service sectors of our society, have meant that faculty at many institutions—and especially those in the public sector—are being called upon to teach more courses and more students.

At the same time, however, institutions have increasingly urged faculty to publish, and they have shaped the reward system accordingly. Faculty who wish to continue to devote time to scholarship and publication—generally seen as the surest route to tenure and promotion—must often do so while carrying teaching loads that are becoming heavier each year. This is cruel to members of the faculty, as individuals, and it is counterproductive for our students' education. Institutions should define their missions clearly and articulate appropriate and reasonable expectations against which faculty will be judged, rather than simply exercise a managerial prerogative of demanding all things from all their men and women.

8. *Service, both institutional and community, is an important component of faculty work.* The institutional service performed by faculty is vital to the functioning of our colleges and universities. We do not urge that the rewards for service be commensurate with those for dedicated teaching and scholarship. On the other hand, we believe that such service is essential to the health of our institutions and can make significant contributions to society. It should be recognized and appropriately rewarded.

Service represents enlightened self-interest on the part of faculty, for whom work on the curriculum, shared governance, academic freedom, and peer review comprise the scholar's and teacher's contributions to the shaping and building of the institution. In addition, it is through service that the professional disciplines communicate and that the exchange of scholarship, by means of conferences and publications, is made feasible. And it is through service that the faculties of our colleges and universities offer their professional knowledge, skills, and advice to their communities. The faculty's commitment to the public welfare, as well as its reinvestment in the health and continuing social and intellectual utility of the academy, is expressed to a considerable extent by what we refer to as service. It is a vital component of our collective lives and of our role in society.

Notes

1. "Statement on Faculty Workload with Interpretive Comments," AAUP, *Policy Documents and Reports*, 11th ed. (Baltimore: Johns Hopkins University Press, 2015), 237–40.

2. The data referred to here and in other places, dating primarily from the 1970s and 1980s, are provided in the longer report from which this report is excerpted. See "The Work of Faculty: Expectations, Priorities, and Rewards," *Academe* 80 (January–February 1994): 35–48.

Mandated Assessment of Educational Outcomes

The report that follows is excerpted from a longer report of the same title, which was approved by the Association's Committee on College and University Teaching, Research, and Publication and adopted by the Association's Council in June 1991.

Background

The American Association of University Professors has long recognized that the practical difficulties of evaluating student learning do not relieve the academic profession of its obligation to attempt to incorporate such evaluation into measures of teaching effectiveness. The Association's *Statement on Teaching Evaluation*[1] contains the following comments on "student learning":

> Evaluation of teaching usually refers to the efforts made to assess the effectiveness of instruction. The most valid measure is probably the most difficult to obtain, that is, the assessment of a teacher's effectiveness on the basis of the learning of his or her students. On the one hand, a student's learning is importantly influenced by much more than an individual teacher's efforts. On the other, measures of before-and-after learning are difficult to find, control, or derive comparisons from. From a practical point of view, the difficulties of evaluating college teaching on the basis of changes in student performance limit the use of such a measure. The difficulties, however, should not rule out all efforts to seek reliable evidence of this kind.

It is also important to note that many of the measures proposed by proponents of mandated[2] assessment—examinations of various kinds, essays, student portfolios, senior theses and comprehensive examinations, performances and exhibitions, oral presentations, the use of external examiners—have been in place for many years. So have certain standardized tests that have become widely accepted for specific ends, such as the SAT or ACT for purposes of admission to undergraduate work, or the GRE and the LSAT for admission to post-baccalaureate programs. Other indicators favored by proponents of assessment, such as alumni satisfaction and job placement, have been used in recurring academic program reviews, some of which have been undertaken through institutional initiatives, others of which have been mandated by state agencies. As a general rule it is safe to observe that undergraduates in American postsecondary education, and their academic programs, are more intensively and perhaps more frequently evaluated than are those in postsecondary education anywhere else in the world. If many of the aforementioned measures have long been in place, the question naturally arises: What is different about the call for mandated assessment in its present form, and why is it seen as necessary by many policy makers, including some within the higher education community itself?

The assessment movement is in part a response to increased demands for public accountability and in part a by-product of various national reports on the state of higher education in the late 1980s which criticized both growing research emphases in the nation's colleges and universities and the quality of undergraduate education. A 1986 report by the National Governors' Association, "Time for Results,"[3] states that, despite "obvious successes and generous funding," "disturbing trends" are evident in both objective and subjective studies of educational effectiveness. The report complains that "not enough is known about the skills and knowledge of the average college graduate," and that the decline in test scores and the frustrations voiced about the readiness of graduates for employment exist in a climate of institutional indifference to educational effectiveness. The opening paragraph of "Time for Results" charges: "Many colleges and universities do not have a systematic way to demonstrate whether student learning is taking place. Rather, learning—and especially developing abilities to utilize knowledge—is *assumed* to take place as long as students take courses, accumulate hours, and progress 'satisfactorily' toward a degree." Such allegations indicate that the call for an increased emphasis on assessment not only will be increasingly linked to subsequent budgetary increments or decrements, but also will, though often inexplicitly, be accompanied by external pressures on the internal academic decision-making processes of colleges and universities.

Critics of mandated assessment have questioned whether the premise of assessment proponents, namely, that higher education has been generously funded in recent years, can withstand the light of scrutiny. Those individuals—board members, administrators, faculty members, students, and staff—who are more directly in touch on a daily basis with the working realities of campus life have noted that support has not kept pace with growth. They see an increased reliance on part-time or short-term faculty, starved scientific and technical laboratories, the deferment of routine maintenance costs, the growth of academic support staffs at a rate that outstrips the number of new tenure-eligible faculty positions, and patterns of funding that follow enrollment trends without regard to the relative priority of subjects in those very liberal arts in which undergraduate unpreparedness has been decried by national study commissions. Under these circumstances, critics question the relevance and importance of assessment when access to higher education has been expanded without a corresponding expansion in the base of support.

In the remainder of this report we examine Association policies that provide a historical context for considering the subject of assessment, and then consider specific issues related to present discussions of mandated assessment. After this review we conclude with a set of recommendations that we believe should govern discussions of the implementation of assessment procedures on particular campuses.

Applicable Association Policies

The Association's long-standing principles relating to academic freedom and tenure, and to college and university government, provide a broad and generally accepted context within which to treat the question of assessment in higher education. These principles are embodied in a number of documents from which the earlier-cited *Statement on Teaching Evaluation* derives its own more specific applicability. The joint 1940 *Statement of Principles on Academic Freedom and Tenure* sets forth in its preamble the principle that "academic freedom in its teaching aspect is fundamental to the protection of the rights of the teacher in teaching and of the student to freedom in learning" and goes on to stipulate that "teachers are entitled to freedom in the classroom in discussing their subject." The *Statement on Government of Colleges and Universities* spells out those areas of institutional

life requiring joint effort, and those falling within the primary responsibility of the governing board, the president, and the faculty, respectively. It also contains a concluding section on student status.

The direct implications of mandated assessment for academic freedom and tenure have not yet become a centerpiece of public discussion. Proponents of mandated assessment argue that the impact of assessment instruments on the conduct of individual classes not only has been, but will remain, negligible in the extreme, and that the complaints that such instruments will force individual faculty members to "teach to the test" misrepresent both the purpose and the techniques of assessment in the crudest and most reductive terms. They deny that mandated assessment would ever be based on a single quantitative instrument. While it is true that, thus far, the assessment movement does not appear to have resulted in any overt infringement of academic freedom as traditionally understood, the question remains whether, in more subtle ways, assessment may begin to shape the planning and conduct of courses. We believe, moreover, that the demand for mandated assessment is related to recent calls for the "post-tenure" review of faculty performance, inasmuch as an increased public demand for "accountability" on the part of colleges and universities, and real or alleged dissatisfaction with their internal processes of decision making, are common themes underlying both movements. This possible interplay between two movements which heretofore have been treated as distinct will be commented upon further below and, in our view, ought to be a continuing subject of discussion and review by the Association.

Our remaining comments in this section focus on the *Statement on Government* as a frame of reference for considering mandated assessment. The statement is premised on the interdependence of governing board, administration, and faculty. It emphasizes the institutional self-definition within which these constituent groups work together, giving recognition to the fact that American higher education is not a unitary system but rather contains many diverse institutions. While unequivocal in its position that "the faculty has primary responsibility for such fundamental areas as curriculum, subject matter and methods of instruction, research, faculty status, and those aspects of student life which relate to the educational process," the statement allows for the possibility that external bodies with jurisdiction over the institution may set "limits to realization of faculty advice." We interpret this proviso to refer to those areas—for example, the allotment of fiscal resources within a statewide system—which are primarily the responsibility of "other groups, bodies, and agencies." It may, for example, be the function of a state agency, and legitimately so, to determine (and provide reasonable grounds to the affected institution for so determining) that the establishment of a new professional school on a particular campus cannot be justified in terms of existing resources. This finding is quite a different matter from external action designed to force particular internal revisions in an existing educational program.[4]

As we see it, the question of most fundamental interest in terms of long-standing Association policy is the extent to which, despite disclaimers by its proponents, the mandatory assessment movement thus far has tended to represent a form of external state intrusion, bypassing the traditional roles of governing board, administration, and faculty, as well as both duplicating and diminishing the role of the independent regional accrediting bodies. A derivative question is whether mandated assessment, to the extent that it is driven by the felt need to compare institutions, requires measures of quantification applicable to all those institutions, and thus tends to diminish the autonomy and discourage the uniqueness of individual campuses. We take up this question as the first of several issues in the section that follows.

Some Specific Assessment Issues

1. Institutional Diversity

The manner in which institutional self-identity is defined varies both within and between the private and public sectors, though the historical basis for such distinctions may have been eroded to some extent in recent years. Thus private institutions may seem to have a greater freedom from direct state intrusion, but in states with scholarship or tuition-assistance programs offered without regard to whether the student is attending a public or a private college or university, it is increasingly difficult for all but the most prestigious "independents" to operate without some attention to state policy. Within public systems most state colleges and universities reflect different missions in their degree programs and student clientele. Many of the proponents of assessment link it to this fact and call for clearer and more distinct descriptions of roles and missions: a particular state assessment plan may indeed specify that Campus A is not necessarily expected to follow the same procedure for assessment as Campus B, and the plan may

therefore seem to endorse the principle of institutional diversity.

Such lip service to diversity, however, obscures some serious issues. Even a reasoned recognition of institutional differences of the sort that mandated assessment plans claim to recognize may result in the stifling of growth and development at an institution in the process of change, or the favoring of one campus with a particular set of goals over another in the same system. The governors' report makes it clear that "universities that give high priority to research and graduate instruction" will be the object of particularly close scrutiny in the assessment of undergraduate educational outcomes, thus raising the question of whether one implication of institutional definition is the homogenization of different campuses within a particular system, and whether there will not be a de facto ascription of superior value to those institutions that have remained devoted primarily to undergraduate teaching. It is doubtless unwise and undesirable for all institutions in a state system to aspire to research university status, but it is equally unwise and undesirable as a matter of social policy to depreciate, directly or indirectly, the research mission of those campuses capable of carrying it out.

Proponents of mandated assessment have also undercut their own assertions of respect for institutional differences by pointing to specific institutions as exemplars of "good practice." They do not pause to consider whether a model devised at one type of institution, for example, a small Roman Catholic liberal arts college or a middle-sized state institution initially founded for the purpose of teacher training and now embracing an expanded purpose, is necessarily—or properly—transferable to other kinds of institutions. Nor do they pause to note that successful assessment tools may be successful not because of their intrinsic merit, but because the ambience and scale of a particular campus already guarantee those conditions of teaching and learning conducive to such an assessment. The findings and conclusions of a study of student progress at a primarily residential four-year liberal arts college with a high rate of successful degree completion may tell us little or nothing about a large urban campus with significant dropout rates and a greater number of student transfers. Either of these institutions might be more appropriately compared to a peer institution in another state than to another institution that happens to be in the same state. To encourage institutions to develop their own instruments for assessment does not necessarily mean that the outcomes of the various assessment instruments will be properly acknowledged as logical extensions of institutional differences, since, as we have already said, higher education agencies tend to want the kinds of data that facilitate comparisons among institutions.

2. *Skills versus Values*

Although any mandated assessment plan might be resisted as an effort to increase external political control over colleges and universities, or dismissed as a cynical public relations ploy, we have no doubt that many supporters and practitioners of mandated assessment are motivated by legitimate and well-intentioned concern for educational quality. But their motivations are diversely grounded and sometimes mutually exclusive. Some educational and political leaders, viewing with alarm the decline in standardized test scores nationwide, tend to focus their attention on the need for colleges and universities to certify that students have attained certain basic educational skills. Others profess primary concern for the student's acquisition of moral values. For them, assessment presents itself as an additional means for achieving curricular change of the sort called for in various books and national reports published in the second half of the 1980s. Though inevitably these goals overlap—indeed, most in either group would probably state their belief in the importance of the purposes espoused by the other—they cannot be reached by similar means or tested by the same instruments. Indeed, as a practical matter, it is not even clear that in a time of budgetary constraints they can both be realized as a part of the same agenda. Given such competing demands, it is likely that mandated assessment will force a change in curriculum, not in order to produce a better-educated student, but to enhance the "measurability" of the outcomes.

As a general rule, those standardized measurement instruments that are the easiest to replicate are the least valid in any context other than the assessment of basic skills. As we have already noted, colleges and universities already employ such standardized tests as the ACT and the SAT to assist them in determining the admissibility of prospective undergraduate students, just as graduate and professional programs employ a variety of other standardized tests to measure undergraduate preparation at their respective entry levels. What lends this process some degree of credibility—despite the well-recognized misuse of these instruments when they are devised without proper regard for persons of varying cultural backgrounds—is that the *interpretation*

of results is usually tailored to the mission of the particular institution. Test scores, if they are used in conjunction with other evaluative instruments such as a student's standing as a graduating senior in high school, may argue for admission to one institution if not to another. This capacity to differentiate among students is the particular genius of American higher education: that in its diversity of institutional purposes, it offers a flexible response to different student needs and abilities while ensuring that access to higher education remains a proper part of education for the citizenry of a democratic society. Historically, faculty members and administrators have assumed that test measurements are retrospective, determining admissibility on the basis of the student's demonstrated pre-collegiate or pre-professional skills.

Standardized outcomes testing in general education directed to the acquisition of values as well as facts is another matter, and it is worth noting that neither of the major national testing services has yet succeeded in devising a standardized general education examination that satisfies either the institutions or the test designers themselves. Though proponents of mandated assessment may wish to pay tribute both to the acquisition of skills and to the acquisition of a broadened general education, it is unlikely that the resources that would be required for a basic improvement in skills *alone* at the collegiate level could also be devoted to enhancing the environment necessary for the transmission of diverse content and the development of critical thinking so central to the preparation of students in the liberal arts. The costs of conducting assessment drain funds away from other institutional needs, such as smaller classes, reduced dependence on part-time faculty, and adequate numbers of full-time faculty members to staff both graduate and undergraduate instruction—needs which are at loggerheads, too, with external demands for remediation at the college level. Assessment carried on without proper attention to the incompatibility of the two goals—the attainment of skills and the learning of values—can have only one result: shifting the burden of blame to the faculty, just as in the K–12 system many teachers and principals are operating under a state mandate for reform without adequate funds to implement it and are now under pressure to show measurable results.

Under these conditions, values are likely to be subordinated to skills, and the quality of higher education as *higher* education, rather than as remediation, will suffer. When the mission of a particular institution dictates that scores be used to determine placement in basic skills courses so as to compensate for inadequate prior preparation at the primary and secondary levels, then the funding of such instruction needs to be provided at a level that protects the viability of instruction appropriate to undergraduates who are ready for a college-level curriculum. Under present conditions, such additional resources as are available would be better devoted to remedying inadequate student preparation than to attempting to assess it.

3. Assessment in the Major Field of Study

Most faculty members agree on the importance of assessing systematically a student's competence in the major, as is shown by the multiplicity of forms of assessment that many departments employ. Yet even in this disciplinary context the range of possible student options after graduation makes it unlikely that an externally mandated assessment instrument would do anything more than gauge the lowest common vocational denominator. The major is properly regarded as a vehicle for deepening the student's general education and for sharpening the student's independent research and study skills, and thus standardized assessment of achievement in the major field raises precisely the same objections it does in general education.

Learning for its own end—for the purpose of developing breadth, intellectual rigor, and habits of independent inquiry—is still central to the educational enterprise; it is also one of the least measurable of activities. Whereas professional curricula are already shaped by external agencies, such as professional accrediting bodies and licensing boards, the liberal arts by contrast are far more vulnerable to intrusive mandates from other quarters; for example, the governors' report professes to find evidence of program decline "particularly in the humanities." To be sure, even in the liberal arts a student's accomplishment in the major can be measured with relative objectivity by admissions procedures at the graduate and professional level that include GRE scores as one of the bases for judgment. But a student majoring in English may wish to pursue a career in editing, publishing, journalism, or arts administration (to name only a few); a political science major may have in mind a career in state or local government or in the US State Department. Either of them may have chosen his or her major simply out of curiosity, or perhaps out of a desire to be a well-educated citizen before going to law school or taking over the family business.

For these reasons we suggest that the success of a program in the major field of study is best evaluated not by an additional layer of state-imposed assessment but by the placement and career satisfaction of the student as he or she enters the world of work. Whereas imposed assessment measurements will at best—and rightly—attract faculty cynicism and at worst lead to "teaching to the test," no responsible faculty member will ignore the kinds of informed evaluation of a program available through a candid interchange with a graduating senior or recent graduate.

4. "Value-Added" Measures

Despite their occasional disclaimers, proponents of mandated assessment frequently desire quantifiable outcome data based on a comparison of students' entrance and exit performance at a postsecondary institution, or their performance at entrance and at the beginning of the junior year, before their attention turns primarily to their work in the major. Our concerns are two: (a) whether the data, based on what are sometimes called "value-added" measures, realistically reflect the diverse structures of American higher education and the different kinds of student involvement in it; and (b) whether value-added measures are sound even in narrow quantitative terms.

Perhaps the crudest form of value-added testing involves the administration of an identical general-education examination to the same body of students twice during their college careers. Even if—which we doubt—the acquisition of knowledge could be measured by the mere repetition of an earlier test, the uncritical implementation of value-added measures is quite simply unsustainable in light of the increasingly migratory, part-time, and drop-in–drop-out patterns of many American undergraduates. Like debates over what constitutes the one true curriculum or reading list, value-added measures ignore the fact that any system which presupposes a particular pace or place for student learning is at best applicable to a diminishing, and in some cases relatively elite, proportion of the student population.

We do not believe that the most important, or even useful, kind of learning that takes place at any level of education is readily quantifiable or results from the accumulation of facts by rote. Yet such an emphasis is implied in value-added measures, since the words themselves betray the assumption that one must add something measurable to something else in order to evaluate educational outcomes.

5. Accountability versus Self-Improvement; or, Does Involving the Faculty in the Process Make It All Right?

Although, as we noted earlier, proponents of assessment have argued that the purpose of assessment is to provide diagnostic tools for self-improvement, both institutional and personal, in some cases direct budgetary consequences may ensue not only from the choice of noncompliance over compliance, but also from the results of the assessment itself. A vivid example of the slippery slope down which higher education could descend can be found in those segments of the K–12 system in which standardized tests have been employed to appraise curricular and teaching effectiveness and to group children by presumed intellectual level. What emerges as the end result of such a process is no longer an educational matter but rather a policy issue external to the schools, with the resulting data being interpreted by persons not necessarily expert in primary and secondary education, and the faculty harboring deep-seated feelings of disenfranchisement in the process.

Proponents of mandated assessment might respond that the historic position of faculties in higher education sufficiently guarantees the continuing primacy of the faculty in the assessment process. If, the argument runs, faculty members develop and administer the assessment instruments, and these are used primarily for pedagogic self-improvement, then what can the objection be?

The second of these points—as to whether pedagogic, curricular, and thus institutional, self-improvement is really the primary reason for mandated assessment—has already been questioned. We have seen sufficient evidence that such a call for self-improvement does not take place in a fiscal or policy vacuum. Most faculty members, in our experience, are perfectly willing to undertake a periodic look at their own effectiveness. Increasing numbers of institutions have been developing programs to devise incentives for such self-examination, which we regard as a continuing faculty responsibility. But self-examination is best conducted in a climate free of external constraint or threats, however vaguely disguised.

The nub of the problem lies, as it has throughout this report, not so much in the noun *assessment* as in the modifier *mandated*. If, indeed, proponents of assessment want to express support for measures of student progress that are based on principles of sound instruction—papers, essay examinations, theses, special projects, or performances or exhibitions—then an informed

dialogue between the institution's representatives and the public may be usefully carried on. But if mandated assessment presupposes instruments that move further in the direction of greater standardization and quantification, then the adoption of such instruments requires not only the participation of testing experts, but also an involvement by faculty members and administrators in the development of discipline-specific or general-education versions of such tests.

The fact that faculty members, rather than external agencies, select or even participate in the design of the test instrument does not substantially diminish the problems of standardization and reductionism inherent in the process of developing a reliable test instrument. And in view of the political forces that drive such demands, the assertion that the faculty can oversee or even control the design is of little meaning if the requesting agency wants to accumulate data susceptible of statistical formulation and translatable into budgetary decisions.

We have already implied that one academic, as opposed to budgetary, consequence of mandated assessment is "teaching to the test," a pressure on faculty members to transmit to their students easily testable nuggets of information rather than broader conceptual issues and methods of reasoning. We must also acknowledge that for some faculty members a move toward standardized outcomes measurement might in fact represent a tempting relief from the exigencies of grading papers and essay examinations. An unwelcome result for both higher education and the public would be the exodus of better faculty members to other careers (as has already happened in certain segments of the K–12 system for much the same reason) or at the very least for other campuses not yet infatuated with "value-added" assessment measures.

Furthermore, faculty participation in the development of mandated assessment instruments— a sine qua non if some degree of faculty control were to be exerted over the process—would represent yet one more burden added to the existing teaching, research, and public service responsibilities that faculty members already carry. The added burden might be acceptable if it contributed to furthering the central academic purposes of a college or university, but, as we have sought to show, mandated assessment is not likely to achieve that result.

To reconnect the discussion briefly with the earlier mention of post-tenure reviews, we believe that both mandated systems of post-tenure review and mandated procedures for assessment, even if they involve faculty collaboration, are strikingly similar both in their demands and in their adverse practical outcome. In both cases it can be said that faculty members have been evaluating each other and assessing their students' learning outcomes for many years. In both cases the faculty is informed that it can participate in, or even control, the procedures and thus retain its traditional role of primary responsibility, whether over faculty status or over academic programs. But in both cases the faculty is also being told that the very instruments it has devised in the past are no longer sufficient to ensure either faculty quality or student learning, and that new mandated instruments are needed to satisfy public demands for greater accountability. Thus the logic of mandated assessment requires that faculty judgment be superseded if some agency external to the campus deems the need for public accountability not to have been met.

Proponents of mandated assessment cannot have it both ways. Either the purpose of mandated assessment is the improvement of teaching and learning in an atmosphere of constructive cooperation, or it shifts the responsibility for educational decisions into the hands of political agencies and others not only at a remove from, but by the nature of their own training and biases not versed in, the purposes and processes of higher education.

Recommended Standards for Mandated Assessment

American higher education has generally encouraged frequent assessment of student learning. The recent movement to mandate such assessment differs, however, in that it emphasizes evaluation of overall instructional and programmatic performance rather than individual student achievement. The American Association of University Professors recognized in its *Statement on Teaching Evaluation* that assessment of student learning outcomes may provide the most valid measure—though also the most difficult to obtain reliably—for the evaluation of teaching effectiveness. The Association has also recognized that such assessment is the responsibility of the faculty, whose primary role in curriculum and instruction has been set forth in the *Statement on Government of Colleges and Universities*.

Where assessment of student learning is mandated to ensure instructional and programmatic quality, the faculty responsibility for the development, application, and review of assessment procedures is no less than it is for the assessment of individual student achievement. Since the *Statement on Teaching Evaluation* was first formulated, increased public attention has

been turned toward various plans for externally mandated assessments of learning outcomes in higher education. Some of the plans have been instituted on short notice and with little or no participation by faculty members who, by virtue of their professional education and experience, are the most qualified to oversee both the details and the implications of a particular plan. Often these plans are the result of external political pressures, and may be accompanied by budgetary consequences, favorable or unfavorable, depending on the actual outcomes the mandated schemes purport to measure.

The Association believes that the justification for developing any assessment plan in a given case, whether voiced by a legislative body, the governing board, or one or more administrative officers, must be accompanied by a clear showing that existing methods of assessing learning are inadequate for accomplishing the intended purposes of a supplementary plan, and that the mandated procedures are consistent with effective performance of the institutional mission. The remaining question involves the principles and derivative policies that should prevail when agencies external to colleges and universities—state legislatures, regional and professional accreditation bodies, and state boards of higher education—insist that assessment take place. We believe that the following standards should be observed:

1. Central to the mission of colleges and universities is the teaching-learning relationship into which faculty members and their students enter. All matters pertinent to curricular design, the method and quality of teaching, and the assessment of the outcome in student learning must be judged by how well they support this relationship.

2. Public agencies charged with the oversight of higher education, and the larger public and the diverse constituencies that colleges and universities represent, have a legitimate stake in the effectiveness of teaching and learning. Their insistence that colleges and universities provide documented evidence of effectiveness is appropriate to the extent that such agencies and their constituencies do not: (a) make demands that significantly divert the energies of the faculty, administration, or governing board from the institution's primary commitment to teaching, research, and public service; or (b) impose additional fiscal and human burdens beyond the capacity of the responding institution to bear.

3. Because experience demonstrates the unlikelihood of achieving meaningful quantitative

measurement of educational outcomes for other than specific and clearly delimited purposes, any assessment scheme must provide certain protections for the role of the faculty and for the institutional mission as agreed upon by the faculty, administration, and governing board, and endorsed by the regional accrediting agency. Specifically:

(a) The faculty should have primary responsibility for establishing the criteria for assessment and the methods for implementing it.

(b) The assessment should focus on particular, institutionally determined goals and objectives, and the resulting data should be regarded as relevant primarily to that purpose. To ensure respect for diverse institutional missions, it is important that uniform assessment procedures not be mandated across a statewide system for the purpose of comparing institutions within the system. For a further development of this point, see (f) below.

(c) If externally mandated assessment is to be linked to strategic planning or program review, the potential consequences of that assessment for such planning and review should be clearly stated in advance, and the results should be considered as only one of several factors to be taken into account in budgetary and programmatic planning.

(d) The assessment process should employ methods adequate to the complexity and variety of student learning experiences, rather than rely on any single method of assessment. To prevent assessment itself from making instruction and curriculum rigid, and to ensure that assessment is responsive to changing needs, the instruments and procedures for conducting assessment should be regularly reviewed and appropriately revised by the faculty. We suggest the following considerations with respect to both quantitative and qualitative measures:

(i) Quantitative performance measures exhibit two specific dangers. First, reliable comparisons between disparate programs, or within individual programs over time, demand narrow and unchanging instruments, and thus may discourage necessary curricular improvement and variety. Second, even where such instruments are ordinarily available or responsive to changing curricula (as with certification and graduate record examinations), they may be unreflective of diverse purposes even within a single discipline or field of study. Thus, such instruments should not be used as the exclusive means of assessment.

(ii) Qualitative performance measures are often pedagogically superior to quantitative tests. These measures include such devices as capstone courses, portfolios, exhibitions, senior essays, demonstrations and work experiences, and the use of external examiners. The use of these measures, however, is costly and implies a curricular decision to shift additional resources to evaluate outcomes rather than to improve student learning. Hence, adoption of such procedures should include a review of costs and benefits compared to other curricular options such as greater investment in the support of first- and second-year students.

(e) If a state agency mandates assessment, the state should bear the staffing and other associated costs of the assessment procedure, either directly or in the form of a supplemental budgetary allocation to the campus for the purpose.

(f) If comparative data from other institutions are required for purposes of assessment, the faculty should have primary responsibility for identifying appropriate peer units or peer institutions for those purposes, and (as with program planning referred to in [c] above) the results of that assessment should be only one of the several factors in arriving at such comparisons.

(g) Externally mandated assessment procedures are not appropriate for the evaluation of individual students or faculty members and should not be used for that purpose.

Notes

1. AAUP, *Policy Documents and Reports*, 11th ed. (Baltimore: Johns Hopkins University Press, 2015), 219–22.

2. Throughout this document the word "mandated" usually implies an external mandate, that is, one imposed by an agency outside the college or university. On occasion, however, institutional governing boards (as opposed to a superboard or coordinating board) or even administrative officers may themselves deliver such a mandate. In such instances the roles of the respective parties should be defined in terms of the broad principles of the Association's "Statement on Government of Colleges and Universities," discussed below.

3. National Governors' Association, *Time for Results: The Governors' 1991 Report on Education* (Washington, DC: National Governors' Association Publication Office, 1986).

4. Under the heading "Joint Effort," the "Statement on Government" (*Policy Documents and Reports*, 118) adds, "Special considerations may require particular accommodations: (1) a publicly supported institution may be regulated by statutory provisions, and (2) a church-controlled institution may be limited by its charter or bylaws. *When such external requirements influence course content and manner of instruction or research, they impair the educational effectiveness of the institution*" (emphasis added).

Statement on Online and Distance Education

This statement was approved under the title *Statement on Distance Education* in March 1999 by the Association's Special Committee on Distance Education and Intellectual Property Issues. It was adopted by the Association's Council and endorsed by the Eighty-Fifth Annual Meeting in June 1999.

Preamble

In distance education (or distance learning) the teacher and the student are separated geographically so that face-to-face communication is absent; communication is accomplished instead by one or more technological media, most often electronic (interactive television, satellite television, computers, and the like).[1] The geographic separation between teacher and student may be considerable (for example, in a course offered over the World Wide Web), or the distance may be slight (for example, from the teacher's computer to the student's in a nearby campus building). Hence distance education may apply to both on- and off-campus courses and programs. For the most part, this statement's focus is on programs and courses offered for credit. It does not, however, exclude noncredit courses, programs of general cultural enrichment, or other programs that support the educational objectives of the institution.

Distance education in its contemporary forms invariably presents administrative, technical, and legal problems usually not encountered in traditional classroom settings. For example, questions arise regarding copyright for materials adapted from traditional classroom settings or created expressly for distance education. In addition, systems of interactive television, satellite television, or computer-based courses and programs are technologically more complex and expensive than traditional classroom instruction, and require a greater investment of institutional resources and more elaborate organizational patterns. These issues not only make more difficult the question who is entitled to claim ownership of materials designed for distance education; they also raise questions about the appropriate distribution of authority and responsibility between the general administration of the college or university, on the one hand, and the separate academic departments or units within a given institution, on the other. The technical and administrative support units responsible for maintaining and operating the means of delivering distance-education courses and programs are usually separate from particular academic departments or units that offer those courses and programs.

More important, the development of distance-education technologies has created conditions seldom, if ever, seen in academic life—conditions that raise basic questions about standards for teaching and scholarship. For example, in distance education the teacher does not have the usual face-to-face contact with the student that exists in traditional classroom settings. Thus, special means must be devised for assigning, guiding, and evaluating the student's work. In order to communicate with the student, the teacher frequently utilizes sophisticated and expensive technological devices that are not under the teacher's exclusive control and that often require special technical knowledge that the teacher may not fully possess. The teacher's syllabus, lectures, examinations, and other course materials may be copied or recorded and reused without the teacher's presence. The teacher's academic and legal rights may not be fully or accurately understood or may be in dispute in this new environment. Also in potential dispute are issues regarding the faculty's overall authority in determining appropriate policies and procedures for the use of these new technologies. Finally, the nature of teacher-student interaction and the preparation and teaching of distance-education classes often require significantly more time than that needed for courses offered in traditional classroom settings; consequently, the teacher should receive commensurate compensation.

It is imperative, therefore, that colleges and universities now using or planning to use the new technologies of distance education consider the educational functions these new media are intended to perform and the specific problems they raise. Traditional academic principles and procedures will usually apply to these new media, either directly or by extension, but they will not be applicable in all circumstances. When they are not, new principles and procedures will need to be developed so that the new media will effectively serve the institution's basic educational objectives. The principal purpose of this statement is to offer guidelines to that end.

Principles

1. *General.* The use of new technologies in teaching and scholarship should be for the purpose of advancing the basic functions of colleges and universities to preserve, augment, and transmit knowledge and to foster the abilities of students to learn. The development of appropriate institutional policies concerning these new technologies as instruments of teaching and scholarship is therefore the responsibility of the academic community.

2. *Areas of Responsibility.* The governing board, administration, faculty, and students all have a continuing concern in determining the desirability and feasibility of utilizing new media as instruments of education. Institutional policies on distance education should define the responsibilities for each group in terms of the group's particular competence. Indeed, a principal role of these groups in devising policies is to find those uses that enhance the institution's performance of its basic functions. These uses will vary depending on (a) the size and complexity of the institution, (b) its academic mission, (c) the potential of the new technological media for scholarship and the delivery of instruction, and (d) the variety and possible combinations of technologies to be employed for education and research.

   As with all other curricular matters, the faculty should have primary responsibility for determining the policies and practices of the institution in regard to distance education. The rules governing distance education and its technologies should be approved by vote of the faculty concerned or of a representative faculty body, officially adopted by the appropriate authorities, and published and distributed to all concerned.

   The applicable academic unit—usually a department or program—should determine the extent to which the new technologies of distance education will be utilized, and the form and manner of their use. These determinations should conform with established institutional policies.

Before they are offered, all programs and courses for academic credit that utilize distance-education technologies should be considered and approved by the faculties of the department, division, school, college, or university, or by representatives of those bodies that govern curricular matters generally. The procedures for approval should apply to all such courses and programs, including those recorded in some way and thus not requiring the teacher's active presence on a regular basis. The faculty should determine the amount of credit toward a degree that a student may earn in courses utilizing the technologies of distance education.

The faculty of the college or university should establish general rules and procedures for the granting of teaching-load credit in the preparation and the delivery of programs and courses utilizing distance-education technologies, for required outside-of-class student contact (office hours), and for the allocation of necessary supporting resources. Within the general provisions of these governing regulations, specific arrangements should be made within the applicable academic unit (usually the department) for courses offered by its members.

Adequate preparation for a distance-education course, whether one that requires the regular, active presence of the instructor, or one that has been recorded, requires considerable time and effort for the creation or adaptation of materials for the new media, and for the planning of assignments, evaluations, and other course materials and their distribution. The instructor will therefore need to have adequate time to prepare such materials and to become sufficiently familiar with the technologies of instruction prior to delivery of the course. Such preparation—depending on the teacher's training or experience, the extent of the use of these technologies in the course, their complexity and the complexity of the materials to be created or adapted—will usually require significant release time from teaching during an academic term prior to the offering of the new course.

To enable them to carry out their instructional responsibilities, teachers assigned to these courses should be given support in the form of academic, clerical, and technical assistance, as well as means of communicating and conferring with students. Sufficient library resources must also be provided to the students to enable them to benefit from the teaching. Since instruction by distance-education technologies does not allow for the same degree of interaction between students and teacher that is possible in a traditional classroom setting, provision should be made for the students to confer personally with the teacher at designated times.

If the institution prepares courses or programs for use by entities outside the institution, whether for academic credit or not, whether recorded or requiring the regular, active presence of the teacher, the faculty should ensure that the same standards obtain as in courses and programs prepared for use in their own institution.

3. *Teaching Appointments.* The precise terms and conditions of every appointment should be stated in writing and be in the possession of the faculty member and the institution before the faculty member is assigned to utilize distance-education technologies in the delivery of instructional material in a course for academic credit. No member of the faculty should be required to participate in distance-education courses or programs without adequate preparation and training, and without prior approval of such courses and programs by the appropriate faculty bodies.

4. *Academic Freedom.* A faculty member engaged in distance education is entitled to academic freedom as a teacher, researcher, and citizen in full accordance with the provisions of the 1940 *Statement of Principles on Academic Freedom and Tenure,* jointly developed by the Association of American Colleges (now the Association of American Colleges and Universities) and the American Association of University Professors and endorsed by more than 200 educational and professional organizations.

5. *Selection of Materials.* Teachers should have the same responsibility for selecting and presenting materials in courses offered through distance-education technologies as they have in those offered in traditional classroom settings. For team-taught or interdisciplinary courses and programs, the faculty involved should share this responsibility.

6. *Technical Considerations.* The institution is responsible for the technological delivery of the course. Faculty members who teach through distance-education technologies are responsible for making certain that they have sufficient technical skills to present their subject matter and related material effectively, and, when necessary, should have access to and consult with technical support personnel. The teacher, nevertheless, has the final responsibility for the content and presentation of the course.

7. *Proprietary Rights and Educational Policies.* The institution should establish policies and procedures to protect its educational objectives and the interests of both those who create new material and those who adapt material from traditional courses for use in distance education. The administration should publish these policies and procedures and distribute them, along with requisite information about copyright law, to all concerned persons. The policies should include provisions for compensating those who create new course materials or who adapt course materials originally prepared for traditional classroom usage, including any use or reuse of recorded material.

Provision should also be made for the original teacher-creator, the teacher-adapter, or an appropriate faculty body to exercise control over the future use and distribution of recorded instructional material and to determine whether the material should be revised or withdrawn from use.

A teacher's course presentation should not be recorded without the teacher's prior knowledge and consent. Recordings of course material are academic documents, and thus, as with other works of scholarship, should have their author or creator cited accordingly.

Note

1. For a more comprehensive definition and explanation, see the report "Distance Learning," *Academe* 84 (May–June 1998): 30–38.

On Conditions of Employment at Overseas Campuses

The statement that follows was issued jointly by the American Association of University Professors and the Canadian Association of University Teachers (CAUT). It was approved for publication in April 2009 by the AAUP's Committee A on Academic Freedom and Tenure and CAUT's Executive Committee.

US and Canadian colleges and universities have been actively expanding their foreign operations in recent years. Overseas branch campuses and degree programs have proliferated, as have the overseas sale of curricular and other instructional materials and the franchising of campuses, online or distance learning, international student recruitment, and study-abroad programs.

The expansion of higher education opportunities is a welcome feature of today's more internationally integrated world. Not surprisingly, these international initiatives are proving attractive both to private investors and to colleges and universities. Advocates of private investment now refer routinely to a multitrillion-dollar global market in educational services, and efforts to open up this lucrative market further are driving bilateral or multilateral trade agreements and negotiations. As a result, globalization has become one of the principal means of privatizing and commercializing higher education.

The leading nations in the field of international education have sought, under the World Trade Organization's General Agreement on Trade in Services[1] and in the name of trade liberalization, to harmonize global standards for providing higher education services. According to the WTO's tenets of free trade, educational services should be treated like any other commodity, and foreign providers should be afforded the same public benefits and privileges as domestic institutions of any member nation. Several international organizations in higher education have voiced their opposition to these tenets:

- the 2001 Joint Declaration on Higher Education and the General Agreement on Trade in Services,[2] issued by four leading academic organizations in the United States, Canada, and Europe (the American Council on Education, the Council for Higher Education Accreditation, the Association of Universities and Colleges of Canada, and the European University Association);
- the 2002 Porto Alegre Declaration (Carta de Porto Alegre),[3] signed by the major Iberian and Latin American associations of higher education;
- the resolutions adopted by Education International (with 394 national teacher and academic staff federations from 171 countries representing 30 million teachers, academic staff, and others who work in education) at its 2001 World Congress in Jomtien, Thailand[4] and at its 2004 World Congress in Porto Alegre, Brazil.[5]

These declarations and resolutions recognize that trade liberalization risks weakening governments' commitment to and investment in public higher education. They also assert that education is not a commodity and that reliance on public mandates (exclusively so in most countries) should make it distinct from other services.

The pace of overseas expansion also threatens to affect the character of higher education in the United States and Canada. The sheer number of faculty employed in foreign operations is increasing, and most are contingent employees on temporary contracts. Because foreign programs and campuses are usually less costly, colleges and universities may make decisions favoring their development over more expensive US- and Canadian-based equivalents staffed by tenure-track faculty. Continued pursuit of this path will accelerate the casualization of the academic workforce, taking its toll on the quality of instruction as well as adversely affecting faculty rights.

Moreover, as the US and Canadian presence in higher education grows in countries marked by authoritarian rule, basic principles of academic freedom, collegial governance, and nondiscrimination are less likely to be observed. In a host environment where free speech is constrained, if not proscribed, faculty will censor themselves, and the cause of authentic liberal education, to the extent it can exist in such situations, will suffer.

Consequently, it is essential that all international initiatives undertaken by US and Canadian colleges and universities respect the UNESCO Recommendation concerning the Status of Higher Education Teaching Personnel,[6] with its emphasis on academic freedom, institutional autonomy, collegial governance, nondiscrimination, and employment security.

The treatment of nonacademic employees involved in the construction, service, and maintenance of foreign campuses is another area of concern. Colleges and universities as employers and contractors should uphold the full observance of internationally recognized standards governing the rights and working conditions of nonacademic employees who build and maintain classrooms and offices and meet other needs that keep the institutions functioning. Universities operating internationally should adopt a code of conduct governing the workplace conditions and rights of all nonacademic employees, even and especially if these workers are employed directly by a local subcontractor.

Education should not be a commodity, bought and sold in the international marketplace and subject to the rules of competitive trade that govern a deregulated global economy. Participating in the movement for international education can rest on laudable educational grounds. But those grounds will be jeopardized if hard-earned standards and protections are weakened rather than exported.

In sum, the AAUP and CAUT expect every US and Canadian college and university in any international initiative undertaken in partnership, or using the institution's name, to honor the provisions in the UNESCO Recommendation concerning the Status of Higher Education Teaching Personnel. For nonacademic employees, we expect each institution and its subcontractors to adopt a code of conduct consistent with International Labor Organization (ILO) standards.

In accordance with the principles of collegial governance, US and Canadian college and university administrations should provide their faculty and staff associations and the institution's senior academic body with information about any international initiative being contemplated. If the initiative proceeds, administrations should provide detailed updates on all aspects of the project, with special emphasis on provisions to ensure academic freedom and tenure and collegial

governance, including policies on approval and regular assessment of programs and curriculum, appointment and evaluation of academic staff, workload, appropriate compensation and working conditions, anti-harassment and -discrimination provisions, intellectual property, occupational health and safety, equity, and rights to appeal procedures characterized by substantive and procedural fairness.

Implementation of these obligations will require vigilance by faculty at US and Canadian institutions. AAUP and CAUT traditions of academic freedom and shared governance make it clear that faculty representatives should have an integral role in drafting and reviewing plans designed to establish satellite programs and branch campuses. Plans for curriculum development and faculty hiring need explicit faculty approval. Compensation, working conditions, and grievance procedures for US- and Canadian-based faculty will be subject to formal negotiation on many campuses with collective bargaining. The state of the law in host countries may necessitate bilateral negotiations in order to ensure fair working conditions for the faculty and staff at an overseas site; domestic faculty should be involved in reviewing such arrangements as an essential safeguard that these conditions are being met.

AAUP local chapters and CAUT member associations can play a key role in making certain that their institutions meet these obligations. AAUP and CAUT stand ready to assist their members and the higher education community more generally in this work.

Notes

1. http://www.wto.org/english/tratop_e/serv_e/gatsintr_e.htm.

2. Signed September 28, 2001. http://www.iau-hesd.net/sites/default/files/documents/2001_-_joint_declaration_on_higher_education_and_the_general_agreement_on_trade_in_services_en.pdf.

3. Signed April 27, 2002. http://www.grupomontevideo.edu.uy/index.php/publicaciones/declaraciones/374-carta-de-porto-alegre.

4. "Resolution on the Status of Higher Education Personnel," Third World Congress of Education International (Jomtien, Thailand), signed July 29, 2001. http://pages.ei-ie.org/library/libraries/detail/75.

5. "Resolution on Education—Public Service or Commodity?," Fourth World Congress of Education International (Porto Alegre, Brazil), signed July 24, 2004. http://pages.ei-ie.org/library/libraries/detail/39.

6. Signed November 11, 1997. http://portal.unesco.org/en/ev.phpURL_ID=13144&URL_DO=DO_TOPIC&URL_SECTION=201.html.

Intellectual Property, Copyright, and Outside Funding

In 1966, the Special Committee on Academic Personnel Ineligible for Tenure addressed concerns over researchers "who are not teachers," whom the committee identified as "relatively new to higher education." Noting that "a researcher is the same thing as a teacher insofar as his right to academic freedom, his status as a faculty member, and his entitlement to tenure are concerned," the committee commented on a separate development regarding the status of researchers:

> Now, however, there are an important number of researchers working in universities and university-operated agencies to whom this assumption does not so clearly apply. Workers on Department of Defense and Atomic Energy Commission projects offer the extreme example; but anyone who works on a project which is defined by a contract between the employing institution and a sponsoring agency, government, industry, or foundation is likely to be more or less limited in his freedom to decide for himself what line of investigation he will pursue. The question arises whether universities ought to be engaged in this kind of contract research at all. The Special Committee regards this as an important question, but not one that can be settled at this time by a component of the AAUP. The fact is that many of the best universities are so engaged, and the question to be answered is what the AAUP policy should be toward the people involved, particularly concerning the conditions of academic freedom and tenure under which they work.

The rapidly increasing concerns of research scholars in the policies and in the related issues of intellectual property, copyright, and conflict of interest led to the publication of the Association's 2014 *Recommended Principles to Guide Academy-Industry Relationships.*

Statement on Intellectual Property

The statement that follows, prepared by a subcommittee of the Association's Committee A on Academic Freedom and Tenure, was approved by Committee A and adopted by the Association's Council in November 2013.

The management of inventions, patents, and other forms of intellectual property in a university setting warrants special guidance because it bears on so many aspects of the university's core missions, values, and functions, including academic freedom, scholarship, research, shared governance, and the transmission and use of academic knowledge by the broader society. Intellectual property refers broadly to patents, copyrights, trademarks, and (according to some definitions) trade secrets, in addition to the underlying subject matter that is controlled by the owner of these property rights established by statute (namely, inventions, works of authorship, and identifiers that distinguish goods and services in the marketplace). Patents provide the owner with the right to exclude others from practicing—making, using, and selling—an invention.[1] A patent, unlike a copyright, goes beyond the protection of written expression to accord an exclusive right to the operational principles that underlie the invention. Copyright prohibits unauthorized copying or modification of particular instances of expression; a patent permits the exclusion of work created independently, is not limited to the precise "expression," and has no "fair use" exception, even for nonprofit purposes. Thus, patents may have an additional and potentially substantial impact on university research, may affect the value and role of scholarly publication, and may influence collaborations and the transfer of technology developed or improved in other research settings. The management of university-generated intellectual property is complex and carries significant consequences for those involved in direct negotiations (faculty inventors, companies, university administrators, attorneys, and invention-management agents) as well as those who may be affected (competing companies, the public, patients, and the wider research community).

Whether ownership of a particular invention resides with the inventors or is assigned by the inventors to a university technology-transfer office, a university-affiliated foundation, or an independent invention-management agency, it is essential that all those involved recognize the distinctive role that inventions arising out of scholarly research should have. Faculty investigators and inventors, together with university administrators, must communicate this role and hold those involved accountable when they are engaged in the development and deployment of patent rights.

One fundamental principle should be clear: inventions are owned initially by their inventors. That principle is established in both the US Constitution and federal patent law. As the US Supreme Court affirmed in its 2011 decision in *Board of Trustees of Leland Stanford Junior University v. Roche Molecular Systems, Inc (Stanford v. Roche)*,[2] faculty inventors in a university setting are also the initial owners of their inventions. Ownership of patent rights that may attach to an invention, however, may be transferred to another party by a written instrument. Thus, control of patent rights may be distinguished from ownership, since the initial patent owner may choose to enter a contract with (or transfer title to) another entity that manages those patent rights on his or her behalf. A university may become the owner of patent rights in a faculty invention by voluntary assignment, as was the case at most universities prior to 1980.

Some universities have sought to make their ownership of all faculty patent rights a condition of employment, citing the use of university facilities as a justification for asserting their ownership. Some also insist that externally funded research contracts specify that the university will manage all the resulting intellectual property. Though these strategies are increasingly preferred by many universities, there is little to indicate that such ownership claims advance university interests, whether taken narrowly as the pursuit of income from patent licenses or broadly in terms of the social value of research and access to its results. The 2011 *Stanford v. Roche* ruling affirmed that such rationales for the nonvoluntary confiscation of faculty intellectual property are often unfounded.

For many years university policies recognized that faculty members owned their intellectual property but required that they share profits with the institution when patentable intellectual property was commercialized. The AAUP regards such policies as fair and reasonable, so long as the faculty inventor or creator determines whether and how the work is to be marketed. Faculty members should have the right to distribute some work—software being a common example—for free if they choose.

Universities have often distinguished between copyrightable and patentable intellectual property, ceding faculty ownership of the former and asserting institutional ownership of the latter. But both are products of scholarship and protected by academic freedom, which provides for control by faculty authors over dissemination of their works.

A fundamental problem that arises from university ownership of patent rights to faculty inventions is that it tends to create institutional conflicts of interest between the university's governance role and its financial and competitive interests in exploiting patented inventions for its own benefit. It is all too easy for universities to conflate royalty income with their public service mission to enhance economic growth while failing to perceive, or to acknowledge, the conflict that arises with respect to other institutional responsibilities and the university's long-standing commitment to the broad dissemination of knowledge.

Inventions—despite distinctions often drawn in university policy statements—are a natural outgrowth of scholarly activities. The scholarly nature of university-based inventions does not simply disappear with the addition of a potential patent or other intellectual property rights. Thus, the fundamental rights of faculty members to direct and control their own research do not terminate when they make an invention or other research discovery; these rights properly extend to decisions involving invention management, intellectual property licensing, commercialization, dissemination, and public use. Faculty inventor "assignment" of an invention to a management agent, including the university that hosted the underlying research, should be voluntary and negotiated, rather than mandatory, unless federal statutes or previous sponsored-research agreements dictate otherwise.[3] Faculty inventors and investigators retain a vital interest in the disposition of their research inventions and discoveries and should, therefore, retain rights to negotiate the terms of their disposition. The university, or its management agents, should not undertake intellectual property development or

take legal actions that directly or indirectly affect a faculty member's research, inventions, instruction, or public service without the faculty member's or inventor's express consent. Of course, faculty members, like other campus researchers, may voluntarily undertake specific projects, including online courses, under explicit and signed work-for-hire contracts. When such work-for-hire agreements are truly voluntary, their contracted terms may legitimately narrow faculty intellectual property rights.

Faculty members have a collective interest in how university inventions derived from academic research are managed. Through shared governance, they also have a responsibility to participate in the design of university protocols that set the norms, standards, and expectations under which faculty discoveries and inventions will be distributed, licensed, and commercialized. The faculty senate, or an equivalent governing body, should play a primary role in defining the policies and public-interest commitments that will guide university-wide management of inventions and other knowledge assets stemming from campus-based research. These management protocols should devote special attention to the academic and public-interest obligations traditionally central to the university mission. Governing bodies should also consider the formation of a specially assigned faculty committee to review the university's invention-management practices regularly, represent the interests of faculty investigators and inventors to the campus as a whole, and make recommendations for reform when necessary.

Standards should be set for the handling of faculty intellectual property rights in the design and subsequent use of instructional materials, including online courses. Course syllabi at many institutions are considered public documents; indeed, they may be posted on universally accessible websites. It is thus to be expected that teachers everywhere will learn from one another's syllabi and that syllabi will be disseminated as part of the free exchange of academic knowledge. Faculty lectures or original audiovisual materials, however, unless specifically and voluntarily created as works made for hire, constitute faculty intellectual property. As components of faculty-designed online courses, they cannot be revised, edited, supplemented, or incorporated into courses taught by others without the consent of the original creator. Nor can an online course as a whole be assigned to another instructor without the consent of the faculty member who created the course, unless, once again, the faculty member agreed to treat the course as a work made for hire with such ownership rights residing in the institution. Faculty governing bodies have a special—and increasing—responsibility to ensure that faculty members are not pressured to sign work-for-hire agreements against their will.

Just as the right to control research and instruction is integral to academic freedom, so too are the rights of faculty members to control the disposition of their research inventions. Inventions made in the context of university work are the results of scholarship. University policies should direct all invention-management agents to represent and protect the expressed interests of faculty inventors along with the interests of the institution and the broader public. Where the interests diverge irreconcilably, the faculty senate, or an equivalent governing body, should adjudicate the dispute with the aim of selecting a course of action that promotes the greatest benefit for the research in question, the broader academic community, and the public good. Students and academic professionals should also have access to grievance procedures if they believe their inventor rights or other intellectual property rights have been violated. Students should never be urged or required to surrender their intellectual property rights (for example, in their dissertations) in advance to the university as a condition of participating in a degree program.

Notes

1. "Practicing an invention" first of all means taking the concept and giving it material embodiment, a key step in its manufacture.

2. 131 S.Ct. 2188 (2011).

3. The term *invention-management agent*, as used in this statement, covers all persons tasked with handling university-generated inventions and related intellectual property, including, for example, university technology-transfer offices, affiliated research foundations, contract invention-management agents, and legal consultants.

Statement on Copyright

This statement was approved in March 1999 by the Association's Special Committee on Distance Education and Intellectual Property Issues. It was adopted by the Association's Council and endorsed by the Eighty-Fifth Annual Meeting in June 1999.

The objective of copyright is, in the words of the US Constitution, to "promote the progress of science and useful arts." To achieve that objective, authors are given exclusive rights under the Copyright Act to reproduce their works, to use them as the basis for derivative works, to disseminate them to the public, and to perform and display them publicly. Institutions of higher learning in particular should interpret and apply the law of copyright so as to encourage the discovery of new knowledge and its dissemination to students, to the profession, and to the public. This mission is reflected in the 1940 *Statement of Principles on Academic Freedom and Tenure:* "Institutions of higher education are conducted for the common good and not to further the interest of either the individual teacher or the institution as a whole. The common good depends upon the free search for truth and its free exposition."

Academic Practice

Within that tradition, it has been the prevailing academic practice to treat the faculty member as the copyright owner of works that are created independently and at the faculty member's own initiative for traditional academic purposes. Examples include class notes and syllabi; books and articles; works of fiction and nonfiction; poems and dramatic works; musical and choreographic works; pictorial, graphic, and sculptural works; and educational software, commonly known as "courseware." This practice has been followed for the most part, regardless of the physical medium in which these "traditional academic works" appear; that is, whether on paper or in audiovisual or electronic form. As will be developed below, this practice should therefore ordinarily apply to the development of courseware for use in programs of distance education.

Unilateral Institutional Policies

Some colleges and universities have promulgated policies, typically unenforced, that proclaim traditional academic works to be the property of the institution. Faculty handbooks, for example, sometimes declare that faculty members shall be regarded as having assigned their copyrights to the institution. The Copyright Act, however, explicitly requires that a transfer of copyright, or of any exclusive right (such as the exclusive right to publish), must be evidenced in writing and signed by the author-transferor. If the faculty member is indeed the initial owner of copyright, then a unilateral institutional declaration cannot effect a transfer, nor is it likely that a valid transfer can be effected by the issuance of appointment letters to new faculty members requiring, as a condition of employment, that they abide by a faculty handbook that purports to vest in the institution the ownership of all works created by the faculty member for an indefinite future.

Other colleges and universities instead proclaim that traditional academic works are "works made for hire," with the consequence that the institution is regarded as the initial owner of copyright. This institutional claim is often stated to rest upon the use by the faculty member, in creating such works, of college or university resources, such as office space, supplies, library facilities, ordinary access to computers and networks, and money.

The pertinent definition of "work made for hire" is a work prepared by an "employee within the scope of his or her employment." In the typical work-for-hire situation, the content and purpose of the employee-prepared works are under the control and direction of the employer; the employee is accountable to the employer for the content and design of the work. In the case of traditional academic works, however, the faculty member rather than the institution determines the subject matter, the intellectual approach and direction, and the conclusions. This is the very essence of academic freedom. Were the institution to own the copyright in such works, under a work-made-for-hire theory, it would have the power, for example, to decide where the work is to be published, to edit and otherwise revise it, to prepare derivative works based on it (such as translations, abridgments, and literary, musical, or artistic variations), and indeed to censor and forbid dissemination of the work altogether. Such powers, so deeply inconsistent with fundamental principles of academic freedom, cannot rest with the institution.

College or University Copyright Ownership

Situations do arise, however, in which the college or university may fairly claim ownership of, or an interest in, copyright in works created by faculty (or staff) members. Three general kinds of projects fall into this category: special works created in circumstances that may properly be regarded as "made for hire," negotiated contractual transfers, and "joint works" as described in the Copyright Act.

1. *Works Made for Hire.* Although traditional academic work that is copyrightable—such as lecture notes, courseware, books, and articles—cannot normally be treated as works made for hire, some works created by college or university faculty and staff members do properly fall within that category, allowing the institution to claim copyright ownership. Works created as a specific requirement of employment or as an assigned institutional duty that may, for example, be included in a written job description or an employment agreement, may be fairly deemed works made for hire. Even absent such prior written specification, ownership will vest with the college or university in those cases in which it provides the specific authorization or supervision for the preparation of the work. Examples are reports developed by a dean or by the chair or members of a faculty committee, or college promotional brochures prepared by a director of admissions. Some institutions appear to treat course examinations as falling within this category, but the stronger case can be made for treating examinations as part of the faculty member's customary instructional materials, with copyright thus owned by the individual.

   The Copyright Act also defines as a "work made for hire" certain works that are commissioned from an individual who is not an employee but an "independent contractor." The institution will own the copyright in such a commissioned work when the author is not a college or university employee, or when the author is such an employee but the work to be created falls outside the normal scope of that person's employment duties (such as a professor of art history commissioned by the institution under special contract to write a catalog for a campus art gallery). In such situations, for the work-made-for-hire doctrine to apply there must be a written agreement so stating and signed by both parties; the work must also fall within a limited number of statutory categories, which include instructional texts, examinations, and contributions to a collective work.

2. *Contractual Transfers.* In situations in which the copyright ownership is held by the faculty (or staff) member, it is possible for the individual to transfer the entire copyright, or a more limited license, to the institution or to a third party. As already noted, under the Copyright Act, a transfer of all of the copyright or of an exclusive right must be reflected in a signed document in order to be valid. When, for example, a work is prepared pursuant to a program of "sponsored research" accompanied by a grant from a third party, a contract signed by the faculty member providing that copyright will be owned by the institution will be enforceable. Similarly, the college or university may reasonably request that the faculty member—when entering into an agreement granting the copyright or publishing rights to a third party—make efforts to reserve to the institution the right to use the work in its internally administered programs of teaching, research, and public service on a perpetual, royalty-free, nonexclusive basis.

3. *Joint Works.* Under certain circumstances, two or more persons may share copyright ownership of a work, notably when it is a "joint work." The most familiar example of a joint work is a book or article written, fully collaboratively, by two academic colleagues. Each is said to be a "co-owner" of the copyright, with each having all the usual rights of the copyright owner (i.e., to license others to publish, to distribute to the public, to translate, and the like), provided that any income from such uses is shared with the other. In rare situations, an example of which is discussed immediately below, it may be proper to treat a work as a product of the joint authorship of the faculty member and his or her institution, so that both have a shared interest in the copyright.

New Instructional Technologies

The development of new instructional technologies has led to some uncertainties with regard to the respective rights of the institution and its faculty members. For example, courseware prepared for programs of distance education will typically incorporate instructional content authored and presented by faculty members, but the college or university may contribute specialized services and facilities to the production of the courseware that go beyond what is traditionally provided to faculty members generally in the preparation of their course materials. On the one hand, the institution may simply supply "delivery mechanisms," such as videotaping, editing, and marketing services; in such a situation, it is very unlikely that the institution will be regarded as having contributed the kind of "authorship" that is necessary for a "joint work" that automatically entitles it to a share in the copyright ownership. On the other hand, the institution may, through its administrators and staff, effectively determine or contribute to such detailed matters as substantive coverage, creative graphic elements, and the like; in such a situation, the institution has a stronger claim to co-ownership rights.

Ownership, Control, Use, and Compensation: Informed Allocation of Rights

Given the varying roles possibly played by the institution and the faculty member, and the nascent state of distance-education programs and technologies, it is not likely that a single principle of law can clearly allocate copyright-ownership interests in all cases. In some instances, the legal rules may warrant the conclusion that the college or university is a "joint author"; in other instances, that the institution should be compensated with royalties commensurate with its investment; and in yet others, that it has some sort of implied royalty-free "license to use" the copyrighted work. It is therefore useful for the respective rights of individual faculty members and the institution—concerning ownership,

control, use, and compensation—to be negotiated in advance and reduced to a written agreement. Although the need for contractual arrangements has become more pressing with the advent of new instructional technologies, such arrangements should be considered even with respect to more traditional forms of authorship when the institution seeks to depart from the norm of faculty copyright ownership. An alternative format—perhaps somewhat less desirable, because less likely to be fully known to and appreciated by individual faculty members—would be detailed and explicit institutional regulations dealing with a variety of pertinent issues, subject to the strictures noted above concerning copyright transfers. Such regulations should, of course, give great weight to the views of the faculty, and may be reflected either in widely available institutional policy documents or in collective bargaining agreements.

Whoever owns the copyright, the institution may reasonably require reimbursement for any unusual financial or technical support. That reimbursement might take the form of future royalties or a nonexclusive, royalty-free license to use the work for internal educational and administrative purposes. Conversely, when the institution holds all or part of the copyright, the faculty member should, at a minimum, retain the right to take credit for creative contributions, to reproduce the work for his or her instructional purposes, and to incorporate the work in future scholarly works authored by that faculty member. In the context of distance-education courseware, the faculty member should also be given rights in connection with its future uses, not only through compensation but also through the right of "first refusal" in making new versions, or at least the right to be consulted in good faith on reuse and revisions.

Statement on Multiple Authorship

The statement that follows was approved for publication by the Association's Committee on Professional Ethics in June 1990.

Over the years, different scholarly fields have evolved different patterns of research and publication. In some areas, the solitary researcher remains the model, an ideal that draws some of its strength from association with the Romantic conception of the creative artist. Even in those fields, however, genuine collaboration is possible and even inescapable as different analytical skills are called upon to illuminate increasingly complex subjects of inquiry. Elsewhere in the scholarly world, collaboration is the norm. This appears to be particularly true in those sciences where separated disciplines must be brought to bear on a novel question, or where complex, articulated laboratory organizations are essential, or where (as in some areas of physics and astronomy) the scale is so large and the expense so vast that any original contribution is beyond the capacity of a scholar working alone or of even small teams of scholars.

In this varied and constantly shifting situation, disciplines have arrived at certain conventions that govern the listing of names of collaborators. This may seem at first glance a sufficiently equitable arrangement: scholars within the field know what to expect and how to evaluate their colleagues' estimate of their respective contributions. But there are times when the wider academic community must become involved in such questions, as will a still-wider world outside the university. Faculty members and administrators making decisions about appointments, promotion and tenure, and salary increases must try to evaluate individual worth and reckon with the significance of authorship. So, too, must granting agencies, public and private, while the government and the press, seeking expertise, must make repeated judgments about the basis of the authority that individual scholars may claim. A vast list of publications, dazzling to the uninitiated, may conceal as much as it reveals, and the conventions of particular disciplines may give rise to the suspicion, if not the actuality, of questionable ethical practices.

It is well known that actors' agents frequently negotiate hard about the order of credits, placement, and size of type; no such excesses need follow from an expectation that scholars who take part in a collaborative project should explain forthrightly—to disciplinary peers as well as to other academic colleagues and to such members of the public as may have occasion to inquire—the respective contributions of those who put their names to the finished work. This clarification might be accomplished in a preface, an extensive footnote, or an appendix; no one format can serve every scholarly combination. But a candid statement would do much to establish degrees of responsibility and authority, to ensure fair credit to junior or student colleagues, and to avoid unseemly later disputes about priority, real or alleged errors, and plagiarism. Purely formal association with the enterprise (such as the headship of a laboratory where no direct research involvement was present) would be noted for what it is, to the benefit of the participants as much as of those outside the field.

Making plain the actual contribution of each scholar to a collaborative work calls for an equivalent recognition in return. That academic decision makers frequently find themselves in a troubling dilemma when faced with genuine substantive collaboration testifies to the strength of the ideal of individual creativity. While in some scholarly activity carried on in tandem it is possible for contributors to make clear the respective contributions of each (as is often, and should be regularly, done by two or three joint authors of a book), in other cases the collaboration is so intimate as to defy disentangling: the creativity is imbedded in, and consequent upon, constant exchange of ideas and insights. This scholarly and psychological reality must be fully recognized in making academic decisions about the accomplishments and careers of single members of such combinations: what they have done must not be reduced to a second order of merit or, worse, dismissed out of hand. This recognition is particularly important in the case of younger scholars who may take a leading role in a collaboration that at first sight is one of subordination. To insist on individual demonstration of the abilities of a young scholar working on a topic where collaboration is inescapable, and where (as is often the case) immense amounts of time are required for fruitful results, may disrupt a promising career, force unneeded and diversionary publication, put undue emphasis on the vexing question of priority of discovery, and distort perceptions of the creative process.

These are questions of immense complexity and subtlety, not to be resolved by an unimaginative application of traditional academic myths or by bureaucratic heavy-handedness. Peer judgment alive to these questions, together with a sensible weighing of merely quantitative measures of accomplishment and reputation, will do much to remedy a problem that through parochialism, misplaced egotism, and inadvertence threatens to become steadily worse and to contribute to tarnishing the scholarly enterprise.

Statement on Conflicts of Interest

The statement that follows was approved for publication by the Association's Committee on Professional Ethics in June 1990 and revised by that committee in November 2013 with the endorsement of Committee A on Academic Freedom and Tenure.

American universities have long been engaged with the institutions of the wider society, to their mutual benefit. Universities have trained ministers, teachers, corporate leaders, and public servants, and have taken on wider responsibilities in research and administration for state and federal governments. The years after World War II brought both quantitative and qualitative change in this relationship as a result of the global responsibilities assumed by the United States and of the strikingly new importance attained by science. This change was symbolized and advanced by an immense increase in federal and state funding for higher education and in investment by private foundations. As universities entered an era of more stringent budgetary limitations, another major shift occurred—to greater reliance on private funding and to a closer symbiosis between universities and industry.

The many opportunities offered to both university researchers and the private sector by sweeping developments in certain areas of science, business, medicine, and technology have led to new concerns in both universities and government. One such concern, about freedom to conduct research and to publish the results, has rightly exercised universities in deliberations about whether to undertake such joint efforts and, if so, on what terms. Questions of conflict of interest have focused on the pressures that financial interests of university personnel participating in extra-university enterprises might exert, consciously or not, on the design and the outcome of the research.

A conflict of interest may most easily be defined as a circumstance in which a person's primary interests and responsibilities (such as the responsibility to analyze research results as dispassionately as possible) may be compromised by a secondary interest (such as financial gain). Identifying a conflict of interest does not entail an accusation of wrongdoing. Conflicts of interest have been shown to affect judgments unconsciously, so a conflict of interest refers to a factual circumstance wherein an impartial observer might reasonably infer that a conflict is present. Not all conflicts of interest are financial in nature, but financial conflicts of interest are not only the ones most easily managed but also the ones most likely to undermine public respect for, and trust in, higher education.

The American Association of University Professors addressed this issue in the past, and in 1990 reaffirmed the 1965 joint statement of the AAUP and the American Council on Education, *On Preventing Conflicts of Interest in Government-Sponsored Research at Universities*,[1] and commended the 1983 report of an Association subcommittee on *Corporate Funding of Academic Research*.[2] The latter report, avowedly tentative and anticipating a fuller statement at a later time, assumed that the initiative must lie with university faculties for drawing up conflict-of-interest guidelines for their campus, with due regard for the proper disclosure of a faculty member's involvement in off-campus enterprises, in terms of investment, ownership, or consultative status; for the use of university personnel, including students; and for the disposition of potential profits. A number of federal agencies, professional associations, and scholarly journals have now taken the view that proper disclosure should also address mounting evidence that research integrity is compromised by financial conflicts of interest.[3]

Since conflict-of-interest policies are designed to be preventive, faculties are well advised to base them not only on local but also on national experience. Higher education could benefit from the adoption of reasonably consistent standards nationwide. Useful federal guidelines for health-related fields were issued by the Department of Health and Human Services in 2011. They define "a significant financial conflict of interest that could affect the design, conduct, or reporting" of Public Health Service–funded research as one that exceeds $5,000 annually. Under the 2011 rule, university plans for managing individual conflicts of interest must be made readily accessible to the public, either on a website or by responding to any request "within five business days." The AAUP recommends that campuses adopt these policies and practices for all conflicts of interest that cannot be eliminated in health fields, even for research not federally funded.

The following considerations should be taken into account when developing, revising, or implementing conflict-of-interest guidelines. Faculties should be centrally involved in establishing conflict-of-interest policies, ensuring clear reporting requirements, and setting forth steps to eliminate conflicts of interest when possible, or to manage them when that is not feasible. Because the central business of the university remains the acquisition and dissemination of knowledge, unfettered by extra-university dictates, faculties should ensure that any cooperative venture between members of the faculty and outside agencies, whether public or private, respects the primacy of the university's principal mission, with regard to the choice of subjects of research and the reaching and publication of results.

The integrity of individual research and the overall reputation of universities make it prudent for institutions and their faculty governing bodies to require disclosure by all faculty, staff, and administrators of such information and documents as consulting contracts, external research support, compensated board memberships, and significant equity holdings or indebtedness in the areas of a person's research or teaching, both public and private. Setting a dollar amount, or percentage of interest in a company, that triggers disclosure may be appropriate. Such requirements for disclosure should be carefully focused on legitimate areas of concern and not improperly interfere with the privacy rights of university personnel and their families. The best way to ensure compliance with that principle is to publicize specific guidelines defining conflicts of interest and to make disclosure a routine aspect of the profession. That normally includes a requirement that university personnel report major equity holdings by a spouse, partner, or dependent child that overlap with the academic responsibilities of teaching, research, service, and administration.

Faculties should make certain that the pursuit of such joint ventures does not become an end in itself and so introduce distortions into traditional university understandings and arrangements. While private and public agencies could once be said to have a direct interest in only a few fields of research and in only certain questions within those fields, government, industry, and private foundations now fund research in a wide variety of disciplines. Accordingly, it is increasingly important that external interests not be allowed to shift the balance of academic priorities in a university without thorough debate about the consequences and without the considered judgment of appropriate faculty bodies. So, too, care must be taken to avoid contravening a commitment to fairness by widening disparities—in teaching loads, student supervision, or budgetary allocation—between departments engaged in such outside activity and those not less central to the nature of a university, which have, or can have, no such engagement.

The ability to procure private or government funding may in certain circumstances be an appropriate consideration in making judgments about salaries, tenure, and promotion, but it must be kept in proper proportion and be consistent with criteria established by the faculty. Guidelines concerning intra-university research support should guard against making its availability dependent, solely or predominantly, on the likelihood that the research so supported will result in obtaining outside funding.

Notes

1. AAUP, *Policy Documents and Reports*, 11th ed. (Baltimore: Johns Hopkins University Press, 2015), 271–73.

2. *Academe* 69 (November–December 1983): 18a–23a. See also the "Statement on Corporate Funding of Academic Research," *Policy Documents and Reports*, 274–76.

3. AAUP, *Recommended Principles to Guide Academy-Industry Relationships* (Washington, DC: AAUP Foundation, 2014), especially "Risk 4: Financial Conflicts of Interest," 95–100; "A Brief History of Efforts to Address COI at US Universities and Academic Medical Centers," 103–12; "General Principles for Management of Conflicts of Interest (COI) and Financial Conflict of Interest (FCOI)," 163–88; and "Targeted Principles: Managing COI in the Context of Clinical Care and Human Subject Research," 189–93.

On Preventing Conflicts of Interest in Government-Sponsored Research at Universities

The many complex problems that have developed in connection with the extensive sponsored research programs of the federal government have been of concern to the government, the academic community, and private industry. The American Association of University Professors, through its Council, and the American Council on Education, working in cooperation with the president's science advisor and the Federal Council of Science and Technology, in 1965 developed a statement of principles formulating basic standards and guidelines in this problematic area.

An underlying premise of the statement is that responsibility for determining standards affecting the academic community rests with that community, and that conflict-of-interest problems are best handled by administration and faculty in cooperative effort. In addition to providing guidelines, the statement seeks to identify and alert administration and faculty to the types of situations that have proved troublesome. Throughout, it seeks to protect the integrity of the objectives and needs of the cooperating institutions and their faculties, as well as of sponsoring agencies.

The increasingly necessary and complex relationships among universities, government, and industry call for more intensive attention to standards of procedure and conduct in government-sponsored research. The clarification and application of such standards must be designed to serve the purposes and needs of the projects and the public interest involved in them and to protect the integrity of the cooperating institutions as agencies of higher education.

The government and institutions of higher education, as the contracting parties, have an obligation to see that adequate standards and procedures are developed and applied; to inform one another of their respective requirements; and to ensure that all parties to the relationship are informed of and apply the standards and procedures that are so developed.

Consulting relationships between university staff members and industry serve the interests of research and education in the university. Likewise, the transfer of technical knowledge and skill from the university to industry contributes to technological advance. Such relationships are desirable, but certain potential hazards should be recognized.

Conflict Situations

1. *Favoring of Outside Interests.* When a university staff member (administrator, faculty member, professional staff member, or employee) undertaking or engaging in government-sponsored work has a significant financial interest in, or a consulting arrangement with, a private business concern, it is important to avoid actual or apparent conflicts of interest between government-sponsored university research obligations and outside interests and other obligations. Situations in or from which conflicts of interest may arise are:

   a. the undertaking or orientation of the staff member's university research to serve the research or other needs of the private firm without disclosure of such undertaking or orientation to the university and to the sponsoring agency;

   b. the purchase of major equipment, instruments, materials, or other items for university research from the private firm in which the staff member has the interest without disclosure of such interest;

   c. the transmission to the private firm or other use for personal gain of government-sponsored work products, results, materials, records, or information that are not made generally available (this would not necessarily preclude appropriate licensing arrangements for inventions, or consulting on the basis of government-sponsored research results where there is significant additional work by the staff member independent of the government-sponsored research);

d. the use for personal gain or other unauthorized use of privileged information acquired in connection with the staff member's government-sponsored activities (the term "privileged information" includes, but is not limited to, medical, personnel, or security records of individuals; anticipated material requirements or price actions; possible new sites for government operations; and knowledge of forthcoming programs or of selection of contractors or subcontractors in advance of official announcements);

e. the negotiation or influence upon the negotiation of contracts relating to the staff member's government-sponsored research between the university and private organizations with which the staff member has consulting or other significant relationships; and

f. the acceptance of gratuities or special favors from private organizations with which the university does, or may conduct, business in connection with a government-sponsored research project, or extension of gratuities or special favors to employees of the sponsoring government agency, under circumstances that might reasonably be interpreted as an attempt to influence the recipients in the conduct of their duties.

2. *Distribution of Effort.* There are competing demands on the energies of faculty members (for example, research, teaching, committee work, outside consulting). The way in which a faculty member divides his or her effort among these various functions does not raise ethical questions unless the government agency supporting the research is misled in its understanding of the amount of intellectual effort the faculty member is actually devoting to the research in question. A system of precise time accounting is incompatible with the inherent character of the work of faculty members, since the various functions they perform are closely interrelated and do not conform to any meaningful division of a

standard work week. On the other hand, if the research agreement contemplates that a faculty member will devote a certain fraction of effort to the government-sponsored research, or the faculty member agrees to assume responsibility in relation to such research, a demonstrable relationship between the indicated effort or responsibility and the actual extent of the faculty member's involvement is to be expected. Each university, therefore, should—through joint consultation of administration and faculty—develop procedures to ensure that proposals are responsibly made and complied with.

3. *Consulting for Government Agencies or Their Contractors.* When the staff member engaged in government-sponsored research also serves as a consultant to a federal agency, such conduct is subject to the conflict-of-interest provisions in the Federal Criminal Code (18 U.S.C. Sec. 202 *et seq.*) and the conflict-of-interest regulations adopted by the National Institutes of Health, the Public Health Service, and the National Science Foundation. When the staff member consults for one or more government contractors, or prospective contractors, in the same technical field as the staff member's research project, care must be taken to avoid giving advice that may be of questionable objectivity because of its possible bearing on the individual's other interests. In undertaking and performing consulting services, the staff member should make full disclosure of such interests to the university and to the contractor insofar as they may appear to relate to the work at the university or for the contractor. Conflict-of-interest problems could arise, for example, in the participation of a staff member of the university in an evaluation for the government agency or its contractor of some technical aspect of the work of another organization with which the staff member has a consulting or employment relationship or a significant financial interest, or in an evaluation of a competitor to such other organization.

University Responsibility

Each university participating in government-sponsored research should make known to the sponsoring government agencies:

1. the steps it is taking to ensure an understanding on the part of the university administration and staff members of the possible conflicts of interest or other problems that may develop in the foregoing types of situations; and

272

2. the organizational and administrative actions it has taken or is taking to avoid such problems, including:

   a. accounting procedures to be used to ensure that government funds are expended for the purposes for which they have been provided, and that all services which are required in return for these funds are supplied;

   b. procedures that enable it to be aware of the outside professional work of staff members participating in government-sponsored research, if such outside work relates in any way to the government-sponsored research;

   c. the formulation of standards to guide the individual university staff members in governing their conduct in relation to outside interests that might raise questions of conflicts of interest; and

   d. the provision within the university of an informed source of advice and guidance to its staff members for advance consultation on questions they wish to raise concerning the problems that may or do develop as a result of their outside financial or consulting interests, as they relate to their participation in government-sponsored university research. The university may wish to discuss such problems with the contracting officer or other appropriate government official in those cases that appear to raise questions regarding conflicts of interest.

The above process of disclosure and consultation is the obligation assumed by the university when it accepts government funds for research. The process must, of course, be carried out in a manner that does not infringe on the legitimate freedoms and flexibility of action of the university and its staff members that have traditionally characterized a university. It is desirable that standards and procedures of the kind discussed be formulated and administered by members of the university community themselves, through their joint initiative and responsibility, for it is they who are the best judges of the conditions which can most effectively stimulate the search for knowledge and preserve the requirements of academic freedom. Experience indicates that such standards and procedures should be developed and specified by joint administration-faculty action.

Statement on Corporate Funding of Academic Research

This report was prepared by a subcommittee of the Association's Committee A on Academic Freedom and Tenure. It was approved by Committee A and adopted by the Association's Council in November 2004.

Research universities have long collaborated with industry to their mutual benefit. The relationship has been the most productive for both parties when scholars are free to pursue and transmit basic knowledge through research and teaching. Learning, intellectual development, and progress—material, scientific, and technological—require freedom of thought and expression, and the right of the researcher to convey the results of inquiry beyond the classroom, laboratory, or institution.

The relationship, however, has never been free of concerns that the financial ties of researchers or their institutions to industry may exert improper pressure on the design and outcome of research. This is especially true of research that has as its goal commercially valuable innovations, which is the most common type of industry-sponsored research. Although corporate funding of academic research accounts for a relatively small percentage of all university research funds—approximately 7 percent of the total—that percentage has grown more rapidly than support from all other sources over the past two decades.[1] It may be expected to continue to grow absent an expansion of federal monies on a scale comparable to 1953–68, the halcyon years of federal funding. Moreover, the impact of corporate funding of university research has greater influence where it is most heavily focused, primarily in the fields of medicine, biology, chemistry, and engineering.

Some recent examples of university-industry and faculty-industry relationships that have drawn public attention are:

1. The death of a patient in a gene-transfer study at the University of Pennsylvania in fall 1999 and claims that the financial ties of the researchers to the company that financed their work biased their judgments.
2. Grants for biomedical research from tobacco companies and the Council for Tobacco Research. Though many recipients of these grants state that they have never been pressured to alter or "cook" data, some critics have questioned whether the availability of such funding lends credibility to company claims that health damage caused by smoking is still an unproven hypothesis and undermines public confidence in the possibility of disinterested science.
3. Research on a thyroid-replacement drug funded by a company with a vested interest in demonstrating the drug's superiority to generic drugs. In this case, the manufacturer intervened to try to prevent publication of an article that had been rigorously vetted by the *Journal of the American Medical Association*.
4. Endowed chairs in which a corporate sponsor retains some measure of control through the device of rotating as opposed to tenured appointments.
5. Activities of a university center on credit research, sponsored by major firms in the retail credit industry, whose findings are used by lawmakers debating changes in federal bankruptcy law.
6. A highly visible whistle-blowing episode in Canada in which a faculty researcher was removed as a principal investigator in a drug study when she broke a gag rule about the toxic risks to some of her patients. The institution denied her legal assistance on grounds that she had not obtained the approval of the administration for her confidential agreement with the drug company, an agreement that an investigator characterized as a "very big mistake."
7. Universities actively encouraging faculty members to form private research companies to promote licensing of innovations, which in turn can induce rivalry among faculty.
8. A study (published in *Science and Engineering Ethics*, II) of 789 journal articles that showed that in 34 percent of the articles one or more author had a financial interest in the subject matter being studied.

Perhaps the most striking example of a new form of university-industry partnership and a possible harbinger of future developments is the 1998 agreement between the Department of Plant and Microbial Biology at the University of California, Berkeley, and the Novartis Corporation, a Swiss pharmaceutical company.[2] Under a five-year, $25-million arrangement, Novartis is funding research in the department and will receive licensing rights to a proportion of the number of discoveries by the department's researchers equal to the company's share of the department's total research budget, whether or not the discoveries result directly from company-sponsored research. Where the financial resources of an academic department are dominated by a corporation there is the potential, no matter how elaborate the safeguards for respecting academic freedom and the independence of researchers, for weakening peer review both in research and in promotion and tenure decisions, for distorting the priorities of undergraduate and graduate education, and for compromising scientific openness.

An additional concern focuses less on research and teaching in a single department than on the ethos of the entire university. President George Rupp of Columbia University has observed that research may become somewhat too domesticated, aimed at short-term objectives dictated by corporate sponsors, or even our own faculty, as their entrepreneurial instincts lead them to try to identify and patent discoveries that will have a payoff. That is a risk that the university as a whole faces. It can involve not only the sciences and engineering, but the humanities and social sciences as well. For example, consider the impact of some of the new media capabilities. There are current commercial attempts to harness the ideas, even the lectures and presentations, of faculty members. The danger exists that universities will be so assimilated into society that we will no longer be the kind of collectors of talent that allow creativity to blossom. We must guard against being harnessed directly to social purposes in any way that undermines the fundamental character of the university.[3]

The increasingly complex and controversial relationships among universities, researchers, and corporations led the federal government in 1995 to require researchers who receive grants from the National Science Foundation or the Public Health Service (the latter includes the National Institutes of Health) to disclose to their institutions any "significant financial interests . . . that would reasonably appear to be affected by [their] research." Specifically, researchers must report any income ("when aggregated for the investigator and the investigator's spouse and dependent children") greater than $10,000 that they receive

from a corporation that could benefit from their research, or any equity interest greater than $10,000 that exceeds 5 percent ownership interest in such a corporation. The government also requires universities to have "adequate enforcement mechanisms," and, as appropriate, to impose sanctions.[4]

Most research universities have adopted policies, with varying degrees of specificity, that reflect the government's requirements. Some have adopted more stringent regulations. At Washington University in St. Louis, for example, there is no monetary minimum for reporting financial ties with a corporation that sponsors research, while researchers at Johns Hopkins University must have the approval of the institution before they accept a fiduciary role with a company, if such a position is related to their academic duties. In addition, at least two professional organizations—the American Society for Gene Therapy and the American Society for Human Genetics—have called on their members not to own stock in any company that funds their research.

These various initiatives rest on the premise that conflicts of interest generated by university-industry ties can thrive if researchers do not know what standards of professional conduct are expected of them.[5]

It is safe to say, however, that the pressures that brought these government and university requirements into being are not likely to diminish for the foreseeable future, and that there will be a continuing need to ensure that conflict-of-interest policies are properly implemented. The primary responsibility for such efforts resides within the academic community and especially with the faculty. The possible efforts are several:

1. Consistent with principles of sound academic governance, the faculty should have a major role not only in formulating the institution's policy with respect to research undertaken in collaboration with industry, but also in developing the institution's plan for assessing the effectiveness of the policy.[6] The policy and the plan should be distributed regularly to all faculty, who should inform students and staff members associated with them of their contents.

2. The faculty should work to ensure that the university's plan for monitoring the institution's conflict-of-interest policy is consistent with the principles of academic freedom. There should be emphasis on ensuring that the source and purpose of all corporate-funded research contracts can be publicly disclosed. Such contracts should explicitly provide for the

open communication of research results, not subject to the sponsor's permission for publication.

3. The faculty should call for, and participate in, the periodic review of the impact of industrially sponsored research on the education of students, and on the recruitment and evaluation of researchers (whether or not they hold regular faculty appointments) and postdoctoral fellows.

4. The faculty should insist that regular procedures be in place to deal with alleged violations by an individual of the university's conflict-of-interest policy. Should disciplinary action be contemplated, it is essential that safeguards of academic due process be respected.[7]

5. Because research relationships with industry are not static, the faculty, in order to ensure that the assessment of conflict-of-interest policies is responsive to changing needs, should regularly review the policies themselves as well as the instruments for conducting the assessment.

Notes

1. National Science Board, *Science & Engineering Indicators—1998* (Arlington, VA: National Science Foundation, 1998), 2.

2. A somewhat similar arrangement in 1982 between Monsanto and the medical school at Washington University in St. Louis produced about $150 million in basic-research money for the university. See Goldie Blumenstyk, "Berkeley Pact with a Swiss Company Takes Technology Transfer to a New Level," *Chronicle of Higher Education,* December 11, 1998, A56.

3. Government-University-Industry Research Roundtable, *A Dialogue on University Stewardship: New Responsibilities and Opportunities. Proceedings of a Roundtable Discussion* (Washington, DC: National Academies, 1998), 22.

4. In 1999, the National Institutes of Health (NIH) issued principles and guidelines to discourage research-

ers from entering into unduly restrictive agreements with corporations about sharing their work with others. The NIH's remarks about "academic freedom and publication" merit full citation:

> Academic research freedom based upon collaboration, and the scrutiny of research findings within the scientific community, are at the heart of the scientific enterprise. Institutions that receive NIH research funding through grants, cooperative agreements, or contracts ("Recipients") have an obligation to preserve research freedom, safeguard appropriate authorship, and ensure timely disclosure of their scientists' research findings through, for example, publications and presentations at scientific meetings. Recipients are expected to avoid signing agreements that unduly limit the freedom of investigators to collaborate and publish, or that automatically grant co-authorship or copyright to the provider of a material.
>
> Reasonable restrictions on collaboration by academic researchers involved in sponsored-research agreements with an industrial partner that avoid conflicting obligations to other industrial partners are understood and accepted. Similarly, brief delays in publication may be appropriate to permit the filing of patent applications and to ensure that confidential information obtained from a sponsor or the provider of a research tool is not inadvertently disclosed. However, excessive publication delays or requirements for editorial control, approval of publications, or withholding of data all undermine the credibility of research results and are unacceptable. (64 *Federal Register* 72090 [December 23, 1999])

5. See, for example, "On Preventing Conflicts of Interest in Government-Sponsored Research at Universities," issued jointly by the AAUP and the American Council on Education, AAUP, *Policy Documents and Reports*, 11th ed. (Baltimore: Johns Hopkins University Press, 2015), 271–73.

6. See "Statement on Government of Colleges and Universities," ibid., 117–22.

7. See Regulations 5 and 7 of the Association's "Recommended Institutional Regulations on Academic Freedom and Tenure," ibid., 79–90.

Recommended Principles for Faculty Handbooks and Collective Bargaining Agreements to Guide Academy-Industry Relationships

These recommendations are extracted from *Recommended Principles to Guide Academy-Industry Relationships* (2014), an initial version of which Committee A on Academic Freedom and Tenure approved for publication in May 2012.

On campuses with academic collective bargaining, those of these 56 principles that concern or affect terms and conditions of academic employment should be incorporated directly or by reference into the academic collective bargaining agreements. These provisions might especially include applicable grievance procedures, academic freedom and publication rights, intellectual property policies, and individual conflict of interest reporting obligations. The academic agreement should also ensure that the academic senate has a substantial role in establishing and implementing those of the recommendations that are not incorporated in the collective bargaining agreement.

Part I—General Principles to Guide Academy-Industry Engagement University-Wide

Handbook Principle 1: Faculty Governance: The university recognizes the primacy of shared academic governance in establishing campus-wide policies for planning, developing, implementing, monitoring, and assessing all donor agreements and collaborations, whether with private industry, government, or nonprofit groups. In these areas, there will be meaningful participation of the appropriate faculty governance bodies, and, to the extent that donor agreements and collaborations relate to the academic mission of the university, the administration should concur with the judgment of these governance bodies regarding these donor agreements and collaborations except in rare instances and for compelling reasons that should be stated in detail. Faculty, not outside sponsors, will retain majority control over the campus management of these agreements and collaborations.

Handbook Principle 2: Academic Freedom, Autonomy, and Control: The university will protect and preserve its academic autonomy—including the academic freedom rights of faculty, students, postdoctoral fellows, and academic professionals—in all its relationships with industry and other funding sources by maintaining majority academic control over joint academy-industry committees and exclusive academic control over core academic functions (such as faculty research evaluations, faculty hiring and promotion decisions, curriculum development, classroom teaching, and course content).

Handbook Principle 3: Academic Publication Rights: Agreements between the university and third parties will fully protect academic publication rights, with only limited delays (a maximum of 30–60 days) to remove corporate proprietary or confidential information or to file for patents or other IP protection prior to publication. The university does not permit either sponsor efforts to obstruct publication or sponsored research agreements that limit or prohibit the free, timely, and open dissemination of research data, codes, reagents, methods, and results. Sponsor attempts to compel a faculty member, student, postdoctoral fellow, or academic professional to edit, revise, withhold, or delete contents of an academic publication (including a master's thesis or doctoral dissertation) or presentation (beyond legally justified claims to protect explicit trade secrets) are prohibited and must be acknowledged in writing as prohibited in all sponsored research contracts. While funders are free to make editorial suggestions, academic researchers are free at all times to accept or reject them.

Handbook Principle 4: The Authenticity of Academic Authorship: To protect the authenticity of academic publishing, the university prohibits faculty, students, postdoctoral fellows, medical residents, and other academic professionals from engaging in practices variously described as industry-led "ghostwriting" or "ghost authorship." Ghostwriting or ghost-authorship occurs when a private firm or an industry group initiates the publication of an "academic" article in a science or medical journal in support of its commercial products or interests, without publicly disclosing that the corporate entity has initiated and also often performed the initial drafting of the article, and then recruited an academic researcher (sometimes referred to as an "academic opinion leader") to sign on as the nominal "author" (frequently in exchange for a fee). This practice violates scholarly standards and is unacceptable in any academic setting.

Handbook Principle 5: Access to Complete Study Data and Independent Academic Analysis: The university prohibits faculty and others on campus from participating in sponsored research that restricts investigators' ability to gain access to the complete study data related to their sponsored research or that limits investigators' ability to conduct free, unfettered, and independent analyses of complete data to verify the accuracy and validity of final reported results. These basic academic freedom rights will be secured within the legal terms of all sponsored research contracts.

Handbook Principle 6: Confidential and Classified Research: The university does not permit classified research to be conducted on campus, and it does not permit confidential corporate, government, or nonprofit research that may not be published. [See the full Principle 6 for further specifications your campus may wish to embody in its handbook.]

Handbook Principle 7: Academic Consulting: To address the potential for conflicts of commitment and other financial conflicts of interest, all consulting contracts worth $5,000 or more a year are to be reported to and reviewed and managed by the university's standing conflict of interest committee(s) that are charged with addressing both individual and institutional conflicts of interest. Neither faculty members nor administrators may sign consulting contracts that undercut their professional ability to express their own independent expert opinions, except when consulting with industry, government, or other parties on explicitly classified or proprietary matters. All such consulting agreements are to be secured in writing.

Part II—General Principles for Academic Education and Training

Handbook Principle 8: Recruiting and Advising Graduate Students, Medical Residents, and Faculty: The admission of graduate students to degree programs and the appointment of medical residents and faculty will be based on their overall qualifications, not on their potential to work under a particular donor agreement or collaborative research alliance, whether commercial, governmental, or nonprofit. A PhD student's main adviser must not have any significant financial interest, including equity, in a company that is funding or stands to profit from the student's thesis or dissertation research. Requests for exceptions will be evaluated with respect to both conflicts of interest and potential conflicts of commitment, all of which should be disclosed orally and in writing to all affected parties and periodically reviewed by [insert name of faculty body].

Handbook Principle 9: Impartial Academic Evaluation: Students, postdoctoral fellows, academic professionals, and junior colleagues are entitled to impartial and fair evaluations of their academic performance. Because of the risk of both real and perceived bias, faculty members with a significant personal financial interest in the outcome of their students' research may not have sole responsibility for evaluating student progress toward a degree.

Handbook Principle 10: Grievance Procedures: Although collective bargaining contracts often include detailed and exemplary grievance procedures, the AAUP as a whole has not endorsed model grievance procedures that go beyond what is called for in Regulation 16 of the *Recommended Institutional Regulations on Academic Freedom and Tenure:* "If any faculty member alleges cause for grievance in any matter not covered by the procedures described in the foregoing regulations, the faculty member may petition the elected faculty grievance committee [here name the committee] for redress. The petition will set forth in detail the nature of the grievance and will state against whom the grievance is directed. It will contain any factual or other data that the petitioner deems pertinent to the case. Statistical evidence of improper discrimination, including discrimination in salary, may be used in establishing a prima facie case. The committee will decide whether or not the facts merit a detailed investigation; if the faculty member succeeds in establishing a prima facie case, it is incumbent upon those who made the decision to come forward with evidence in support of their decision. Submission of a petition will not automatically entail investigation or detailed consideration thereof. The committee may seek to bring about a settlement of the issue(s) satisfactory to the parties. If in the opinion of the committee such a settlement is not possible or is not appropriate, the committee will report its findings and recommendations to the petitioner and to the appropriate administrative officer and faculty body, and the petitioner will, upon request, be provided an opportunity to present the grievance to them. The grievance committee will consist of three [or some other number] elected members of the faculty. No officer of the administration will serve on the committee." Faculty with financial conflicts related to a grievance filing will recuse themselves from its adjudication in formal proceedings. (See Principle 10 in the main report for specific guarantees that might be included in a handbook or collective bargaining agreement.)

Part III—General Principles for Management of Intellectual Property (IP)

Handbook Principle 11: Faculty Inventor Rights and IP Management: Faculty members' fundamental rights to direct and control their own research do not terminate when they make a new invention or other research discovery; these rights extend to decisions about their intellectual property—including invention management, IP licensing, commercialization, dissemination, and public use. Faculty assignment of an invention to a management agent, including the university that hosted the underlying research, will be voluntary and negotiated, rather than mandatory, unless federal statutes or previous sponsored research agreements dictate otherwise. Faculty inventors retain a vital interest in the disposition of their research inventions and discoveries and will, therefore, retain rights to negotiate the terms of their disposition. Neither the university nor its management agents will undertake IP decisions or legal actions directly or indirectly affecting a faculty member's research, inventions, instruction, or public service without the faculty member's and the inventor's express consent. Of course, faculty members, like other campus researchers, may voluntarily undertake specific projects as "work for hire" contracts. When such work for hire agreements are truly voluntary and uncoerced, their contracted terms may legitimately narrow faculty IP rights.

Handbook Principle 12: Shared Governance and the Management of University Inventions: The faculty senate or an equivalent body will play a primary role in defining the policies and public-interest commitments that will guide universitywide management of inventions and other knowledge assets stemming from campus-based research. University protocols that set the norms, standards, and expectations under which faculty discoveries and inventions will be controlled, distributed, licensed, and commercial-ized are subject to approval by the faculty senate or an equivalent governance body, as are the policies and public-interest commitments that will guide universitywide management of inventions and other knowledge assets stemming from campus-based research. A standing faculty committee will regularly review the university's invention management practices, ensure compliance with these principles, represent the interests of faculty investigators and inventors to the campus, and make recommendations for reform when necessary.

Handbook Principle 13: Adjudicating Disputes Involving Inventor Rights: Just as the right to control research and instruction is integral to academic freedom, so too are faculty members' rights to control the disposition of their research inventions. Inventions made in the context of university work are the results of scholarship. Invention management agents are directed to represent and protect the expressed interests of faculty inventors, along with the interests of the institution and the broader public to the maximum extent possible. Where the interests diverge insurmountably, the faculty senate or an equivalent body will adjudicate the dispute with the aim of recommending a course of action to promote the greatest benefit for the research in question, the broader academic community, and the public good. Student and other academic professional inventors have access to grievance procedures if they believe their inventor or other IP rights have been violated. Students will not be urged or required to surrender their IP rights to the university as a condition of participating in a degree program.

Handbook Principle 14: IP Management and Sponsored Research Agreements: In negotiating outside sponsored-research agreements, university administrators will make every effort to inform potentially affected faculty researchers and to involve them meaningfully in early-stage negotiations concerning invention management and IP. In the case of large-scale corporate sponsored research agreements like strategic corporate alliances (SCAs), which can have an impact on large numbers of faculty members, not all of whom may be identifiable in advance, a special faculty committee will be convened to participate in early-stage negotiations, represent collective faculty interests, and ensure compliance with relevant university protocols. Faculty participation in all institutionally negotiated sponsored research agreements will always be voluntary.

Handbook Principle 15: Humanitarian Licensing, Access to Medicines: When lifesaving drugs and other critical public-health technologies are developed in academic laboratories with public funding support, the university will make a strong effort to license such inventions in a manner that will ensure broad public access in both the developing and the industrialized world. When issuing an exclusive license to a company for the development of a promising new drug—or any other critical agricultural, health, or environmental safety invention—the university will always seek to include provisions to facilitate distribution of these inventions in developing countries at affordable prices.

Handbook Principle 16: Securing Broad Research Use and Distribution Rights: All contracts and agreements relating to university-generated inventions will include an express reservation of rights—often known as a "research exemption"—to allow for academic, nonprofit, and governmental use of academic inventions and associated intellectual property for non-commercial research purposes. Research exemptions will be reserved and well publicized prior to assignment or licensing so that faculty members and other academic researchers can share protected inventions and research results (including related data, reagents, and research tools) with colleagues located at this university or at any other nonprofit or governmental institution. The freedom to share and practice academic discoveries, for educational and research purposes, whether legally protected or not, is vitally important for the advancement of research and scientific inquiry. It also enables investigators to replicate and verify published results, a practice essential to scientific integrity.

Handbook Principle 17: Exclusive and Nonexclusive Licensing: The university, its contracted management agents, and faculty will always work to avoid exclusive licensing of patentable inventions, unless such licenses are absolutely necessary to foster follow-on use or to develop an invention that would otherwise languish. Exclusive and other restrictive licensing arrangements will be used sparingly, rather than as a presumptive default. When exclusive licenses are granted, they will have limited terms (preferably less than eight years), include requirements that the inventions be developed, and prohibit "assert licensing," sometimes referred to as "trolling" (aggressively enforcing patents against an alleged infringer, often with no intention of manufacturing or marketing the product oneself). Exclusive licenses made with the intention of permitting broad access through reasonable and nondiscriminatory sublicensing, cross-licensing, and dedication of patents to an open standard should meet

public-access expectations. However, the preferred methods for disseminating university research are nonexclusive licensing and open dissemination, to protect the university's public interest mission, open-research culture, and commitment to advancing research and inquiry through broad knowledge sharing. To enhance compliance and public accountability, the university requires all invention-management agents to report publicly and promptly any exclusive licenses issued together with written statements detailing why an exclusive license was necessary and why a nonexclusive one would not suffice. The faculty senate, or another designated governance body, has the authority to review periodically any exclusive licenses and corresponding statements for consistency with the principle.

Handbook Principle 18: Upfront Exclusive Licensing Rights for Research Sponsors: The university will refrain from signing sponsored research agreements, especially multi-year, large-scale SCA agreements, granting sponsors broad title, or exclusive commercial rights, to future sponsored research inventions and discoveries unless such arrangements are narrowly defined and agreed to by all faculty members participating in, or foreseeably affected by, the alliance. If this arrangement is not feasible, as in the case of larger SCAs, the faculty senate (or another designated governance body) will review and approve the agreement and confirm its consistency with principles of academic freedom and faculty independence and with the university's public interest missions. Special consideration will be given to the impact exclusive licenses could have on future, as-yet-unimagined uses of technologies. When granted, exclusive rights will be defined as narrowly as possible and restricted to targeted fields of use only, and every effort will be made to safeguard against abuse of the exclusive position.

Handbook Principle 19: Research Tools and Upstream Platform Research: The university and its contracted management agents will undertake every effort to make available and broadly disseminate research tools and other upstream platform inventions in which they have acquired an ownership interest. They will avoid assessing fees, beyond those necessary to cover the costs of maintaining the tools and disseminating them, and avoid imposing other constraints that could hamper downstream research and development. No sponsored research agreement will include any contractual obligations that prevent outside investigators from accessing data, tools, inventions, and reports relating to scholarly review of published research, matters of public health and safety, environmental safety, and urgent public policy decisions.

Handbook Principle 20: Diverse Licensing Models for Diverse University Inventions: Faculty investigators and inventors and their management agents will work cooperatively to identify effective licensing or distribution models for each invention with the goal of enhancing public availability and use.

Handbook Principle 21: Rights to "Background Intellectual Property" (BIP): University administrators and their agents will not act unilaterally when granting sponsors rights to university-managed background intellectual property (BIP) related to a sponsor's proposed research area but developed without the sponsor's funding support. The university will be mindful of how BIP rights will affect faculty inventors and other investigators who are not party to the sponsored research agreement. University administrators and managers will not obligate the BIP of one set of investigators to another's sponsored research project, unless that BIP is already being made available under nonexclusive licensing terms or the affected faculty inventors and investigators have consented.

Part IV—General Principles for Management of Conflicts of Interest (COI) and Financial Conflicts of Interest (FCOI)

Handbook Principle 22: [This principle asks that campuses develop their own financial COI policies. We have identified key elements of what such a policy should include, but campus implementation will require integrating the policy with local committee responsibilities and governance structures. However, a policy might begin with COI definitions, as suggested under the full Principle 22 discussion, and proceed to general statements (the university COI policy specifies how FCOI will be reported, reviewed, managed, or eliminated, along with our enforcement policies) before proceeding to details.]

Handbook Principle 23: Consistent COI Enforcement across Campus: University COI policies apply consistently across the whole institution, including affiliated medical schools, hospitals, institutes, centers, and other facilities; they apply to faculty, students, administrators, and academic professionals.

Handbook Principle 24: Standing COI Committees: The COI committee oversees implementation of policies to address individual and institutional COI. At least one member is from outside the institution and has been approved by [insert the name of the appropriate faculty

governance body]. Members must be free of conflicts of interest related to their COI oversight functions. After faculty financial COI disclosure statements have been reviewed by an appropriate campus standing committee, they will be made available to the public.

Handbook Principle 25: Reporting Individual COI: Faculty members and academic professionals are required to report to the standing campus COI committee all significant outside financial interests relating directly or indirectly to their professional responsibilities (research, teaching, committee work, and other activities), including the dollar amounts involved and the nature of the services compensated—regardless of whether or not they believe their financial interests might reasonably affect their current or anticipated university activities. Faculty members must also report family member patent royalty income and equity holdings related to their own teaching and research areas. All administrators will report similar financial interests both to their superiors and to the standing COI committee. Presidents and chancellors will also report such information to the standing committee.

Handbook Principle 26: Inter-office Reporting and Tracking of Institutional COI: To keep track of institutional conflicts of interest, our institutional COI committee has a campuswide reporting system that requires the technology transfer office, the office of sponsored programs, the development office, the grants office, institutional review boards (IRBs), purchasing operations, and corresponding offices at affiliated medical institutions to report, at least quarterly, to the standing COI committee on situations that might give rise to institutional conflicts.

Handbook Principle 27: Strategies for Reviewing, Evaluating, and Addressing COI: Our strategies for addressing individual financial COI include divesting troublesome assets, terminating consulting arrangements, resigning corporate board seats, and withdrawing from affected projects. Our methods for addressing institutional financial COI include divesting equity interest in companies doing campus research, placing conflicted equity holdings in independently managed funds with explicit firewalls to separate financial from academic decisions, recusing conflicted senior administrators from knowledge of, or authority over, affected research projects, and requiring outside committee review or oversight. Because of conflicting fiduciary responsibilities, the university prohibits senior administrators from receiving compensation for serving on corporate boards during their time in office.

Handbook Principle 28: Developing a Formal, Written COI Management Plan: If the university's standing COI committee finds compelling circumstances for allowing a research project, or other professional activity, to continue in the presence of a significant financial COI—without the elimination of the conflict—the committee will document the circumstances and write a formal management plan for each case. The plan will detail how the university will manage the financial COI and eliminate or reduce risks to its affected constituents (students, collaborating researchers, faculty, patients), its pertinent missions (research integrity, informed consent, and recruitment of research volunteers), and its reputation and public trust.

This policy is consistent with the Department of Health and Human Services (DHHS)–National Institutes of Health (NIH) rules implemented in 2011 to address financial conflicts, requiring all universities that receive DHHS or NIH grants to prepare and enforce such management plans.

Handbook Principle 29: Oversight and Enforcement of COI Rules: The university's COI policy details our oversight procedures, as well as our available sanctions for noncompliance. These are essential for ensuring compliance with university rules and maintaining public trust in the university's ability to regulate itself.

Handbook Principle 30: University-Vendor Relationships and COI: The university will ensure that vendor evaluation, selection, and contracting for university products and services are consistent with our academic mission and do not jeopardize the best interests of our students. Vendors must not be asked to make, or be coerced into making, financial contributions to the university, either through direct university donations or through the recruitment of other contributing donors, in exchange for winning university contracts. All university bidding for contracts and services related to such areas as banking and student loans will be conducted through a fair, impartial, and competitive selection process.

Handbook Principle 31: COI Transparency: Public Disclosure of Financial Interests and COI Management Plans: University COI policy requires faculty, administrators, students, postdoctoral fellows, and academic professionals to disclose to all journal editors all significant personal financial interests that may be directly or indirectly related to the manuscripts they are submitting for consideration. COI disclosure on publications is to summarize funding sources for the last five years, not just for the project at hand. The same COI disclosure requirements apply to oral presentations, including those presented in conferences, courts, and legislative chambers. After the university's standing COI committee reviews faculty COI disclosure statements, they will be posted to a public website, and the information on the website will remain publicly accessible for at least a decade. This measure addresses growing demands from Congress, state governments, journal editors, the media, and public-interest groups for increased reporting and transparency of faculty COI. It is also consistent with DHHS-NIH (2011) rules, which require universities to disclose all significant financial COI (as per the DHHS-NIH definition) related to a faculty member's DHHS-funded research on a public website or to provide the information upon public request within five days. Disclosure of financial COI also extends to affected patients and to volunteers for human subject research projects.

Part V—Targeted Principles: Managing COI in the Context of Clinical Care and Human Subject Research

Handbook Principle 32: Individual and Institutional COI and Human Subject Research: To maximize patient safety and preserve public trust in the integrity of academic research, the university operates with a strong presumption against permitting financial COI related to clinical medical research and experimental studies involving human subjects. A "rebuttable presumption" against permitting clinical trial research that may be compromised by financial COI will govern decisions about whether financially conflicted researchers or financial conflicts involving the institution will be allowed in pursuing a particular human subject research protocol or project, unless a compelling case can be made to justify an exception.

Handbook Principle 33: Institutional Review Boards (IRBs) and COI Management: An institutional review board (IRB) must review all proposed human clinical trial protocols, paying careful consideration to all related financial COI, before research is allowed to proceed. First, financially conflicted IRB members will recuse themselves from deliberations related to studies with which they have a potential conflict. Second, the institution's standing COI committee will prepare summary information about all institutional and individual financial COI related to the research protocol under review. The summary will accompany the protocol when it is presented to the IRB. The IRB will take the COI information into account when determining whether, and under what circumstances, to approve a protocol. Neither the IRB nor the standing COI committee is to reduce the stringency of the other's management requirements. Finally, if a research protocol is allowed to proceed, the IRB will disclose any institutional or investigator financial COI as well as the university's management plans for addressing them to all patient volunteers (in informed consent documents) and all investigators and units involved with the research protocol.

Handbook Principle 34: COI, Medical Purchasing, and Clinical Care: The university's COI policy requires all personnel with financial interests in any manufacturer of pharmaceuticals, devices, or equipment, or in any provider of services, to disclose such interests and to recuse themselves from involvement in related purchasing decisions. To the extent an individual's expertise is necessary in evaluating a product or a service, the individual's financial ties will be disclosed to those responsible for purchasing decisions.

Handbook Principle 35: COI Transparency in the Context of Medical Care: University policy requires all physicians, dentists, nurses, pharmacists, and other health professionals, as well as investigators, to disclose their financial COI to both patients and the broader public.

Part VI—Targeted Principles: Strategic Corporate Alliances (SCAs)

Handbook Principle 36: Shared Governance and Strategic Corporate Alliances (SCAs): The planning, negotiation, approval, execution, and ongoing oversight of new SCAs formed on campus require the involvement of the faculty senate. The senate will appoint a committee to review a first draft of a confidential memorandum of understanding (MOU) pertaining to newly proposed SCAs. The direct and indirect financial obligations of all parties will be made clear from the outset. Before a final agreement is reached on a broad SCA, the full faculty senate will review it. Formal approval of broad SCAs must await both stages in this process. All approved SCA agreements will be made available to all faculty and academic professionals as well as to the public. If the SCA designates specific funding for new full-time faculty appointments (FTEs), all normal university and departmental procedures for academic searches and appointments—as well as advancement and promotion decisions—will be followed to honor and protect academic self-governance. Temporary employees may not exclusively staff, administer, or supervise SCAs. Normal grievance procedures and due process will govern complaints regarding interference with academic freedom or other faculty or academic rights that may arise under SCAs.

Handbook Principle 37: SCA Governance and Majority Academic Control: The university will retain majority academic control and voting power over internal governance bodies charged with directing or administering SCAs in collaboration with outside corporate sponsors. The SCA's main governance body will include members who are not direct stakeholders of the SCA and are based in academic disciplines and units that do not stand to benefit from the SCA in any way. A joint university-industry SCA governance body may have a role in awarding funding, but it will have no role in such exclusively academic functions as faculty hiring, curriculum design, and course content.

Handbook Principle 38: Academic Control over SCA Research Selection (for Broad SCAs): In the case of broad SCAs, university representatives will retain majority representation and voting power on SCA committees charged with evaluating and selecting research proposals or making final research awards. These committees must also employ an independent peer-review process.

Handbook Principle 39: Peer Review (for Broad SCAs): Using a standard peer-review process, independent academic experts will evaluate applications and award funding whenever SCAs issue a request for proposals (RFP) in a new grant cycle. Any expert involved in the peer-review and grant-award process should be free of personal financial COI related to the area of research being reviewed to ensure that research selection is scientifically driven, impartial, and fair. Appointees to committees charged with research selection are prohibited from awarding commercial research funding to themselves, their departments, or their labs and should not be past recipients of funding from that SCA.

Handbook Principle 40: Transparency regarding the SCA Research Application Process (for Broad SCAs): SCA agreements will clearly and transparently detail their methods and criteria for research selection and will explain how academic researchers may apply for SCA grant funding.

Handbook Principle 41: Protection of Publication Rights and Knowledge Sharing in SCA Agreements: All the provisions of Principle 3 apply to strategic corporate alliances as well.

Handbook Principle 42: SCA Confidentiality Restrictions: To protect the university's distinctively open academic research environment, restrictions on sharing confidential corporate information and other confidentiality restrictions will be minimized insofar as possible in SCA agreements.

Handbook Principle 43: SCA Anti-competitor Agreements: Restrictions in SCA agreements on faculty, academic professionals, postdoctoral fellows, and students interacting or sharing information and research with private-sector competitors of SCA sponsors, or receiving separate research support from outside firms—often embodied in anti-competitor or noncompete agreements—will be avoided or minimized to the greatest extent possible.

Handbook Principle 44: Exclusive Licensing and SCA Agreements: All the provisions of Principles 17 and 18 apply to strategic corporate alliances as well.

Handbook Principle 45: Limits on Broader Academic Disruption by SCAs: SCAs can be approved only if faculty members and students within all academic units will, as a practical as well as a theoretical matter, retain the freedom to pursue their chosen research topics, including avenues of inquiry that are outside the purview of, not in conformity with, or even in opposition to the SCA's research agenda. All SCA agreements must strive to limit to the greatest extent possible negative financial, intellectual, or professional impacts on other academic units, colleges, and the university as a whole, as well as on faculty members, academic professionals, postdoctoral fellows, and students engaged in research and activities outside the purview of the collaborative SCA arrangement. No faculty member, postdoctoral fellow, academic professional, or student will be coerced into participating in a sponsored project; all participation will be entirely voluntary.

Handbook Principle 46: Early Termination of SCA Sponsor Funding: All SCA legal contracts must include provisions to prohibit sudden, early termination of the agreement. If the negotiating process leads to inclusion of an early-termination option, it must prohibit the sponsor from arbitrarily or suddenly terminating the agreement or decreasing pledged funding prior to the expected term, without at least three months of advance notification. Salaries and research costs associated with the project must be continued for that period.

Handbook Principle 47: Independent, Majority Faculty Oversight of the SCA, and Post-agreement Evaluation: An independent, majority faculty oversight committee consisting of faculty members with no direct involvement in the SCA will be established at the start of a new SCA agreement to monitor and at least annually review the SCA and its compliance with university policies and guidelines. A post-agreement evaluation plan will also be included in the formal SCA contract so the campus can reflect and draw on the experience in organizing future campus-based academy-industry alliances. External evaluation may be appropriate for broad SCAs and will be initiated as appropriate. Evaluation reports will be public documents.

Handbook Principle 48: Public Disclosure of SCA Research Contracts and Funding Transparency: No SCA or other industry-, government-, or nonprofit-sponsored contract may restrict faculty members, students, postdoctoral fellows, or academic professionals from freely disclosing their funding source. A signed copy of all final legal research contracts formalizing an SCA and any other types of sponsored research agreements formed on campus will be made freely available to the public—with discrete redactions only to protect valid commercial trade secrets, not for other reasons.

Part VII—Targeted Principles: Clinical Medicine, Clinical Research, and Industry Sponsorship

Handbook Principle 49: Access to Complete Clinical Trial Data and the Performance of Independent Academic Analysis: All the provisions of Principle 5 apply to clinical trial data as well.

Handbook Principle 50: Registry of Academic-Based Clinical Trials in a National Registry: All clinical trials conducted by the university's academic investigators will be entered into ClinicalTrials.gov (http://www.clinicaltrials.gov/) —the national clinical trial registry maintained by the US National Library of Medicine and the National Institutes of Health. The entry will be made at or before the onset of patient enrollment.

Handbook Principle 51: Safeguarding the Integrity and Appropriate Conduct of Clinical Trials: All clinical trials affiliated with the university are required to use independent data safety monitoring boards (DSMBs) and/or publication and analysis committees to protect the integrity and appropriate conduct of academic-based clinical trial research.

Handbook Principle 52: Patient Notification: Industry-, government-, and nonprofit-sponsored research agreements may not restrict faculty members or academic professionals from notifying patients about health risks and/or lack of treatment efficacy when such information emerges and patients' health may be adversely affected.

Handbook Principle 53: Undue Commercial Marketing Influence and Control at Academic Medical Centers: Educational programs, academic events, and presentations by faculty members, students, postdoctoral fellows, and academic professionals must be free of industry marketing influence and control. Both academics and administrators are prohibited from participating in industry-led "speakers bureaus" financed by pharmaceutical or other industry groups.

Handbook Principle 54: Appropriate Use of Facilities and Classrooms at Universities and Academic Medical Centers: Pharmaceutical, medical-device, and biotechnology companies may not distribute free meals, gifts, or drug samples on campus or at affiliated academic medical centers, except under the control of central administration offices for use by patients who lack access to medications. Academic facilities and classrooms may not be used for commercial marketing and promotion purposes unless advance written permission from academic institutional authorities has been explicitly granted and academic supervision arranged. (Commercial marketing of services would, for example, be appropriate at a job fair.) All marketing representatives are required to obtain advance authorization before site visits. Finally, faculty members, physicians, trainees, and students are prohibited from directly accepting travel funds from industry, other than for legitimate reimbursement of contractual academic services. Direct or indirect industry travel funding for commercial marketing junkets, which may include trips to luxury resorts and expensive dinners, are prohibited.

Handbook Principle 55: Marketing Projects Masquerading as Clinical Research: Faculty members, students, postdoctoral fellows, and academic professionals based at our academic-affiliated institutions are prohibited from participating in marketing studies that masquerade as scientifically driven clinical trial research.

Handbook Principle 56: Predetermined Research Results: Faculty members and other academic investigators are prohibited from soliciting research funding from outside sponsors with the implied suggestion or promise of predetermined research results.

Budgets, Salaries, and Benefits

Throughout its history, the Association has been concerned with the role of the faculty in budgetary matters and with the economic welfare of faculties in the setting of proper institutional management and finance, including salaries, taxes, provision for retirement, and incidental arrangements such as insurance, treatment of outside income or other legal claims of faculty members, and education of faculty children and spouses. Of special concern when the national economy has demanded it has been the concept of "financial exigency" and the impact of economic crises on the profession.

Calling the high inflation after World War I a situation "which makes it impossible that this, the only general professional society of university teachers, should any longer ignore the economic side of the teacher's calling," AAUP president Arthur Lovejoy announced the creation of the Committee on the Economic Condition of the Profession in 1919. Since 1948, the Association has regularly published reports on professorial salaries.

The Association, often through its Committee on Women in the Academic Profession, has addressed the disparate treatment of men and women faculty in salary and benefits. Commenting on the claim that differential salaries between men and women were based on "supply and demand," the committee noted in 1921, "On this point, we would also call attention to the fact that the demand in this case comes, or fails to come, mainly from the very ones who cite the lack of it as their reason for not giving faculty women even-handed justice in matter of rank and salary."

The Association's interest in pensions dates back to 1916, when the Committee on Systems of Pensions and Insurance for University Teachers was created. The committee negotiated with the Carnegie Foundation for the Advancement of Teaching over the creation of the Teachers Insurance and Annuity Association. In the 1970s, the Committee on Women in the Academic Profession also advocated an end to the provision of lower pension benefits to academic women because of their longer average life expectancy. (The US Supreme Court, in a 1983 ruling, put an end to this practice.)

The AAUP has recognized financial exigency as a legitimate reason for terminating tenure since it issued the *Conference Statement on Academic Freedom and Tenure* in 1925. The invocation of financial exigency has naturally increased during times of economic crisis, and the Association has regularly responded when such crises affected higher education. For instance, in 1937, Committee Y on Effect of Depression and Recovery on Higher Education published a detailed study of the Great Depression, *Depression, Recovery and Higher Education*, and in 2013, Committee A on Academic Freedom and Tenure released the report *The Role of the Faculty in Conditions of Financial Exigency*, included in this volume, in response to the 2008 financial crisis that led to a large number of department and program closures.

The Role of the Faculty in Budgetary and Salary Matters

This statement was approved by the Association's Committee on College and University Governance, adopted by the Association's Council in May 1972, and endorsed by the Fifty-Eighth Annual Meeting.

General Principles

The purpose of this statement is to define the role of the faculty in decisions as to the allocation of financial resources according to the principle of shared authority set forth in the *Statement on Government of Colleges and Universities,* and to offer some principles and derivative guidelines for faculty participation in this area. On the subject of budgeting in general, the *Statement on Government* asserts:

> The allocation of resources among competing demands is central in the formal responsibility of the governing board, in the administrative authority of the president, and in the educational function of the faculty. Each component should therefore have a voice in the determination of short- and long-range priorities, and each should receive appropriate analyses of past budgetary experience, reports on current budgets and expenditures, and short- and long-range budgetary projections. The function of each component in budgetary matters should be understood by all; the allocation of authority will determine the flow of information and the scope of participation in decisions.

Essentially two requirements are set forth in this passage:

1. *Clearly understood channels of communication and the accessibility of important information to those groups which have a legitimate interest in it.*
2. *Participation by each group (governing board, president, and faculty) appropriate to the particular expertise of each.*[1] Thus the governing board is expected to husband the endowment and obtain capital and operating funds; the president is expected to maintain existing institutional resources and create new ones; the faculty is expected to establish faculty salary policies and, in its primary responsibility for the educational function of the institution, to participate also in broader budgetary matters primarily as these impinge on that function. All three groups, the *Statement on Government* makes clear, should participate in long-range planning.

Faculty Participation in Budgeting

The faculty should participate both in the preparation of the total institutional budget and (within the framework of the total budget) in decisions relevant to the further apportioning of its specific fiscal divisions (salaries, academic programs, tuition, physical plant and grounds, and so on). The soundness of resulting decisions should be enhanced if an elected representative committee of the faculty participates in deciding on the overall allocation of institutional resources and the proportion to be devoted directly to the academic program. This committee should be given access to all information that it requires to perform its task effectively, and it should have the opportunity to confer periodically with representatives of the administration and governing board. Such an institution-level body, representative of the entire faculty, can play an important part in mediating the financial needs and the demands of different groups within the faculty and can be of significant assistance to the administration in resolving impasses that may arise when a large variety of demands are made on necessarily limited resources.

Such a body will also be of critical importance in representing faculty interests and interpreting the needs of the faculty to the governing board and president. The presence of faculty members on the governing board itself may, particularly in smaller institutions, constitute an approach that would serve somewhat the same purpose, but does not obviate the need for an all-faculty body that may wish to formulate its recommendations independent of other groups. In addition, at public institutions there are legitimate ways and means for the faculty to play a role in the submission and support of budgetary requests to the appropriate agency of government.

Budgetary decisions directly affecting those areas for which, according to the *Statement on*

Government, the faculty has primary responsibility—curriculum, subject matter and methods of instruction, research, faculty status, and those aspects of student life that relate to the educational process—should be made in concert with the faculty. Certain kinds of expenditures related to the academic program, such as the allocation of funds for a particular aspect of library development, student projects under faculty sponsorship, or departmental equipment, will require that the decision-making process be sufficiently decentralized to give the various units of the faculty (departments, divisions, schools, colleges, special programs) autonomy in deciding upon the use of their allocations within the broader limits set by the governing board, president, and agencies representative of the entire faculty. In other areas, such as faculty research programs or the total library and laboratory budget, recommendations as to the desirable funding levels for the ensuing fiscal period and decisions on the allocation of university funds within the current budget levels should be made by the university-level, all-faculty committee as well as by the faculty agencies directly concerned.[2] The question of faculty salaries, as an aspect of faculty status, is treated separately below.

Circumstances of financial exigency obviously pose special problems. At institutions experiencing major threats to their continued financial support, the faculty should be informed as early and as specifically as possible of significant impending financial difficulties. The faculty—with substantial representation from its nontenured as well as its tenured members, since it is the former who are likely to bear the brunt of any reduction—should participate at the department, college or professional school, and institution-wide levels in key decisions as to the future of the institution and of specific academic programs within the institution. The faculty, employing accepted standards of due process, should assume primary responsibility for determining the status of individual faculty members.[3] The question of possible reductions in salaries and fringe benefits is discussed in the section below. The faculty should play a fundamental role in any decision that would change the basic character and purpose of the institution, including transformation of the institution, affiliation of part of the existing operation with another institution, or merger, with the resulting abandonment or curtailment of duplicate programs.

Before any decisions on curtailment become final, those whose work stands to be adversely affected should have full opportunity to be heard.

In the event of a merger, the faculties from the two institutions should participate jointly in negotiations affecting faculty status and the academic programs at both institutions. To the extent that major budgetary considerations are involved in these decisions, the faculty should be given full and timely access to the financial information necessary to the making of an informed choice. In making decisions on whether teaching and research programs are to be curtailed, financial considerations should not be allowed to obscure the fact that instruction and research constitute the essential reason for the existence of the university. Among the various considerations, difficult and often competing, that have to be taken into account in deciding upon particular reductions, the retention of a viable academic program necessarily should come first. Particular reductions should follow considered advice from the concerned departments, or other units of academic concentration, on the short-term and long-term viability of reduced programs.

Faculty Participation in Decisions Relating to Salary Policies and Procedures

The *Statement on Government* asserts that "the faculty should actively participate in the determination of policies and procedures governing salary increases." Salaries, of course, are part of the total budgetary picture; and, as indicated above, the faculty should participate in the decision as to the proportion of the budget to be devoted to that purpose. However, there is also the question of the role of the faculty as a body in the determination of individual faculty salaries.

1. The Need for Clear and Open Policy
Many imagined grievances as to salary could be alleviated, and the development of a system of accountability to reduce the number of real grievances could be facilitated, if both the criteria for salary raises and the recommendatory procedure itself were (a) designed by a representative group of the faculty in concert with the administration, and (b) open and clearly understood.[4] Such accountability is not participation per se, but it provides the basis for a situation in which such participation can be more fruitful.

Once the procedures are established, the person or group that submits the initial salary recommendation (usually the department chair, alone or in conjunction with an elected executive committee of the department) should be informed of its status at each further stage of the salary-determination process. As the *Statement on Government* points out, the chief competence for the judgment of a colleague rests in the department, school, or program (whichever is the smallest applicable unit of faculty government within the institution), and in most cases the salary recommendation presumably derives from its judgment. The recommending officer should have the opportunity to defend that recommendation at a later stage in the event of a serious challenge to it.

2. Levels of Decision Making

Not all institutions provide for an initial salary recommendation by the department chair or the equivalent officer; the Association regards it as desirable, for the reasons already mentioned, that the recommendation normally originate at the departmental level. Further review is normally conducted by the appropriate administrative officers; they should, when they have occasion to question or inquire further regarding the departmental recommendation, solicit informed faculty advice by meeting with the department head or chair and, if feasible, the elected body of the faculty. It is also desirable that a mechanism exist for review of a salary recommendation, or of a final salary decision, by a representative elected committee of the faculty above the department level in cases involving a complaint.[5] Such a committee should have access to information on faculty salary levels. Another faculty committee, likewise at a broader level than that of the department, may be charged with the review of routine recommendations.

Of the role of the governing board in college and university government, the *Statement on Government* says: "The governing board of an institution of higher education, while maintaining a general overview, entrusts the conduct of administration to the administrative officers, the president and the deans, and the conduct of teaching and research to the faculty. The board should undertake appropriate self-limitation." The *Statement* adds that "in the broadest sense of the term" the board "should pay attention to personnel policy." The thrust of these remarks is that it is inadvisable for a governing board to make decisions on individual salaries, except those of the chief administrative officers of the institution. Not only do such decisions take time that should be devoted to the board's functions of overview and long-range planning, but such decisions also are in most cases beyond the competence of the board.

When financial exigency leads to a reduction in the overall salary budget for teaching and research, the governing board, while assuming final responsibility for setting the limits imposed by the resources available to the institution, should delegate to the faculty and administration concurrently any further review of the implication of the situation for individual salaries, and the faculty should be given the opportunity to minimize the hardship to its individual members by careful examination of whatever alternatives to termination of services are feasible.

3. Fringe Benefits

The faculty should participate in the selection of fringe-benefit programs and in the periodic review of those programs. It should be recognized that of these so-called fringe benefits, at least those included in the definition of total compensation set forth by the Association's Committee on the Economic Status of the Profession, have the same standing as direct faculty salaries and are separated for tax purposes. They should be considered and dealt with in the same manner as direct payment of faculty salary.

Notes

1. The participation of students in budgetary decisions affecting student programs and student life is taken for granted in this document, but no attempt is made to define the nature of that participation here.

2. For obvious reasons, the focus here is on funding from the resources of the institution, and not from external agencies such as private contractors or the federal government. Even in these cases, however, it may be possible in certain circumstances for the faculty to play a part in deciding further on the allocation of a particular grant to various purposes related to the project within the institution. There should be careful faculty and administrative scrutiny as to the methods by which these funds are to be employed under the particular contract.

3. On the question of due process and appropriate terminal settlements for individual faculty members (on tenure or prior to the expiration of a term appointment) whose positions are being abolished, see Regulation 4c of the "Recommended Institutional Regulations on Academic Freedom and Tenure," AAUP, *Policy Documents and Reports*, 11th ed. (Baltimore: Johns Hopkins University Press, 2015), 81–82.

4. This section does not take into account those situations in which salaries are determined according to a step system and/or a standard salary is negotiated for each rank. The salary policy and, in effect, individual salaries are public information under such systems.

5. See Regulation 16 of the "Recommended Institutional Regulations on Academic Freedom and Tenure," *Policy Documents and Reports*, 88.

The Role of the Faculty in Conditions of Financial Exigency

The report that follows is excerpted from a longer report of the same title, which was prepared by a subcommittee of the Association's Committee A on Academic Freedom and Tenure, approved by Committee A in May 2013 and adopted by the Council in June 2013.

Introduction

The past forty years have witnessed a decisive shift in power in American colleges and universities.[1] Increasingly, institutions that were once governed jointly by faculty members and administrators have become overwhelmingly or wholly dominated by their administrations, as the faculty senates at these institutions have withered into insignificance. For the most part, the faculty retains jurisdiction over systems of peer review and the protocols of scholarly communication, but, astonishingly, faculty members have begun to lose control over the one central element of higher education where they have long been presumed to have invaluable expertise—the curriculum. Administrators are making unilateral budgetary decisions that profoundly affect the curricula and the educational missions of their institutions; rarely are those decisions recognized as decisions about the curriculum, even though the elimination of entire programs of study (ostensibly for financial reasons) has obvious implications for the curricular range and the academic integrity of any university.

As decision-making power has shifted to administrators, public universities have felt intensified financial pressures, especially in the wake of the financial crisis of 2008. Because the effects of the crisis have been especially pronounced for state budgets, public universities from coast to coast have seen severe if not draconian cuts in state appropriations and corresponding increases in tuition. States for a generation have been gradually shifting costs from state funding to tuition payments, but the new pressures have arrived at a time when public and legislative complaints about college tuition are on the rise and when concerns over student debt have become national news. The perfect storm thus generated—declining financial support combined with rule to a larger degree by administrative fiat—affords administrations the potential to manufacture a sudden "crisis" where none exists. For example, shifting costs from state revenues to student tuition payments does not in itself constitute an immediate financial crisis. We believe doing so is bad public policy, but it is a way of avoiding a funding shortfall, not creating one. Similarly, although many university endowments suffered substantial losses during the recession, very few institutions actually rely on endowment income for a major portion of their budgets. For that matter, endowments have by now largely recovered, as have the markets on which they are dependent. Claims of financial crisis based on the performance of the market should thus be met with skepticism.

As the AAUP discovered in its investigation of how New Orleans institutions responded to the effects of Hurricane Katrina, public perception of a crisis has opened a window of opportunity for campus managers to make some of the cuts and programmatic changes they have in fact long wanted to make.[2] An institution's desire to shift priorities is not the same as a fiscal crisis, and one should not mistake the former for the latter. As we will detail below, claims that a campus is facing either a crisis or a form of slow fiscal starvation need to be investigated thoroughly, and neither the faculty nor the staff can conduct such an investigation without access to detailed financial data. There are widely accepted metrics for analyzing an institution's financial health, metrics that make objective, reliable conclusions possible. We stress *objective* conclusions, because administration assertions about financial challenges cannot always be accepted at face value. That is not to say that small liberal arts colleges and some public institutions are not facing real financial pressures. It is to say that all members of the university community deserve to participate in relevant discussions of those pressures—and to do so with the aid of sound and detailed information.

The immediate occasion of this report is the decision of some university administrations to cut costs by eliminating entire programs—and terminating the positions of tenured faculty members in those programs. The University at Albany, State University of New York, made international news in 2010 when it announced the closing of its classics, French, Italian, Russian, and theater degree programs; the AAUP had begun an investigation but suspended it after two potentially affected French professors agreed to retire and the closing of the several degree programs was not followed by the involuntary termination of any tenured faculty appointments. Though it received much less national attention at the time, Southeastern Louisiana University also eliminated its undergraduate French majors (in French and French education) in 2010, dismissing the program's three tenured professors with a year's notice—and then offering one of them a temporary instructorship at a sharply reduced salary. In April 2012, an AAUP investigating committee's report on the University of Louisiana system, with its focus on Southeastern Louisiana University and Northwestern State University, was published online, and Committee A presented statements on these two institutions in the nine-university system to the 2012 annual meeting, which imposed censure.[3] In addition to the discontinuance of the French majors at Southeastern, with the resulting action against the three tenured professors, the chemistry major at the University of Louisiana at Monroe was discontinued, but without notification of termination to anyone among five threatened chemistry professors; and the discontinuance of the doctoral program in cognitive sciences at the University of Louisiana at Lafayette, while followed by notification of appointment termination to two tenured professors, resulted in steps to avoid implementation. At Northwestern State, however, a wide range of programs suffered discontinuance and more than twenty tenured professors suffered termination of appointment through the ending of programs, including economics, German, journalism, philosophy, and physics.

In 2010, at the University of Nevada, Reno, twenty-three degree programs were closed and dozens of faculty members released, including nearly twenty tenured professors. At the University of Nevada, Las Vegas, the president contemplated seeking a declaration of financial exigency in spring 2011 because of massive cuts in state financing. He eliminated over three hundred total positions and eighteen degree programs but avoided layoffs of tenured professors and of most faculty members with appointments probationary for tenure.

In March 2012, the University of Northern Iowa announced the elimination of more than fifty programs. An AAUP investigation at Northern Iowa resulted in a report that was published online in January 2013.[4] Subsequent corrective action, however, resulted in deferral of censure consideration by the 2013 annual meeting. Massive layoffs at National Louis University, a private institution in Chicago, also triggered an AAUP investigation that led to censure in 2013, and multiple layoffs at Southern University in Baton Rouge, Louisiana's flagship historically black institution, similarly became the subject of investigation and 2013 censure.[5]

In most of these cases, however, the institutions declined to issue declarations of financial exigency, the sole recent exception being Southern University in Baton Rouge. It therefore became clear that the AAUP needed to address program closures that are made in the absence of declarations of exigency and to revisit our *Recommended Institutional Regulations on Academic Freedom and Tenure*.[6]

The current Recommended Institutional Regulation 4c sets a very high bar for terminations on grounds of financial exigency: "Termination of an appointment with continuous tenure, or of a probationary or special appointment before the end of the specified term, may occur under extraordinary circumstances because of a demonstrably bona fide financial exigency, i.e., an imminent financial crisis that threatens the survival of the institution as a whole and that cannot be alleviated by less drastic means."

Regulation 4d, by contrast, provides procedures for tenure terminations as a result of program closings not mandated by financial exigency: "Termination of an appointment with continuous tenure, or of a probationary or special appointment before the end of the specified term, may occur as a result of bona fide formal discontinuance of a program or department of instruction." Regulations 4d(1) and 4d(2) set out the conditions for discontinuing programs and tenure commitments:

(1) The decision to discontinue formally a program or department of instruction will be based essentially upon educational considerations, as determined primarily by the faculty as a whole or an appropriate committee thereof.

[Note: "Educational considerations" do not include cyclical or temporary variations in enrollment. They must reflect long-range judgments that the educational mission of the institution as a whole will be enhanced by the discontinuance.]

(2) Before the administration issues notice to a faculty member of its intention to terminate an appointment because of formal discontinuance of a program or department of instruction, the institution will make every effort to place the faculty member concerned in another suitable position. If placement in another position would be facilitated by a reasonable period of training, financial and other support for such training will be proffered. If no position is available within the institution, with or without retraining, the faculty member's appointment then may be terminated, but only with provision for severance salary equitably adjusted to the faculty member's length of past and potential service.

[Note: When an institution proposes to discontinue a program or department of instruction, it should plan to bear the costs of relocating, training, or otherwise compensating faculty members adversely affected.]

Neither of these regulations appears adequate to the situation in which many institutions now find themselves—in part because the standard of "exigency" was initially drawn from small, private, impecunious institutions, not large state universities, few of which can plausibly be said to face imminent crises that threaten their very existence. In recent decades, and especially in recent years, colleges and universities in the public sector have more commonly experienced intermediate conditions that may fundamentally compromise the academic integrity of the institution but do not threaten the survival of the institution as a whole. Thus most colleges and universities are not declaring financial exigency even as they plan for widespread program closings and terminations of faculty appointments. They are refusing to declare exigency for ostensibly good reasons (namely, that their financial conditions are not so dire as those invoked by Regulation 4c or that a declaration of financial exigency would itself worsen the institution's financial condition) and for arguably bad reasons (namely, so that they can operate in severe-financial-crisis mode, bypassing AAUP standards of faculty consultation and shared governance without the bad publicity of declaring exigency). This report seeks to address this phenomenon and to propose sound procedures for program review under conditions captured by neither Regulation 4c nor Regulation 4d as currently written.

As we note in more detail below, this report is in some respects a continuation of a debate begun in the mid-1970s, the last era of major retrenchment in American higher education. Then,

W. Todd Furniss, a staff officer of the American Council on Education (ACE), had criticized the gap between Regulations 4c and 4d, writing, "Good sense tells us that in the real world there are far more conditions between imminent bankruptcy on the one hand and, on the other, program change that would 'enhance' the 'educational mission of the institution as a whole' in the absence of a financial emergency."[7] At the time, Committee A chair and former AAUP president Ralph S. Brown had replied that " 'discontinuance' may be invoked in hard times as a substitute, perhaps a subterfuge, for an exigency crisis that cannot be convincingly asserted."[8] The relevance of Furniss's and Brown's concerns to current conditions is obvious. But the widespread and systemic nature of the challenges facing American universities in the second decade of the twenty-first century compels us to revisit and revise the terms of the debate begun a generation ago. We are therefore proposing a new definition of "financial exigency" that is more responsive to actual institutional conditions and that will extend the standard of exigency to situations not covered by the AAUP's current definition. Under this new definition, an institution need not be on the brink of complete collapse in order to declare exigency. Rather, it needs to demonstrate that substantial injury to the institution's academic integrity will result from prolonged and drastic reductions in funds available to the institution, and it needs to demonstrate dispositively that the determination of its financial health is guided by generally accepted accounting principles.

We want to make it clear at the outset that many current "crises" represent shifts in priorities rather than crises of funding. Financial exigency is not a plausible complaint from a campus that has shifted resources from its primary missions of teaching and research toward employing increasing numbers of administrators or toward unnecessary capital expenditures. A campus that can reallocate resources away from teaching and research is not a campus that can justify cuts in its core mission on financial grounds. Discussions of a campus's financial state cannot be fairly or responsibly conducted without faculty consultation about budgetary priorities. Our definition of "financial exigency" is as follows: *financial exigency entails a severe financial crisis that fundamentally compromises the academic integrity of the institution as a whole and that cannot be alleviated by less drastic means.* We will expand on this definition and provide detailed recommendations for the faculty deliberations necessary for a legitimate declaration of exigency that warrants program closure.

Cuts in teaching and research must be a last resort, after, among other actions, the administrative budget is reviewed and reduced and supplements for athletics and other nonacademic programs are eliminated. Moreover, colleges and universities need more objective, quantitative standards for claiming financial exigency—such as an index that uses ratios that incorporate institutional debt level and reserves, along with other data, to come up with a composite score to assess and establish institutional financial health. The Ohio Board of Regents (OBR), for example, uses such an index and requires that the composite score fall below a certain level for two consecutive years before classifying an institution as being in serious financial difficulty. (The appendix to our report describes the components of an index that is similar to the OBR index and can be used to guide determinations of an institution's financial condition.)

This report provides guidance for how legitimate claims of financial exigency can be reviewed and substantiated and for how institutions should proceed with program closures under such a condition. Nothing in it weakens academic freedom, tenure, and shared governance as they are now understood and protected in the AAUP's current *Recommended Institutional Regulations*. On the contrary, the report urges that institutions increase the level of faculty consultation and deliberation at every stage of the process, beginning with the guideline that is currently a note to Regulation 4c(1), stipulating that "there should be a faculty body that participates in the decision that a condition of financial exigency exists or is imminent and that all feasible alternatives to termination of appointments have been pursued."

To close this introduction, we want to make explicit the reasons why the faculty should be centrally involved in deliberations about exigency. Certainly, such involvement is not the model in the corporate world, where downsizings and layoffs are simply announced and severance packages issued. Why then should academe be any different? The answer goes to the heart of the rationale for tenure as the basis for academic freedom, and indeed to the heart of the rationale for institutions of higher education. As Matthew Finkin and Robert Post have written,

> [I]nstitutions of higher education serve the public interest and . . . promote the common good. The common good is not to be determined by the arbitrary, private, or personal decree of any single individual; nor is it to be determined by the technocratic calculation of rational and predictable profit incentives. The common good is made visible only through open debate and discussion in which all are free to participate. *Faculty, by virtue not only of their educational training and expertise but also of their institutional knowledge and commitment, have an indispensable role to play in that debate.*[9]

Program closures are matters of curriculum, central to the educational missions of colleges and universities—missions over which the faculty should always have primary responsibility. Closures ordered by administrative fiat—even, or especially, when they are ordered by administrators who believe they have done due diligence in program review—are therefore inimical not only to the educational mission of colleges and universities but also to the social contract according to which faculty expertise, academic freedom, and tenure serve the public good.

We believe it is crucial to keep the larger picture in view. After World War II, the United States embarked on the world's most extensive experiment in mass higher education. That experiment was a success, if one measures success by the fact that the American system of higher education was commonly described, over the ensuing decades, as the envy of the rest of the world; it was a success as an expansion of the promise of democracy as well. But in recent years the social contract underwriting that experiment has been largely rewritten. Tenure has been eroded by the growth of the ranks of the non-tenure-track faculty, and it is no coincidence that academic decision making has moved more and more emphatically into the hands of administrations. Tenure itself has increasingly been understood as a private, individual affair, a merit badge signifying that a faculty member has undergone peer review and is entitled to academic freedom in his or her teaching and research; few in academe, much less those outside of it, appreciate the broader principle that tenure serves the public good by allowing for independence of inquiry and by providing an incentive to intellectual exploration. At the same time, state legislatures have steadily disinvested in institutions of higher education, offloading costs onto individuals and families and characterizing education as a private investment rather than a public good.

The recent wave of program closures represents the confluence of all these long-term trends: the erosion and redefinition of tenure, the massive growth in the ranks of the contingent faculty outside the tenure system, and the nationwide disinvestment in public higher education. It is time for faculty members to reclaim and reassert their proper roles as the stewards and guardians of the educational missions of their institutions—for the good of American higher education and the greater good of all.

Recommendations for Institutions Experiencing Financial Exigency

As will be seen, with the focus of financial exigency now to be on the survival of the institution's academic integrity, the determining role of the institution's faculty becomes truly crucial.

A. Determination of the Financial Condition of the Institution

In what follows, we review AAUP policy on the role of faculty members in the determination of their institutions' financial condition. We believe that our policy documents and reports provide decisive guidance in these matters, and we note at the outset that it seems to be increasingly difficult to find institutions in which the faculty has been afforded the primary responsibility—or, if that phrase is ambiguous, *any* responsibility—to conduct those determinations. Once again, this is not to say that the crises facing many institutions are not real; it is to say only that the critical protocol established in a note to Regulation 4c(1), that "there should be a faculty body that participates in the decision that a condition of financial exigency exists or is imminent and that all feasible alternatives to termination of appointments have been pursued," is often being ignored. Frequently, a crisis is simply declared, and steps are taken to meet it—steps that sometimes, but not regularly, involve substantial consultation with an appropriate faculty body. In too many cases, "faculty consultation" seems to consist of merely informing faculty members of what will be done to them.

The *Statement on Government of Colleges and Universities* was jointly formulated in 1966 by the AAUP, the ACE, and the Association of Governing Boards of Universities and Colleges. The AAUP adopted the document as official policy, and the other two organizations commended it to the attention of their membership. The statement recognizes a division of labor among trustees, presidents, and faculty members and offers the following recommendation with regard to budgeting: "The allocation of resources among competing demands is central in the formal responsibility of the governing board, in the administrative authority of the president, and in the educational function of the faculty. Each component should therefore have a voice in the determination of short- and long-range priorities, current budgets and expenditures, and short- and long-range budgetary projections."[10] The statement further specifies that the judgment of the faculty "is central to general educational policy" and that the faculty therefore "has primary responsibility for such fundamental areas as curriculum, subject matter, and methods of instruction, research, faculty status, and those aspects of student life which relate to the educational process."[11] We hold that program closure is very much a matter of educational policy and that the faculty should therefore be accorded an *initial and decisive* role in any deliberations over program closure and release of tenured faculty members.

Additionally, the AAUP's statement *The Role of the Faculty in Budgetary and Salary Matters*, adopted in 1972, reads as follows:

> The faculty should participate both in the preparation of the total institutional budget and (within the framework of the total budget) in decisions relevant to the further apportioning of its specific fiscal divisions (salaries, academic programs, tuition, physical plant and grounds, and so on). The soundness of resulting decisions should be enhanced if an elected representative committee of the faculty participates in deciding on the overall allocation of institutional resources and the proportion to be devoted directly to the academic program. *This committee should be given access to all information that it requires to perform its task effectively, and it should have the opportunity to confer periodically with representatives of the administration and governing board.*[12]

Established AAUP policies therefore provide clear and unambiguous support for the position that faculty consultation and participation should be integral to the budget process, quite apart from any consideration of the financial status of the institution. Faculty consultation and participation in budget matters should simply be part of the ordinary course of business, in good times or in bad. In other words, we are not proposing a radical new platform of emergency measures whereby faculty committees are summoned to review university budgets only when institutions are experiencing financial exigency; we are reaffirming the principles that inform policies that have existed for forty years and more, recommending that faculty participate in the budget process at every stage—even as we acknowledge that on many campuses, these policies would in fact lead to radical changes in business as usual.

But AAUP policy also speaks specifically to occasions in which institutions are experiencing financial exigency and in response to which emergency measures are contemplated. The first recommendation in the Association's statement *On Institutional Problems Resulting from Financial Exigency: Some Operating Guidelines* reads as follows: "There should be early, careful, and meaningful faculty involvement in decisions relating to the reduction of instructional and research programs. The financial conditions that bear on such decisions should not be allowed to obscure the fact that instruction and research constitute the essential reasons for the existence of the university."[13] Although the call for "early, careful, and meaningful faculty involvement" might seem to be clear on its face, we believe that recent developments with regard to program closures have rendered it necessary for us to specify "faculty involvement" in greater detail. We therefore propose the following procedures for faculty involvement in program closures.

Before any proposals for program discontinuance on financial grounds are made or entertained, the faculty must be afforded the opportunity to render an assessment in writing on the institution's financial condition. The faculty body performing this role may be drawn from an elected faculty senate or elected as an ad hoc committee by the faculty; it should not be appointed by the administration. At institutions governed by collective bargaining agreements, the leadership of the union is an elected body of its faculty members and should have a role in the assessment as well. (Should the faculty refuse to participate in a process that might result in faculty layoffs, they effectively waive their right to do so.) We recommend, in order to make those determinations, that the faculty should have access to, at minimum, five years of audited financial statements, current and following year budgets, and detailed cash flow estimates for future years. Beyond that, in order to make informed proposals about the financial impact of program closures, the faculty needs access to detailed program, department, and administrative-unit budgets; but *the determination of the financial position of the institution as a whole must precede any discussion of program closures.* As stated in Regulation 4c(1), the faculty should determine whether "all feasible alternatives to termination of appointments have been pursued," including expenditure of one-time money or reserves as bridge funding, furloughs, pay cuts, deferred-compensation plans, early-retirement packages, and cuts to noneducational programs and services.

We note ruefully that this recommendation speaks to practices to which few institutions now adhere and will doubtless be read as a radical departure from business as usual—even though it follows clearly from AAUP principles. We also anticipate that it will meet with resistance from some administrators who will claim that faculty members do not have requisite expertise in these matters. We acknowledge that faculty members who engage in detailed consultation of this kind will necessarily have to be or become literate in budgetary matters. But there are two critical points that need to be considered. The first is that every institution of higher education that offers a full curriculum of instruction necessarily includes faculty members who specialize in accounting, finance, and economics more generally. Their expertise is directly relevant to the determination of financial exigency. The second is that outside the disciplines of accounting, finance, and economics, faculty members long experienced in the analysis of complex data relevant to their particular disciplines as well as to their own departments and schools can be expected to bring seasoned judgment to bear on institutional finances and their impact on the future of educational programs.

However, when we speak of "the financial position of the institution as a whole" we are not simply returning to the standard of "an imminent financial crisis that threatens the survival of the institution as a whole and that cannot be alleviated by less drastic means" than the termination of appointments. Again, we are proposing a new definition of "financial exigency" that we believe corresponds more closely to the facts on the ground for most institutions of higher education. Financial exigency can be catastrophic and corrosive even when it does not threaten (as it rarely does) the survival of the institution as a whole. But because this definition of "financial exigency" does not require that an institution be faced with the prospect of immediate closure and bankruptcy, it must be accompanied by greater safeguards for faculty members and more stringent guarantees that it will not be abused.

Neither Regulation 4c nor Regulation 4d requires an institution to consult with or seek input from faculty members in programs slated for termination. This seems to us a significant omission, particularly since our guidelines on institutional problems resulting from financial exigency insist that such consultation is imperative: "Given a decision to reduce the overall academic program, it should then become the primary responsibility of the faculty to determine where within the program reductions should be made. Before any such determination becomes final, those whose life's work stands to be adversely affected should have the right to be heard."[14] It may be objected that the results of such a recommendation would be predictable, insofar as very few affected faculty members would argue for their own program's elimination or their own release. However, some arguments for a program's elimination or preservation are better than others, and we believe that faculty members must be entrusted with the right to make and assess those arguments. Regulation 4c(2) affords a faculty member whose position is terminated "the right to a full hearing before a faculty committee," and Regulation 4d(3) provides that a faculty member whose position is terminated for reasons other than exigency "may appeal a proposed relocation or termination resulting from a discontinuance and has a right to a full hearing before a faculty committee." But there is no provision for consultation with such faculty members before the decision is made. In the future, we propose, faculty members in a program being considered for discontinuance because of financial exigency should be informed in writing that it is being so considered and given at least thirty days in which to respond. We recommend that Regulations 4c and 4d be revised accordingly.

B. Another Suitable Position Elsewhere within the Institution
Regulation 4d(2) states,

> Before the administration issues notice to a faculty member of its intention to terminate an appointment because of formal discontinuance of a program or department of instruction, the institution will make every effort to place the faculty member concerned in another suitable position. If placement in another position would be facilitated by a reasonable period of training, financial and other support for such training will be proffered. If no position is available within the institution, with or without retraining, the faculty member's appointment then may be terminated, but only with provision for severance salary equitably adjusted to the faculty member's length of past and potential service.

This provision is crucial to determining whether a program is being discontinued for sound, legitimate educational reasons or whether it is being discontinued simply in order to shed its tenured faculty members: an institution that makes no substantial effort (or, as is often the case, no effort at all) to find "another suitable position" for faculty members affected by program closure is effectively using program

closure as a convenient way to terminate tenured appointments.

The problem, of course, lies in specifying what "another suitable position" might be. It is obviously beyond the capacity of this subcommittee to imagine every kind of possible program discontinuance and the potentially suitable positions for which affected faculty members should be considered; the challenge lies in developing overarching principles that can have numerous specific applications. The question is further complicated when one considers the case of *Browzin v. Catholic University*, as Ralph Brown explained in 1976:

> What is a program? What is a department? Here also we must rely on good faith, and on faculty involvement. An example of questionable judicial definition, albeit to a good end, is found in the *Browzin* case. . . . The issue was whether an adequate attempt had to be and had been made to place Professor Browzin in another suitable position. The trial in the lower court had concentrated on financial exigency. An ambiguity in the 1968 [*Recommended Institutional Regulations on Academic Freedom and Tenure*] seemed to relate the obligation to seek a suitable position only to cases of abandonment of program. Judge Wright, striving to give effect to what he thought were underlying goals, concluded that "financial exigency is in the case, but so is *abandonment of a program of instruction*" (italics Judge Wright's). Since courses in Soil Mechanics and Hydrology, "Browzin's particular responsibility," were given up, "The University did discontinue Browzin's program of instruction." If the issue had been solely whether Browzin could be terminated because of a program discontinuance, I do not think we would want to accept this notion of a one-man program. The case would then seem to be a simple breach of tenure, in the absence of financial exigency.
>
> Why then is a larger carnage acceptable? Only because it does not seem to be right to require a university to maintain a program, and the people in it, when a serious educational judgment has been made, in the language of [Regulation 4d(1)'s] note, that "the educational mission of the institution as a whole will be enhanced by the discontinuance."[15]

We see no reason to abandon or revise the AAUP's long-standing position on one-person programs, which seem to us administrative devices for cherry-picking tenured faculty members for release. In the AAUP's 1983 report on Sonoma State University, for instance, the investigating committee commented decisively on that institution's use of "Teaching Service Areas" to define individual faculty members as one-person programs. "Through the device of the Teaching Service Area," the committee wrote, "the newly engaged nontenured faculty members may be reappointed while the appointment of a tenured professor with many years of service may be terminated. The administration need only decide to reduce the 'biology' Teaching Service Area by one person and leave 'microbiology' and 'molecular biology' alone."[16] The committee therefore found, and we concur, that such a procedure "is prone to abuse by the administration and serves to undermine academic freedom, tenure, and due process."[17] Whatever name such procedures go under (or, as is more likely, when they carry no official designation at all), we hold that they are not "program closures" as we understand the term, but, rather, an illegitimate means for targeting and terminating individual faculty appointments.

We therefore want to try to answer Brown's question—*what is a program?*—without relying exclusively on good faith and faculty involvement (though both are clearly necessary). First and foremost, programs cannot be defined ad hoc, at any size; programs must be recognized academic units that existed prior to the declaration of financial exigency. The term "program" should designate a related cluster of credit-bearing courses that constitute a coherent body of study within a discipline or set of related disciplines. Ideally, the term should designate a department or similar administrative unit that offers majors and minors; at the University of Northern Iowa in 2012, by contrast, the administration's definition of "program area" was not agreed to by United Faculty, the local AAUP collective bargaining unit, and was indeed so fluid and capricious as to allow for multiple cherry-picking operations. One way to determine whether a program closure is bona fide is to ask whether the courses in the program continue to be offered, as was the case at Southeastern Louisiana University after it "closed" its majors in French and French education. In other words, the elimination of a major or minor in a course of study is, of itself, no excuse for the release of tenured faculty members if courses are still on the books (presumably to be taught instead by non-tenure-track faculty members, or by faculty members who have been stripped of tenure).[18]

As the court in *Browzin* held,

[T]he obvious danger remains that "financial exigency" can become too easy an excuse for dismissing a teacher who is merely unpopular or controversial or misunderstood—a way for the university to rid itself of an unwanted teacher but without according him his important procedural right. The "suitable position" requirement would stand as a partial check against such abuses. An institution motivated only by financial considerations would not hesitate to place the tenured professor in another suitable position if one can be found, even if this means displacing a nontenured instructor.[19]

We note, however, that in the years since *Browzin*, and Brown's response thereto, academic programs themselves have undergone substantial transformation. The change has brought about both danger and opportunity. First, with the post–World War II expansion of American higher education, the meaning of "another suitable position" has changed radically. Second, since the 1970s, in every field of intellectual endeavor— from the arts and humanities to the social, speculative, and applied sciences—colleges and universities have heralded the virtues of interdisciplinarity and have created a wide variety of innovative interdepartmental programs, centers, and institutes in order to encourage interdisciplinary research, teaching, and collaboration. On the one hand, this transformation of the curricular landscape would appear to have made it easier for administrations to define "programs" whose proposed discontinuance is simply a means of terminating one troublesome tenured professor. On the other hand, the expansion or redefinition of the traditional disciplines, together with the creation of new interdisciplinary programs, should also have made it easier for institutions to find "another suitable position" for faculty members in discontinued programs.

Two examples will help illustrate what we are suggesting. At SUNY-Albany, the tenured professors in classics, French, Italian, and Russian could very well have been consolidated in a department of languages and literatures that would also have included Spanish and less-taught other languages. If the SUNY-Albany administration did not consider this possibility, it would be but one of many ways in which AAUP standards were ignored. At Pennsylvania State University, the termination of the university's science, technology, and society program—itself created, in 1969–70, by faculty members from the colleges of earth and mineral sciences, engineering, liberal arts, and science—affected five tenure-track professors working on a wide variety of subjects, such as the history of autism and networks created by families with autistic children, the politics of food security, and the history of Chinese ecological science and environmental governance, with a focus on climate policy and urban development. The faculty members involved clearly can be housed in any number of academic units, from the traditional Department of Human Development and Family Studies to newer interdisciplinary units such as the Huck Institutes of the Life Sciences, the Penn State Institutes of Energy and the Environment, and the International Center for the Study of Terrorism.[20] American universities have found many ways of creating such centers and institutes, using them as devices for establishing new areas of research and teaching and for engaging new faculty members. We are aware that few of these centers and institutes were created with the intention that they would include tenure-track faculty lines. But because the AAUP maintains that tenure is held in the institution rather than any department, college, program, or other subdivision within the institution, we believe that it is incumbent upon institutions to be at least as creative in finding ways to relocate faculty members whose programs have been discontinued. In some cases, relocating a faculty member may involve provost-level negotiations, if, for instance, the faculty member's line is to be transferred between colleges. But in all cases, the first sentence of Regulation 4d(2) must be observed: the institution must make every effort to place the faculty member concerned in another suitable position before the administration issues notice to a faculty member of its intention to terminate an appointment because of formal discontinuance of a program or department of instruction. The effort to find another suitable position must *precede* the announcement of an institution's *intent* to terminate a program; it cannot follow the announcement as faculty members and administrators scramble to put together a Plan B.

If an undergraduate major or a graduate program is eliminated but lower-level courses continue to be offered (as is the case with many reductions of foreign-language programs), the professor who is reassigned from upper-level to lower-level courses is not considered to be relocated "elsewhere." Tenure rights enable the professor to assume the teaching of lower-level courses that have been taught by nontenured faculty members; departments and colleges should not assume that if upper-level courses are eliminated, the tenured faculty members who taught them need to be released as well. All relocations of tenured faculty members should allow those faculty members to retain their tenure rights, including eligibility for service on department, college, and institution-wide committees; no relocated professor should suffer a

reduction in his or her salary, unless across-the-board salary reductions are part of an institution's response to its financial condition, and no relocated professor should suffer demotion from his or her previously earned academic rank.

Again, the AAUP holds that the locus of tenure is in the institution as a whole, not in any subdivision (department, college, program) thereof. Therefore, the elimination of a program in which a faculty member has tenure does not entail the elimination of that faculty member's tenure rights, and it is for this reason that he or she has the right to be relocated.

We note also that an increasingly common justification for program closure is "low completion rates," that is, low numbers of graduates per year. We believe that gauging enrollment simply by counting the number of student majors is especially inimical to sound academic judgments. Often, modern languages such as French and German are unduly penalized by such calculations, because they discount the number of students who meet language requirements by taking courses in French and German without majoring in those subjects; but in the University of Louisiana system and at the University of Northern Iowa, this kind of bean counting affected the sciences as well, as when the UNI administration slated a physics program for closure without considering how many majors in the other sciences needed to take courses in physics. So-called "data-driven" program closures should be eschewed in favor of comprehensive, orderly reviews of the full profile of an institution's curricular offerings, reviews that are guided not solely by enrollment numbers but also by sound, rational, and justifiable determinations of the intellectual strengths and weaknesses of each program.

Lastly, we reaffirm the provisions of Regulations 4d(2) and 4d(3), requiring institutions to offer a reasonable period of training for faculty members affected by program discontinuance, financial and other support for such training, severance pay equitably adjusted to the faculty member's length of past and potential service, the right to appeal a proposed relocation or termination, and the right to a full hearing before a faculty committee.

C. Personnel Priorities

Regulation 4c(1) states that "judgments determining where within the overall academic program termination of appointments may occur involve considerations of educational policy, including affirmative action, as well as of faculty status, and should therefore be the primary responsibility of the faculty or of an appropriate faculty body. The faculty or an appropriate faculty body should also exercise primary responsibility in determining the criteria for identifying the individuals whose appointments are to be terminated. These criteria may appropriately include considerations of length of service." In earlier versions, this clause read "considerations of age and length of service," but it was revised to conform to the Age Discrimination in Employment Act of 1967. Since the end of mandatory retirement in academe, this issue has become only more complex, and it is complicated still further by the multiple demographic changes in the academic workforce over the past four decades: the professoriate contains far more women and minorities than it did in 1970 (a development we welcome) and far fewer faculty members with tenure as a proportion of all faculty members (a development we deplore). Forty years ago, roughly three-quarters of all faculty members were tenured or probationary for tenure; today, roughly three-quarters of all faculty members do not have, and have little hope of gaining, the protections of tenure.

When programs are discontinued and faculty members face relocation or release, priority must be given to the tenured, or tenure itself will lose meaning. It is worth reviewing this imperative with regard to the consideration of "seniority" in our revised definition of financial exigency. Thanks to the dramatic expansion and institutionalization of the nontenured ranks, it is possible to find non-tenure-track faculty members with significant seniority—amounting even to decades—over newly tenured members of the faculty. Similarly, our operating guidelines on institutional problems resulting from financial exigency state that "as particular reductions are considered, rights under academic tenure should be protected. The services of a tenured professor should not be terminated in favor of retaining someone without tenure who may at a particular moment seem to be more productive."[21]

However, Regulation 4c(3) complicates matters somewhat: "The appointment of a faculty member with tenure will not be terminated in favor of retaining a faculty member without tenure *except in extraordinary circumstances where a serious distortion of the academic program would result*" (emphasis added). Matters are complicated still further by AAUP policy holding that all full-time faculty members who have exceeded seven years of service are considered to be within the cohort of the tenured, regardless of whether they have undergone formal tenure procedures. As a result,

their rights to the protections of academic due process that accrue with tenure are identical to those of faculty members with tenure. It is only for the purpose of defining professional standards for relocating or releasing tenured faculty members in programs facing discontinuance that we draw a distinction between these categories. When programs are discontinued, institutions must make every effort to relocate both formally and informally tenured faculty members to other academic programs. What should be strictly forbidden, in any case, are decisions to terminate faculty appointments based on quantitative or otherwise reductive assessments that do not consider the breadth and versatility of a faculty member's research and teaching, since these determinations effectively create a system of punishment and reward that does not answer to essentially educational considerations and is easy to manipulate by appeal to evanescent fluctuations in enrollments and research funding, or evanescent fluctuations in the productivity of individual faculty members.

Further, we want to enhance the role of all faculty members in decision making. We call attention to a critical passage in the AAUP statement *The Role of the Faculty in Budgetary and Salary Matters*, which grants to contingent faculty members a key role in the determination of financial exigency, consonant with the role we recommend for tenured faculty members:

> Circumstances of financial exigency obviously pose special problems. At institutions experiencing major threats to their continued financial support, the faculty should be informed as early and as specifically as possible of significant impending financial difficulties. The faculty—*with substantial representation from its nontenured as well as its tenured members, since it is the former who are likely to bear the brunt of any reduction*—should participate at the department, college or professional school, and institution-wide levels in key decisions as to the future of the institution and of specific academic programs within the institution.[22]

The reference to the faculty's being "informed as early and as specifically as possible" is potentially misleading; although administrators have a fiduciary responsibility to alert the campus to impending challenges, in a properly collaborative and consultative environment, the faculty would have a detailed and ongoing sense of the institution's financial health. In a similar vein, AAUP operating guidelines on institutional problems resulting from financial exigency specify that "the granting of adequate notice to nontenured faculty should also be given high financial priority." We propose that "adequate notice" be understood in relation to a non-tenure-track faculty member's length of service. For instance, in Regulation 13e(1), the following provision is made for "part-time faculty members who have served for three or more terms during a span of three years": "Written notice of reappointment or nonreappointment will be issued no later than one month before the end of the existing appointment. If the notice of reappointment is to be conditioned, for example, on sufficiency of student enrollment or on financial considerations, the specific conditions will be stated with the issuance of the notice." We propose that this provision be extended to all nontenured faculty members who are released as a result of a declaration of financial exigency; nontenured faculty members with more than seven years of service have long-standing affiliations with an institution, and they may have to make major life changes—switching careers, moving families—in order to seek new positions. Nontenured faculty members with three or more years of service but less than seven should be granted six months of additional appointment after notice of termination on the same grounds. Tenured faculty members, if they are released on the ground that they are not as qualified to execute the fullest possible range of the program's educational and institutional mission as others in their cohort, should be provided with an additional year of appointment after they have been given notice of termination for financial considerations.[23] We note that this provision is especially germane to our revised definition of financial exigency, insofar as a campus that is not experiencing an imminent financial crisis that threatens the survival of the institution as a whole (but, rather, a *severe* financial crisis that fundamentally compromises the *academic integrity* of the institution as a whole) presumably will have the time and resources necessary to give its long-serving faculty members adequate long-term notice of termination.

Finally, there is the question of how departments should prioritize terminations of tenured faculty appointments with regard to educational considerations. Particularly in fields that have undergone substantial intellectual transformations in recent decades, these decisions can pit established fields against emerging fields—to the detriment of the former, if too much weight is given to recent developments in a discipline, or to the detriment of the latter, if too much weight is given to traditional areas and forms of scholarship. This committee finds it exceptionally difficult to recommend specific courses of action in such cases; we cannot say, as a general rule,

whether (to take a salient example from the Furniss-Brown exchange) a department should prefer to keep its three senior tenured scholars of European history or terminate one of them in favor of keeping the younger tenured scholar in Asian studies. Such decisions will be wrenching regardless of their outcomes and may lead to substantial redefinition of a department's or program's core educational mission. We propose, therefore, that any decisions about the priority of subfields within a discipline be made with respect to the long-term health and viability of the discipline as an educational enterprise, as determined by deliberations in good faith, balancing the virtues of both established and emerging fields and asking which areas of study, and which methodologies, will best serve the discipline and prospective student populations for the foreseeable future.

There are good reasons for our hesitation in this matter. We do not wish to compel, or to give administrators the right to compel, individual departments to accept refugees from closed programs. We consider it illegitimate to try (for example) to force a chemistry department to appoint a pharmacist from a discontinued program or to expect law schools or economics departments to accept business professors who teach law or economics if the law school or economics department in question deems those professors to be unqualified for appointment. However, *every good faith effort must be made to find another suitable position for displaced faculty members with tenure*, and if one department blocks an appointment, it should provide a written statement of its rationale.

Whenever a department refuses the reappointment of a faculty member, the burden remains on the administration to try to find another plausible department as a home. Every presumption should be in favor of preserving the tenured position; as we noted above, interdisciplinary programs, centers, and institutes might well accommodate displaced faculty members, particularly if their work crosses disciplinary boundaries. No invidious reasons should be accepted for a department's decision not to accept a displaced faculty member; a department cannot insist that it does not want to hire another woman or demur on ideological grounds that would violate a faculty member's academic freedom. If a faculty member believes that his or her rejection by a proposed relocation department is invidious, spurious, or in violation of AAUP principles, that faculty member should have the right to appeal to an appropriate faculty committee. But that committee's recommendation should be advisory, not binding; and we do not grant deans and provosts the right to override the wishes of departments if those departments' decisions are based on legitimate educational and intellectual grounds.

D. Proposed Changes for Individual Institutions

At institutions not covered by collective bargaining agreements, the foregoing policy statements, like all AAUP guidelines, are recommendations: they represent our careful consideration of best practices for colleges and universities, and they offer a definitive measure by which institutions can gauge their adherence to the standards that should govern American higher education. The faculty and administrations at institutions not governed by collective bargaining should therefore work together to include the report's policy statements and recommendations in their institutional regulations and faculty handbooks.

Collective bargaining representatives that incorporate some or all of the AAUP's previous recommendations related to this report into their collective agreements, or that seek in the future to negotiate new or revised agreements that incorporate these recommendations, should also seek to ensure that disputes regarding the interpretation and enforcement of the policies and procedures are resolved through a grievance process that includes binding arbitration. In the best cases, the enforceable procedures that result will include an opportunity for the faculty, acting through the union or the faculty senate, to participate in the determination of whether a bona fide financial exigency exists. In such cases, the parties may need to determine whether to continue with their existing understanding of "financial exigency" or to adopt our revised definition. Similarly, those institutions whose agreements specifically include AAUP-recommended program review and closure procedures that entail faculty participation in these decisions, or incorporate such AAUP-recommended procedures by reference, should update their agreements to incorporate these revised recommendations. We recommend, further, that collective bargaining representatives take special care to ensure that faculty members without tenure are granted the right to participate in determinations of financial exigency and program discontinuance, since they are likely to bear the brunt of program closures and layoffs.

Too often, however, the imposition of excessively narrow interpretations of negotiable terms and conditions of employment means that faculty collective bargaining agreements fall short of the faculty involvement that constitutes best practice. Contracts that do not provide the safeguards afforded by faculty participation in decisions respecting financial exigency and program closure typically must then rely entirely on layoff and recall provisions to protect academic integrity and faculty rights. In view of the flexibility provided by the vast increase in instruction by part-time and short-term appointees, and the deleterious consequences for academic freedom and educational quality that may be expected to result, there is no excuse for layoff procedures that permit routine reliance on the layoff of faculty members within the term of their appointments in order to meet short-term financial or enrollment concerns. Where proposed layoffs involve dismissal of faculty members with tenure, faculty members whose length of service entitles them to the protections of tenure, or term appointees within the term of their appointments, agreements should adopt at minimum AAUP-recommended procedures regarding order of layoff, length of notice, fair consideration for alternative suitable positions, and severance pay. These agreements ought particularly to ensure, through seniority provisions and appeal procedures, that layoffs cannot be based on considerations inconsistent with academic integrity and academic freedom.

Conclusion

This report has sought to address the gap between Regulation 4c on financial exigency and Regulation 4d on program discontinuance by redefining "financial exigency." As we set forth in the introduction, our new definition names a condition that is less dramatic than that in which the very existence of the institution is immediately in jeopardy but is significantly more serious and threatening to the educational mission and academic integrity of the institution than ordinary (short- and long-term) attrition in operating budgets. Financial exigency can legitimately be declared only when fundamental compromise of the institution's academic integrity will result from prolonged and drastic reductions in funds available to the institution, and only when the determination of the institution's financial health is guided by generally accepted accounting principles. In proposing this new definition, however, we insist again that financial exigency is not a plausible complaint from a campus that has shifted resources from its primary missions of teaching and research toward the employment of increasing numbers of administrators or toward unnecessary capital expenditures.

In order to ensure that our definition of "financial exigency" does not become an excuse for program elimination and the termination of tenured faculty positions when less drastic responses to institutional crisis are available, this report urges that faculty members be involved in consultation and deliberation at every stage of the process, beginning with a determination that a state of financial exigency exists. We offer specific recommendations for such faculty involvement:

1. Before any proposals for program discontinuance on financial grounds are made or entertained, the faculty should have the opportunity to render an assessment in writing on the institution's financial condition.
2. Faculty bodies participating in the process may be drawn from the faculty senate or elected as ad hoc committees by the faculty; they should not be appointed by the administration.
3. The faculty should have access to, at minimum, five years of audited financial statements, current and following-year budgets, and detailed cash-flow estimates for future years.
4. In order to make informed proposals about the financial impact of program closures, the faculty needs access to detailed program, department, and administrative-unit budgets.
5. The faculty should determine whether "all feasible alternatives to termination of appointments have been pursued," including expenditure of one-time money or reserves as bridge funding, furloughs, pay cuts, deferred-compensation plans, early-retirement packages, deferral of nonessential capital expenditures, and cuts to noneducational programs and services, including expenses for administration.
6. Faculty members in a program being considered for discontinuance because of financial exigency should be informed in writing that it is being so considered and given at least thirty days in which to respond. Tenured, tenure-track, and contingent faculty members should be involved.

We reaffirm the AAUP's long-standing opposition to the elimination of "one-person" programs, which allows for selective, arbitrary termination of tenured faculty members; and we reaffirm the principle that tenured faculty members hold tenure in the institution as a whole, not in any college, department, program, or other subdivision thereof. We also affirm long-standing AAUP policy that all full-time faculty members who have taught at an institution for over seven years are considered to be within the cohort of the tenured, whether or not they have undergone formal tenure procedures. It is precisely because tenure resides in the entire institution that tenured faculty members have the right to another suitable position within the institution, and we urge institutions to be creative in finding ways to relocate faculty members whose programs have been discontinued. Most important, we reiterate that the institution must make every effort to place the faculty member concerned in another suitable position *before* the administration issues notice to a faculty member of its intention to terminate his or her appointment because of formal discontinuance of a program or department of instruction. We reaffirm the principle that tenured faculty members must not be released and then replaced with nontenured faculty members. And we recommend that faculty members without tenure who are released as a result of program closure be given notice of nonreappointment commensurate with their length of service to the institution. Finally, we recommend that collective bargaining representatives adopt the recommendations of this report to the fullest extent possible.

We affirm these principles and make these recommendations not as a rearguard measure, not as a last-ditch attempt to keep the flickering flame alive before the forces of austerity engulf American higher education. We do believe that the forces of austerity are threatening to engulf American higher education; certainly this is why institutions are closing programs that should be part of any serious educational institution's curricular portfolio and implementing policies that further erode the ranks and the discretionary authority of the tenured professoriate. But we do not issue this report in a defensive mode. On the contrary, we believe that the erosion of the ranks and of the discretionary authority of the tenured professoriate is not only bad for American higher education but also bad for society as a whole and for the future of the United States. Program closures on the scale we have recently witnessed represent a massive transfer of power from the faculty to the administration *over curricular matters that affect the educational missions of institutions,* for which the faculty should always bear the primary responsibility. In most cases the decisions to close programs are made unilaterally and are driven by criteria that are not essentially educational in nature; they are therefore not only procedurally but also substantively illegitimate.

Moreover, program closures on this scale appear to reflect—and to implement—a widespread belief that faculty positions and instructional costs are the first expenditures an institution should seek to trim, as opposed to expenditures on administration or capital projects.

We cannot say this strongly enough: the widespread closure of academic programs, when undertaken by administrations unilaterally or on occasion with a fig leaf of faculty participation, represents a significant threat to the foundations of American higher education. These initiatives essentially transform colleges and universities from educational to managerial institutions, in which instruction in a course of study is simply another "deliverable" and where programs are so many inventory items to be discounted, downsized, or discontinued according to a reductive logic of efficiency and the imperative to lower labor costs whenever possible. We are not as a rigid matter of principle opposed to program closures. The AAUP has long acknowledged that a college or university can discontinue a program of instruction, but our standard has been that if the discontinuation is not undertaken for financial reasons, it must be shown to enhance the educational mission of the institution as a whole; we have long acknowledged that programs can be cut in times of financial exigency, but only if an appropriate faculty body is involved in the decision-making process, beginning with the determination of whether an institution is experiencing bona fide financial exigency. But by and large, the program closings of recent years do not meet any of these standards. They represent a violation of the principles on which American higher education should operate and must be contested by a vigorous, principled, and informed faculty.

Appendix: Measuring Financial Distress

The purpose of this appendix is to provide faculty members with some guidance in understanding the financial condition of their institutions. While no single number can capture the entire financial condition of an institution, the composite index described below is designed to indicate whether an institution may be facing financial distress.

This index can be used to analyze how the financial condition of one institution has changed over time and to compare similar institutions. If the index falls below the threshold discussed in this appendix, it may indicate that the institution is facing financial exigency. However, the index's merely falling below the threshold does not automatically indicate that a state of financial

exigency exists; falling below the threshold should instead be seen as necessary but not sufficient to declare that an institution is in severe financial distress. Even if an institution's composite index falls below the level that could indicate the existence of a state of severe financial distress, appropriate faculty committees as well as administrators at an institution should examine financial statements and other budgetary materials with great care to ensure that the factors causing the index to fall are real and not transient.

The index described below is a variant of the index used by the Ohio Board of Regents to assess the financial health of public institutions of higher education in Ohio. The index uses four ratios: a solvency ratio, an activity ratio, and two margin ratios. A *solvency ratio* measures the ability of an institution to meet its debt obligations. An *activity ratio* measures the ability of an institution to cover its operating expenses. *Margin ratios* measure the relationships between the inflow and outflow of resources at an institution.

There are several differences between how reserves, cash flow, and net assets are measured at public and private institutions. The Governmental Accounting Standards Board governs financial statements for public institutions, whereas the Financial Accounting Standards Board governs financial statements for private institutions.

The *solvency ratio* used in the index is known as the viability ratio, and it measures the ratio of reserves to the institution's long-term debt. At public institutions, reserves are defined as unrestricted net assets plus restricted expendable net assets. At private institutions, reserves are defined as unrestricted net assets plus temporarily restricted net assets. If a private institution does not separately report value of assets invested in physical plant net of accumulated depreciation minus the liability for long-term debt (net assets invested in plant), then the value of assets invested in plant net of accumulated depreciation minus the liability for long-term debt should be subtracted from unrestricted net assets. In addition, at institutions that offer postretirement benefits, the liabilities for these postretirement benefits should be subtracted from unrestricted net assets. The viability ratio shows the percentage of the institution's debt that could be paid off using reserves and is a primary indicator of solvency.

The activity ratio used in the composite index is known as the *primary reserve ratio*. It is the ratio of reserves (as defined in the previous paragraph) to operating expenses plus interest on

Table 1. Ratio Scores

	0	1	2	3	4	5
Viability ratio	< 0	0 to .29	.30 to .59	.6 to .99	1.0 to 2.5	> 2.5 or n/a
Primary reserve ratio	< −.1	−.1 to .049	.05 to .099	.10 to .249	.25 to .49	.5 or greater
Cash flow ratio	< −.05	−.05 to 0	0 to .009	.01 to .029	.03 to .049	.05 or greater
Net asset ratio	< −.05	−.05 to 0	0 to .009	.01 to .029	.03 to .049	.05 or greater

capital-asset related debt. The *primary reserve ratio* shows how many months an institution could continue its operations even if it had no sources of revenue.

The first margin ratio used in the composite index is the *cash-flow ratio*, which is the ratio of operating cash flow to total revenue. Institutions of higher education use accrual accounting, which means that they have certain "non-cash" expenses such as depreciation and the losses on the disposal of assets. In addition, unrealized changes in the value of assets (such as changes in the value of investments held in an endowment) can result either in gains that are booked as income or in losses that are booked as expenses. The existence of non-cash expenses and unrealized gains and losses on investments means that the income (or losses) before other revenues (net income) is not always a reliable indicator of net resources gained or lost by an institution. The operating cash-flow ratio is therefore at times a better indicator of the inflow and outflow of resources that can support operations. At public institutions, operating cash flow is the sum of net cash used by operations and net cash provided by noncapital financing activities minus interest paid on capital debts and leases. At private institutions, operating cash flow is net cash provided by operating activities minus interest payments on capital debts and leases.

The second margin ratio is the *net-asset ratio*, which is the change in net assets divided by the total revenue. The change in net assets is the most comprehensive indicator of the difference between revenues and expenses and is therefore one of the primary performance indicators for institutions.

To create a composite index, each of the ratios listed above is converted into a continuous score between 0 and 5 using ranges from table 1 and the piecewise linear function shown in the equation below. (If one wishes, an index can be calculated with a step function simply by assigning scores for the various ratios using the table below and then taking a weighted average of those scores using the weights in table 2.) The advantage of using the piecewise linear function $s(X)$ is that it

results in a score for each ratio that changes continuously as each underlying ratio changes. Without the piecewise linear function, a very small change in a ratio can lead to a large change in the score when the underlying ratio crosses a threshold.

The following piecewise linear function creates a continuous score by using a linear function between the points where the $a_0 \ldots a_4$ represent the viability, primary reserve, and cash-flow and net-asset ratios:

$$
s(X) = \begin{cases}
0 & \text{if } X \le a_0 - \dfrac{a_1 - a_0}{2} \\[2ex]
\dfrac{X - a_0}{a_1 - a_0} + .5 & \text{if } a_0 - \dfrac{a_1 - a_0}{2} \le X \le a_1 \\[2ex]
\dfrac{X - a_1}{a_2 - a_1} + 1.5 & \text{if } a_1 \le X \le a_2 \\[2ex]
\dfrac{X - a_2}{a_3 - a_2} + 2.5 & \text{if } a_2 \le X \le a_3 \\[2ex]
\dfrac{X - a_3}{a_4 - a_3} + 3.5 & \text{if } a_3 \le X \le a_4 + \dfrac{a_4 - a_3}{2} \\[2ex]
5 & \text{if } X \ge a_4 - \dfrac{a_4 - a_3}{2}
\end{cases}
$$

The scores generated for each of the ratios using either the piecewise linear function or the step function are then weighted as follows:

Table 2. Weights

Score	Weight
Viability score	0.225
Primary reserve score	0.450
Cash flow score	0.20
Net asset score	0.125

Multiplying each weight times its respective score and summing creates a composite index. In general, a score of 1.75 or below for two consecutive years would indicate a condition of severe financial distress.

Discussion of Ratios

VIABILITY RATIO

Definition: Reserves divided by debt

Public-sector reserves = Unrestricted net assets plus restricted expendable net assets

Private-sector reserves = Unrestricted net assets plus temporarily restricted net assets

What the ratio tells us:

Whether the institution has sufficient reserves in relation to the amount of debt. If the ratio is greater than 1.0, then reserves are greater than debt, which indicates financial strength.

PRIMARY RESERVE RATIO

Definition: Reserves divided by total expenses

What the ratio tells us:

Whether the institution has sufficient reserves to handle unexpected declines in revenues or unexpected increases in expenses. If the ratio is 33%, then the institution can cover expenses for four months (33% of twelve months). A ratio above 25% indicates that the institution is in a relatively strong position with respect to operating reserves.

CASH-FLOW RATIO

Definition: Operational cash flows divided by total revenues

What the ratio tells us:

Whether the institution is generating sufficient cash flows to meet obligations. Cash from operating activities includes cash inflows from tuition, grants, and contracts and from sales and outflows for compensation, payments to suppliers, and payments for scholarships and fellowships. Cash flows from noncapital financing activities include state appropriations, grants for noncapital purposes (for example, Pell grants), and gifts. This ratio gives us a pure measure of cash flows.

NET-ASSET RATIO

Definition: Change in net assets divided by total revenues

What the ratio tells us:

The change in net assets is total revenues less total expenses, so this ratio tells us whether there was a "profit" or "loss" during the year.

Technical Definitions

Unrestricted net assets are those for which the institution has financial freedom and flexibility. There is not a pot of cash sitting around, but if there are unrestricted net assets, then the institution has liquid assets (cash, investments, receivables) that it can tap.

Restricted expendable net assets are reserves that have been set aside for a particular purpose, such as paying future debt obligations. The institution cannot use these reserves for any other purpose, but an institution is much better off having a fund set aside to cover future obligations than not to have one.

Temporarily restricted net assets are donations that have a time component (as, for example, when a donor states that the principal of a gift cannot be used for ten years).

Debt is interest-bearing debt.

Public-sector operating cash flows consist of net cash (used) by operating activities plus net cash provided by noncapital financing activities (mostly the state appropriation) minus interest expense.

Private-sector operating cash flows consist of cash flows from operations minus interest expense.

Notes

1. In this report we will henceforth use the term "universities" interchangeably with "institutions," although we are aware that the term often applies to institutions that would ordinarily be designated as "colleges."

2. "Report of an AAUP Special Committee: Hurricane Katrina and New Orleans Universities," *Academe* 93 (May–June 2007): 59–125.

3. "Academic Freedom and Tenure: Northwestern State University of Louisiana and Southeastern Louisiana University," *Bulletin of the American Association of University Professors.* Special issue, *Academe* 98 (July–August 2012): 6–29.

4. "Academic Freedom and Tenure: University of Northern Iowa," *Bulletin of the American Association of University Professors.* Special issue, *Academe* 99 (July–August 2013): 4–16.

5. "Academic Freedom and Tenure: National Louis University (Illinois)," ibid., 17–29; "Academic Freedom and Tenure: Southern University, Baton Rouge," ibid., 30–39.

6. AAUP, *Policy Documents and Reports*, 11th ed. (Baltimore: Johns Hopkins University Press, 2015), 79–90.

7. W. Todd Furniss, "The 1976 AAUP Retrenchment Policy," *Educational Record* 57, no. 3 (1976): 135.

8. Ralph S. Brown Jr., "Financial Exigency," *AAUP Bulletin* 62 (April 1976): 13.

9. Matthew W. Finkin and Robert C. Post, *For the Common Good: Principles of American Academic Freedom* (New Haven, CT: Yale University Press, 2009), 125; emphasis added.

10. *Policy Documents and Reports*, 119.

11. Ibid., 120.

12. Ibid., 289; emphasis added.

13. Ibid., 309.

14. Ibid.

15. Brown, "Financial Exigency," 13.

16. "Academic Freedom and Tenure: Sonoma State University," *Academe* 69 (May–June 1983): 8.

17. Ibid., 9.

18. This is not to say that a faculty member should be guaranteed the same courses he or she taught prior to the declaration of financial exigency. If the elimination of a major or minor entails the elimination of advanced courses in a subject, so be it. We will not seek to uphold the right of a Spanish professor to continue teaching small seminars on Cervantes instead of lower-division language-instruction courses. We are concerned here only with preserving the positions of tenured faculty members, not with dictating the content of their course loads.

19. *Browzin v. Catholic University*, 527 F.2d 843 (US App. D.C.) at 847.

20. Penn State conducted its program closures, which were announced in 2011, by means of a "Core Council" that included minimal faculty input, none of which concerned the financial state of the university. There was no attempt to find "another suitable location" for the probationary faculty members in the science, technology, and society program until after its closure had been decreed, though arrangements were eventually made for some—not all—of the faculty members affected.

21. *Policy Documents and Reports*, 309.

22. Ibid., 290; emphasis added.

23. We find it exceptionally vexing to have to set a standard for providing adequate notice of nonreappointment for non-tenure-track faculty members with more than seven years of service when our policies do not recognize the legitimacy of an institution's having any full-time faculty members in this category. But we want to provide some protection for the full-time non-tenure-track faculty members even though we do not accept the legitimacy of their positions off the tenure track.

On Institutional Problems Resulting from Financial Exigency: Some Operating Guidelines

The guidelines that follow reflect Association policy as set forth in the *Recommended Institutional Regulations on Academic Freedom and Tenure*,[1] *The Role of the Faculty in Budgetary and Salary Matters*,[2] and other policy documents. They were formulated by the Association's staff, in consultation with the Joint Committee on Financial Exigency, Committee A on Academic Freedom and Tenure, and the Committee on College and University Governance. They were first issued in 1971 and reissued in slightly revised form in 1972. The current text includes revisions approved by Committee A in 1978.

1. There should be early, careful, and meaningful faculty involvement in decisions relating to the reduction of instructional and research programs. The financial conditions that bear on such decisions should not be allowed to obscure the fact that instruction and research constitute the essential reasons for the existence of the university.

2. Given a decision to reduce the overall academic program, it should then become the primary responsibility of the faculty to determine where within the program reductions should be made. Before any such determination becomes final, those whose life's work stands to be adversely affected should have the right to be heard.

3. Among the various considerations, difficult and often competing, that have to be taken into account in deciding upon particular reductions, the retention of a viable academic program should necessarily come first. Particular reductions should follow considered advice from the concerned departments, or other units of academic concentration, on the short-term and long-term viability of reduced programs.

4. As particular reductions are considered, rights under academic tenure should be protected. The services of a tenured professor should not be terminated in favor of retaining someone without tenure who may at a particular moment seem to be more productive. Tenured faculty members should be given every opportunity, in accordance with Regulation 4c of the Association's *Recommended Institutional Regulations on Academic Freedom and Tenure*,[3] to readapt within a department or elsewhere within the institution; institutional resources should be made available for assistance in readaptation.

5. In some cases, an arrangement for the early retirement of a tenured faculty member, by investing appropriate additional institutional funds into the individual's retirement income (ordinarily feasible only when social-security benefits begin), may prove to be desirable if the faculty member is agreeable to it.

6. In those cases where there is no realistic choice other than to terminate the services of a tenured faculty member, the granting of at least a year of notice should be given high financial priority.

7. The granting of adequate notice to nontenured faculty should also be given high financial priority. The nonreappointment of nontenured faculty, when dictated by financial exigency, should be a consideration independent of the procedural standards outlined in Regulation 4c, with one exception: when the need to make reductions has demonstrably emerged after the appropriate date by which notice should be given, financial compensation to the degree of lateness of notice should be awarded when reappointment is not feasible.

8. A change from full-time to part-time service, on grounds of financial exigency, may occasionally be a feature of an acceptable settlement, but in and of itself such a change

should not be regarded as an alternative to the protections set forth in Regulation 4c or as a substitute for adequate notice.[4]

9. When, in the context of financial exigency, one institution merges with another, or purchases its assets, the negotiations leading to merger or purchase should include every effort to recognize the terms of appointment of all faculty members involved. When a faculty member who has held tenure can be offered only a term appointment following a merger or purchase, the faculty member should have the alternative of resigning and receiving at least a year of severance salary.

10. When financial exigency is so dire as to warrant cessation of operation, the institution should make every effort in settling its affairs to assist those engaged in the academic process so that, with minimal injury, they can continue their work elsewhere.

Notes

1. AAUP, *Policy Documents and Reports*, 11th ed. (Baltimore: Johns Hopkins University Press, 2015), 79–90.

2. Ibid., 289–91.

3. Ibid., 81–82.

4. See also note 3 of "Senior Appointments with Reduced Loads," ibid., 169.

Governance Standards in Institutional Mergers and Acquisitions

The statement that follows is excerpted from a longer draft statement, *On Institutional Mergers and Acquisitions*, which was prepared by a joint subcommittee of the Association's Committee A on Academic Freedom and Tenure and the Committee on College and University Governance and approved for publication by the parent committees and by the Association's Council in November 1981. The Committee on College and University Government in February 1983 approved the separate publication of the following section of that statement entitled *Procedural Standards in Implementation*, which deals with the faculty's role.

Protection of faculty rights and prerogatives in a merger situation requires early and full faculty involvement in any discussions leading to a merger. The role of the faculty, first in the planning of an institutional merger or acquisition and then in implementing it, derives from the principles of shared responsibility and authority as set forth in the *Statement on Government of Colleges and Universities*. Because, according to the *Statement on Government*, "the faculty has primary responsibility for such fundamental areas as curriculum, subject matter and methods of instruction, research, faculty status, and those aspects of student life which relate to the educational process," and because these areas will inevitably be affected by a merger or acquisition, it is imperative that the faculty of the concerned institutions be afforded a meaningful role in the planning and implementation of mergers and acquisitions. This role is set forth with additional particularity in the Association's statement on *The Role of the Faculty in Budgetary and Salary Matters*:[1]

> The faculty should play a fundamental role in any decision that would change the basic character and purpose of the institution, including transformation of the institution, affiliation of part of the existing operation with another institution, or merger, with the resulting abandonment or curtailment of duplicate programs.

Before any decisions on curtailment become final, those whose work stands to be adversely affected should have full opportunity to be heard. In the event of a merger, the faculties from the two institutions should participate jointly in negotiations affecting faculty status and the academic programs at both institutions.

The essential point is that the faculty of both institutions should be involved before decisions or commitments to affiliate have been made, or before any decisions on curtailment of programs (if such decisions are an aspect of the affiliation) become final. Preliminary or exploratory discussions about the possibility of institutional affiliation may in some instances occur without full faculty involvement, but full involvement of the faculties of both institutions should begin early in any course of discussion that appears likely to eventuate in an affiliation; any final commitment bearing on institutional affiliation made without full faculty involvement would be inimical to the principles set forth in the *Statement on Government* and the statement on *The Role of the Faculty in Budgetary and Salary Matters*.

The possibility for abuse of the merger situation is greatest in those cases in which a condition of imminent or existing financial exigency is offered as the basis for exceptional treatment of the tenure commitment as outlined above. As in any instance in which a condition of financial exigency is offered as a justification for modification of tenure obligations, the decision on the financial situation of the institution is too grave, and its consequences too far-reaching, to be made solely in restricted administrative circles. Any decision to seek merger in a context of financial exigency should be made with the fullest possible participation of the faculty in the institution that would be acquired. The faculty of the institution that is experiencing severe financial difficulties should be informed as early and as specifically as possible of those difficulties, and that faculty should participate fully in any decision to seek merger as an alternative to possible extinction.

Merger of two institutions when one is experiencing financial exigency may present opportunities to preserve faculty positions and protect faculty status. At the same time, care must be taken that merger is not employed as a means of breaching tenure obligations. The Association offers its advice and assistance, as early as possible in the course of merger negotiations, to ensure compliance with the standards set forth in this statement. In all merger situations, the Association is prepared to enforce adherence to these standards, in accordance with its established procedures for processing complaints and cases.

Note

1. AAUP, *Policy Documents and Reports*, 11th ed. (Baltimore: Johns Hopkins University Press, 2015), 290. See also item 9 in "On Institutional Problems Resulting from Financial Exigency: Some Operating Guidelines," ibid., 310.

Salary-Setting Practices That Unfairly Disadvantage Women Faculty

The report that follows, prepared by a subcommittee of the Association's Committee W on the Status of Women in the Academic Profession, was approved for publication by Committee W in April 1992 for the information of the profession. Statistical information in the report was updated in 2014.

Background

That male faculty members outearn their female colleagues is well established. In 1975, male professors across all institutions outearned females by 9.2 percent; male instructors' advantage was 4.5 percent. By the 1990–91 academic year, the disparity for full professors had climbed to 11.5 percent and for instructors to 6.7 percent.[1] Almost two decades after scholars first called attention to it, the wage gap among faculty has widened, testifying to the continuing need for procedures to identify sex disparities in faculty salaries that need correction.

In 1977, the American Association of University Professors began distributing a *Higher Education Salary Evaluation Kit*,[2] and Committee W members and others have detailed strategies for documenting and rectifying the male-female pay gap in academia.[3] Faculty on many campuses have conducted salary studies and negotiated remedies, although sometimes only after litigation.[4] For example, after a 1988 University of Connecticut study found that women faculty members earned on average $1806 less than what men with similar characteristics earned, the university allotted $1800 per woman faculty member in every administrative unit for pay adjustments.

Until now, attention to salary disparities by sex in higher education has largely been restricted to statistical studies showing the failure of universities to compensate female faculty for factors that affect pay at the same rate they did men in the same departments. However, such studies, and the remedies they have motivated, have failed to address the problem of interdepartmental differentials that disadvantage women. Nor have they addressed problems caused by certain common salary-setting practices that systematically and unfairly disadvantage women. These practices need to be examined on every campus and modified. Unless that occurs, the salary gap will persist.

Pay Equity

Differences in pay between specialties can be an important source of disadvantage for women. When occupational segregation by sex is present, it opens the way for employers to structure pay scales in such a way that predominantly male occupations pay more than predominantly female ones.

The social scientists who have made empirical studies of this issue in the whole economy have concluded that the sex composition of an occupation does in fact affect its rate of pay, with the pay being lower the higher the proportion of women in the occupation.[5] These systematic differences in the pay of male- and female-dominated occupations persist after factors that legitimately affect compensation are taken into account.

The underpayment of female-dominated specialties is plausibly associated with the propensity, observed in many cultures, to put a low value in terms of esteem and recompense on work associated with women. The recognition of this phenomenon by social science research has given rise to a call for equal pay for jobs that can be shown, through job evaluation, to make similar demands on the worker in terms of responsibilities and other requirements. The demand for "pay equity" (also known as "comparable worth") calls for removing from compensation schemes any bias associated with the sex composition of jobs or their sex labels.[6]

Although an increasingly conservative judiciary has dealt harshly with plaintiffs' claims for pay equity brought under the Civil Rights Act of 1964, a large number of state and local governments have responded to the call for pay equity by analyzing wages of sex-typed occupations in the public sector, and some have implemented remedies that have reduced the pay gap between male and female public employees.[7] However, remedies have rarely extended to disparities among university professors across disciplines or administrative units.

Pay Equity for University Professors

In the university context, differentials between and among departments on a given campus may be legitimate if they are the result of differences in the cost and length of required training, of off-campus possibilities for lucrative use of the skills involved, or of the rarity of the necessary talent. Inequities in pay occur if the sex composition of a discipline affects faculty salaries, net of legitimate determinants of salary, or if tasks that are disproportionately assigned to female faculty members (e.g., teaching large service courses, advising students) are systematically under-rewarded. That considerable sex segregation exists in academic institutions makes possible substantial pay inequity.

The tendency for salaries to be lower in disciplines with higher proportions of women is well known,[8] although only a few researchers have directly investigated pay equity among faculty. In an important study, Staub found that the sex composition of disciplines affected both salaries and salary increases among institutional members of the National Association of State Universities and Land-Grant Colleges.[9] Moreover, her time-series analyses showed that a substantial increase of women in a discipline was associated with a drop in the relative salaries paid to jobholders. In a subsequent study of both NASULGC institutions and those included in salary surveys conducted by the College and University Personnel Association, Bellas found that greater proportions of women in academic disciplines were associated with lower entry-level salaries, even after controlling for labor-market conditions appropriate to the discipline.[10]

Women's Pay and "the Market"

It is sometimes claimed that all pay differences between men and women, including those within and between occupational specialties, can be explained by the operations of "the market." Those who make this point go on to explain that attempts to revoke the market's verdict, for example by rearranging occupational pay scales, are bound to cause damage: shortages of labor in some occupations, and oversupplies in others, with resulting unemployment.

But market-determined wages and discrimination that merits correction are by no means mutually exclusive. The prices or salaries that a market sets depend on supply and demand. If persons operating on the demand side of the market—those with the power to make salary offers and to hire—behave in a discriminatory manner because of societal tradition, and if competition is not rigorous enough to eliminate such discriminatory behavior, then the market itself will produce discriminatory results.[11]

The correction of intradepartmental differentials resulting from the undervaluation of women's traditional fields will work best if the movement for reform is widespread and coordinated. If this occurs, the demand side of "the market" will quickly come to consist of a majority of nondiscriminatory employers. The more involved colleges and universities are in pay equity adjustments, the sooner the market itself will come to support nondiscriminatory salaries. However, the failure of others to reduce discrimination should not serve as an excuse to delay adjustments in any institution.

Within disciplines, female faculty members may be "less marketable" than male colleagues of equal merit, because discriminatory attitudes on other campuses reduce their likelihood of getting an outside offer. Moreover, a higher proportion of women than of men belong to two-career couples, so that the ability of women to seek and accept outside offers is on average lower. These facts suggest that salary gaps between equally meritorious people can open up if outside offers result in salary adjustments without attention to internal equity in pay-setting. One solution would be to review internal equity analyses whenever pay adjustments are made to meet outside offers.

Further Common Practices That Disadvantage Women

On many campuses salaries are adjusted with reference to the previous year's activities. Those who are judged to have an equally meritorious year are given the same percentage increase. This practice can sometimes perpetuate inequities. For example, consider the case of a man and a woman hired as beginning professionals at different salaries, who then have identically meritorious careers. The year-by-year increment process will perpetuate the original percentage gap, and widen the absolute gap, despite the fact that their merit, based on their entire career, is equal.

Adjusting salaries based on the faculty member's total scholarly record will correct inequities across cohorts such as those stemming from being hired in periods of budget stringency, as well as any legacy of sex inequity in starting salaries or in past raises. Paying women faculty members lower salaries than men simply because they started at lower salaries is illegal, even if women and men have received equal percentage raises (*Bazemore v. Friday* 478 US 385, 1986).

Other practices may disadvantage women faculty in salary-setting. Individualized bargaining in fixing entry salaries may result in candidates judged of identical merit starting at differing salaries. As noted above, such differences, which may have little to do with merit, get perpetuated if year-to-year adjustments are based solely on reviews of the previous year.

Maintaining the confidentiality of salaries (and in some instances even of the routinely updated CVs used in the determination of salary) may spare people with low salaries from embarrassment vis-à-vis their colleagues and students. However, such confidentiality also serves to mask and thus perpetuate inequities. Experience has shown that allowing access to data almost always reveals inequities by sex, and within sexes as well. Therefore, on balance, openness is to be preferred.

Wage compression—allowing people who have been in the institution longest to lag in salary—may have a disparate impact on women because they are perceived as less mobile. Institutions sometimes underpay for the "invisible" work that some teaching and service involve, because it is disproportionately assigned to women.

Recommendations

Based on the considerations above, we make the following recommendations:

1. The national AAUP and campus chapters should gather and publicize data on salary disparities across disciplines, departments, and other administrative units to call attention to such differentials and their association with units' sex composition.

2. Every institution should work toward achieving a just compensation system. Differentials between and among departments should be carefully examined, and those that derive merely from a traditional devaluation of "women's fields" should be eliminated, even if the "market" remains largely unreformed.

3. In particular, internal institutional departmental differences should be compared with survey data from other institutions. If an institution reflects larger differentials than the external market, adjustments may be in order.

4. Institutions should examine differing faculty work loads in teaching, advising, and service across departments as well as within departments and correct inequities.

5. In fixing entry salaries, institutions should discourage individualized bargaining, which favors men owing to their advantage in a discriminatory market. Similarly, rewarding a woman less than a man judged to be of equal merit who is receiving more outside offers

reproduces within the institution the market's discriminatory behavior. Institutions should consider standardizing pay practices across constituent units.

6. Institutions should acknowledge, measure, and reward the various contributions they expect of faculty, and should not unfairly downgrade the reward of contributions disproportionately assigned to women faculty. Whenever possible, institutions should develop objective indicators of such activities (e.g., number of hours student contact), as well as of vital services faculty perform for their institutions, communities, and professions (e.g., hours of committee service per semester).

7. Institutions should disseminate criteria for the setting of pay standards widely, both to those who determine salary and to all faculty members.

8. In making regular yearly salary adjustments, and in implementing remedies to reduce inequity, institutions should compare faculty members' total scholarly record when adjusting salaries, rather than simply basing raises on recent productivity.

9. In reviewing salary structures, institutions should address issues of equity by age and experience. Institutions should not exploit the inability of faculty members to move because of discrimination in the academic labor market or because they belong to two-career couples.

10. Campus Committees W should:
    a. Work to conduct salary-equity studies at regular intervals. Committees conducting such studies should involve faculty from disproportionately female fields such as nursing, library science, and social work.
    b. Press their universities to review personnel practices to ensure that they do not disproportionately relegate women to non-tenure-track positions, to demanding service courses, or to heavy advising and committee assignments.
    c. Press their universities to review promotion practices to identify any tendency to deny tenure disproportionately to women or to promote them more slowly than men.
    d. Make all faculty and administration salaries and all CVs readily accessible to faculty.
    e. Ask that job candidates be given data on departmental salary structures and salaries of recent appointees and as long as a university's salaries are not standardized encourage candidates to negotiate for starting salaries in line with those of other faculty members with similar credentials.

f. Encourage their universities to take into account in evaluating the performance of administrators their progress in achieving equitable salary structures and salary-setting practices.

g. Cooperate in pay-equity campaigns with non-faculty employees and (where they exist) their unions.

Notes

1. Figures for 1974–75 are from "Academic Women and Salary Differentials," *Academe* 74 (July–August 1988): 33. Those for 1990–91 are from *Academe* 77 (March–April 1991): 22, Table 5. According to the 2013–14 AAUP report, men professors across all institutions were paid salaries 14.7 percent higher in that year than women professors, on average. Among associate professors, men were paid 7.4 percent more on average, and among assistant professors 8.6 percent more. For instructors, the disparity in favor of men was 3.3 percent. (John W. Curtis and Saranna Thornton, "Losing Focus: The Annual Report on the Economic Status of the Profession, 2013–14," *Academe* 100 [March–April 2014]: 26, survey report, Table 5.)

2. Elizabeth L. Scott, *Higher Education Salary Evaluation Kit* (Washington, DC: AAUP, 1977).

3. Jane Loeb and Marianne A. Ferber, "Representation, Performance, and the Status of Women on the Faculty," in Alice S. Rossi and Anne Calderwood (eds.), *Academic Women on the Move* (New York: Russell Sage Foundation, 1973), 239–54; Mary W. Gary and Elizabeth L. Scott, "A 'Statistical' Remedy for Statistically Identified Discrimination," *Academe* 66 (May 1980): 174–81; Mary W. Gray, *Achieving Pay Equity on Campus* (Washington, DC: AAUP, 1990).

4. "Representation, Performance, and the Status of Women" (unpublished, n.d.); Deana Finkler, David T. Van Dyke, and Jeffrey D. Klawsky, "How Statistics, Law, and Politics Influence the Evaluation of Gender Salary Disparity in Higher Education" (unpublished paper, University of Nebraska, Omaha, n.d.); Dale Baum and Harry Jones, "Salary Equity: Statistically Identified Discrimination Against Texas A & M Female Faculty Members" (unpublished report, March 5, 1987).

5. Donald J. Trieman and Heidi I. Hartmann, *Women, Work, and Wages* (Washington, DC: National Academy of Sciences, 1981); Helen Remick (ed.), *Comparable Worth and Wage Discrimination* (Philadelphia: Temple University Press, 1984); Robert T. Michael, Heidi I. Hartmann, and Brigid O'Farrell (eds.), *Pay Equity: Empirical Inquiries* (Washington, DC: National Academy of Sciences, 1989). Only Randall Filer ("Occupational Segregation, Compensation Differentials, and Comparable Worth," in *Pay Equity*, 153–70) finds no significant effect on wages of proportion of the occupation that is female. This paper was subjected to strong criticism by discussants on grounds of its methodology.

6. Note that the meaning of the term "pay equity" differs from the term "equal pay," which refers to paying persons in the *same* job equally.

7. Ronnie Steinberg, "Radical Challenges in a Liberal World: The Mixed Success of Comparable Worth," *Gender & Society* 14 (December 1987): 466–75; Linda Ames, "Pay Equity: What Works?," *First Annual Women's Policy Research Conference: Proceedings, May 19, 1989, Washington, DC* (Washington, DC: Institute for Women's Policy Research, 1990); Joan Acker, *Doing Comparable Worth* (Philadelphia: Temple University Press, 1989); Sara M. Evans and Barbara J. Nelson, *Wage Justice* (Chicago: University of Chicago Press, 1989).

8. Lois Haignere, "Salary Equity Four Cell," *Collective Bargaining in Higher Education: The 1990's. Proceedings of the 18th Annual Conference* (New York, NY, April 23–24, 1990).

9. Kay Staub, "Level of Female Participation: An Overlooked Factor in Salary Differences among Faculty Disciplines?" (lecture, Annual Conference of the Southern Association for Institutional Research, New Orleans, October 28–30, 1987).

10. Marcia Bellas, "Comparable Worth in Academia: Analysis of the Effects of Faculty Salaries on the Sex Composition and Labor-Market Conditions of Academic Disciplines" (PhD diss., University of Illinois, Champaign, 1992).

11. William P. Bridges and Robert L. Nelson, "Markets in Hierarchies: Organizational and Market Influences on Gender Inequality in a State Pay System," *American Journal of Sociology* 95 (November 1989): 616–58; Marlene Kim, "Gender Bias in Compensation Structures: A Case Study of Its Historical Basis and Persistence," *Journal of Social Issues* 45 (1989): 39–50; Alice Kessler-Harris, *A Woman's Wage: Historical Meanings and Social Consequences* (Lexington: University Press of Kentucky, 1990).

Statement of Principles on Leaves of Absence

The statement that follows, prepared by a special committee of the American Association of University Professors and the Association of American Colleges (now the Association of American Colleges and Universities), was adopted by the Association of American Colleges at its annual meeting in January 1972. In May 1972, it was adopted by the Council of the American Association of University Professors and endorsed by the Fifty-Eighth Annual Meeting.

The statement, designed to emphasize the value of leaves of absence and to give guidance to institutions in making or improving provisions for them, offers what the two associations believe to be sound standards for flexible and effective leave programs. Though limited financial resources at an individual institution may delay the immediate establishment of an ideal leave policy, careful consideration should be given to possible steps toward the early development of such a policy.

Purposes

Leaves of absence are among the most important means by which the teaching effectiveness of faculty members may be enhanced, their scholarly usefulness enlarged, and an institution's academic program strengthened and developed. A sound program of leaves is therefore of vital importance to a college or university, and it is the obligation of faculty members to make use of available means, including leaves, to promote their professional competence. The major purpose is to provide opportunity for continued professional growth and new, or renewed, intellectual achievement through study, research, writing, and travel. Leaves may also be provided in appropriate circumstances for projects of direct benefit to the institution and for public or private service outside the institution.[1] Leaves should also be granted for illness, recovery of health, and maternity.

Development of Leave Policies

Leave policies and procedures should be developed with full faculty participation. Faculty members, acting through appropriate representatives, should also have a key role in the selection of the recipients of individual leaves. The institution and the individual faculty member have a common responsibility for endeavoring to achieve the objective of the leave program—the institution by establishing an effective program, the faculty member by making appropriate use of it. Leave

policies should be flexible enough to meet the needs of both the individual and the institution.

Eligibility and Procedures

The purpose of a leave program is to promote the professional development of all faculty members—those who are likely to stay at the institution for a long period but also, although not necessarily to the same degree, those for whom there is no such assurance.

Previous service and leaves at other institutions should be taken into consideration in determining eligibility for leave. Persons nearing retirement should be eligible for leave with pay if it is clear that the leave will achieve its purposes both for the individual and for the institution.

For a nontenured faculty member on scholarly leave for one year or less, the period of leave should count as part of the probationary period as if it were prior service at another institution.[2] Exceptions to this policy should be mutually agreed to in writing prior to the leave.

Faculty members should apply for a leave at a reasonable time in advance and through established procedures, so that the institution can more readily care for their work in their absence and so that they can plan to make the best use of the opportunity. All evidence that the leave will increase individual effectiveness or produce academically or socially useful results should be considered in evaluating applications. A leave may either involve specialized scholarly activity or be designed to provide broad cultural experience and enlarged perspective. Administrators and faculty agencies concerned with implementation of leave policies may reasonably require faculty members to submit such advance plans as are likely to ensure productive results.

Individual and Institutional Obligations

Faculty members have an obligation to return for further service following a leave of absence when the circumstances of granting the leave indicate that this is the equitable action, as is often the case when a leave with pay is granted. A faculty member should of course honor an agreement to return to the institution, unless other arrangements are mutually agreed upon. The precise terms of the leave of absence should be in writing and should be given to the faculty member prior to the commencement of the leave.

Even when there is no obligation to return, the faculty member who resigns while on leave should give notice according to accepted standards. Moreover, a college or university should not knowingly invite a person to join its staff at a time when the individual cannot properly accept the invitation. In most instances, an institution that invites a faculty member to accept a new appointment while on leave should feel obligated to pay at least a portion of the cost of the leave.

Frequency and Duration of Leaves

Leaves should not be considered as deferred compensation to which a faculty member is entitled no matter what other opportunities the faculty member may have had for professional development. They should, however, be provided with reasonable frequency and preferably be available at regular intervals, because they are important to the continuing growth of the faculty member and the effectiveness of the institution.

Ordinarily, leaves of absence, whatever the source of funding, should not be more than one year in length, but exceptions to this rule should be possible in cases involving health, public service, overseas appointments, or other special circumstances.

Financial Arrangements

Leaves of one semester at full salary or an academic year at half salary are commonly provided. The institution is not obliged to assume the financial burden of all types of leaves. It does have the obligation, however, to use its own leave funds in such a manner as to balance the opportunity for professional development among and within academic fields.

Whatever the source of funding, the amount paid to the faculty member on leave should not depend on the cost of caring for the person's work in his or her absence, nor should a leave of absence of a year or less interfere with the opportunity for promotion or increase in salary.

Continuous coverage under various types of insurance programs should be provided while a faculty member is on leave. When the faculty member is on leave with pay, both the institution and the individual should continue contributions toward that person's retirement annuity. If a faculty member, on leave without pay, takes a temporary but full-time appointment at another institution or organization, it is reasonable to expect the appointing institution or organization to assume the cost of institutional contributions to the individual's retirement annuity and group-insurance programs.

Foundations, government agencies, and other organizations supporting leaves for scholarly purposes should include in their grants an amount sufficient to maintain institutional annuity and group-insurance contributions as well as salaries.

Notes

1. Leave for the purpose of engaging in political activity is discussed in the "Statement on Professors and Political Activity" (AAUP, *Policy Documents and Reports*, 11th ed. [Baltimore: Johns Hopkins University Press, 2015], 39).

2. Credit for prior service toward fulfillment of the probationary period is discussed in the 1940 "Statement of Principles on Academic Freedom and Tenure" (ibid., 13–19). See the section on "Academic Tenure," paragraph numbered 2.

Institutional Responsibility for Legal Demands on Faculty

The statement that follows, a revision and expansion of a 1984 statement, was approved by the Association's Committee A on Academic Freedom and Tenure and adopted by the Association's Council in November 1998.

There has been in recent years a steady growth in lawsuits filed against faculty members over the discharge of their professional responsibilities. Legal actions have been initiated by colleagues, by rejected applicants for faculty positions, by students, and by persons or entities outside the academic community. Litigation has concerned, among numerous issues, admissions standards, grading practices, denial of degrees, denial of reappointment, denial of tenure, dismissals, and allegations of defamation, slander, or personal injury flowing from a faculty member's participation in institutional decisions or from the substance of a faculty member's research and teaching. The increasing number of these lawsuits, which often reflect a lack or misuse of appropriate procedures for evaluation and review within an academic institution, is much to be regretted. The parties concerned are subject not only to damage to reputation but also to significant financial liability, which may include cost of legal representation, loss of time, court costs and expenses, and judgments of the court or out-of-court settlements. Moreover, faculty members have increasingly been summoned by legal process to disclose or account for their research and teaching in lawsuits to which they are not parties. Colleges and universities have a responsibility for ensuring legal representation and indemnification to members of their faculties who are subject to lawsuits stemming from their professional performance in institutional service or their conduct of research and teaching.

Statement

The Association recommends that colleges and universities adopt a comprehensive general policy on legal representation and indemnification for members of their faculties. The policy should ensure effective legal and other necessary representation and full indemnification in the first instance for any faculty member named or included in lawsuits or other extra-institutional legal proceedings arising from an act or omission in the discharge of institutional or related professional duties or in the defense of academic freedom at the institution. It should also include specific provisions as follows:

1. The policy should include all stages of such legal action, threatened or pending, in a judicial or administrative proceeding, and all aspects of the use of compulsory process whether or not the faculty member is a party in the proceeding.
2. The policy should ensure effective legal representation of the faculty member's interests, whether by the institution's regular counsel or by specially retained counsel, with due attention to potential conflicts of interest.
3. The policy should be applicable whether or not the institution is also named or included in the legal action, though the institution might consider joining in the action as a party if it has not been named.
4. The policy should provide for all legal expenses, for all other direct costs, and for court judgments and settlements.
5. The policy may provide for legal representation and indemnification through insurance.
6. The policy may provide for a faculty committee to make recommendations on the application of the policy to extraordinary circumstances not foreseen at the time of promulgating the policy of general application.

Collective Bargaining

The relationship of the activities of the Association to those of unions has been a subject of discussion since the AAUP's founding. However, the AAUP did not face the issue of collective bargaining directly until the 1960s. Discussing the events that led to the establishment of a Special Committee on the Representation of Economic Interests, the chair of that committee, Yale law professor Clyde Summers, recalled,

> In 1964, two organizations made moves toward obtaining recognition as the exclusive representative of the faculty of the City University of New York. . . . The moves by these two organizations for exclusive recognition presented the Association with the question of what position it should take in the matter. To explore the problem, the Association held a two-day conference in December, 1964, attended by 25 Association officers, staff members and guests. As a result of this conference the Council decided to create a Special Committee on Representation of Economic Interests to develop recommendations.
>
> By the time the committee was constituted, intervening events had made the problem even more pressing. A number of state legislatures passed statutes providing for collective bargaining by public employees, encompassing within the statutes faculty members of tax-supported colleges and universities. . . .
>
> The Committee on Representation of Economic Interests, composed of eight members of whom four had participated in the initial Conference, was named in late October [1965] and met one month later. The pressing problem was to develop guides for the Washington Office to follow in responding to situations [at several institutions].

In 1966, the Special Committee presented its report on the Representation of Economic Interests to the Council, which approved it. While at that point still tentative about extending the activities of the Association into collective bargaining, the committee recommended that chapters of the Association should receive approval "to become the exclusive representative of the faculty" only under certain conditions, the most prominent of which was the absence of a working governance system that provides for an "effective faculty voice and adequate protection and promotion of faculty economic interests."

In 1973, the annual meeting adopted the AAUP's first *Statement on Collective Bargaining*, which recognized formal bargaining as a "major additional way of realizing [the Association's] goals in higher education." Revisions to the statement were adopted in 1984. Ten years later, in 1994, the Committee on Representation of Economic and Professional Interests approved further revisions, affirming that "faculties at public and private institutions are entitled, as professionals, to choose . . . to engage in collective bargaining to ensure effective faculty governance." The revised statement was adopted by the Council in June 1994 and endorsed by the Eightieth Annual Meeting. Committees of the

Association have periodically developed policy statements to guide implementation of Association standards in collective bargaining settings.

The Association's collective bargaining chapters have used formal negotiation and enforcement of contractual agreements to advance professional standards and to bring legally binding protections to the rights and prerogatives of faculty members, as collective bodies and as individuals. These chapters are the members of the AAUP-CBC, a union that makes up one part of the tripartite structure that resulted from the Association's 2013 reorganization. (The other two components of this structure are the AAUP, a professional organization, and the AAUP Foundation, a charitable organization.)

In 2005, the Council endorsed the adoption by the Collective Bargaining Congress, the predecessor organization of the AAUP-CBC, of a statement on *Academic Unionism*, which noted,

> Commentators sometimes mistake unions for special interest groups. But AAUP unions are public interest groups. The Collective Bargaining Congress believes that they provide the best way for tenured and tenure-track faculty, contingent faculty, academic professionals, and graduate assistants to work for their institutions and so fulfill that "duty . . . to the wider public" that the AAUP's founders affirmed in 1915 in their first declaration of the faculty's mission in American democracy.

Statement on Collective Bargaining

The statement that follows, a further revision of a statement initially adopted in 1973 and revised in 1984, was approved by the Association's Committee on Representation of Economic and Professional Interests, adopted by the Association's Council in November 1993, and endorsed by the Eightieth Annual Meeting. In 2009, the AAUP Council approved a minor revision of the statement.

The basic purposes of the American Association of University Professors are to protect academic freedom, to establish and strengthen institutions of faculty governance, to provide fair procedures for resolving grievances, to promote the economic well-being of faculty and other academic professionals, and to advance the interests of higher education. Collective bargaining is an effective instrument for achieving these objectives.

The presence of institutions of faculty governance does not preclude the need for or usefulness of collective bargaining. On the contrary, collective bargaining can be used to increase the effectiveness of those institutions by extending their areas of competence, defining their authority, and strengthening their voice in areas of shared authority and responsibility. The Association therefore affirms that faculties at both public and private institutions are entitled, as professionals, to choose by an election or comparable informal means to engage in collective bargaining in order to ensure effective faculty governance. Trustees and administrators are of course free publicly to question the desirability of collective bargaining, but they should not resort to litigation or other means having the purpose or effect of restraining or coercing the faculty in its choice of collective bargaining. Where a faculty chooses collective bargaining, the trustees and administration have a corresponding obligation to bargain in good faith with the faculty-selected representative and should not resort to litigation or any other means intended to avoid this obligation.

As a national organization that has historically played a major role in formulating and implementing the principles that govern relationships in academic life, the Association promotes collective bargaining to reinforce the best features of higher education. The principles of academic freedom and tenure, fair procedures, faculty participation in governance, and the primary responsibility of the faculty for determining academic policy will thereby be secured. More-over, collective bargaining gives the faculty an effective voice in decisions that vitally affect its members' professional well-being, such as the allocation of financial resources and determination of faculty salaries and benefits. For these reasons, the Association supports efforts of local chapters to pursue collective bargaining.

Policy for Collective Bargaining Chapters

1. When a chapter of the Association enters into collective bargaining, it should seek to
    a. protect and promote the professional and economic interests of the faculty as a whole in accordance with the established principles of the Association;
    b. maintain and enhance within the institution structures of representative governance that provide full participation by the faculty in accordance with the established principles of the Association;
    c. obtain explicit guarantees of academic freedom and tenure in accordance with the principles and stated policies of the Association; and
    d. create orderly and clearly defined procedures for prompt consideration of problems and grievances of members of the bargaining unit, to which procedures any affected individual or group shall have access.
2. In any agency shop or compulsory dues check-off arrangement, a chapter or other Association agency should incorporate provisions designed to accommodate affirmatively asserted conscientious objection to such an arrangement with any representative.
3. The principle of shared authority and responsibility requires a process of discussion, persuasion, and accommodation within a climate of mutual concern and trust. Where that process and climate exist, there should be no need for any party to resort to devices of economic pressure such as strikes, lockouts, or unilateral changes in terms and conditions of

employment by faculty or academic management. Normally, such measures are not desirable for the resolution of conflicts within institutions of higher education.

Therefore, the Association urges faculties and administrations in collective bargaining to seek mutual agreement on methods of dispute resolution, such as mediation, fact-finding, or arbitration. Where such agreement cannot be reached, and where disputes prove themselves resistant to rational methods of discussion, persuasion, and conciliation, the Association recognizes that resort to economic pressure through strikes or other work actions may be a necessary and unavoidable means of dispute resolution.

Participation in a strike or other work action does not by itself constitute grounds for dismissal or nonreappointment or for imposing other sanctions against faculty members. Permanent replacement of striking or locked-out faculty members is equivalent to dismissal solely for participation in a strike or other job action. Moreover, if action against a faculty member is proposed on the basis of participation in a strike, as on any ground encompassed by the 1940 *Statement of Principles on Academic Freedom and Tenure*, the proceedings must satisfy the requirements of academic due process supported by the Association. The Association will continue to protect the interests of members of the profession who are singled out for punishment on grounds that are inadequate or unacceptable, or who are not afforded all the protections demanded by the requisites of academic due process.

Statement on Academic Government for Institutions Engaged in Collective Bargaining

The statement that follows was approved by the Association's Committee on Representation of Economic and Professional Interests and the Committee on College and University Governance in 1988 and adopted by the Association's Council in June of that year.

The Association's *Statement on Government of Colleges and Universities* affirms that effective governance of an academic institution requires joint effort based on the community of interest of all parties to the enterprise. In particular, the statement observes that:

> The variety and complexity of the tasks performed by institutions of higher education produce an inescapable interdependence among governing board, administration, faculty, students, and others. The relationship calls for adequate communication among these components and full opportunity for appropriate joint planning and effort. Joint effort in an academic institution will take a variety of forms appropriate to the kinds of situations encountered.

The various parties engaged in the governance of a college or university bring to higher education differing perspectives based on their differing, but complementary, roles in the academic effort. Traditional shared governance integrates those differing roles into productive action that will benefit the college or university as a whole. It is in the best interest of all parties to ensure that the institutions of shared governance function as smoothly and effectively as possible. Collective bargaining is one means to that end. As the Association's *Statement on Collective Bargaining*[1] asserts, "collective bargaining can be used to increase the effectiveness of [institutions of faculty governance] by extending their areas of competence, defining their authority, and strengthening their voice in areas of shared authority and responsibility."

Collective bargaining should not replace, but rather should ensure, effective traditional forms of shared governance. The types of governance mechanisms appropriate to a particular college or university are dictated by that institution's needs, traditions, and mission. Since those basic factors are not necessarily affected by the emergence of

collective bargaining at a campus, bargaining does not necessarily entail substantive changes in the structure of shared governance appropriate for that institution.

Collective bargaining on a campus usually arises at least in part in response to agencies or forces beyond the scope of institutional governance. When problems in institutional governance do contribute to the emergence of collective bargaining, these problems generally stem less from inadequacy in the structure for shared governance than from a failure in its proper implementation. Bargaining can contribute substantially to the identification, clarification, and correction of such difficulties.

Collective bargaining contributes to problem solving in three primary ways. Formal negotiation can improve communication between the faculty and the administration or governing board. Such communication is essential if the joint planning and effort urged by the *Statement on Government* is to be productive. Collective bargaining can secure consensus on institutional policies and procedures that delineate faculty and administrative participation in shared governance. Finally, collective bargaining can ensure equitable implementation of established procedures.

Collective bargaining should ensure institutional policies and procedures that provide access for all faculty to participation in shared governance. Employed in this way, collective bargaining complements and supports structures of shared governance consistent with the *Statement on Government*. From a faculty perspective, collective bargaining can strengthen shared governance by specifying and ensuring the faculty role in institutional decision making. Specification may occur through bargaining of governance clauses that define faculty responsibilities in greater detail; assurance of the faculty's negotiated rights may be provided through a grievance procedure supporting the provisions of the negotiated contract. From an administration perspective, contractual clarification and arbitral review of shared governance can reduce the conflicts occasioned by ill-defined or contested allocation of responsibility and thereby enhance consensus and cooperation in academic governance.

The sharing of authority in the governance of colleges and universities, as the *Statement on Government* asserts, is sound practice for academic institutions to follow. Any process for refining and enforcing proper practice should be viewed by all parties concerned with the welfare of higher education as a welcome addition to academic problem solving. Collective bargaining can be such a process. To be effective, bargaining must allow the parties to confront all aspects of their common problems, without encountering externally imposed barriers to possible solutions. Each party must be free to address matters of legitimate concern, and bargaining should provide an inclusive framework within which the parties will be encouraged to move toward resolution of their differences. For this reason, the scope of bargaining should not be limited in ways that prevent mutual employment of the bargaining process for the clarification, improvement, and assurance of a sound structure of shared governance.

Thus, effective collective bargaining can serve to benefit the institution as a whole as well as its various constituencies. Faculty, administrations, governing boards, and state and federal agencies should cooperate to see that collective bargaining is conducted in good faith. When legislatures, judicial authorities, boards, administrations, or faculty act on the mistaken assumption that collective bargaining is incompatible with collegial governance, they do a grave disservice to the very institutions they seek to serve. The cooperative interaction between faculty and administration that is set forth as a workable ideal in the *Statement on Government* depends on a strong institutional commitment to shared governance. By providing a contractually enforceable foundation to an institution's collegial governance structure, collective bargaining can ensure the effectiveness of that structure and can thereby contribute significantly to the well-being of the institution.

Note

1. AAUP, *Policy Documents and Reports,* 11th ed. (Baltimore: Johns Hopkins University Press, 2015), 323–24.

Arbitration of Faculty Grievances

This report, prepared by a joint subcommittee of the Association's Committee on Representation of Economic and Professional Interests and Committee A on Academic Freedom and Tenure, was approved by the respective committees in March and April 1973.

Introduction

Collective bargaining by faculties in higher education has been accompanied by the use of arbitration[1] for the resolution of disputes involving questions of contractual application or interpretation that may include matters of faculty status and rights. It should be noted that the use of arbitration does not wholly depend on the existence of a collective bargaining relationship. It may be provided for in institutional regulations, agreed to between an internal faculty governing body and the administration, or utilized on an ad hoc basis in a particular case. The enforceability of agreements to arbitrate future disputes, however, is a legal question involving both federal and state law. Since arbitration developed in the industrial context, it must be given the closest scrutiny when applied to the needs of higher education. Accordingly, this joint subcommittee was given the task of providing an initial review of that application.

Preliminary Considerations

The Association has been committed, since its founding in 1915, to securing a meaningful role for the faculty in decisions on matters of faculty status, rights, and responsibilities. The Association's *Statement on Government of Colleges and Universities* provides a brief discussion of the bases for this position:

> The primary responsibility of the faculty for such matters is based upon the fact that its judgment is central to general educational policy. Furthermore, scholars in a particular field or activity have the chief competence for judging the work of their colleagues; in such competence it is implicit that responsibility exists for both adverse and favorable judgments. Likewise, there is the more general competence of experienced faculty personnel committees having a broader charge. Determinations in these matters should first be by faculty action through established procedures, reviewed by the chief academic officers with the concurrence of the board. The governing board and the president should, on questions of faculty status, as in other

matters where the faculty has primary responsibility, concur with the faculty judgment except in rare instances and for compelling reasons which should be stated in detail.

The *Statement* does not suggest a formal device to resolve disputes between faculty and governing board. Indeed, resort to any body outside the institution, such as the courts, for an official resolution of disputes in matters of faculty status, rights, and responsibilities poses a serious challenge to accepted notions of institutional autonomy. Moreover, a survey of current practices, admittedly limited, reveals that arbitration has been used not solely to break impasses between faculty and governing board but to review the soundness of faculty decisions themselves. This suggests an additional problem of the relationship of arbitration to faculty autonomy.

The Use of Arbitration

In many situations, administrators are responsive to faculty recommendations and indeed may welcome them. In such cases the resort to arbitration will probably not be perceived as necessary. In some situations, however, administrators or trustees are unresponsive to Association standards and faculty actions, and final legal authority to resolve matters of faculty status usually lies with the governing board concerned. In such cases, outside impartial review may well be useful. It must also be recognized that in many situations faculty members do not enjoy or exercise a degree of independence adequate to the assurance of protections embodied in Association standards. In these situations also, independent impartial review may play a role.

For example, disputes regarding the appropriateness of individual salaries, or the imposition of penalties for alleged violations of institutional regulations, or the termination of academic appointments for reason of financial exigency, or decisions affecting a faculty member's teaching duties or programs of instruction are the sorts of controversies resolution of which may be fostered in varying degrees by arbitration.

It seems clear that, where resort to a formal external agency is deemed necessary, arbitration affords some advantages over judicial proceedings. In a court challenge, the procedure and substance are prescribed by federal and state constitutions, statutes, and judicial decisions in whose formulation the profession has almost no role. In contrast, arbitration procedures and substantive rights are largely within the joint power of the administration and the faculty's collective representative to prescribe. Hence the parties to the academic relationship can shape procedures to their special needs, formulate substantive rules embodying the standards of the profession, and select decision makers with special competence in the field. In addition, arbitration may prove a quicker and less expensive remedy.

Thus, where the faculty does not share in the making of decisions or its voice is not accorded adequate weight, arbitration may have particular utility. However, the finality of arbitral review also has its hazards, especially in the present nascent state of arbitral doctrine, and because of the slight experience of arbitrators in academic settings. Accordingly, arbitration may play a useful role in an academic setting to the extent it can foster rather than impair the sound workings of institutional government.

It is suggested that four factors are essential for the effective use of arbitration: (1) sound internal procedures preliminary to arbitration that enjoy the confidence of both faculty and administration; (2) careful definitions of both arbitral subjects and standards to be applied by the arbitrator; (3) the selection of arbitrators knowledgeable in the ways of the academic world, aware of the institutional implications of their decisions, and, of course, sensitive to the meaning and critical value of academic freedom; and (4) the assurance that the hearing will include evidence relating to the standards and expectations of the teaching profession in higher education and that appropriate weight will be given to such evidence.

1. Preliminary Procedures

Arbitration should be used most discriminatingly. It is not a substitute for proper procedures internal to the institution but should serve only as a final stage of that procedure. The availability of this forum should assist in rendering the earlier procedures more meaningful. Indeed, the submission of an inordinate number of grievances to arbitration may be significantly erosive of healthy faculty-administration relations.

The Association has suggested preliminary procedures for the adjustment of general faculty complaints and grievances.[2] With more detail, the Association has crystallized procedures to be utilized in dismissal proceedings,[3] proposed procedures to be used in hearing allegations of violations of academic freedom or discrimination in the nonreappointment of nontenured faculty,[4] and adopted detailed provisions dealing with decisions on nonreappointment and review therefrom not raising issues of academic freedom or discrimination.[5]

The subcommittee recognizes that a wide variety of institutional practices exists in American higher education, and that the degree to which faculties actually possess the decision-making authority recommended in the foregoing varies accordingly. It may not be possible, then, to propose a single model of arbitration responsive to these varying institutional patterns and the many kinds of issues which could conceivably be presented for an arbitral determination. The subcommittee believes it to be of critical importance, however, that, in the agreement to arbitrate any matter affecting faculty status, rights, and responsibilities, the judgment of the faculty, as the professional body properly vested with the primary responsibility for such determinations, be accorded a strong presumption in its favor.

2. Arbitral Standards

The definition of the arbitral standards requires the most careful attention. In some instances arbitration has been used to correct only procedural departures, while in others arbitral review of the merits of a decision has been afforded. The latter has proceeded under broad standards such as "just cause" for a particular action or more rigorous ones such as determining whether the questioned decision was "arbitrary and capricious."

A tentative review of arbitral decisions under the varying approaches has revealed widely differing results and in some cases a degree of arbitral unresponsiveness to the underlying academic values. Accordingly, the subcommittee believes it to be requisite to the use of arbitration as a means of enhancing internal governance that fairly rigorous arbitral standards be established in those cases in which norms and procedures unique to higher education are implicated.

3. Selection and Education of Arbitrators

Much depends on the qualities of the individual selected to serve as the arbitrator and the degree to which he or she is educated by the parties to the issues for adjudication in the context of professional practice and custom and to the importance of the decision to the life of the institution. Here the Association can make a valuable contribution, whether or not a local affiliate is serving as a collective representative. As the preeminent organization of college and university faculty in the United States, the Association should share its expertise in reviewing the qualifications of proposed arbitrators and should consider, jointly with other organizations, consulting on the establishment of a national panel or regional panels of qualified individuals. Further, the Association may prepare model briefs or other materials dealing with accepted norms of academic practice to be used as educational materials before an arbitrator and should consider sponsoring, again possibly with other organizations, workshops for arbitrators on these issues. The Association should also maintain an up-to-date file of awards and provide detailed comments on their academic implications, perhaps in some published form. Since the use of arbitration in this setting is so novel, it is clear that for higher education, unlike for the industrial sector, no well-defined set of doctrines has been developed. It is incumbent on the Association to assist directly in shaping such doctrines through all available means. Toward this end the Association should establish a joint subcommittee of the national committees having an interest in this area. A detailed study of the actual effects of arbitration under the varying approaches currently practiced and the drafting of model arbitration clauses would fall within the purview of such a body.

Two final issues require attention: the rights of the individual under a collective agreement providing for arbitration as the terminal stage of the grievance procedure; and the Association's role in the event an arbitral award departs significantly from fundamental substantive standards sponsored by it. Where there is an exclusive collective representative, the agent almost invariably controls access to arbitration. The subcommittee believes that this approach may be inappropriate in an academic setting and recommends that individual faculty members have access to arbitration on their own behalf if the collective representative refuses to press their claims. Because the issue placed before an arbitrator may touch deeply an individual's basic academic rights or freedoms, the individual should have the opportunity of participating in the selection of the arbitrator and have full rights to participate in all phases of the procedure, includ-

ing all preliminaries, on a parity with the collective representative, if any, and the administration. Experimentation with the allocation of costs of proceedings where the representative does not itself desire to proceed to arbitration would be useful. Costs may be assessed by the arbitrator between the parties according to the gravity of the injury, if one is found, or could be borne equally by the administration and the complaining faculty member.

The Association has traditionally viewed itself as supporting basic standards and has not viewed its processes as being limited because of contrary provisions in an institution's regulations, or, for that matter, an adverse judicial determination. Equally, the Association should continue to challenge significant departures from elemental academic rights, whether or not these departures have warrant in a collective agreement or an arbitrator's award.

Summary

Arbitration can be a useful device for resolving some kinds of disputes and grievances that arise in academic life. Especially when collective bargaining is practiced, resort to arbitrators who are sensitive to the needs and standards of higher education may be the preferred way to avoid deadlocks or administrative domination. But arbitration is not a substitute for careful procedures that respect the autonomy of the faculty and the administration in their respective spheres. A system of collective bargaining that routinely resorts to arbitration is an abdication of responsibility. This is especially true of the faculty's primary responsibility to determine who shall hold and retain faculty appointments.

Notes

1. Arbitration is a term describing a system for the resolution of disputes whereby the parties consent to submit a controversy to a third party for decision. The decision may be advisory only but is usually agreed to be binding. The parties participate in the selection of the arbitrator and may shape the procedure to be used; costs are usually borne equally between them.

2. Regulation 16, "Recommended Institutional Regulations on Academic Freedom and Tenure," AAUP, *Policy Documents and Reports*, 11th ed. (Baltimore: Johns Hopkins University Press, 2015), 88.

3. "Statement on Procedural Standards in Faculty Dismissal Proceedings," ibid., 91–93.

4. Regulation 10, "Recommended Institutional Regulations," ibid., 85–86.

5. "Statement on Procedural Standards in the Renewal or Nonrenewal of Faculty Appointments," ibid., 94–98.

Arbitration in Cases of Dismissal

This report was approved for publication by the Council of the American Association of University Professors in June 1983.

In 1973, the Association's Committee A on Academic Freedom and Tenure and the Committee on Representation of Economic and Professional Interests approved publication in the *AAUP Bulletin* of a report which was addressed to the topic, *Arbitration of Faculty Grievances*.[1] That report, prepared by a joint subcommittee, was viewed by the committees as a first statement on the relationship of arbitration of faculty grievances to established Association policies. The present report amplifies the development of arbitral practices in higher education, with particular emphasis on the question of arbitration of dismissal cases.[2] Consistent with the Association's longstanding obligations to the profession to define sound academic practice, this report was prepared after analysis of collective bargaining agreements reached by agents, AAUP and otherwise, and of the relationship of contractual provisions for dismissal to the 1940 *Statement of Principles on Academic Freedom and Tenure*, the *Statement on Procedural Standards in Faculty Dismissal Proceedings*,[3] and the *Statement on Government of Colleges and Universities*. It should be added parenthetically that arbitration of faculty status disputes is not limited to institutions with collective bargaining agreements. Members of the subcommittee were aware of one large public system and one large private university that do not have collective bargaining, but that do have faculty regulations that provide for arbitration of certain faculty status matters.

As was noted in the 1973 report, the *Statement on Government of Colleges and Universities* gives to the faculty primary responsibility for making decisions on faculty status and related matters. The *Statement on Government* asserts, "The governing board and president should, on questions of faculty status, as in other matters where the faculty has primary responsibility, concur with the faculty judgment except in rare instances and for compelling reasons which should be stated in detail."

Any discussion of Association policy on dismissals should, of course, begin with the provisions of the 1940 *Statement of Principles* and the *Statement on Procedural Standards*. Both documents are joint policies of the AAUP and the Association of American Colleges (now the Association of American Colleges and Universities). The "Academic Tenure" section of the 1940 *Statement* includes a basic outline of the procedural steps necessary for review of the dismissal for cause of a teacher previous to the expiration of a term appointment. The *Statement on Procedural Standards* supplements the 1940 *Statement* by describing the academic due process that should be observed in dismissal proceedings. The Association has also provided a fuller codification of appropriate dismissal procedures in Regulations 5 and 6 of its *Recommended Institutional Regulations on Academic Freedom and Tenure*.

Collective Bargaining Modification

Collective bargaining normally results in a formally negotiated contract governing terms and conditions of employment; the provisions of the collective agreement define the legal rights and duties of faculty, administrators, and trustees. Customarily, the collective agreement authorizes a neutral third party, an arbitrator, to resolve disputes which arise under it. In contrast to most litigation, negotiated arbitration clauses afford the administration and the faculty opportunity to prescribe the procedures and standards that apply and, most important, jointly to select the decision maker.

It is appropriate to restate here the four factors that the 1973 subcommittee noted as essential for the effective use of arbitration:

1. sound internal procedures preliminary to arbitration which enjoy the confidence of both faculty and administration;
2. careful definition of both arbitral subjects and standards to be applied by arbitration;
3. the selection of arbitrators knowledgeable in the ways of the academic world, aware of the institutional implications of their decisions, and, of course, sensitive to the meaning and critical value of academic freedom; and
4. the assurance that the hearing will include evidence relating to the standards and expectations of the teaching profession in

higher education and that appropriate weight will be given to such evidence.

This subcommittee concludes that in cases of dismissal the faculty member may properly be given the right, following a proceeding in accordance with the *Statement on Procedural Standards* and the *Recommended Institutional Regulations,* to appeal a negative decision to an arbitrator. The subcommittee believes that the *Statement on Procedural Standards* provides the most appropriate model for faculty dismissal proceedings. However, where alternatives are implemented, it urges that they should at least make provision for meaningful faculty participation in the dismissal process and for compliance with the requirements of academic due process in the formal dismissal hearing.

Essential Preliminary Faculty Participation

Before any formal procedures are invoked, the subcommittee believes that the essential faculty procedures preliminary to any contemplated dismissal, already set forth in Association policy statements,[4] should be followed. The subcommittee is particularly disturbed by contractual dismissal procedures that do not provide in any way for formal faculty participation in a mediative effort prior to the formulation of dismissal charges. It is the subcommittee's opinion that such participation is necessary both to resolve disputes short of formal proceedings and to advise the administration on the wisdom of further pursuit of a particular matter.

In the event that an administration, after receiving faculty advice, chooses to formulate charges for dismissal of a tenured member of an institution's faculty or a non-tenured faculty member during the term of appointment, a hearing on the charges should be held, whether or not the faculty member exercises the right to participate in the hearing. A dismissal is not simply a grievance which may not be pursued. A dismissal is a sanction of the highest order requiring a demonstration of cause regardless of the faculty member's individual action or inaction in contesting the charge.

Arbitration Following a Faculty Hearing

It is common practice within the profession that, following a hearing before a faculty committee, the hearing committee presents a report to the president who, in turn, either accepts the report or returns it to the committee with reasons for its rejection prior to transmittal of the report to the governing board. The governing board, in turn,

has traditionally made the final decision after study of the recommendations presented to it. In the event that the board disagrees with the faculty committee's recommendations, the board should remand the matter to the committee and provide an opportunity for reconsideration. This subcommittee recommends that, after the board's ruling, a faculty member who has pursued these traditional procedures should be given the right to proceed to arbitration. If the collective bargaining agreement provides for arbitration of faculty status disputes, it would be anomalous to deny the right to arbitrate a dismissal, while lesser matters dealing with faculty status may be arbitrated. More important, arbitration in this setting is not a substitute for unfettered trustee judgment, but for the courts; thus, it is not a question of whether institutional officers will be subject to external review, but of what forum is best equipped to perform the task.

It is normally the collective bargaining representative's responsibility to control access to arbitration. The subcommittee believes, however, that the issue of dismissal is of such magnitude that an individual against whom dismissal charges have been sustained by the institutional review processes up to and including the institution's board of trustees should have an unfettered right to seek arbitral review. Moreover, the nature of a dismissal charge against an individual is such, with each case standing on its own merits, that arbitration decisions in dismissal cases should not be considered to have created precedent for other arbitrations dealing with dismissals.

Thus, the subcommittee recommends that, in cases where the collective bargaining representative decides not to appeal a dismissal to arbitration, the individual be given the right to seek arbitral review independently. In that event, the individual would be expected to bear those costs of the arbitration normally assumed by the collective bargaining representative.

As the 1973 subcommittee noted, it is of critical importance ". . . that in the agreement to arbitrate any matter affecting faculty status, rights, and responsibilities, the judgment of the faculty as a professional body properly vested with the primary responsibility for such determinations be afforded a strong presumption in its favor." This subcommittee agrees and accordingly recommends that, particularly on questions of academic fitness and the norms of the profession, the arbitrator should give great weight to the findings and recommendations of the faculty hearing committee.

The subcommittee recommends that the collective bargaining agreement not limit the scope of the issues that may come to an arbitrator in a dismissal case. The arbitration decision should, of course, be based on the record. The subcommittee recommends that the collective bargaining agent have the right to participate in the proceedings in order to inform the arbitrator fully about the standards applicable to the case under review. The recommendation to permit the arbitrator to examine the procedures leading to the dismissal charges, the procedures for review of the charges, and the substance of the record developed in the hearings before the faculty committee as well as the arbitration is based on the expectation that the parties will select an arbitrator sensitive to the standards and practices of the local and national academic communities.

The procedures of the actual arbitration proceeding should be codified in advance and either spelled out in the collective bargaining agreement or, if there is a known policy that would guide the proceeding, referred to in the agreement. One policy often referred to in agreements at private institutions is the *Labor Arbitration Rules* of the American Arbitration Association;[5] agreements at public institutions often cite the arbitration rules of the agency that administers the state's collective bargaining statute.

Alternative Arbitration Procedures

The above proposal contemplates the addition of arbitration to procedures already required by the *Statement on Procedural Standards* and the *Recommended Institutional Regulations*. The proposal does no violence to the basic fabric of the 1940 *Statement,* for the basic dismissal decision is arrived at with full due process within the local academic community. Arbitration merely substitutes an expert neutral—jointly selected—for the judiciary in any subsequent contest over whether the decision was procedurally deficient or substantially in error under standards widely recognized in the academic world.

The subcommittee recognizes that, in the interest of expeditious adjudication of dismissal charges, some institutions in collective bargaining have devised alternative dismissal procedures. Such procedures range from direct arbitration of dismissal cases to modifications of the *Statement on Procedural Standards* procedures that incorporate arbitration as part of the formal hearing process, thereby obviating the need for an additional arbitration step upon completion of the internal institutional process.

The subcommittee cannot embrace a position that abandons a model of the faculty as a professional body passing judgment upon its members. Thus, it must reject resort to arbitration as a permissible alternative to the *Statement on Procedural Standards* procedures unless certain additional requirements are met. Alternative procedures, designed to comply with the spirit of the *Statement on Procedural Standards,* would have to be examined on a case-by-case basis. At a minimum, the subcommittee would expect such procedures to comply with the *Statement on Procedural Standards* in the following respects:

1. There should be specific provision for faculty participation in a mediative effort prior to the formulation of dismissal charges.
2. There should be significant faculty representation on the hearing panel in a formal hearing of any charges.
3. The formal hearing procedures should comply with the requirements of academic due process as outlined in the *Recommended Institutional Regulations.*

Summary

In summary, the subcommittee has concluded that it is permissible to have the potential dismissal of a faculty member subject to review by an outside arbitrator who may make a binding decision. Disputes concerning the dismissal of a faculty member from a tenured position or of a nontenured faculty member during the term of appointment require faculty participation in an effort to mediate the dispute and require a formal hearing.

Consistent with the *Statement on Procedural Standards* and the *Recommended Institutional Regulations,* we believe arbitral review may be appropriate after presidential and board review. Alternate procedures providing for arbitration at an earlier stage may be acceptable, provided they ensure faculty participation in a mediative effort prior to formulation of dismissal charges, significant faculty participation in a hearing of such charges, and adherence in the formal hearing to the procedural requirements of academic due process.

Notes

1. AAUP, *Policy Documents and Reports,* 11th ed. (Baltimore: Johns Hopkins University Press, 2015), 327–29.
2. The comments on arbitration of dismissal cases are also applicable to those instances in which an administration seeks not to dismiss but to impose a severe sanction; see Regulation 7a of the Association's

"Recommended Institutional Regulations on Academic Freedom and Tenure," ibid., 85.

3. Ibid., 91–93.

4. See "Statement on Procedural Standards" and Regulation 5b of the "Recommended Institutional Regulations on Academic Freedom and Tenure," ibid., 83.

5. *Labor Arbitration Rules (Including Expedited Labor Arbitration Rules)* (New York: American Arbitration Association), July 1, 2013. https://www.adr.org/cs/idcplg?IdcService=GET_FILE&dDocName=ADRSTAGE2012805&RevisionSelectionMethod=LatestReleased.

Dismissal Proceedings in a Collective Bargaining Setting Where Arbitration Substitutes for a Faculty Hearing

The statement that follows was approved for publication by the Association's Committee A on Academic Freedom and Tenure and the Committee on Representation of Economic and Professional Interests and adopted by the Association's Council in June 1991.

In 1973, the Committee on Academic Freedom and Tenure and the Committee on Representation of Economic and Professional Interests approved the publication of a report on *Arbitration of Faculty Grievances.*[1] The committees viewed that report as a first statement on the relationship of arbitration of faculty grievances to established Association policies. A second report, *Arbitration in Cases of Dismissal,* approved for publication by the Council in June 1983, was prepared in response to the increased acceptance of arbitration as a means of resolving disputes in higher education in the intervening ten years.[2]

The 1983 report emphasized the importance "of the faculty as a professional body passing judgment upon its members." The exercise of such judgment forms an essential aspect of the "traditional shared governance" affirmed in the Association's 1988 *Statement on Academic Government for Institutions Engaged in Collective Bargaining.*[3] The responsibility of exercising collective faculty judgment is most importantly present in the goal of faculty participation in proceedings to dismiss faculty members, a goal stressed in the 1940 *Statement of Principles on Academic Freedom and Tenure.*

The Association recognizes, however, that circumstances may arise in which such participation is not feasible. Where circumstances dictate that arbitration substitute for faculty judgment on issues of faculty dismissal, certain key requirements must be met before the procedures can reasonably be regarded as compatible with basic standards of academic freedom and tenure.

These requirements are:

1. Preliminary Procedures. Designated representatives of the faculty should inquire into the situation informally, may attempt mediation, and, if a mutually acceptable adjustment cannot be effected, may advise the administration on whether formal proceedings should be instituted. The faculty member should not be placed on suspension during the preliminary proceedings or any ensuing formal proceedings unless immediate harm to the faculty member or others is threatened by the faculty member's continuance. Any such suspension should be with pay.

2. Formal Proceedings. Formal proceedings may begin only after the administration has formulated a statement of charges against the faculty member, framed with reasonable particularity.

The process for selecting an arbitrator should ensure the appointment of someone familiar with the standards and practices of the academic community, versed in the meaning of academic freedom, and appreciative of its central value. Tripartite arbitration, in which the arbitrator serves as one member of a hearing panel together with a member of the faculty and a member of the academic administration, may enhance attentiveness to appropriate academic standards.

The arbitration hearing should encourage the inclusion of faculty testimony on disputed matters relating to academic performance and on whether the stated cause, if demonstrated, warrants the penalty of dismissal. The burden of demonstrating adequacy of cause should rest with the administration.

In those dismissal cases where arbitration is the only available forum for a formal proceeding and where the collective bargaining representative decides against going to arbitration, the faculty member should be permitted to proceed to arbitration independently, bearing those costs that the collective bargaining representative would normally assume. The faculty member should have the opportunity to select counsel of his or her choice, at the faculty member's expense.

The proceedings should provide procedural due process as called for in Regulation 5 of the Association's *Recommended Institutional Regulations on Academic Freedom and Tenure*,[4] including the keeping of a verbatim record of the hearing to be made available to the concerned parties and a requirement that the arbitrator's decision be accompanied by a written explanation.

The faculty member's dismissal should not become effective unless and until the arbitrator hands down a decision calling for dismissal.

Whether dismissal proceedings are conducted through a process of faculty hearing or arbitration, cause for dismissal should be decided on the basis of the faculty member's entire record and be related, directly and substantially, to the faculty member's professional fitness as a teacher or researcher; and dismissal after two years of service should, in all cases not involving moral turpitude, be with the affordance of at least one year of terminal notice or severance pay.

Notes

1. AAUP, *Policy Documents and Reports*, 11th ed. (Baltimore: Johns Hopkins University Press, 2015), 327–29.

2. Ibid., 330–33.

3. Ibid., 325–26.

4. Ibid., 83–84.

Work and Family

Upon its reactivation in 1970, the Committee on Women in the Academic Profession identified three policy issues for its immediate attention: antinepotism rules, maternity leaves, and part-time appointments. While the committee's report on the third topic, *Senior Appointments with Reduced Loads*, is included elsewhere in this volume, the two reports in this section build on and extend the initial reports by the committee on the other two topics, which were completed in 1971 and 1974, respectively.

The committee also commented on the absence of women in positions of leadership and on key committees of the Association and made recommendations to address these concerns. Speaking at the end of the first year of the committee's reactivation, its chair, Goucher College sociology professor Alice S. Rossi, made an impassioned plea for the AAUP to address the concerns of academic women with greater urgency. Identifying the issue of affirmative action in addition to the concerns listed above, Rossi noted,

> Up to this point I have reported in formal terms on the work of Committee W, written before coming to this convention. I would like to supplement them with a few additional remarks about events during the convention itself, most importantly concerning the workshop held last night under Committee W sponsorship. The workshop adjourned at 11:30 p.m. but could easily have continued for several more hours, so keen was the interest in and the sense of shared commitment to the issue of academic women. It was a difficult but encouraging experience to chair that meeting, for it helped, more than any experience I have had as chairman of the Committee this year, to dispel the image of AAUP that is held in the world in which I have moved in academe over the past decade—a ponderously slow-moving, tedious establishment with an early twentieth century liberalism that wears thin in the late twentieth century world we live in. It has been a complex first year trying to get accustomed to the structure and procedures of the Association, made tolerable by the conviction I brought to the chairmanship of Committee W that it was a natural springboard for action that is long overdue in behalf of American academic women.

> It was a bracing experience last night to meet women and men from local chapters and conferences and to sense in them the same bitter edge of frustration and impatience I brought to the Committee last fall. While I think the Committee has made progress this year, it has been an uphill battle not always successful in resisting the pressure to be mild and bland in the AAUP style. With the encouragement provided by last night's workshop, I would like to say that I do not think my Committee has fought hard enough in saying loudly and clearly that the time is now past when we can do business as usual in the old familiar ways where the problems facing academic women are concerned.

Yesterday afternoon we spent two hours on the St. John's case, clearly an instance on which the delegates felt strongly about righting the wrongs suffered by twenty-one dismissed faculty members. It was called the most serious case of the decade; if I recall correctly, someone suggested it was the case of the century. I understand a resolution will be presented today protesting the denial of academic freedom to professors in Greece. But, my friends, far more serious denial of rights—in hiring, in salary scale, in promotion—has been a regular, persistent, and continuing experience for thousands of American women in higher education. There are many in this ballroom who could match the St. John's case a dozen times over with equally horrifying experiences that women have had on your faculties over the past hundred years, and which, if anything, are increasing as colleges and universities trim their staffs of their easiest "expendables."

It is not sufficient to say that AAUP stands ready to help in individual cases submitted to Committee A. There are growing numbers of academic women in this Association who are articulately and poignantly angry. *If* AAUP hopes to retain them as members or attract new younger women members, it will have to move at a quicker pace and with firmer commitment than has been its usual style in the past. With the renewed sense of confidence from last night's meeting, I shall in future urge my Committee to step up the pace of its work and sharpen its demands for action by the Association.

As the reports in several sections of this volume show, some of the concerns of academic women have remained the same, while others have changed in response to the growing presence of women in the academic workplace.

Statement of Principles on Family Responsibilities and Academic Work

The statement that follows was approved in May 2001 by the Association's Committee on the Status of Women in the Academic Profession and its Subcommittee on Academic Work and Family. In June 2001 the Association's Committee A on Academic Freedom and Tenure endorsed the substance of this statement. The committee noted that the statement is a departure from the 1940 *Statement of Principles on Academic Freedom and Tenure*, but one that provides an important relief for probationary faculty in their child-rearing years. In November 2001 the AAUP Council adopted this statement as Association policy. Statistical information in the report was updated in 2014.

In 1974 the Association issued a statement, *Leaves of Absence for Child-Bearing, Child-Rearing, and Family Emergencies*,[1] which presciently called for

> [a]n institution's policies on faculty appointments [to be] sufficiently flexible to permit faculty members to combine family and career responsibilities in the manner best suited to them as professionals and parents. This flexibility requires the availability of such alternatives as longer-term leaves of absence, temporary reductions in workload with no loss of professional status, and retention of full-time affiliation throughout the child-bearing and child-rearing years.

Since 1974 there have been significant demographic and legal changes affecting the academic profession. Notably, the percentage of women faculty has increased: in 1975 women made up 22.5 percent of full-time faculty, while in 2000–01, women constituted 36 percent of full-time faculty, according to the AAUP's Annual Report on the Economic Status of the Profession, known as the "salary survey," which is published in the March–April issue of the Association's journal, *Academe*.[2] Many of the policies promoted in the AAUP's 1974 statement are now federal law, such as the Pregnancy Discrimination Act of 1978, which prohibits discrimination based on pregnancy, and the Family and Medical Leave Act of 1993, which provides for up to twelve weeks of unpaid leave a year for employees (women and men) to care for a newborn or a newly adopted child; to care for a parent, spouse, or child with a serious health condition; or to deal with the employee's own serious health condition. Accordingly, the Committee on the Status of Women in the

Academic Profession revisited the 1974 statement to address some of the current issues facing faculty members as they seek to integrate their family obligations and their work responsibilities in today's academic community.

Although increasing numbers of women have entered academia, their academic status has been slow to improve.[3] Women remain disproportionately represented within instructor, lecturer, and unranked positions: more than 57 percent of those holding such positions are women, according to the AAUP's annual salary survey. In contrast, among full professors, only 26 percent are women, and 74 percent are men. Women remain significantly underrepresented at research institutions; this is in stark contrast to their significant representation at community colleges. The proportion of full-time women faculty at two-year institutions increased from 38 percent in 1987 to approximately 50 percent in 1998. At the same time, among full professors at doctoral institutions, the proportion of faculty members who are women is only 19 percent. A salary advantage held by male faculty members over female faculty members exists at all ranks and institutional types. The salary gap is largest at the rank of full professor where, for all institutional types combined, women are paid, on average, only 88 percent of what their male colleagues are paid.[4] Most important, the percentage of women who hold tenured positions remains low. The 2000–01 AAUP salary survey reported that among full-time faculty women, only 48 percent are tenured, whereas 68 percent of full-time men are tenured.

The conflict between work and family obligations that many faculty members experience is more acute for women faculty than for men. Giving birth and raising children are distinctive events. Only women give birth, and it is an event that interrupts the career of a higher percentage of professors than any other "physical disability" or family obligation. Eighty-seven percent of women become parents during their working lives.[5] Pregnancy, childbirth, and child rearing are also age-related, and most commonly occur during the same years that college faculty are seeking tenure in their jobs. In 1995 the average PhD recipient was thirty-four years old.[6] Although many men take substantial responsibility for the care of children, the reality is that women still assume more responsibility for child rearing than do men:

> Raising a child takes 20 years, not one semester. American women, who still do the vast majority of child care, will not achieve equality in academia so long as the ideal academic is defined as someone who takes no time off for child-rearing. With teaching, research, committee assignments, and other responsibilities, pre-tenure academics commonly work many hours of overtime. Defining job requirements in this way tends to eliminate virtually all mothers, so it is not surprising the percentage of tenured women in U.S. colleges and universities has climbed so slowly.[7]

Thus, the development and implementation of institutional policies that enable the healthy integration of work responsibilities with family life in academe require renewed attention.

The Association suggests that the following principles and guidelines be used to construct appropriate policies and practices regarding family leaves, modified teaching schedules, "stopping the tenure clock," and institutional assistance for family responsibilities. The policies fall into two categories: (1) general policies addressing family responsibilities, including family-care leaves and institutional support for child and elder care; and (2) more specific policies, such as stopping the tenure clock, that specifically relate to pretenure faculty members who are primary or coequal caregivers for newborn or newly adopted children, responding to the special and age-related difficulty of becoming a parent during the pretenure years.

Transforming the academic workplace into one that supports family life requires substantial changes in policy and, more significantly, changes in academic culture. These changes require a thorough commitment from the leaders of educational institutions as well as from the faculty.[8] No template of policies fits every institution, but it is essential that the priorities, workloads, rewards structure, and values of the academy permit and support an integration of family and work. Without such support, the commitment to gender equity, for both women and men, will be seriously compromised.

Because of the unique characteristics of academic life, particularly the flexibility of schedules, tremendous potential exists for achieving a healthy work-family integration. At the same time, academic culture poses a special challenge. The lack of a clear boundary in academic lives between work and family has, at least historically, meant that work has been all pervasive, often to the detriment of family. As Lotte Bailyn of the Massachusetts Institute of Technology accurately observed:

> The academic career . . . is paradoxical. Despite its advantages of independence and flexibility, it is psychologically difficult. The lack of ability to limit work, the tendency to compare oneself primarily to the exceptional giants in one's field, and the high incidence of overload make it particularly difficult for academics to find a satisfactory integration of work with private life. . . . It is the unbounded nature of the academic career that is the heart of the problem. Time is critical for professors, because there is not enough of it to do all the things their job requires: teaching, research, and institutional and professional service. It is therefore impossible for faculty to protect other aspects of their lives.[9]

As educational institutions seek to support faculty members in integrating work responsibilities and family life, they should recognize that families are varied and that they change in structure and needs over time. Therefore, institutions should adopt policies that contemplate, for example, the existence of blended families created by divorce and remarriage, and policies that include domestic partners, adopted and foster children, and other household members who live in a family group. Administrators and faculty members should be alert to the many forms that discrimination may take against those with a variety of family responsibilities throughout their careers.

Family-Care and Disability Leaves

Federal and state laws provide for a variety of paid and unpaid leaves for family responsibilities. These legal requirements establish minimum benefits only. The Association encourages institutions to offer significantly greater support for faculty members and other academic professionals with family responsibilities.

Pregnancy Disability Leave

Under the federal Pregnancy Discrimination Act of 1978, which is part of Title VII of the Civil Rights Act of 1964, universities as employers must provide the same disability benefits for pregnancy and childbirth as they provide for any other physical disability. If professors are entitled to paid disability leaves under institutional benefit programs, then women professors are entitled to paid pregnancy leaves. Physicians routinely certify six to eight weeks as the physical disability period for a normal pregnancy and birth. Some states, local governments, and, where applicable, collective bargaining agreements, go beyond federal law and require pregnancy disability leaves regardless of the availability of other disability leaves. The AAUP recommends that all educational institutions offer paid disability leaves for pregnancy.

Family Care Leave

The federal Family and Medical Leave Act (FMLA) requires employers with fifty or more employees to provide unpaid leave to both women and men for care of newborn or newly adopted infants, or for the care of children, spouses, or parents with serious health conditions. Employees can take up to twelve weeks of FMLA leave within a twelve-month period.

Although the FMLA is an important first step, it is inadequate, because it does not require that such family-care leave be paid, and it fails to provide for leave to care for same-sex or other domestic partners, and other ill family members who are not spouses or parents. In addition, the twelve-week annual time limit may, in certain circumstances, be inadequate. (Some states, local governments, and collective bargaining agreements provide more generous family leave.) The Association encourages both public and private educational institutions to go beyond the minimum coverage prescribed by the FMLA and provide also some form of paid family-care leave. (There are a number of ways institutions may finance the cost of family leave. For example, some institutions provide faculty members with the option of using their paid annual or sick leave concurrently with their unpaid leave.)

Emergency Care and Other Short-Term Leave

Family emergencies can be disruptive professionally as well as personally. Nevertheless, they can be accommodated based on familiar models of sick leave. Options include extending sick leave to include leave to care for an ill family member in cases of short-term illnesses not covered by the federal FMLA or other laws. Other alternatives include allowing use of short-term emergency leaves for contingencies connected to unusually adverse weather conditions or other emergency situations, such as the unavailability of usual child- or elder-care services.

Longer-Term Leave for Child Rearing or Other Family Responsibilities

Institutions frequently grant extended unpaid leaves of absence to faculty members for a variety of purposes.[10] Rearing children should be recognized as one appropriate ground for a leave of absence, and such leaves should be available to both men and women on the same terms and conditions as other unpaid leaves of absence. Other family responsibilities, such as caring for an ailing family member, should also be considered a legitimate reason for allowing unpaid leaves of absence.

The timing and duration of such leaves should be determined by mutual agreement between the faculty member and the administration. Faculty members on family leaves should receive consideration with respect to salary increments, insurance coverage, retirement annuities, and the like, comparable to the benefits available to faculty members on other types of unpaid leaves, such as those for public or private service outside the institution. Individual and administrative obligations connected with such leaves, including the timing of a tenure decision, should be those set forth in the applicable provisions of the AAUP's *Statement of Principles on Leaves of Absence* (1972).[11]

In accommodating the family needs of faculty members, whether through paid or unpaid leaves of absence of short or long duration, institutions should be careful in assigning the duties of the faculty member on leave. To avoid creating resentment among faculty members toward the professor on leave, disproportionate burdens should not be placed on other faculty members.

Active Service with Modified Duties

Many institutions of higher education have responded to the need for faculty to take care of newborn or newly adopted children by creating modified duty policies to allow faculty to obtain relief from some teaching or service obligations while remaining in active-service status. Active-service status allows faculty members to continue research or other obligations and receive full pay. For example, the University of California system's "active service–modified duties" policy allows faculty partial or full relief from teaching for one quarter (or semester) if the faculty member has "substantial responsibility" for care of a newborn or newly adopted child under the age of five. This period of modified duties is not considered a leave, and the faculty member receives full pay.[12] Other universities allow faculty to reduce semester- or year-long teaching loads for child-care purposes with proportional reductions in pay.[13]

In 1974 the AAUP recommended in *Leaves of Absence for Child-Bearing, Child-Rearing, and Family Emergencies* that "[t]he alternative of temporarily reduced workload should be available to faculty members with child-rearing responsibilities." Subsequently, in 1987 the AAUP recognized in *Senior Appointments with Reduced Loads*[14] the importance of "policies and practices that open senior academic appointments to persons with reduced loads and salaries without loss of status." The statement acknowledged that such "[m]odified appointments would help meet the special needs of individual faculty members, especially those with child-rearing and other personal responsibilities." The AAUP now recommends that the possibility of appointments with reduced loads be extended to all full-time faculty members, irrespective of their tenure status. The AAUP encourages institutions to explore the possibility of adopting policies providing for short-term periods of modified duties at full pay for family responsibilities.

The Tenure Clock

The resolution of pretenure family-work conflicts is critical to ensuring that academic opportunities are truly equitable. Such conflicts often occur just when the research and publication demands of the tenure process are most onerous, and when many faculty members have responsibilities for infants and young children. Institutions should adopt policies that do not create conflicts between having children and establishing an optimal research record on the basis of which the tenure decision is to be made.

Tenure remains a fundamental requirement for protecting academic freedom. The administration and the faculty of an institution must determine the specific academic standards governing the tenure decision at their institution. Academic standards, however, can and, in this instance, should be distinguished from the amount of time in which an institution's academic standards can be met.[15] Specifically, institutions should allow flexibility in the time period for achieving tenure to enable faculty members to care for newborn or newly adopted children.

A probationary period of seven or fewer years allows faculty members to establish their record for tenure. Historically, this probationary period was based on the assumption that the scholar was male and that his work would not be interrupted

by domestic responsibilities, such as raising children. When the tenure system was created, the male model was presumed to be universal.[16] It was assumed that untenured faculty—whether men or women—were not the sole, primary, or even coequal caretakers of newborn or newly adopted children.[17] An inflexible time factor should not be used to preclude women or men who choose to care for children from pursuing tenure within a reasonable period of years. One study found that 80 percent of "leadership campuses" enable faculty members to exclude a certain amount of probationary time for specific reasons, such as the birth or adoption of a child.[18]

The 1974 AAUP statement *Leaves of Absence for Child-Bearing, Child-Rearing, and Family Emergencies* provided for "stopping the tenure clock" for purposes of child bearing or rearing when a professor takes a full or partial leave of absence, paid or unpaid. The AAUP now recommends that, upon request, a faculty member be entitled to stop the clock or extend the probationary period, with or without taking a full or partial leave of absence, if the faculty member (whether male or female) is a primary or coequal caregiver of newborn or newly adopted children.[19] Thus, faculty members would be entitled to stop the tenure clock while continuing to perform faculty duties at full salary. The AAUP recommends that institutions allow the tenure clock to be stopped for up to one year for each child, and further recommends that faculty be allowed to stop the clock only twice, resulting in no more than two one-year extensions of the probationary period.[20] These extensions would be available whether or not the faculty member was on leave.

In extending the probationary period in recognition of the time required for faculty members to care for newborn or newly adopted children, institutional policies should clearly provide that the tenure candidate be reviewed under the same academic standards as a candidate who has not extended the probationary period.[21] Institutions should guard against imposing greater demands on a faculty tenure candidate as a consequence of his or her having extended the absolute time from the year of appointment to the year of tenure review.[22] To ensure that any modification of the probationary time limits does not create or perpetuate historic gender discrimination, administrations should monitor tenure decisions to ensure that different standards are not imposed in practice through the application of policies that appear neutral. Institutions should also take care to see that faculty members are not penalized in any way for requesting and receiving extensions of the probationary period.

When a faculty member requests and receives an extension of the probationary period, the appropriate university official should clearly inform the faculty member, in writing, that existing academic standards will govern the future tenure decision. Administrators and faculty members are encouraged to disseminate the stop-the-tenure-clock policy widely, and to monitor the policy's use by both women and men.

The stopping of the tenure clock should be in the form of a clear entitlement under institutional policies, rather than in the form of an individually negotiated agreement or informal practice. Written employment policies designed to support the raising of children should not create a separate "track" that may stigmatize faculty members. Studies of junior tenure-track faculty indicate that the pressures result not only from time demands created by conflicting responsibilities, but also from uncertain or conflicting expectations on the part of senior faculty concerning the standards for tenure. On some campuses, an implicit model of total dedication still exists, requiring faculty members to demonstrate that work is one's primary, even sole, commitment. Such expectations must be clarified and modified to recognize the realities of the lives of faculty members who wish to raise children while pursuing an academic career.[23]

Additional Institutional Support
Child Care
Although many institutions recognize the need for child care, fewer offer or subsidize it.[24] The AAUP recommends an institutional commitment to the provision of quality child care for the children of faculty and other academic professionals. As with other benefits, recommendations on the extent and form of such institutional support (whether through subsidized on-campus care or through a benefit plan) should be sought from an appropriate body of the faculty in consultation with other groups on campus, such as staff and students.

Child care is an issue for both men and women. The AAUP believes that for faculty members with child-rearing responsibilities to participate successfully in teaching, research, and service to their institution, they must have access to quality child-care facilities. Furthermore, the availability of child care is a crucial issue in recruiting and retaining faculty. Employers in and out of academe have found that the provision of on-site facilities has led to stronger and more contented families and increased productivity.[25] Some of the benefits that accrue for faculty parents from child-care arrangements on campus include the ability to be reached easily in an emergency, the time and money saved in transportation, and the opportunity to share an occasional lunch or other daytime activity with their children. Faculty members derive peace of mind from knowing that their children are receiving quality care and that the facility has long-term stability. If the institution has an early childhood education program, the opportunity to use the facility for training students provides an additional benefit and contributes to high standards of child care.

Universities and colleges should assume a share of the responsibility for the provision of child-care services. Some institutions, because of their size or other considerations, may choose not to support on-site child care. Such institutions should explore alternatives, such as cooperative arrangements with other nearby employers, resource and referral services, and financial assistance.

Elder and Other Family Care
Increasingly, faculty members are called upon to care for elderly parents and other family members. This tends to be more characteristic of mid-career or senior faculty than of junior faculty.[26] Some faculty members may also be "sandwiched" between responsibilities for children and parents at the same time.

Just as the Association recommends an institutional commitment to providing quality child care, it also strongly recommends an institutional commitment to supporting faculty members in providing quality care to elderly parents or to other family members. Colleges and universities should consider affording financial support to faculty members to cover expenses necessary to allow family members to attend existing centers and programs that provide for elder care or the care of family members with special needs. Institutions should consider providing benefit plans that afford faculty members various options in meeting their family responsibilities.

Flexible Work Policies and Schedules
In addition to formal leave policies, faculty members and academic professionals should have flexibility in scheduling to enable them to respond to family needs as they arise. Flexible work policies allow faculty members to participate in a child's scheduled school activities or to handle the conflicts between school and academic calendars. Colleges and universities should, to the extent possible, coordinate academic-year calendars with

other local educational institutions, or provide child-care support when conflicts occur.[27]

Both child and other family-care needs of faculty members should be included among the many legitimate considerations in scheduling classes, meetings, and other faculty obligations.[28] Likewise, institutional financial support for the expenses of providing substitute care should be considered when faculty members attend professional conferences.

Conclusion

Because institutional policies may be easier to change than institutional cultures, colleges and universities should monitor the actual use of their policies over time to guarantee that every faculty member—regardless of gender—has a genuine opportunity to benefit from policies encouraging the integration of work and family responsibilities. The goal of every institution should be to create an academic community in which all members are treated equitably, families are supported, and family-care concerns are regarded as legitimate and important.

A more responsive climate for integrating work and family responsibilities is essential for women professors to participate on an equal basis with their male colleagues in higher education. Recognizing the need for broader and more inclusive policies represents a historic moment of change. The Association encourages both women and men to take advantage of legal and institutional change so that all faculty members may participate more fully in the care of their children, and may provide the necessary care for parents and other family members.

Notes

1. *AAUP Bulletin* 60 (June 1974): 164–65.

2. In data collected for the 2013–14 AAUP report, women made up 43 percent of all full-time faculty members (John W. Curtis and Saranna Thornton, "Losing Focus: The Annual Report on the Economic Status of the Profession, 2013–14," *Academe* 100 [March–April 2014]: 35, survey report, Table 12).

3. Robin Wilson, "Percentage of Part-Timers on College Faculties Holds Steady after Years of Big Gains," *Chronicle of Higher Education*, April 23, 2001. According to the 2013–14 AAUP report, women held exactly 57 percent of full-time instructor, lecturer, and unranked faculty positions. Women were 29 percent of full professors overall, and 24 percent of full professors at doctoral universities. Among the full-time faculty members in associate's degree (or "two-year") colleges, 53 percent were women (John W. Curtis and Saranna Thornton, "Losing Focus: The Annual Report on the Economic Status of the Profession, 2013–14," *Academe* 100 [March–April 2014]: 35, survey report, Table 12).

4. Marcia Bellas, *AAUP Faculty Salary and Faculty Distribution Fact Sheet*, 2000–2001 (April 2001). Data from the 2013–14 AAUP report show that women full-time faculty members continue to experience a salary disadvantage at all ranks and all types of institutions. The salary gap remains largest at the rank of full professor, with women receiving salaries that are 87 percent of those of men (survey report: 26, Table 5). Tenure rates for both men and women have declined since 2000–2001, but the gender gap remains: 45 percent of women full-time faculty members have tenure, compared with 62 percent of men (survey report: 34, Table 1).

5. Jane Waldfogel, "The Effect of Children on Women's Wages," *American Sociological Review* 62 (1997): 209. Similarly, 81 percent of men become fathers at some point in their lives. See Nancy E. Dowd, *Redefining Fatherhood* (New York: New York University Press, 2000), 22. Men, however, do not give birth, and some become fathers at later ages, some even after retirement.

6. Robert Drago and Joan Williams, "A Half-Time Tenure-Track Proposal," *Change* (November–December 2000): 47–48. In 2012, the median age for doctorate recipients was 31.8 years ("Survey of Earned Doctorates, 2012," National Science Foundation, http://www.nsf.gov/statistics/srvydoctorates/, Table 27).

7. Ibid.

8. Cornell University provides an example of such an institutional commitment: "Cornell University is committed to policies, practices, and programs supportive of the members of its diverse community as they traverse the interlocking worlds of work and family. The University encourages, at all levels, an environment which is supportive of and sensitive to the needs and mutual dependence of the workplace and working families."

9. Lotte Bailyn, *Breaking the Mold: Women, Men, and Time in the New Corporate World* (New York: Free Press, 1993), 51.

10. This section incorporates portions of the text of the AAUP's 1974 "Leaves of Absence for Child-Bearing, Child-Rearing, and Family Emergencies."

11. AAUP, *Policy Documents and Reports*, 11th ed. (Baltimore: Johns Hopkins University Press, 2015), 317–18.

12. Similarly, the School of Science at the Massachusetts Institute of Technology provides that the school "will normally offer a one-semester release from teaching and administrative activities at full pay to faculty members who act as the primary caretaker at home for a new child." The University of Michigan also provides for "modified duties for childbearing," which

> enable a faculty member to recover fully from the effects of pregnancy and childbirth by allowing a pregnant faculty member, on request to her dean, [to] be granted a period of modified duties without a reduction in salary. At a minimum, modified duties means relief from direct teaching responsibilities for the academic term that includes the actual sick leave time the faculty member expects to take in connection with the birth. This policy is available to non-tenured as well as tenured faculty, but

is available only in conjunction with pregnancy or childbirth. The tenure clock is not stopped during the period of modified duties unless the faculty member also has an appointment of less than 80 percent during the time she is on modified duties.

13. For example, the Wayne State University AAUP-AFT collective bargaining agreement (1999b–2002) provides for modified duty assignments at full or partial pay, depending on whether a full or reduced teaching load is arranged.

14. *Policy Statements and Reports*, 169.

15. The AAUP statement "On Crediting Prior Service Elsewhere as Part of the Probationary Period," ibid., 167–68, recognizes that "in specific cases the interests of all parties may best be served through agreement at the time of initial appointment to allow for more than four years of probationary service at the current institution (but not exceeding seven years), whatever the prior service elsewhere." Just as adjustments may be made to the probationary clock regarding prior service, so, too, should institutional policies allow for adjustment of the probationary period for the "specific cases" of faculty members who are primary or coequal caregivers to newborn or newly adopted children.

16. As Susan Kolker Finkel and Steven G. Olswang have noted, the traditional tenure system was based on a model designed for men who were professors with wives at home caring for children. See Finkel and Olswang, "Child Rearing as a Career Impediment to Women Assistant Professors," *Review of Higher Education* 19 (1996): 130. Accordingly, few of the early women professors married or had children. See Jessie Bernard, *Academic Women* (University Park: Pennsylvania State University Press, 1964). In 1973 the Carnegie Commission on Higher Education wrote,

> Probably the most serious handicap facing married women desirous of a teaching career in higher education, especially in research-oriented universities, is that in the very age range in which men are beginning to achieve a reputation through research and publication, 25 to 35, married women are likely to be bearing and rearing their children.

Opportunities for Women in Higher Education; Their Current Participation, Prospects for the Future, and Recommendations for Actions (New York: McGraw Hill, 1973), 139–40.

17. Nor did the traditional tenure system take into account the increased likelihood of medical problems associated with delayed childbirth or the age-related obstacles to adoption. See Amy Varner, "The Consequences and Costs of Delaying Attempted Childbirth for Women Faculty" (2000), and Joan Yang, "Adoption Issues for Faculty" (2000).

In 1995 the median age for the completion of a PhD was thirty-four, which places the age of tenure at around forty; thus, "[a]sking women to delay having children until such a late age seems unfair and unkind, and involves health and infertility risks." Drago and Williams, "A Half-Time Tenure-Track Proposal."

A recent University of Michigan report found that the university's "women assistant professors were more likely than men either to have children prior to beginning their academic careers or to delay child bearing and rearing until after they receive tenure or until they are well established in their careers." *University of Michigan Faculty Work-Life Study Report* (Ann Arbor: Regents of the University of Michigan, 1999), 18.

In a survey of 124 women assistant professors in 1996, 43 percent viewed time required by children as a serious impediment to tenure; among those with children under age six, the figure rose to 82 percent. Finkel and Olswang, "Child Rearing as a Career Impediment to Women Assistant Professors," 133.

18. "Leadership campuses" are defined as the ninety-four campuses that were in the top 25 percent of respondents to a survey on "family-friendly" policies conducted by the College and University Personnel Association (CUPA). The report found that "these policies were put into effect in order to recognize that circumstances beyond the faculty member's control may hinder the performance of responsibilities such as teaching, research, and service to the school or community." Dana E. Friedman et al., *The College and University Reference Guide to Work-Family Programs* (Washington, DC: CUPA Foundation, 1996), 120.

19. A growing number of institutions of higher learning already provide policies that extend the pretenure clock without requiring the faculty member to be on leave. For example, the University of Michigan faculty handbook provides for automatically stopping the tenure clock upon faculty request for up to one year for child rearing: "The one-year exclusion for pregnancy, childbirth, and related medical conditions is automatic on request, but requests must be made prior to the initiation of the tenure review." Similarly, the University of California policy provides that "the Chancellor may grant to a faculty member who has substantial responsibility for the care of a newborn child or newly adopted child under the age of five up to one year off the tenure clock for each birth or adoption, provided that all time off the tenure clock totals no more than two years. . . . [T]he campus will accept no requests to stop the tenure clock after the tenure review has begun."

20. One survey found that of those higher education institutions that offer "stop-the-tenure-clock" policies, "nine out of ten allow the exclusion of up to two semesters." See Friedman et al., *College and University Reference Guide to Work-Family Programs.* The University System of Georgia recently amended its board of regents policies on tenure to "enhance the family-friendly work environment." In so doing, it adopted a stop-the-tenure-clock policy that provides that "the total time granted for suspension of the tenure clock . . . shall not ordinarily exceed two years."

21. Institutions should inform external reviewers that the candidate's probationary period has been extended under institutional policy and that the candidate's record should be reviewed as if he or she had only the normal probationary period.

22. The *1997–2000 Master Agreement* between Northern Michigan University and the university's AAUP chapter provides that "the taking of [family] leave shall not otherwise prejudice future tenure or promotion consideration." Similarly, Pennsylvania State University's policy provides that a "staying of the provisional tenure period should not penalize or adversely affect the faculty member in the tenure review." In addition, the University of Wisconsin policy provides that if "the faculty member has been in probationary status for more than seven years, the faculty member shall be evaluated as if he or she had been in probationary status for seven years, not longer."

23. Similar requests should be considered during the pre-tenure period. So, for example, requests by tenure-track candidates to extend the time period for a third-year review, because of the birth or adoption of a newborn child for whom he or she is the primary or coequal caregiver, should be considered and, if granted, clearly documented so that the candidate is reviewed under the proper standard.

24. This section incorporates the substance and most of the text of the AAUP's 1989 statement "Faculty Child Care," *Academe* 76 (January–February 1990): 54.

25. In 2001 there were approximately 2,500 campus-based child care centers in the United States, according to the National Coalition for Campus Children's Centers.

26. Elder-care responsibilities appear to fall most heavily on tenured professors, especially tenured women faculty. Thirty-seven percent of employees who assume elder-care responsibilities are fifty or older. See James T. Bond, Ellen Galinksy, and Jennifer E. Swanberg, *1997 National Study of the Changing Workforce* (New York: Families and Work Institute, 1997).

According to the National Academy on Aging, 72.5 percent of all informal caregivers are women. See Amy Varner and Robert Drago, "The Changing Face of Care: The Elderly" (2000). Accordingly, career advancement may be jeopardized by such caregiving responsibilities, including the continued advancement of women faculty. See M. M. Robinson, B. L. Yegidis, and J. Funk, *Faculty in the Middle: The Effects of Family Caregiving in Universities*, Wellesley College Center for Research on Women, Working Paper 296 (Wellesley, 1999).

27. The University Park campus of Pennsylvania State University and the town of State College, for example, coordinate their spring breaks to enable faculty parents to care for their children during the break. See *Final Report to the Alfred P. Sloan Foundation for the Faculty and Families Project*, Pennsylvania State University, Work-Family Working Paper #01-02 (State College, 2001).

28. A 1996 study found that two-thirds of women and close to one-third of men experienced family difficulties when faculty meetings were scheduled after 5 p.m. on weekdays or during the weekend. See Linda P. Fried et al., "Career Development for Women in Academic Medicine," *Journal of the American Medical Association* 276 (September 1996): 898–905.

Recommendations on Partner Accommodation and Dual-Career Appointments

The recommendations that follow were prepared by a subcommittee of the Committee on Women in the Academic Profession and approved by the full committee in April 2010.

Introduction

In 1971, the AAUP issued a statement on *Faculty Appointment and Family Relationship* to address the problem of nepotism rules that prevented immediate family members from serving in the same department or school at many institutions. The statement, prepared by Committee W on the Status of Women in the Academic Profession, called for the elimination of those rules because they were "wholly unrelated to academic qualifications" and limited opportunities for qualified candidates "on the basis of an inappropriate criterion."[1] The committee took issue with nepotism rules because of their disparate impact on women entering the profession who found their path to full-time positions barred by institutional policies based on outdated assumptions regarding faculty couples. In the decades since that statement was issued, the demographics of the academic profession have changed markedly. What might have been a rare occurrence in the 1970s, an academic couple seeking appointments in the same university, or even in the same department, has become much more common. Research has shown that faculty members are increasingly likely to have academic partners, particularly in the case of women academics.[2] In addition, the recognition of domestic partnerships, civil unions, and, in some states, gay marriage, has broadened the definition of the couple beyond the traditional notion of the 1970s.

As a result of this increase in the number of women seeking academic employment, hiring practices have changed markedly, while studies since the 1990s have noted expanding concern over the issue of accommodating the partners of those under consideration for faculty appointments.[3] As a University of Oregon report on dual careers states, "increasingly, university professionals are part of dual-career couples, and this phenomenon has emerged as a critical recruitment and retention issue in higher education," particularly for research universities.[4] Research universities have appointed women as faculty members at significantly lower rates than have other sectors of higher education and may view dual-career accommodation as a key strategy to increase diversity or retain qualified women faculty. Research suggests that faculty members may choose a position based on the availability of assistance for an academic partner or leave a position out of dissatisfaction at the lack of such accommodation. As the Clayman Institute for Gender Research study of faculty appointments at thirteen research universities suggests, "couples more and more vote with their feet, leaving or not considering universities that do not support them."[5] In addition, partner accommodation may be particularly important in "attracting more women to underrepresented fields."[6] As a result, many colleges and universities are wrestling with the issue whether, and, if so, how, to provide partner accommodation.

The AAUP has a long-standing interest in this issue based on its concern for faculty governance, gender equity, and work-family balance. Policies on partner accommodation touch on issues raised in the *Statement of Principles on Family Responsibilities and Academic Work* regarding healthy work-family integration, and the special challenges raised by academic culture.[7] The provision of support for partners has a direct impact on the ability of dual-career academic couples to integrate successful careers with family responsibilities.[8] Thus, assistance for academic partners can be an important part of any work/life balance initiatives. In the absence of such accommodations, academic couples may find themselves faced with long-distance relationships or the subordination of one career to the partner who succeeds in securing a position. Evidence, such as the high proportion of women in part-time and contingent positions, and the relative lack of women in tenure-track positions in research universities, suggests that the lack of such arrangements may be having an adverse impact on the careers of academic women.

The development of sound partner-accommodation policies can benefit significantly from attention to AAUP faculty governance policies, especially those pertaining to faculty appointments. According to the Association's *Statement on Government of Colleges and Universities*, "faculty status and related matters are primarily a faculty responsibility," including appointments and reappointments.[9] Because procedures permitting dual-career appointments may circumvent usual university practices, issues related to faculty responsibility for personnel decisions become paramount. Care should therefore be taken to consult adequately with appropriate faculty bodies. Respect for faculty governance, however, must be balanced against the competing demands of gender equity and work-family balance, which require sensitivity to the needs of dual-career couples. Creating a reasonable compromise between the demands of academic work and family responsibilities can be complicated if one member of a couple either has limited employment options or must seek a job at a distance. These recommendations, therefore, are designed to assist colleges and universities in understanding the complex issues raised by dual-career academic appointments, and to develop equitable policies responsive to changes in academic demographics.

Any institution considering the development of partner-accommodation policies must also consider the potential impact of these policies on collective bargaining agreements. Collective bargaining agreements may, for example, mandate specific search procedures or set strict policies for adding department lines that would limit the options for dual-career appointments. In addition, some institutions may find extensive partner accommodation, especially arrangements involving positions for partners of new appointees, to be difficult given their size, geographic location, or institutional type. A large research university, for example, may have greater ability to find positions for partners than a smaller institution with fewer potential faculty positions or fewer departments and programs.

Types of Partner Accommodation
Many institutions already offer varying types of assistance to dual-career couples including:

Membership in an HERC (Higher Education Recruitment Consortium) or other network: HERCs are formal organizations of area colleges already established in some regions and states, such as Southern California, New England, Missouri, and New Jersey.[10] HERCs provide a variety of services for listing and sharing open positions that can be invaluable in assisting academic partners. HERC membership costs vary by the size of the institution, making this option, where available, particularly useful for smaller institutions without the resources to establish a partner-accommodation program. Institutions may also establish less formal networks for information sharing about openings at nearby colleges and universities or in local businesses and non-profit organizations. Such arrangements represent the least controversial option for offering accommodation to academic partners, and may be particularly useful for those colleges and universities that are unable to offer extensive assistance because of limited resources. In some regions, however, the lack of urban concentrations or the absence of nearby universities may make these options less workable.

Assistance for relocating partners: Human resource offices or specialized partner-assistance offices can also provide help with résumés and interview preparation as well as provide other assistance to relocating partners such as identifying child-care facilities or assisting with locating housing. Such help can ease the transition to a new region.

Bridging positions: Some institutions offer the possibility of a "bridging" position or a temporary fellowship to allow the institution time to identify a full-time line or to provide short-term support while a partner searches for a position.[11] These can be particularly useful for academic partners because of the timetable of faculty searches. Such positions should be clearly described as temporary so as not to raise expectations about the provision of permanent employment.

Provision of a permanent position for a faculty partner: An institutional offer of a new tenure-track (or equivalent position) line for a partner has been called the "holy grail of dual-career accommodation."[12] In other cases, an institution may offer full- or part-time contingent positions to the partners of newly appointed faculty. At least one study has shown that faculty members with positions at the same institution may experience greater satisfaction and find it easier to balance work and family responsibilities, making this option attractive from the candidate's perspective.[13] Such positions, however, while providing the most direct assistance for dual-career couples can also present problems for both the institution and the newly appointed faculty member. Of particular concern is any policy that would increase the number of faculty on contingent appointments for the sake of partner accommodation, or that would limit the benefits or the opportunities for promotion for those partners appointed under such arrangements.

Assistance to graduate students: When the partner is completing graduate studies, an institution can provide teaching opportunities, library privileges, or other assistance toward completing the degree. This is temporary assistance, however, and may not satisfy the long-term needs of a dual-career couple.

Shared positions: In this type of arrangement, partners share a tenure-track position with defined responsibilities for teaching, research, and service. The shared position may be 100 percent or more of a full-time position with, for example, each partner appointed at 50 percent of a full-time position, or perhaps an arrangement in which one partner is appointed at 60 percent and the other at 50 percent for a slightly more than full-time position. This form of accommodation, however, is usually limited in its applicability to those faculty members in the same or closely related disciplines, and for those who do not require two full-time salaries. Because the tendency among academics to form couples based upon similar or related areas of specialization appears to be on the rise, shared position may become even more desirable in the near future.

Both shared positions and dual-career appointments can present problems. The most important considerations when devising shared-position arrangements involve treating the faculty members as individuals who are equally eligible for benefits, and opportunities for tenure and promotion. With respect to shared tenure-track positions, institutions must carefully define responsibilities and standards for evaluation so that individuals are not treated differently from other faculty because they are in a less-than-full-time position. Potential problems with shared positions must also be considered carefully, including the possibilities of a split tenure decision denying tenure to one partner, while granting it to the other, the departure of one member of the couple to assume a position at a different institution, or the couple's separation or divorce.

Clearly, different accommodation policies offer potential benefits but also present potential problems. We recognize that careful study and due consideration are required to develop policies regarding shared positions and dual-career appointments. Most institutions, however, could provide partner accommodation through assistance with the job search, or access to university resources for graduate study, both of which involve fewer resources and less potential controversy.

Developing Policies for Dual-Career Appointments

The offer of a tenure-track position to the partner of a job candidate is often the most satisfactory solution from the candidate's point of view. Such positions may also present benefits to the institution. Some universities have identified dual-career accommodation as an opportunity to enhance their programs. At Princeton University, Professor Joan Girgus, special assistant to the dean of faculty, has stated: "At Princeton, we recruit families, not individuals," giving the accommodation of faculty couples a central place in the university's faculty recruitment program.[14] The University of Northern Arizona Partner Assistance Program noted that "implementation of a dual-career program is crucial to successful recruitment and retention of employees."[15] Institutions have also argued that such policies are important to ensure competitiveness in hiring the best talent or to ensure gender and/or ethnic diversity. The Harvard Task Force on Women, for example, recommended establishment of a "Dual-Career Program" as one way to increase progress toward gender equity and diversity.[16] A 2008 report by the University Committee on Women Faculty and Students at the University of Notre Dame noted that exit interviews with female faculty members leaving the institution often cited "spousal hiring issues" as important in their decisions.[17] In the sciences, where gender equity has been particularly difficult to achieve, partner appointments may prove a useful tool.[18]

Such offers, however, need to be made carefully, since the method of proceeding with a dual-career appointment is crucial to its success, and the timeframe for such offers is often limited. Universities will thus benefit from carefully thought-out policies that can serve as applicable guidelines for dual-career faculty appointments, rather than attempt to make arrangements on a case-by-case basis. Also institutions with collective bargaining agreements will have to reconcile any procedures with contractual language on searches or modify those agreements.

Partner-accommodation policies that involve additional faculty lines or replacement of existing contingent positions may present other difficulties that must be anticipated. Most commonly cited are problems within departments that are pressured to accept the appointment of a faculty partner. Individuals appointed under such difficult circumstance may feel marginalized by their new departments, or face difficulties achieving tenure or promotion because of lingering resentment over the initial appointment procedures. This problem can be exacerbated if the position takes funding away from other departmental priorities or when the partner appointment replaces a long-serving faculty member on a contingent appointment. A proposal from the ADVANCE (Increasing the Participation and Advancement of Women in Academic Science and Engineering Careers) Working Group of the Earth Institute at Columbia University points out that "[a]ttempts to accommodate partners can be futile if the partner does not feel wanted by the institution."[19] Additional problems may arise when the partner appointed is referred to as a "trailing spouse," or in other ways as a less-qualified adjunct to a faculty "star." Much of the resistance to partner accommodation is based on a perceived threat to the "quality" of faculty appointments.[20] When the accommodated partner is a woman, the circumstances of appointment can exacerbate potential gender bias. The best safeguard against a proliferation of complaints regarding partner accommodation arrangements is the observance of well-considered and consistently applied policies relevant to all qualified candidates without regard for faculty rank or status. Special emphasis should be placed on respecting the rights of long-serving faculty members on contingent appointments. Every effort should be made not to replace a contingent faculty position with a partner accommodation appointment.

Recommendations on Dual-Career Appointments

This document provides guidelines on developing policies on partner accommodation, but it is not necessarily an endorsement of a particular policy or of the practice of dual-career appointments as appropriate for all institutions. Such programs are becoming more common in research universities where women have been consistently underrepresented among the tenure-track and tenured faculty. On the other hand, accommodating dual-career couples may be problematic for smaller institutions or those with collective bargaining agreements. It is important to note that many universities have search and/or affirmative-action procedures that would prevent any modification of the formal appointment process, thereby making a quick decision on a dual-career appointment impossible.[21] In all cases, partner-accommodation policies must meet the strictest tests for transparency and good governance practices.

- Institutions that provide any form of partner accommodation should have a clearly worded policy that covers all full-time appointments rather than rely upon ad hoc arrangements available only on select bases. Such policies should also be available to all couples, not just those in heterosexual marriages.
- Such policies should be developed by appropriate faculty bodies or committees, not by the administration in the absence of meaningful faculty participation. The process for developing such procedures is arguably as important as the procedures themselves, and must take into account local conditions and institutional particularities.
- Policies should address important issues such as the process by which decisions on dual-career appointments are reached, and the budgetary impact of those decisions. They should also include provision for maintaining open communication with the prospective faculty members, who should be kept informed of the process, and for adequate consultation on the arrangements with the department, if the latter is not directly responsible for employment negotiations.
- All appointment decisions should be made as part of a process driven by consideration of merit. Faculty appointed under accommodation policies should be subject to the same evaluative procedures as all other faculty members.
- Departments asked to consider a dual-career appointment must be permitted to follow reasonable departmental hiring procedures, and must be free to refuse the appointment. Potential accommodation appointments must consider departmental hiring priorities and programmatic needs.
- Normal search procedures may have to be modified to take into account the limited time frame for making an offer to a candidate's partner. Such modifications should not, however, infringe upon good governance practices or limit faculty involvement in the search process nor should they violate campus affirmative-action policies. Collective bargaining agreements may need to be modified to accommodate dual-career appointments, and the impact on those agreements should be considered carefully.
- Whenever possible, appointments should be made to tenure-track positions. Dual-career appointments should not be the occasion for increasing the number of faculty members on contingent appointments at an institution.

- Every effort should be made not to replace faculty members on contingent appointments with partner-accommodation appointees.
- Information on these policies should be made available to all candidates for faculty positions as a regular part of the recruitment process. Discrimination guidelines limit questioning candidates about their marital and family status, but candidates should be made aware of campus policies so they can raise the issue.
- Policies should leave the question of initiating discussions of dual-career appointments up to the candidate to avoid intrusive and possibly illegal inquiries about a candidate's family situation. Institutions can, however, make information about an institution's dual-career policies readily available on a website or in a brochure given to all candidates to encourage these discussions to occur in a timely manner. Once a candidate has inquired about the possibility of dual-career accommodation, however, that inquiry should not be used as an excuse to eliminate the candidate from consideration for the position.
- Universities may find it preferable to have a third party handle the negotiations for dual-career appointments, rather than have the arrangements directly negotiated by department chairs who may not be fully aware of the procedures and issues involved, in which case chairs should be kept fully informed of the progress of negotiations. Such a third party could be a designated individual within the administration or a specific office within the university.[22]
- Funding for any dual-career appointment should be clearly accounted for and consonant with institutional conditions and budgetary requirements.
- Dual-career appointment procedures should be evaluated regularly, and data collected frequently, to provide an objective basis for subsequent modifications to the policies, and so that these evaluations do not depend upon anecdotal evidence.
- Institutions should take every care to ensure that faculty members appointed as part of a dual-career arrangement are treated as separate individuals valuable in their own right.

Underlying all of these recommendations are some basic principles that institutions should keep in mind. According to the AAUP's *Statement on the Ethics of Recruitment and Faculty Appoint-*ments, the principle of "openness and shared responsibility" should inform all policies. Where partners are appointed to the same department, "reasonable restrictions" on the role of an immediate family member should apply, particularly in areas where conflicts of interest may arise, such as evaluation for tenure or promotion, setting of salaries, or, more generally, where one partner is in a position to serve as "judge or advocate" of a family member.[23] Appropriate safeguards must also be put in place should one partner become chair of a department in which his/her partner holds an appointment. Universities establishing such positions should also be clear about state nepotism laws, as well as be cognizant of Association-recommended standards and procedures as set forth in the 1940 *Statement of Principles on Academic Freedom and Tenure* and the applicable provisions of the *Recommended Institutional Regulations on Academic Freedom and Tenure.*[24]

In sum, these recommendations call for policies that balance the needs of departments and institutions with the needs of faculty members. Individual faculty appointments, above all, should be based on the candidate's potential contribution to the position, the department, and the institution. Sensitivity to work/life balance must also be tempered by attention to good governance and the protections of tenure.

Notes

1. "Faculty Appointment and Family Relationship," *AAUP Bulletin* 57 (June 1971): 221.

2. See for example, Londa Schiebinger, Andrea Davies Henderson, and Shannon K. Gilmartin, *Dual-Career Academic Couples: What Universities Need to Know* (Stanford: Michelle R. Clayman Institute for Gender Research, Stanford University, 2008), 4; and Lisa E. Wolf-Wendel, Susan Twombly, and Suzanne Rice, "Dual-Career Couples: Keeping Them Together," *Journal of Higher Education* 71 (May–June 2000): 291–321.

3. See, for example, Carla Hesse, "Do We Need a Spousal/Partner Hiring Policy? An Open Forum Sponsored by the Committee on Women Historians," *Perspectives on History* 36 (May 1998). They noted that "departments are engaging in heated debates over this issue; they are improvising and regularly express the need for guidance from the AHA" about partner-accommodation policies. The best introduction to this issue is Lisa Wolf-Wendel, Susan B. Twombly, and Suzanne Rice, *The Two-Body Problem: Dual-Career Couple Hiring Practices in Higher Education* (Baltimore: Johns Hopkins University Press, 2003).

4. University of Oregon, "Dual Career Guidelines," http://ups.uoregon.edu/node/61.

5. *Dual-Career Academic Couples*, 2.

6. Ibid., 74.

7. "Statement of Principles on Family Responsibilities and Academic Work," AAUP, *Policy Documents and Reports*, 11th ed. (Baltimore: Johns Hopkins University Press, 2015), 339–46.

8. For results of one study suggesting this, see Elizabeth M. O'Laughlin and Lisa G. Bischoff, "Balancing Parenthood and Academia: Work/Family Stress as Influenced by Gender and Tenure Status," *Journal of Family Issues* 26 (January 2005): 101–2.

9. *Policy Documents and Reports*, 121.

10. For information on New Jersey–Eastern Pennsylvania–Delaware HERC, for example, see http://www.hercjobs.org/nj_east_pa_delaware, and for the New England HERC, see http://www.hercjobs.org/new_england. The national HERC site can be found at http://www.hercjobs.org. HERC websites also have links to additional resources and research material on dual-career issues.

11. See, for example, the Partner Opportunities Program, begun at UC Davis in the mid-1990s (http://popprogram.ucdavis.edu), and the Faculty Fellowship Program at the University of Oregon, "Dual Career Guidelines."

12. *Two-Body Problem*, 103.

13. Robin Wilson, "Academic Couples Said to Be Happier Working at Same University," *Chronicle of Higher Education*, August 2, 2002, A12; the study conducted by Cornell University's Careers Institute was entitled "Intimate Academics: Co-Working Couples in Two American Universities."

14. Joan Girgus, "Dual Career Academic Couples at Princeton." Talk at Dual-Career Academic Couples Conference: Strategies & Opportunities, Clayman Institute for Gender Research, Stanford University, Palo Alto, CA, June 2009.

15. University of Northern Arizona, "Partner Assistance Program," http://hr.nau.edu/node/2277.

16. "Harvard Task Forces on Women Release Findings and Recommendations," *Harvard Gazette*, May 16, 2005, http://news.harvard.edu/gazette/story/2005/05/harvard-task-forces-on-women-release-findings-and-recommendations/.

17. University Committee on Women Faculty and Students, University of Notre Dame, "Enhancing the Recruitment and Retention of Female Faculty: A Comprehensive Report," Spring 2008, http://president.nd.edu/assets/4766/ucwfs_final_report_publish_version.pdf.

18. For a discussion of this issue in one science field where gender equity is a problem, see Marc Sher, "Dual-Career Couples—Problem or Opportunity," *CSWP Gazette: The Newsletter of the Committee on the Status of Women in Physics of the American Physical Society* 25 (Fall 2006): 1.

19. Earth Institute ADVANCE Working Group on Science & Technology Recruiting to Increase Diversity, Columbia University, "A Proposal for Recruiting and Retaining Dual-Career Couples," issued October 7, 2005, http://www.hercjobs.org/metro_ny_southern_ct/_template_assets/docs/Earthinstitute.pdf.

20. For a discussion of some of these issues, see Robin Wilson, "The Backlash against Hiring Couples," *Chronicle of Higher Education*, April 13, 2001, A16; and Joseph Kay (pseud.), "Too Many Couples," Chronicle Careers, *Chronicle of Higher Education*, April 9, 2007, http://chronicle.com/article/Too-Many-Couples/46466.

21. Open search requirements were first mandated under federal affirmative-action programs beginning in the 1970s in order to open up the faculty hiring process so that white women and women and men of color had a better opportunity to compete for faculty positions. Under Federal Executive Order 11246, colleges and universities that receive federal funds are still required to maintain affirmative-action programs, and research universities continue to have numerous goals to appoint more women and minority faculty. Under these campus programs a search may be waived if the potential appointee will meet an affirmative-action "goal." Because women continue to be underrepresented on the faculties of research universities, search requirements are sometimes waived in order to accommodate dual-career couples.

22. Many institutions with dual-career hiring policies use the provost's office for coordinating such offers, but a few have separate dual-career offices that perform this service.

23. "The Ethics of Recruitment and Faculty Appointments," *Policy Documents and Reports*, 155–56.

24. Ibid., 79–90.

Discrimination

The Association's official concern with issues of discrimination can be traced to 1918 and the establishment of a committee charged with "investigat[ing] and report[ing] upon . . . the present or the desirable status of women in college and university faculties." That committee issued two reports and then fell into a period of quiescence. The reactivation of that committee in 1970, now called the Committee on Women in the Academic Profession, and the creation a year later of a special Council Committee on Discrimination, marked the start of an active program "against invidious distinctions based on . . . nonrelevant characteristics" of various sorts. As the Council Committee stated in its initial report, it was calling on the Association, and through it the academic community, to "expand its traditional concern for the freedom of academics to include explicitly concern for the opportunity to be an academic."

Reflecting positions taken by successive annual meetings, the Association's Council in 1976 adopted a brief formal statement, *On Discrimination*, modified in 1994 and further in 1995:

> The Association is committed to use its procedures and to take measures, including censure, against colleges and universities practicing illegal or unconstitutional discrimination, or discrimination on a basis not demonstrably related to the job function involved, including, but not limited to, age, sex, disability, race, religion, national origin, marital status, or sexual orientation.

Primarily through the Committee on Women in the Academic Profession and Committee A on Academic Freedom and Tenure, the Association has developed and issued several policy statements and reports that address potential inequities and discriminatory treatment facing faculty members in colleges and universities. The documents in this section include procedural standards for processing complaints of discrimination and recommended criteria and procedures for advancing affirmative action and for dealing with sexual harassment and sexual assault. The *Recommended Institutional Regulations on Academic Freedom and Tenure*, found in an earlier section, provide safeguards of academic due process to those making allegations of discrimination (see, in particular, Regulations 10 and 16).

On Processing Complaints of Discrimination

This report, a revision of a report originally adopted in 1977, was approved by the Association's Committee A on Academic Freedom and Tenure and adopted by the Association's Council in November 1991. It was endorsed by the Seventy-Eighth Annual Meeting in June 1992.

Introduction

The Association has, through its statement *On Discrimination*, declared its opposition to improper discrimination in colleges and universities and has resolved to work toward correcting inequities:

> The Association is committed to use its procedures and to take measures, including censure, against colleges and universities practicing illegal or unconstitutional discrimination, or discrimination on a basis not demonstrably related to the job function involved, including, but not limited to, age, sex, disability, race, religion, national origin, marital status, or sexual orientation.[1]

With respect to procedures within colleges and universities suitable for identifying and processing complaints of discrimination in a decision against reappointment, the Association, in Regulation 10 of its *Recommended Institutional Regulations on Academic Freedom and Tenure*, sets forth the following provisions:

> If a faculty member on probationary or other nontenured appointment alleges that a decision against reappointment was based significantly on considerations that violate (a) academic freedom or (b) governing policies on making appointments without prejudice with respect to race, sex, religion, national origin, age, disability, marital status, or sexual orientation, the allegation will be given preliminary consideration by the [insert name of committee], which will seek to settle the matter by informal methods. The allegation will be accompanied by a statement that the faculty member agrees to the presentation, for the consideration of the faculty committee, of such reasons and evidence as the institution may allege in support of its decision. If the difficulty is unresolved at this stage, and if the committee so recommends, the matter will be heard in the manner set forth in Regulations 5 and 6, except that the faculty member making the complaint is responsible for stating the grounds upon which the allegations are based, and the burden of proof will rest upon the faculty member. If the faculty member succeeds in establishing a prima facie case, it is incumbent upon those who made the decision against reappointment to come forward with evidence in support of their decision. Statistical evidence of improper discrimination may be used in establishing a prima facie case.[2]

This report examines evidentiary issues of proof of discrimination and provides guidance to faculty, administrators, and the Association's staff on handling complaints raising claims of discrimination. While the report was drafted specifically to address allegations of discrimination on the basis of sex, it has over the years proven useful for complaints of improper discrimination based on other attributes as well.

The Nature of Sex-Discrimination Claims

Sex discrimination can occur at every stage of decision making in an individual's teaching career (e.g., entry, salary, fringe benefits, assignments, academic rank, reappointment, tenure, and retirement). At each stage, some complaints of sex discrimination may be accompanied by supporting evidence of a relatively conventional kind. More often than not, however, sex-discrimination claims present the special difficulty of proving motivation.

1. The Importance of Motivation

Most complaints involving sex discrimination require proof of an improper motive for an otherwise proper action. The need to assess motivation in processing complaints is not limited to those alleging sex discrimination. Many other complaints involving a faculty member's status, such as allegations that the faculty member's appointment was not renewed for reasons violative of academic freedom or that a termination for financial exigency was in bad faith, rest upon demonstration of improper motivation. To a significant extent, evidence to support allegations of sex discrimination must be sought in much the same way as in other complaints of violations of Association-supported standards. Proving improper motivation can, however, be more difficult in the area of sex discrimination, because it is the kind of discrimination that often relates to who a person is rather than to what a person says or does.[3] In a complaint involving academic freedom, for example, the complainant will generally assert that the adverse action which allegedly constitutes a violation of academic freedom is in retaliation for something the complainant did or said and that, but for the protected speech or conduct, the adverse action would not have occurred. Sex discrimination, on the other hand, may not result from anything someone says or does. The involuntary characteristic of sex may itself motivate discrimination. It is difficult in such circumstances to point to an "incident" to which the alleged discrimination can be traced, a fact which ordinarily makes proof of discrimination much more elusive.

Principles and standards relating to academic freedom, moreover, have gained more widespread acceptance in the academic community than any analogous principles and standards in the area of sex discrimination in academic life. Consequently, it seems reasonable to anticipate that some faculty members and administrative officers may be less sensitive to, and less supportive of, complaints of sex discrimination than experience has shown them to be concerning complaints raising issues of academic freedom.

2. Evidence of Sex Discrimination

Ascertaining whether improper motive was involved in a given case becomes more manageable when the general search for bias is made more concrete. The categories listed below are intended to specify the types of evidence from which sex discrimination can be inferred. While descriptive, they are not intended to be exhaustive.

These categories consist, in general, of evidence specifically related to sex, and evidence reflecting general institutional deficiencies not specifically related to sex. Direct evidence of sexual bias and unequal application of standards are examples of evidence specifically related to sex. Vague criteria for appointment and promotion, failure to give reasons for nonrenewal upon the faculty member's request, inadequate grievance mechanisms, and deviations from procedures normally employed by an institution are examples of evidence reflecting general deficiencies in procedure. This second type of evidence, while not necessarily as probative of sex discrimination as evidence that is specifically related to sex, might, where there is more direct evidence, be considered part of the totality of circumstances from which sex discrimination can be inferred.

A. DIRECT EVIDENCE OF SEX DISCRIMINATION

Criteria that are themselves discriminatory, and sexist statements or conduct, provide direct evidence of sex discrimination. Criteria used for making decisions in colleges and universities are rarely discriminatory on their face. It is highly unlikely that such criteria would be used to select for or against a sexual characteristic.[4] Sexist statements or conduct, whether or not well intentioned, also constitute direct evidence of sex discrimination, and are much more common than obviously discriminatory criteria. Such evidence would be present, for example, if a member of a tenure committee were to state: "Women make bad engineers," or "I will resign if a woman is granted tenure."

B. UNEQUAL APPLICATION OF STANDARDS

Unequal treatment of men and women provides one of the most telling forms of evidence of sex discrimination. A criterion might be applied to a member of one sex but not to a similarly situated member of the opposite sex; or the same criterion might be applied more rigorously to a member of one sex than to a similarly situated member of the opposite sex. For example, a woman may be denied tenure (1) for lack of a PhD in a department that has recently granted tenure to a man without one; (2) because of "inadequate teaching" when her teaching evaluations are virtually identical to those of a male faculty member who has been granted tenure; or (3) where standards traditionally considered important by the institution would have strongly suggested a different result.

Because sex discrimination is seldom overt, statistical evidence is an essential tool. Statistics may not, alone, establish discrimination, but they can provide an adequate basis for requesting an explanation from the institution. In approving the "relevance of statistics as a means of shifting the burden to come forward with evidence," the Association's Council Committee on Discrimination pointed to the historically effective application of statistics in detecting and remedying racial discrimination in the composition of juries. The committee noted that, because it was virtually impossible to prove that the persistent absence of blacks from juries was the result of discrimination in each particular case, federal courts came to regard the significant disparity in the proportion of blacks on juries as permitting a prima facie inference that racial discrimination was a contributing element. This inference shifted the burden to the state, even though overt discrimination could not be proved in an individual case.

The following types of statistical data, while not individually or collectively determinative, may be meaningful in cases involving allegations of sex discrimination at the college or university level: (1) salary differentials between men and women (comparisons should, where possible, take into account factors such as institution, department, rank, and years of experience); (2) numerical differentials between men and women (comparisons should, where possible, take into account the same factors as in salary differentials, and also tenured or nontenured status); (3) the proportion of women on the faculty in relation to (i) the number of qualified women available for appointment, and (ii) affirmative-action goals; (4) changes in the percentage of women on the faculty; (5) the number and distribution of women on decision-making bodies; and (6) differential promotion and tenuring rates. The Association should intensify its work in gathering and developing such statistical data to the extent that they are not already available from other sources.

C. GENERAL DEFICIENCIES IN PROCEDURE
The general deficiencies in procedure summarized above are familiar to the Association's work. The operating assumption that procedural irregularities often indicate substantive violations has guided traditional Committee A work. The Association, when presenting its concern about an academic freedom case to administrative officers, often refers to inadequate evaluation procedures and provisions for due process, the failure to state reasons for nonreappointment, or the statement of vague reasons, as increasing its concern.[5] The Association, on occasion, has also expressed concern over a substantive decision that is an inexplicable departure from results generally reached in similar circumstances. The importance of circumstantial evidence in establishing sex discrimination suggests careful attention to this factor.

It is important to reiterate that these types of evidence from which sex discrimination can be inferred are not exhaustive, and that they cannot be fitted into an abstract formula that might indicate in advance the precise combination of relevant criteria that would create a presumption of sex discrimination in a particular case. The identification and processing of complaints involving sex discrimination must depend on accumulated precedent and on the sensitivity and judgment of those responsible for seeing them to a conclusion.

The Association's Processing of Complaints of Sex Discrimination
This section of the subcommittee's report, while it may also be applicable in part to review bodies at colleges and universities, discusses particular aspects of the processing by the Association's staff of complaints of sex discrimination. As in the subcommittee's specification of evidence of sex discrimination, this discussion is not intended to be exhaustive.

1. The Complaint
A. COMPLAINT EVALUATION
The faculty member who believes that his or her rights as an academic have been infringed and who seeks the assistance of the Association is expected to present relevant evidence. Faculty colleagues and members of the Association's staff can often be helpful in clarifying issues and identifying the kind of evidence that may be pertinent. Staff members should help faculty members recognize and develop complaints involving sex discrimination by explaining what constitutes "evidence" and by guiding complainants in collecting such evidence. Inquiries currently made of complainants who allege certain procedural violations (for example, seeking, inter alia, letters of appointment, the faculty handbook, the current contract, and a letter of nonreappointment) provide an appropriate analogy.

B. "MIXED" COMPLAINTS
Complaints by faculty members will often include the possibility of both sex discrimination and other violations of Association policy. Thus, for example, the complaint may involve late notice or excessive probation as well as sex discrimination. Although the former grounds may more easily be established, any evidence of sex discrimination should be carefully collected and weighed. The more obvious violation, standing alone, may ultimately be deemed an inadequately serious matter to warrant further action. The complaint of sex discrimination, on the other hand, may reflect serious problems that should be pursued. Collecting evidence of sex discrimination is therefore important even when the complaint could be processed on some other, more easily established, ground.

C. MULTIPLE JURISDICTIONS
Complainants should be systematically informed by the staff of their right to go to the Equal Employment Opportunity Commission (EEOC), to other state and federal administrative agencies, and to the courts. The Association in principle is willing to proceed even if an EEOC complaint or a judicial action is also initiated, but it is often more difficult for the Association to pursue a complaint which is simultaneously pending before an administrative or judicial body. College and

university officials are less likely to cooperate with representatives of the Association in both the production and assessment of relevant evidence when other proceedings have been instituted.

These facts should be conveyed to complainants, but without any suggestion that the complainant's election of institutional, administrative, and/or judicial remedies would preclude the Association's involvement in a complaint of sex discrimination any more than in a complaint involving academic freedom. In appropriate circumstances, the Association should pursue the complaint and attempt to discover the relevant evidence even though institutional officials may decline to cooperate in the inquiry.

2. Case Status
A "complaint" becomes a "case" in Association terminology when the general secretary, or a staff member acting on behalf of the general secretary, communicates with a college or university administration to express the Association's concern, usually with a recommendation for corrective action.

A. Informal Assistance
The Association's staff may, and often should, take a variety of steps before deciding whether the evidence warrants opening a case, including the collection and analysis of data, letters or calls of inquiry, informal efforts to resolve the difficulty, and assistance in helping the complainant pursue remedies through institutional channels. Institutional channels, including hearings before faculty committees as called for in the *Recommended Institutional Regulations*, are in many instances the best forum for an initial review of the range of complaints brought to the attention of the Association. The particular difficulties inherent in proving sex discrimination underline the value of such hearings, which give institutions an opportunity to resolve disputes internally and produce a record upon which the institution's own action can later be reviewed by the Association under a standard of reasonableness. The test for taking any of these steps should be the same for complaints alleging sex discrimination as for any other complaint: whether the action contemplated is an appropriate measure under the circumstances. The complainant need not provide the Association with any specific quantum of proof to gain informal assistance.

B. Standards for Opening a Case
A case may be opened when the information available to the staff permits a reasonable

inference of a significant departure from principles or procedural standards supported by the Association. This is no magical moment, clear to all involved. It is the point at which the staff can reasonably state to the administration that a credible claim appears to exist. The initial approach to the administration should explain that the assessment offered has been based primarily on information received from other sources and should invite the administration to comment and to provide information which might add to the Association's understanding of the matter.

This procedure for opening a case applies to the entire range of Committee A complaints and, in essence, reflects the judgment that an adequate basis exists for asking the college or university to provide a valid explanation. Placing a burden of explanation on the institution can be justified on two grounds: (1) sufficient evidence exists to enable the Association's staff to make a reasonable inference that a lack of adherence to standards supported by the Association may have occurred, and (2) the administration has better access to the reasons for its position.

C. The Response of the Administration
On some occasions, an administration will respond by accepting the staff's recommendation for corrective action. On other occasions, the administration's explanation of its position will prove, after further discussion with the complainant, to meet the Association's concerns. On still other occasions, an administration may state reasons that appear valid on their face, but are in fact a pretext that camouflages a departure from principles or procedural standards supported by the Association. As in establishing an inference that a departure may have occurred, it will often be necessary to rely on circumstantial evidence to demonstrate that an apparently valid reason is actually a pretext. These determinations are difficult and must be made carefully. The Association does not, for example, substitute its own judgment for the professional judgment of an academic department. Nor does it do so in evaluating a claim of sex discrimination. In an assessment of whether a stated reason is valid, it is not the right to judge that is being questioned, nor the expertise of the judges, but whether the judgment was, in fact, professional and nondiscriminatory. Thus, an administration's apparently valid explanation of an action against a complainant, like the staff's expression of its reasonable inference that sex discrimination was actually a factor in such a decision, is rebuttable rather than conclusive.

3. Formal Investigation
A. STANDARDS FOR AUTHORIZING AN INVESTIGATION

The degree of importance of the principles and procedural standards at issue in a particular case, the degree of seriousness of the case itself, and the utility of an investigation and a potential published report, are major factors in a decision by the general secretary to authorize an investigation by an ad hoc committee. The resolutions passed by the 1971 and 1975 annual meetings emphasize that the Association has committed itself to use all its applicable procedures and sanctions, including censure, in appropriate cases involving sex discrimination. The importance of clarifying and elaborating Association policy in the area of sex discrimination is an additional factor to consider in a decision to investigate.

B. INVESTIGATION DURING LITIGATION

The 1965 *Report of the Special Committee on Procedures for the Disposition of Complaints under the Principles of Academic Freedom and Tenure* pointed out that the pendency of litigation often makes it difficult for the Association to conduct a formal investigation. Institutional officials may, on the advice of counsel, decline to cooperate.[6] As the 1965 report noted, this position may be justified, or it may unreasonably be used as an obstructive device.[7] Moreover, the importance of such cooperation may vary from case to case. In determining whether to authorize a formal investigation while litigation is pending, the interests of the Association, which are based on its own standards of proper academic practice, may be different from the issues before the courts.

C. COMPOSITION AND BRIEFING OF INVESTIGATING COMMITTEES

The Association properly strives to have at least one person on each investigating committee who has previously served on such a committee. The need for experience likewise suggests that an ad hoc committee investigating a case potentially involving sex discrimination have a member adequately experienced and that the committee be well briefed on the nature of such claims and how they are handled by courts and agencies.

D. "MIXED" CASES

Investigating committees are likely to be presented with cases involving both sex discrimination and other issues of concern to the Association. In addition, investigating committees may encounter general practices of sex discrimination unrelated to the case that originally prompted the investigation. The question arises whether in these situations the committee should address the sex-discrimination issues even though a report might be written without reference to sex discrimination. While decisions on the scope of an investigation rest in the last analysis with the ad hoc committee itself, the 1965 report concluded that reports of investigating committees should not be restricted to the particular issues that prompted the investigation.

> The Association's functions in freedom and tenure cases are not restricted to judging the particular case of the aggrieved professor. We are not merely an academic legal aid society, but a force for academic freedom and tenure throughout American higher education. When that force can be exerted by dealing generally with the health of the institution under investigation or by dealing with issues of a potentially recurrent character, we believe the opportunity should be taken. An investigation should be regarded as an occasion for the advancement of the principles of the Association rather than as a step in a grievance process; while reports of this character may take somewhat longer, they are worth the cost. And where the pursuit of not strictly material issues carries the committee to areas of uncertain and fruitless speculation, the staff and Committee A may be relied upon to reduce the report to its proper dimension.

The subcommittee reaffirms this view, with the caveat that the investigating committee must in each situation determine whether the facts are so unclear that comment might be premature. The inquiries and reports of investigating committees in cases involving claims of sex discrimination, therefore, should address these claims, as they relate both to the individual complainant and to the institution generally, even though other aspects of the complaint could be addressed without reaching them.

General Patterns of Sex Discrimination in the Absence of an Individual Complaint

Investigations normally are not authorized unless the Association has received an individual complaint. The 1965 report, however, concludes that in certain circumstances investigations should proceed in the absence of an individual complaint. The report points out that conditions in general may be so bad that it would be artificial to dwell on a single offense, that professors may be too intimidated to initiate a complaint, and that severe violations may occur that do not cost anyone a job. It notes with approval a particular investigation that was authorized because of reports of generally poor conditions rather than as a result of a specific complaint and expresses the hope that further investigations will be authorized in this manner.

The reasons stated in the 1965 report for supporting investigations in the absence of specific cases apply with special force to matters of sex discrimination. Statistical evidence might identify situations that are generally so bad that adequate grounds to justify an investigation already are present. Professors who feel discriminated against, and those who might have evidence of discrimination, seem especially likely to feel intimidated, particularly by the threat of adverse future actions. Further, these cases are more likely than most to place the individual faculty member in opposition to colleagues, rather than only to the administration. In addition, the merits of an individual's case would not be at issue in analyzing a general pattern—a significant consideration given the difficulty of proving discrimination in particular cases. Finally, investigations based on statistical data would enable the Association to focus on the basic source of the problem. The relevant statistical base for a general pattern would often be larger, and might therefore provide more meaningful comparisons than are possible in individual cases.

Investigations based on statistical data, once adequately developed, should be a useful supplement to the case method and, in some respects, could deal with the available evidence more effectively than the case method. Egregious patterns and examples of sex discrimination, as revealed by statistical data and proper investigation and analysis, should be brought to the attention of the profession.

Notes

Editor's Note (2014): The law in this area is evolving, and interested parties should consult legal counsel regarding current laws. The AAUP report "Sexual Harassment: Suggested Policy and Procedures for Handling Complaints" (AAUP, *Policy Documents and Reports*, 11th ed. [Baltimore: Johns Hopkins University Press, 2015], 363–65) should also be consulted.

1. AAUP, *Policy Documents and Reports*, 10th ed. (Baltimore: Johns Hopkins University Press, 2006), 229.

2. *Policy Documents and Reports*, 11th ed., 85–86.

3. See the "Report of the Council Committee on Discrimination," *AAUP Bulletin* 58 (June 1972): 160–63.

4. An exception would be an improper "anti-nepotism" regulation. See "Faculty Appointment and Family Relationship," *AAUP Bulletin* 57 (June 1971): 221.

5. See "Statement on Procedural Standards in the Renewal or Nonrenewal of Faculty Appointments," *Policy Documents and Reports*, 11th ed., 94–98.

6. "Report of the Special Committee on Procedures for the Disposition of Complaints under the Principles of Academic Freedom and Tenure," *AAUP Bulletin* 51 (May 1965): 210–24.

7. Committee A has periodically reviewed this issue. The difficulties in proceeding with the investigation are noted in "The Report of Committee A, 1971–72," *AAUP Bulletin* 58 (June 1972): 145–55. In 1974, the committee "reaffirmed its position that litigation and investigation can be pursued simultaneously under certain circumstances." See *AAUP Bulletin* 61 (April 1975): 16.

On Freedom of Expression and Campus Speech Codes

The statement that follows was approved by the Association's Committee A on Academic Freedom and Tenure in June 1992 and adopted by the Association's Council in November 1994.

Freedom of thought and expression is essential to any institution of higher learning. Universities and colleges exist not only to transmit knowledge. Equally, they interpret, explore, and expand that knowledge by testing the old and proposing the new. This mission guides learning outside the classroom quite as much as in class, and often inspires vigorous debate on those social, economic, and political issues that arouse the strongest passions. In the process, views will be expressed that may seem to many wrong, distasteful, or offensive. Such is the nature of freedom to sift and winnow ideas.

On a campus that is free and open, no idea can be banned or forbidden. No viewpoint or message may be deemed so hateful or disturbing that it may not be expressed.

Universities and colleges are also communities, often of a residential character. Most campuses have recently sought to become more diverse, and more reflective of the larger community, by attracting students, faculty, and staff from groups that were historically excluded or underrepresented. Such gains as they have made are recent, modest, and tenuous. The campus climate can profoundly affect an institution's continued diversity. Hostility or intolerance to persons who differ from the majority (especially if seemingly condoned by the institution) may undermine the confidence of new members of the community. Civility is always fragile and can easily be destroyed.

In response to verbal assaults and use of hateful language, some campuses have felt it necessary to forbid the expression of racist, sexist, homophobic, or ethnically demeaning speech, along with conduct or behavior that harasses. Several reasons are offered in support of banning such expression. Individuals and groups that have been victims of such expression feel an understandable outrage. They claim that the academic progress of minority and majority alike may suffer if fears, tensions, and conflicts spawned by slurs and insults create an environment inimical to learning.

These arguments, grounded in the need to foster an atmosphere respectful of and welcoming to all persons, strike a deeply responsive chord in the academy. But, while we can acknowledge both the weight of these concerns and the thoughtfulness of those persuaded of the need for regulation, rules that ban or punish speech based upon its content cannot be justified. An institution of higher learning fails to fulfill its mission if it asserts the power to proscribe ideas—and racial or ethnic slurs, sexist epithets, or homophobic insults almost always express ideas, however repugnant. Indeed, by proscribing any ideas, a university sets an example that profoundly disserves its academic mission.

Some may seek to defend a distinction between the regulation of the content of speech and the regulation of the manner (or style) of speech. We find this distinction untenable in practice because offensive style or opprobrious phrases may in fact have been chosen precisely for their expressive power. As the United States Supreme Court has said in the course of rejecting criminal sanctions for offensive words:

> [W]ords are often chosen as much for their emotive as their cognitive force. We cannot sanction the view that the Constitution, while solicitous of the cognitive content of individual speech, has little or no regard for that emotive function which, practically speaking, may often be the more important element of the overall message sought to be communicated.

The line between substance and style is thus too uncertain to sustain the pressure that will inevitably be brought to bear upon disciplinary rules that attempt to regulate speech.

Proponents of speech codes sometimes reply that the value of emotive language of this type is of such a low order that, on balance, suppression is justified by the harm suffered by those who are directly affected, and by the general damage done to the learning environment. Yet a college or university sets a perilous course if it seeks to differentiate between high-value and low-value speech, or to choose which groups are to be protected by curbing the speech of others. A speech code unavoidably implies an institutional competence to distinguish permissible expression of hateful thought from what is proscribed as thoughtless hate.

Institutions would also have to justify shielding some, but not other, targets of offensive language—proscribing uncomplimentary references to sexual but not to political preference, to religious but not to philosophical creed, or perhaps even to some but not to other religious affiliations. Starting down this path creates an even greater risk that groups not originally protected may later demand similar solicitude—demands the institution that began the process of banning some speech is ill equipped to resist.

Distinctions of this type are neither practicable nor principled; their very fragility underscores why institutions devoted to freedom of thought and expression ought not adopt an institutional-ized coercion of silence.

Moreover, banning speech often avoids consideration of means more compatible with the mission of an academic institution by which to deal with incivility, intolerance, offensive speech, and harassing behavior:

1. Institutions should adopt and invoke a range of measures that penalize conduct and behavior, rather than speech—such as rules against defacing property, physical intimidation or harassment, or disruption of campus activities. All members of the campus community should be made aware of such rules, and administra-tors should be ready to use them in preference to speech-directed sanctions.
2. Colleges and universities should stress the means they use best—to educate—including the development of courses and other curricu-lar and co-curricular experiences designed to increase student understanding and to deter offensive or intolerant speech or conduct. These institutions should, of course, be free (indeed encouraged) to condemn manifesta-tions of intolerance and discrimination, whether physical or verbal.
3. The governing board and the administration have a special duty not only to set an outstand-ing example of tolerance, but also to challenge boldly and condemn immediately serious breaches of civility.
4. Members of the faculty, too, have a major role; their voices may be critical in condemning intolerance, and their actions may set examples for understanding, making clear to their students that civility and tolerance are hallmarks of educated men and women.
5. Student-personnel administrators have in some ways the most demanding role of all, for hate speech occurs most often in dormitories, locker rooms, cafeterias, and student centers. Persons who guide this part of campus life should set high standards of their own for tolerance and should make unmistakably clear the harm that uncivil or intolerant speech inflicts. To some persons who support speech codes, measures like these—relying as they do on suasion rather than sanctions—may seem inadequate. But freedom of expression requires toleration of "ideas we hate," as Justice Holmes put it. The underlying principle does not change because the demand is to silence a hateful speaker, or because it comes from within the academy. Free speech is not simply an aspect of the educational enterprise to be weighed against other desirable ends. It is the very precondition of the academic enterprise itself.

Sexual Harassment: Suggested Policy and Procedures for Handling Complaints

The report that follows, a further revision of a report adopted initially in 1984, first revised in 1990, and subsequently revised in 2014, was approved by the Association's Committee on Women in the Academic Profession, adopted by the Association's Council in June 1995 and February 2014, and endorsed by the Eighty-First Annual Meeting.

The American Association of University Professors has traditionally opposed every kind of practice that interferes with academic freedom. In recognition of the profession's own responsibility to protect that freedom, moreover, the Association has frequently spoken to the need for colleges and universities to provide appropriate ethical standards and to provide suitable internal procedures to secure their observance.

Recently, national attention has focused on complaints of sexual harassment in higher education. These particular complaints invoke the Association's more general commitment to the maintenance of ethical standards and the academic freedom concerns these standards reflect. In its *Statement on Professional Ethics*,[1] the Association reiterates the ethical responsibility of faculty members to avoid "any exploitation of students for . . . private advantage." The applicability of this general norm to a faculty member's use of institutional position to seek unwanted sexual relations with students (or anyone else vulnerable to the faculty member's authority) is clear. Similarly, the Association's *Statement on Freedom and Responsibility*[2] states that "intimidation and harassment" are inconsistent with the maintenance of academic freedom on campus. This statement is no less germane if one is being made unwelcome because of sex, rather than because of race, religion, politics, professional interests or other irrelevant characteristics. The unprofessional treatment of students and colleagues assuredly extends to sexual discrimination and sexual harassment, as well as to other forms of intimidation.

It is incumbent upon a university or college to make plain the general policy we have just described, with an established procedure for its implementation. Educational programs about sexual harassment may be very useful in preventing its occurrence.[3]

The institution should also make clear that sexual harassment and attempted sexual duress are included under the heading of unprofessional conduct threatening to the academic freedom of others. At the same time, it is incumbent upon a university or college to provide due process for those accused of harassment.[4]

Not all institutions find it sufficient to treat sexual harassment under existing policy and procedures. Some have developed definitions of exceptional detail. Whatever policy is adopted, it should be made clear that the institution does not condone abuses by faculty members of the academic freedom of others, whether in respect to sexual harassment or otherwise, and that genuine internal recourse is available against such misconduct.[5] It should also be made clear that these procedures will provide due process for those accused. As advice to colleges and universities desiring a separate statement of policy on sexual harassment, the Association proposes the following.

Statement of Policy

It is the policy of this institution that no member of the academic community may sexually harass another.[6] Sexual advances, requests for sexual favors, and other conduct of a sexual nature constitute sexual harassment when:

1. such advances or requests are made under circumstances implying that one's response might affect educational or personnel decisions that are subject to the influence of the person making the proposal;[7] or
2. such speech or conduct is directed against another and is either abusive or severely humiliating, or persists despite the objection of the person targeted by the speech or conduct; or
3. such speech or conduct is reasonably regarded as offensive and substantially impairs the

academic or work opportunity of students, colleagues, or co-workers. If it takes place in the teaching context, it must also be persistent, pervasive, and not germane to the subject matter. The academic setting is distinct from the workplace in that wide latitude is required for professional judgment in determining the appropriate content and presentation of academic material.[8]

Applicable Procedures

1. Bringing a Complaint

a. Any member of the college or university community who believes that he or she has been the victim of sexual harassment as defined above (the complainant) may bring the matter to the attention of the individual(s) designated to handle complaints of discrimination (such as the grievance officer or another officer on campus sensitive to the issues involved).[9]

b. The complainant should present the complaint as promptly as possible after the alleged harassment occurs. One consequence of the failure to present a complaint promptly is that it may preclude recourse to legal procedures should the complainant decide to pursue them at a later date. Another possible consequence is greater difficulty in conducting an investigation.

c. If the complainant decides to proceed, the complainant should submit a written statement to the grievance officer.[10] Cases involving sexual harassment are particularly sensitive and demand special attention to issues of confidentiality. Dissemination of information relating to the case should be limited, in order that the privacy of all individuals involved is safeguarded as fully as possible.

d. The grievance officer should inform the alleged offender of the allegation and of the identity of the complainant. A written statement of the complaint should be given to both parties. Every effort should be made to protect the complainant from retaliatory action by those named in the complaint.

2. Resolution of a Complaint

a. Promptly after a complaint is submitted, the grievance officer should initiate whatever steps he or she deems appropriate to effect an informal resolution of the complaint acceptable to both parties.[11]

b. The complainant, if unsatisfied with the resolution proposed by the grievance officer, should have access to the grievance procedures at the institution upon prompt submission of a written request to the grievance officer.

c. *Review by a faculty committee of a complaint against a faculty member.*[12] Members of the faculty review committee should meet to discuss the complaint. Unless the committee concludes that the complaint is without merit, the parties to the dispute should be invited to appear before the committee and to confront any adverse witnesses. The committee may conduct its own informal inquiry, call witnesses, and gather whatever information it deems necessary to assist it in reaching a determination as to the merits of the allegations. Once such a determination has been reached, it should be communicated in writing to both parties and to the grievance officer. A summary of the basis for the determination should be provided to either party upon request.

d. *Corrective action and/or disciplinary measures.* If the review committee's findings do not lead to a mutually acceptable resolution, and if the committee believes that reasonable cause exists for seeking sanctions against a faculty offender, the grievance officer should forward the recommendation immediately to the chief administrative officer or his or her designate. The chief administrative officer shall then proceed in the manner set forth in Regulations 5 and 7 of the Association's *Recommended Institutional Regulations on Academic Freedom and Tenure,*[13] except that the need for a preliminary review will be precluded.

Well-publicized procedures such as these will help to create an atmosphere in which individuals who believe that they are the victims of harassment are assured that their complaints will be dealt with fairly and effectively. It is more important still to create an atmosphere in which instances of sexual harassment are discouraged. Toward this end, all members of the academic community should support the principle that sexual harassment represents a failure in ethical behavior and that sexual exploitation of professional relationships will not be condoned.

Notes

1. AAUP, *Policy Documents and Reports,* 11th ed. (Baltimore: Johns Hopkins University Press, 2015), 145–46.

2. "A Statement of the Association's Council: Freedom and Responsibility," *AAUP Bulletin* 56 (December 1970): 375–76.

3. The United States Supreme Court has established strong incentives for colleges and universities to create and disseminate policies on sexual harassment and to conduct training. See *Faragher v. City of Boca Raton,* 524 US 775 (1998); *Burlington Industries, Inc. v. Ellerth,* 524 US 742 (1998). Policies and training on sexual violence are similarly important campus initiatives. Campus SaVE Act, P.L. 113-4, March 7, 2013, amending sec. 485(f) of the Higher Education Act; "Dear Colleague Letter," US Department of Education, April 11, 2011. Available at www2.ed.gov/about/offices/list/ocr/letters/colleague-201104.html.

4. *Federal Register* 62 (March 13, 1997): 12034, at 12045.

5. Institutions are well advised to check that their anti-harassment policies and procedures address all the personal characteristics that their nondiscrimination policies protect. A complaint might arise, for example, about racial harassment.

6. For the state of the law as it pertains to sexual harassment in the employment context, see the cases cited in note 3, as well as *Burlington Northern & Santa Fe Railway Co. v. White,* 548 US 53 (2006), and *Oncale v. Sundowner Offshore Services, Inc.,* 523 US 75 (1998).

7. See the Association's 1995 "Consensual Relations between Faculty and Students," *Policy Documents and Reports,* 149.

8. See the Association's statement, "On Freedom of Expression and Campus Speech Codes," ibid., 361–62. The Office for Civil Rights (OCR) in the US Department of Education, which enforces the prohibition of sexual harassment under Title IX, has explicitly stated that institutions "in regulating the conduct of students and faculty to prevent or redress discrimination must formulate, interpret, and apply their rules in a manner that respects the legal rights of students and faculty, including those court precedents interpreting the concept of free speech. OCR's regulations and policies do not require or prescribe speech, conduct or harassment codes that impair the exercise of rights protected under the First Amendment." OCR applies the same academic freedom concept to private institutions. "Dear Colleague Letter" dated July 28, 2003. Available at www2.ed.gov/print/about/offices/list/ocr/firstamend.html.

9. The grievance officer should counsel the complainant about other avenues for pursuing the complaint, such as state or local government human-rights or law enforcement agencies, the federal Equal Employment Opportunity Commission, or the Office for Civil Rights of the US. Deadlines for filing complaints with these agencies should be explained.

10. If the complainant decides not to proceed, the institution might enhance educational efforts or take other non-disciplinary steps. See Revised Sexual Harassment Guidance: Harassment of Students by School Employees, Other Students, or Third Parties under Title IX, at sec. VII B. Available at www2.ed.gov/about/offices/list/ocr/docs/shguide.html.

11. The Office for Civil Rights in the US Department of Education has, however, cautioned that mediation is inappropriate in matters involving sexual violence. See "Dear Colleague Letter" dated April 11, 2011, cited above in note 3.

12. The Association seeks through these guidelines to urge the adoption by colleges and universities of adequate due-process provisions for all members of the academic community—students, faculty, and staff—where there has been an allegation of sexual harassment. It has developed specific review procedures to handle complaints involving faculty members. See "Due Process in Sexual-Harassment Complaints," *Academe* 77 (September–October 1991): 47.

13. *Policy Documents and Reports,* 79–90.

Campus Sexual Assault: Suggested Policies and Procedures

The statement that follows was approved in October 2012 by the Association's Committee on Women in the Academic Profession and its Subcommittee on Sexual Assault on Campus. It was adopted by the Association's Council in November 2012.

The American Association of University Professors has long recognized that the freedom to teach and to learn is inseparable from the maintenance of a safe and hospitable learning environment. Several Association documents identify important elements of such an environment. The *Joint Statement on Rights and Freedoms of Students*, states that the "freedom to learn depends upon appropriate opportunities and conditions in the classroom, on the campus, and in the larger community." The *Statement on Professional Ethics* emphasizes the responsibility of faculty members to "avoid any exploitation . . . of students." *Sexual Harassment: Suggested Policy and Procedures for Handling Complaints* reiterates this ethical responsibility, asserting that acts of harassment clearly violate expected standards of campus conduct. The same statement emphasizes that the success of any policy requires campus leadership to "provide appropriate ethical standards and to provide suitable internal procedures to secure their observance."[1]

National attention has recently turned to sexual violence and the problems it poses for the classroom, campus, and community.[2] Actual or threatened sexual assault raises issues for colleges and universities that go beyond those of sexual harassment. Whereas the prevention and management of sexual-harassment incidents are generally considered to fall within the purview of campus policy and procedures, incidents of sexual violence and sexual assault may constitute criminal offenses, require medical attention, and raise special concerns about reporting, record keeping, media attention, and police involvement. Because definitions of various acts and their status differ widely by state, community, research study, and institution, colleges and universities are urged to determine the terms and conditions applicable in their localities.[3]

Some colleges and universities choose to incorporate sexual assault into existing policies governing professional ethics, sexual harassment, or campus violence. Institutions that wish to have a separate statement on the prevention and management of campus sexual assault may find the suggestions presented in this report useful in developing policy and procedures. Drawing on research findings and other sources, we first outline the scope of the problem, the consequences, and the management of sexual assault. We then summarize federal law pertaining to sexual assault, including the provisions of the Jeanne Clery Act and its reporting requirements for institutions of higher education. We then outline what a robust sexual-assault policy might look like, noting institutional and procedural elements that authorities consider promising as well as those that pose special challenges for the development of sound policy and procedures. We discuss the special role and responsibility of faculty members, a group often overlooked in campus sexual-assault prevention and training programs. We conclude by emphasizing the importance of coherent and consistent policy throughout the institution.

I. Scope of the Problem

Campus sexual assault is a significant problem.[4] Women in the traditional age range for college students—from eighteen to twenty-one—are four times more likely to be sexually assaulted than women in any other age group, and college-bound women are at greater risk than their non-college-bound peers.[5] Between 20 and 25 percent of college women and 4 percent of college men report having been sexually assaulted during their college years.[6] The rate for gay, lesbian, bisexual, transgender, and queer students is estimated to be slightly higher.[7] Studies of campus sexual assault indicate that many—perhaps most—assaults and attempted assaults are never reported or, if reported, not consistently counted as official.[8] The fact that sexual assaults on campuses largely take place between acquaintances blurs understandings both of consent and of assault, and lessens the likelihood of reporting.[9] Unlike "stranger rape," acquaintance rape may not even be perceived by those involved as "rape," a perception that may discourage or delay disclosure (which may occur days, weeks, even years after the event).[10]

II. Consequences of Sexual Assault

The consequences of sexual assault are potentially very serious. An immediate concern is physical injury, which may be extensive enough to require medical treatment or hospitalization.[11] Pregnancy and sexually transmitted diseases (STDs), including HIV, are additional concerns.[12] Emotional damage may be serious and equally requiring of treatment. Sexual assault may affect students' academic achievement as well as their capacity to contribute to the campus community. College students who have survived sexual assault rarely perform at their prior academic levels, are sometimes unable to carry a normal course load, and frequently miss classes. These changes stem sometimes from social withdrawal, sometimes from a desire to avoid the perpetrator. Assaulted students regularly drop courses altogether, leave school, or transfer. Along with decline in academic performance and social withdrawal, long-term outcomes may include increased risk of depression, substance abuse, self-harm, eating disorders, post-traumatic stress, personality disorders, and suicide.[13]

Beyond their destructive effects on individuals, incidents of sexual assault may have negative consequences for colleges and universities. First, they harm the institution's educational mission by undermining the safe and hospitable learning environment necessary for learning and teaching. Second, they cast doubt on stated commitments by campus leaders to end campus violence. Third, cases exposed in the national media may bring scandal to the institution and its leaders, create distrust toward the administration among parents and alumni, and erode fundraising efforts as well as legislative and philanthropic support. Fourth, institutions found in violation of basic preventive measures may be fined.[14] Finally, even incidents that stay local are likely to damage the institution's standing in the community.

III. Management of Campus Sexual Assault

As we suggest in this document, sound campus policy and procedures should aim to eliminate sexual assault and its devastating consequences. Closer coordination with trained law-enforcement officials, for example, increases the likelihood that incidents will be more fully investigated and adjudicated. In terms of the conviction and punishment of perpetrators, however, the outcomes are not much better for cases handled by the criminal justice system. A 2011 *Chicago Tribune* investigation of six midwestern universities tracked 171 alleged campus sex crimes reported by students and investigated by police over the previous five years; twelve of the accused perpetrators were arrested, of whom four were convicted. In only one of those four cases was the attacker another student, though student-to-student assault is the most common form of sexual assault on campuses.[15] Thus the rate of arrests and convictions in these cases is not only low—7 percent and 2 percent, respectively—but also well below the average reported nationally. As the *Tribune* article concludes, "The trend leaves untold numbers of college women feeling betrayed and vulnerable, believing that their allegations are not taken seriously."

Such findings are disappointing. Despite progress over recent decades in public and professional understanding of sexual assault and sexual violence, recent research makes clear the persistence and influence of several entrenched myths: it is the victim's fault; most allegations of sexual assault and rape are false and typically motivated by revenge against particular men or against men in general; the presence of drugs or alcohol makes it difficult to investigate allegations or even establish whether an incident actually took place; and acquaintance rape is not rape.[16] Below we note additional factors that appear to influence the reporting, tracking, counting, investigating, classifying, and adjudicating of incidents of sexual assault.

IV. Federal Laws on Sexual Assault and Related Crimes

Title IX requires institutions of higher education to report incidents of sexual violence and to track patterns of sexual misconduct and other behaviors that create a hostile environment for women. In spring 2011, the Office for Civil Rights offered additional guidance for interpreting Title IX in its "Dear Colleague Letter." The letter states that institutions are required to "take immediate action to eliminate the harassment, prevent its recurrence, and address its effects."[17]

Title IX lays out the investigative process to be used in such instances. In 1990, Congress enacted a law that requires all two- and four-year colleges and universities to file annual reports with the federal government on campus crime, and campus security amendments passed in 1992, 1998, and 2008 further require campuses to develop and disseminate prevention policies, make specific assurances to victims, and report an expanded set of crime categories, including hate crimes.

Together, these federal regulations on campus crime are now known as the Jeanne Clery Disclosure of Campus Security Policy and Campus Crime Statistics Act, or the Clery Act.[18] Yet, as we have noted, sexual violence encompasses a broad array of activities, including sexual harassment, sexual assault, and stalking. Definitions and classifications differ according to state, jurisdiction, investigatory agency, and institution; so do the campus, legal, and criminal status of specific acts and their penalties. This patchwork of laws and definitions confuses efforts to address campus sexual assault; indeed, roughly two-thirds of campuses file Clery Act reports incorrectly.[19] The same differences and inconsistencies muddy the activities of reporting, record keeping, researching, and bringing attackers to justice. A further complication is identified in a 2005 report on Clery to Congress: "the dual jurisdiction of campus administration and law enforcement."[20] As the report notes, campus sexual assault is potentially subject to two parallel but not fully commensurate systems of investigation and adjudication: the campus disciplinary process, which seeks to determine whether the institution's sexual misconduct policy was violated, and the criminal justice system, which seeks to determine whether the alleged attacker is guilty of a criminal act. Most reports of sexual assault on campus are handled administratively. A perpetrator found in violation of campus policy may be disciplined in a variety of ways, including suspension or expulsion.[21] However, if the campus does not consider the incident a crime, it will not be counted in Clery statistics. At the same time, campus authorities are often reluctant to refer incidents to the criminal justice system and thereby yield control of the proceedings, opening them to public as well as media scrutiny.[22]

While the requirements of the Clery Act have undoubtedly alerted many campus and public officials to the problem and extent of campus sex crimes, continuing confusion remains on several points. In the aftermath of the 2011 Penn State scandal, for example, media reports as well as statements to the press by college and university leaders revealed uncertainty about the meanings of and distinctions among such terms as *sexual assault*, *sexual abuse*, *sexual harassment*, and *rape*. Given the state-by-state patchwork of terms and statutes, this uncertainty is perhaps to be expected. Research on Clery reporting, however, also indicates confusion over the meaning of *student*, *campus*, *crime*, and other terms central to Clery reporting mandates.[23] Obviously, terminological confusion confounds statistical estimates as well as meaningful cross-campus comparisons.

While a small number of institutions have put in place rigorous procedures for obtaining, collating, tracking, processing, and reporting Clery statistics, a standardized model for the overall process does not yet exist. Accordingly, as with terminology, practices may be very different from one campus to the next. This inconsistency is confirmed by a 2011 study by the Center for Public Integrity: comparing sexual-assault data submitted in universities' annual Clery security reports with data collated from the records of service and advocacy agencies connected to or near campuses, the center found "troubling discrepancies in Clery Act numbers."[24] Numerous cases of student assaults reported by the advocacy agencies, though sent to the universities, were routinely omitted from the Clery summaries.

Accordingly, it seems clear that closer collaboration with local law enforcement, greater knowledge of what constitutes "a crime," and better coordination between campus and community service providers would aid many colleges and universities in more effectively addressing the problems of campus sexual assault. As of this writing, however, such coordination is the exception rather than the rule.

V. Development of Robust Policy and Procedures

Several points emerge from our comments thus far: terms and definitions matter; policies and procedures should be coherent across the institution and consistent with state and federal law; coordination across relevant campus and noncampus units will encourage better understanding of the problem; policies and procedures should be consistent with collective bargaining agreements, if applicable; and the effective management of campus sexual assault will be aided by broader changes in campus culture. In addition to these general principles, a number of policy and procedural measures are recommended by most experts on campus sexual assault.[25]

1. All members of the campus community—faculty members, administrators, staff members, and students—share responsibility for addressing the problem of campus sexual assault and should be represented in the policy-development process. Once policies and procedures are in place, the institution must make them widely available.[26]
2. Early in the policy-development process, the institution needs to determine the rules, definitions, laws, reporting requirements, and penalties that pertain to sexual assault in the local criminal justice system.[27] More broadly,

because incidents of campus sexual assault may be reported to noncampus authorities and may in fact take place off campus, the institution is advised to consult and coordinate procedures with campus and noncampus police, health-care providers, and community service providers experienced in dealing with sexual assault. Establishing and maintaining an ongoing network will help coordinate campus policy with off-campus law enforcement and facilitate the important activities of counseling, treatment, referral, record keeping, investigation, adjudication, and Clery reporting.

3. Policies and procedures must be clear, readable, and accurate; information must be widely disseminated and readily accessible to all members of the campus community; and materials must include descriptive (operational) definitions of sexual assault, rape, and other forms of sexual violence, explaining why these actions violate acceptable standards of conduct and, in some cases, constitute criminal offenses. Potential campus and criminal penalties should be made equally clear.

4. Guidelines for reporting an incident of sexual assault should be clear and explicit and include names, titles, and contact information. They should state when and where to report an incident, file a complaint, or press a charge. The policy should encourage victims to report the incident to campus authorities and to off-campus police, and should generally indicate what each procedure entails and what purpose the reporting will serve. Procedural options following the report of an incident should likewise be clear and explicit. The policy should include an official statement prohibiting retaliation against individuals who report incidents of assault and specify the disciplinary actions that will follow threats and attempts to retaliate.

5. The reporting of sexual assault is essential for accurate record keeping and to prevent repeat offenses. Given the widespread underreporting of sexual assault, reporting should be facilitated as much as possible—for example, by providing for direct reporting by name, confidential reporting, and anonymous reporting. Some campuses provide for third-party reporting; others have developed systems for centrally collating reported incidents from all sources without double-counting.[28] Mental health and religious counselors are explicitly exempted from Clery reporting requirements, but the legislation encourages institutions to establish a confidential or anonymous reporting procedure to which counselors may refer their clients.[29]

6. Ideally, a single official or office should be charged with overseeing and coordinating the many responsibilities associated with allegations of sexual assault.[30] This office or individual should be one with appropriate experience, established authority, and sufficient resources. Such duties would include responding to incident reports, coordinating communication and record keeping among offices and agencies, disseminating information to the campus through materials and training sessions, ensuring that the victim receives whatever immediate care and follow-up are needed, establishing procedures for classifying and counting incidents, and filing Clery reports that are as comprehensive and accurate as possible. The name and contact information for the individual and office should be widely publicized; preferably a live responder would be available round the clock.

7. Campus policy and procedures should be publicized through a multimedia approach that includes press releases, brochures, posters, radio and video spots, and web-based messages. Again, all information should include the name and contact information of experienced campus officers as well as contact information for campus and appropriate off-campus law-enforcement officials. Contact information should also be provided for relevant campus, community, and online resources (for example, ride services, the local mass-transit system, emergency phone locations, rape hotlines, and Twitter alerts). Some campuses post stickers with emergency information on the doors of all campus buildings.

8. Prevention programs, required on some campuses for all entering and transfer students, aim to work "proactively to end sexual violence."[31] Often using trained peer educators, such programs may focus on healthy relationships, the meaning of consent, and strategies for bystander intervention. Workshops and training sessions should play a continuing role in campus education.

9. Physical and electronic prevention and security measures include improved campus lighting; trimming of vegetation; trained student and security officer patrols; carded access to residence halls; presentations by campus police to student, faculty, and staff groups; and widespread distribution and publication of campus security information.[32]

10. While education and prevention efforts typically focus on women, the most likely

victims of sexual assault, campuses should also direct education toward men, the most likely perpetrators. Education and training programs for men have the potential to change the culture of the campus with respect to sexual violence of all forms.[33] Among the most promising practices are prevention and intervention programs designed for all-male campus groups (male athletes, fraternity brothers, and male members of the Reserve Officers' Training Corps). Such programs explore what men can do, individually and collectively, to prevent these crimes. For example, a University of California, Santa Cruz, program identifies intervention strategies available to bystanders (such as friends, roommates, or fraternity brothers) when a male peer seems on the verge of committing a potentially criminal sexual offense.

11. Recent educational projects aimed at "bystanders" may sound casual or unlikely to succeed. In fact, such projects are aimed at the peers and peer groups of potential perpetrators and potential victims and thus may provide significant education to the campus community and have an impact on the larger campus culture.[34]

12. Though students are the focus of the current document, a campus assault policy should eventually cover all campus constituencies.

VI. Faculty Responsibilities

While the foregoing suggestions are generally applicable to campuswide strategies for managing sexual assault, the role of faculty members in protecting student rights and freedoms is distinctive and merits further discussion. As advisers, teachers, and mentors, faculty members may be among the most trusted adults in a student's life and often are the persons in whom students will confide after an assault. A faculty member may also be the first adult who detects changes in a student's behavior that stem from a sexual assault and can encourage the student to talk about it. Faculty members may thus find themselves in the role of "first responders" to reports of sexual assault, yet few consider themselves adequately equipped for the role—in part because they are the least likely campus constituency to receive information about sexual assault and guidance about reporting and responding to it.

The reporting question is important. The Clery Act mandates that campus crime statistics be gathered from "campus police or security, local law enforcement, and other school officials who have 'significant responsibility for student and campus activities' such as judicial affairs directors." It is the view of this committee that faculty members, as a general rule, do not fall into this category and are therefore not mandated Clery reporters.[35] As a consequence, faculty members are thus usually not expected to be trained investigators, nor, except in specific circumstances as defined by individual institutions, are they normally expected to be mandated reporters of incidents about which they are told or happen to learn.[36] But they can provide other important forms of support and assistance:

1. They can listen to the student's disclosure and then make a referral to an experienced campus official or service provider; obviously, the more information the faculty member has about the quality and track record of available services, the better the advice and referral will be.

2. They can state explicitly that they take it seriously and help the student clarify points of doubt or confusion.

3. They can consider whether any immediate action (such as medical attention) may be wanted or needed.

4. They can describe campus policy, procedures, and reporting options; urge the student to file a report (while making clear that the decision to do so is ultimately the student's); and offer to accompany the student in taking any actions.

5. They can help the student think through immediate and longer-term options (the immediate collection of medical evidence, for example, makes future reporting possible) and offer assistance in navigating the campus bureaucracy.

6. Faculty members who are knowledgeable about and committed to principles of justice and due process are well equipped to help develop policy and see that its procedures protect the victim while ensuring due process for the accused perpetrator. They can also advise and support student activist groups that are pressing the campus to respond more forcefully to the problem of sexual assault.[37]

7. Knowledgeable faculty members can serve on student discipline panels (where such panels include faculty).

8. Faculty members with appropriate expertise can help provide training on campus sexual assault and reporting procedures.

9. Qualified faculty members can promote through their research a better understanding of the issues surrounding campus sexual assault. David Lisak, a leading authority on sexual assault, observes that the heated public discourse in this controversial field "often

makes no reference to actual research." "It is remarkable," he writes, "how little research has been done in the United States," noting that the major government-funded studies of rapes and their low rate of prosecution come from the United Kingdom and Australia, where the field is less characterized by confidentiality and fragmentation.[38]

10. Faculty members should be aware that they could be called to testify in a criminal proceeding about a conversation with a student regarding sexual assault and may want to consider professional liability insurance as a safeguard.

VII. Final Considerations

In this document, we have presented suggestions culled from research, media commentary, higher education policy, local and national women's advocacy groups, and law-enforcement models. Yet despite intense concern and some progress, campus sexual assault remains a field, as Lisak has put it, "fraught with controversy" and "enmeshed in dispute and in the politics of gender and sexuality."[39] We have mentioned many of the issues that fuel controversy and dispute and that in many ways impede the just and fair resolution of incidents of campus sexual assault. As we have noted, the widely accepted estimate is that fewer than 5 percent of completed and attempted sexual assaults on college students are brought to the attention of campus authorities or law enforcement. Even fewer of these incidents are rigorously adjudicated. While the difficulties of reporting, counting, sorting, and record keeping could presumably be reduced by sound policy and procedures, it is less clear how investigation, adjudication, and resolution might best be improved. The stark fact is that alleged attackers almost uniformly go unpunished, and many victims of sexual assault believe that no reporting or disciplinary process will produce justice.[40] Moreover, in the words of the Center for Public Integrity, campus proceedings are typically "shrouded in secrecy," and neither the public nor the victim is likely to be told how the case was resolved. And, as we have noted, the outcomes are little improved when handled by the criminal justice system.

In an effort to improve the likelihood of bringing perpetrators to justice, the Office for Civil Rights has proposed lowering the standard of proof in disciplinary proceedings involving sexual assault. The office argues in its "Dear Colleague Letter" that replacing the prevailing standard of "clear and convincing evidence" with a "preponderance-of-the-evidence" standard

would help level the playing field for victims of sexual violence. The proposal has in general been favorably received by women's advocacy groups and sexual-assault support agencies but has been opposed by many organizations representing both progressive and conservative values. The AAUP advocates the continued use of "clear and convincing evidence" in both student and faculty discipline cases as a necessary safeguard of due process and shared governance. The committee believes that greater attention to policy and procedures, incorporating practices we have suggested here, is the more promising direction.

Approaches to the critical problem of campus sexual assault will continue to evolve, and the growing body of research and experience may eventually make possible the identification of a definitive set of best practices. In the meantime, careful attention to policy demonstrates the institution's resolve to reduce rates of campus sexual assault on a continuing and sustained basis. Attention to the procedures that implement policy is no less important: well-designed procedures strengthen a campus culture of respect and safety, ensure an appropriate institutional response to incidents of assault, and add to our knowledge of incidents and outcomes. In turn, that knowledge enables an institution to measure the effectiveness of its policy and procedures over time.

Notes

1. AAUP, *Policy Documents and Reports*, 11th ed. (Baltimore: Johns Hopkins University Press, 2015), 381, 145, 363.

2. Christopher P. Krebs et al., *Campus Sexual Assault (CSA) Study* (Washington, DC: US Department of Justice, 2007), https://www.ncjrs.gov/pdffiles1/nij /grants/221153.pdf. The April 4, 2011, "Dear Colleague Letter" from the US Department of Education's Office for Civil Rights addresses the scope and significance of sexual violence in educational settings, and the accompanying fact sheet provides widely accepted statistics. "Dear Colleague Letter," Office for Civil Rights, US Department of Education, http://www2.ed .gov/about/offices/list/ocr/letters/colleague-201104 .html.

3. We use *sexual violence* as a blanket term for sexual harassment, sexual abuse, sexual assault, rape, stalking, domestic violence, and other forms of sexual misconduct. We use *sexual assault* to denote coercive physical contact of a sexual nature, including rape. *Rape*, a common legal term denoting forced sexual intercourse (with oral, vaginal, or anal penetration), has in many states been replaced by statutes defining and prohibiting activities encompassed by the more inclusive term *sexual assault*; we retain the term *rape* when used in cited documents. For more on definitions and terminology, see Heather M. Karjane, Bonnie S. Fisher, and Francis T. Cullen, *Campus Sexual Assault:*

How America's Institutions of Higher Education Respond (Washington, DC: US Department of Justice, 2002), 2–3, https://www.ncjrs.gov/pdffiles1/nij/grants/196676.pdf.

4. See "Sexual Assault on Campus Statistics," American Association of University Women (AAUW), accessed February 2, 2014, http://www.aauw.org/what-we-do/legal-resources/know-your-rights-on-campus/campus-sexual-assault/#stats; and Krebs et al., *Campus Sexual Assault Study.*

5. See, for example, Heather M. Karjane, Bonnie S. Fisher, and Francis T. Cullen, *Sexual Assault on Campus: What Colleges and Universities Are Doing about It* (Washington, DC: US Department of Justice, 2005), http://www.ncjrs.gov/pdffiles1/nij/205521.pdf.

6. Centers for Disease Control and Prevention, *Sexual Violence Facts at a Glance 2012,* accessed January 17, 2013, http://www.cdc.gov/Violence Prevention/pdf/SV-DataSheet-a.pdf.

7. Lee van der Voo, "Sexual Violence on Campus: Not Just a Crime of Men against Women," *Investigate West,* February 25, 2010, http://invw.org/node/941; "National Statistics about Sexual Violence on College Campuses," New York University Student Health Center, accessed February 2, 2014, http://www2.binghamton.edu/counseling/services/sexual-assault-peer-education/campus-stats.html. See also Ann Fleck-Henderson et al., *Beyond Title IX: Guidelines for Preventing and Responding to Gender-Based Violence in Higher Education* (San Francisco: Futures without Violence and Avon Foundation for Women, 2012), 5, http://www.acha.org/topics/docs/Futures_Without_Violence_Beyond_Title_IX.pdf: "Those on campus who may be marginalized, underrepresented, or especially vulnerable warrant special attention. These groups will differ from campus to campus, but may include LGBTQ individuals, women of color, women with disabilities, immigrant women, or international students."

8. Based on statistical extrapolation from many sources, some researchers estimate that only 5 percent of campus sexual assaults are officially reported: "Sexual assault is widely considered to be the most underreported crime in America." Karjane, Fisher, and Cullen, *Sexual Assault on Campus,* ii.

9. It has been estimated that 90 percent of campus women who are victims of sexual assault know the person who assaulted them. Krebs et al., *Campus Sexual Assault Study.*

10. "Half of all student victims do not label the incident 'rape.'" Karjane, Fisher, and Cullen, *Sexual Assault on Campus,* 2.

11. Sexual-assault advocacy groups recommend that all victims of physical sexual assault, even those reluctant to file an official report, undergo a medical exam and forensic evidence collection; this makes it feasible to file an official report or charge in the future. See http://safercampus.org, the website of the national activist organization Students Active for Ending Rape.

12. The AAUW states that 40 percent or more of sexual-assault incidents involve transmission of a sexually transmitted disease. Some states mandate testing of convicted attackers for HIV and other STDs. See AAUW, "Sexual Assault on Campus Statistics."

13. Connie J. Kirkland, *Academic Impact of Sexual Assault* (Fairfax, VA: George Mason University, 1994).

14. Recent cases are highlighted on the AAUW's website at http://www.aauw.org/what-we-do/legal-resources/know-your-rights-on-campus/campus-sexual-assault/#cases.

15. Todd Lighty, Stacy St. Clair, and Jodi S. Cohen, "Few Arrests, Convictions in Campus Sex Assault Cases," *Chicago Tribune,* June 16, 2011, http://articles.chicagotribune.com/2011-06-16/news/ct-met-campus-sexual-assaults-0617-20110616_1_convictions-arrests-assault-cases. The convicted student had pleaded guilty to sexual battery and criminal confinement.

16. Two forums on campus sexual assault held in Virginia in spring 2011 and 2012 brought together leaders in research, higher education, policy, and law enforcement. Among the presenters was David Lisak, a clinical psychologist and leading authority on interpersonal violence, including sexual assault. Lisak documented the influence and pervasiveness of such myths and stereotypes in all aspects of campus sexual assault. Two of his papers, along with other useful presentations from the 2012 forum, can be downloaded from the Virginia Department of Criminal Justice's website at http://www.dcjs.virginia.gov/vcss/training/SAForum/.

17. See http://www2.ed.gov/about/offices/list/ocr/letters/colleague-201104.html.

18. The act was renamed in 1998 to honor Jeanne Clery, a student sexually assaulted and murdered in her dormitory room on the Lehigh University campus in 1986. At the same time, her parents founded the nonprofit foundation Security on Campus, Inc.; see http://www.securityoncampus.org/summary-jeanne-clery-act for a summary of the Jeanne Clery Act. Institutions that fail to comply with the Clery Act may be fined or lose eligibility for federal student-loan programs.

19. See Karjane, Fisher, and Cullen, *Sexual Assault on Campus*; and Krebs et al., *Campus Sexual Assault Study.* Four-year institutions and historically black colleges and universities are more likely to report correctly; four-year public institutions do better than their private counterparts.

20. Karjane, Fisher, and Cullen, *Sexual Assault on Campus,* 10.

21. Alternatively, accusers found in violation may be censured, required to pay restitution, lose privileges, issued a no-contact order, or placed on probation.

22. This "parallel judicial universe" is believed by some to have contributed to the scandal at Pennsylvania State University and to the poor handling of other cases. See, for example, Nina Bernstein, "On Campus, a Law Enforcement System to Itself," *New York Times,* November 12, 2011, http://www.nytimes.com/2011/11/12/us/on-college-campuses-athletes-often-get-off-easy.html.

23. "Sexual Assault on Campus," US Department of Justice, last modified October 1, 2008, http://www.nij.gov/topics/crime/rape-sexual-violence/campus/pages/welcome.aspx.

24. "Campus Sexual Assault Statistics Don't Add Up," Center for Public Accountability, last modified June 5, 2012, http://www.publicintegrity.org /2009/12/02/9045/campus-sexual-assault-statistics -don-t-add.

25. Obviously, an institution's size, financial situation, and resources will affect its capacity to carry out these recommendations. Nonresidential institutions and those governed by collective bargaining agreements, for example, may need to adapt these suggestions to their own circumstances.

26. Some institutions have policies and procedures on the books but do not widely publicize them.

27. For specific information, consult the state-by-state listings on the website of the Rape, Abuse, and Incest National Network at http://rainn.org/public -policy/laws-in-your-state.

28. Institutions that conscientiously count and report Clery sex crimes note that their diligence may backfire, making their campuses appear less safe than those that file more casual reports. See Karjane, Fisher, and Cullen, *Sexual Assault on Campus*, 12–14.

29. The issues posed by different campus reporting requirements and the need for confidentiality are complex and may actually discourage faculty and staff cooperation.

30. Oversight for these multiple responsibilities seems most often to be assigned to campus security, women's programs and services, or student services.

31. The quoted statement and examples of prevention programming are from the Campus Acquaintance Rape Education (or CARE) program, founded in the 1990s at the University of Illinois at Urbana-Champaign.

32. See Westat, Diane Ward, and Janice Lee Mann, *The Handbook for Campus Safety and Security Reporting* (Washington, DC: US Department of Education, 2011), http://www2.ed.gov/admins/lead /safety/handbook.pdf.

33. According to the AAUW, 43 percent of college men said that during their college years they had used some form of coercion to obtain sex. Attention to men can clarify for them the meaning of consent and of the phrase "no means no"; it can also help identify behavioral precursors to assault (such as sexual harassment and stalking). AAUW, "Sexual Assault on Campus Statistics."

34. Karjane, Fisher, and Cullen, *Sexual Assault on Campus*, 12. See also J. Katz, "Reconstructing Masculinity in the Locker Room: The Mentors in Violence Prevention Project," *Harvard Educational Review* 65 (Summer 1995): 163–74.

35. The phrase "significant responsibility for student and campus activities" will have different meanings at different institutions. Clearly there may be circumstances in which faculty members do have significant supervisory responsibilities for students—for example, when they lead field trips or trips abroad or sponsor debate or music competitions or athletic events. Each campus must clarify oversight and reporting responsibilities as activities require. Where faculty members have student advising as an assigned responsibility in their job description, mandated reporting might be required. Other conditions may prevail at nonresidential campuses, community colleges, and institutions working under collective bargaining agreements.

36. The faculty and staff web page of the Office of Women's Affairs at the University of Illinois at Chicago, which addresses sexual-assault and sexual-harassment issues for the campus, states that "all faculty and staff who supervise student activities are considered Jeanne Clery–mandated reporters. If you are given information about the occurrence of a crime on campus, you are required to make a report. In [the] future the Office of Women's Affairs will offer an online training program for all mandated reporters." Here the key phrase is "supervise student activities," but there is no real explanation of what these activities encompass. See "Faculty and Staff," University of Illinois at Chicago Office of Women's Affairs, accessed January 18, 2013, http://www.uic.edu/depts/owa /facstaff.html.

37. The national activist organization Students Active for Ending Rape (http://safercampus.org) identifies additional ways in which faculty members can support efforts to establish policy and procedures for handling campus sexual assault.

38. David Lisak et al., "False Allegations of Sexual Assault: An Analysis of Ten Years of Reported Cases," *Violence against Women* 16 (December 2010): 1319, 1331.

39. Ibid., 1318.

40. See http://www.publicintegrity.org/accountability /education/sexual-assault-campus.

Accommodating Faculty Members Who Have Disabilities

The report that follows is excerpted from a longer report of the same title, which was prepared by a subcommittee of Committee A on Academic Freedom and Tenure. In November 2011, Committee A approved the report for publication.

Introduction

In recent years the rights and responsibilities of students who have disabilities have received considerable attention. Professors routinely accommodate students with a front-row seat in class or extended time on an examination. Faculty members who have disabilities have received far less attention. This report from a subcommittee of Committee A on Academic Freedom and Tenure addresses practical and legal issues concerning faculty members who have disabilities.[1]

In higher education, as in American society generally, one still often encounters the stereotype that disability necessarily equates with diminished professional competence. With suitable accommodations, a faculty member who has a physical or mental disability may perform equally well as, or even better than, a colleague who does not have a disability. As an expert on these issues observed in 2009, "So far, professional groups have not fully incorporated disability in their diversity agendas."[2] In promoting access and success for faculty members with disabilities, the AAUP highlights the significant talents of an important group, promotes a diverse professoriate, and expands role models for students.

A faculty member may have a disabling condition at the time of his or her appointment or may develop a disability later. The onset can be rapid or gradual. A disability may be a physical or mental condition, and a faculty member may have multiple disabilities. Comprehensive data are not readily available on the incidence of disability among the American professoriate.[3]

Federal, state, and local laws establish basic requirements for the protection of faculty members who have disabilities. Federal laws include the Americans with Disabilities Act and Section 504 of the Rehabilitation Act of 1973. While this report incorporates some core legal principles and expands upon them for the academic setting, it is not a substitute for legal advice tailored to particular situations.

Steps in Accommodation

Most institutions have well-developed procedures for managing the needs of students who have disabilities.[4] Procedures for managing faculty accommodation requests, while used less frequently, are equally important.

Raising the Issue of Disability. If a faculty member believes that a disabling condition impedes his or her discharge of professional responsibilities, it is incumbent on the individual to bring the matter to the attention of appropriate institutional authorities. Someone who has an obvious disability, such as blindness or a missing limb, need not provide notice. Unless a disability is obvious, the institution must not initiate discussion with an individual about a potential disability. This is a fundamental requirement— that the faculty member alone has the right and responsibility to raise the issue of disability.

Once a faculty member indicates, whether orally or in writing, that he or she has a disability, a structured process involving several steps begins. If it has not already done so, the institution must identify the "essential functions" of the faculty member's position. The nature and extent of the disability may be examined. Most importantly, the individual and institution must engage in good-faith discussions about how best to accommodate the limiting conditions. The following sections address the steps in accommodation.

Throughout the process, institutional authorities must respect the individual's privacy interests and confine information about the matter to those with professional responsibility for addressing or resolving it. Under federal law, information about a disability must not be included in the faculty member's regular personnel file. This separation limits the possibility that the information might improperly and negatively influence decisions regarding the individual.

A search committee should only raise disability when asking all candidates whether they may need an accommodation in the application or interview process. If the candidate does need accommodation, the institution should be thorough and gracious. The Modern Language Association has prepared advice on interviewing candidates with disabilities.[5]

Defining Essential Functions. A faculty member who has a disability needs to accomplish the essential functions of his or her position, either with or without an accommodation. Essential elements common to all faculty positions would be requirements such as

- mental agility, including capacity for analysis and evaluation;
- mastery of a complex subject;
- initiative;
- creativity;
- strong communication skills;
- ability to work cooperatively with others; and
- ethical behavior.

If an institution has a standard teaching load, fulfilling the load could be an essential function. Research and service expectations may also be essential functions at many institutions.

Beyond essential functions common to all faculty appointments, a particular position may have its own requirements. The demands of an academic position that involves performing on violin with the music department's faculty string quartet differ from those of a position in theoretical mathematics. Apart from obvious differences in subject matter, the violinist needs the capacity to play in public quartet performances.[6] The mathematician, in contrast, might require sophistication in highly specialized computer functions. The hours each devotes to working directly with students would likely differ. Such variations shape the essential functions of particular faculty positions.

At what point should a university define the essential functions of its faculty positions? Some institutions define essential functions for the purpose of, and in the process of, posting and eventually filling open positions. Such institutions routinely include the essential functions in the vacancy announcements, typically listed as "required qualifications." Other institutions have proceeded more comprehensively, establishing essential functions for all faculty positions. But some colleges and universities, perhaps most, have not undertaken to define the essential functions of their faculty positions. We encourage appropriate faculty bodies, including departments and faculty governing bodies, to define the essential functions of faculty positions, subject to review by administrative authorities.

Articulating essential functions provides a useful framework for professional responsibility and reduces for all faculty members the prospect of arbitrary charges of neglect of duties or incompetence.

Nonessential functions are those that may be absorbed by other people. Leading student field trips may, for example, be an essential function for a geology professor. Driving the van, however, may be a nonessential function that someone else could perform. Nonessential functions are also called marginal functions.

A position's essential functions provide the starting point for considering a faculty member's request for accommodation on the basis of a disability. Briefly stated, an individual who has a disability must perform the essential functions, either with or without an accommodation. If a faculty member requests an accommodation and the institution has not previously defined his or her essential functions, the institution must promptly perform the analysis. The analysis at this point is only of the *position*—what are its core responsibilities, without regard to the individual situation prompting the analysis. That is, the essential functions of a position are independent of any individual who may hold it.

If an institution has defined essential functions of faculty positions before a professor requests an accommodation, the institution avoids possible charges that it manipulated the analysis to the detriment of the individual. Written position descriptions and detailed vacancy announcements provide evidence of essential functions. Faculty members should lead the effort to create fair descriptions of essential functions of faculty positions.

Establishing the Nature and Extent of the Disability. An individual who has a disability may first raise the issue in a request for leave for medical treatment or rehabilitation. Unless a disability and the limitations it creates are obvious, the institution may need information about the nature and extent of the disability. The goal is an objective analysis of the individual's condition and capacity to fulfill the position's essential functions.

The faculty member typically seeks documentation from his or her own health-care provider or other appropriate professional.[7] The institution may write to the professional to share a description of the essential functions of the individual's position. The institution might solicit from the professional specific information, such as the diagnosis, the expected duration of and prognosis for the disabling condition, the individual's general limitations and specific capacity to perform the essential functions, and suggestions for possible accommodations.

The institution may have an appropriate professional of its choice review the documentation. If after review the institution requires additional information, it may seek further guidance and clarification from the professional who provided the original documentation for the faculty member. In unusual situations, central issues may remain unresolved even after further exchange with this professional. The institution may take the final step of arranging for a health-care provider or other appropriate professional of its choice to evaluate the faculty member's capacity to fulfill the position's essential responsibilities. The faculty member should not bear any expense for an evaluation by a health-care provider or other appropriate professional selected by the institution.

It is useful to bear in mind that the term disability has a technical, legal meaning. It does not cover all limiting conditions.[8] A bad cold and a broken leg are not disabilities because they are transitory and typically last fewer than six months. A disability is a long-term physical or mental impairment that significantly impedes an individual in performing an activity that is of central importance to life.[9] Central activities include sleeping and eating, for example, and also bodily processes such as function of the immune system and normal cell growth. A disability may be continuous, episodic, or intermittent. Intermittent disability would include cancer in remission, if when active the disease would be an impairment. The statute, regulations, and case law all elaborate on the definition.

The Americans with Disabilities Act protects a person *without* a disability if the employer treats him or her as impaired. This is informally known as the statute's "regarded as" clause. Caution requires that we avoid making comments suggesting that faculty members or others have a mental or physical problem.

Discussing Accommodation. Once a faculty member has raised a disability issue, the essential functions of the position have been identified, and the nature and extent of the disabling condition have been established, the process of discussing and structuring accommodations begins. Federal law mandates an interactive process. The faculty member and the department are typically well informed about possible adjustments that would permit the individual to succeed in meeting the essential functions. Experts from a campus disability-support office or human resources often provide valuable assistance. They may have considerable experience in translating diagnoses into pragmatic considerations and suggesting accommodations.

An experimental scientist with a disabling back condition might need higher laboratory countertops. A professor who loses his eyesight might need a reader and a specially equipped computer. The options are nearly infinite, and a reasonable solution should be selected to fit the circumstances. The essence of the interactive process is that each party solicits and considers the other's suggestions. The solution must be effective and reasonable, and the institution must be prepared to defray reasonable expenses.[10]

Sometimes persons who have disabilities privately and quietly bear the burden of making their own accommodations. They should, however, be encouraged to avail themselves of the institution's resources, to which they have a legal right.

Some accommodation requests may be inherently unreasonable. These might include, for example,

- demand for the creation of a part-time position with a full-time salary,
- refusal to serve on committees with specific individuals,
- removal of the department chair,
- refusal to teach undergraduates, or
- refusal to participate in department meetings.

Even some of these requests, though, should be evaluated in the context of the position's essential functions. If travel to campus for meetings is problematic, perhaps a faculty member could participate remotely. If attendance at department meetings is not an essential function, then an individual might be excused entirely.

The US Department of Labor sponsors the Job Accommodation Network, which provides online resources and telephone advice on workplace accommodations.[11] Structuring reasonable accommodations calls for creativity, flexibility, and open dialogue. A successful accommodation redounds to the mutual benefit of the institution and the faculty member.

Addressing Evaluation and Performance Issues. In past decades, the first female or minority professor in a department may not have received effective mentoring and evaluations.[12] Faculty members who have disabilities should not suffer the same fate. They should be evaluated on the same schedule and basis as their colleagues who are not disabled.[13] Those responsible for the evaluation should take care to be candid and to avoid paternalism. Evaluators should not assume a faculty member's disability is the cause of any performance problems. Like any other faculty member, a faculty member who has a disability may fail to fulfill professional responsibilities. The basis for discipline or dismissal must be the individual's performance. Institutions must avoid speculating on medical causes for performance problems. If a faculty member appears to be exhibiting mild dementia, for example, the evaluation should address the problematic behavior and its consequences. Such an evaluation might appropriately state: "You did not meet your class three times last semester and did not provide an explanation. Students report that your lectures are disorganized. You failed to turn in grades by the deadline. These problems harm current students and impede the department's efforts to attract more students to the major."

While some might criticize such an approach as insensitive, it focuses on performance and addresses core institutional concerns. Were the evaluation to suggest, for example, that "some early-stage dementia may be contributing to your problems," it could constitute disability discrimination. Were the evaluation to urge the individual to consider retirement, it would likely run afoul of age discrimination laws.

To protect the dignity of faculty members unable to fulfill their professional responsibilities, institutions are well advised to seek negotiated resolutions.[14] Failing a mutually satisfactory resolution, in serious cases the institution should proceed under Regulation 5 of the Association's *Recommended Institutional Regulations on Academic Freedom and Tenure.*[15]

A faculty member who has a disability is entitled to the same due-process protections as a faculty member who does not have a disability. Equity requires use of the standard criteria and procedures. In special circumstances, however, an institution might wish to offer an abbreviated process on a voluntary basis. This could be appropriate if, for example, the subject matter of the proceeding were of a highly sensitive personal nature. An abbreviated process might involve a representative standing in for the individual or mutually agreed-upon stipulations of facts about the faculty member's performance. The choice between the full process and an abbreviated one must be left entirely to the individual.

Conceivably, a faculty member facing dismissal might for the first time indicate that he or she has a disability and might request an accommodation. In its discretion, the institution may proceed as discussed above, obtaining an objective opinion from the individual's health-care provider or other appropriate professional about the nature and extent of the disability. The information may form the basis for discussion of accommodations

that would allow the faculty member better to fulfill his or her professional responsibilities, thus postponing or eliminating the need for dismissal proceedings. But an institution bears no legal obligation to accommodate retroactively a disability of which it was unaware. The faculty member who first raises a disability issue during a dismissal proceeding may be entitled to a reasonable accommodation in order to participate effectively in the proceeding itself.[16]

An institution must avoid requiring psychological counseling or medical treatment as a condition for a faculty member with a disability to retain his or her position. Mandatory counseling or treatment is inconsistent with using performance as the sole basis for judging professional fitness.

Conclusion

A final cautionary note is in order. It is important to avoid casual use of words such as "disabled" or "handicapped" unless circumstances warrant the technical application of such terms. Similarly, the speculative or pejorative labeling of an individual as having a mental or physical challenge perpetuates negative stereotypes and may even create a presumption that the speaker regards the individual as having a disability.

The academy welcomes and supports qualified faculty members with disabilities, who deserve the same opportunities and protections as their colleagues who are not disabled.

Notes

1. The subcommittee's original task was to review Regulation 4(e) of the AAUP's "Recommended Institutional Regulations on Academic Freedom and Tenure," "Termination Because of Physical or Mental Disability," which, on the advice of the subcommittee, Committee A then withdrew, inviting further comment. The language of the withdrawn regulation can be found in *Academe* 93 (March–April 2007): 124–25.

2. Carrie G. Basas, "Lawyers with Disabilities Add Critical Diversity to the Profession," in John W. Parry and Williams J. Phelan IV (eds.), *The Second National Conference on the Employment of Lawyers with Disabilities: A Report from the American Bar Association for the Legal Profession* (Washington, DC: American Bar Association, 2009), 26–29.

3. The National Science Foundation (NSF) tracks the careers of persons with disabilities who hold doctorates in the sciences and engineering. The NSF reported that, in 2008, 7.3 percent had a disability (http://www.nsf.gov/statistics/wmpd/). As to the general lack of data, regulations limit the kinds of queries employers may make of applicants regarding disability.

4. The many ways in which faculty members can support students who have disabilities are beyond the

scope of this report. We simply note the option of including a syllabus statement such as: "My goal is to make this course accessible to all students. If you think you need an accommodation for a disability, please let [the appropriate party—for example, 'me,' 'the disability services office,' or 'the associate dean'] know at your earliest convenience. Some aspects of this course—the assignments, the in-class activities, and the way I teach—may be modified to facilitate your participation and progress. The sooner you make [the appropriate party] aware of your needs, the sooner we can determine appropriate accommodations. I will treat any information you provide about your disability or accommodations with respect."

5. MLA Committee on Disability Issues in the Profession, *Disability and Hiring: Guidelines for Departmental Search Committees* (New York: Modern Language Association, September 2006), http://www .mla.org/dis_hiring_guidelines.

6. If a violin pedagogue, not involved in the faculty string quartet, lost the use of her hands, her teaching career would not necessarily come to an end. Some professors teach instrumental music orally to avoid having their sound and interpretation unduly influence their students. Alternatively, an assistant might demonstrate on the violin during lessons. The issue is whether the faculty member can perform the essential functions of her position in violin instruction, either with or without an accommodation.

7. Consider the situation of a faculty member who has attention deficit disorder or attention deficit hyperactivity disorder. She may furnish documentation about her condition from an expert in learning disabilities, although the expert may not be a "healthcare provider" as that phrase is commonly understood.

8. Questions often arise on the legal status of alcohol abuse and illegal drug use. Federal law covers past or current alcoholism as a disability. Illegal drug use is not a covered disability. Federal law, however, protects individuals undergoing treatment for drug addiction. An institution may prohibit faculty and staff from consuming or possessing alcohol or illegal drugs on campus. It may also prohibit faculty and staff from arriving at work impaired by alcohol or illegal drugs. See, for example, the Drug-Free Schools and Communities Act of 1989, 20 US Code §1011(I).

9. Here is the statutory definition. Definition of disability (42 US Code §12102):

As used in this chapter:
(1) Disability. The term 'disability' means, with respect to an individual
   (A) a physical or mental impairment that substantially limits one or more major life activities of such individual;
   (B) a record of such an impairment; or
   (C) being regarded as having such an impairment (as described in paragraph (3)).
(2) Major Life Activities
   (A) In general. For purposes of paragraph (1), major life activities include, but are not limited to, caring for oneself, performing manual tasks,

seeing, hearing, eating, sleeping, walking, standing, lifting, bending, speaking, breathing, learning, reading, concentrating, thinking, communicating, and working.
   (B) Major bodily functions. For purposes of paragraph (1), a major life activity also includes the operation of a major bodily function, including but not limited to, functions of the immune system, normal cell growth, digestive, bowel, bladder, neurological, brain, respiratory, circulatory, endocrine, and reproductive functions.
(3) Regarded as having such an impairment.
For purposes of paragraph (1)(C):
   (A) An individual meets the requirement of "being regarded as having such an impairment" if the individual establishes that he or she has been subjected to an action prohibited under this chapter because of an actual or perceived physical or mental impairment whether or not the impairment limits or is perceived to limit a major life activity.
   (B) Paragraph (1)(C) shall not apply to impairments that are transitory and minor. A transitory impairment is an impairment with an actual or expected duration of 6 months or less.

10. As Appendix C of the full report discusses, feasibility, cost, and effect of program adjustments are related factors. The institution must reach a reasonable, justifiable conclusion in balancing competing considerations.

11. See http://askjan.org.

12. See, for example, *Kunda v. Muhlenberg College*, 621 F.2d 532 (3d Cir. 1980), a case involving a female faculty member who was not advised about a requirement of an advanced degree.

13. For sound faculty evaluation guidelines, see *Good Practice in Tenure Evaluation: Advice for Faculty, Department Chairs, and Academic Administrators* (Washington, DC: American Council on Education, American Association of University Professors, and United Educators Insurance, 2000).

14. In severe situations, an institution may require a faculty member to undergo a fitness-for-duty medical evaluation. The healthcare provider performing the evaluation should receive information about the essential functions of the individual's position. Merely requiring such an evaluation does not, as a matter of federal law, constitute discrimination on the basis of disability. State laws may also bear on such examinations.

15. AAUP, *Policy Documents and Reports*, 11th ed. (Baltimore: Johns Hopkins University Press, 2015), XXX–XXX.

16. Students facing disciplinary procedures sometimes raise an issue of disability for the first time during the discipline process. Should the same pattern occur for a faculty member facing dismissal or other severe sanction, the institution might examine how it has handled comparable student disability accommodation requests.

Students

Although the Association has been involved in issues that relate to student concerns throughout its history, in 1960 Committee A on Academic Freedom and Tenure began to address the topic of academic freedom of students in response to "recent events around the country, and particularly in the South," which confronted students "with many questions which in some fashion relate to their general claim to academic freedom," including "students' activities in connection with the desegregation controversy." Upon request by Committee A, the Council authorized the appointment of a Committee on Faculty Responsibility for the Academic Freedom of Students in 1960, which issued the *Statement on the Academic Freedom of Students* in 1965. Recognizing the still tentative nature of the conclusions drawn by the committee, the Council authorized the committee to seek out other interested educational associations with which to collaborate on a potential joint statement. These efforts resulted in the *Joint Statement on Rights and Freedoms of Students*.

Two additional statements, one on graduate students and one on intercollegiate athletics, which specifically addresses concerns of student athletes, are also included in this section. A related document not included here—the draft *Statement on Student Participation in College and University Government*, published in 1970 and included in some previous editions of the Redbook before 1984—is of historical interest but was not further revised by the Committee on College and University Governance.

Joint Statement on Rights and Freedoms of Students

In June 1967, a committee composed of representatives from the American Association of University Professors, the United States National Student Association (now the United States Student Association), the Association of American Colleges (now the Association of American Colleges and Universities), the National Association of Student Personnel Administrators, and the National Association of Women Deans and Counselors formulated the joint statement. The document was endorsed by each of its five national sponsors, as well as by a number of other professional bodies. The governing bodies of the Association of American Colleges and the American Association of University Professors acted in January and April 1990, respectively, to remove gender-specific references from the original text; references were updated in 2006.

In September 1990, September 1991, and November 1992, an interassociation task force met to study, interpret, update, and affirm (or reaffirm) the *Joint Statement*. Members of the task force agreed that the document had stood the test of time quite well and continued to provide an excellent set of principles for institutions of higher education. The task force developed a set of interpretive endnotes to incorporate changes in law and higher education which had occurred since 1967. A list of associations endorsing the annotations appears as an appendix.

Preamble

Academic institutions exist for the transmission of knowledge, the pursuit of truth, the development of students, and the general well-being of society. Free inquiry and free expression are indispensable to the attainment of these goals. As members of the academic community, students should be encouraged to develop the capacity for critical judgment and to engage in a sustained and independent search for truth. Institutional procedures for achieving these purposes may vary from campus to campus, but the minimal standards of academic freedom of students outlined below are essential to any community of scholars.

Freedom to teach and freedom to learn are inseparable facets of academic freedom. The freedom to learn depends upon appropriate opportunities and conditions in the classroom, on the campus, and in the larger community.[1] Students should exercise their freedom with responsibility.

The responsibility to secure and to respect general conditions conducive to the freedom to learn is shared by all members of the academic community. Each college and university has a duty to develop policies and procedures that provide and safeguard this freedom. Such policies and procedures should be developed at each institution within the framework of general standards and with the broadest possible participation of the members of the academic community. The purpose of this statement is to enumerate the essential provisions for students' freedom to learn.

Freedom of Access to Higher Education

The admissions policies of each college and university are a matter of institutional choice, provided that each college and university makes clear the characteristics and expectations of students that it considers relevant to success in the institution's program.[2] While church-related institutions may give admission preference to students of their own persuasion, such a preference should be clearly and publicly stated. Under no circumstances should a student be barred from admission to a particular institution on the basis of race.[3] Thus, within the limits of its facilities, each college and university should be open to all students who are qualified according to its admissions standards. The facilities and services of a college or university should be open to all of its enrolled students, and institutions should use their influence to secure equal access for all students to public facilities in the local community.

In the Classroom
The professor in the classroom and in conference should encourage free discussion, inquiry, and expression. Student performance should be evaluated solely on an academic basis, not on opinions or conduct in matters unrelated to academic standards.

1. Protection of Freedom of Expression
Students should be free to take reasoned exception to the data or views offered in any course of study and to reserve judgment about matters of opinion, but they are responsible for learning the content of any course of study for which they are enrolled.

2. Protection against Improper Academic Evaluation
Students should have protection through orderly procedures against prejudiced or capricious academic evaluation.[4] At the same time, they are responsible for maintaining standards of academic performance established for each course in which they are enrolled.

3. Protection against Improper Disclosure
Information about student views, beliefs, and political associations that professors acquire in the course of their work as instructors, advisers, and counselors should be considered confidential. Protection against improper disclosure is a serious professional obligation. Judgments of ability and character may be provided under appropriate circumstances, normally with the knowledge and consent of the student.

Student Records
Institutions should have carefully considered policy as to the information that should be part of a student's permanent educational record and as to the conditions of its disclosure. To minimize the risk of improper disclosure, academic and disciplinary records should be separate, and the conditions of access to each should be set forth in an explicit policy statement. Transcripts of academic records should contain only information about academic status. Information from disci-

plinary or counseling files should not be available to unauthorized persons on campus, or to any person off campus without the express consent of the student involved, except under legal compulsion or in cases where the safety of persons or property is involved. No records should be kept that reflect the political activities or beliefs of students. Provision should also be made for periodic routine destruction of non-current disciplinary records. Administrative staff and faculty members should respect confidential information about students which they acquire in the course of their work.[5]

Student Affairs
In student affairs, certain standards must be maintained if the freedom of students is to be preserved.[6]

1. Freedom of Association
Students bring to the campus a variety of interests previously acquired and develop many new interests as members of the academic community. They should be free to organize and join associations to promote their common interests.

a. The membership, policies, and actions of a student organization usually will be determined by vote of only those persons who hold bona fide membership in the college or university community.
b. Affiliation with an extramural organization should not of itself disqualify a student organization from institutional recognition.[7]
c. If campus advisers are required, each organization should be free to choose its own adviser, and institutional recognition should not be withheld or withdrawn solely because of the inability of a student organization to secure an adviser. Campus advisers may advise organizations in the exercise of responsibility, but they should not have the authority to control the policy of such organizations.
d. Student organizations may be required to submit a statement of purpose, criteria for membership, rules of procedure, and a current list of officers. They should not be required to submit a membership list as a condition of institutional recognition.
e. Campus organizations, including those affiliated with an extramural organization, should be open to all students without respect to race, creed, or national origin, except for religious qualifications which may be required by organizations whose aims are primarily sectarian.[8]

2. Freedom of Inquiry and Expression

a. Students and student organizations should be free to examine and discuss all questions of interest to them and to express opinions publicly and privately. They should always be free to support causes by orderly means that do not disrupt the regular and essential operations of the institution. At the same time, it should be made clear to the academic and larger community that in their public expressions or demonstrations students or student organizations speak only for themselves.

b. Students should be allowed to invite and to hear any person of their own choosing. Those routine procedures required by an institution before a guest speaker is invited to appear on campus should be designed only to ensure that there is orderly scheduling of facilities and adequate preparation for the event, and that the occasion is conducted in a manner appropriate to an academic community. The institutional control of campus facilities should not be used as a device of censorship. It should be made clear to the academic and larger community that sponsorship of guest speakers does not necessarily imply approval or endorsement of the views expressed, either by the sponsoring group or by the institution.[9]

3. Student Participation in Institutional Government

As constituents of the academic community, students should be free, individually and collectively, to express their views on issues of institutional policy and on matters of general interest to the student body. The student body should have clearly defined means to participate in the formulation and application of institutional policy affecting academic and student affairs.[10] The role of student government and both its general and specific responsibilities should be made explicit, and the actions of student government within the areas of its jurisdiction should be reviewed only through orderly and prescribed procedures.

4. Student Publications

Student publications and the student press are valuable aids in establishing and maintaining an atmosphere of free and responsible discussion and of intellectual exploration on the campus. They are a means of bringing student concerns to the attention of the faculty and the institutional authorities and of formulating student opinion on various issues on the campus and in the world at large.

Whenever possible the student newspaper should be an independent corporation financially and legally separate from the college or university. Where financial and legal autonomy is not possible, the institution, as the publisher of student publications, may have to bear the legal responsibility for the contents of the publications. In the delegation of editorial responsibility to students, the institution must provide sufficient editorial freedom and financial autonomy for the student publications to maintain their integrity of purpose as vehicles for free inquiry and free expression in an academic community.

Institutional authorities, in consultation with students and faculty, have a responsibility to provide written clarification of the role of the student publications, the standards to be used in their evaluation, and the limitations on external control of their operation. At the same time, the editorial freedom of student editors and managers entails corollary responsibilities to be governed by the canons of responsible journalism, such as the avoidance of libel, indecency, undocumented allegations, attacks on personal integrity, and the techniques of harassment and innuendo. As safeguards for the editorial freedom of student publications the following provisions are necessary:

a. The student press should be free of censorship and advance approval of copy, and its editors and managers should be free to develop their own editorial policies and news coverage.

b. Editors and managers of student publications should be protected from arbitrary suspension and removal because of student, faculty, administration, or public disapproval of editorial policy or content. Only for proper and stated causes should editors and managers be subject to removal and then only by orderly and prescribed procedures. The agency responsible for the appointment of editors and managers should be the agency responsible for their removal.

c. All institutionally published and financed student publications should explicitly state on the editorial page that the opinions there expressed are not necessarily those of the college, university, or student body.

Off-Campus Freedom of Students

1. Exercise of Rights of Citizenship

College and university students are both citizens and members of the academic community. As citizens, students should enjoy the same freedom of speech, peaceful assembly, and right of petition that other citizens enjoy and, as members of the academic community, they are subject to the obligations that accrue to them by virtue of this membership. Faculty members and administration officials should ensure that institutional powers are not employed to inhibit such intellectual and personal development of students as is often promoted by their exercise of the rights of citizenship both on and off campus.

2. Institutional Authority and Civil Penalties

Activities of students may upon occasion result in violation of law. In such cases, institutional officials should be prepared to apprise students of sources of legal counsel and may offer other assistance. Students who violate the law may incur penalties prescribed by civil authorities, but institutional authority should never be used merely to duplicate the function of general laws. Only where the institution's interests as an academic community are distinct and clearly involved should the special authority of the institution be asserted. Students who incidentally violate institutional regulations in the course of their off-campus activity, such as those relating to class attendance, should be subject to no greater penalty than would normally be imposed. Institutional action should be independent of community pressure.

Procedural Standards in Disciplinary Proceedings

In developing responsible student conduct, disciplinary proceedings play a role substantially secondary to example, counseling, guidance, and admonition.[11] At the same time, educational institutions have a duty and the corollary disciplinary powers to protect their educational purpose through the setting of standards of scholarship and conduct for the students who attend them and through the regulation of the use of institutional facilities. In the exceptional circumstances when the preferred means fail to resolve problems of student conduct, proper procedural safeguards should be observed to protect the student from the unfair imposition of serious penalties.

The administration of discipline should guarantee procedural fairness to an accused student.[12] Practices in disciplinary cases may vary in formality with the gravity of the offense and the sanctions that may be applied. They should also take into account the presence or absence of an honor code, and the degree to which the institutional officials have direct acquaintance with student life in general and with the involved student and the circumstances of the case in particular. The jurisdictions of faculty or student judicial bodies, the disciplinary responsibilities of institutional officials, and the regular disciplinary procedures, including the student's right to appeal a decision, should be clearly formulated and communicated in advance.[13] Minor penalties may be assessed informally under prescribed procedures.

In all situations, procedural fair play requires that a student charged with misconduct be informed of the nature of the charges and be given a fair opportunity to refute them, that the institution not be arbitrary in its actions, and that there be provision for appeal of a decision. The following are recommended as proper safeguards in such proceedings when there are no honor codes offering comparable guarantees.

1. Standards of Conduct Expected of Students

The institution has an obligation to clarify those standards that it considers essential to its educational mission and its community life. These general behavioral expectations and the resultant specific regulations should represent a reasonable regulation of student conduct, but students should be as free as possible from imposed limitations that have no direct relevance to their education. Offenses should be as clearly defined as possible and interpreted in a manner consistent with the aforementioned principles of relevancy and reasonableness.[14] Disciplinary proceedings should be instituted only for violations of standards of conduct formulated with significant student participation and published in advance through such means as a student handbook or a generally available body of institutional regulations.

2. Investigation of Student Conduct

a. Except under extreme emergency circumstances, premises occupied by students and the personal possessions of students should not be searched unless appropriate authorization has been obtained. For premises such as residence halls controlled by the institution, an appropriate and responsible authority should be designated to whom application should be made before a search is conducted. The application should specify the reasons for the search and the objects or information sought. The student should be present, if possible, during the search. For premises not controlled by the institution, the ordinary requirements for lawful search should be followed.

b. Students detected or arrested in the course of serious violations of institutional regulations, or infractions of ordinary law, should be informed of their rights.[15] No form of harassment should be used by institutional representatives to coerce admissions of guilt or disclosure of information about conduct of other suspected persons.

3. Status of Student Pending Final Action
Pending action on the charges, the status of a student should not be altered, or the student's right to be present on the campus and to attend classes suspended, except for reasons relating to the student's physical or emotional safety and well-being, or for reasons relating to the safety and well-being of other students, faculty, or institutional property.

4. Hearing Committee Procedures
When the misconduct may result in serious penalties, and if a penalized student questions the fairness of disciplinary action, that student should be granted, on request, the privilege of a hearing before a regularly constituted hearing committee. The following suggested hearing committee procedures satisfy the requirements of procedural due process in situations requiring a high degree of formality.

a. The hearing committee should include faculty members or students, or, if regularly included or requested by the accused, both faculty and student members. No member of the hearing committee who is otherwise interested in the particular case should sit in judgment during the proceeding.

b. The student should be informed, in writing, of the reasons for the proposed disciplinary action with sufficient particularity, and in sufficient time, to ensure opportunity to prepare for the hearing.[16]

c. The student appearing before the hearing committee should have the right to be assisted in his or her defense by an adviser of the student's choice.

d. The burden of proof should rest upon the officials bringing the charge.

e. The student should be given an opportunity to testify, to present evidence and witnesses, and to hear and question adverse witnesses. In no case should the committee consider statements against the student unless he or she has been advised of their content and of the names of those who made them and has been given an opportunity to rebut unfavorable inferences that might otherwise be drawn.

f. All matters upon which the decision may be based must be introduced into evidence at the proceeding before the hearing committee. The decision should be based solely upon such matters. Improperly acquired evidence should not be admitted.

g. In the absence of a transcript, there should be both a digest and a verbatim record, such as a tape recording, of the hearing.

h. The decision of the hearing committee should be final, subject only to the student's right of appeal to the president or ultimately to the governing board of the institution.[17]

Appendix
The following associations endorsed the interpretive notes below:

American Association of Community Colleges
American Association of University Administrators
American Association of University Professors
American College Personnel Association
Association for Student Judicial Affairs
National Association for Women in Education
National Association of Student Personnel Administrators
National Orientation Directors Association
Southern Association for College Student Affairs
United States Student Association

Notes
1. In order to protect the freedom of students to learn, as well as enhance their participation in the life of the academic community, students should be free from exploitation or harassment.

2. In order to enable them to make appropriate choices and participate effectively in an institution's programs, students have the right to be informed about the institution, its policies, practices, and characteristics. Institutions preparing such information should take into account applicable federal and state laws.

3. The reference to race must not be taken to limit the nondiscrimination obligations of institutions. In all aspects of education, students have a right to be free from discrimination on the basis of individual attributes not demonstrably related to academic success in the institution's programs, including, but not limited to, race, color, gender, age, disability, national origin, and sexual orientation. Under *Grutter v. Bollinger*, 539 US 306, 330 (2003), "student body diversity"—including racial diversity—"is a compelling state interest that can justify the use of race in university admissions." This means that, when colleges and universities determine that achieving diversity within the student body is relevant to their academic mission, their admissions offices may take an applicant's race into account as one factor among many in making an admission decision.

4. The student grievance procedures typically used in these matters are not appropriate for addressing charges of academic dishonesty or other disciplinary matters arising in the classroom. In these instances, students should be afforded the safeguards of orderly procedures consistent with those set forth in "Procedural Standards in Disciplinary Proceedings." (In 1997,

the AAUP's Committee A on Academic Freedom and Tenure approved a statement on "The Assignment of Course Grades and Student Appeals," AAUP, *Policy Documents and Reports*, 11th ed. [Baltimore: Johns Hopkins University Press, 2015], 29–30.)

5. The Family Educational Rights and Privacy Act (FERPA) provides for the protection of student records. Consistent with FERPA, institutions should have a statement of policy on the content of a student's educational record, as well as the conditions for its disclosure. Institutions should also have policies and security practices to control access to student records that may be available or transmitted electronically.

6. As in the case of classroom matters, students shall have protection through orderly procedures to ensure this freedom.

7. "Institutional recognition" should be understood to refer to any formal relationship between the student organization and the institution.

8. The obligation of institutions with respect to nondiscrimination, with the exception noted above for religious qualifications, should be understood in accordance with the expanded statement on nondiscrimination in note 3. Exceptions may also be based on gender as authorized by law.

9. The events referred to in this section should be understood to include the full range of student-sponsored activities, such as films, exhibitions, and performances.

10. "Academic and student affairs" should be interpreted broadly to include all administrative and policy matters pertinent to students' educational experiences.

11. The student conduct that may be subject to the disciplinary proceedings described in this section should be understood to include alleged violations of standards of student academic integrity.

12. In addition, student organizations, as well as individual students, may be subject to institutional disciplinary sanctions, and in those circumstances, student organizations should also be guaranteed procedural fairness.

13. Like other practices in disciplinary cases, the formality of any appellate procedures should be commensurate with the gravity of the offense and the sanctions that may be imposed.

14. The institution should state as specifically as possible the sanctions that may be imposed through disciplinary proceedings.

15. This provision is intended to protect students' rights under both institutional codes and applicable law. Where institutional regulations are violated, students should be informed of their rights under campus disciplinary procedures. Where arrests are made for infractions of the law, students must be informed of their rights by arresting authorities.

16. The student should also be informed of the specific sanctions that may be imposed through the disciplinary proceeding.

17. As a matter of responsible practice, the decision of the hearing committee, as well as grounds and procedures for appeal, should be communicated to the student in writing within a reasonable period of time.

Statement on Graduate Students

The statement that follows was approved by the Association's Committee on Teaching, Research, and Publication in October 1999. It was adopted by the AAUP's Council in June 2000 and endorsed by the Eighty-Sixth Annual Meeting.

Preamble

Graduate programs in universities exist for the discovery and transmission of knowledge, the education of students, the training of future faculty, and the general well-being of society. Free inquiry and free expression are indispensable to the attainment of these goals.

In 1967 the American Association of University Professors participated with the National Student Association, the Association of American Colleges, and others in the formulation of the *Joint Statement on Rights and Freedoms of Students.*[1] The *Joint Statement* has twice been revised and updated, most recently in November 1992. The AAUP's Committee on Teaching, Research, and Publication, while supporting the Association's continuing commitment to the *Joint Statement*, believes that the distinctive circumstances of graduate students require a supplemental statement.

The statement that follows has been formulated to reflect the educational maturity and the distinguishing academic characteristics and responsibilities of graduate students. These students not only engage in more advanced studies than their undergraduate counterparts, but often they also hold teaching or research assistantships. As graduate assistants, they carry out many of the functions of faculty members and receive compensation for these duties. The statement below sets forth recommended standards that we believe will foster sound academic policies in universities with graduate programs. The responsibility to secure and respect general conditions conducive to a graduate student's freedom to learn and to teach is shared by all members of a university's graduate community. Each university should develop policies and procedures that safeguard this freedom. Such policies and procedures should be developed within the framework of those general standards that enable the university to fulfill its educational mission. These standards are offered not simply to protect the rights of affected individuals but also to ensure that graduate education fulfills its responsibilities to students, faculty, and society.[2]

Recommended Standards

1. Graduate students have the right to academic freedom. Like other students, they "should be free to take reasoned exception to the data or views offered in any course of study and to reserve judgment about matters of opinion, but they are responsible for learning the content of any course of study for which they are enrolled."[3] Moreover, because of their advanced education, graduate students should be encouraged by their professors to exercise their freedom of "discussion, inquiry, and expression."[4] Further, they should be able to express their opinions freely about matters of institutional policy, and they should have the same freedom of action in the public political domain as faculty members should have.

   Graduate students' freedom of inquiry is necessarily qualified by their still being learners in the profession; nonetheless, their faculty mentors should afford them latitude and respect as they decide how they will engage in teaching and research.

2. Graduate students have the right to be free from illegal or unconstitutional discrimination, or discrimination on a basis not demonstrably related to job function, including, but not limited to, age, sex, disability, race, religion, national origin, marital status, or sexual orientation, in admissions and throughout their education, employment, and placement.[5]

   Graduate students should be informed of the requirements of their degree programs. When feasible, they should be told about acceptance, application, and attrition rates in their fields, but it is also their responsibility to keep themselves informed of these matters. If degree requirements are altered, students admitted under previous rules should be able to continue under those rules. Graduate students should be assisted in making timely progress toward their degrees by being provided with diligent advisers, relevant course offerings, adequate dissertation or thesis supervision, and periodic assessment of and clear communication on their progress. Students should understand that dissertation or thesis work may be constrained by the areas of interest and specialization of available faculty supervisors.

If a graduate student's dissertation or thesis adviser departs from the institution once the student's work is under way, the responsible academic officers should endeavor to provide the student with alternative supervision, external to the institution if necessary. If a degree program is to be discontinued, provisions must be made for students already in the program to complete their course of study.

3. Graduate students are entitled to the protection of their intellectual-property rights, including recognition of their participation in supervised research and their research with faculty, consistent with generally accepted standards of attribution and acknowledgment in collaborative settings. Written standards should be publicly available.

4. Graduate students should have a voice in institutional governance at the program, department, college, graduate school, and university levels.

5. Under the Association's *Recommended Institutional Regulations on Academic Freedom and Tenure*, graduate-student assistants are to be informed in writing of the terms and conditions of their appointment and, in the event of proposed dismissal, are to be afforded access to a duly constituted hearing committee.[6] They should be informed of all academic or other institutional regulations affecting their roles as employees. Graduate-student employees with grievances, as individuals or as a group, should submit them in a timely fashion and should have access to an impartial faculty committee or, if provided under institutional policy, arbitration. Clear guidelines and timelines for grievance procedures should be distributed to all interested parties. Individual grievants or participants in a group grievance should not be subjected to reprisals. Graduate-student employees may choose a representative to speak for them or with them at all stages of a grievance.

6. Good practice should include appropriate training and supervision in teaching, adequate office space, and a safe working environment. Departments should endeavor to acquaint students with the norms and traditions of their academic discipline and to inform them of professional opportunities. Graduate students should be encouraged to seek departmental assistance in obtaining future academic and nonacademic employment. Departments are encouraged to provide support for the professional development of graduate students by such means as funding research expenses and conference travel.

7. Graduate students should have access to their files and placement dossiers. If access is denied, graduate students should be able to have a faculty member of their choice examine their files and, at the professor's discretion, provide the student with a redacted account. Graduate students should have the right to direct that items be added to or removed from their placement dossiers.

8. As the Association's Council affirmed in November 1998, graduate-student assistants, like other campus employees, should have the right to organize to bargain collectively. Where state legislation permits, administrations should honor a majority request for union representation. Graduate-student assistants must not suffer retaliation from professors or administrators because of their activity relating to collective bargaining.

9. In order to assist graduate students in making steady progress toward their degrees, the time they spend in teaching or research assistantships or other graduate employment at the institution should be limited in amount—a common maximum is twenty hours per week—and should afford sufficient compensation so as not to compel the student to obtain substantial additional employment elsewhere.

10. Graduate-student assistants, though they work only part time, should receive essential fringe benefits, and especially health benefits.

Notes

1. AAUP, *Policy Documents and Reports*, 11th ed. (Baltimore: Johns Hopkins University Press, 2015), 381–86.

2. We recognize that the responsibilities of graduate students vary widely among individuals, courses of study, and institutions. Some provisions of this statement may not apply to students in professional schools who may have different types of responsibilities from those of students in other disciplines.

3. "Joint Statement," *Policy Documents and Reports*, 11th ed., 382.

4. Ibid.

5. "On Discrimination," AAUP, *Policy Documents and Reports*, 10th ed. (Washington, DC: AAUP, 2006), 229.

6. Regulation 14, "Recommended Institutional Regulations on Academic Freedom and Tenure," *Policy Documents and Reports*, 11th ed., 87.

Statement on Intercollegiate Athletics

The statement that follows was prepared by a special committee of the Association's Council. It was adopted by the Council in June 1991.

Introduction

On many campuses the conduct of intercollegiate athletic programs poses serious and direct conflicts with desired academic standards and goals. The pressure to field winning teams has led to widely publicized scandals concerning the recruitment, exploitation, and academic failure of many athletes.

Expenditures on athletics may distort institutional budgets and can reduce resources available for academic functions. Within some academic programs faculty members have been pressured to give preferential treatment to athletes. Coaches and athletic directors are themselves often trapped in the relentless competitive and financial pressures of the current system, and many would welcome reform.

Not all institutions have problems with athletics of the same type or to the same degree. Nevertheless, we believe that all colleges and universities would benefit from the adoption of a national set of standards that would protect athletes from exploitation and would place expenditures on and administration of athletic programs under the regular governance procedures of the institution.

We urge faculty participation in the cause of reform. We urge our administrators to enter into national efforts to establish new standards through the National Collegiate Athletic Association (NCAA) or other regulatory agencies. We specifically endorse the following proposed reforms and ask faculty colleagues, administrators, and athletic department staff throughout the country to join with us in working to implement them on their campuses, in their athletic conferences, through the NCAA, and nationally.

Admissions and Academic Progress

1. Institutions should not use admissions standards for athletes that are not comparable to those for other students.
2. A committee elected by the faculty should monitor the compliance with policies relating to admissions, the progress toward graduation, and the integrity of the course of study of students who engage in intercollegiate athletics. This committee should report annually to the faculty on admissions, on progress toward graduation, and on graduation rates of athletes by sport. Further, the committee should be charged with seeking appropriate review of cases in which it appears that faculty members or administrators have abused academic integrity in order to promote athletic programs.

Avoidance of Exploitation

Students who are athletes need time for their academic work. Participation in intercollegiate athletics in the first year of college is ill-advised. Athletes should have at least one day a week without athletic obligations. Overnight absences on weekday evenings should be kept to a maximum of one per week, with rare exceptions. The number of events per season should be periodically reviewed by the faculty. Student athletes should be integrated with other students in housing, food service, tutoring, and other areas of campus life.

Financial Aid

Financial-aid standards for athletes should be comparable to those for other students. The aid should be administered by the financial-aid office of the institution. The assessment of financial need may take account of time demands on athletes which preclude or limit employment during the academic year. Continuation of aid to students who drop out of athletic competition or complete their athletic eligibility should be conditioned only on their remaining academically and financially qualified.

Financing Athletics: Governance

1. Financial operations of the department of athletics, including all revenues received from outside groups, should be under the full and direct control of the central administration of the campus. Complete budgets of the athletic department for the coming year and actual expenditures and revenues for the past year should be published in full detail. Annual budgets as well as long-term plans should be approved under the regular governance

procedures of the campus, with meaningful involvement of elected faculty representatives.

2. Particular scrutiny should be given to use of the institution's general operating funds to support the athletic department. Institutions should establish regulations governing the use of, and the payment of fees for, university facilities by private businesses, such as summer athletic camps. Fees charged to coaches should be assessed on the same basis as those charged to faculty members and other staff engaged in private business on campus. Published budgets should include an accounting of maintenance expenses for sports facilities, activities of booster groups, payments by outsiders for appearances by coaches and other athletic staff, payments by sports-apparel companies, and sources of scholarship funds.

3. Elected faculty representatives should comprise a majority of the campus committee that formulates campus athletic policy, and such a committee should be chaired by an elected faculty member.

Conflicts of Interest

Paid-for trips to games, and other special benefits for faculty, administrators, or members of governing boards involved in the oversight of athletics, whether offered by the university or by outside groups, create conflicts of interest and should be eliminated.

Implementation

1. In order to avoid the obstacles to unilateral reform efforts, the university's chief administrative officer should join with counterparts in other institutions to pursue these reforms and report annually to the academic community on the progress of such efforts.

2. Beginning five years from adoption of these principles at an institution, athletic events should be scheduled only with institutions, and within conferences and associations, that commit themselves to the implementation of these principles.

Final Comment

Institutions should redouble their efforts to enroll and support academically able students from disadvantaged backgrounds regardless of their athletic ability. Athletic programs never should have been considered as a major way of supporting students from disadvantaged backgrounds in institutions of higher education. If these recommendations are adopted, athletes who lack academic skills or interests will no longer be enrolled, and some of those excluded will be from such backgrounds. In the interest of such athletes, institutions and the NCAA should avoid regulations that interfere with the creation of other channels of entry for these athletes into professional athletics.

Appendix: Investigative Procedures of the Association

Association Procedures in Academic Freedom and Tenure Cases

The following procedures were initially approved by Committee A on Academic Freedom and Tenure in August 1957. Subsequent revisions were approved by Committee A in June 1982, November 1999, and June 2000. To reflect a change in title for the Association's chief of staff, "general secretary" was updated in 2014 to "executive director."

1. The executive director[1] is authorized to receive, on behalf of Committee A, complaints from faculty members at duly accredited colleges and universities about departures from the Association's recommended standards concerned with academic freedom and tenure and related principles and procedures which are alleged to have occurred or to be threatened at their institutions. Incidents coming to the executive director's attention through other channels may also be subject to examination, if in the executive director's judgment the incidents in question are likely to be of concern to the Association. In cases where attention by the Association seems justified, the executive director shall make a preliminary inquiry and, where appropriate, communicate with the administration of the institution concerned in order to secure factual information and comments.

2. The executive director should attempt to assist the complainant(s) and the institution in arriving at a satisfactory resolution of the situation, if that appears to be possible.

3. If there is substantial reason to believe that a serious departure from applicable Association-supported standards has occurred, and if a satisfactory resolution of the situation does not appear to be possible, the executive director shall determine, upon the advice of the staff's committee on investigations and of others as appropriate, whether an ad hoc committee should be established to investigate and prepare a written report on the situation. In an exceptional case in which a violation of the 1940 *Statement of Principles on Academic Freedom and Tenure* or related Association standards is clearly established by incontrovertible written evidence, the executive director may authorize the preparation of a report without an onsite investigation.

4. If a decision is made to establish an investigating committee, the executive director shall designate a committee of two, three, or occasionally a larger number of members of the Association, depending on the importance and complexity of the case. One of the members ordinarily shall be designated as chair. In selecting the members, the executive director shall take account of such relevant factors as their experience and expertise in academic freedom and tenure issues, their subject matter fields in relation to those of the faculty member(s) involved in the incident(s), and the relation of their home institutions to the institution where the investigation will occur.

5. The executive director shall provide the committee with an advisory briefing on the procedures it will be expected to follow, on the existing information about the situation to be reported upon, and on the issues that appear to call for analysis, accompanied by available documentary evidence relevant to the investigation. The task of the investigating committee is to ascertain the facts involved in the incident(s) under investigation and the positions of the principal parties. The committee will determine whether the 1940 *Statement of Principles on Academic Freedom and Tenure* and/or related standards as interpreted by the Association have been violated, whether the institution's own stated policies have been disregarded, and whether conditions for academic freedom and tenure, as well as related conditions, are generally unsatisfactory. The executive director shall assist the committee so far as possible in making arrangements for its work and in providing it with clerical and editorial services.

6. The investigating committee shall, at Association expense, visit the institution where the incident(s) under investigation occurred, for

the purpose of securing information and interviewing the parties concerned and others who may possess relevant information or views.

7. The investigating committee should inquire fully into the violation(s) of AAUP standards alleged to have occurred, into conditions of academic freedom and tenure in the institution that form the background of the particular case(s) or that may have given rise to related incidents, and into relevant subsequent developments. The investigating committee may seek to secure such facts and viewpoints as it may deem necessary for the investigation, through onsite interviews, written documents, or correspondence or interviews both before and after the campus visit. In communications with the principal parties and on its visit to the institution, the investigating committee should make clear that it acts not in partisanship, but as a professional body charged with ascertaining the facts and respective positions as objectively as possible and as related to applicable Association-supported standards.

8. In an institution where a local chapter of the Association exists, the executive director should consult with the chapter officers when an investigation is being considered, when one is authorized, and when the visit of the investigating committee is being arranged. Either the executive director or the committee may seek the assistance of these officers in making local arrangements. The appropriate officer of the state conference shall also be consulted.

9. The investigating committee should not accept hospitality or any form of special treatment from the administration, from a faculty member whose case is being investigated, or from anyone else who has had a direct involvement in the case. The AAUP chapter should be alerted to the need to avoid situations, such as social events, which might compromise the integrity of the investigation. If the administration provides a room or other facilities for the committee's interviews, the committee may accept the arrangements if this will serve the convenience of the investigation.

10. The investigating committee may interview any persons who might be able to provide information about the matter(s) under investigation, and it must afford the subject faculty member(s) and the chief administrative officers the opportunity to meet with the committee. The committee should set up personal interviews with individuals who

have firsthand information, whether members of the faculty, members of the governing board, or officers of the administration. The committee should also seek meetings with officers of faculty bodies and of the AAUP chapter. Such persons should ordinarily be interviewed separately from each other, but exceptions may be made upon the wishes of those interviewed and at the discretion of the committee. In order for the Association's investigative and mediative processes to be most effective, faculty members, board members, and administrators alike need to be able to communicate freely with the investigating committee. Accordingly, the committee should encourage candor from all interviewees by protecting their confidentiality to the fullest extent possible consistent with the committee's need to prepare its report to Committee A. Information gathered in the course of an investigation should be kept confidential to the maximum extent permitted by law.

11. The function of the investigating committee is to prepare a report for submission to Committee A. The members of the investigating committee should not express opinions on the matter(s) under investigation, either confidentially to the parties concerned or publicly. If questions about a potential resolution of the situation under investigation should arise, the committee should refer the matter promptly to the executive director.

12. The investigating committee should determine its plan for the writing of its report. The report should include a sufficiently full statement of the evidence to enable the reader to understand the situation and judge the adequacy of the information in support of the committee's findings and conclusions. The report should state definite conclusions, either on the issues suggested to the committee by the executive director or on its own alternative formulation of the issues involved. The committee should determine whether the administration's actions that were investigated were in procedural and substantive compliance with principles and standards supported by the Association. The committee may set forth recommendations for or against publication of its report and for or against Association censure of the administration concerned, but the decision on these matters will rest with Committee A and, as to censure, with the annual meeting of the Association. Hence, any recommendation as to censure will not be published as part of the report. The

report should be transmitted in confidence to the executive director.

13. As soon as possible after receiving the report of the investigating committee, the executive director shall review it and communicate with the committee regarding any suggestions for revision. The committee's completed draft shall be transmitted to the members of Committee A, who may call for further revisions prior to the report's release to the principal parties and its potential publication. With Committee A's approval, the revised text shall then be transmitted on a confidential basis to the persons most significantly involved in the report, and to the local chapter president, with the request that they provide corrections of any errors of fact that may appear in it and make such comments as they may desire on the findings and conclusions reached. The appropriate state conference officer shall be provided with the prepublication report on a confidential basis and be invited to offer comments. The executive director shall invite the investigating committee to revise its report in the light of comments received. If significant revisions are to be made, the executive director shall seek Committee A's approval. The final text shall be published through its posting on the Association's website and subsequently in printed form in the annual *Bulletin of the American Association of University Professors*. The members of the investigating committee shall be listed as the authors of the published report unless they withhold their names because of disagreement with changes required by Committee A or as a result of comments from the principal parties.

14. At any time during the process described above, the Association remains open to the possibility of a resolution agreeable to all parties that will serve to confirm the administration's acceptance of Association-supported policies and procedures and provide corrective measures for the events that gave rise to the investigation.

Note

1. As used in this statement, "executive director" means the executive director or another professional staff member of the Association who may be delegated to perform the duties of the executive director in relation to a particular matter.

Standards for Investigations in the Area of College and University Governance

In 1991, the Association's Council adopted a proposal from the Committee on College and University Governance that makes it possible for an AAUP annual meeting to sanction an institution for "substantial non-compliance with standards of academic government." The following procedures, initially approved by the Committee on College and University Governance in May 1994 and revised by the committee in November 2010, set out the steps along the path that could lead from an expression of faculty concern at an institution to the imposition of an Association sanction. To reflect a change in title for the Association's chief of staff, "general secretary" was updated in 2014 to "executive director."

1. The executive director[1] is authorized to receive, on behalf of the Committee on College and University Governance, complaints of departures from the Association's recommended standards relating to academic governance at a particular college or university.

2. Such complaints should include a description of the situation and specific information on the past or contemplated use of local remedies. They should be accompanied by supporting documentation.

3. The executive director shall, in each instance where attention by the Association seems justified, make a preliminary inquiry and, where appropriate, communicate with the administration and involved faculty bodies at the institution to secure information and comments.

4. When feasible, the executive director shall attempt, by correspondence and discussion, to assist the parties in arriving at a resolution compatible with AAUP principles and standards. When significant departures from those principles and standards appear evident, the executive director shall write to the parties to convey the Association's concerns and invite a response to them.

5. If there is substantial reason to believe that a serious departure from applicable Association-supported standards has occurred, and if a satisfactory resolution of the situation does not appear to be possible, the executive director shall determine, upon the advice of the staff's committee on investigations, the chair of the Committee on College and University Governance, and others as appropriate, whether an ad hoc committee should be established to investigate and produce a written report.

6. In determining whether to proceed to investigation and report on situations related to college or university governance, the Association looks to the condition of faculty status and of faculty-administrative relations. The Association will investigate when it appears that corporate or individual functions of the faculty, as defined in the *Statement on Government of Colleges and Universities*, have been seriously threatened or impaired. Administrative actions such as the abolition of an existing faculty senate, the thorough restructuring of an institution, or the imposition of a faculty handbook, which occur without meaningful faculty involvement, are examples of situations that might be the basis for the authorization of an investigation. In reaching a decision on whether or not to undertake an investigation, the executive director will consider the magnitude of the problem for the faculty involved, for the institution as a whole, and for the Association in its capacity as an organization representing faculty interests in higher education.

7. The Association will ordinarily investigate only after local means for correction—formal as well as informal—have been pursued without satisfactory result. This precondition may not apply where local remedies are inadequate or where recourse to them would worsen the situation or expose individual faculty members to harm.

8. If a decision is made to establish an investigating committee, the executive director shall

appoint the members of the committee, designating one of them as chair. In selecting the members, the executive director shall consider such relevant factors as their experience and expertise in governance matters and the relation of their home institutions to the institution where the investigation will occur.

9. The task of the investigating committee is to determine the relevant facts and the positions of the principal parties and to reach findings on whether the standards enunciated in the *Statement on Government* and in derivative Association documents have been violated, and whether unacceptable conditions of academic governance prevail. The executive director shall provide the investigating committee with an advisory briefing on the procedures it will be expected to follow during a campus visit and on the facts, issues, and available documentary evidence relevant to the investigation. The executive director shall also assist the committee so far as possible in making arrangements for its work and in providing it with clerical and editorial support.

10. The investigating committee's report, to be submitted in confidence to the executive director, should include sufficient facts for the reader to understand the situation and judge the adequacy of the evidence in support of the committee's findings and conclusions. The committee should determine whether actions by the principal parties were reasonable under the circumstances and consistent with applicable Association-recommended procedural and substantive standards. The committee may offer advice to the Committee on College and University Governance as to whether the Association should impose a sanction on the institution concerned, but such advice is not to be included in either the draft report sent to the principal parties or the final published report. It is the responsibility of the Committee on Governance to determine whether a recommendation to impose a sanction should be presented to the annual meeting of the Association.

11. As soon as possible after receiving the report of the investigating committee, the executive director shall review it and communicate any suggestions for revision to the investigating committee. When the report has been satisfactorily revised, the executive director shall send it to the members of the Committee on College and University Governance for comment and a decision concerning its publication. As a condition of approving

publication, or by way of suggestion to the authors of the report, the members of the Committee on Governance may propose changes in the draft text. After further revision, the text shall then be transmitted confidentially to the persons most significantly affected by or implicated in the report, including the chief administrative officers of the institution, with the request that they provide corrections of any errors of fact that may appear in it and make such comments as they may desire upon the findings and conclusions reached. If their responses indicate a need for significant changes in the report, the text with the resulting revisions may be resubmitted to the Committee on College and University Governance. With that committee's concurrence, and after the investigating committee has been consulted as to final revisions, the report will be published through its posting on the Association's website and subsequently in printed form in the annual *Bulletin of the American Association of University Professors*. An advance copy of the published report shall be transmitted to the principal parties.

12. If the Committee on College and University Governance judges, based on the published report and any subsequent developments, that the administration and/or governing board of the institution under investigation have seriously infringed standards of college and university governance endorsed by the Association, it may recommend to the next annual meeting that the institution be sanctioned for "substantial non-compliance with standards of academic government." In reaching its decision, the Committee on Governance shall again invite comment from the investigating committee, though it is not bound to follow the investigating committee's recommendation. If the annual meeting concurs with the recommendation of the Committee on College and University Governance, notice of "non-compliance" will be published regularly in *Academe*, for the purpose of informing Association members, the profession at large, and the public that unsatisfactory conditions of academic governance exist at the institution in question.

13. After a notice of sanction has been published by the Association, the executive director, acting on behalf of the Committee on College and University Governance, will correspond periodically with the administration and appropriate faculty groups at the institution, seeking to ascertain whether stated policies

and procedures have been brought into substantial conformity with standards of college and university governance endorsed by the Association, and whether evidence exists of meaningful faculty participation in academic governance. So long as a particular college or university remains under sanction, the Committee on College and University Governance will monitor and report on developments at the institution.

14. When evidence has been obtained that a sanctioned institution has achieved substantial compliance with Association-supported governance standards, the Committee on College and University Governance will review the information and determine whether to recommend to the annual meeting of the Association that the sanction be removed. Notice of the recommendation and the action will be published in *Academe*.

Note

1. As used in this statement, the "executive director" may be another member of the Association's professional staff to whom the executive director has assigned the particular responsibility.

Index

graduate student employees (*cont.*)
  and collective bargaining, 388; dismissal of, 87;
  teaching workloads for, 240, 388
Gratz v. Bollinger, 162n4
grievance procedures: for academic professionals,
  215; and access to faculty personnel files, 100–104;
  and access to university records, 61; for graduate
  students, 87, 388; for minor sanctions, 85; in
  nonreappointment cases, 85–86, 94, 96, 97, 98;
  recommended standards, 88; in salary disputes, 88,
  290; in sexual-harassment cases, 364; university
  records of, 62
Grutter v. Bollinger, 128n, 163n4, 385n3

Hadzi-Antich, In Re, 166
hearings, faculty: arbitration as substitute for, 334–35;
  arbitration following, 331–32; committee membership and procedures, 89n11, 92; on complaints of
  academic freedom violation in nonreappointment,
  86–87, 97; on complaints of discrimination in
  nonreappointment, 86–87, 97; in dismissal for
  cause, 12, 14, 83–84, 92–93; for extramural
  utterances, 14–15n6, 31; politically controversial
  personnel decisions and, 34, 35, 36; record of, 14–15,
  84, 93; in sexual-harassment complaints, 364; on
  termination of appointment for financial exigency,
  15, 82, 297–98; on termination of appointment for
  program discontinuance, 83, 297–98
hearings, student, 385
Hong v. Grant, 127, 128n6, 129n9

Imposition of Tenure Quotas, On the, 68–70
inadequate consideration, nonreappointment and
  complaints of, xviii, 80, 86, 87, 94, 96, 97–98, 101,
  103, 214
*Inclusion in Governance of Faculty Members Holding
  Contingent Appointments, The*, 197–209
incompetence, xvii, xviii, 52, 125, 128, 217, 230, 231,
  375; hearing on charges of, 14–15, 84; post-tenure
  review and, 230
indemnification, faculty, 319
indoctrination, 20, 21, 22, 25, 25n2, 26n5, 34
*Institutional Problems Resulting from Financial
  Exigency, On: Some Operating Guidelines*,
  309–10
*Institutional Responsibility for Legal Demands on
  Faculty*, 319
institutional review board (IRB), 72, 72n3, 281, 282–83.
institutions, academic: accreditation of, 132–33;
  autonomy of, 119–20, 122n3, 158, 159, 258, 327;
  budgeting at, responsibility for, 119, 289–91;
  child-care arrangements of, 343–44, 346n24,
  348; communication among components of,
  118–19, 121; copyright issues for, 264–66; and
  corporate-funded research, 274–76, 277–85;
  electronic communications and, 42–57; and
  enforcement of faculty ethical standards, 145;
  and ethics of faculty recruitment, 153–54,
  155–56; external relations of, 119; and faculty
  background investigations, 164–66; faculty
  liability, responsibility for, 319; freedom of
  artistic expression, responsibility for protecting,

40–41; governance of, 117–122; government-
  sponsored research and, 271–73; and intercollegiate athletics, 134–41, 389–90; limitations on
  use of faculty for contingent appointments by,
  177–78; mergers and acquisitions of, 290, 310,
  311–12; overseas campuses of, 257–58; and
  political activities of faculty, 38, 39, 86; public
  funding of, 41, 172, 178–79, 271–73, 292;
  recommended regulations on academic freedom
  and tenure and, 79–90; speaking officially for,
  14, 31, 40, 49–50, 119, 128; and standards and
  criteria for tenure, 68, 70, 94–95, 98, 160, 161,
  169, 199, 211, 219–20, 224; and student records,
  disclosure of, 382. *See also* religiously affiliated
  institutions
insurance plans: coverage during leaves of absence,
  318; for faculty liability, 319
intellectual property, 46, 258, 261; academic professionals' right to, 263; copyright issues, 264; and
  corporate-funded research, 274–76; faculty
  handbook principles on, 279–81; graduate
  students' rights to, 263, 388; online and distance
  education and, 254–56
investigations: AAUP committee reports of, xiv, xvii,
  2, 4, 359, 394, 395, 397; of discrimination complaints, 359; "limitations" clause and, 66; and
  pending litigation, 359; procedures for, in academic
  freedom and tenure cases, 393–95; standards for,
  in governance cases, 396–98

joint effort, in academic governance, 116, 118, 119,
  246, 325
*Joint Statement on Faculty Status of College and
  University Librarians*, 210–11
Joint Statement on Rights and Freedoms of Students,
  381–86
joint works, copyright of, 265. *See also* authorship:
  multiple

Keyishian v. Board of Regents, 13–14n1, 127
Knight Foundation Commission on Inter-collegiate
  Athletics, 135, 140, 141n3
Kunda v. Muhlenberg College, 378n12

Labor Arbitration Rules, 332, 333n5
leaves of absence: annuity contributions and, 318;
  crediting of prior service elsewhere, 80; for family
  responsibilities, 340–41; for health reasons, 339;
  for librarians, 211; for political activities, 39, 86;
  during probationary period, 80, 317; statement of
  principles on, 317–18
legal demands on faculty, institutional responsibility
  for, 319
liability, faculty, 319
librarians, 43, 44, 53, 108, 201, 202, 204, 210–11,
  213, 214
"limitations" clause, 14, 14n5, 64–67
litigation: AAUP investigation during, 359; against
  faculty members, 319; on personnel files access,
  100–101
*Los Angeles Department of Water and Power v.
  Manhart*, 162n2

presidents: budgetary matters and, 119, 289–91; duties and powers of, 120; evaluation and retention of, 131; governance of athletic programs and, 135, 137; removal of, arbitrary, 131; role of, in faculty dismissal proceedings, 35, 83, 84, 85, 92–93, 121, 331; selection of, 119, 130; students' right of appeal to, 385

Preventing Conflicts of Interest in Government-Sponsored Research at Universities, On, 271–73

prior service elsewhere: crediting of, 14, 15n8, 167–68, 345n15; leaves of absence and, 80

privacy, personal: and electronic communications, 44, 50, 52, 54, 55; and faculty background investigations, 164, 165, 166

Privacy Act of 1974, 164

Privacy Protection Study Commission, 165

probationary faculty appointments: academic freedom and, 14, 85, 94; automatic termination of, 68–69; conversion of contingent faculty appointments to, 178–81, 187–88, 209n19; evaluation during, 16n10, 80, 95, 219, 223, 278, 342; leaves of absence during, 80, 317; and length of probationary period, 14, 15–16nn8–9, 68, 69, 75, 76, 80, 88nn1–2, 94, 151, 156, 167–68, 176, 177, 188n1, 199, 230, 342; in medical schools, 74–75; prior service elsewhere and, 14, 15n8, 167–68; and standards and criteria for tenure, 68, 70, 94–95, 98, 160, 161, 169, 199, 211, 219–20, 224; and standards for notice of nonreappointment, 15–16n9, 85, 89n12, 94, 99, 215; and "stopping the tenure clock," 340, 342, 343, 345n19; tenure quotas and, 68–70; terms and conditions of, 14, 15n8, 79, 80, 86, 94–95, 168, 177. *See also* nonreappointment; tenure

Processing Complaints of Discrimination, On, 355–60

professional staff. *See* academic professionals

programs, academic: discontinuance of, xvii, xviii, 81, 82–83, 89n8, 161–62, 169n3, 231, 292–305; reduction of, 309

promotion, 59, 60, 62, 70, 89n7, 94, 101, 102, 103, 112n9, 119, 121, 151, 155, 159, 160, 161, 162, 169, 179, 186, 187, 191, 199, 204, 205, 211, 215, 219, 221, 223, 227, 229, 231, 232, 243, 267, 270, 275, 277, 283, 285, 315, 318, 338, 346n22, 349, 350, 351, 356, 357

Protecting an Independent Faculty Voice: Academic Freedom after Garcetti v. Ceballos, 126–29

publications, student, 383

public funding of higher education, 41, 172, 178–79, 271–73, 292, 295–96

Public Health Service, 269, 272, 275

publishing. *See* research

quotas: hiring, and affirmative action, 158, 163n8; tenure, 68–70

rank, faculty, xvii, 12, 12n6, 14, 15n7, 76, 77, 78, 80, 86, 89n14, 151, 153, 155, 156, 162, 167, 168n1, 169, 176, 177, 179, 183n3, 188n1, 190–91, 192, 197, 207, 208n17, 210, 242, 287, 291n4, 300, 339, 344nn3–4, 350, 355, 357; for faculty on contingent appointments, 176, 177, 179, 183n3,

188n1, 190–91, 197, 207, 208n17, 339, 344n3; for librarians, 211

reasonable accommodation, 376, 377

Recommendations on Partner Accommodation and Dual-Career Appointments, 347–52

Recommended Institutional Regulations on Academic Freedom and Tenure, 79–90

Recommended Principles for Faculty Handbooks and Collective Bargaining Agreements to Guide Academy-Industry Relationships, 277–85

recruitment, faculty, 153–54, 155–56, 278; affirmative action and, 160; and background investigations, 164–66; and corporate funding of researchers, 276; ethics of, 153–54, 155–56

reduction of academic programs or departments, 309

Regents of the University of California v. Bakke, 158, 162n4

Relationship of Faculty Governance to Academic Freedom, On the, 123–25

religious affiliation, academic appointments and, 158

religiously affiliated institutions: academic freedom and, 4–5, 14, 14n5, 64–67; admission to, 381–82; appointments to, 158; governing boards of, 119; "limitations" clause and, 14, 14n5, 64–67

reprimand, of faculty, 50, 85, 110, 112nn9–10

research: academic freedom and, 14, 21, 43–46; appointments, 74, 76; conflicts of interest in government-sponsored, 275–76; corporate funding of, 274–76; electronic communications and, 42, 43–46, 47, 49, 51, 52, 54; full-time non-tenure-track faculty and, 191–92, 192–93; institutional review board and, 72, 72n3, 281, 282–83; in medical schools, 71, 284–85; multiple authorship and, 267–68; post-tenure review and, 231–32; sponsored, 145, 262, 265, 269, 271–73, 274–76, 277–81, 284

research institutions, 174, 176, 180, 186, 205, 247, 274, 275, 339, 347, 348, 350; and corporate funding of research, 274–76. *See also* medical schools

resignation, faculty, 80–81, 153–54, 156

retirement: academic professionals and, 215; accelerated, as alternative to tenure quotas, 70; for age, 185n29; contributions for, during family leave, 341; contributions for, during leave of absence, 318; and disability, 377; early, 81, 231, 297, 304, 309; faculty on contingent appointments and, 174, 185n31; mandatory, xvii, 14, 185n29, 301; phased, 169

retrenchment. *See* discontinuance of program or department; financial exigency

Rights and Freedom of Students, Joint Statement on, 381–86

Role of the Faculty in Budgetary and Salary Matters, The, 289–91

Role of the Faculty in Conditions of Financial Exigency, The, 292–308

Role of the Faculty in the Accrediting of Colleges and Universities, The, 132–33

romantic relationships between faculty and students, 149

sabbatical leaves. *See* leaves of absence

salary: of academic professionals, 215; department chair recommendations on, 290, 291; faculty role in decisions on, 289–91; full, dependent on external funding, 74–75, 76; leaves of absence and, 318, 340–41; market-determined, 313–16; notice of, for following academic year, 79, 80–81, 154; recruitment and offer of, 156; reductions in, and financial exigency, 291, 297, 300, 304; report, AAUP annual, 187, 190, 208n17, 339; during suspension, 16n11, 83, 92, 106–7, 334; terminal, 14–15, 85, 335; of women faculty members, 313–16, 339, 357. *See also* compensation; severance salary

Salary-Setting Practices That Unfairly Disadvantage Women Faculty, 313–16

sanctions, AAUP, on institution, 396–98

sanctions, on faculty: for abuse or misuse of institution's computer system, 48; arbitration and, 332–33n2; for conflicts of interest, 276; other than dismissal, xix, 85, 110–11; procedures for imposition of, 85; in sexual-harassment cases, 364; strikes as grounds for, 324; suspension during dismissal proceedings, 16n11, 83, 92, 106–7, 334. *See also* dismissal; reprimand, of faculty; suspension from duties

sectarian institutions. *See* religiously affiliated institutions

Senior Appointments with Reduced Loads, 169

service, faculty, 170, 174, 175, 176, 177, 179, 180, 181, 183n5, 186, 187, 188, 191, 197–209, 210–11, 219, 222, 227, 228, 229, 232, 235, 239, 240, 241, 242, 243–44, 250, 251. *See also* workloads, faculty

severance salary: in dismissal cases, 14–15, 85, 335; in financial exigency, 82, 85, 294, 295; in institutional mergers, 310; in terminations for program discontinuance, 83, 85, 297–98, 300, 303

sex discrimination: and access to faculty personnel files, 100–104; and athletics programs, 140; claims of, 355; general patterns of, 359–60; processing complaints of, by AAUP, 358–60; sexual harassment, 363–65; statistical evidence of, 85–86, 88, 97, 98, 278, 355, 356, 360

sexual assault, campus: faculty responsibilities related to, 369–71; federal laws on, 367–68; institutional policies related to, 368–70

sexual harassment, 363–65; due process in handling complaints of, xix, xxin32, 364

Sexual Harassment: Suggested Policy and Procedures for Handling Complaints, 363–65

sexual relations between faculty and students, 149

shared governance. *See* governance, academic; joint effort, in academic governance

Silva v. New Hampshire, 113n26

Simonson v. Iowa State University, 113n23

Smith v. University of Washington Law School, 162–63n4

speakers, outside: statement on academic freedom and, 37–38; students' choice of, 122, 383

special and emergency appointments. *See* non-tenure-track appointments, full-time; part-time faculty

Special Committee on Distance Learning and Intellectual Property Issues, 254, 264

speech codes, 23, 361–62; sexual harassment and, 365n8

sponsored research, copyright and, 265. *See also* works made for hire, and copyright

standard of proof: in disciplinary proceedings involving sexual assault, 371; in dismissal proceedings, xviii, 84, 229, 233; in politically controversial academic personnel decisions, 35–36. *See also* burden of proof in dismissal proceedings

Standards for Investigations in the Area of College and University Government, 396–98

standards for notice of nonreappointment, 15–16n9, 85, 89n12, 94, 99, 215; for full-time non-tenure-track faculty, 89n12, 99n1; for part-time faculty, 86

Standards for Notice of Nonreappointment, 99

Stanford v. Roche, 261

Statement of Principles on Academic Freedom and Tenure with 1970 Interpretive Comments, 1940, 13–19; on academic freedom, 14; endorsers of, 15–17; history of, 13; "limitations" clause in, 14, 14n5, 64–67; on probationary period, 14; on tenure, 14–15

Statement of Principles on Family Responsibilities and Academic Work, 339–46

Statement of Principles on Leaves of Absence, 317–18

Statement on Academic Government for Institutions Engaged in Collective Bargaining, 325–26

Statement on Collective Bargaining, 323–24

Statement on Conflicts of Interest, 269–70

Statement on Copyright, 264–66

Statement on Corporate Funding of Academic Research, 274–76

Statement on Extramural Utterances, Committee A, 31

Statement on Faculty Workload with Interpretive Comments, 237–40

Statement on Government of Colleges and Universities, 117–22

Statement on Graduate Students, 387–88

Statement on Intellectual Property, 261–63

Statement on Intercollegiate Athletics, 389–90

Statement on Multiple Authorship, 267–68

Statement on Online and Distance Education, 254–56

Statement on Plagiarism, 147–48

Statement on Procedural Standards in Faculty Dismissal Proceedings, 91–93

Statement on Procedural Standards in the Renewal or Nonrenewal of Faculty Appointments, 94–98

Statement on Professional Ethics, 145–46

Statement on Professors and Political Activity, 39

Statement on Recruitment and Resignation of Faculty Members, 153–54

Statement on Teaching Evaluation, 219–22

statistical evidence of sex discrimination, 85–86, 88, 97, 98, 278, 355, 356, 360

"stopping the tenure clock," 340, 342, 343, 345n19

strikes, faculty, 90n18, 323, 324

students: academic freedom of, 382, 383, 387; and admissions policies, 122n4, 137–38, 381–82, 389; and appeals of course grades, 29–30, 382; athletics and, 134–41, 389–90; and budgetary matters, role in, 291n2; as citizens, 119, 383–84; in the classroom, 20, 23, 382; conduct of, standards relating to, 384; confidentiality and, 382; consensual relations with faculty, 149; as "customers," 224; disciplinary proceedings against, 384–85; discrimination against, 87, 385n3, 386n8, 387;

students (*cont.*)

educational records of, 382; effects on, of excessive use of contingent faculty appointments, 173–74, 193–94; and electronic communications, 42, 43, 46, 47, 48, 49, 51, 52, 54; evaluation of faculty, 205, 223–26, 229, 356; and financial aid policies, 137–38, 389–90; governance and, 121–22, 379, 383, 388; graduate, 87, 387–88; institutional authority over, and civil penalties, 384, 386n15; legal counsel for, 385; mandated assessment and, 245–53; and number of degrees conferred, 172; organizations of, 382; performance evaluation of, 29, 138, 231, 382; plagiarism and, 148; publications of, 383, 388; records of, 382, 386n5; at religiously affiliated institutions, 381; rights and freedoms of, 381–86; speaker choices of, 122, 383; status of, 122–23; university records and, 61. *See also* graduate student employees

suspension from duties, 51, 105–113, 368; during dismissal proceedings, 16n11, 83, 92, 106–7, 334; as severe sanction, xix, 85, 107, 110–11

Sweezy v. New Hampshire, 57n39

teaching: academic freedom and, 7, 9, 14, 20–27, 28, 29, 40, 46–47, 72, 128, 145, 256; and assignment of course grades, 29–30, 382; and course materials, 9, 20, 22, 24, 28, 33, 46, 47, 72, 147, 225, 231, 254, 255, 256, 266; evaluation of, 205, 223–26, 229, 356; expectations, priorities, and rewards, 241–44; mandated assessment and, 245–53; methods, post-tenure review and, 229–34; multi-section courses, 28; online and distance, 254–56. *See also* workloads, faculty

teaching assistants, 14–15n6, 70, 192, 197, 199, 240. *See also* graduate student employees

teaching-intensive appointments, 186–89

teaching loads. *See* workloads, faculty

temporary faculty. *See* non-tenure-track appointments, full-time; part-time faculty

tenure: academic freedom and, 14, 68–70, 94, 167, 170, 175–76, 177, 186, 187, 190, 192–94, 213, 342; accreditation standards and, 132–33; clock, stopping of, 340, 342, 343, 345n19; and conversion of contingent faculty appointments, 178–81, 187–88, 209n19; and crediting prior service elsewhere, 14, 15n8, 167–68; definition of, 12, 14–15; denial of (*see* nonreappointment); of department chairs or heads, 121; economic security and, 14, 75, 76, 77, 183, 213; excessive probation and, 167, 357; for faculty on contingent appointments, 86–87, 176, 186–88, 301; faculty responsibility in decisions on, 121; financial exigency and, 81–82, 169n3, 300–302, 309, 311–12; institutional mergers and, 290, 310, 311–12; for librarians, 211; locus of, 167, 300; mandatory retirement and, xvii, 14, 185n29, 301; in medical schools, 73–78; and post-tenure review, 229–34; probationary period of fixed length and, 14,

15–16nn8–9, 68, 69, 75, 76, 80, 88nn1–2, 94, 151, 156, 167–68, 176, 177, 188n1, 199, 230, 342; quotas, 68–70; standards and criteria for, 68, 70, 94–95, 98, 160, 161, 169, 199, 211, 219–20, 224; written statement of terms of, initial appointment and, 14, 15n8, 79, 80, 94–95, 156, 182, 219–20. *See also* dismissal; due process, academic; non-tenure-track appointments, full-time; part-time faculty; termination of faculty appointments

Tenure and Teaching-Intensive Appointments, 186–89

Tenure in the Medical School, 73–78

term contracts, 68, 78n8, 171, 193, 199, 202, 203

termination of faculty appointments: in discontinuance of program or department, 82–83, 169n3; by faculty member, 80–81, 153–54, 156; for financial exigency, 81–82, 296–305; by institution, xviii–xix, 81–83. *See also* dismissal; severance salary

Title IX of the Education Amendments of 1972, 137, 365n8, 365n10, 367

trustees. *See* governing boards

United States Student Association (formerly United States National Student Association), joint statement with AAUP, 381–86

University of Pennsylvania v. EEOC, 100, 101

university records, access to, 58–63; for graduate students, 388; presumptions about, 60–62; for students, 61

Use and Abuse of Faculty Suspensions, The, 105–13

Verification and Trust: Background Investigations Preceding Faculty Appointment, 164–66

women faculty: at community colleges, 339; and contingent appointments, 172, 184nn15–16, 191, 196n6; and family responsibilities, 339–40; at research institutions, 339; salary of, vs men, 313–16, 339, 357. *See also* sex discrimination

workloads, faculty, 39, 61, 169, 178, 182, 188, 220, 231, 235, 237–40, 241–44, 258, 315, 339, 340, 342; in community colleges, 240; of full-time non-tenure-track faculty, 180, 186, 191, 192–93; of graduate student employees, 240, 388; inequity in distribution of, 237, 238–39, 241; and modified duties, 341–42, 344n12; online and distance education and, 240; of part-time faculty, 240; policies for family responsibilities, 339–46; procedures for determining, 238; reduction of, for family responsibilities, 341–42, 344n12; for senior appointees, 169, 178, 182, 342; teaching assignments, maximum, 237–38; teaching assignments, preferred, 237; teaching evaluation and, 220. *See also* faculty: work of

Work of Faculty, The: Expectations, Priorities, and Rewards, 241–44

works made for hire, and copyright, 262–63, 264, 265, 279